Britain and the Ending of the Slave Trade

Britain
and the ending of the
slave trade

Suzanne Miers

Longman

LONGMAN GROUP LIMITED

London
Associated companies, branches and
representatives throughout the world

First published 1975

ISBN 0 582 64079 2

Printed in Great Britain by
Western Printing Services Ltd, Bristol

Contents

Acknowledgements

A complete acknowledgement of all the help I have received in the course of this long study is virtually impossible, but first and foremost I have to thank Professor Roland Oliver, who supervised the doctoral dissertation, completed in 1969, upon which this work is based and whose help and encouragement induced me to complete it. I owe also a great debt to Professor Philip Curtin, who made it possible for me to spend two years teaching at the University of Wisconsin and who opened my eyes to so many facets of African history, to Professor Jean Stengers, who first called my attention to the Brussels Conference and was ever ready to discuss it, and to Drs Colin Newbury, Cyril Northcote Parkinson and Professor William Roger Louis, who have helped me in innumerable ways over the years, and initially to the late Professor Dame Lillian Penson who first introduced me to historical research. I would like to thank particularly Professor A. J. Hanna who exceeded the heights of friendship by reading and commenting on the whole text and Professors Jan Vansina, Igor Kopytoff, Roger Anstey, Joseph C. Miller, Gerald Hartwig, James Vaughan, Boniface Obichere, Kingsley Ogedengbe, Martin Klein, Norman Bennett and Paul Lovejoy, Dr Humphrey Fisher, Dr John Grace, Miss Ylvisaker and Mr Frederick Cooper who all read and commented on parts of it. The Reverend Dr A. J. Arkell generously made available his papers to me and discussed his work against the slave trade in the Sudan in the 1920s. Mrs Trudy Newbury gave me great assistance with German sources. Mrs Gwendolin Cowe and Mr Rotemeyer translated the Dutch documents for me. Mlle Fernande Baetens translated a Flemish article, Mr Donald Hart and Mr David Cummings checked numerous references and Mr Claude Bernard drew the maps. Mrs Foskett kindly allowed me to use the papers of her grandfather, Sir John Kirk, and gave me much generous hospitality. Mr Gona Kazungu, Mr John Maliti, Mr Thomas Chibunga, Miss Christine Cornell, Mr Elton Jando and Mr Simon Reuben were invaluable assistants during my interviewing in East Africa. I must mention, too, the students in my seminars at the University of Wisconsin in 1967–8 and 1969–70 and at Ohio University in 1970–1 and 1971–2, whose interest and comments were a source of great stimulation and amongst whom I wish in particular to mention Dr Vera Reber.

My debt to the African informants who so generously gave me their time and helped me to recreate the world of their fathers and grandfathers is immense, although little oral material has been used in this particular volume. I am grateful too to my friends Mr and Mrs Mohammad Bashrahil of Lamu and their relations and friends who did much to increase my understanding of slavery on the Swahili coast, to Mr Neville Chittick, Dr Godfrey Muriuki and Mr James Allen who gave me so much valuable assistance in East Africa, and to Chief Benjamin Shaha who gave me much help with interviews in the Tezo/Roka location.

It is impossible to acknowledge all the help that I have had from the archivists of the many archives and libraries in which I collected my material, but I would like to express my particular appreciation of the assistance given me by Mr Desneux of the Ministère des Affaires Etrangères in Brussels and his assistant the late Madame Christine Nisole, M. Maurel of the archives of Afrique Occidentale Française in Dakar and Mr Neville Chittick and the staff of the British Institute in Eastern Africa.

This work was substantially aided by research grants from the Central Research Fund of the University of London for work in Paris and Brussels in 1963–4 and in West Africa in 1966, from the Joint Committee on African Studies of the American Council of Learned Societies and the Social Science Research Council, and Ohio University Baker Fund, financed by Mr and Mrs Edwin Kennedy, for work in East Africa in 1972–3. In addition, Ohio University International Studies Centre paid for microfilms and certain other expenses in London, Paris, Brussels and The Hague in the summers of 1970 and 1971, and I particularly wish to thank Dr Alan Booth who, as Director of African Studies at Ohio University, did much to assist me.

In conclusion I owe a very special debt to my husband, the late Brigadier Richard Miers who first insisted I return to historical studies, to my children, Caroline and Charles, without whom I should have had no incentive to embark on this book, to Lavinia Doris Hall who looked after us with devotion during the trying years when it was in the making, to my brother and sister-in-law, Anne and David Doyle, for their hospitality and generosity and to my mother Joyce Doyle for her unfailing support as well as constant reminders of the passage of time (expressed by 'wrap it up, for God's sake') without which this work might never have seen the light of day.

Illustrations

The author and publishers would like to express their gratitude to the following for permission to reproduce photographs: to the *Illustrated London News* for the photographs between pages 96 and 97 and facing page 112; to the Radio Times Hulton Picture Library for the photographs between pages 224 and 225 (except for the portrait of Sir John Kirk) and also on the cover; to the National Portrait Gallery for the portrait of Sir John Kirk facing page 225; to the Musée Royal de l'Afrique Centrale for the photograph facing page 240; and to Frank Cass, publishers of *Fighting the Slave Hunters in Central Africa*, by Alfred J. Swann, for the photographs facing page 241. The publishers have been unable to trace the copyright owner of the illustration facing page 113.

The maps were drawn by Clive Gordon Associates.

Slavery you say is bad. I agree that it is bad, but slave labour is to the interior of Africa what steam-power is to your country. In your great factories where steam is used, is all well with the employees? Is there not much misery and suffering? ... Well, if the angel of God came and saw the unhappiness of your factories and said: 'This must not continue—abolish steam', would you think it a wise decree?

Zubayr Pasha

(Quoted in Lord Lugard—*The Dual Mandate*, London 1965, 5th ed., p. 365.)

Preface

Lord Salisbury described the Brussels Conference of 1889–90 as the first in the history of the world to meet 'for the purpose of promoting a matter of pure humanity and goodwill'. Humanitarians regarded it as a triumph and found it fitting that it was held in the year the British and Foreign Anti-Slavery Society celebrated its half-centenary. For Britain it was the climax of a struggle upon which she had embarked a full eighty years before —a struggle to associate all the major powers in a comprehensive agreement to end the African slave trade. The conference was a unique event in its day and it established precedents for the future.

Yet when I began my work it took little time to discover that most people had never heard of it. Perhaps this is hardly surprising for it had received but scant attention from historians. It was the subject of a little known work by Henry Queneuil, presented as a doctoral thesis in Paris in 1907, when the wealth of archival sources, now open, was not available and before the invaluable memoirs of Emile Banning, who took part in the meeting, had been published. Recently Father Ceulemans considered the conference from the point of view of the aims of King Leopold II in *La Question Arabe et le Congo*. Otherwise it has been touched upon in many books but systematically studied in none.

The few people I consulted who knew enough not to confuse the meeting with King Leopold's famous conference of 1876 had merely wondered in passing what it had all been about. Why had so many diplomats and some of the leading Africanists of the day spent many weary months hammering out an act against the slave trade at a critical moment in the scramble for Africa? In the cynical age in which we live the stated aims of the meeting could not be taken at their face value as they had been in the past. But if the participants were not primarily interested in suppressing the slave traffic, what were they doing?

This was the question I set out to answer. I soon discovered that a complete history of the conference would require work in the archives of all the colonial powers and in some of the others as well. This was beyond my resources and not all these archives were open at the time. I therefore limited the field to a study of Britain's policy. She was after all the instigator of the meeting and the country which took the most interest in it. Happily another scholar, Mr Tshimanga of the University of Aix, is now working on French policy at the conference and doubtless other studies will follow to enlighten us on the aims of the other participants.

I had intended to start with the conference and then consider the results of the Brussels Act in Africa but at every turn I found I was having to go back into the nineteenth century for the origins of the various questions debated in Brussels. For instance, the Act confirmed existing treaties against the slave trade. These agreements were easy enough to find, but when it came to discovering why they were all different, whether they were working satisfactorily and why France and Morocco were not bound by treaty, I not only had to consult a large number of secondary works but also had to make sallies into the archives to find the answers. I concluded, therefore, that it would be useful to start with a discussion of the building of the British treaty network.

Equally, since the slave trade supplied a vast market in Africa, it was necessary to understand something of African slavery to appreciate the difficulties facing the various governments and other agencies bent on destroying it, as well as the problems raised by the freeing of slaves and the harbouring of fugitives. Few secondary works dealt with either slavery or African economic history but information was scattered through a large number of 'micro-histories' of different African peoples, anthropological and ethnographic studies and the invaluable publications of explorers, missionaries and early administrators. My work was virtually complete before Father Renault published his *Lavigerie, l'Esclavage Africain et l'Europe*, with its wealth of information on the slave traffic. Slavery itself is only now being systematically studied and the rich source of oral tradition being exploited. In fact I was driven, in conjunction with Professor Igor Kopytoff, to edit a book on African slavery to bring together at least a selection of studies in this vast, fascinating and virtually untapped field.

These explanatory chapters on the treaty network and African slavery form Part I of this volume. Although some oral and other primary sources have been used, they are largely based on secondary works and were originally intended to be a short introduction to a study of the Brussels conference. As my research proceeded, however, they showed the same irresistible tendency to expand as the empire with the 'turbulent frontier' and they now form about half the book. I considered pruning them radically to produce a more balanced work but eventually decided that since no synthesis of this type existed they would at least guide the reader to the main issues of the period before 1888 and to existing sources. They are offered here with all the frustration of knowing that they are introductory and necessarily superficial.

The second half of this work deals with British policy towards humanitarian issues at the Berlin Conference, traces the events leading to the Brussels Conference and ends with a discussion of this meeting and the act it so laboriously hammered out and the aims of the colonial powers then engaged in the scramble for Africa. This too threatened to become 'open-ended' for it involved consideration of the arms and spirits traffic. I have made some use of British customs records but, to keep this study to manageable proportions and bring it to the point of publication, I have had to concentrate on the diplomatic issues and the slavery question. Much interesting work remains to be done in both these fields, as well as on the role of the humanitarians as a pressure group. In fact throughout my difficulty has been to focus this study and to avoid digressing into the many fascinating avenues it opens up.

The epilogue covers the later history of the Brussels Act and of the slave, spirits and arms trades based on a selective use of primary sources. I am planning a further work on this subject and a sketch is included here simply to round off the story.

As the sequence of events is always important in diplomatic history I have kept on the whole to the chronological approach, but to help the reader who may want to trace a particular issue I have resorted to sub-headings and a table of contents which reads rather like the nineteenth-century travelogues to which I owe so great a debt, but without such vignettes as 'Pork highly esteemed—a Human Bartered for a Fat Hog', 'Tribe of Corpses', 'Overboard to avoid the Rain' or 'Caterpillars for Supper'.

But if my tale is duller, I trust it is still worth the telling. There has been much debate between scholars since Eric Williams published his controversial book, *Capitalism and Slavery*, in 1944 as to whether Britain's long battle against the slave trade and slavery was inspired and sustained primarily by philanthropic or by economic and political considerations. It is my conviction that only a series of studies of the type undertaken in part II of this work based on a close scrutiny of the documentary evidence will eventually provide the information from which conclusions can be drawn. Such studies are needed for each stage in the struggle and particularly necessary are economic histories. Although this is the story of a diplomatic episode of the last century, it sheds light on the way in which a cause considered noble at the time can be used by interested parties to further their own ends.

Abbreviations

Ad.	Admiralty, British
AEB	Archives du Ministère des Affaires Etrangères, Brussels
AG de B. Adhes.	Acte Générale de Bruxelles, Adhesions
CAE	Conférence Anti-Esclavagiste
Af.	Africa
AGR	Archives Générales du Royaume, Brussels
VE	Van Eetvelde papers
AOF	Archives de l'Afrique Occidentale Française, Dakar
APR	Royal Archives, Palais Royal, Brussels
ASS	Anti-Slavery Society papers, Rhodes House, Oxford
AS & APS	Anti-Slavery and Aborigines' Protection Society
BFASS	British and Foreign Anti-Slavery Society
BFSP	*British and Foreign State Papers*
CAB	Cabinet Papers in the Public Record Office, London
CAE	Conférence Anti-Esclavagiste de Bruxelles
CO	Colonial Office and also Colonial Office archives in the Public Record Office, London
COCP	Colonial Office confidential print
conf.	confidential
EHR	*English Historical Review*
EIC	Archives of the État Indépendant du Congo, Brussels
Enc.	Enclosed, enclosing, enclosure (according to context)
FMAE	Archives du Ministère des Affaires Etrangères, Paris
AQG	Afrique Questions Générales
CC	Correspondance commerciale
CP	Correspondance politique
All.	Germany
Belg.	Belgium
Brt.	Britain
Hol.	Holland
MDA	Mémoires et Documents, Afrique
N.S.	New Series
Port.	Portugal
Russ.	Russia
Trip.	Tripoli
Turk.	Turkey
FMM	Archives du Ministère de la Marine, Paris
FMO	Archives Nationales, Section d'Outre-Mer, Paris

FO	Foreign Office, also denotes Foreign Office archives in the Public Record Office, London
FOCP	Foreign Office confidential print
IO	India Office
JAH	*Journal of African History*
KP	Kirk Papers
BASC	Folder marked Brussels Anti-Slavery conference
Misc.	Folder marked Uganda railway, etc.
STE	Folder marked Slave Trade and Egypt 1875–9
STZ	Folder marked Zanzibar 1868–73
MBZ	Archives of the Ministerie van Buitenlandsche Zaken, The Hague
MP	Papers of Sir William Mackinnon, School of Oriental and African Studies, London
PL	Papers of Baron Lambermont, Ministère des Affaires Etrangères, Brussels
Plens.	Plenipotentiaries to the conference
PP	*British Parliamentary Papers*
PRO	Public Record Office, London
NAN	National Archives of Nigeria
sec.	secret
SP	Papers of Robert Cecil, 3rd Marquess of Salisbury
ST	Slave Trade
STC	Slave trade conference, Brussels 1889–1890
THSG	*Transactions of the Historical Society of Ghana*
US M	Archives of the United States Department of State, Washington D.C. on microfilm

Dedication

To Nanny
(Miss Lavinia Doris Hall)

Part One

The Results of Britain's Anti-slavery Policy by 1884

Introduction

The Abolition of the British Slave Trade

The transatlantic slave trade was a vast forced labour migration providing workers for the plantations, mines, factories and houses of the New World. Slavery kept them in subjection, preventing them from sharing in the fruits of their labour and taking their rightful place in society. A constant flow of new slaves was needed as disease and ill treatment took a heavy toll[1] and the rate of natural increase was usually low.[2] Beginning late in the fifteenth century the trade lasted some four hundred years during which an estimated nine to ten million people were brutally torn from their homes in Africa and landed in the Americas.[3] The merchants of many nations participated in this nefarious traffic but the British were the greatest slavers of the eighteenth century. In 1807, however, they outlawed the trade to British subjects[4] and became at a blow its arch-enemies—a metamorphosis which has still to be completely explained.

Until the mid-eighteenth century there had been little opposition to slavery in Britain but thereafter it was increasingly denounced, on both moral and rational grounds by intellectuals, Christian evangelists, Quakers and others.[5] This reform movement, which had its counterparts in France

1 Treatment varied according to time, place and occupation but in some instances it was considered more economic to work a slave to death and replace him rather than to look after him, see for instance F. W. Knight, *Slave Society in Cuba during the Nineteenth Century*, Wisconsin 1970, pp. 75–6; L. Bethell, *The Abolition of the Brazilian Slave Trade*, Cambridge 1970 (henceforth *Abolition*), p. 4. For examples of differences in treatment see L. Foner and E. D. Genovese, *Slavery in the New World*, Prentice-Hall, 1969.

2 Reproduction rates also varied with time and place but were generally low as fewer women were imported than men and bad living conditions and ill-treatment contributed to high infant mortality. Slaves were sometimes bred but often it was regarded as cheaper to buy new slaves rather than to care for mothers and young children. See E. Phillip LeVeen, 'British Slave Trade Suppression Policies 1821–65: Impact and Implications', Ph.D. Chicago (Economics) 1971, pp. 70–3.

3 The exact number of slaves transported is unknown. This estimate is taken from P. D. Curtin, *The Atlantic Slave Trade: A Census* (henceforth *Slave Trade*), Wisconsin 1969, pp. 265–9.

4 By the Abolition Act, 47. Geo. III, Cap. 36, March 1807.

5 They included people as diverse as the Quaker leaders, the Scottish moralists— Hutcheson, Beattie and Reid—John Wesley, Bishop Warburton, Adam Smith, John

3

and North America and was not limited to slavery, sprang from the cultural climate of the eighteenth century, the age of 'enlightenment', religious revival and rapid economic change, which witnessed the growth of humanitarianism and of faith in the 'natural rights' and fundamental equality of all men. A notable victory was won in 1772, when it was declared illegal to take a slave out of England by force, a restriction on masters' rights which heralded the end of slavery in Britain.[6] This did not apply to the colonies, but henceforth the slave trade, as opposed to slavery, was attacked ever more vociferously by a small but dedicated group of philanthropists, foremost among whom were the Quakers and the Clapham Sect',[7] including William Wilberforce, who led the movement in Parliament where he and his followers were derisively called the 'Saints'.

They worked in propitious times for political and economic changes were eroding the strength and cohesiveness of their opponents who included the merchants and seamen of the port towns, particularly Liverpool,[8] who conducted the traffic, the West Indian planters who relied on it for labour and various allied business interests.[9] The majority of the electorate and most members of Parliament had no personal stake in the trade but supported it because they thought it a lucrative commerce vital to the prosperity

Locke, Jeremy Bentham and the jurist William Blackstone. For the history of the anti-slavery movement see David Brion Davis, *The Problem of Slavery in Western Culture*, Cornell 1966; B. Fladeland, *Men and Brothers: Anglo-American Antislavery Cooperation*, (henceforth *Men and Brothers*) University of Illinois, 1972; Dale H. Porter, *The Abolition of the Slave Trade in England, 1784–1807*, Archon 1970; Howard Temperley, *British Antislavery 1833–1870*, London 1972; Roger Anstey, 'A reinterpretation of the abolition of the British slave trade 1806–7' (henceforth 'Reinterpretation'); *English Historical Review* (henceforth *EHR*), lxxxvii, April 1972, 343, pp. 304–32; G. R. Mellor, *British Imperial Trusteeship 1783–1850*, London 1951; Eric E. Williams, *Capitalism and Slavery*, London 1964 (first published Chapel Hill 1944). See also older works, e.g. F. J. Klingberg, *The Anti-Slavery Movement in England*, Yale 1926 (henceforth *Anti-Slavery Movement*), and 'The Evolution of the Humanitarian Spirit in Eighteenth Century England', *Pennsylvania Magazine of History and Biography*, lxvi, 1942, pp. 260–78; R. Coupland, *The British Anti-Slavery Movement* (henceforth *British Anti-Slavery Movement*), London 1933.
6 This famous judgement by Lord Chief Justice Mansfield applied to England and Ireland. Similar decisions followed in Scotland. For a discussion of the legal aspects of this case see H. Fischer, 'The Suppression of Slavery in International Law', 1, *The International Law Quarterly*, 3, Jan. 1950, pp. 28–51, 31–2.
7 So called because some of the leading 'Abolitionists' lived in Clapham. For a definition of abolitionist see below, p. 7, fn. 24.
8 In the late eighteenth century Liverpool conducted 70 to 85 per cent of the English slave trade, personal communication from Professor Anstey. For this traffic see also C. Northcote Parkinson, *The rise of the port of Liverpool*, Liverpool 1952; Gomer Williams, *History of the Liverpool Privateers and Letters of Marque with an account of the Liverpool Slave Trade*, part 2, London and Liverpool 1897; F. E. Hyde, B. B. Parkinson and S. Marriner, 'The Nature and Profitability of the Liverpool Slave Trade', *Economic History Review*, 2nd series, v, 3, 1953, pp. 368–77.
9 These included manufacturers of goods bartered for slaves in Africa, sugar factors and others.

of the West Indies and hence of Britain.[10] The great wealth of the planters had not only given them a political influence out of proportion to their numbers but had contributed to the popular belief that the West Indies, producing vital tropical staples, were particularly valuable to the Empire as a whole.[11] The traffic was also regarded as a training ground for the seamen essential to the navy in time of war and there was a general and well-founded fear that if it was outlawed it would simply pass into foreign hands to the benefit of Britain's commercial rivals.

By the late eighteenth century, however, the expansion of commerce was bringing opportunities and wealth to merchants and manufacturers unconnected with the Caribbean or the slave trade, which became proportionately less important even to Liverpool;[12] while the British West Indian sugar producers, faced with competition from more fertile foreign colonies, suffered an economic decline.[13] In the past, preferential duties had given them a virtual monopoly of the English market[14] but this advantage was largely lost during the French Revolutionary and Napoleonic wars, when Britain conquered some of the French, Dutch and Spanish Caribbean colonies and not only allowed them to be developed with English capital and supplied with labour by English slavers but permitted them to sell their sugar in Britain on the same terms as her own islands.[15] Moreover, British sugar was undersold in Europe by foreign sugar crossing the ocean in neutral ships, free from the expenses of convoying which forced up British prices.[16] By 1804 there was an overall glut in Caribbean produce, West Indian sugar was piling up in England and British planters, importing few slaves themselves and facing ruin, were anxious to cut off the supply of labour to their rivals.[17] Since the war had given Britain command of the seas and the bulk of the slave trade was conducted by her merchants, she had the

10 Porter, ch. 4; R. A. Austen and W. D. Smith, 'Images of Africa and British Slave Trade Abolition: The Transition to an Imperialist Ideology 1787–1807', *African Historical Studies*, ii, 1, 1969, p. 74. For a discussion of the actual value of the islands to Britain see Robert Paul Thomas, 'The Sugar Colonies of the Old Empire: Profit or Loss for Great Britain?', *Economic History Review*, 2nd series, xxi, 1, 1968, pp. 30–45.
11 Eric E. Williams, pp. 85 ff.; pp. 69–83, pp. 71–3; Porter, p. 16
12 Klingberg, *Anti-Slavery Movement*, p. 101
13 See Porter, pp. 8–15, 108 ff. They were faced increasingly with competition from the French colonies, the Dutch colonies in Guyana, the Spanish island of Cuba and Portuguese Brazil, and a number of causes weakened their economy.
14 For the effect of these duties in the late eighteenth and early nineteenth centuries see *ibid.*, pp. 108 ff.; for their later history see P. D. Curtin, 'The British Sugar Duties and West Indian Prosperity', *Journal of Economic History*, xiv, 2, 1954, pp. 157–64. They were out of keeping with the nascent free trade movement in England and against the interests of certain groups such as the East India Company which from 1787 sought to develop sugar production in its own territories.
15 Porter, p. 113
16 *Ibid.*, pp. 113 ff.; Anstey, 'Re-interpretation'
17 Porter, pp. 125 ff.

power and incentive, temporarily at least, to restrict the traffic without fear of merely diverting it into foreign hands.[18]

In 1805 therefore an Order-in-Council restricted the import of slaves into the conquered colonies.[19] This measure, striking at rival producers, did not require parliamentary sanction and was sufficiently in the national interest not to arouse serious opposition. The following year an Act of Parliament prohibited British participation in the slave trade to any foreign territory.[20] Though aimed at Britain's competitors like the Order-in-Council, this law actually killed a large part of the British slave traffic[21] and prepared the way for the *coup de grâce* of 1807—which outlawed the transport of slaves in British ships and forbade their import into any British colony.

This final step, bitterly opposed by many planters and traders hoping for better times, was apparently due to a combination of circumstances including the economic difficulties of the British West Indies, the decline of their importance to Britain,[22] the peculiar conditions created by the war, the fact that the greater part of the British slave trade had been banned by the Act of 1806 and last, but not least, the advent of a government with a number of ministers determined to end the traffic.

Much of the credit, however, must go to the small but vocal body of philanthropists who had opposed the trade through two decades of bitter conflict because they thought it inhuman and morally indefensible and whose ultimate aim became the suppression of slavery itself. They are usually called humanitarians since their concern was for the plight of the slaves and not with any material reward for themselves. Their altruism has, of course, been questioned. Doubtless their motives were as mixed as their personalities and since many of them were inspired by religious sentiments, their philanthropy was surely often tempered by the hope of reward after death.[23] Nevertheless, as human affairs go, these were men of principle, who

18 The French, Dutch and Spanish as enemies had been virtually driven out of the slave trade. The Danish trade was outlawed from 1803 and the U.S. trade was due to be abolished by 1808. The Portuguese traffic could not be touched but Portugal was a small power and an ancient ally who might be expected to yield to British pressure.
19 This included all colonies captured since 1802. It prohibited import of slaves unless their numbers were severely reduced by natural causes and then only in limited numbers, Porter, p. 132.
20 46 Geo. III, Cap. 52, 23. May 1806
21 Professor Anstey believes that some two thirds of the British trade was outlawed by this Act, personal communication.
22 Some West Indian planters also alienated British supporters by failing to respond to an official request to improve conditions on their estates to encourage natural reproduction and render the slave trade unnecessary. They also lost the support of some of their business allies by illegal trading with the United States, see Porter, pp. 98 ff., 120–4.
23 For a further discussion of humanitarians see section on the Anti-slavery Society below, pp. 30–3.

gave a high moral tone to the propaganda campaigns the abolitionists[24] conducted all over the country.

Their role in the history of the anti-slavery movement is of peculiar importance. It was they who fired the public imagination[25] and gave the movement a wide popular appeal, implanting in the mind of the average Briton an enduring conviction that here was a great and altruistic cause worthy of his support. This was to be reflected in the willingness of the electorate, year after year and even when there was no obvious economic return from it, to sanction the expenditure of a certain amount of public money and effort to suppress the slave traffic.

Humanitarianism, however, was only one factor in the intricate complex of motives which began and sustained the long battle against the African slave trade. There were always those, and they included statesmen, politicians, businessmen, planters, shippers, manufacturers, merchants and even missionaries, who supported the movement because it suited their interests to do so. Only because of such support was the triumph of 1807 possible and it was to be a necessary ingredient of all future important victories in the anti-slavery game.[26] As will be seen again and again in the pages which follow, humanitarianism, although a vital and enduring force in the long international struggle upon which Britain was now to embark, was not usually by itself sufficiently powerful a motive to move either the British or other governments to effective action. Fortunately, however, the suppression of the slave traffic often dovetailed in well with Britain's other interests, and with those of other powers.

24 The term abolitionist is used here to describe active members and supporters of anti-slavery societies. For a discussion of definitions see Fladeland, *Men and Brothers*, pp. xi–xii; Howard Temperley, p. ix.

25 See below, pp. 30–3, for a discussion of public opinion and the suppression of the slave trade.

26 For many years British historians regarded the suppression of the British slave trade in 1807 and the outlawing of slave holding by Europeans in the British Empire in 1833 as the triumphs of humanitarianism over vested interests, see for example, Coupland, *Anti-Slavery Movement*. This was challenged by Eric E. Williams in *Capitalism and Slavery*, in which he attributes British policy to changing economic conditions. Fallacies in his argument have been pointed out. See for instance R. Anstey, 'Capitalism and Slavery: a Critique', *The Economic History Review*, 2nd series, xxi, 2, 1968, pp. 307–20, and *Re-interpretation*; LeVeen, pp. 99 ff.; C. Duncan Rice, 'Critique of the Eric Williams Thesis—The Anti-Slavery Interest and the Sugar Duties, 1841–53', 'The Trans-Atlantic Slave Trade from West Africa', cyclostyled paper of the Centre of African Studies, University of Edinburgh, 1965, pp. 44–60; Howard Temperley, pp. 44–5, 73–6. Nevertheless Williams' work was seminal and has stimulated a re-examination of the question. For a further discussion of this point see Conclusion below, pp. 315 ff.

Chapter One

The Attack from the Periphery I: British Treaties with European Powers

Origins of the treaty network

Once Britain had renounced the slave traffic she had to force the same sacrifice on other nations to prevent this important commerce from simply passing into foreign hands for the benefit of rival merchants, shippers and planters. Henceforth it became an object of national policy to end the foreign slave trade. This could only be achieved, however, if all the maritime powers passed adequate laws and, of equal importance, saw that they were enforced, for slavers were safe from arrest as long as they could sail under the protection of even one national flag. From 1807 therefore successive British governments tried with varying degrees of persistence to secure the necessary foreign co-operation.

While the Napoleonic wars lasted Britain was able to reduce the export of slaves from West Africa by exercising her rights as a belligerent to seize enemy ships and search neutral vessels for contraband of war.[1] Exploiting her command of the seas, she exceeded her powers by searching for slaves and by arresting and trying slavers, often with questionable legality.[2] Her interpretation of belligerent rights was hotly contested by other nations and her high-handed actions left an unfortunate legacy of ill will and saddled her with a number of claims for compensation for wrongful arrest. The groundwork for the long struggle against the slave traffic was nevertheless laid. A squadron was sent out to the coast of Africa to intercept slavers.[3] A system

1 The export of slaves could not be completely stopped as Britain never had enough ships to spare for patrolling the coast and could not arrest Portuguese slavers plying between Portuguese ports, although for a while she illegally intercepted those found north of the equator; see Leslie Bethell, *Abolition*, pp. 6–11; Pierre Verger, *Flux et reflux de la traite des Nègres entre le Golfe de Benin et Bahia De Todos os Santos du XVIIe au XIXe siècles*. Paris and the Hague 1968, pp. 295–7.

2 Denmark and the United States had both outlawed the slave traffic and the British seized slavers flying their flags and charged them with breaking their own laws. Britain also arrested Swedish slavers although the trade was still legal in Sweden. For a discussion of these cases see Elsie I. Herrington, 'British Measures for the Suppression of the Slave Trade from the West Coast of Africa, 1807–33', M.A., London, 1923; Fischer, pp. 32 ff.

3 For the role of the navy see Christopher Lloyd, *The Navy and the Slave Trade*, London 1949; and W. E. F. Ward, *The Royal Navy and the Slavers*, London 1969.

of bounties was instituted to reward sailors for every captive they liberated as well as to compensate them for the dangers and tedium of the work. A vice-admiralty court was established in Sierra Leone to try offenders and provision was made for the care of freed slaves.[4] Britain was also able to extort the first treaties against the slave trade from her allies as and when the fortunes of war made them dependent upon her help.[5] These were of limited value[6] but were nevertheless a step towards securing essential foreign co-operation.

The end of the war, however, threw everything back into the melting pot. Belligerent rights lapsed, Britain gave back some of the colonies she had conquered and her powers of cajolery faded. With the resumption of normal commerce, a recrudescence of the traffic could clearly be expected in view of the great demand for slaves after so long a period of reduced supplies. The peace negotiations of 1814–15, however, presented a unique opportunity for securing an international agreement against the trade.

The Foreign Secretary, Lord Castlereagh,[7] spurred on by the abolitionists, brought the question before the eight great powers[8] at the Congress of Vienna, hoping that the support of Austria, Prussia and Russia, who were not directly interested in the trade, would strengthen his hand against the colonial nations. He wanted the traffic outlawed within three years, a permanent ambassadorial conference set up to supervise the effectiveness of measures taken against it, and reciprocal rights given to the powers to

4 For the measures taken to provide for freed slaves in Sierra Leone see Johnson U. J. Asiegbu, *Slavery and the Politics of Liberation 1787–1861*, London 1969, pp. 23 ff.; see ch. 3 below for a discussion of the problem of freed slaves.

5 Treaties were signed with Portugal, 19 Feb. 1810, see Bethell, *Abolition*, p. 8; with Sweden, 3 March 1813, see *British and Foreign State Papers* (henceforth *BFSP*), I, pt. 1, p. 302; with the Netherlands, 15 June 1814, *BFSP* III, pp. 889–90; with Spain, 5 July 1814, *BFSP* III, pp. 921–2; with France, 30 May 1814, *BFSP* I, pt. 1, pp. 172–3.

6 Spain and France (under Louis XVIII) merely agreed to limit the traffic to the supply of their own colonies, although France agreed to outlaw it completely in five years. Portugal agreed to allow the traffic only between her own colonies. Only Sweden and Holland engaged to outlaw it completely. Test cases made it clear that even if a foreign power had signed a treaty with Britain outlawing the slave traffic, the Royal Navy could not arrest slavers flying its flag unless this was specifically sanctioned in the treaty and the foreign power had outlawed the trade, see Lloyd, p. 44; Herrington, p. 97; Fischer, pp. 32 ff.; S. Daget, 'L'abolition de la traite des noirs en France de 1814 à 1831', *Cahiers d'Etudes Africaines*, 1971, pp. 14–58, pp. 18 ff.

7 For Castlereagh's policy see C. K. Webster, *The Foreign Policy of Castlereagh*, I, *1812–15*, London 1931, II, *1815–22*, London 1947, 2nd ed.; K. Mackenzie, 'Great Britain and the Abolition of the Slave Trade by the Other Powers (1812–22)', B.Litt. Oxford 1952; B. Fladeland, 'Abolitionist Pressures on the Concert of Europe, 1814–22', *Journal of Modern History*, 38, 4, 1966, pp. 355–73 (henceforth 'Abolitionist Pressures'). Castlereagh, intent on the reconstruction of Europe after the long period of war, found the slave trade question hampered his diplomacy and that the agitation in England designed to force his hand encouraged foreign powers to raise the price of their concessions.

8 Britain, France, Austria, Prussia, Russia, Portugal, Spain and Sweden.

search each others' ships. France, Spain and Portugal objected vigorously to these proposals and Castlereagh only succeeded in getting a declaration appended to the Act of Vienna, condemning the slave trade as 'repugnant to the principles of humanity and universal morality'.[9] It was not declared illegal, no time limit was fixed for its abolition, no international machinery against it was established, there was no commitment to definite action and even the arrest of slavers was not sanctioned. Such questions were to be the subject of individual negotiations between interested nations.

Nevertheless the declaration was a milestone in the struggle against the traffic, for it marked the general acceptance by the great powers of the principle that the trade was an evil, which, however profitable, must be ended for humanitarian reasons. It was thus the beginning of the process by which 'native welfare' became an accepted matter of international concern.

The discussions of 1814–15 set the pattern for the future attitudes of the various powers towards the slave traffic. Britain had emerged as the great protagonist of a cause she regarded as morally right, quite apart from the fact that it was to her obvious advantage to prevent the trade being simply diverted to the benefit of rival merchants and colonial powers. The strength of public feeling on the subject had been clearly demonstrated by a flood of petitions from all over the country containing nearly a million signatures[10] and by addresses carried in both Houses of Parliament. Henceforth it was clear that the abolition of the foreign slave traffic was an important political issue which no British government could afford to ignore. Castlereagh, normally more secretive, was careful to see that his efforts to secure it were fully recorded in Blue Books and other publications for all to see.[11] His successors followed suit. As time went on this became increasingly irritating to other powers, who found themselves in the invidious position of appearing to defend the slave trade when they opposed British policy.

Other nations were from the first sceptical of British humanitarianism. In France, as in England, an anti-slavery movement had developed in the late eighteenth century. Slavery had actually been abolished, at least in theory, during the French Revolution, largely in the vain hope of regaining St Domingue, the greatest of the sugar-producing colonies, which had been lost as a result of a slave revolt in 1792. However, colonial pressure and conservative reaction at home led to its restoration under Napoleon.[12] Only

9 Declaration of the Eight Powers, relative to the Universal Abolition of the Slave Trade, 8, Feb., 15; Annexe XV to the Treaty of Vienna, 9, June, 15; E. Hertslet, *Commercial Treaties*, I, p. 9.

10 This was particularly impressive since Britain's total population was thirteen million. For British public feeling and the activities of the abolitionists at this time, see Klingberg, *Anti-Slavery Movement*, pp. 131 ff., and Fladeland, 'Abolitionist Pressures', pp. 355 ff.

11 Harold Temperley and L. M. Penson, *A Century of Diplomatic Blue Books*, 2nd Impression, London 1966, p. 3

12 For a brief outline of the movement and the events of the revolution and empire see A. G. Hopkins, *Economic History of West Africa*, London 1973, p. 114; Daget;

the outbreak of war with England in 1803 had prevented a significant revival of the French slave traffic.[13] In 1814, the king, Louis XVIII, and his ministers may have been reasonably sympathetic to the anti-slave trade cause or at least, have appreciated the need to defer to British pressure,[14] but the planters and commercial classes thought Britain merely wanted to prevent a revival of French trade and colonial prosperity. They believed that she was able to afford the luxury of abolition because her colonies were well stocked with slaves whereas theirs, ravaged as they had been by wars, disorders and foreign occupation, were in dire need of labour,[15] particularly St Domingue, which they still hoped to recover.[16] France therefore was willing to accept abolition in principle but only after she had had time to restock her dependencies.[17]

Portugal and Spain were equally suspicious of British motives. Portugal was deeply involved in the slave traffic. Not only was she a major carrier[18] but in her African colonies, particularly Angola, the trade was an important branch of commerce and source of revenue.[19] In addition during the war her Brazilian empire had found a new prosperity producing tropical goods for a growing export market and was badly in need of labour. The Spanish island of Cuba was also developing into an important sugar producer and likewise suffered from an acute shortage of slaves. Both powers feared that

Gaston-Martin, *Histoire de l'esclavage dans les colonies françaises*, Paris 1948, pp. 166 ff. In some colonies the abolition of slavery during the Revolution was not implemented. For the evolution of French opinion and the growth of the anti-slavery movement in the early nineteenth century see Y. Debbasche, 'Poésie et Traite: L'Opinion Française sur le Commerce Négrier au Début du XIXe Siècle', *Revue Française d'Histoire d'Outre-Mer*, xlviii, 1961, pp. 311–52.

13 During most of the eighteenth century France was, with Britain and Portugal, a major carrier of slaves. However, with the outbreak of war during the French Revolution, her slave traffic dropped to insignificance. For a discussion of the French traffic see Curtin, *Slave Trade*, ch. 6.

14 The king had gained his throne with the help of Britain and her allies, who had defeated Napoleon, and his position was far from secure.

15 For French views see Daget, p. 18; Debfasche, pp. 311–16; Gaston-Martin, p. 248; Webster I, p. 271, II, p. 461; Fladeland, 'Abolitionist Pressures', pp. 355–66. It was widely believed abroad that British planters had deliberately stocked up with slaves during the period when the traffic was under attack and that only when they were well supplied and there was also a sugar glut, had abolition been carried. British abolitionists found this accusation embarrassing, see A. F. Corwin, *Spain and the Abolition of Slavery in Cuba 1817–86*, Texas 1967, pp. 26–7.

16 Gaston-Martin, pp. 251, 262; Fladeland, 'Abolitionist Pressures', pp. 364–5

17 Hence her agreement to limit the traffic to her own colonies and accept abolition in 5 years.

18 Curtin, *Slave Trade*, ch. 7

19 James Duffy, *Portuguese Africa*, Harvard 1959, p. 142; Richard J. Hammond, *Portugal and Africa, 1815–1910*, Stanford 1966, p. 42; Mabel V. Jackson (Haight), *European Powers and South-East Africa*, New York 1967 (2nd ed.), pp. 62 ff. For the role of the traffic in Angola see Jan Vansina, *Kingdoms of the Savanna*, Wisconsin 1966, pp. 185 ff.

any attack on the trade would damage the economy of their possessions and alienate their colonists.[20]

France, Spain and Portugal therefore fiercely opposed the British proposals, particularly the suggestion that reciprocal rights to search merchant ships be granted to the navies of the powers who signed the Act of Vienna. Since only Britain had sufficient naval forces to take effective action against slavers, this would be tantamount to giving her the right to police the seas.[21] Such a concession would have been viewed, especially in France, as an affront to the national dignity[22] and Britain was suspected of asking for it in order to interfere with the trade of rival commercial and maritime powers by harassing their shipping, the memory of her high-handed actions during the war encouraging such beliefs.

The stage was thus set for the next seventy years. On the one side was England, determined to wipe out the slave trade, convinced of the righteousness of her cause, willing and able to police the seas, demanding the co-operation of the maritime nations and the moral support of those powers not directly concerned with the traffic. On the other were France and Portugal, opposing Britain's demands, deeply suspicious of her motives and firmly convinced that her anti-slavery policy cloaked political and economic ambitions in Africa and elsewhere. For many years the United States, Spain and Brazil, independent from 1822, also resisted British pressure.[23] Each power had its own reasons for countenancing the traffic and none believed in British humanitarianism. Consequently measures proposed to combat the trade were rarely considered on their merits but were inextricably bound up with questions of maritime rights, colonial and commercial rivalry and national pride.

To the end of his life,[24] Castlereagh worked for an international treaty along the lines he had laid down at Vienna. In 1816 he convoked a conference of the ambassadors of France, Austria, Prussia and Russia, hoping that it would constitute itself into a permanent bureau to collect information about the slave traffic, negotiate with recalcitrant powers and organise a Christian league against the trade.[25] His efforts were in vain. The conference petered

---

20 For a discussion of the whole position with regard to Brazil see Bethell, *Abolition*, pp. 1–15; for Cuba see Corwin, pp. 22 ff.; see also Webster, II, p. 416; W. L. Mathieson, *Great Britain and the Slave Trade 1839–65*, London 1929, pp. 7–8. Wartime developments had seriously weakened the power of both countries over their colonies.

21 Reciprocity would be a myth anyway, as few if any slavers used the British flag and direct British participation in the traffic waned rapidly, especially after it became a felony in 1811; see Herrington, p. 72.

22 In France, recently humiliated by her defeat in the Anglo-French wars, concessions to Britain were regarded as unpatriotic and the slave trade issue was thus tied up with the question of national revival, Daget, p. 30.

23 For the winning of their co-operation see below, pp. 14–20.

24 In 1822

25 The protocols of this conference, which held a number of meetings, are in

out, foundering on the opposition of France, supported by Russia.[26] Spain and Portugal never co-operated, Austria and Prussia paid only lip service to the cause. No power, it was clear, would surrender any of its rights unless it was directly in its interests to do so. Castlereagh's hopes of an international agreement carried out under the supervision of a permanent bureau were not to come near to realisation for another seven decades.

However, concessions which could not be obtained as part of a general treaty could still be extracted by negotiations with individual powers. By bribery and cajolery,[27] agreements were eventually reached with Spain and Portugal allowing the right to search, reciprocal in theory, and providing for the establishment of mixed commission courts for the trial of slavers.[28] A similar treaty was signed with Holland. These agreements only partially outlawed slaving. Portugal's traffic between her own ports south of the Equator remained legal; so did the Spanish trade south of this line until 1820. This greatly handicapped the British anti-slave trade squadron as Spanish (until 1820) and Portuguese slavers found north of the Equator could claim that they had been blown off course or make other excuses for their presence. The treaties also had grave defects. For instance, a slaver could not be convicted unless captives were actually found on board. Cornered vessels could therefore escape conviction by landing their slaves, or even by throwing them overboard; while, on the other hand, naval officers shadowing slavers on the African coast were tempted to wait until they loaded, or even to force them to load their cargoes in order to arrest them. To remedy this, later agreements allowed ships to be condemned if they were found to be equipped for the traffic.[29] This made the transatlantic voyage more ghastly as slavers, to minimise incriminating evidence, now sailed with open gratings instead of air scuttles and used split bamboo stalks instead of planks for slave decks.[30]

FO 84/1 and 2. Among its objects was the suppression of the operations of the 'Barbary' pirates who captured Christians in the Mediterranean and held those who were not ransomed in slavery in Muslim North Africa.

26 For the French part in this British defeat see Daget, p. 24.

27 Spain was paid £400,000 for agreeing to prohibit the traffic north of the Equator from 1817 and south of it from 1820 and accepting the right to search. British methods of cajolery employed at various times to secure treaties included threats of unilateral action against slavers, refusal to ratify treaties on other issues or to help negotiate loans on the London money market, and the withholding of diplomatic recognition from newly independent Latin American states, see Corwin, pp. 28–32.

28 These courts contained representatives from the signatory powers. For their functioning see L. Bethell, 'The Mixed Commissions for the Suppression of the Trans-Atlantic Slave Trade in the Nineteenth Century', *Journal of African History* (henceforth *JAH*) vii, 1, 1966, pp. 79–93.

29 All these treaties are in Hertslet, *Commercial Treaties*, I and II.

30 Herrington, pp. 155–6. For descriptions of the horrors of the Atlantic crossing, or middle passage, see Lloyd, pp. 31 ff.; D. P. Mannix and M. Cowley, *Black Cargoes: A History of the Atlantic Slave Trade 1518–1865*, New York 1962, ch. 5. For a discussion of the mortality rates on the voyage see Curtin, *Slave Trade*, ch. 10.

These treaties were of considerable importance, however, for they brought into being an international maritime police force, the Royal Navy, armed with its right to search, and international courts for the suppression of the slave trade. They were the foundations upon which Castlereagh's successors were to build, until finally Britain was at the centre of a great network of treaties which made her, as far as the slave trade went, the undisputed policeman of the high seas. No other nation had such far-reaching powers, or for that matter had assumed such responsibilities. Gradually all the maritime states of Europe and America were drawn permanently into the net with one vital exception—France.

France and the treaty network

On his escape from Elba Napoleon had made a bid for British support by outlawing the French slave traffic.[31] This had forced King Louis XVIII, when he regained his throne in 1815, to declare it illegal[32] and to agree to co-operate with the other great powers to bring it to an end.[33] This engagement, however, was not honoured. The traffic under the French flag revived. The French navy did little to suppress it and the government contented itself with passing ineffectual laws.[34] In spite of the appeals of abolitionists the general public remained on the whole apathetic.[35]

The fall of the Bourbons, however, brought abolitionists to power, with a parliament sympathetic to the cause.[36] New laws were passed in 1831 and the same year the new king, Louis Philippe, anxious for British support,[37] signed a treaty accepting a very restricted right to search, to be exercised within a defined zone by warships individually authorised to do the job for a specific time only. This right could be revoked in case of abuse and slavers were to be tried by their own national tribunals under their own laws and not in mixed commission courts. The number of cruisers to be used against

31 *BFSP* III, p. 196, decree of 29 March 1815
32 *BFSP* III, pp. 198–9, letter of 30 July 1815 from Talleyrand to Castlereagh; Daget, p. 22
33 *BFSP* III, pp. 292–3, additional article to the 2nd Treaty of Paris, 20 Nov. 1815
34 Daget, pp. 25 ff.; Gaston-Martin, pp. 253 ff.; Herrington, p. 152; E. Maugat, 'La traite clandestine à Nantes au XIXe siècle', *Bulletin de la Société Archéologique et Historique de Nantes*, 1954, pp. 162–9. French courts usually acquitted slavers.
35 The abolitionist movement was of little importance until 1819 but thereafter some headway was made as people became more aware of the horrors of the trade. The abandonment in the late 1820s of the hope of regaining St. Domingue removed a powerful stimulus to supporting the traffic. However, maritime, colonial and commercial circles remained opposed to any concessions to Britain and the anti-slavery movement did not have the popular support it had in Britain, see Daget, p. 49; Debbasche; Gaston-Martin, pp. 261–4.
36 Hubert Deschamps, *Histoire de la traite des noirs de l'antiquité à nos jours*, Fayard 1971 (henceforth *La traite*), pp. 198–9; Daget, pp. 53–7
37 Daget, pp. 56–7; Gaston-Martin, pp. 262 ff

the trade by either power was not to be more than double that employed by the other and the whole agreement had to be renewed annually. These clauses were designed to disarm any suspicion that France was giving Britain jurisdiction over her shipping. To avoid friction in the execution of the treaty, a supplementary convention concluded in 1833 laid down rules of procedure for search in the form of detailed instructions for naval officers, and provided for the prompt payment of damages and compensation for wrongful arrest.[38]

Taken together these two conventions set the pattern for later treaties with European powers. The British Foreign Secretary, Lord Palmerston, dreaming of a league of all Christian states, hoped that other nations, particularly the U.S.A., Russia, Prussia and Austria would adhere to them.[39] By 1838, however, only such minor powers as Denmark, the Hansa Towns, Sardinia, Tuscany and the Kingdom of the Two Sicilies had done so, and in spite of British efforts the Atlantic slave trade was still a large-scale operation, taking between thirty and forty thousand slaves across the ocean annually.[40] At this point Thomas Fowell Buxton launched his campaign for an onslaught on the traffic by new methods which included increasing and concentrating the anti-slavery squadron, developing trade with Africa and signing treaties with African and Asian rulers.[41] He aroused considerable support mainly in non-conformist circles.[42] This fitted in well with Palmerston's policy of securing British strategic interests against French encroachments on the route to India, and of promoting British trade with the interior of Africa.[43]

38 Treaties of 30 Nov. 1831 and 22 March 1833, Hertslet, *Commercial Treaties*, IV, pp. 109, 115
39 Palmerston to Hummerlauer, 11 Nov. 1839, FO 84/291; for Palmerston's policy see R. J. Gavin, 'Palmerston's Policy towards East and West Africa 1830–65' (henceforth 'Palmerston's Policy'), Cambridge Ph.D. 1958, pp. 74 ff.
40 Curtin, *Slave Trade*, pp. 233–8. Professor Curtin estimates the annual average of slaves imported into the Americas in the nineteenth century as follows:

1811–20: 39,500	1841–50: 40,700
1821–30: 50,600	1851–60: 15,900
1831–40: 36,600	1861–70: 6,700

This may be compared with an estimated 60,000 a year during the peak period in the eighteenth century. The decline began in the 1790s probably due to the Anglo-French wars. After 1815 British abolition and the various anti-slave trade measures prevented a revival of the traffic to its old heights.
41 T. F. Buxton, *The African Slave Trade and its Remedy*, London 1968. This is a reissue, with an introduction by G. E. Metcalfe, of the 2nd edition, first published 1840. See below pp. 42 ff. for the results of his campaign in Africa.
42 See Howard Temperley, pp. 42–61; J. Gallagher, 'Fowell Buxton and the New African Policy 1838–42' (henceforth 'Buxton'), *Cambridge Historical Journal*, x, 1950, pp. 36–58.
43 *Ibid.* and Gavin, 'Palmerston's Policy', pp. 128 ff. These were the years when Mohammed Ali, the ruler of Egypt, was threatening his overlord, the Ottoman emperor, in the Middle East and Britain feared that he might triumph with French support. She also feared French designs in Ethiopia and North Africa. For the interaction of 'legitimate' trade with the slave trade see ch. 3.

He, therefore, pressed for agreements with Asian and African rulers as well as with the European powers.

Eventually, he concluded the treaty of 20 December, 1841 with France, Austria, Prussia and Russia. It followed the lines of the conventions with France except that it was a permanent agreement, the zone in which the right to search might be exercised was larger and there was no limit on the number of ships which any power might use on anti-slave trade operations.[44]

This treaty was a British triumph, but victory was short-lived, for the agreement stirred up a veritable hornets' nest in France where Britain was accused of trying to establish maritime supremacy and control world trade by getting a permanent right to search—a right which in practice would only be exercised against French vessels, since the other signatories had no shipping in the zone. The freedom of the seas, France's position as the champion of the lesser naval powers against British pretensions and French trade[45] were all said to be endangered. Although anti-slavery feeling was growing in the country as a whole, there was a great outcry in the Atlantic ports and the press, led by interested parties and supported by the parliamentary opposition. French opinion was already roused by cases of alleged British misuse of the right to search and by the unfavourable outcome of the Egyptian crisis.[46] The French parliament refused to ratify the treaty which thus fell victim to national pride and Anglo-French rivalry.

It remained in force for the other four signatories, however, and was still in force in the 1880s, having been acceded to by Belgium in 1848 and extended to the new German empire in 1879.[47]

The French agitation brought home to statesmen on both sides of the Channel the repugnance with which Frenchmen viewed the delegation to Britain of the right to search their merchant vessels. France was further alarmed by events on the West African coast, where Britain was signing treaties with African leaders providing for the suppression of the slave traffic

44 Hertslet, *Commercial Treaties*, VI, p. 2, the search zone ran from the American coast to 80 E. between 32 N. and 45 S. in the west and 45 S. and the coast of India in the east. It did not include the Mediterranean. The reasons for this omission are discussed on pp. 70–1 below.

45 French merchants were afraid that delays to merchant shipping might result in heavy losses, see Douglas Johnson, *Guizot: Aspects of French History 1787–1874*, London and Toronto 1963, p. 290.

46 For the treaty question see Johnson, pp. 193, 286–91; Gaston-Martin, pp. 271 ff.; B. Schnapper, *La politique et le commerce français dans le Golfe de Guinée de 1838 à 1871*, Paris 1961, pp. 28–9; G. Wozencroft, 'The Relations between England and France during the Aberdeen–Guizot Ministries (1841–6)', London Ph.D. 1932. For a discussion of Anglo–French rivalry see Henri Brunschwig, *L'avènement de l'Afrique noire du XIXe siècle à nos jours*, Paris 1963, pp. 53 ff.

47 Treaties with Belgium, 24 Feb. 1848, and Germany, 29 March 1879, Hertslet, *Commercial Treaties*, VIII, p. 61, XIV p. 1212. The treaty was modified in 1845 to allow for the fact that certain articles of equipment hitherto considered *prima facie* evidence of slaving were also carried on emigrant ships, 3 Oct. 1845, *ibid.*, VII, p. 79.

and the protection of legitimate trade[48] and where her naval officers had evolved a new and highly effective technique against slavers. Instead of cruising offshore in hopes of falling in with an offender, they now blockaded the rivers where cargoes were collected and loaded and they even landed and destroyed the barracoons where slaves awaited shipment. Considerable success had been achieved before the Law Officers of the Crown declared such action illegal since it involved the destruction of foreign property on foreign soil. To remedy this, the later treaties with Africans specifically authorised the British to suppress the slave trade by force in their domains. The preventive squadron was also strengthened. When in 1842 a Select Committee urged the government to sign more treaties, to reoccupy some abandoned forts and to take over the Gold Coast settlements, which had been run by a committee of merchants since 1825, the French took fright.

These events clearly heralded an era of greater British involvement in Africa. The French navy urged the government to counteract the growth of British power and prestige[49] and merchants complained of the activities of the British preventive squadron.[50] France decided to sign more treaties with African leaders herself, to increase her West African bases and end the right to search which still existed under the conventions of 1831 and 1833.[51] With some difficulty she persuaded Britain to accept a new agreement modelled on the Anglo-American treaty of 1842.[52] The right to search was abrogated, except for rights acquired by treaty to search the ships of other nations.[53] Instead each power was to keep at least twenty-six cruisers on the West African coast to operate against the slave trade but they could only

48 See below, pp. 46 ff.

49 For the role of the navy as the spearhead of French nationalism and centre of anti-British feeling see Brunschwig, pp. 53 ff.

50 Gavin, 'Palmerston's Policy', pp. 149–50   51 Schnapper, pp. 73 ff.

52 The Webster–Ashburton treaty of 9 Aug. 1842, articles 8 and 9, Hertslet, *Commercial Treaties*, VI, p. 859. This treaty bound each power to keep a force of 80 guns on the African coast to operate against slavers. They were to co-operate with each other, to exchange copies of instructions to naval officers on anti-slave trade operations and to enforce laws against slave trading. The U.S.A. had been singularly remiss about enforcement, and slaving under her flag increased in the late 1830s when the spread of the British treaty network prevented slavers from sheltering under other flags. Britain retaliated by illegally arresting American ships and taking them to New York. These articles were designed to stop such interference with American merchant shipping and the American squadron sent out to West Africa was instructed to use force against the British if necessary. The United States refused to concede the right to search, fearing Britain might use it to harass American shipping and being reluctant to abandon her traditional policy of policing her own flag. See Warren S. Howard, *American Slavers and the Federal Law 1837–62*, Berkeley and Los Angeles 1963, pp. 30 ff.; Alan R. Booth, 'The United States African Squadron 1843–1861' in J. Butler (ed.), *Boston University Papers in African History*, I, Boston 1964, ch. 5; H. G. Soulsby, *The Right of Search and the Slave Trade in Anglo-American Relations, 1814–62*, Baltimore 1933, pp. 118 ff.

53 In the case of France this was limited to those minor powers who had acceded to the conventions of 1831 and 1833.

stop each other's merchant vessels to verify their right to fly their flag, and the procedure to be followed on such visits was laid down in joint instructions to naval officers. Any anti-slave trade treaties concluded with African leaders by either France or Britain might be adhered to by the other power and if force was to be used they were to co-operate. This convention was to run for ten years.[54]

As a measure against the slave trade it proved disappointing.[55] Both nations were intent on building up their power on the coast but, whereas the British regarded the suppression of the slave traffic as directly in their interests and necessary to the growth of their already flourishing legitimate trade,[56] the French with slighter commercial interests, were generally unwilling to interfere with a traffic which often complemented legitimate commerce.[57] Unlike Britain, France failed to negotiate treaties with Spain, Portugal and Brazil enabling her to search their ships, nor did she assume powers to deal with slavers who flew no national flag.[58] The value of her West African squadron was thus very limited. There is even evidence that at times it deliberately kept out of the way of slavers[59] and in 1849 its size was reduced.[60] When the convention expired in 1855 neither power considered it worth renewing.

By this time, however, the transatlantic slave trade had been much reduced by the closure of most of the markets of the western world, as one by one the various powers either took effective measures to suppress it or abolished slavery.[61] Cuba was the only remaining bastion of the traffic and most slavers bound for the island flew the American flag as the United States

54 Convention of 29 May 1845, Hertslet, *Commercial Treaties*, VII, pp. 338 ff
55 Schnapper, pp. 78 ff
56 For the connection between the two see chapters 2 and 3 below.
57 For example see C. W. Newbury, *The Western Slave Coast and Its Rulers* (henceforth *Slave Coast*), Oxford 1961, pp. 42–3.
58 Britain signed a comprehensive treaty with Spain in 1835, see Hertslet, *Commercial Treaties*, IV, pp. 440 ff. She assumed the right to deal with vessels not using a national flag by Act of Parliament in 1839 after it was found that slavers could avoid conviction by this means. For the treaties with Portugal see below, pp. 23–4. The French did, however, on occasion apprehend slavers without flags, see Denise Bouche, *Les villages de liberté en Afrique noire française 1887–1910*, Paris and The Hague 1968, p. 48.
59 Bouche, p. 56 note 28
60 Hertslet, *Commercial Treaties*, VIII, pp. 1061–2. This was after the revolution of 1848. However, Bethell states that the use of the French flag by European slavers had declined as a result of the conventions of 1831 and 1833 and that there was no significant revival after 1849, see *Abolition*, pp. 96, 263 note 1.
61 The traffic to the British, Dutch and Danish colonies had long ceased. Imports into the French colonies declined in the 1830s and slaves were emancipated in 1848, see Curtin, *Slave Trade*, pp. 80–4, 234; Bethell, *Abolition*, p. 25. The Latin-American republics outlawed the traffic after they won their independence from Spain, see Corwin, pp. 30–2; J. F. King, 'The Latin American Republics and the Suppression of the Slave Trade', *Hispanic American Review*, xxiv, 1944, pp. 387–411. The U.S.A. imported few slaves in the nineteenth century, see Curtin, *Slave Trade*, pp. 72–5, 234. The greatest single importer of the century was Brazil and in 1850, impelled by

had shown little zeal in carrying out the agreement of 1842.[62] Matters took a new turn in 1857-8 when Britain began to seize American slavers and harass American merchant shipping in the Caribbean. She admitted that she had no right to search genuine American ships but maintained, as she had always done, that she must be allowed to visit all vessels to establish their true identity. There was an outcry in America and the United States countered with claims for compensation.[63] Britain ceased her harassment but opened negotiations with America and France to find a method of preventing slavers from fraudulently using their flags.[64] Eventually they agreed that there could be no right of search unless sanctioned by treaty, but a vessel must show her flag to a foreign man-of-war and, if the commander had reason to suspect that she was not entitled to it, he might visit her. Detailed instructions on procedure were issued to the naval officers of all three powers.[65]

On the eve of the American Civil War, the United States finally began to take active measures against slavers[66] and after the outbreak of hostilities, when her cruisers were needed for other duties, she signed a treaty with Britain granting her the long sought right to search.[67] This, together with measures taken by the Cuban authorities to end smuggling, virtually ended the Atlantic slave trade.[68]

The British treaty network was retained, however, as a safeguard against its revival and because slaves were still being exported from Africa to the Middle East and the islands of the Indian Ocean. The arrangement with France also remained unchanged and the instructions to naval officers,

domestic considerations and spurred on by unremitting British pressure including high-handed operations against slavers in her territorial waters, she finally took effective action against the trade which had been illegal since 1831. This dramatically reduced the numbers of slaves crossing the ocean, see above, p. 16, note 40. For the long struggle against the Brazilian traffic see Bethell, *Abolition*.

62 The treaty failed to stop slaving under the American flag for while it stopped the British from arresting suspect 'American' slavers who stood on their rights, the American squadron on the African coast was rarely an effective policing force. The U.S. navy was too small and had too many commitments to spare adequate ships for the job and much time was wasted sailing to and fro from the Cape Verde Islands where the squadron was based until 1858, to the slaving coasts and on cruises to Madeira to keep up the health and morale of the crews. A number of captures, however, were made on both sides of the Atlantic and slavers had to resort to various devices in order to use American ships. The British also seem to have arrested some American slavers, presumably when their right to fly the flag was in doubt. For a full discussion and lists of captures see Howard, pp. 41 ff. and appendices; see also Booth; Soulsby, pp. 118 ff.

63 For a discussion of the whole question see Soulsby, pp. 157 ff.

64 Soulsby, pp. 168 ff.   65 *BFSP*, 1859-60, pp. 706-9

66 She built up her forces in the Caribbean and made seven captures in 1860.

67 Treaty of Washington, 7 April 1862, Hertslet, *Commercial Treaties*, XI, pp. 621 ff. Slavers subsequently again resorted to the French flag, Howard, p. 64.

68 Although small numbers of slaves continued to be smuggled over until near the end of the century.

redrawn in 1867, were still in force in the 1880s and were applied on the eastern shores of Africa.[69]

Their whole tenor was to discourage visiting and thus minimise friction between Britain and France. British officers were warned not to visit a French vessel unless they had good grounds for suspecting that she had no right to fly the flag—a matter in which a trained seaman, it was said, should make no mistake. A suspect might be hailed, warning shots fired and a commissioned officer, if possible, might then be sent to examine her papers. He made the visit at his own risk, and was to proceed 'with all possible courtesy and consideration', causing the minimum delay. On no account was he to search the vessel or ask about her cargo and commercial operations. His job was strictly to look at the papers which established her identity.[70] If these were in order he and her master were to draw up a full report of his visit. If it was deemed unjustified or had been incorrectly conducted, indemnity might be claimed. If there were grounds for suspicion, the merchantman was to be taken to the most accessible French port and turned over to the authorities for trial. If condemned, she was to be returned to the captor, but if she was acquitted compensation was to be paid.

There was a glaring defect in the whole arrangement. If a slaver was entitled to fly the French flag, British naval officers could take no action against her. As the British Consul-General in Zanzibar, Colonel Euan Smith,[71] complained:

> However great may be the certainty that a French dhow[72] is carrying a large cargo of slaves, the English officer stopping her upon the high seas has no right whatever either to take steps for the liberation of the slaves or even to interfere with the voyage of the dhow. . . . Though the dhow be full of slaves, and although these were to clamour for assistance, the English officer would be wholly unauthorized to do anything to assist them.[73]

Britain had to rely on France to police her own flag and this was not adequately done.

In the early 1880s a flourishing slave trade existed in eastern African waters. Slaves were exported from the mainland to Zanzibar, Pemba,

69 The British version of these instructions is in *Instructions for the Guidance of H.M. Naval Officers Engaged in the Suppression of the Slave Trade* (henceforth *Instructions*), 1882 edition.

70 In the case of French ships the *acte de francisation* and the *congé*. In the case of British ships, French officers were to see the certificate of registry and the ship's articles. French vessels also carried lists of crews and passengers, which together with the *congé* authorising the voyage, had to be renewed. The *acte de francisation* was a permanent document.

71 Later Sir Charles Euan Smith, Consul-General, Zanzibar, 1887–91

72 Strictly a single-masted ship of *c.* 200 tons used in the Arabian sea, but the term is used commonly to denote any Arab ship in East African waters.

73 Memo by Euan Smith, 31 July 1889, FOCP 5977

Madagascar and the Comoro Islands, and across the Red Sea to Arabia.[74] This was a smuggling traffic usually carried on by small African or Arab craft.[75] Residents of the French island of Nossi Bé, off the west coast of Madagascar, of Mayotta in the Comoros, and of the French base at Obock on the Gulf of Aden, might sail under the protection of the French flag. French local officials, anxious to build up their small carrying trade and to increase their influence, did not enquire too carefully into the origins, character, or real residence, of those to whom they granted the use of their colours, nor did they ensure that regulations to prevent their abuse were carried out or even understood.[76] Thus in 1881, when Captain Brownrigg and four members of the crew of the British depot ship, H.M.S. *London*,[77] were killed off Zanzibar by the occupants of a dhow flying French colours, it transpired that the master of the craft had had his flag and papers a long time and, believing they were issued to him personally and not to the vessel, he took them with him to whatever dhow he commanded.[78] France, whose supervision was clearly lax, disclaimed responsibility on the grounds that the dhow was not the precise one for which the papers had been issued.[79] The French squadron in the Indian Ocean was too small and had too many other commitments to police so large an area[80] and in 1889 Euan Smith could not recall a single case of a French cruiser capturing a slaver in East African waters.

The French made certain that the masters of their vessels knew that Britain had no power over them. In fact Monsieur Lacau, French Consul-General in Zanzibar in 1889, admitted to Euan Smith that it had been customary to tell them that it was their duty to treat British officers who stopped them 'with as much rudeness and resistance as could be safely indulged in.'[81] When the British, taking the only recourse open to them against a French slaver, reported it to the nearest French authorities, not only had the culprit time to escape, but French officials usually proved unwilling to admit the charges.[82] As in the days of the Atlantic Trade, France appeared more concerned to protect the dignity of her flag than to suppress the slave traffic. In her defence it must be said that Britain could point to comparatively few actual cases of French dhows known to have

74 See below ch. 2.
75 These vessels might be owned by Indians. Occasionally a European-built schooner was captured in Madagascan waters.
76 François Renault, *Lavigerie, l'esclavage Africain et l'Europe*, 2 vols., Paris 1971, I, pp. 129–30
77 For the work of the *London* see below, ch. 2.
78 Report from C.-in-C. E. Indies, no 257, 3 June 1882, enc. in Admiralty to F.O., 5 July 1882, FO 84/1625
79 *Ibid.*
80 Some correspondence took place on this subject between the Ministry of Foreign Affairs and the Ministry of Marine in 1888, see FMAE to Krantz, 22, 24 and 26 Nov. 1888. FMAE/MDA/111.
81 Memo by Euan Smith, 31 July 1889. FOCP 5977
82 *Ibid.*

been slave trading and the French genuinely believed that Britain would use the right to search to interfere with their commerce.[83]

Clearly the whole question must be viewed in the light of the Anglo-French rivalry of the time. British officials certainly feared and opposed French expansion in the Indian Ocean. Clement Hill's[84] comment on the death of Brownrigg was revealing:

> Good may come of this after all. The French cannot support the action of their subject without laying themselves open to a heavy claim for damages for such an outrage on a boat of our navy; if they do not support it, it will show that their flag is no protection, and be a heavy blow to the influence they are striving to establish in East Africa.[85]

The French dilemma was clear. They had no wish to incur the odium and expense of effectively policing their flag and they could not delegate the task to Britain without damaging their prestige in Africa or arousing strong public feeling at home. In the early 1880s, therefore, they did little to solve the problem. The British fully believed that the slave trade flourished under the protection of the French flag, but representations to Paris were ineffective and, on the eve of the Berlin conference of 1884–5, not only was there no treaty with France, but the prospects of getting one seemed more remote than in 1815.

Portugal and the treaty network

The lack of a treaty with France was not the only loophole in Britain's agreements against the slave trade. The position with regard to Portugal was equally unsatisfactory. The treaties of 1815 and 1817 had left Portuguese slavers free to conduct the traffic between Portuguese colonies south of the equator.[86] This concession ended after 1822 when Brazil became independent, but it was years before Portugal recognised the fact. In the late 1830s slaving under her flag was flagrant and there was little public support for the anti-slavery movement. When the government, headed by an abolitionist, the Marqués de Sá da Bandeira, partially outlawed the traffic

83 For such suspicions see, for instance, Lacau to FMAE, 17 Feb. 1889, FMAE/MDA/111; Michel to Ministre, 21 June 1889, FMM/BB4/1229. Lacau believed that Britain might harass French dhows in order to get their trade into the hands of British Indians.

84 Later Sir Clement Hill, he did much of the 'spade work' on slave trade questions at the Foreign Office. He had accompanied Frere on his mission to Zanzibar in 1872 (see below), was a member of the commission which revised the instructions to naval officers in 1881 and again in 1891. He became an assistant clerk in 1886, senior clerk in 1894 and superintendent of African protectorates 1900–1905. He then retired and was elected to Parliament, and in 1911–12 was President of the African Society.

85 Minute by Hill, on Admiralty to FO, 13 Dec. 1881, FO 84/1607

86 *BFSP*, II, p. 348, IV, pp. 85–115

in 1836,[87] there was such violent opposition in both Angola and Mozambique that the Portuguese feared they might secede.[88] With a weak navy and an empty treasury Portugal was in no position to force the issue. Palmerston tried in vain to negotiate a new treaty and finally took the radical step of having Britain simply assume by Act of Parliament the right to arrest and try Portuguese slavers. Portugal deeply resented this gross infringement of her sovereignty[89] but was too weak to resist and eventually agreed in 1842 to a new treaty,[90] which followed the lines of the conventions of 1831 and 1833 with France and the treaty of 1841.[91]

The results were disappointing. From Angola the traffic was reduced and the Portuguese navy made occasional captures,[92] but many slavers simply moved their operations further north into the regions between 5° 12″ S and 8° S, which Portugal had long claimed but not occupied, and the slave trade became a pawn in the game of imperial expansion.[93] When Portugal condemned vessels caught in this area for slaving in her dominions Britain protested that she did not recognise Portuguese territorial claims. Portugal offered to take vigorous action against the traffic in return for such recognition but the British, who had a growing trade in the area, particularly around the Congo River, feared that once in control the Portuguese would impose protective tariffs which would drive out their merchants.[94]

The question cannot quite be seen as a straightforward weighing in the balance of the slave trade issue against British commercial interests with the scales coming down in favour of the latter, because Portugal's poor anti-slavery record, her military and naval weakness and the notorious corruption of her ill-paid officials made it doubtful that she could suppress the slave traffic even if her government sincerely wished to do so. She was not only a poor risk but her expansion would close the coast to British treaty-making and patrolling,[95] thus preventing Britain from acting herself.

87 Slaves could still be imported into Portuguese possessions by land and colonists could take up to ten with them from one colony to another, James Duffy, *A Question of Slavery*, Harvard 1967 (henceforth *Slavery*), p. 7.
88 F. Latour Da Veiga Pinto, *Le Portugal et le Congo au XIXe siècle*, Paris 1972, pp. 100–2. Portugal even asked Britain to guarantee her colonies in return for a treaty.
89 *Ibid.*, p. 102; Bethell, *Abolition*, pp. 164–5
90 The treaty is in Hertslet, *Commercial Treaties*, VI, p. 625. A measure of Portugal's weakness was that the treaty, unlike those with great powers, provided for mixed commission courts and for the care of freed slaves. These were annulled after Portugal abolished slavery in 1869, a concession later regretted in the Foreign Office, see Lister minute 27 April 1881, FO 84/1938.
91 See above, pp. 15–17, 23.
92 Duffy, *Slavery*, pp. 10–12, 33
93 Pinto, pp. 7 ff.; Roger Anstey, *Britain and the Congo in the Nineteenth Century*, Oxford 1962 (henceforth *Congo*), pp. 37 ff.
94 Anstey, *Congo*, pp. 44, 51–3
95 For a few years Portugal allowed the British to patrol her territorial waters but this right was revoked in 1853 on the grounds that it had been abused. She was anxious to prevent Britain from making treaties in areas she claimed.

The issue therefore remained unresolved and slaves continued to be shipped from the disputed coast. Many were also exported to French and Portuguese colonies from Angola and the Congo under guise of contract labourers.[96]

In Mozambique, which supplied slaves for Cuba and Brazil until these markets closed and thereafter still sent them to Madagascar and the Comoros and supplied contract labourers to Réunion, the trade was equally entrenched and flourished under the very eyes of officials. Governors who attempted to stop it provoked violent opposition from the colonists, were criticised by nationalists in the *Cortes* and received scant support from their home government.[97] British offers of help were rarely accepted and British cruisers, able to stop ships on the high seas only, found themselves virtually powerless. As the Consul complained in 1880:

> Locked out from the coast of supply, with little or no means of information at their command, they are condemned to cruise, either at random over a sea area of more than 500 miles square, in the hope of dropping perchance upon a dhow, in such a waste of waters a veritable 'needle in a bundle of hay', or to endeavour to cover a line of over 1000 miles in length, stretching from Cape Delgado, round by the Comoro Isles and the coast of Madagascar, to Cape St. Vincent.[98]

Generally only one, or at most two, ships were all that could be spared for this thankless task and often they were called away for other duties.

As in Angola, the Portuguese had neither the military nor the naval power even to occupy the lands they claimed, let alone to suppress the traffic. Even on the coast their hold was tenuous and in the Zambesi valley they held only a few posts.[99] The interior frontiers of Mozambique had not been defined by international agreement and their extensive claims had not been recognised by Britain.[100]

The slave trade had long been a cause of friction between Britain and Portugal when a new dimension was introduced into the situation by the arrival in the 1870s of the first British missions successfully to establish themselves in the Nyasa area in the hinterland of Portuguese Mozambique. They came in response to David Livingstone's impassioned plea to combat the slave trade by introducing Christianity, commerce and 'civilisation' to the source of the evil, the heart of Africa from which the slaves came.[101]

96 For this traffic see below, pp. 28–30.
97 A. J. Hanna, *The Beginnings of Nyasaland and North-Eastern Rhodesia 1859–95*, Oxford 1956, pp. 50 ff
98 O'Neill to Granville, no. 55 ST, 31 Dec. 1880, FO 84/1565
99 Hanna, ch. 1; see also M. D. D. Newitt, 'Angoche, the Slave Trade and the Portuguese c. 1844–1910', *JAH*, xiii, 4, 1972, pp. 659–72.
100 Portuguese sovereignty on the coast was defined by Article 2 of the Anglo-Portuguese Treaty of 28 July 1817, but there was no agreement on interior frontiers and Portugal claimed the Zambesi and Shiré valleys; see Hanna, ch. 2.
101 Roland Oliver, *The Missionary Factor in East Africa*, London 1965 (2nd ed.),

His appeal and subsequent writings in which he castigated Portugal for allowing the traffic in her territories,[102] attracted much public attention and interest in Britain. This was doubly dangerous for the Portuguese as the arrival of British missionaries in their hinterland was bound to set limits on their expansion if it went unchallenged and Livingstone's plans necessitated the opening of the country to free trade and allowing freedom of transit on the Zambesi, the highway to the interior. These were concepts contrary to the protectionist and monopolistic colonial policy of Portugal.

Several British missions established themselves in the Nyasa area in the late 1870s and early 1880s[103] and a Glasgow firm, the African Lakes Company, supplied them with stores and traded on the lake.[104] The British Government regarded the region as independent and made no claim to it. British subjects were there as private individuals operating at their own risk. Portugal, however, claimed both the Shiré river and tentatively Lake Nyasa. If the slave trade was to be combated by Livingstone's methods, these claims had to be resisted or the Portuguese must be persuaded to change their policy.

In this situation the initiative passed to the British Minister in Lisbon, the forceful Robert Morier.[105] Here was a man of vision determined to break the eternal round of British nagging and Portuguese parrying and procrastination, which built up resentment on both sides. He set out to enlist Portuguese co-operation in the twin tasks of opening the African interior to European commerce and ending the slave trade. He was fortunate that Ãndrade Corvo, the Portuguese Foreign Minister, had long been convinced that his country should cultivate good relations with Britain, the only nation who could protect her territories both at home and over-seas.[106]

By 1879 they had negotiated a masterly treaty admitting the principle of free transit on the water highways of Africa, including, of course, the Zambesi, providing for joint naval operations against slavers, and even permitting the Royal Navy to operate separately in the territorial waters of Mozambique at the discretion of the Governor-General, who was to be obliged to act on any information received from the British. In the interior combined action

(henceforth *Missionary Factor*), pp. 9–13; Hanna, pp. 3 ff. For Livingstone's own plea see David Livingstone, *Missionary Travels and Researches in South Africa*, London 1857 (henceforth *Missionary Travels*), pp. 673 ff.

102 See David and Charles Livingstone, *Narrative of an Expedition to the Zambesi and its Tributaries*, London 1865 (henceforth *Zambesi*).

103 Missions were sent out by the Free Church of Scotland, the Established Church of Scotland and the Universities Mission to Central Africa.

104 This company, originally called the Livingstonia Central Africa Company, was founded in 1878 and was closely allied to the missions. See Hanna, pp. 20 ff.; Oliver, *Missionary Factor*, pp. 37–8.

105 Later Sir Robert Morier, Minister in Lisbon 1876–81. For his policy, see Hanna, pp. 110 ff.; Anstey, Congo, ch. 5.

106 Pinto, pp. 123–8

against the traffic was to be considered and information exchanged by the two powers.[107] The whole idea, Morier explained,[108] was to:

> foster the idea of joint action and joint responsibility and *pro tanto* to remove the prevalent idea that we desire to monopolise not only the loaves and fishes but also the philanthropy of South Africa.

Morier was surely overestimating the value of treaties and underestimating the proven powers of the colonial authorities to resist directives from Lisbon, but his views were not to be put to the test. The Portuguese Government, at odds over the policy of co-operation with Britain, resigned and its successor, supported by the press and public, failed to ratify the agreement.[109] Thereafter the British Consul in Mozambique was again doomed to remain a helpless spectator of the slave traffic. His information and advice, freely tendered to Portuguese officials, went unheeded, and his only recourse was to the time-honoured but futile practice of exhortation and representation.

An abortive attempt to revive Morier's policy, based on the belief that Portugal could serve Britain's purpose in Africa, was made in 1884. The British Government, fearing that France's ratification of a treaty with a Tio ruler at Stanley Pool[110] was the prelude to French annexations on the upper Congo and the closure of that river to British trade, signed the famous Anglo-Portuguese treaty of 1884,[111] recognising Portuguese claims to the mouth of the Congo which she had long disputed for fear that Portugal would keep both the anti-slave trade squadron and British commerce out of the river. Now she preferred to recognise the sovereignty of the weak state of Portugal, her oldest ally in Europe, to that of stronger rivals. In return Portugal made tariff concessions, agreed to open the Congo and Zambesi to the trade of all nations,[112] promised to suppress slavery and the slave trade, granted Britain the right to search in the territorial waters of Mozambique,[113] undertook not to extend her East African frontiers beyond the confluence of the Ruo and the Shiré and agreed to protect missionaries of all denominations.

However, if the Foreign Office was prepared to advance hand in hand with Portugal in a dual effort to open Africa to civilisation, commerce and

---

107 In return for these and other concessions Britain was to combine with Portugal to build a railway from Lourenço Marques to the Transvaal. See Hanna, pp. 115–16; Pinto, p. 134.
108 Morier to Salisbury, no. 6 ST, 27 Jan. 1879, quoted Hanna, p. 116
109 Pinto, pp. 134–48
110 See below, pp. 53–4
111 Treaty of 26 Feb. 1884. For the negotiations leading to this treaty, see Anstey, *Congo*, pp. 100 ff.; Pinto, pp. 184 ff.; for the texts see Anstey, *Congo*, appendix A, pp. 241 ff.; Pinto, pp. 319–27.
112 A provision from which Britain as the foremost trading nation had most to gain, while avoiding the expense of taking over the riverain territories herself.
113 A face-saving proviso was made here allowing Portugal the same rights in Britain's South African waters.

Christianity, British traders, missionaries and abolitionists were not. In view of her past record they refused to trust her, and organised an agitation, which delayed the signature of the treaty until its rejection by Germany, finally killed it.[114] At the time of the Berlin conference, therefore, the only anti-slavery agreement with Portugal was the one signed in 1842 and it concerned only the export slave traffic which in spite of it still flourished on the coast of Mozambique.

The contract labour traffic

Britain treaties had also failed to stop a traffic which grew up in the nineteenth century in contract labourers, called by the French *libres engagés*. This arose out of the continuing need for workers in the West Indies, the Mascarenes and elsewhere as the slave trade declined and slavery was outlawed.[115] In determining whether the traffic was legitimate, the recruiting grounds were all-important. In areas where slavery and the slave trade existed[116] Britain believed the operation was simply a disguised form of slave dealing. Slaves were captured up-country, brought to the coast or to the Comoros, sold to recruiting agents, ostensibly freed, sometimes even furnished with a contract, and then shipped off to serve in distant lands. Alternatively, those already in captivity might be bought from their masters, the transaction being disguised as an advance of wages. The owners would then replace them with new slaves, or, if the labourers returned, demand the bulk of their earnings.[117] Either way the proceeding stimulated the slave trade.

The question had long been a cause of friction both at home and abroad. Britain herself recruited labour for her Caribbean colonies and Mauritius in India and elsewhere. In the middle decades of the nineteenth century she enlisted freed slaves and other peoples in West Africa, but soon found this gave rise to abuses including slaving.[118] Victims were kidnapped and sold to dealers in Sierra Leone, or bought from local chiefs on the Kroo coast by recruiting agents[119] and in the receiving colonies employers often failed to honour the terms of their contracts. In face of humanitarian, Parliamentary and international protest, Britain tried various ways of controlling this traffic but finally abandoned enlistments in West Africa.[120] She went on recruiting

114 See below, pp. 169–70
115 Britain abolished slavery in her colonies but not her protectorates in 1833, France in 1848, Portugal in 1876. The last western power to do so was Brazil in 1888.
116 Even if illegally as in the Portuguese territories.
117 There were many opportunities for fraud. For the methods resorted to by the Portuguese planters of São Tomé and Princípe see Duffy, *Slavery*, pp. 26 ff.; for French proceedings see Renault, I, pp. 132–6.
118 Howard Temperley, pp. 124–36, 234–5; for a detailed discussion of recruiting in West Africa see Asiegbu, pp. 34 ff.
119 Asiegbu, pp. 147–8
120 *Ibid.*, pp. 149–56. Asiegbu suggests that the desire to see labour employed in the

elsewhere, however, and abuses continued in spite of government regulations.[121]

The traffic from Africa was a serious bone of contention between Britain on the one hand and France and Portugal on the other during the 1850s, when the French were sending workers to the West Indies from the Congo[122] and West Africa,[123] and to the Mascarenes from Mozambique, Madagascar and the Comoros[124] and the Portuguese were shipping them to the Atlantic islands of São Tomé and Princípe.[125] In spite of intermittent scandals, British protests and even temporary renunciations,[126] the traffic continued in the early 1880s. At this time planters in Mayotta, for instance, were engaged in a brisk trade from Grand Comoro in victims enslaved on the island or obtained from the mainland especially to meet their demands.[127]

The argument as to the legality of these operations was continuous if sporadic. Britain herself enlisted labourers in the hinterland of Delagoa Bay and sent them to South Africa. Her officials denied that this was slave trading as the recruits came from areas where slavery was unknown and had themselves begun a spontaneous migration overland into British territories.[128] They protested volubly on the other hand when the French tried to enlist workers in Mozambique, saying that no African would willingly go to the French islands and that enlisting at the terminus of a great slave route such as Ibo was bound to stimulate slaving.[129] By 1884, the French authorities were trying to prevent abuses and the Portuguese were regulating the traffic to the French islands but, significantly, few labourers were forthcoming.[130] Recruiting in the Comoros, however, was unchecked. Moreover the Portuguese still sent over a thousand workers a year to Princípe and São Tomé, mostly from Angola but some came from further afield—Dahomey for instance.[131] Once on the islands they were virtual slaves and they never returned. With the development of the scramble for Africa, an escalation in recruitments could be expected as new colonial powers began

production of cash crops in West Africa was an important reason for the government's eventual obstruction of emigration schemes.

121 Howard Temperley, pp. 234–5. See also I. M. Cumpston, *Indians Overseas in British Territories 1834–54*, London 1953 and O. W. Parnaby, *Britain and the Labour Trade in the Southwest Pacific*, Durham, N. C. 1964.

122 Duffy, *Slavery*, pp. 21–2; Pinto, pp. 115–21

123 S. O. Biobaku, *The Egba and Their Neighbours 1842–1872*, Oxford 1957, p. 60

124 Duffy, *Slavery*, pp. 42 ff

125 *Ibid.*, pp. 8 ff.; Pinto, pp. 118–21

126 Napoleon III abandoned recruiting on the eastern coast of Africa in 1859 for instance.

127 O'Neill to Granville, no. 55, 31 Dec. 1880, FO 84/1565; Renault, I, pp. 133–4

128 O'Neill to Granville, no. 52 ST conf., 26 Nov. 1880, FO 84/1565; Duffy, *Slavery*, pp. 64–5 note 10, p. 71

129 O'Neill to Granville, no. 52 ST conf., 26 Nov. 1880, FO 84/1565. As O'Neill pointed out, slaves who had been some time on the coast could easily pass as free men for recruitment and their masters would replace them with 'raw' slaves from the interior.

130 Duffy, *Slavery*, pp. 89–91   131 *Ibid.*, pp. 96 ff

to look for troops and workers on the continent itself. As early as 1879 King Leopold II of Belgium was enlisting soldiers and labourers in Zanzibar.[132]

Under existing treaties this traffic could be carried on with impunity in both European and African vessels. Naval officers could not interfere even if victims were kidnapped and forced on board under their very eyes.[133] Ships carrying recruits could not be stopped and searched as slavers since technically the passengers were not being consigned into slavery. They had agreed, or so it was said, to contracts, and were travelling, often under official sponsorship, to countries controlled by European powers where slavery was illegal. The traffic from Grand Comoro escaped British interference for the additional reason that there was no valid anti-slave trade treaty with the ruler[134] selling the 'workers', and because they were transported in French dhows, which could not be searched.

The role of the British and Foreign Anti-Slavery Society

Where the treaties failed, however, Britain had evolved another way of dealing with the matter. The failure of others to observe their treaty obligations or to show zeal in the anti-slavery cause was proclaimed to the world through the medium of diplomatic Blue Books, the press and the British and Foreign Anti-Slavery Society[135] in the hope that public opinion in the offending nation might spur its government to action as well as to make it clear at home that Britain was doing all she could.

The society, founded in 1839 by the Quaker Joseph Sturge, was neither the first nor the only anti-slavery body but it was the only one to survive into the 1870s.[136] By the time of its foundation, slavery had been outlawed to Europeans in British colonies[137] and the apprenticeship system which replaced it in the West Indies had been abolished. The major battle in Britain had thus been won. Slavery still existed, however, in India and other

132 For King Leopold II's recruiting operations see thesis for the Université Libre de Bruxelles being prepared by Mr E. Vandewoude.
133 See Hill's minute on the revision of instructions to naval officers, 9 May 1882, FO 84/1630, in which he discussed the decision of the Privy Council on the case of the Portuguese vessel *Ovarense*, stopped by a British cruiser while carrying recruits from Sierra Leone to São Tomé, but subsequently released; see Duffy, *Slavery*, p. 82, fn. 45.
134 He was a rebel who had captured part of the island.
135 Henceforth this will be referred to as the Anti-Slavery Society in the interests of brevity.
136 For the early history of the society see Howard Temperley, pp. 62 ff. For its constitution see its own publication, *Slavery in British Protectorates*, London 1897. The archives of the society are in Rhodes House, Oxford. The society is still in existence and maintains offices in London.
137 This was outlawed in 1833. It is often erroneously said that all slavery was outlawed in the British Empire at this time.

British dependencies[138] and was widespread in foreign territories. The society was specifically formed to combat it everywhere but by means which were 'moral, religious and pacific' only—a reflection of its strongly Quaker membership.

It was essentially a middle class organisation, financed by the modest annual contributions of its members and larger donations from a few rich Quaker or non-conformist business and professional men, who often supported a wide range of philanthropic causes perhaps because they suffered from a sense of guilt at their wealth and believed that it should be used for social and moral improvement.[139] Members of the society often passed the torch on to their descendants. Peases, Sturges, Buxtons and Gurneys, for instance, served on the committee in the 1880s just as they had done forty years earlier.[140]

The society's motto was a picture of an African in chains, kneeling with arms raised in a gesture of supplication and inscribed 'Am I not a man and a brother'. It was truly the keeper of the national conscience as far as slavery was concerned. The only comparable body, the Aborigines' Protection Society, tended not to interfere in the question.[141] The secretary kept up a voluminous and far-flung correspondence with explorers, officials, business-men, and missionaries abroad, collecting information on slavery and the slave trade, which it disseminated through public meetings, lectures, letters to the press and its own periodical, the *Anti-Slavery Reporter*. It kept close watch on British policy freely tendering the government both criticism and advice. Moreover, it called several international conventions, thus gaining for itself the image of leading a world-wide crusade against slavery, and it kept in close touch with abolitionists abroad, made appeals to foreign rulers, and sometimes sent out its own fact-finding missions.

When necessary it could function as an important pressure group, using the techniques evolved by its predecessors in the early days of the movement —the calling of mass meetings, the circulation of petitions for signature and the sending of propaganda to the press and leading public figures. Of prime importance, through its members on both sides of the House, it could get questions raised and debated in Parliament and in the 1880s several members of Parliament actually served on its committee,[142] together with

138 For abolition in India and Africa see below, pp. 157 ff.
139 Howard Temperley, pp. 66 ff. Temperley also suggests that many of them enjoyed a sense of *richesse oblige* from their philanthropic work.
140 Lists of committee members were published in the *Anti-Slavery Reporter*. For a discussion of early members see Howard Temperley, pp. 66 ff.
141 This society was founded in 1838 by a Quaker. For its influence and activities see H. C. Swaisland, 'The Aborigines' Protection Society and British Southern and West Africa', Oxford D.Phil. 1967. Some persons belonged to both societies.
142 These included the president of the society, Arthur Pease, Alfred Pease, Sir R. N. Fowler, a Lord Mayor of London, and Sidney Buxton. In addition, among its non-member supporters was Sir John Kennaway, a prominent member of the Conservative Party and lay head of the Church Missionary Society. The Prince of Wales was

missionaries, prominent churchmen, retired consuls and other officials with experience of the slave trade.[143] Furthermore its correspondents and honorary members usually included the leading Africanists of the day.[144] Thus, although it was a small-scale enterprise run by a minute staff from modest offices in London, operating on a budget of from £1,000 to £2,000 a year in the 1880s[145] and with only a few hundred members[146] its close connections with official, parliamentary, business and ecclesiastic circles made it vocal and influential out of all proportion to its size. Foreign Office officials, aware of its nuisance potential, preferred to keep it friendly and often sought its advice, although they regarded its leaders as well-meaning busybodies.

In the early 1880s, with the Atlantic slave trade dead and slavery no longer legal in British India and its dependencies, much of the fire had gone out of the anti-slavery movement. Indeed, the society's secretary, Charles Allen, complained that neither the British Government nor the public were 'hearty in the cause'. He wrote:

> Our experience, during the last 50 years is that the Anti-Slavery enthusiasm of England among the general public has almost died out, and even when spasmodically excited seldom reaches to the point of opening their purse strings.[147]

The degree to which the movement was ever a truly popular one has still to be investigated, but it seems to have had considerable support earlier in the

Patron of the Society. For the lists of the committee and a commentary on the parliamentary activities of the society see the *Anti-Slavery Reporter*.

143 They included C. P. Rigby, formerly Consul in Zanzibar, J. V. Crawford, formerly Consul in Cuba, W. H. Wylde, a former head of the Slave Trade Department of the Foreign Office, the Rev. Horace Waller of the Universities Mission to Central Africa, and the Roman Catholic Cardinal Manning.

144 In the 1880s these included General Charles Gordon, H. M. Stanley, Emin Pasha, Dr. Schweinfurth and the Nyasaland missionaries Archdeacon Marples and Dr. J. Williams. In 1889 Commander C. Lovett-Cameron, H. H. Johnston and Cardinal Lavigerie were added to the list.

145 In 1884 for instance the society received £638 7s in subscriptions, £54 10s in legacies, £118 10s 4d in collections from churches in Britain and the West Indies and from its own meetings, £46 10s 1d from sales of the *Anti-Slavery Reporter* to non-members and the sale of advertising space. In addition it received an exceptional sum of £685 in donations to the Jubilee fund instituted to mark the fiftieth anniversary of the abolition of slavery in the West Indies and certain other colonies. It also received money from the rental of premises. Its total working budget in that year was some £2,000. In 1887 income was only £1,001 3s 5d, donations being only £129 7s 11d and subscriptions £634 2s 10d. The *Anti-Slavery Reporter*, V, 2, Feb. 1885, p. 305, and VIII, 1, Jan.–Feb. 1888, p. 28.

146 The society had under 200 subscribing members in 1882, about 300 in 1887 and just over 300 in 1888. Some of these subscribers, however, were societies, often women's groups such as the Evesham Ladies' Association which gave £1 2s 6d in 1882, and the Ladies' Negro Friend Society which gave £15.

147 Quoted in E. Glyn-Jones, 'Britain and the End of Slavery in East Africa', Oxford, B.Litt. 1956, p. 29.

nineteenth century.[148] Sustained interest, however, was limited to the middle and at times upper classes.[149] But these although numerically small were the vocal and politically important sections of the population. Until late in the century, they formed the bulk of the electorate, and by the time full adult male suffrage had broadened the base of political power the expansion of missionary activity in Africa and its close connections with the anti-slavery cause doubtless brought the movement support from at least the church-going members of the lower classes.[150] Certainly successive governments believed that action against the slave trade was popular in Britain, although it was clearly not a major concern of the electorate.

That the society was a factor to be reckoned with was shown in 1872 when Sir Bartle Frere enlisted its aid in launching a campaign to force the government to take action against the East African slave traffic. This led to the signing of the treaty of 1873, which outlawed the export of slaves from the territories of the Sultan of Zanzibar and to the subsidising of a monthly mail service between Aden and Zanzibar ostensibly to encourage legitimate trade in East Africa.[151] Frere was as much concerned with the protection of British interests in the Indian Ocean and Middle East as he was with the suppression of the slave trade and the episode well illustrates how a policy designed to secure British paramountcy could be presented as an anti-slavery measure (which it also was) and as such gain the support of the Anti-Slavery Society, sections of the public and Parliament. It also proved that public opinion could still be effectively aroused against the slave traffic.

The slave trade in international relations

Because it was often impossible to distinguish between a policy aimed at suppressing the slave traffic and one designed to further British commercial, strategic or political interests, the slave trade was an invidious factor in international relations. The subsequent history of the East African mail service subsidy is a good illustration of this point and merits some examination. In 1882 when the contract was due for renewal, the Post Office protested that it was not worth their while to pay £10,000 a year for a service which had little postal value.[152] But it soon became clear that it was wanted

148 The million signatures collected on petitions at the end of the Napoleonic wars bear testimony to this, see above, p. 11.
149 The British and Foreign Anti-Slavery Society drew its main support from the middle classes. However, earlier societies and Buxton's African Civilisation Society had aristocratic support, Howard Temperley, pp. 66 ff.
150 This subject has still to be investigated but for popular support of the missionary cause and the response to Livingstone's appeal see Oliver, *Missionary Factor*, pp. 9 ff.
151 See below, pp. 89 ff.
152 Postal revenue from the service was only £250 and the Post Office thought it unnecessary particularly as telegraphic communications had been established with

by the Foreign Office not for postal reasons, nor even primarily to combat the slave trade. The main object was to keep 'the carrying trade of East Africa and the influence it confers' in British hands.[153] The real fear was French competition. One official wrote:

It is no doubt important to save £10,000 a year, but if the result is to let Messageries Maritimes supplant the British Company on the East African Coast I fear it may prove a 'penny wise and pound foolish' policy.[154]

France, it was feared, would also take over the Zanzibar Post Office if the subsidy lapsed and possession of the Post Office 'is one of the causes that has given us our present commanding position'.[155] Sir John Kirk[156] thought it vital to keep 'the mainlines of merchant steamers in the Indian seas under our flag'. He said:

We will be very remiss, if we give the French a chance of extending their lines to the African coast in the direction of the Cape . . .

Kirk admitted that the British India Steam Navigation Company's offer to extend their service to make fortnightly calls at ports from Suez to Natal was beyond the 'requirements of a Slave Trade policy', but in view of the British operations in Egypt[157] he considered it most important not to leave the Red Sea ports 'in other hands'.[158]

The subsidy was recommended to Parliament once more as a means of combating the slave traffic by developing legitimate trade, but the discussions in the Foreign Office clearly show that it was not just the slave traffic that was being attacked, but also the commercial and political expansion of France. It could be, and was, argued that an increase of French influence at Zanzibar would be followed by a revival of the slave trade,[159] but against this one must set Kirk's belief that the *engagés* trade in the Comoros would

Zanzibar in 1879, see Alan Smith, 'History of the East African Posts and Telecommunications Administration 1837–1967,' Ph.D. Nairobi, 1971.

153 Hill minute, 9 June 1882, FO 84/1657

154 Pauncefote minute on Treasury to F.O., 22 March 1882, *ibid*. Messageries Maritimes was a French shipping line.

155 Miles to Granville, no. 55, 24 June 1882, *ibid*. For a discussion of the importance of the Post Office see Alan Smith.

156 Sir John Kirk, 1832–1922, accompanied Livingstone on the Zambesi expedition 1858–63, became Vice-Consul, Zanzibar, in 1866 and Consul-General, 1873–87. For his career see Sir Reginald Coupland, *The Exploitation of East Africa 1856–1890*, London 1939.

157 Britain attacked Egypt, defeated the Egyptian army on 13 Sept. 1882 and subsequently occupied the country.

158 Kirk to Hill, 16 Sept. 1882, FO 84/1657

159 As Kirk wrote: 'You may be quite sure that if we give France the opportunity she will not fail to run ships via Zanzibar to Madagascar. All that is then needed to ruin our work would be for France to make an arrangement with Zanzibar similar to the

be stopped if France annexed the islands. He thought that the planters of Mayotta and Nossi Bé were responsible for the abuse and that closer control by the French Government would end it.[160] Nevertheless, he opposed any encouragement of French designs on the Comoros, as this would bring under French protection the Comorans living in Zanzibar, an important section of the island's population, including most of the overseers and confidential servants.[161] One is left with the impression that, while the suppression of the slave trade was undoubtedly desired by vocal sections of the British public and was a clear British objective, those whose job it was to defend British interests abroad did not let humanitarian questions dictate their policy. They were happy, however, to present that policy to the world in an anti-slavery guise.

Other powers had always suspected British motives, sometimes unfairly. No documentary evidence exists, for instance, to show that the right to search was really wanted to hamper the trade of other nations. On the other hand, the fleet stationed in African waters to suppress the slave trade protected and was ordered to promote British commerce, and the treaties with African rulers often had hidden political implications[162] and might even open the way to thinly veiled British domination as, for example, in Lagos in 1851 and Zanzibar in 1873.[163] British pressure on Portugal and France to give up the *engagés* trade could be construed as an attempt to prevent Portuguese and French planters from getting essential labour, particularly as Britain herself controlled a vast pool of labour in India from which she supplied some of her own colonies. At times she allowed other nations to recruit there but the whole operation was regulated and watched with suspicion, and in 1882 she stopped Indian coolies from going to the French island of Réunion.[164] Yet at the time the activities of Queenslanders recruiting workers in the western Pacific, 'blackbirding', were probably as iniquitous as anything attempted by the French in Africa,[165] and contract labourers suffered ill-treatment in Britain's own colonies.

French suspicions of British motives were of such long standing and so universally held that Sir Villiers Lister, Assistant Under-Secretary at the

one she has with Portugal for the supply of native labour. We might then as well retire.' *Ibid.*
160 Mayotta was the only island in the Comoro group which was French at this time, the others being still independent. Kirk's view is substantiated by Father Renault's research which makes it clear that the French Government by the 1880s was trying to stamp out the abuses inherent in the system. See Renault, I, pp. 133–5.
161 Kirk to Granville, no. 121, 23 Nov. 1883, FO 84/1645
162 See below, pp. 46 ff. for the situation in West Africa. Kirk thought that the treaties signed with the Comoro chiefs in 1882 were useful proof that the islands were independent, Kirk memo, 29 Dec. 1882, FO 84/1623.
163 See below, 48–50, pp. 88 ff. The French were duly suspicious of both treaties.
164 Renault, I, pp. 134–5
165 Lloyd, appendix G, pp. 290–1; Anderson minute, 12 March 1884, FO 84/1683; Report enclosed in Ad. to FO 23 Dec. 1882 FO 84/1625. For the labour traffic in the Pacific see O. W. Parnaby. This traffic drew protests from the Anti-Slavery Society, see *Anti-Slavery Reporter*, iii, 6, June 1883, pp. 162–3.

Foreign Office, thought that any approach to France to end abuses in the *engagés* system on humanitarian grounds would simply meet with 'an incredulous sneer'. The French Ambassador in London was, he believed:

> probably the only Frenchman living who can understand the strong humanitarian feeling in Britain ... and who would not mistake it for hypocrisy concealing national and commercial jealousy.[166]

and he, after all, was of British ancestry and had had a British education.[167]

Portugal had equally strong reasons for believing that Britain was trying to force her to pursue a policy against the best interests of her colonies. The coffee plantations of São Tomé, for instance, depended on the supply of contract labourers, mainly from Angola. In Mozambique as late as the early 1880s the British Consul, O'Neill, thought the Portuguese were afraid to take action against the slave traffic lest it create 'bad blood and a desire for reprisal' among African chiefs. This they could not risk for their power was so nominal over most of their colony that security depended on the goodwill of these very chiefs, and Portuguese finances were so precarious that they could not afford the loss of revenue from any diminution of legitimate trade.[168]

The Portuguese colonists of Mozambique entertained the direst suspicions of the British in Nyasa, believing that every missionary and explorer was playing a political role with the ultimate aim of driving Portugal out of eastern Africa.[169] There is no evidence that the British Government had such intentions, but doubtless suspicion was increased by the appointment of a British Consul to Nyasa in 1883, to fight the slave traffic by exerting 'influence' over African rulers.[170] Influence could be all important in a situation where settlers were few and far from home and had no forces at their command. The extension of British influence depended upon the suppression of the slave trade. Portugal's influence, on the other hand, was actually being carried up country far beyond the territory she controlled, by *africanos*[171] trading in slaves and arms. O'Neill found them on the shores of Lake Shirwa (Lake Chilwa) in the far interior in 1883 and noted the ominous fact that they were teaching the Africans to look upon the British, who dealt in neither commodity, as enemies determined 'to subvert their customs and prevent them from getting those supplies which they are most eager to obtain'.[172]

In these circumstances it was hopeless to expect active co-operation from

---

166 Lister minute, 13 March 1884, FO 84/1683
167 W. H. Waddington, who went to Rugby and Cambridge.
168 O'Neill to Granville, no. 55, 31 Dec. 1880, FO 84/1565
169 Hanna, pp. 120–1   170 See below, p. 107
171 *Africanos* were Portuguese of colonial descent—often of mixed blood.
172 Quoted in Hanna, p. 61, although by the late 1880s the African Lakes Company was said to be in the habit of supplying guns and ammunition to African hunters to shoot elephants for ivory and other game for food, Johnston to Salisbury, no. 12 Af., 16 March 1890. FO 84/2051. For the arms trade see below, pp. 182 ff.

Britain's colonial rivals, at least until their rule was secure, their frontiers defined and their colonies more prosperous or, if they flourished, until they were assured of an adequate supply of labour to maintain their prosperity. It was natural that they should resent her 'holier than thou' attitude, her constant harping on treaty obligations, or the need for a treaty, her assumption of a watching brief over their labour policies, and her infuriating habit of making public the shortcomings of their anti-slavery efforts. This last practice had certain advantages, as Lister pointed out in connection with the Comoro labour traffic: The plan of speaking the truth and shaming the French ... saves H[er] M[ajesty's] G[overnment] from all apparent complicity in their malpractices.[173] It often failed, of course, in its main aim, for the French, or whichever nation was being pilloried, could, and did, simply deny the charges. When relations were good this could degenerate into a diplomatic game played by governments to save face and avoid more drastic action. Before the mid-1880s, when Britain's paramountcy over much of the African coast was resented but not seriously challenged, she indulged in the practice with impunity, but in times of tension it could be dangerous.

The slave trade and the scramble for Africa

By 1884 changes were taking place in Europe and Africa which were to put a different complexion on Britain's policy of suppressing the slave trade. New colonial powers had appeared on the scene. Germany, Italy, and King Leopold now had footholds in Africa and were competing with Britain, France and Portugal for territorial empires, while in Europe there was developing a tighter system of alliances and alignments[174] which made it questionable whether Britain could continue to play the game in the old way. Henry Percy Anderson,[175] who took charge of the African Department of the Foreign Office when it was formed in 1883[176] to replace the old Slave Trade Department, which had been in a state of suspended animation for two years, expressed his doubts when he received evidence from Consul Holmwood about French malpractices in the *engagés* trade:

> The question arises—what is to be done with Holmwood's evidence. According to what I am told in the old practice of the Slave Trade Department it would have been published in the Blue Book and have been given as food to the Anti-Slavery Societies, the risk being taken of French irritation. It seems to me personally doubtful whether at the present day we can treat Slave Trade questions as outside the ordinary rules of

173 Lister minute, 13 March 1884, FO 84/1683
174 See William L. Langer, *European Alliances and Alignments 1871–1890*, New York 1931, for the European background.
175 Later Sir Percy Anderson, 1831–96, in charge of the African Department from 1883, promoted Assistant Under-Secretary, 1894.
176 The Slave Trade Department dealt with African questions until this time—a significant reflection on British priorities in Africa.

diplomatic caution and courtesy, but I know this is not the view of those who have been trained in the Anti-Slavery traditions, who would advocate publicity—*coûte que* [?] *coûte* . . .[177]

In fact the appointment of Anderson opened a new era in Britain's African policy. Gone were the days when her main concern was the suppression of the slave trade. The era of patrolling the coasts and publicising the shortcomings of others now gave way to a period in which Britain defended her interests against other powers on the continent of Africa itself, but with one eye on the European situation. Anderson, determined to uphold British power and prestige, equipped with what has been called a 'first class chessboard mentality'[178] set out to counter all moves made by other nations with whatever means came readily to hand. This is not to imply that he was not genuinely interested in the suppression of the slave trade, but simply that, like others before him, he was prepared to use humanitarian questions when it suited him in the diplomatic game of chess.

In this he was assisted by the traditions which had grown up during the long struggle against the traffic. The fact that in the mind of the British public the trader plying his business, the missionary spreading the gospel and the consul watching over British interests were as much concerned in its suppression as the sailor patrolling the coast, gave an anti-slavery complexion to almost anything the British might do in those regions of Africa where slavery existed or raids took place. On the other hand, Britain's two greatest rivals on the continent, France and Portugal, were regarded as inveterate countenancers of the trade. Their records in this field contributed, together with their fondness for differential duties, to the British belief that they were bad rulers. Lister expressed typical views when he compared the Portuguese unfavourably with the 'worst savages' because they stopped 'all progress and legitimate trade and either connive at the S[lave] T[rade] or are powerless to prevent it';[179] while the French were:

> jealous and bad colonists, they oppress the natives, repel foreign capitalists and have to fall back upon Slavery, slightly disguised, for the labour required on their plantations.[180]

British rule, on the other hand, in British eyes, conferred two inestimable benefits upon subject peoples, free trade and the end of the slave traffic. The British public also took it for granted that Britain's rightful place was at the head of the anti-slavery movement, or indeed of any humanitarian movement, and Parliament was prepared to sanction at least a modest expenditure for the cause which would not have been countenanced for other reasons.

177 Anderson minute, 12 March 1884, FO 84/1683
178 Wm. R. Louis, 'Sir Percy Anderson's Grand African Strategy 1883–96', *EHR*, lxxxi, 1966, pp. 292–314
179 Lister minute, 29 Jan. 1876, FO 63/1116
180 Lister minute, 13 March 1884, FO 84/1683

In the situation created by the scramble for Africa, it was clear that Britain's traditional methods of combating the slave traffic were no longer adequate. The appropriation of the seaboard by new colonial powers closed to the Royal Navy waters in which, hitherto, it had reigned supreme. These now became the territorial waters of European possessions and so were inviolate. There was no certainty that any of these countries would take any action against the export slave trade. In fact, unlike Britain, they had few treaty rights to stop the vessels of other countries on the high seas. Germany, for instance, could only search ships of the nations who had signed the treaty of 1841, Italy[181] and France could only police vessels of signatories to the conventions of 1831 and 1833. None of these agreements applied to the Red Sea, where both France and Italy were extending their rule.[182] The international situation made it no longer politic to expose the lapses of other powers in order to shame them into co-operation. But that co-operation was now more necessary than ever. In the long run it could perhaps be assumed that all the colonial powers would want to put down the traffic. They would not wish their territories to be used as raiding grounds and would probably not find it in their interests to allow slave caravans to cross their dominions or large-scale slave dealing to continue in view of the likelihood of international protests and public outcry at home, particularly as more sophisticated methods of mobilising labour were open to them. In the immediate future, however, they would all be anxious to make their new possessions viable and, in the peculiar conditions of African trade, rigorous action against the slave traffic might drive away the commerce vital to their settlements, deprive them of an important source of labour and alienate peoples whose friendship was essential. The temptation to countenance the trade might therefore be considerable and at the same time the expansion of European rule would give slave traders more opportunities to acquire European flags.

Britain was bound to continue her traditional policy of suppressing the slave trade, but it was now more than ever essential to force other powers to share the odium, expense and difficulties. At the same time she was to find opportunities of presenting certain of her policies in unwarranted humanitarian guise, which made them popular at home and difficult for foreign powers to oppose—opportunities which, under the able guidance of Anderson,[183] and with the surer hand of his master, Lord Salisbury,[184] she was quick to grasp.

181 Italy's rights derived from Sardinia's accession to the conventions of 1831 and 1833, on 8 Aug. 1834, Hertslet, *Commercial Treaties*, IV, p. 384.
182 See below, pp. 110 ff
183 Anderson's power varied with the character of the Foreign Secretary, but as a permanent official with great knowledge of his subject, his influence was important.
184 Robert Cecil, 3rd Marquess of Salisbury, Prime Minister and Foreign Secretary, June 1885–February 1886, Prime Minister, August 1886–January 1887, Prime Minister and Foreign Secretary, January 1887–August 1892.

Chapter Two

The Attack from the Periphery II:
British Treaties with
African Rulers and Leaders to 1884[1]

Origins of the treaty network

Britain only gradually became involved in the suppression of the slave trade on the African continent and to the Middle East. Originally she simply tried to cut off the supply of slaves to European colonies in the Mascarenes and India and the first treaties with African and Asian rulers were signed for this purpose.[2] No attack was launched against the traffic in Africa itself until after 1825 when the explorers Hugh Clapperton and Dixon Denham, back from an official mission to sound out possibilities of trading with West Africa, brought home the welcome news that two Muslim rulers in the far interior, Sultan Muhammad Bello of Sokoto and Shaikh Muhammad al-Kanemi of Bornu,[3] would stop selling slaves if Britain would supply them with European goods in exchange for other commodities.[4] Both recognised the potential value of contacts with Britain and hoped she would furnish them with arms. Bornu was believed to be the greatest supplier of slaves for the traffic across the Sahara to Muslim North Africa and the Middle East. Denham did not think the Shaikh or his people even knew that slaves were also sold to Christians on the Guinea coast,[5] which was against the tenets of Islam. Al-Kanemi had expressed disgust even at the Saharan trade. 'But,'

1 Including the Ottoman empire, Muscat and Madagascar.
2 Treaties with Radama (Madagascar) 23 Oct. 1817 and with Muscat 10 Sept. 1822, Hertslet, *Commercial Treaties*, I, p. 354, III, p. 265; see also R. Coupland, *East Africa and its Invaders*, Oxford 1938, chs. 5, 7; Sir John Gray, *History of Zanzibar from the Middle Ages to 1856*, London 1962, ch. 2; C. S. Nicholls, *The Swahili Coast, Politics, Diplomacy and Trade on the East African Littoral 1798–1856*, London 1971, pp. 218–224. An exception was the clause against the kidnapping and enslaving of Somalis in the General Treaty of 1820 with the pirates of the Persian Gulf but this was inserted on the initiative of the interpreter, did not prohibit the buying of slaves and was not enforced, see John B. Kelly, *Britain and the Persian Gulf 1795–1880*, Oxford 1968, pp. 420, 426; Nicholls, pp. 230–1.
3 The titular ruler of Bornu was Mai Ibrahim but real power was exercised by al-Kanemi.
4 For a summary of the aims and results of this mission see A. A. Boahen, *Britain, the Sahara and the Western Sudan 1788–1861*, Oxford 1964, pp. 54 ff.; for the explorers' own account see D. Denham and H. Clapperton, *Narrative of Travels and Discoveries in Northern and Central Africa, in the years 1822, 1823 and 1824*, London 1826, 2 vols.
5 Denham and Clapperton, II, p. 170

he had asked Denham, 'what are we to do? The Arabs who come here will have nothing else but slaves.' Then he had suggested a remedy: 'Why do you not send us your merchants?'[6]

The idea of combating the slave trade by developing legitimate or 'innocent' commerce was not new[7] but only now did it become official policy. Clapperton went back to Africa to sign a treaty with the Sultan of Sokoto, cement relations with Bornu and explore the routes into the interior from the Gulf of Guinea. It was hoped that consuls would be established in both states and that the rulers would end the slave traffic in the hope of growing rich by trading indigo, gum, ivory and ostrich feathers for European wares. The plan had a dual attraction: not only would the supposedly large trade of the western and central Sudan be diverted southwards into British hands but a blow would also be struck at one of the sources of the slave traffic of both the Sahara desert and the Niger coast. The mission was a tragic failure. Most of its members died *en route*. Clapperton himself succumbed to fever in Sokoto, having quarrelled with the Sultan, who was now at war with Bornu and rather naturally seized the arms intended for his enemies. Britain lost all confidence in him, and Bornu was never reached.[8] However, Richard Lander, the sole survivor of this ill-fated expedition, subsequently returned to Africa to make the vital discovery that the Niger and the Oil rivers of its delta could provide the long sought highway along which trade might flow from the Atlantic into the heart of the continent.

Private attempts to establish trading posts on the Niger soon followed,[9] supported by humanitarians in a marriage of commerce and philanthropy. As Macgregor Laird, the moving spirit behind one of these expeditions declared, his aims were 'nobler' than mere profit. He hoped to bring legitimate trade 'with all its attendant blessings' to the heart of Africa and thus destroy the slave traffic, the curse of the continent.[10] But these ventures were all defeated by the instability of the region and the fevers, which took a high toll of European lives. The task of opening the river to European trade proved too great for private enterprise and the government for many years refused further assistance. By 1837 all attempts to open direct trade with the interior had failed. Legitimate commerce at the coast, however, was

6 *Ibid.*, p. 172
7 P. D. Curtin, *The Image of Africa: British Ideas and Action 1780–1850* (henceforth *Image of Africa*), Wisconsin 1964, pp. 68–70, 125; Boahen, pp. 71–2.
8 Boahen, pp. 80–3. For Clapperton's account see H. Clapperton, *Journal of a Second Expedition into the Interior of Africa from the Bight of Benin to Soccatoo*, London 1966 (first published 1829).
9 Boahen, pp. 93–7; K. O. Dike, *Trade and Politics in the Niger Delta 1830–85*, Oxford 1966, 5th ed., pp. 60–4; C. C. Ifemesia, 'British Enterprise on the Niger 1830–1869', Ph.D. London 1959.
10 Macgregor Laird and R. A. K. Oldfield, *Narrative of an Expedition into the Interior of Africa by the River Niger, in the Steam Vessels Quorra and Alburka in 1832, 1833 and 1834*, 2 vols., London 1971 (first published 1837), pp..1–3.

increasing rapidly as a result of a growing demand for palm oil in Britain,[11] but against all expectations it flourished side by side with the slave traffic,[12] which was still a large-scale operation in spite of all the treaties, special courts and anti-slavery patrols, which tied up a substantial part of the British navy, cost money and took their toll in seamen's lives.[13]

Spurred on by this, Buxton launched his famous campaign. Claiming, erroneously, that the slave traffic was greater than it had ever been,[14] he called on Britain to save Africans from 'darkness and debasement' by showing them that men were worth more as labourers than as merchandise.[15] He advocated sending out freed slaves, who he believed had a better chance of survival than white men, to start farms and factories, introduce modern technology and spread Christianity.[16] They were to be financed and directed by Europeans. At the same time African rulers at the coast and in the interior were to be asked to sign treaties against the slave traffic and to allow free trade in their dominions, while the anti-slavery squadron was to be strengthened. He persuaded the government, which, coincidentally, needed the support of the humanitarians in Parliament, to send an expedition to the Niger to implement his plans.[17] It was a disaster. The Europeans suffered heavy mortality, the cause lost favour as a result and the mission was withdrawn.[18]

Nevertheless the campaign had far-reaching effects. It gave wide publicity to the slave traffic and popularised the idea that it might be eradicated by legitimate commerce and the spread of Christianity. It also gave an impetus

11 For the rise of this trade see N. H. Stilliard, 'The Rise and Development of Legitimate Trade in Palm Oil with West Africa', M.A. Birmingham 1938, p. 15.

12 See below pp., 54, 146 ff. for further discussion on this point.

13 LeVeen, pp. 99–102, estimates the annual average cost of the African squadron alone at £60,000 for the decade 1831–40. This does not count the cost of ships patrolling in the western hemisphere, the costs of bounties for naval crews, of special courts or the care of freed slaves, or the sums paid to Spain and Portugal to secure treaties. He gives an annual average of 500 men to 8.8 ships employed on anti-slavery work during this decade. Ward, p. 190, states that anti-slavery work occupied 1/5th of the navy. This includes the ships in the western hemisphere.

14 Buxton believed that 150,000 slaves were crossing the Atlantic annually, see Buxton pp. 204–5, whereas Curtin estimates that the annual average for the decade 1831–40 was 36,600, see *Slave Trade*, p. 234.

15 See Buxton, pp. 277 ff. Buxton's ideas were not new but he devised a coherent plan and persuaded the government to take some steps towards implementing it.

16 Chances for survival were greatest for people brought up in a tropical environment who had thereby acquired some immunity to tropical diseases. This was not known in the nineteenth century when survival was believed to be a question of race. For a discussion of this question see P. D. Curtin, 'Epidemiology and the Slave Trade', *Political Science Quarterly*, 83, 1968, pp. 190–216.

17 Howard Temperley, pp. 42–61

18 Since high mortality was to be expected and missionaries continued to go out to Africa in spite of it, Metcalfe suggests that there was perhaps an 'element of party spite ' in the withdrawal by a Tory government of a project initiated by their Whig predecessors, Buxton, p. xxiii.

to missionary work in Africa, particularly in modern Nigeria, and it encouraged freed slaves from the West Indies and Sierra Leone to return to their homelands.[19] Most important for the history of anti-slavery operations, it led to an increase in the preventive squadron and a systematic policy of signing treaties against the slave traffic with Africans and Asians—the initiation of a concerted move to gain their co-operation.[20] These agreements were to have unforeseen results.

Treaties with western African peoples

From the Senegal river in the north to Benguela in the south, African societies, great and small, had long sold their fellow men to European traders for textiles, beads, tobacco, cowrie shells, iron bars, brass rods, arms, ammunition, spirits, old military uniforms and other sundries.[21] Europeans also bought ivory, gold, gums, woods, pepper, beeswax, indigo, palm products, hides and other merchandise, but from the late seventeenth century they came primarily for slaves. To meet this demand Africans organised a system of supply which brought victims, mostly prisoners of war,[22] from areas where disturbances made them most readily available.[23] Thus the civil strife which followed the fall of the Oyo empire in the nineteenth century sent thousands of Yoruba across the Atlantic.[24] The rise and expansion of the Fulani[25] empire of Sokoto produced many Hausa and other captives, the fruits of wars, raids and kidnappings, while Dahomey's forays against her weak northern neighbours or the hapless Yoruba to the east provided further victims. Slaves came from far and near. Prisoners of the Fulani from the far interior as well as coastal Ijaw and nearby Igbo were exported from the Niger delta while unfortunates from the lower Congo, the Bihé plateau or even remote Katanga came through the ports of West Central Africa.

Slaves were simply one of many commodities traded back and forth in

19 See J. F. Ade Ajayi, *Christian Missions in Nigeria 1841–91*, London 1965, pp. 10 ff
20 Treaties had been signed earlier but not as part of a concerted attack on the slave traffic.
21 For a discussion of the arms and spirits traffic see ch. 4.
22 For other causes of enslavement see ch. 3.
23 For nineteenth century sources, see Curtin, *Slave Trade*, pp. 251–64; P. D. Curtin and J. Vansina, 'Sources of the Nineteenth Century Atlantic Slave Trade', *JAH* v, 2, 1964, pp. 185–208.
24 Thus apparently fulfilling a spine-chilling curse attributed by tradition to Alafin Aole, who when faced with revolt and forced to commit suicide, is said to have shot arrows to the north, south and west, saying: 'To all the points I shot my arrows will ye be carried as slaves. My curse will carry you to the sea and beyond the seas, slaves will rule over you, and you their masters will become slaves'. Samuel Johnson, *The History of the Yorubas, from the Earliest Times to the Beginning of the British Protectorate*, Lagos 1956 (first published 1921) (henceforth *Yorubas*), p. 192.
25 More correctly Fulbe. Nigerian usage is followed here.

the markets of western Africa. On their journeys down the footpaths and waterways to the coast they might pass through few or many hands and travel singly, in small lots or in large caravans. Europeans bought them from individual merchants,[26] from African corporations such as the trading houses of the Niger delta states[27] or from rulers, either directly or through agents. In the nineteenth century victims were usually gathered together in large lots near the coast and delivered to European factors who kept them in barracoons until they could be loaded onto slave ships for the last grim leg of their sad journey. These factors were a motley collection of Frenchmen, Spaniards, Portuguese, Creoles from Brazil and other adventurers, some employed by shipowners, others independent. Some settled on the coast and a few gained considerable local influence, even enlivening coastal society with their fine living and lavish entertainment.[28] Englishmen, prohibited from dealing in slaves, often supplied slavers with barter goods or even with the capital to finance their operations.[29]

There were a number of European colonies and posts scattered along the western shores of Africa at the time of Buxton's campaign. The British were established on the Gambia, in Sierra Leone and on the Gold Coast, the French on the Senegal river and the island of Gorée off Cape Verde, while Portugal had some posts on the shores of Guinea, a colony in Angola and grandiose claims to vast areas including the coast up to the Congo river.[30] These territories, all small enclaves surrounded by independent African peoples, were militarily weak and dependent upon trade for their revenues.

26 Most of these were African but some were Mulattos like Sam Kanto Brew who served as middlemen between Ashanti and the Spanish slavers in Fanti country in the early nineteenth century; see Margaret Priestley, *West African Trade and Coast Society*, London 1969, ch. 3. In the nineteenth century a number of returned slaves from the New World and Sierra Leone also took part in the trade, see examples in Newbury, *Slave Coast*, pp. 37–38.

27 For these operations see Dike; G. I. Jones, *The Trading States of the Oil Rivers*, London, 1963

28 For the career of two notorious Brazilians who made fortunes on the coast in the nineteenth century see David A. Ross, 'The Kingdom of Dahomey 1818–94', London Ph.D., 1967, pp. 3 ff. and 'The Career of Domingo Martinez in the Bight of Benin 1833–64' *JAH* vi, 1, 1965, pp. 79–90 (henceforth 'Martinez').

29 Ward, pp. 194–5; Newbury, Slave Coast, pp. 38, 42–3; Ross, 'Martinez', p. 81; Anstey, *Congo*, pp. 22–3

30 It is perhaps useful to enumerate here the changes which took place before 1884. Britain's settlements on the Gold Coast were extended in 1850 when she acquired the Danish forts and in 1871 when she bought the Dutch ones. In 1861 she annexed the island of Lagos. From 1857 the French began to colonise the Cape Verde and in the 1840s occupied posts on the Ivory Coast and enlarged a naval base in Gabon by settling a consignment of freed slaves there. They occupied Porto Novo from 1863 to 1866. Portugal's authority in Angola did not stretch far beyond the towns of Luanda and Benguela. She occupied Ambriz in 1855. Black Americans began to colonise Liberia in the 1820s and it was recognised as independent in 1847. Spain re-occupied the island of Fernando Po in the 1840s and subsequently began to explore the mainland of Rio Muni.

They had little influence over the long coastline up and down which slavers ranged collecting cargoes wherever they were available.

Against this long established and often profitable trade[31] the Royal Navy also had little success while the treaty network had significant gaps. However, the tightening of this net, the closing of legal loopholes and the adoption of more effective naval tactics, especially the close blockade of outlets and operations ashore, gradually diverted the traffic away from the more exposed harbours, the open roadsteads and better known markets[32] as well as from the neighbourhood of British and French posts[33] and may have encouraged a shift towards suppliers south of the equator as long as the trade below the line remained legal.[34] It also forced slavers to change their

31 The profitability of the trade is now being investigated, all too little being known about African operations. The profits were unevenly distributed among African producers and middlemen, European factors and shippers, distributors in the New World and officials who were bribed for ignoring or conniving at the trade once it became illegal. Profits fluctuated greatly and are difficult to calculate, particularly after the traffic was outlawed. It can be shown that the selling price of slaves in the western hemisphere was often many times higher than the real price of the goods for which they were obtained in Africa but a high profit on a successful slaving venture was necessary to offset losses on unsuccessful ones. Even in the eighteenth century the risk of loss was high. A slaver might arrive at a port with the barter goods most wanted there but find no slaves and have to go elsewhere where her goods were not in such demand and consequently more were needed to pay for her cargo, or she might have to visit several places to obtain a full load. Competitors might force up the price of slaves in Africa or force it down when a slaver arrived in the New World. The risks and the costs of slaving were thus high and in the nineteenth century naval action made them even higher. For a discussion of this question see LeVeen, pp. 20 ff.; for eighteenth century profits see S. Rottenberg; Roger Anstey, 'The Volume and Profitability of the British Slave Trade, 1761–1807' in S. Engerman and E. Genovese (eds.), *Race and Slavery in the Western Hemisphere: Quantitative Studies*, Princeton (forthcoming). For a general discussion see P. D. Curtin, 'The Slave Trade and the Atlantic Basin: Intercontinental Perspectives' in N. I. Huggins, Martin Kilson and Daniel M. Fox (eds.), *Key Issues in the Afro-American Experience*, New York 1971, pp. 74–93, pp. 85–9.

32 Vansina and Curtin state that this was the reason why there was little or no slaving from the exposed shores of the Ivory Coast and Eastern Liberia in the nineteenth century, Curtin and Vansina, p. 189. Whydah in modern Dahomey also became more difficult to use and slaves were taken to collecting points on neighbouring coasts, Newbury, *Slave Coast*, pp. 40–1; Ward, p. 203. Badagri, situated on a lagoon where concealment was difficult, also lost trade, Ajayi, p. 22; while the trade from Aboh took new routes to new outlets, K. O. Ogedengbe, 'The Aboh Kingdom of the Lower Niger c. 1650–1900', Ph.D. Wisconsin, 1971 (henceforth 'Aboh Kingdom'), p. 302.

33 The Gambia and Senegal rivers were now avoided, Curtin and Vansina, p. 189. Slaving from the Gold Coast became negligible, Curtin, *Slave Trade*, p. 258; Patrick Manning, 'Slaves, Palm Oil and Political Power on the West African Coast', *African Historical Studies*, ii, 2, 1969, pp. 280–8, p. 283.

34 See Curtin, *Slave Trade*, pp. 231 ff. Although interestingly some Portuguese and Brazilians continued to come to West Africa for slaves rather than to Central Africa, apparently because they had good trading contacts and Bahian tobacco was popular in the Bight of Benin.

methods. Where in the eighteenth century they had cruised in leisurely fashion along the coast, waiting off-shore or in rivers and lagoons for cargoes to be brought to them, transacting their business with African suppliers on board ship, they now loaded up quickly in out-of-the-way places and fled hastily out to sea, relying on their factors ashore to buy up captives and keep them pending shipment.[35] They also adopted various subterfuges to avoid detection such as making decoy runs along the coast inviting search before they loaded slaves, or making incriminating equipment in Africa rather than carrying it across the ocean.[36] They used fast, small manoeuvrable ships able to hide in the waterways and lagoons and to out-distance pursuers. These also carried fewer slaves so that less was lost in case of capture.[37] In the last decade, when large vessels were cheap as the result of a commercial depression, they began to use bigger ships, some of them steamers, hoping to make a rich killing on a single voyage.[38] Thus naval operations forced up the costs of slaving,[39] harassed slavers and led to the recapture and liberation of perhaps eight per cent of the victims shipped from Africa.[40] They doubtless also prevented many more from ever embarking. But they failed to stop the traffic.

Naval action was complemented by treaties with Africans. A treaty network, which eventually covered the whole coast from which slaves were exported, was built up slowly. Initially African suppliers received the news that Britain had abolished the slave traffic with frank incredulity.[41] They were ready enough to deal in legitimate goods but were reluctant, even where slaving was unimportant, to give up the freedom to trade as they wished. However, they accepted the treaties for various reasons. Some were cajoled, a few were bribed.[42] Some hoped for help against enemies or rivals, others valued their British customers or wanted better terms of trade.[43] At Old Calabar, on the Cross River, for instance, palm oil had replaced slaves as the main export and the traders wanted British help in diversifying their economy,[44] whereas at Bonny, where the slave trade was still important, it

35 LeVeen, pp. 18 ff. discusses these questions at length.
36 *Ibid.*; Newbury, *Slave Coast*, pp. 38–40; Ward, p. 203.
37 Howard, p. 30; LeVeen, pp. 111–20, 130–1. For a discussion of the inadequacies of naval ships which were outsailed by slavers in the earlier days of anti-slavery operations, see Lloyd, pp. 124–6, and Ward, ch. 2. By the 1840s, however, the West Africa squadron was equipped with faster sailing ships and some steamers. Slavers were also beginning to use steamers which carried large cargoes. Lloyd, p. 128.
38 Lloyd, p. 128; Howard, pp. 56–7   39 LeVeen, pp. 11 ff
40 Curtin, *Slave Trade*, p. 250. This estimate includes captures made by other navies but the majority were made by the Royal Navy.
41 H. Crow, *Memoirs*, London 1970 (reprint—first published 1830) p. 137. Some thought it simply a British move against rival merchants; Ajayi, p. 54.
42 Compensation, usually in the form of goods, was only offered in a few cases.
43 Dike, p. 112, points out that Africans were increasingly aware of the value of their exports and of the low quality of goods offered in return. For the treaties with the Delta States and examples of British methods see Dike, ch. 5.
44 At Old Calabar chiefs received a subsidy and asked for machinery for sugar

took cajolery, bribery and many years of effort before a treaty was obtained.[45] Often, no doubt, Africans expected to break the agreements with impunity and many were more honoured in the breach than the observance. Africans were neither pliant nor helpless in the face of demands for a treaty, but the British had obvious powers of coercion. Naval officers were told not to use threats or intimidation,[46] but the mere arrival of a warship was itself a show of force and if necessary, trade could be paralysed by a blockade until the desired agreement was obtained.

The terms of these treaties varied. Most gave the Royal Navy the right to seize slaves destined for export both on land and in territorial waters.[47] Nearly all provided for free trade and 'most favoured nation' treatment for British subjects. Some contained clauses for the protection of missionaries, for the outlawing of piracy or the elimination of 'barbarous practices' such as human sacrifice.

These agreements played a part in the building of British paramountcy along the western coast. They brought the Africans who signed them within the British orbit. They were regarded as clients rather than allies[48] and the treaties were considered sufficient to prevent a foreign power from taking them under its protection.[49] The agreements were seen as 'arrangements' with 'barbarous chiefs' in no way comparable to the treaties with European powers. Most important they opened the way to interference in local affairs, which was not limited to measures against slavers. Steps were also taken to promote that other pillar of anti-slave trade policy—legitimate commerce. Naval officers enforcing the treaties were instructed to use 'every endeavour to encourage' it, to protect British subjects and to collect all possible information about the country, its resources and its trade.[50]

As long as the British presence on the coast was limited to three small scattered colonies and a naval squadron, interference was sporadic but from 1849 consuls and consular agents were based in West Africa and kept a much closer watch on British interests. Paradoxically this was the result of an attack in the House of Commons on the preventive squadron, on the grounds that it was expensive, ineffective, poisoned relations with other powers and increased the sufferings of slaves, who had to be transported under much worse conditions than they had been when the trade was legal. This attack

processing and teachers to show them how to use it together with cotton and coffee seed. They explained they would need to employ the slaves they could no longer export, see Ajayi, pp. 55–6 and Kannan K. Nair, *Politics and Society in South Eastern Nigeria 1841–1906*, London 1972, pp. 81–3.
45 Dike, pp. 83–93   46 *Instructions*, 1844, section 7
47 The treaties are conveniently collected in *Instructions*, updated editions of which appeared in 1844, 1865, 1882 and 1892. Draft treaties are printed in C. W. Newbury, *British Policy Towards West Africa: Select Documents 1786–1874*, I, Oxford 1965 (henceforth *Documents*), pp. 150–1, 164–5 with an introductory note pp. 133–5.
48 Newbury, *Documents*, pp. 20, 226
49 Gavin, 'Palmerston's Policy', p. 156
50 *Instructions*, 1844, para. 1

was supported by a cross-section of British interests,[51] including radical free traders,[52] Quakers opposed to the use of force, manufacturers and merchants trading with Brazil, or with West Africa and even planters from labour-starved Trinidad and British Guiana, who despaired of ending the slave trade and wanted the squadron to supervise the buying of Africans so as to free them in the Caribbean and build up the labour force in their colonies. The defenders of the squadron, who included some West Coast traders,[53] the planters of Jamaica and Barbados,[54] missionaries,[55] naval officers, philanthropists and the leaders of both political parties, eventually prevailed and as a result the squadron was strengthened, more treaties were signed and consuls were sent to West Africa.

Thus with little formal increase in British territory, naval officers and consuls, backed by ships of the preventive squadron and armed with orders to enforce the treaties, came to assume the role of policeman of the western shores of Africa. At times French, American and Portuguese squadrons also operated on the coast, but the British were a constant force. The fight against the slave traffic provided the moral justification for their proceedings in the eyes of the British electorate and the treaties gave them a claim to legality. Thus a policy sanctioned by Parliament for humanitarian purposes facilitated increasing intervention in the affairs of the coast and furnished some support for growing British trading and missionary activities.

By the mid-nineteenth century the main centres of the traffic were the Bights of Benin and Biafra and the ports to the south, including those around the Congo river. Events at Lagos on the Bight of Benin may be taken as an example of the way in which the abolition issue was interwoven with other interests when it came to formulating policy. Lagos was neither the only, nor even the most important, slave port in the region[56] and in 1851 slaving there was actually in decline and a British legitimate trader, Thomas

51 For summaries of the long discussions see Bethell, *Abolition*, pp. 296–309; Lloyd, ch. 8; Ward, pp. 189–201. Most of those who opposed the squadron advocated other methods of suppression, including the imposition of prohibitive tariffs on slave-grown sugar. Foreign sugar had been taxed at a higher rate than British sugar and slave-grown sugar had paid still higher duties until 1846 when these differential duties were reduced. By 1854 foreign and British sugar paid the same duties. During the debates on the future of the squadron in 1848–50 it was argued that it was hypocritical to remove the tax on slave-grown sugar while claiming a humanitarian role for the preventive squadron.

52 Some free traders argued that an unrestricted trade in slaves would lead to a quicker end to the traffic by satisfying the demand.

53 Traders with West Africa were not unanimous in their views on the value of the squadron; some welcomed its presence, while others, perhaps engaged in supplying slavers with trade goods, wanted it to be withdrawn, Lloyd, p. 110; Ajayi, pp. 59–61; Ward, pp. 194–5.

54 Bethell, *Abolition*, p. 300. They feared competition from Trinidad and British Guiana as much as from foreign producers.

55 The missionaries conducted an active campaign in support of the squadron, see Ajayi, pp. 59–65.

56 Newbury, *Slave Coast*, p. 49

Hutton, had secured a footing.[57] Yet in that year the Royal Navy drove out the ruler, Kosoko, together with Brazilian slavers, and replaced him with a rival, Akitoye, who was willing to sign a treaty against the traffic. This high-handed action was prompted by missionaries working in the hinterland among the Egba at Abeokuta. They described Kosoko, an enemy of the Egba, as an inveterate slaver, and Akitoye, a friend of the Egba, as a reliable ally. They also claimed that if slaving could be stamped out at Lagos legitimate commerce would flow up the valley of the Ogun river as far as the Niger through country 'abounding in cotton'[58]—a raw material essential to the English textile industry. The missionaries mounted a campaign in England to secure government, public and parliamentary support. They were backed by Thomas Hutton, anxious to clear Lagos of Brazilian rivals whose high profits on the slave traffic enabled them to undercut him in the palm oil trade;[59] while the Foreign Secretary, Palmerston, saw a chance of furthering his own cherished schemes for opening Africa to British trade.[60] Lagos was, therefore, attacked and the neighbouring coasts were blockaded, including the shores of Dahomey whose ruler Ghezo, another enemy of the Egba, was believed to be wedded to slaving. Help was sent also to the Egba.[61] As a result of these operations treaties were secured with Dahomey, Lagos, nearby Porto-Novo and Badagri, as well as Abeokuta, all of which were promptly broken.

Thus Britain interfered in a dynastic dispute in Lagos and in the political struggles of the Egba at the behest of traders and missionaries. The cabinet recognised that there was no legal basis for her actions,[62] but considered them morally justifiable because they were directed against 'slave trading chiefs'.[63] But the French firm of Victor Regis, against whom Hutton had competed unsuccessfully for limited supplies of palm oil in the Daho-mean port of Whydah, thought Britain was using the slave trade as a thin cloak to gain commercial advantages at Lagos, and France duly protested.[64]

There followed a decade of consular and naval domination after which

57 Ross, 'Martinez', p. 84, note 32
58 Ajayi, pp. 72–3
59 Ross, 'Martinez', p. 82; Newbury, *Slave Coast*, pp. 52–3
60 R. Gavin, 'Nigeria and Lord Palmerston' (henceforth 'Nigeria'), *Ibadan*, 12 June 1961, p. 26
61 Biobaku, pp. 45–6; Ajayi, pp. 74–5
62 No British property or lives were in jeopardy but the Prime Minister was persuaded by Palmerston to 'wink at any violation of Vattel's rules in regard to a slave trading chief', Gavin, 'Nigeria' p. 25. See also Ajayi, pp. 71–4.
63 This was a gross oversimplification. Akitoye himself had the support of the Brazilian slave factor Martinez, while neither Kosoko nor Ghezo could end the traffic without endangering their thrones, see Ross, 'Martinez', p. 84 note 32; 'Dahomey' pp. 81 ff.; Newbury, *Slave Coast*, pp. 51–3; C. Coquery-Vidvrovitch, 'De la traite des esclaves à l'exportation de l'huile de palme et des palmistes au Dahomey: XIXe siècle' in C. Meillassoux (ed.), *The Development of Indigenous Trade and Markets in West Africa* (henceforth Meillassoux), Oxford 1971, pp. 107–123, p. 112.
64 Newbury, *Slave Coast*, p. 55

Lagos was annexed, officially to safeguard the population from the 'slave traders and kidnappers who formerly oppressed them', to foster legitimate trade and protect Abeokuta against Dahomey.[65] But it was also to establish stable government, forestall any French designs on the island, encourage the production of cotton in the hinterland and open trade routes to the Niger.[66] Annexation, however, brought problems of its own. Lagos merely became another small British colony struggling to attract trade and keep peace in its hinterland,[67] and slaving in the Bights continued. The closing of the markets of the New World in the late 1860s and French renunciation of the recruitment of contract labourers for the West Indies and Réunion, which had stimulated the traffic between 1857 and 1861,[68] reduced the export traffic, but contract labourers were still being exported in the 1880s and 1890s[69] and slave dealing among Africans continued, causing friction between the British colony and surrounding peoples.[70]

Lagos is an extreme example of the way in which, given the right man at the helm,[71] Britain's dual policy of suppressing the slave traffic and promoting legitimate trade led to high-handed action in Africa and roused the suspicions of other powers. In the other strongholds of the nineteenth century slave trade, the Niger and its delta and the Congo, British domination was informal but no less real. Developments in both these areas are important in setting the scene for the Berlin conference and, therefore, merit some attention here.

On the lower Niger and in the delta, the export slave traffic was brisk in the 1830s[72] but declined with the extension of the treaty system, consular supervision and naval action to a small trade which probably continued

65 Russell to Foote, 22 June 1861, FO 84/1141, quoted in Biobaku, p. 68

66 Gavin, 'Palmerston's Policy', pp. 244–5; Ajayi, pp. 167 ff.; Newbury, *Slave Coast*, pp. 64–5; Biobaku, p. 68; Dike, pp. 175–6. American cotton supplies were threatened by the outbreak of the civil war.

67 Newbury, *Slave Coast*, pp. 66 ff.; A. A. B. Aderibigbe, 'Expansion of the Lagos Protectorate, 1863–1900', London Ph.D. 1959; W. D. McIntyre, 'Commander Glover and the Colony of Lagos, 1861–73', *JAH*, iv, 1, 1963, pp. 57–79. Like the other settlements, it had a constant tendency to expand along the coast as administrators, trying to raise revenue, imposed customs duties and then tried to prevent Africans from taking their goods to ports beyond British control.

68 Biobaku, pp. 60–1. For the connection between the contract labour traffic and the slave trade see above, pp. 20–30.

69 B. I. Obichere, *West African States and European Expansion*, New Haven and London, 1971, pp. 90–3; A. G. Hopkins, 'Economic Imperialism in West Africa: Lagos 1880–92', *Economic History Review*, xxi, 1968, pp. 580–606, p. 589. Some of the slaves exported by the Portuguese were sent via Luanda to Brazil where slavery was legal until 1888 (personal communication from Dr B. I. Obichere).

70 See ch. 3 for a discussion of African slavery and of the way it led to friction with the British.

71 In this case, Palmerston, who was Foreign Secretary in 1851 and Prime Minister in 1861. He was an advocate of gun-boat diplomacy and sympathetic to the anti-slavery cause.

72 Dike, pp. 52 ff.

until the closing of the transatlantic market.[73] It was in the Oil Rivers that legitimate trade particularly in palm oil made its most spectacular strides and led to ever-increasing British interference. Consuls, seeking to suppress the slave traffic and safeguard British merchants, as well as to control their lawlessness and settle their endless disputes with Africans, came, with naval support, to dominate the waterways by the 1880s, supporting co-operative rulers, opposing recalcitrant ones, even appointing African officials in a search for local authorities willing and able to protect British trade.[74]

The reports of the explorer, Heinrich Barth, who travelled in the western Sudan between 1849 and 1855,[75] rekindled official interest in trade with the interior, and led to the first successful trading venture up the Niger in 1854, organised by MacGregor Laird with the aid of a government subsidy. The journey was epoch-making, for it was found that quinine, used as a prophylactic, saved the Europeans from the usual ravages of fever and removed a great obstacle to white penetration of Africa.[76] By 1859 posts had been established as far as Lokoja at the confluence with the Benue. This move up river was opposed by European coastal traders and by the African middlemen who supplied them with palm oil from the producing regions in the interior. The latter found their livelihood threatened by the appearance of the British in their traditional markets. British traders had to fight their way up the waterway, escorted by gunboats of the Royal Navy. Africans who resisted found their towns bombarded and their homes destroyed by punitive expeditions.[77] Matters were exacerbated by cut-throat competition between the European merchants themselves.

In 1879 in an effort to strengthen their position, the principal British firms on the Niger amalgamated to form the United African Company under the leadership of George Goldie,[78] only to be challenged by French traders backed by a French consular agent, as well as by new English competitors

73 It seems that slaves from the lower Niger were exported from Lagos and the ports to the west after slaving in the Oil Rivers declined and this may have continued until the demise of the Atlantic trade. Ogedengbe, 'Aboh Kingdom', pp. 302–3.

74 In their search for Africans willing and strong enough to protect British traders, the British sometimes failed to understand the real powers of a particular office thus causing misunderstandings, see for instance Obaro Ikime, *Niger Delta Rivalry*, London 1969, pp. 69 ff., for a discussion of the office of 'Governor of the River' in Itsekiri country.

75 Barth was a member of an expedition under James Richardson sent out to explore prospects for legitimate trade and armed with treaties against the slave trade. For his account see *Travels and Discoveries in North and Central Africa: Being a Journal of an Expedition undertaken under the Auspices of H.B.M.'s Government in the Years 1849–1855*, London 1857, 5 vols.

76 For an account of this expedition by its leader see W. B. Baikie, *Narrative of an Exploring Voyage up the rivers Kw'ora and Binne (Commonly known as the Niger and Tsadda) in 1854*, London 1856.

77 Dike, pp. 206–8

78 Originally George Goldie-Taubman, knighted in 1887 and known as Sir George Goldie. For his career see John Flint, *Sir George Goldie and the Making of Nigeria*, London 1960 (henceforth *Goldie*).

and Africans from Sierra Leone and Lagos.[79] Moreover, middlemen from Brass in the delta began a price war in a bid to save their markets. Goldie decided to apply for a royal charter which would enable him to rule the whole region north of the delta and incidentally to exclude all competitors. He reorganised the firm as the National African Company,[80] with more influential directors and more capital than its predecessor, and began in the early 1880s to sign treaties with African rulers, giving the company political power and a commercial monopoly. He also opened negotiations to acquire the rival French business.

The British Consul in the Oil Rivers, as alarmed as Goldie at the French intrusion, urged his government to assume political control of the delta.[81] The Foreign Office showed little concern until it was discovered that France, advancing from her base in Senegal, had concluded a treaty with Segou on the upper Niger giving special privileges to French merchants. By 1882 the French threat was explicit and it seemed that British commerce on the river and in the delta could no longer be safeguarded by the old system of informal domination. This commerce was but a small fraction of the total volume of British trade, but it was still sizable and there was a clear expectation that it would become much greater when the riches of the interior could be tapped.

The same menace now appeared on the Congo, where informal empire took a somewhat different form. Serious naval operations against the slave traffic did not begin until the 1840s when the squadron was increased after Britain acquired the power to deal with Spanish, Portuguese and Brazilian slavers south of the equator.[82] Treaties were signed with Africans along this coast just as they were elsewhere, but little use seems to have been made of the right to operate on land. No consular officer visited the area regularly and the British presence was limited to naval patrols, which seized slavers, punished those responsible for occasional attacks on the property of British traders and fought the pirates who harassed traffic on the river. For many years slaves remained a major export and British merchants supplied slavers with barter goods. Legitimate trade did not reach sizable proportions until after the Atlantic slave traffic died down and a large-scale offensive had been mounted against pirates in 1865. Thereafter growth was steady, although naval protection against piracy was necessary for a further decade.[83]

By the early 1880s the value of British trade in the Congo region was

79 Flint, pp. 30 ff
80 *Ibid.* pp. 41 ff
81 *Ibid.*, pp. 47–8
82 For the whole subject of British activities around the Congo, see Anstey, *Congo*, and 'British Trade and Policy in West Central Africa between 1816 and the early 1880's', *Transactions of the Historical Society of Ghana*, iii, 1, 1957, pp. 47–71.
83 Anstey, *Congo*, pp. 27–8. An interesting reflection on the contention that legitimate trade would eventually drive out the slave trade is provided by the fact that one pirate leader and Portuguese slavers believed in the 1860s that if they could drive legitimate traders from the river the slave traffic would revive.

comparable with that on the Niger and Oil rivers.[84] Not only were several English firms operating on and around the river but foreign traders used British-made guns, powder, hardware and textiles. Moreover, the epic journey of the explorer, Commander Cameron, across Africa,[85] closely followed by that of Henry Morton Stanley, who reached Boma from the east coast in 1877,[86] had revealed that once the cataracts on the lower river were passed, the Congo and its tributaries formed a navigable highway for steam boats stretching far into the heart of Africa.

Already there existed a vast interior commercial network along which goods flowed from market to market, carried in canoes or by porters.[87] Stanley had found four Portuguese muskets at Rubunga nine hundred and sixty five miles up the Congo, and had seen evidence of an extensive traffic in the far interior in European wares traded side by side with local products.[88] The major staples of the long distance trade were slaves and ivory but with the demise of the Atlantic trade, only the latter was exported. It was brought to the coast by merchants travelling singly, in small groups or in great caravans of up to five hundred people bearing two or three hundred tusks.[89] From the nearer hinterland Europeans obtained palm products. Trading conditions were far from ideal. Tolls and dues were exacted at markets and along the trade routes, pirates were a hazard on the interior waterways[90] while at the coast Europeans sometimes committed depredations on Africans, which went unpunished and so poisoned relations.[91] Nevertheless, the system functioned satisfactorily enough and there was on the Congo, as on the Niger, not only an established trade to be protected, but the potential commerce of the great river basin to be exploited.

Hence Britain's alarm at the totally unexpected news that an officer in the French Navy, Savorgnan de Brazza, had concluded a treaty[92] giving France sovereign rights with Iloo, ruler of the Tio, an important trading people occupying strategic lands around Stanley Pool, at the head of the navigable river.[93] The ratification of this agreement by France in 1882 raised the spectre of French tariffs excluding Britain from the trade of the upper Congo and

84 *Ibid.*, pp. 29–34. Anstey suggests that the total British stake may have been worth some £2,000,000 in 1884 compared with an estimated £3,000,000 for the Bights of Benin and Biafra together. These are rough estimates only. See also Pinto, pp. 79–81.
85 See V. L. Cameron, *Across Africa*, 2 vols., London 1877.
86 See H. M. Stanley, *Through the Dark Continent*, 2 vols. 1899, first published in 1878 (henceforth *Dark Continent*).
87 Jan Vansina, *The Tio Kingdom of the Middle Congo 1880–92*, Oxford 1973 (henceforth *Tio*), ch. 10
88 Stanley, *Dark Continent*, II, pp. 224, 278–9
89 Vansina, *Tio*, p. 260
90 *Ibid.*, p. 259
91 Like the cold-blooded drowning of 32 Africans by European traders who accused them of arson.
92 This is often called the Makoko Treaty.
93 Vansina, *Tio*, ch. 10 and preface. An estimated one-sixth of Africa's ivory production passed through Tio hands.

as has been seen, led England to negotiate the abortive Anglo-Portuguese treaty of 1884.[94]

In sum, by the early 1880s, Britain's paramountcy, which had long been established over western Africa, outside the regions under French and Portuguese control, was being challenged. Her anti-slavery policy had played its part in the development of this paramountcy leading her to patrol the coasts and to sign treaties which gave her a special relationship with the people and enabled her to operate in their territories. It had been used to justify, even if it had not prompted, certain high-handed actions, such as the seizure of Lagos. At the outset it had forced her merchants to turn to alternative forms of trade. Her operations against slavers were not responsible for the growth of legitimate commerce. This developed in response to the great increase in the demand for African products on the world market, an increase encouraged by the removal of restrictive duties and navigation acts in the western world, by a fall, as a result of the industrial revolution, in the real costs of manufactures bartered in Africa and by the growing availability of cheaper and surer forms of transport.[95] British policy, however, had encouraged its growth while increasing the risks, costs and difficulties of slavers. The expansion of legitimate trade did not kill the export slave traffic. In fact in many places the two flourished side by side and were conducted by the same people. The palm oil trade grew fastest, for instance, between 1817 and 1835, a period of active slaving[96] in the very areas east of the Volta where it was particularly rife.[97] Nevertheless in the long run growth of legitimate trade perhaps made suppression easier by furnishing Africans with alternative means of acquiring western products.

British proceedings had built up strong foreign suspicions as to the real motives of her crusade against the Atlantic slave trade, but it is doubtful whether the long struggle, which cost over £13,000,000 of the taxpayers' money,[98] really resulted in a direct economic benefit to Britain, at least as far as her African trade was concerned.[99] Her merchants, barred from direct participation in a lucrative commerce, suffered sometimes from the hostility of African and European slavers[100] and complained of costly delays

94 For the outcome of these negotiations see below, pp. 169 ff.
95 C. W. Newbury, 'Prices and profitability in early nineteenth century West African trade' (henceforth 'Trade') in Meillassoux, pp. 91–106, pp. 91–4.
96 LeVeen, pp. 94–5
97 Stilliard, p. 15
98 LeVeen, p. 99. This includes naval costs from 1811–70, the expenses of the court at Freetown and the sums paid to obtain treaties from Spain and Portugal.
99 LeVeen, ch. 2, discusses the effect on Britain's economy as a whole and concludes that no private interests actually gained. There are some unanswered questions as to the effect of the campaign on the sugar production of Britain's rivals, whose labour costs were raised, and as to whether British manufacturers would have sold more goods in Africa had the slave trade been allowed to continue untrammelled. There is, too, the problem of how far in the long run the unrestricted export of labour from Africa would have reduced the supply of legitimate exports.
100 See examples in Dike, p. 54; Anstey, *Congo*, p. 24

as customers abandoned them to find cargoes for slave ships,[101] which had to clear port quickly to avoid the navy.[102] There is evidence too, that trade was sometimes diverted into new channels from which they reaped no benefit.[103] Counterbalancing these basic tribulations, her traders, particularly on the Niger, sometimes secured some advantages from naval and consular protection[104] and from official efforts to open new avenues of trade, a fact not lost upon their rivals. The extent to which this aided them has still to be fully investigated. By the 1880s, however, legitimate commerce was by no means all British. Some areas, for instance, were dominated by French and German merchants, and the Dutch were established on the Congo, but, as the leading industrial and commercial power, Britain had a large share of it and could hope for more.

It was in her long battle against the Atlantic slave trade that Britain served, as it were, her apprenticeship in the anti-slavery game. It was on the shores and waterways of Western Africa that naval officers experimenting with different methods of suppression, learnt the tricks of the trade and discovered their own limitations. It was to check the Atlantic traffic that the treaty network first took shape and that animosities with European powers were first built up—animosities and suspicions which, in the case of France and Portugal, coloured their outlook in the 1880s.

If the Atlantic traffic was now dead, slaving was by no means ended. An export trade still existed across the Sahara desert. Contract labourers were still shipped to the Portuguese and other colonies. Throughout the vast interior of western and central Africa and even at the coast, Africans continued to enslave and sell each other, virtually unaffected by the treaties and beyond the range of British action. Their victims were supplied by the numerous wars and disturbances which marked the times. Ironically this traffic was encouraged in some areas by the growth of legitimate trade which presented new opportunities for utilising slave labour in Africa.[105]

Muslim slavery

Elsewhere the results had also been disappointing. The first serious attempts

101 Dike, pp. 53–54

102 LeVeen, pp. 93–98, suggests that this explanation is more likely than the opinion prevalent among traders that Africans preferred to deal in slaves rather than in legitimate goods because profits were higher.

103 The Asante, finding their export of slaves curtailed by British surveillance, turned their efforts to producing kola nuts for Hausa caravans from the north to the detriment of British merchants on the Gold Coast, Ivor Wilks, 'Asante Policy towards Hausa Trade in the Nineteenth Century', Meillassoux, pp. 124–41, p. 130.

104 Such protection was not always forthcoming. At times the navy refused to interfere on behalf of traders of whose proceedings officers disapproved, while consular protection also meant supervision and control.

105 The role of slavery and the slave trade among Africans are discussed below together with the results of the development of legitimate trade, see pp. 118 ff.

to check the traffic across the Sahara desert and from eastern Africa were made after Buxton's campaign. Britain was now tackling the complex question of slavery in the Muslim world.[106] The Islamic religion sanctioned the enslavement of infidels captured in war but in practice many others also suffered this fate,[107] including Muslims, and slavery was widespread. In the nineteenth century the institution was deeply entrenched in the social structure of Islam, and many of the slaves came from Africa.

This was the great reservoir of manpower where they were captured in wars or raids, kidnapped, paid as tax or tribute, presented as gifts, or simply bought.[108] Slaves came from many different places and often travelled great distances. From the western and central Sudan they crossed the Sahara on the great caravan routes to northern Africa, and many were sent on to the markets of the Ottoman empire and beyond.[109] From the Sudan and Ethiopia, they came northwards, overland or down the Nile to the North African littoral or were shipped eastwards, as were Somalis, to Arabia, the Persian Gulf and India.[110] From eastern Africa even beyond the great lakes they were carried away to Persian and Arabian markets.[111] Many were dispersed through the Muslim world by pilgrims going to or returning from Mecca and their destinies were as varied as their origins.

The function of slavery in the Islamic world was both social and economic, and the market was selective and sophisticated. Different types of slaves were wanted for different purposes. The most highly prized were not Africans but 'white' slaves, usually Circassian or Georgian girls, wanted as concubines in harems as far apart as Zanzibar and Morocco, but they were expensive and their numbers small.[112] Light-skinned 'red' Ethiopian girls,

106 For an introduction to Muslim slavery see 'Abd' by R. Brunschvig, *Encyclopedia of Islam*, 1960, I.
107 Sometimes victims were imported from abroad under the fiction that they had been captured in a *jihad*, or holy war.
108 For a fuller discussion of why and how people were enslaved, see below, pp. 118 ff.
109 For the nineteenth century traffic see Boahen, ch. 5; E. W. Bovill, *Golden Trade of the Moors*, London 1968 (2nd ed.), ch. 25; J. L. Miège, *Le Maroc et l'Europe (1830–94)*, 4 vols., Paris 1961, II, pp. 146 ff.; Renault, II, pp. 4 ff.
110 R. Gray, *A History of the Southern Sudan 1839–89*, pp. 5 ff., London 1961; M. F. Shukry, *The Khedive Ismail and Slavery in the Sudan (1863–79)*, Cairo 1938; G. Baer, 'Slavery in Nineteenth Century Egypt', *JAH*, viii, 3, 1967, pp. 417–47; M. Abir, *Ethiopia During the Era of the Princes*, London 1968, ch. 2; Renault, II, pp. 24 ff. Further sources are cited below, pp. 75 ff.
111 Kelly, pp. 412–13; Coupland, *East Africa*, pp. 500 ff.; *Exploitation*, ch. 7; Renault, I, pp. 12 ff. Further sources are cited below, pp. 86 ff.
112 Expensive as they were, however, white girls were despised by the Ethiopians in the harem of Sayyid Sa'id of Zanzibar and called 'cats' because of their blue eyes. (Princess Salme) Emily Ruete, *Memoirs of an Arabian Princess*, New York 1888, p. 34. In earlier centuries there was a flourishing trade in white male slaves wanted as state officials or soldiers in certain countries, notably Egypt where Mamluke slaves formed a ruling caste. But by the mid-nineteenth century this traffic had dwindled and only a few white males were bought as domestic servants, as playfellows for the sons of the

usually Galla or Sidama, served the same purpose and were in greater supply but they, too, commanded high prices and were sent far afield.[113] Black women were also widely used as concubines and, being cheaper, they were also wanted as servants.

To attend the women or to serve as officials, eunuchs were required. They were particularly valued as officials since they could not found rival dynasties of their own. They were rare and expensive. Mutilation was against the tenets of Islam and only certain African peoples practised it. The crude operation was usually performed outside, or in the remoter parts of, the Muslim world upon small boys. Many died from haemorrhage on the spot,[114] but the value of the survivors might be as much as eight times that of an ordinary slave boy.[115] Boys aged from four to ten had the highest chance of survival. Men were sometimes gelded for the trade, or as punishment for crime or because it was the custom to mutilate prisoners of war. Eunuchs were obtained from parts of Ethiopia, from Mossi country, from Bagirmi and other states in the Sudanic belt,[116] and the operation was also said to be performed in Morocco,[117] upper Egypt, Hijaz and Yemen.[118]

Ethiopian men cost more than 'Negroes', at least in Arabia, where they were considered 'more refined and intelligent' but also less suited to heavy work. They were used in the cities as personal servants or employed in trade and light jobs. In upper Arabia, they were the armed retainers of the Emirs. The desert nomad and the employers of heavy labour, however, wanted hardy 'Negroes', and there was a market in Arabia for black slaves from as far afield as modern Malaŵi, who could be worked harder and were cheaper than those from nearby Ethiopia.[119] On the other hand, in Morocco, slaves from remote Bornu were considered stronger than those from the nearer parts of the western Sudan and were, therefore, sometimes imported through Cairo and sold at higher prices.[120]

Clearly then the market for slaves might be quite selective. Sometimes they were trained for a particular destiny. Those bound for North Africa and the Middle East might be kept a year or two in the oases of the northern

rich or for the practice of sodomy, see Baer, pp. 417–18; C. Snouck Hurgronje, *Mekka in the latter Part of the Nineteenth Century*, II, trans., London and Leyden 1931, p. 10.
113 They were much prized in Morocco, Miège, II, p. 157.
114 Burton to Granville, 7 Feb. 1881, FOCP 4626
115 *Ibid.* According to Burton, boys valued at £5 to £10 before the operation were worth from £25 to £80 afterwards.
116 For further references see, *inter alia*, Renault, II, pp. 60–2; G. B. Alan and Humphrey J. Fisher, *Slavery and Muslim Society in Africa*, London 1970, pp. 143–8; Bovill, p. 246.
117 See below, p. 62 ff.
118 Borchgrave to Chimay, 21 Oct. 1889, 25 Oct. 1889, AEB/CAE/6 no. 6
119 For slavery in Arabia see Hurgronje, pp. 10 ff.; Kelly, ch. 10; C. M. Doughty, *Travels in Arabia Deserta*, London 1888, 2 vols., I, pp. 553 ff. Most of the slaves Doughty saw came from the upper Nile, however.
120 Miège, II, p. 157, quotes prices for 1866, when Bornu slaves cost 50% more than those from the western Sudan.

Sahara while they learnt Arabic and the rudiments of Islam.[121] Egyptian girls were sometimes groomed for concubinage.[122] Circassian concubines learnt to sew and read, but not to write, and they studied religion and music.[123]

Obviously the slave trade was a means of supplying the demand for labour. Slaves were to be found working the clove plantations of Zanzibar, tending dates in the Hijaz, or coffee in the Yemen, growing food in the oases of the Sahara and Arabia, tilling the fields in Egypt, building in Mecca, diving for pearls in the Red Sea and the Persian Gulf, serving as sailors in the eastern seas, or acting as agents for Arab traders. They also swelled the armies of certain states, such as Egypt and Hyderabad, of Arab rulers or of merchant princes such as Tippu Tip in East Africa and Al-Zubayr in the Sudan. The majority, however, were probably used as domestic servants in households from Morocco to India, and many were concubines. For this reason the number of women probably exceeded the number of men, and females usually cost more.[124]

Possession of slaves was not limited to the rich. They were usually the only owners of the more expensive concubines and eunuchs, and of rare slaves, such as dwarfs wanted as playthings or deaf mute girls prized as servants because their discretion could be relied upon.[125] But in areas where the price was not too high quite humble people might own slaves.[126] In a poorer household in Arabia a black slave woman might be a maid of all work as well as her master's concubine.[127]

Slaves, however, were not usually simple instruments of production. They were valued for more than their labour. Slavery had important social functions. It was the means by which a man might build up his family. The number of legal wives he might have was limited to four but he could have all the concubines he could afford, and their children were free and usually, but not always, had the same standing as his other progeny.[128]

121 M. Emerit, *La Révolution de 1848 en Algérie*, Paris 1949, p. 31; Ross Dunn, 'The Trade of Tafilalt: Commercial Change in Southeast Morocco on the Eve of the Protectorate', *African Historical Studies*, iv, 2, 1971, pp. 271–304, 281–2.

122 E. W. Lane, *Manners and Customs of Modern Egyptians*, London 1954 edition (first published 1836), pp. 200–1.

123 Baer, pp. 423–4. It was desirable that as Muslims they should be able to read the Koran but writing was not considered necessary.

124 It is true that men were more likely to be killed in the wars and raids that produced slaves but the market must have been the controlling factor as the number of male slaves exported to the Western world far exceeded that of females.

125 Nachtigal cited in Fisher and Fisher, p. 163

126 For instance, in the nineteenth century Egyptian *fellahin* owned them, see Baer, p. 421, and the working classes in the Sudan, see R. C. Slatin, *Fire and Sword in the Sudan*, London and New York, 1896, p. 557.

127 Hurgronje, p. 13

128 Only a man's children by his own slave were free, those by the slave of another belonged to her master. Among some peoples, such as the Tuareg, the children of slaves were not accepted as equal to those of free women.

Furthermore his choice of wives might be limited by political and other considerations but concubines could be chosen for their charms.[129] Moreover slaves were a status symbol.

Thus in Morocco, Aubin recorded that:

In all the houses black slaves are employed as domestics . . . negroes and negresses, whose numbers and costume reveal the style of the house.[130]

In nineteenth-century Egypt it was said that:

the possession of one or more slaves is as essential to 'respectability' amongst one's neighbours as is that of a servant for menial work in a European family; and this social consideration has, probably, more to do with the maintenance of the institution than any question as to the relative cost of slave and free labour.[131]

Hurgronje testified that in Mecca the rich liked to fill their houses with slaves, who consequently led an easy life.[132]

To the rich and powerful the institution offered the opportunity of obtaining retainers whose fortunes were dependent upon those of their master. Some slaves occupied positions of trust and power and were free in all but name.[133] Many were emancipated by their masters but the bond between them was theoretically unbroken, for in the Muslim world a freedman and his descendants remained in a state of clientage towards his former owner and his heirs in perpetuity. The ex-slave was bound to pay certain benefits to his late master who, in return, was bound to give him patronage and protection.[134]

The advantages of slavery were not entirely on the side of the master. The slave, it is true, suffered grave disabilities. Legally he was a chattel, who could be sold, given away or inherited, and his services could be pledged or hired out—all without his consent. He could neither own nor inherit property. He was an inferior, whose life was considered less valuable than that of a free man and whose evidence was seldom accepted in a court of law.[135] He could not marry without his master's consent. In practice, however, there is ample testimony that most slaves were integrated into society and often their situation differed little from and was even some-

129 In Morocco, for instance, the Sultan's wives were chosen from different branches of the ruling dynasty.
130 E. Aubin (pseudonym), *Morocco of Today* (trans.), London 1906. Aubin made his observations in 1902–3.
131 J. C. McCoan, *Egypt as It Is*, London 1877, p. 307
132 Hurgronje, p. 12. Hurgronje was in Mecca in 1884–5.
133 For a discussion of the definition of slavery see below, pp. 143–5 ff.
134 In practice such customs were not always observed. The master and his progeny had a claim to a share of anything left by freed slaves and their descendants upon their deaths.
135 Conversely, since he was an inferior, his punishment for crime might be less than that of a free man, who was held to be fully responsible for his actions.

times preferable to that of a free man. They had considerable social mobility. Emancipation was considered a meritorious act and was widely practised, slaves being freed on their master's death, or because he wished to atone for some misdeed or to mark Ramadan, or simply after a number of years of faithful service.[136] They were also allowed to earn the money to buy their freedom. Some were freed for practical reasons. Hurgronje reported that male house slaves in Mecca were usually freed at the age of 20 since their duties brought them into close contact with women and this was undesirable.[137] A concubine could usually not be sold after she had borne her master children and she was free when he died.[138] It was considered wrong to separate young children from their mothers. Slave children were usually brought up along with their master's offspring, and those who were born and raised in the household were generally only sold for exceptional faults such as habitual drunkenness.[139]

It was a master's duty to marry off his slaves suitably and to clothe, feed and treat them well. Much stress was laid on this in Muslim ethics and Muslim law required that a slave should be sold if he was not adequately provided for. By Maliki law emancipation was compulsory if a slave was mutilated and, in certain countries, slaves could demand to be sold if they were not satisfied with the way they were treated.[140] Freedmen were often helped to establish themselves.[141] In general the slave had one great blessing denied to the free man: security in time of trouble. In an uncertain world he had a patron and protector.[142] There was an old Turkish proverb to the effect that it was better to be a rich man's slave than a poor man's son. It was also safer to be a concubine than to be a wife, for a wife could be divorced, whereas a concubine would be sold or otherwise provided for.[143]

If Muslim slavery at its best was a benign institution, far better than its transatlantic counterpart, the system was nevertheless open to abuse. A

136 In Africa emancipation was perhaps rare in some places. For African slavery see below, pp. 113–14, 118 ff., but it was widely practised in Turkey, Arabia, Morocco.
137 Hurgronje, p. 13
138 Services, however, were still expected of her during the master's lifetime. Practice varied, however, with different Islamic sects. Among the Ibadi in Zanzibar a slave who had borne her master children could be sold at his death, Hardinge to Kimberley, 26 Feb. 1895, *PP* Africa no. 6 (1895), LXXI, 1895, p. 143, C 7707.
139 Reuben Levy, *The Social Structure of Islam*, Cambridge, 2nd ed., 1969, p. 77
140 Practice varied considerably, but Aubin says that in Morocco a slave had only to take refuge at a shrine and claim the right to be sold, while Hurgronje testifies that in Arabia discontented slaves could demand to be sold and the request was usually complied with.
141 Doughty, I, p. 554
142 Hurgronje, p. 12, states that labourers often refused emancipation. The Moorish government also claimed that slaves refused their freedom in order to retain security.
143 Informants in Lamu confirmed this point. Concubines are also reported to have on occasion refused marriage, which automatically conferred freedom, for this reason. See Brunschvig, pp. 107 ff.

slave's welfare basically depended on the benevolence of his master. All too often the laws and sanctions for his protection proved inadequate. Evidence of harsh treatment abounds. Probably the worst feature of Islamic slavery, however, was the misery to which it gave rise in the heart of Africa—the raids, the killing, the separation of husband and wife, of parent and child. Every slave sold in the markets of North Africa, the Middle East or Zanzibar, like every slave sold in the western world, left a gap in an African town, village or homestead. Every journey to the coast and across the sea left in its wake a trail of desolation and death.

Some journeys such as that across the Sahara desert were particularly ghastly. This voyage was always hazardous. Whole caravans were sometimes buried by sandstorms or perished from thirst when vital wells were found to be silted up. But the slaves, without shoes or clothes and often forced to walk, suffered most. Barth recorded the death from exposure of forty in a single night between the Fezzan and Benghazi and terrible tales were told of slaves left to die in the desert when their feet were so swollen that they could no longer stand or they were so exhausted that incessant beating could spur them no further.

The Sahara journey, like the Atlantic crossing, caused terrible suffering and took a high toll of human life. As late as 1886, the British Consul in Benghazi believed that two thirds of the slaves who started the voyage from the Sudanic belt to Cyrenaica died on the way.[144] Every slave who found an acceptable fate in a Muslim household had suffered the miseries of capture, or the degradation of being sold or condemned to a lifelong loss of freedom.

When Palmerston opened negotiations to close the slave markets of the Middle East and North Africa, he faced a formidable task. He was not dealing, as in Europe, with governments who had accepted the principle that slave trading was wrong. On the contrary, Muslim rulers thought it normal. Furthermore, they regarded the enslavement of an unbeliever, upon whom they might confer the blessing of Islam, as morally justified.[145] He was fighting the social system of whole peoples. It is true that he was attacking the slave trade and not slavery, but since, in some countries few people were born in bondage[146] and emancipation was prevalent, the institution was bound to die if the supply of slaves was stopped.[147]

Palmerston's negotiations were hampered by his policy of protecting the

144 Dupuis to the Duke of Edinburgh, 11 July 1886 enc. in Awdry to Lister, 24 Aug. 1886, FOCP 5459.

145 There is evidence that slaves also sometimes gave thanks for their capture and conversion, see Doughty, I, p. 555; Hurgronje, p. 17; Hay to Rosebery, no. 24, 13 May 1886, FOCP 5459.

146 Since a man could not be his father's slave the only people born into slavery normally were the children of two slaves, or the children of a slave woman by someone other than her own master. Practice varied, but it was said that few people were born into slavery in Egypt and the Ottoman empire.

147 It might, of course, also change for the worse if masters became less willing to emancipate their slaves.

routes to the east by bolstering up the declining Ottoman empire and preventing other powers from acquiring too great an influence in the Barbary states, East Africa and the Middle East. His success, therefore, varied with the degree of pressure he thought it wise to exert on any of the nations involved and with their own particular international position.

Morocco and the treaty network

Palmerston failed to negotiate any treaty with Morocco. The Sultan, certain that Britain would not push matters to extremes in view of his country's strategic position on the straits of Gibraltar, turned a deaf ear to all representations.[148] No agreement had been reached in the 1880s[149] when the Moroccan slave trade attracted considerable attention in Europe. Sensational and often garbled accounts of the ill-treatment of individual slaves appeared in the local foreign press and were reported in European newspapers.[150] These denounced the hawking of slaves through the streets of Tangier[151] and the separation of young children from their mothers,[152] and reported that boys were being castrated in Morocco.[153] The Anti-Slavery Society took up the matter with gusto and sent its own commissioners to investigate.[154] Questions were asked in Parliament. Particular attention was drawn to the holding of slaves by persons under British protection[155] and

148 Boahen, pp. 141 ff
149 It appears that little was done by Britain after 1842 to get a treaty. Sir John Drummond Hay who had been her representative in Morocco from 1845 maintained in 1872 that he had never had instructions to raise the question with the Moorish Government, although he had sometimes done so on his own initiative, Hay to Granville, no. 1, ST, 10 Jan. 1872, FO 84/1354.
150 The *Anti-Slavery Reporter* published many extracts from the three Tangier foreign language papers, the Spanish *Al-Moghreb al-Aksa*, the French *Réveil du Maroc* and the *Times of Morocco*. These papers, founded in 1883 and 1884, were essentially the mouthpieces of the European business community in Tangier, see Miège, pp. 324 ff. The English papers which carried articles on the subject included *The Times*, *Evening Standard*, *Daily News*, *Pall Mall Gazette*, and *Daily Chronicle*.
151 For an emotional account see *Anti-Slavery Reporter*, IV, 10, 16 Dec. 1884, pp. 228–9.
152 *Anti-Slavery Reporter*, VII, 2, March-April 1887 pp. 50–1
153 *Ibid.*, and III, 7, July 1883; *Evening Standard*, 19 June 1883
154 Reports on Moroccan slavery appeared in the *Anti-Slavery Reporter* before 1883, but from May of that year almost every issue devoted space to it. The secretary and treasurer of the society visited Morocco in 1884, and the secretary and Mr J. V. Crawford in 1885. They founded an anti-slavery society in Tangier. For their findings see *Anti-Slavery Reporter*, IV, 6, 16 June 1884, pp. 120–5; *The Times*, 12 May 1884; C. H. Allen and J. V. Crawford, *Morocco—Report to the Committee of the BFASS*, London 1886. The society urged the government to take action and saw to it that questions were raised in Parliament, where Mr Arthur Pease, MP, president of the society, looked after much of their business.
155 *Anti-Slavery Reporter*, III, 11, 21 Nov. 1883, p. 274, IV, 6, 16 June 1884, p. 125;

much stress was laid on the fact that public slave dealing—a 'scandal to civilisation'—went unchecked on the very threshold of Europe, 'almost within sight of a British possession'.[156]

This campaign, however, was only part of a much more important agitation in business and humanitarian circles for the reform of the whole archaic and corrupt system of government and the opening of Morocco to foreign investment and commerce.[157] Foreign trade, hampered by export duties and prohibitions, was confined to certain ports, foreign enterprise was discouraged and diplomats were relegated to Tangier away from the capitals. Port and transport facilities were poor. Government was arbitrary, and officials poorly paid, if at all, resorted to corruption and extortion. Moroccans sought security in foreign protection which was freely extended by powers anxious to increase their influence. As a result large numbers of the Sultan's subjects escaped his jurisdiction and avoided taxes.

In addition, Morocco had no frontiers in the European sense—the Sultan counted as his subjects all who mentioned his name in Friday prayers, and over much of the vast region he claimed his rule was purely nominal. European businessmen trying to establish themselves in territories beyond his effective control, where he could give them little protection, found their activities hampered by his opposition.[158] Sultan Mulay Hassan I[159] had shown some inclination towards reform, but he had been checked by an economic depression, which crippled his finances from 1877. By the early 1880s the abuse of the protection system and rising fears of European, particularly French, intervention, made him reluctant to make any changes which might increase foreign interference in Morocco.

In this situation humanitarian questions were but pawns in a greater game. Slavery and the slave trade were only two of the many institutions under attack. Much stress was also laid by foreign businessmen and humanitarians on the terrible conditions in prisons, on brutal punishments, on the treatment of the Jews and on the extortions of officials. The picture built up in England was of a backward, barbarous but rich country in dire need of reform, and the government was urged to pursue a more active policy.[160] Britain's main interest, however, was to maintain the independence and integrity of Morocco to prevent her coasts from falling into the hands of a rival European power. Reform was of secondary concern. The architect and principal instrument of British policy was Sir John Drummond Hay,[161]

Hay to Granville, no. 3 Af., 13 Mar. 1884, FO 84/1668; *The Times*, 12 and 14 May 1884.

156 *Pall Mall Gazette*, 16 April 1883. There are many other references in the same vein.

157 For a full discussion of Morocco in this period see Miège, III, IV.

158 Miège, III, pp. 293 ff.; F. V. Parsons, 'The North-West African Company and the British Government, 1875–95', *Historical Journal*, i, 2, 1958, pp. 136–53.

159 Mulay Hassan I, 1873–94

160 Miège, IV, pp. 146–7

161 See *ibid.*, pp. 67 ff. for his policy.

who at this time had no desire to see the Sultan take steps which might weaken his authority, and no wish to jeopardise his own position as a trusted advisor by pressing unpopular measures. The slavery issue was a particularly delicate one, being a social and, in the eyes of the Moors, a religious question.

Nevertheless the Foreign Office ordered an inquiry into slavery in Morocco and made a 'friendly' appeal to the Sultan to consider abolition.[162] He replied that it was impossible:

> It would endanger us with our subjects, for it touches, not on customs alone, but also religion. This Empire is not as other countries, which are civilized and whose inhabitants dwell in cities; they ... are mostly Bedouins and Nomads, and do not always occupy the same place, ... but change with every wind. They cannot be bound by anything; and it is very difficult for them to forsake their customs—much more so to forsake what concerns their religion. They do not obey what is ordered them— they obey in words, but not in deeds. If their obedience in acts is required, troops and an army must be sent to them, until they obey though with repugnance, and then when the troops are withdrawn they revert to their customs.[163]

When it is remembered that the Sultan frequently had to enforce his authority by military force, that he owed his throne to the fact that he was a religious leader and was expected to uphold the faith,[164] that his subjects were highly conservative,[165] particularly the Muslim clerics and powerful religious fraternities,[166] and that all men of influence were probably slave owners, this argument seems reasonable. Certainly Hay thought any attempt at abolition might provoke revolution.[167]

The Anti-Slavery Society, however, denounced the reply as unsatisfactory and the religious objections as untrue.[168] Grist was added to the mill when, early in 1884, a spiritual leader, the Sharif of Ouezzane, who had recently put himself under French protection, freed his slaves, renounced slave trading and declared that slavery was not inherent in the Muslim faith.[169] France moreover decreed that none of her protégés or employees

162 White to Granville, no. 6, Af., 13 Aug. 1883, and enc., FO 84/1638

163 Vizier to White, 28 Aug. 1883, enc. White to Granville, no. 7 Af., 11 Sept. 1883, *ibid.*

164 The Sultan claimed to be the true Caliph of the Muslim world, owing no allegiance to Constantinople.

165 A fact noted by all contemporary travellers, Miège, IV, p. 135.

166 Further evidence is needed to establish the actual importance on the policy of the Sultan of the resistance to reform in religious and intellectual circles, *ibid.*

167 Hay to Rosebery, no. 3 Af., 23 April 1886, FO 84/1764.

168 *Anti-Slavery Reporter*, IV, 5, 17 May 1884, pp. 107–8

169 For a discussion of the relations between France and the Sharif see Miège, IV, pp. 44 ff.

might own slaves. This provoked a typical reaction from the secretary of the Anti-Slavery Society:

> Would that the initiative had been taken by England, who ought to be second to none in her efforts to raise aloft the banner to human freedom[170]

Britain hastened to follow the French example.

Britain also urged the Sultan to stop the public sale of slaves at seaports, warning him that it was repugnant to Europeans, and that stories in the press might lead to pressure to end Moroccan independence if slave dealing was not kept out of the sight of foreigners.[171] To this request he eventually agreed, but no other steps were taken to check the traffic.

The actual extent of the trade at this time is hard to estimate, at present, but as the Sultan imposed a tax on every sale, the archives of the Makhzen may eventually yield the necessary information.[172] Morocco was not believed to export any slaves[173] but she imported them from the south mainly through Tuat and Tindouf. Contemporaries gave figures which seem to accord with their own predilections. Hay, who consistently played down the slavery issue, thought that there were few slaves in the country[174] and that not more than 300 to 500 were imported annually,[175] while the correspondents of the Anti-Slavery Society, who probably exaggerated, believed there were 50,000 slaves in Morocco,[176] and that around 4,000 came in across the desert every year.[177] In addition a few Circassians and Ethiopians came from the east in European ships,[178] and so, according to the Moroccans, did eunuchs,[179] and some slaves came in with caravans of pilgrims returning from Mecca.[180]

170 *The Times*, 12 May 1884; *Anti-Slavery Reporter*, IV, 6, 16 June 1884, p. 124
171 Hay to Cid Mohammed Bargash, 7 Jan. 1884, enc. in Hay to Granville, no. 2 Af., 5 Feb. 1884, FO 84/1668
172 Miège, I, p. 22, III, p. 365
173 Hay denied press reports that slaves for sale were taken to the east in European ships. They sometimes accompanied their masters on pilgrimages, he said, but as the price was higher in Morocco than in the east they were not sold, Hay to Rosebery, no. 3 Af., 23 April 1886. FO 84/1764.
174 Hay to Granville, no. 1, ST, 10, Jan 1872, FO 84/1354
175 Hay to Rosebery, no. 24, Af., 13 May 1886, FOCP 5459
176 *Anti-Slavery Reporter*, V, 2, 22 Feb. 1885, p. 289, article by Donald Mackenzie
177 Allen and Crawford, article by Rolleston, correspondent of the *Globe* in Tangier. Miège considers this question at length and states that the numbers of slaves imported through Tuat cannot be estimated but from information in the French archives in Rabat he quotes the figure arriving annually at Tindouf between 1875 and 1885 at 500 to 1,000, and remarks that the numbers seem to decline after 1882 with a general decline of trans-Saharan trade, Miège, III, pp. 363 ff.
178 Hay to Rosebery, no. 24, 13 May 1886, FOCP 5459
179 Cid Mohammed Bargash to Hay, 31 Jan. 1884, enc. in Hay to Granville, no. 2, Af., 5 Feb. 1884, FO 84/1668. The Moors denied that boys were castrated in Morocco but according to the Tangier press the operation was performed on 50 boys in Meknès in 1883, *Anti-Slavery Reporter*, III, 7, July 1883, and the British Consul in Safi had heard rumours of the operation being performed by a 'Shereef residing in the Atlas

These imports, however, represent only part of the trafficking which went on in Morocco. In hard times, and times were very hard indeed between 1877 and 1885 when a series of bad harvests reduced thousands of people to destitution and drove many of them into the cities, peasants were obliged to sell their children to keep them from starving,[181] and masters were forced to sell their slaves.[182] Even in prosperous years slaves changed hands for a variety of reasons such as their own misconduct or because their owner went bankrupt or ill-treated them, and free children were kidnapped and sold.[183] Sales included persons of every colour and age and both sexes.[184] Most of those imported from the south were young children,[185] some so young that the auctioneers carried them through the streets on their shoulders. A major dispersal point for these slaves seems to have been the market at Marrakesh, but many small markets existed in towns and in the countryside.[186]

Opinions varied considerably on the treatment of slaves. Moroccans insisted that they were well cared for and that their lot was far preferable to that of a free poor person or a freed slave both of whom were liable to starve in time of trouble.[187] Hay was inclined to agree with them and maintained that the plight of the free peasants should give greater cause for anxiety than that of slaves.[188] On the other hand the Consul in Mazagan thought they were 'invariably badly treated'.[189] Where Hay believed that the life of a concubine was:

Mountains' with few casualties, report by Hunot, 30 May 1883, enc. no. 5 in Hay to Granville, 16 June 1883, *PP* LXVI, 1883, C–3700. T. E. Zerbib visited Messfouia in 1887 and reported seeing many very sick-looking 'negro boys'. He was told castration was practised there and that 28 out of 30 victims died, *Anti-Slavery Reporter*, VII, 2, March-April 1887, p. 50.

180 Dunn, p. 283

181 This was deplored by good Muslims but nevertheless was admitted practice, Cid Mohammed Bargash to Hay, 31 Jan. 1884, enc. in Hay to Granville, no. 2. Af., 5 Feb. 1884, FO 84/1668.

182 Hay believed the destitution in the countryside had trebled sales in Tangier, Hay to Granville, no. 2. Af., 5 Feb. 1884, *ibid*. The reports of 1883 stress the exceptional number of slaves being offered for sale and the consequent drop in prices; report by Payton, 30 May 1883, enc. 3 in Hay to Granville, no. 5, 16 June 1883, *PP* LXVI, 1883, C–3700; report by Hunot, 30 May 1883, enc. 5, *ibid*.; Redman to Hay, May 1883, enc. 1, *ibid*.

183 Report by Hunot, 30 May 1883, enc. 5 in Hay to Granville, no. 5, 16 June 1883, *ibid*.

184 *Ibid*.

185 Report by Payton, 30 May 1883, enc. 3 in Hay to Granville, no. 5, 16 June 1883, *ibid*.

186 Where there was no special market for slaves, as in Mogador, they simply followed the auctioneer around the town while he called out the latest bid, *ibid*.

187 Cid Mohammed Bargash to Hay, 31 Jan. 1884, enc. in Hay to Granville, no. 2, Af., 5 Feb. 1884, FO 84/1668. It would appear that the client relationship between slave and master did not function to protect the freed slave in Morocco, perhaps because times were exceptionally bad.

188 Hay to Rosebery, no. 3 Af., 23 April 1886, FO 84/1764

189 Redman to Hay, May 1883, enc. no. 1 in Hay to Granville, no. 5, 16 June 1883, *PP* LXVI, 1883, C–3700.

far preferable and less immoral than that of thousands of girls in Europe who are sold by their parents or sell themselves and fall into the lowest state of degradation,[190]

Consul Hunot thought that they were 'subjected to the most degrading treatment that can be conceived', and added

imagine unprotected young females, some of whom are handsome, in the hands of savage barbarians, who have virtually the power of life and death over their victims, for no inquiries are ever made into the cause of death; and the only restraint, therefore, is the slave-owner's pecuniary interest in his slave.[191]

Harems could not be penetrated and such judgements were clearly subjective.

These examples illustrate the difficulty of assessing the value of contemporary literature on slavery, not just in Morocco but everywhere. A consul faced with a case of brutality to a slave might consider it as a rare incident on a par with wife-beating in England, or he might take it as proof positive that the whole institution lent itself to abuse and should be abolished. Even slave markets found their defenders. Hurgronje, for instance, claimed that the market in Mecca was a jovial, happy place, where slaves laughed among themselves at the questions of inquisitive buyers and no more objected to being physically examined than a European minded a medical examination.[192] Most observers, however, found the sight repulsive.[193]

The weight of contemporary evidence suggests that most slaves in Morocco were domestic servants, leading a reasonably easy life.[194] Some acquired skills and were allowed to make money for themselves and even buy their freedom, and emancipation was not uncommon. Compared with a free man the slave had greater protection against hunger and the exactions of an arbitrary government. Aubin commented that the servant women could often come and go as they wished,[195] and so had more liberty than their mistresses in their harems, while a concubine who had children by her master was free and inherited part of his property on his death.[196] But whatever the condition of the slaves, given the strategic position of Morocco,

190 Hay to Rosebery, no. 24, 13 May 1886, FOCP 5459
191 Hunot report, 30 May 1883, enc. 5 in Hay to Granville, no. 5, 16 June 1883, *PP* LXVI, 1883, C-3700.
192 Hurgronje, p. 15. Slatin also thought few slaves in Omdurman minded examination, p. 557.
193 See for instance, Allen and Crawford, pp. 10–11; Aubin, p. 35; *Anti-Slavery Reporter*, II, 6, June 1882, pp. 166–7.
194 See reports enc. in Hay to Granville, no. 5, 16 June 1883, *PP* LXVI, C-3700. Some slaves were owned by desert nomads and were used as servants or shepherds, Dunn, p. 276.
195 Aubin, pp. 253–4
196 Renault, II, p. 10

the international rivalry of the 1880s and the refusal of the Sultan to take any measures against slavery or the slave trade, there was little Britain could do about it.

France and Algeria and Tunis

In the other North African states the position was very different. Algeria was already French when Palmerston opened his campaign and all discussions, therefore, had to be conducted with France. Slavery legally ended when it was abolished in all French colonies in 1848. It is believed that there were relatively few slaves in the colony at the time. Owing to the working of Muslim law and custom, they were outnumbered by free blacks.[197] Those that existed were mainly women domestic servants, who had come across the desert from the south. After abolition, slavery is said to have died out slowly as masters, fearing their slaves would escape, lost interest in buying them.[198] In any case supplies were limited as tribal rivalry, followed by French military action and the establishment of customs posts in southern Algeria diverted the main trans-Saharan caravan trade to markets in Morocco or to Ghadames.[199] Beyond French borders, especially around Mzab, slavery persisted and slaves were freely imported until the French conquest of 1883. Thereafter the trade declined to a small smuggling traffic.[200]

Tunis, on the other hand, did not come under French protection until the early 1880s. When Palmerston began negotiations, her ruler feared both French and Turkish aggression and wanted British support to maintain his independence. By 1846, therefore, he had actually prohibited both slavery and the slave trade. This was confirmed in a treaty between Britain and Tunis in 1875,[201] but no penalties for slave holding were mentioned and in the eyes of the population it was not a crime. In the 1880s, when the French were in general control, the position with regard to slavery was curious. Although it was forty years since it had been abolished, slaves were still being smuggled in from the Sudanic belt, probably mainly for concubinage, and any who fled to the British Consulate were given protection and freed through British intercession with the authorities. From 1879 to 1884 between sixty and seventy slaves a year obtained their freedom in this way, most of them women and many belonging to members of the ruling family.[202]

197 Emerit, p. 33   198 *Ibid.*, p. 42
199 C. W. Newbury, 'North African and Western Sudan Trade in the Nineteenth Century: a Re-Evaluation', *JAH*, vii, 2, 1966, pp. 233–46, p. 235; Renault, II, p. 12; Dunn, pp. 297–303
200 Renault, II, pp. 10–11
201 Tunisian decrees against the slave trade and slavery are in Hertslet, *Commercial Treaties*, VIII, pp. 914, 917 and the treaty of 1875 is in *ibid.*, XIV, p. 553.
202 Reade to Granville, no. 15, 16 April 1884, FO 84/1673. See also G. Jobard, *L'esclavage en Tunisie*, Tunis 1890.

Some eunuchs also took refuge at the Consulate.[203] Generally the Tunisian authorities made no difficulty about granting them manumission certificates.

However, some cases took place in the mid-1880s which gave rise to discussions between England and France, and are worth quoting for the light they throw both on the futility of the anti-slavery laws as administered in Tunisian courts[204] and on the curious position in which the British found themselves. In 1884 two women took refuge at the Consulate. The Consul had already obtained certificates of freedom for them, when two of their owner's black servants claimed them as wives. Wives would have had to be returned to their husbands, while slaves could remain under British protection. The case came before the Muslim judge, or Cadi, who, on very doubtful evidence pronounced the marriages valid. The French supported him. The British Consul, however, refused to surrender the women, pleading that if he did:

> all further intervention on behalf of slaves who come to the Consulate for protection against the arbitrary and generally brutal treatment of their masters, and are, for the most part females, in a state of abject distress and bearing the marks of corporal punishment on their bodies, would be useless.[205]

The matter was allowed to drop and the women remained free.

Two years later another fugitive was claimed first as a slave and later by the same man as his wife. By prevailing Muslim law a man's wife could not be his slave. When the Cadi heard that the girl had not been freed on marriage, he liberated her on the spot but then declared the marriage valid. The British considered this flagrant corruption.[206] Again the French upheld the Cadi and the English refused to return the slave.

Such cases show the curious role of British Consuls in states where slavery existed, whether it was legal, as in Morocco, or illegal but clearly practised, as in Tunisia. They were self-appointed policemen in the midst of an alien population with very different social ideas, and they were interfering in domestic, even, the French claimed, matrimonial affairs. Since a Muslim household was a very private place and little could be known about what really went on inside it, such intervention required great caution and was liable to be resented. However, Britain could congratulate herself on the fact that slavery was at least illegal in Tunisia and that its suppression was now a French responsibility, even if it appeared unlikely that France would risk upsetting her new subjects by any determined attack on the remaining vestiges of the institution.[207]

203 Sandwich to Salisbury, no. 2, 30 Jan. 1886, FO 84/1768
204 Slavery cases did not come before French courts but were exclusively dealt with in Tunisian courts.
205 Reade to Granville, no. 15, 16 April 1884, FO 84/1673, and encs.
206 Report by Rothery, 16 June 1886, enc. in Welby to Lister, 25 June 1886, FOCP 5459. Most of the other documents in this case are in FO 84/1768.
207 The attitude of the French was expressed by d'Estournelles when he wrote to

The Turks and the slave trade in Tripoli and Cyrenaica

Tripoli came under effective Turkish rule in 1842 and henceforth all negotiations had to be conducted at Constantinople and were part of the long struggle to end the Ottoman slave traffic. This struggle was conducted with caution, since it was feared that the social upheavals resulting from an attack on slavery might deal the *coup de grâce* to the crumbling Turkish empire. Not only were the sultans the sons of slave mothers, but most officials had started life as slaves, and the institution was said to be intimately bound up with the habits and religion of all classes from the Sultan 'down to the lowest peasant'.[208]

Concessions would imply an acceptance by the Sultan, the head of much of the Muslim world, of the British view that slave dealing was wrong, and this he was far from believing. Gradually, however, concessions were wrung from the Turks. In 1847 they agreed to prohibit their ships from taking part in the slave traffic to the Persian Gulf[209] and they closed the slave markets of Constantinople. During the Crimean War when Britain and France were fighting to defend the Ottoman empire against the Russians, revelations of an extensive trade in white slaves across the Black Sea and in black slaves from North Africa led to strong representations.[210] As a result, the Turks prohibited the white slave traffic in 1854 and three years later outlawed the trade in blacks everywhere except in the 'holy' province of the Hijaz, where Muslim feeling ran high, slave dealing was rife and Turkish control nominal. Elsewhere it was still legal to own slaves but not to buy or sell them, and light penalties were prescribed for doing so.[211] The declared aim of the law or *firman* was the eventual abolition of slavery itself.

This was a great step forward but the law remained a dead letter in many parts of the empire, including Tripoli and Cyrenaica. In the 1880s slaves were still being exported to Turkish and other ports. Britain had no powers to search ships in the Mediterranean and when she eventually negotiated a treaty with Turkey in 1880, she still did not acquire this right, presumably for the same reasons as those given by W. H. Wylde in 1869:

> The steamers that carry slaves also carry passengers of all denominations, pilgrims of all shades of colour, free blacks who are domestic servants of some of the passengers, and free blacks travelling on their own account.

Reade that unfortunately he was told that: 'le Cadi est seul compétent pour décider si un mariage entre indigènes est valable ou non. Si vous pouvez m'aider à repliquer à cet argument je ne demande pas mieux', 20 Mar. 1884, enc. Reade to Granville, no. 15, 16, April 1884, FO 84/1673.
208 Kelly, p. 586, quoting from Ponsonby to Palmerston, ST no. 1, 27 Dec. 1840, FO 84/333.
209 *Ibid.*, p. 587. Turkish ships were barely involved in this traffic.
210 Boahen, pp. 152 ff.
211 Confiscation for the first offence, confiscation and a year's imprisonment for the second, Hertslet, *Commercial Treaties*, X, pp. 1097 ff.

How could the Commander of a cruiser discriminate between the slaves and the free blacks, when, as I hear is the case, the former are dressed up the same as their free countrymen ? And suppose a mistake did take place, and one of our cruisers were either to detain a vessel or take out of her an individual under French protection, what correspondence we should probably have with the French government on the subject.[212]

All that Britain could do, therefore, to stop the export of slaves across the Mediterranean, was to make representations to the territorial authorities.

In Cyrenaica in the 1880s Turkish officials allowed slaves to be smuggled on board steamers of the Mahsoussa line under their very eyes. Victims were disguised as domestic servants or euphemistically described as 'refugees' from the Sudan. Small batches of captives were also shipped out secretly on little coastal schooners from collecting points east of Benghazi beyond the range of telegraphic communication.[213] Others were exported overland to Egypt.[214]

Only a minority of the slaves reaching Tripoli and Cyrenaica in the late nineteenth century were exported. Most remained in the vilayets scattered through town and country as domestic servants. Every Bedouin who owned land or a camel was said to have one or more. They were of all ages and both sexes but the greatest demand was for women and girls. They came mainly from Darfur and Wadai, through the oases of Kufra, in the Libyian desert, or Selimeh and Siwa in Egypt to Awjilah and Jalo, in Cyrenaica, suffering all the terrible privations and high mortality of the desert crossing.[215]

Slaves were among the few profitable commodities exported across the Sahara. They were believed earlier in the century to be the only goods going north on the eastern routes.[216] The trade on these routes was given a great impetus by the establishment of the puritanical Muslim religious brotherhood, the Sanusiya, in Cyrenaica in 1843.[217] This order forged links with Wadai, established religious centres, or *zawiya*, far and wide across the Sahara, kept the peace among desert peoples, sheltered and protected traders and virtually ruled the hinterland of Turkish Cyrenaica.

212 Quoted in Boahen, p. 157. Wylde was head of the Slave Trade Department of the Foreign Office. The Mediterranean was politically a very sensitive area throughout the nineteenth century and any interference with its shipping was liable to cause diplomatic complications.
213 Dupuis to Duke of Edinburgh, 11 July 1886, enc. in Awdry to Lister, 24 Aug. 1886, FOCP 5459; Richard to d'Estrées, no. 78, 22 Feb. 1889, FMAE/CC/Trip/45; Grande to Crispi, 8 June 1889, enc. in Catalani to Salisbury, 25 June 1889, FOCP 6010; Cameron Report, 11 May 1889, enc. in White to Salisbury, no. 10, Af., conf., 8 July 1889, FO 84/1971; Wood to Rosebery, no. 2, Af., 10 July 1886, and enc., FO 84/1768.
214 See Renault, II, p. 15.
215 *Ibid.* For the horrors of the desert crossing see p. 61 above.
216 Boahen, p. 127, gives this information but cites no source.
217 For a history of the Sanusi see E. E. Evans-Pritchard, *The Sanusi of Cyrenaica*, Oxford 1949.

Far from stopping the slave traffic into Cyrenaica, the Turkish authorities, from the chief of police down, were reported to be conniving at it.[218] Caravans from central Africa arrived unhindered at Awjilah, although the Turks had a police force there about fifty strong in 1889. From this oasis, slaves were distributed all over the province.[219] They were brought into Benghazi in small groups of two or three.[220] It was left to the British Consul to denounce slave dealers, but, when he did, convictions could not be obtained in local courts.[221] An average of a hundred slaves a year obtained their freedom by taking refuge at the British Consulate[222] but they were then persecuted by the police until they went back to their master, or they were sold by officials.[223]

When the British protested, Turkish governors simply denied that the slave trade existed.[224] By 1889, however, they were pleading inability to cope with the situation. Cyrenaica was poor, its treasury empty, communications were bad and the oases of Jalo and Awjilah were not under effective control.[225] This was doubtless true.[226] But the question must be related to the Turkish position in North Africa. There, by the 1880s, the French were established to the west and were pushing down into the Sahara trying to divert caravans back to Algeria by wooing the desert peoples. To the east the British had occupied Egypt. The Mahdi,[227] Muhammad Ahmad ibn' Abdallah, was in control of the Sudan, and the whole hinterland of Cyrenaica was dominated by the Sanusi. The Turks claimed sovereignty and hoped to extend their rule far out into the Sahara. The best buffers against French, British or Sudanese aggression were the Sanusi and the independent desert peoples.

218 Wood to Rosebery, no. 1, Af., 22 April 1886, no. 2, Af., 10 July 1886, no. 3, Af., 30 July 1886, FO 84/1768. For examples of the connivance of ill-paid Turkish officials in the Fezzan earlier in the century see G. Nachtigal, *Sahara and Sudan*, I, Berlin 1879, pp. 132–3, 480–1, 701, cited in Fisher and Fisher, p. 167.
219 Cameron report, 11 May 1889, enc. in White to Salisbury, no. 10, Af., conf., 8 July 1889, FO 84/1971
220 Memo by Marinitch, 6 July 1889, enc. in White to Salisbury, no. 10, Af., conf., 8 July 1889, *ibid.*
221 Cameron report, 11 May 1889, enc. in White to Salisbury, no. 10, Af., conf., 8 July 1889, *ibid.*
222 *Ibid.* Cameron to Salisbury, no. 1, 1 Jan. 1889, FO 84/1971. 47 were freed in 1884, 54 in 1885, 94 in 1886, 108 in 1887 and 115 in 1888.
223 Numbers of slaves were also freed by the consulate in Tripoli. See ch. 3 below for the freed slave question.
224 Cameron report, 11 May 1889, enc. in White to Salisbury, no. 10, Af., conf., 8 July 1889, FO 84/1971.
225 Marinitch memo., 6 July 1889, enc. *ibid.*; Cameron to White, 24 Dec. 1888, enc. in White to Salisbury, no. 39, conf., 30 Jan. 1889, *ibid.*
226 Certainly the British Consul agreed, Cameron report, 11 May 1889, enc. in White to Salisbury, no. 1, Af., conf., 8 July 1889, *ibid.*
227 Muhammad Ahmad ibn 'Abdallah launched a religious revolution in the Sudan in 1881 which drove out the Egyptians. See p. 81 below.

A determined attack on the slave traffic could only alienate them[228] and deal a blow to the small trade of Benghazi, probably ending its long distance contacts.[229] In the local North African situation, it was simply not in the Ottoman interest to adopt a vigorous policy of suppression and the Turkish administrator of Benghazi was actually reported to have presented the Sanusi leader with five slaves when he visited Jaghbub in 1889.[230] On the other hand in the international field, France and Italy were suspected of casting covetous eyes on Tripoli, and Turkey could not afford to offer an excuse for intervention by openly protecting the slave traffic. This may account for the more active steps taken in this very year in Tripoli where there were more foreign observers and Turkish power was greater.[231] Whereas the policy of pleading weakness and taking no effective action was doubtless a reasonable response to the position in Cyrenaica.

The slave trade of the Sahara Desert

Thus over forty years after Palmerston had launched his attack on the North African slave trade, slaves still found a ready market in Cyrenaica, Tripoli and Morocco and a smaller one in Tunis, and were still being exported from the coast of Cyrenaica to Ottoman ports in the Mediterranean and Middle East. In the Sahara itself the trade went unchecked. A vast area of desert and tundra stretching from the Atlantic to the borders of Egypt was inhabited mainly by Muslim nomads. Slavery was of particular importance in the lives of these people, for desert conditions put a great strain on their limited manpower.

Not only did they have to cover great distances to graze their animals, but they often had several kinds of animals requiring different types of pasture found many miles apart.[232] In addition, as they could not live off their flocks and herds alone, they were forced to grow dates, vegetables and

228 For a discussion of Turkish policy in the Sahara see A. Martel, *Les confins saharo-tripolitains de la Tunisie 1881–1911*, 2 vols., Paris 1965, I, pp. 801, ff.
229 The trade of the Awjilah oasis with Benghazi was so small that the British Consul pointed out that if the people were pressed too hard for arrears of tax, they might simply fall back on Kufra. Cameron to Salisbury, no. 19, 19 Aug. 1889, FO 84/1971. The trade of Tripoli with the Sudanic belt was declining in the 1880s. The French consul wrote in 1889 that only 600 camels were required for the Sudanic caravan as against 2000 in about 1883, Profits had dropped from 80%–150% to 10%–20%. Imports into the Sudanic belt had halved. He attributed this to the fall in the demand for Sudanese ostrich feathers in Europe. The main Sudanese exports were now hides, skins and ivory. This information is for Tripoli but it would follow that if slaves could be marketed they would be the most profitable of the goods, and perhaps the only ones, making the whole journey from the central Sudan to Benghazi. D'Estrées to Spuller, no. 32, 29 July 1889, FMAE/CC/Trip./45.
230 D'Estrées to Spuller, 9 Dec. 1889, *ibid*.   231 See ch. 6, p. 246.
232 J. Nicolaisen, 'Slavery Among the Tuareg in the Sahara', *KUML* 1957, pp. 93–113. English summary, pp. 107–113, pp. 107–8. The author points out that the Tuareg of the Ahaggar mountains may graze their animals on pastures as much as

millet in the oases. Sometimes more food had to be obtained from the desert fringes to the north or south. Raiding for slaves and animals was a normal method of increasing their wealth and provided them with the necessary trade goods. Some nomads also supplemented their resources by running caravans across the desert. For all these occupations men were required, and they would often be away from home for long periods of time.

Desert people sometimes solve manpower shortage by close co-operation between families, but to the nomad of the Sahara in the last century, slavery was an obvious and time-hallowed solution. He acquired slaves to use as barter or to do the chores around the tents or on the march, to watch the animals, sometimes to fight for him or to help cultivate the oases,[233] or to collect or carry goods such as gum copal for trade.[234] The Sanusi used many slaves as servants or agricultural labourers in their zawiya.[235]

In the desert slavery was normally practised in accordance with Muslim law although with some interesting variations. Some of these may be mentioned briefly here since they show the wide differences in the institution even among Muslims. Among the Tuareg, for instance, marriages between free men and slave women were rare and concubinage was not widely practised, but if a man did have a child by a female slave, the child remained a slave and took the status of his mother as did all Tuareg.[236] Slaves thus usually married other slaves and remained a separate caste. Barth commented upon the fact that the Tuareg encouraged them to wed and seemed to 'take great pains to rear slaves'.[237]

However, they were integrated into the family of their owner and stood in the same relationship to members of that family as other people of their generation. Thus a master would treat an older slave with much the same deference as he treated his own father but would expect the same obedience from a young slave as from his own children.[238] If a slave wished to change

500–600 kilometres apart at any one time. He also discusses the extent to which they need to supplement their food by trade. This is a recent study but the manpower problem must have been great in the unsettled conditions of the nineteenth century.
233 Nicolaisen, p. 110; F. R. Rodd, *People of the Veil*, London 1926, pp. 134–6. Both discuss the uses of slaves among the Tuareg. Nomads despise the settled life of the oases and in many cases cultivation is done by a depressed class of apparently mixed descent, *haratin*, who are distinct from slaves, but there is also evidence that slaves were sometimes used for agricultural work. See, for instance, Nachtigal, I, p. 91, cited in Fisher and Fisher, p. 114; Barth, I, pp. 387–8.
234 Fisher and Fisher, p. 114, citing, the use of slaves by the Trarza Moors. There are also numerous references in AOF K 14 to Moorish gum traders coming with their slaves to French posts in Senegal.
235 Renault, II, p. 15
236 Marriages between slaves and free women were forbidden. The child of a free man and a slave while remaining a slave would not however remain in the lowest caste, the *ikelan*, but would be a more respected *buzu*, a herdsman rather than a cultivator, and his descendants might rise into the class of vassals—*imghad*, Rodd, pp. 134–6.   237 Barth, II, p. 151
238 Fictive kin bonds were ascribed so that the older slave was considered as his

74

masters he could do so by nicking the ear of the riding camel of the man he wished to serve. His owner would then be obliged to give him to that man in compensation for the damage to the camel.[239] To lose a slave in this way was considered a great disgrace. Customs such as these discouraged cruelty but life in the desert was generally harsh for everyone. Barth thought the Tuareg treated their slaves better than the Arabs or Tebu, although he was appalled to see slaves harnessed to a plough and driven with a whip in Air.[240] A French observer on the other hand thought that all the slaves who travelled with the nomads, Moors, Tuareg, or Arabs, had hard lives,[241]

Britain had attempted to check the desert slave trade in the 1840s and 1850s by establishing vice-consuls at Murzuk and Ghadames to promote legitimate commerce and watch the traffic, and by sending missions to sign treaties with the desert peoples.[242] Although much useful information was collected, these efforts came to nothing and long before 1880 the consulates were closed and Britain concentrated on exhorting the Moroccans and Turks, who made such extensive claims to suzerainty, to suppress it. A British company which established itself briefly at Cape Juby on the Atlantic coast to open up legitimate trade received scant official support, and its applications for a charter to administer the area were turned down.[243] The only serious efforts against the desert trade in the 1880s were made by the French as they advanced southwards into the northern Sahara,[244] but over most of the vast interior, the trade flourished beyond the range of European interference.

Egypt and the treaty network

Egypt, like Tripoli, was part of the Ottoman empire, and although her viceroy the Khedive was a virtually independent hereditary ruler, he was

father. The wife of a young slave had the same avoidance relationship with her husband's master as the master's own daughter-in-law would have. Nicolaisen, pp. 110–112.

239 *Ibid.*, p. 109
240 Barth, I, pp. 387–8, II, pp. 23, 151, V, p. 415
241 *Commandant de Cercle* of Timbuktu to the Governor of the Sudan, 29 Sept. 1894, AOF/K/14.
242 For this whole subject see Boahen, pp. 135 ff.
243 Britain feared the grant of a charter would precipitate a 'scramble' for Morocco although the area in question was not recognised by the powers as being part of Morocco. See Parsons; Miège, III, pp. 293 ff.; Donald MacKenzie, *The Khalifate of the West*, London 1911.
244 For an example of French action see Martel, I, pp. 421–3. He cites the arrival at Douz (Nefzaoua) in southern Tunisia in 1887 of Tuareg traders bringing slaves. They had no other trade goods and had been driven by famine in Tripolitania into French territory for the first time since France had occupied the oasis. The French escorted them out of the country, together with their slaves, and invited them to return again as legitimate traders. See also Renault, II, p. 11, for French suppression of the traffic in southern Algeria.

not given the right to negotiate separate treaties with foreign powers until 1873. The country was one of the great importers of both black and white slaves.[245] The vast majority, however, were black, and women outnumbered men by about three to one. Most were domestic servants, but large numbers of men were recruited into the army[246] and some were agricultural labourers.[247] Owners ranged from the ruler himself down to humble fellahin, many of whom bought slaves to work in the fields or to do military service for them when they made large profits from the cotton boom of the 1860s. Slaves were both status symbols and instruments of production and were much prized. In households where both free and slave servants were kept, the coarsest work was done by the free. A recent study suggests that there were about thirty thousand slaves in Egypt around 1880, nearly half living in Cairo. Muslim law was in full operation and emancipation was common after only a few years of servitude; a fact which kept up the demand for new slaves.[248]

Egypt was geographically well placed to draw upon a steady supply of African captives, particularly after her conquest of the Sudan early in the nineteenth century. They came from Bornu and Wadai across the western desert through the Siwa oasis from Cyrenaica.[249] Great numbers also came from south and west of Darfur, travelling overland to the Nile at Asyut or after 1850 through Kordofan and Khartoum.[250] From slaving grounds in the Sudan, the Nuba mountains or Ethiopia, they came also down the river or up the Red Sea.[251] Some were re-exported to various markets in the Ottoman empire often disguised as domestic servants and travelling openly on steamships of the Egyptian Aziziyya company. But most stayed in Egypt or the northern Sudan, where slavery was also widespread even amongst peasants and Bedouins, and where slaves served much the same purposes as in Egypt.[252]

245 Small numbers of white males continued to be imported until quite late in the century for use as officials, army officers or even as companions for the sons of the rich and there was a steady demand for white concubines, who were sometimes acquired even by peasants.
246 They were used mainly in the Sudan.
247 For slavery in Egypt I have relied heavily on Baer who is the source of my information unless other sources are cited.
248 Baer believes that the number of slaves in Egypt remained fairly constant through the nineteenth century partly for this reason, p. 423.
249 They came from the Sudanic belt either on the Kufra-Benghazi route, or through the Fezzan. In the late 1870s British consuls estimated that 2,000 slaves a year were entering Egypt across the western desert, Baer, p. 426, citing Cookson to Malet, 17 May 1880, FO 141/138, and they were still coming in 1890, see Renault, II, p. 15.
250 For slavery and the slave trade in Darfur see R. S. O'Fahey, 'Slavery and the Slave Trade in Darfur', *JAH*, xiv, 1, 1973, pp. 29–43.
251 Estimates suggest that 1,500 a year came through Korodofan and Darfur in the early 1870s, while 500–600 came up the Red Sea in 1869, Baer, p. 426.
252 For slavery in the Sudan see P. F. M. McLoughlin, 'Economic Development and

Egypt's conquest of the Sudan in the years after 1820 offered unique opportunities for slaving. From 1853 traders established themselves on the White Nile and the Bahr al-Ghazal to deal in ivory.[253] They soon found that their profits depended on the slave trade.[254] Known as 'Khartoumers' they swiftly built up private empires beyond the range of Egyptian authority establishing armed encampments or *zariba*, recruiting their own armies and dominating large tracts of country. By the 1860s they were the spearhead of Egyptian expansion but were not under Egyptian control and their activities sent a steady stream of victims to markets in the northern Sudan, Egypt, Turkey and Arabia. They also used slaves themselves as armed retainers, servants, concubines, porters and agricultural labourers and paid them as wages to their followers.

Britain exhorted the Viceroy to stop the import of slaves into the country[255] and made representations about the traffic on the White Nile.[256] The rulers of Egypt themselves banned public slave markets in 1854 and took a few measures against the traffic particularly after the issue of the Ottoman *firman* against it in 1857. The only results, however, were that markets were moved to discreet places and more slaves were transported overland instead of down the Nile and various deceptions were practised by slavers.[257] This was scarcely surprising, since most people approved of the trade, considerable numbers made their living by it, and the majority of officials, even at the highest level, were implicated in it.[258] Furthermore, slaving was encouraged by the fact that slaves continued to be recruited into the Egyptian army. Only really energetic measures, carried out by incorruptible officers, could be expected to root out a traffic that had become so firmly, apparently permanently, entrenched in the economic and social systems of Egypt and the Sudan.

the heritage of slavery in the Sudan Republic', *Africa*, 32, Oct. 1962, pp. 355–91. Information scattered through G. B. Hill (ed.), *Colonel Gordon in Central Africa 1874–79*, London 1884, 2nd ed., Slatin, and many other sources.

253 Until 1853 the commerce of the White Nile was a government monopoly.

254 For the slave trade from the Sudan and the operations of slave and ivory traders, see Gray, pp. 46 ff.; G. Schweinfurth, *The Heart of Africa*, 2 vols., London 1873 (trans.).

255 Baer, pp. 431–2

256 Gray, p. 167

257 Gray, pp. 52–3, 73; P. M. Holt, *A Modern History of the Sudan*, New York 1961 (henceforth *Modern History*), pp. 64–6; Renault, II, pp. 24–5. Nachtigal, who was travelling with a caravan of merchants from Darfur to el Obeid in 1874, recorded their dismay when they heard that slaves could no longer be sold in Egypt, but a Nile merchant came to meet them and took some of their captives, confident that he could hide them in villages and bribe the authorities until such time as the law was less rigorously enforced, G. Nachtigal, *Sahara and Sudan*, IV, translated by A. G. B. Fisher and H. J. Fisher, London 1971 (first published as volume III, Leipzig 1889), pp. 381–9.

258 See example cited in Renault, II, p. 24, fn. 4; Nachtigal, III, pp. 489, 495, 502–3, 505, cited in Fisher and Fisher, p. 168.

In 1863, however, an event took place which gave the Khedive Ismail[259] the incentive to take effective action against the traffic. This was the arrival in Egypt of the British explorers, J. H. Speke and J. A. Grant, with the news that beyond the area of 'utter savagedom' on the White Nile lay the rich, populous and thriving inter-lacustrine kingdoms, eager to do legitimate trade with Europe. Hitherto these regions had only been approached by Arab traders operating from Zanzibar. It was now suggested that they could more easily be reached up the Nile, and Ismail determined to extend his rule southwards to these promising fields.

Two years later another British explorer, Sir Samuel Baker, returning from his discovery of Lake Albert, roundly denounced the pillaging and slaving around the White Nile,[260] which he wrongly thought was preventing the development of a profitable legitimate trade in ivory. In 1869, Ismail appointed Baker to lead an expedition up the river to open the way to the great lakes, drive the slave traders from the area, and establish Egyptian control.

Whatever Ismail's private views on the morals of slave dealing may have been, he was now to become increasingly aware of the political advantages of playing the anti-slavery game. Not only was he extending his empire overland towards the inter-lacustrine kingdoms but he was also advancing along the western shores of the Red Sea. He had obtained the ports of Suakin and Massawa from his overlord the Sultan of Turkey and laid claim to the north-eastern coast of Africa down to Cape Guardafui.[261] To implement his plans he wanted British support and when Frere called on him on his way to Zanzibar late in 1872, Ismail offered to end the slave trade in central Africa but explained that as a Muslim ruler he would have to justify this to his own subjects. He suggested that a demonstration in England against the Egyptian slave trade would strengthen his hand.[262] This was an interesting statement of his dilemma, a dilemma also facing other Muslim rulers. He needed British support but this could only be had if the slave trade was suppressed, and this might cost him the allegiance of his subjects and would certainly arouse the anger of those with vested interests in the traffic. The demonstration he wanted was easily arranged and in due course he received a memorial from the Anti-Slavery Society.[263]

Within a few months of this conversation with Frere, the Sultan of Turkey granted Egypt the right to conclude non-political agreements with foreign powers. Almost immediately Britain proposed a convention against the slave trade.[264] The Khedive, still eager for British support, agreed and

259 Ismail 1863–79. The first measures against the slave trade were taken in the reign of his predecessor Said, 1854–63.

260 See Gray, pp. 82 ff. and Baker's own story in his account of his journey, *Albert Nyanza, Great Basin of the Nile*, London 1886, 2 vols., I, pp. 17–24, 91–5.

261 He was to obtain Zeila in 1875.

262 Memo. enc. in Frere to Granville, no. 1, 1 Jan. 1873, FO 84/1389

263 Gray, pp. 176–7

264 Elliot to Granville, 8 July 73, no. 19, ST, FO 84/1370. It had to be a convention between governments as opposed to a treaty between independent sovereigns.

talks began.[265] They were to drag on for four years and to become inextricably bound up with the question of Egyptian territorial expansion. By 1875 Britain was anxious to recognise Egyptian sovereignty along the western shore of the Red Sea as a safeguard against the extension of the French and Italian footholds at Obock and Assab.[266] She regarded Egypt as a more pliant and therefore preferable guardian of this coast, strategically placed on the short route to India.

However, the slave trade was attracting considerable attention in England.[267] The reports of the British Consul at Jidda and of Colonel Charles Gordon, who had succeeded Baker as Governor of Egypt's southernmost province, Equatoria, all indicated a flourishing traffic, carried on with the connivance of Egyptian officials. Recruits for the army were obtained in raids and sent in chains to Khartoum, tax collectors swept women and children off into bondage, and customs officers were implicated in transporting them across the Red Sea.[268]

Clearly Britain could not recognise any extension of Egyptian rule unless strong measures were taken.[269] The Khedive tried to bargain for a port on the Indian Ocean, within the territories claimed by Zanzibar and wanted the limits of Egyptian sovereignty defined in exchange for signing a slave trade convention.[270] This was brushed aside and he was warned that as long as the traffic continued he would find no support in Britain for his cherished schemes of extending his dominions in central Africa.[271] The response was all that could be desired. Gordon was appointed Governor-General of the whole Sudan with a free hand to suppress the trade, a retired British officer was placed in charge of policing the Red Sea and, in August 1877, a far-reaching convention was signed.[272]

Egypt undertook to prevent the import, export and transit of black and

265 Ismail wanted British support for judicial reforms, which the French opposed, and in his disputes with the Suez Canal Company as well as for his territorial ambitions.
266 See A. Ramm, 'Great Britain and the Planting of Italian Power in the Red Sea 1868–85', *EHR* lix, 1944, pp. 211–36; David Hamilton, 'Imperialism Ancient and Modern: a study of English attitudes to the claims to sovereignty to the Northern Somali Coastline', *Journal of Ethiopian Studies*, v, July 1967, pp. 9–35.
267 Gray, p. 181; the Anti-Slavery Society attacked it and in the House of Commons the Opposition was making capital out of it.
268 Vivian to Derby, no. 5, ST, 8 Dec. 1876, FO 84/1450
269 In October 1873, Frere had headed a deputation to the Foreign Office proposing that Egyptian rule in the Nile valley should only be recognised provided the slave trade and slavery were abolished in his territories, Gray, p. 177.
270 In 1875 he seized a port at the mouth of the Juba from the Sultan's garrisons, so as to support Gordon's advance down the Nile—the Nile route was proving difficult and an easier supply line was needed. This caused an outburst of indignation in Britain, for the Sultan was proving a worthy ally against the slave trade (see below, pp. 92 ff.) and Ismail withdrew. For this incident see A. I. Salim, *The Swahili Speaking Peoples of Kenya's Coast, 1895–1965*, Nairobi 1973, pp. 43–6.
271 Gray, p. 182; Derby to Vivian, no. 8 ST, 2 Mar. 1877, FO 84/1472; Vivian to Derby, no. 4 ST, 18 Feb. 1877, FO 84/1472 and no. 6, 27 Dec. 1876, FO 84/1450
272 Hertslet, *Commercial Treaties*, XIV, p. 321

Ethiopian slaves and to punish slave dealers severely. To stop fraud, blacks and Ethiopians were only to leave the country if they were free and armed with manumission papers. Private sales from family to family were to become illegal in Egypt in 1884 and in the Sudan in 1889. Dealing in white slaves was to be outlawed from 1883.[273] A bureau was to be set up to deal with slavery matters, with power to free slaves and provide for them. Britain and Egypt were to have reciprocal rights to search on the high seas and in territorial waters in the Red Sea, the Gulf of Aden and off the coasts of Africa and Arabia. Suspected slavers were to be tried by their own national courts and compensation was to be paid for wrongful arrest. Freed slaves were to be handed over to their liberators.

This agreement not only foreshadowed an early end to the slave trade, it also dealt a blow to slavery. Not only was the supply of slaves to be cut off, but after the prescribed dates they would cease to be a marketable commodity and the manumission bureau would make it easier for them to obtain their liberty and fend for themselves as free men.[274] In these circumstances they would cease to be an attractive investment. After the convention was signed, Britain recognised Egyptian sovereignty as far as Ras Hafoun, but only on condition, which was never met, that Turkey agreed not to cede any of this coast to a foreign power. Egypt further agreed to make Berber and Bulhar free ports and to charge only moderate duties elsewhere. Thus it was hoped that the Khedive would serve the British purpose by suppressing the slave traffic and promoting legitimate commerce.

Events, however, were to prove him unequal to the task. In the Sudan, the convention multiplied his difficulties. Gordon took vigorous measures against slavers[275] which swelled the rising tide of discontent with Egyptian rule, alienating important sections of the population. Furthermore he

---

273 The distinction between black slaves and white had been drawn on the insistence of Ismail, who had not wanted to interfere with the trade in whites, as he feared Turkey would object. The British also viewed it in a different light as Wylde explained: 'We have in fact always shut our eyes to this Traffic as far as we could possibly do so, in as much as it is carried on under circumstances differing entirely from those which characterize the African Slave Trade . . . in one case the Slaves are procured in the first instance by a system of murder and bloodshed which depopulate the country where slave hunting is carried on—in the other victims, if victims they can be called, are voluntary ones, and look forward with pleasure to the change in destiny which awaits them', minute on Vivian to Derby, no. 21 ST, 21 April 1877; see also no. 19, 14 April 1877, FO 84/1472. Kirk recorded that efforts to free white slaves bound for the Sultan of Zanzibar's harem always failed as the women would not co-operate, minute, 6 Nov. 1882, FO 84/1623. However, if more usually white slaves were bought from their Circassian owners or their parents, some at least initially were victims of raids. Princess Salme (Emily Ruete), daughter of a Circassian concubine and Sayyid Sa'id of Zanzibar, states that her mother and uncle were captured as children in a raid in which their parents were killed, Ruete, p. 6.

274 For the freed slave question, see below, pp. 160 ff.

275 See Shukry, ch. 10; Gray, pp. 123 ff.; P. M. Holt, *The Mahdist State in the Sudan 1881–98*, Oxford 1958 (henceforth *Mahdist State*).

employed European senior officers, believing that Egyptians could not be trusted to suppress the traffic. This gave the operation a Christian character, fatal in a land where Muslim feeling was strong, slave dealing was not considered wrong and the trade lay at the root of the prosperity of many people. Gordon broke the power of the greatest traders and drove out many lesser dealers but had not the resources to eradicate slaving completely and he left the Sudan in 1879 certain that the convention could not be carried out.[276] Two years later, Egyptian forces at Fashoda were still selling slaves to pay the taxes which had to be remitted to Khartoum,[277] while slaves still crossed the Red Sea although the Egyptian patrol service was organised by English officers. This was hardly surprising as one gunboat and three small steamers struggled to police a thousand miles of coast[278] and in fact the service was soon abandoned as a failure.[279]

In 1882, faced with the Mahdist rebellion in the Sudan, the Egyptian governor resorted again to buying black slaves for the army.[280] With the situation deteriorating, Gordon returned to Khartoum to evacuate Egyptian forces. En route, he rescinded the law forbidding the sale of slaves from family to family, due to come into force in 1889. Soon afterwards Khartoum fell and he was murdered. Thereafter until the British conquest of 1898 the northern Sudan was in the hands of the Mahdi and his successor Khalifa Abdullahi Ibn Muhammed.[281] Slaving was now unchecked but the export traffic declined. It was forbidden by the Madhists, who had religious scruples about selling slaves to people of other Muslim sects and were anyway short of supplies as the traders, no longer able to export their ivory, ceased operations. Slaves, therefore, continued to be exported across the Red Sea, but in smaller numbers.[282]

In Egypt, however, the convention of 1877 marked the start of a more determined effort to prevent the import of slaves. A special department, the Service for the Abolition of Slavery, was set up under a European official, measures were taken to intercept caravans, numbers of captives were freed and slave dealers punished.[283] But, with the population sympathetic to the slavers and officials deeply implicated in the trade,[284]

276 Baer, p. 435. Indeed Gordon thought that Ismail had merely agreed to the convention as a 'sop' to the British Government to counterbalance 'the cries of his creditors', Gordon to Northbrook, private, 15 Nov. 1881 FOCP/4619.
277 Gray, p. 154
278 Gray, p. 126
279 Baer, p. 432, fn. 5
280 Renault, II, pp. 37–8
281 Abdullahi Ibn Muhammed, 1846–99, ruled the Madhist state from 1885 to 1898.
282 Renault, II, pp. 38–9; Holt, *Modern History*, pp. 121–2
283 Punishment for slave dealing varied from 5 months' to 5 years' hard labour Baer, p. 433; Baring to FO, 7 March 1884, FOCP 5155.
284 When a caravan from Darfur was intercepted at Asyut in 1880, for instance, the notables and shaikhs tried to hide the slaves, and those implicated ranged from the 'umda' (headman) of the town to one of the richest merchants, who was the French Consular Agent, and a friend of the governor. Baer, p. 436.

evidence was difficult to come by and convictions hard to obtain. Moreover as long as slaves could still move about the country legally and be sold from one family to another, opportunities for fraud were limitless. Captives could be imported armed with certificates of manumission or marriage obtained by bribery in Darfur, or disguised as the servants, concubines or wives of pilgrims returning from Mecca.[285] Experience in Egypt made it clear that, unless the general public condemned slavery, government action could diminish the trade but not eradicate it.

Nevertheless, Britain could pride herself on the fact that the first important steps had been taken and after 1882, when she occupied the country herself, she was able to take more effective measures. Slavers were tried by court martial under British supervision.[286] No returning pilgrim could bring back more wives and slaves than he had taken with him.[287] Of great importance, efforts were made to help and protect freed slaves and all who applied for freedom were granted it.[288] It was uphill work but the position improved steadily, until, by the late 1880s, British officials claimed that slavery was moribund.[289]

The Ottoman empire and the treaty network

The Anglo-Egyptian convention led naturally to negotiations for a similar agreement with Turkey—the essential first step towards reducing the trade in slaves from the Sudan, Ethiopia and the Somali coast across the Red Sea and Gulf of Aden to Arabia and the Persian Gulf. This traffic was particularly brisk at the time of the *Haj*, when pilgrims from all over the Muslim world assembled in the ports of Western Arabia and many took the opportunity to buy slaves to take home.

Britain had tried to cut down the market by her treaties with the rulers of the Gulf and South Arabia,[290] by trying to stop the import of slaves into India and Persia and by continual pressure on the Turks to carry out the *firman* of 1857. This *firman*, however, did not apply to the Hijaz, which was the great distributing centre, and where an attempt to close the slave market

285 Baer, pp. 437–8. The difficulties of checking on the slaves and wives returning from pilgrimage were considerable, ships stopped for only a few hours and proper inquiries could not be made; the authorities anyway had to find proof that the slaves were intended for sale. Portal to Rosebery, no. 7 Af., 22 July 1886, FOCP 5459; Baring to Kitchener, no. 136, 5 Mar. 1887, FO 633/5.
286 Baring to Rosebery, no. 3 Af., conf., 19 April 1886, FOCP 5459
287 Portal to Rosebery, no. 7 Af., 22 July 1886, *ibid.*, and Baring to Kitchener, no. 136, 5 March 1887, FO 633/5.
288 Baring to Salisbury, no. 10 Af., 2 April 1889, FO 84/1972. For the problem of freed slaves and the measures taken in Egypt, see below, pp. 160 ff.
289 Shaefer to Baring, 10 Feb. 1887, *PP* Africa, no. 4 (1887), p. 9; Baring to Salisbury, no. 10 Af., 2 April 1889, FO 84/1972
290 See below, pp. 86 ff.

in 1855 had caused a riot.[291] Britain had failed to negotiate a treaty with Ethiopia,[292] but nearer to her base at Aden, she had obtained agreements with chiefs around Berbera in 1855 and 1856, prohibiting the slave trade and allowing her to arrest slavers, demand the release of slaves, and appoint an official to reside in Berbera during the annual trade fair to see that the treaties were observed.[293]

When Frere passed through the Red Sea on his way to Zanzibar in the winter of 1872, he pointed out that an agreement with Turkey against the slave traffic was necessary for political as much as humanitarian reasons. The opening of the Suez Canal in 1869 and the Turkish conquest of the Arabian peninsula between 1871 and 1873[294] had led to a great increase in the number of Ottoman vessels in the Red Sea and to pressure on the coastal tribes to submit to Turkish rule. He feared the Turkish advance, seeing it as a threat to Aden and even India, where the large Muslim population might respond to a call from the Sultan to overthrow their infidel British rulers. He warned that the maritime Arabs had a strong inducement to accept Turkish rule which would give them the right to fly the Ottoman flag and thus protect slavers from molestation by the Royal Navy. 'I fear,' he wrote, 'few of the maritime Slave Trading Chiefs will resist the Temptation even at the Cost of their Independence.'[295] He also thought the slave trade was being conducted in steamers subsidised by the Turkish Government with the connivance of Ottoman officials.

At the time of Frere's visit the Red Sea traffic was believed to be fairly small, and he estimated that about 2000 slaves a year came into Jidda, the biggest port near Mecca.[296] The Turkish hold on Arabia was precarious. In fact a British Consul, investigating the import of slaves into India by pilgrims returning from Mecca, reported that the Turks were so unpopular in the Hijaz that any action against the slave trade would provoke a rebellion.[297] In these circumstances, Turkey, beset as she was by financial crises and revolts in the Balkans, could hardly be expected to launch an attack on the traffic. Britain contented herself with appointing a Consul to Jidda to watch the trade and concentrated her efforts on negotiating the convention with Egypt.

During the Egyptian talks the British Ambassador in Turkey warned his government that the Porte would object if Egypt granted Britain the right to search, as Egyptian vessels flew the Ottoman flag and were indistinguish-

291 Renault, II, p. 68   292 See below, pp. 110 ff.

293 Hertslet, *Commercial Treaties*, XIII, pp. 9–11

294 The Turks conquered Asir and Yemen between 1871 and 1873, installed a protégé as ruler of Najd and occupied the western coast of the Persian Gulf.

295 Frere to Granville, no. 5, 10 Jan. 1873, FO 84/1389. For Frere's views see also R. J. Gavin, 'The Bartle Frere Mission to Zanzibar, 1873', *The Historical Journal*, v, 2, 1962, pp. 122–48.

296 Frere to Granville, no. 7, 10 Jan. 1873, *ibid.* There were of course many other ports of import.

297 *Ibid.*

able from Turkish ships.[298] This concession, however, was a *sine qua non* for the British recognition of Egyptian sovereignty along the north-eastern littoral.[299] Once the convention was signed the Khedive undertook to urge the Sultan to follow his example.

By this time the reports of the Jidda Consulate revealed that the Red Sea traffic was not the small trade in domestic servants that Frere had visualised, but a large-scale operation supplying labour for the date gardens of Medina and north Hijaz, the coffee plantations of Yemen and the pearl fisheries of the Red Sea and Persian Gulf, as well as domestic servants, concubines and eunuchs wanted all over the Muslim world. Slaves bought in the markets of western Arabia were being re-exported by sea to Egypt, Constantinople and even Morocco, or sent by caravan across the desert to the Persian Gulf, where their value had increased recently as a result of the measures taken against the Zanzibar traffic.[300] Reliable figures for the trade are impossible to obtain, but Vice-Consul A. B. Wylde believed in 1876 that some thirty thousand slaves a year were crossing the Red Sea.[301] When the British Consulate was set up in Jidda in 1874, the slave market was in the centre of the bazaar. The Consul persuaded the Turks to close it,[302] but slave dealing continued unabated in private. Captives were landed in broad daylight under the guns of Ottoman cruisers and brought into the walled city under the eyes of officials. At Hodeida (al Hudaydah) in the Yemen, the Turkish authorities were reported to be enriching themselves by charging duties on each slave imported.[303]

By 1878, this traffic was attracting considerable attention in Britain, and was an embarrassment to the government, which based its Middle Eastern policy on the defence of Asiatic Turkey against Russian encroachment. The Turks had just been defeated in war with Russia and needed British support. They, therefore, responded to hints that co-operation against the slave trade would have a favourable effect on English public opinion,[304] already much disturbed by reports of Ottoman atrocities in Bulgaria. Negotiations were opened which ended in the signature of the convention of 1880.[305]

Turkey reaffirmed her prohibition of the slave trade, engaged to stop the import and export of black slaves[306] and to punish offenders in accordance

298 Elliot to Granville, no. 1 ST, 4, Jan. 1874, FO 84/1397. The Turks did protest in 1877.

299 Minute by Wylde (undated), on Porte to Musurus Pasha, 4 Oct. 1877, communicated to the Foreign Office, 22 Oct. 1877, FO 84/1482.

300 See below, pp. 86 ff

301 Memo, by Wylde, 25 Nov. 1876, FO 84/1450

302 Derby to Beyts, no. 2, 18 Feb. 1875, FO 84/1412. An Ottoman Circular of 1872 had ordered all public slave markets closed.

303 Derby to Beyts no. 2, 18 Feb. 1875, FO 84/1412.

304 Vivian to Derby, 20 Dec. 1877, no. 70 ST, most conf. FOCP 3686. Minute by Wylde, 2 March 1878, on Layard to Derby, tel. no. 283, 2 March 1878, FO 84/1658

305 Hertslet, *Commercial Treaties*, XV, p. 417

306 The question of white slaves was not raised on the advice of the British Ambassador, Layard to Granville, no. 10 ST, 21 Feb. 1880, FO 84/1658.

with the *firman* of 1857. African slaves were only to leave the Ottoman empire if they were travelling with their masters as domestic servants and carried appropriate documents. Free blacks leaving the country had to have manumission papers. Adequate measures were to be taken to protect freed slaves.[307] Persons dealing in, or responsible for, the mutilation of children were to be treated as criminals. Britain was granted the right to search Turkish vessels on the high seas, in the Red Sea, the Gulf of Aden, the Indian Ocean and the Persian Gulf, and in territorial waters where there were no constituted Ottoman authorities. Where these existed, British officers might insist on their acting against slavers. The right to search was, of course, mutual in theory. The Mediterranean was excluded for fear of diplomatic complications.[308] Suspected offenders were to be tried in their own national courts and compensation was to be paid for wrongful arrest. To prevent slaves from being fraudulently passed off as members of a ship's company, any vessel with slave sailors was to carry papers listing and describing them.

The Foreign Office regarded this treaty as the 'small end of the wedge' to be driven home later.[309] The Anti-Slavery Society feared that trial by Ottoman courts might be a mere farce and they urged a return to the system of mixed commissions, but this would have been an affront to Turkish dignity and was regarded as unnecessary. As Hill put it:

> Ottoman tribunals may be untrustworthy, but we can keep so close a watch and exercise such a supervision over them that I do not anticipate any flagrant case of injustice.[310]

Events were to prove him over-sanguine. The Turks did not set up the tribunals necessary to deal with slavers. No new law was enacted for the trial and sentencing of slave dealers, and in its absence they normally escaped with a light fine, because the *firman* of 1857 was not usually considered to carry sufficient authority to be acted upon. The necessary draft law and a recommendation for the establishment of tribunals in Hodeida and Jidda were sent by the council of ministers to the Sultan in 1883, but he had taken no action upon them in 1889.[311] The article in the convention which allowed slaves to travel with their masters enabled them to be smuggled across the Red Sea or Mediterranean disguised as servants. The stipulation that if an offender was not an Ottoman subject and had not committed his crime in Turkish territory, he must be handed over to his own national authorities, meant that, for some years to come, dealers from

307 For the freed slave question see below, pp. 160 ff.
308 Hill minute, 14 Dec. 1881, FO 84/1658, and see above, pp. 70–1
309 Minute on Layard to Salisbury, no. 21 tel. 13, Jan. 1880, *ibid.*
310 Hill minute on BFASS to Granville, 7 Oct. 1881, FO 84/1658
311 Memos by Marinitch, 23 July 1889, enc. in White to Salisbury, no. 14, Af., 9 Sept. 1889, FO 84/1971, and 13 Jan 1890, enc. in White to Salisbury, no. 2, Af., 15 Jan. 1890, FO 84/2056.

the western shores of the Red Sea escaped punishment. The necessary papers were never issued to Ottoman vessels with slave crews, and this simple expendient prevented British naval action against Turkish slavers. The whole situation remained thoroughly unsatisfactory and on the eve of the Berlin conference there was still a ready market for slaves in the Ottoman empire even in Constantinople and Turkish co-operation against the trade existed on paper only.[312]

The East African slave trade and the treaty network

More satisfactory treaties were obtained against the East African slave traffic, but only after many years of effort. In the early days, Britain contented herself with trying to cut off the supply of slaves to the Mascarenes[313] and, from the late 1830s, to western India. Interference with the trade to Arabia and the Persian Gulf was limited for fear of alienating Sayyid Sa'id, ruler of Muscat and Zanzibar, and the shaikhs of the Trucial coast, and thereby undermining her influence in a region of great importance to her empire in India.[314] The traffic was mainly in the hands of the Arabs of Muscat, subjects of Sayyid Sa'id, who settled permanently in Zanzibar from 1840 and presided over a growing commercial empire largely financed by Indians and based principally on the export of ivory and slaves from the East African mainland and cloves from Zanzibar and Pemba.[315] The slaves were usually exported to Muscat by the Omanis and some were carried up the Gulf or to the northern coasts of the Indian Ocean and to India itself, by other traders.[316] Merchants from Mukalla and other Hadhrami ports also came to Zanzibar and the Swahili coast and collected slaves to sell in the ports of the Hadramawt or western Arabia.

In 1841, Palmerston launched an attack on this Arab trade after reports from India revealed its dimensions.[317] Sayyid Sa'id was in an invidious position. He wanted the British to support him in Oman and recognised their considerable powers of coercion but he feared that measures against the slave traffic would alienate his subjects and reduce his revenues, which were partially raised from taxes on slaves. Constant pressure, together with British political support and the fact that the economy of Zanzibar was sufficiently diversified to give him a large income independent of the slave trade, finally induced him in 1845 to agree to a treaty to end the import of slaves in his Arabian territories and their export from his African ones,

312 See A. B. Wylde, *'83–'87 in the Soudan*, London 1888, 2 vols., II, ch. 9; Renault, II, pp. 65–9.
313 See above, p. 40.
314 See Kelly, ch. 10, for a full discussion of this subject and Nicholls, ch. 9.
315 For Omani expansion in East Africa and the economic development of the coast see Nicholls.
316 Kelly, pp. 413–14
317 Nicholls, p. 233

except to the islands of Zanzibar, Pemba and Mafia.[318] The Royal Navy was given the right to search vessels flying his flag, unless they were bound only for the islands. The treaty was followed by further agreements with the shaikhs of the Persian Gulf and eventually with Mukalla and Shuhr, all conceding Britain powers to search and to try slavers in her own courts.[319] Persia also signed a treaty against the maritime slave trade but did not allow the British to search her vessels unless they were accompanied by Persian officers and she retained the right to try her own nationals.[320]

Treaties were also made with Johanna in 1844, after the French occupied Nossi-Bé, Nossi-cumba and Mayotta, to prevent them from recruiting labourers on the island, who would inevitably have been replaced by slaves from the mainland.[321] Similar agreements followed with Grand Comoro and Mohilla. These gave Britain the right to search, to try slavers and dispose of freed slaves.[322] A treaty with the Queen of the Hova kingdom in Madagascar in 1865 forbade the import of slaves and confirmed Britain's right to search in Madagascan waters.[323]

These treaties, which made Britain the policeman of the Indian Ocean and Persian Gulf, had serious limitations. Their greatest failing was that slaves could still legally be transported along the coast between Kilwa and Lamu as well as exported to Zanzibar, Pemba and Mafia. Slavers could, therefore, still lawfully embark and once at sea, ostensibly bound for the islands, it was easy enough to elude the few British cruisers available to patrol the Indian Ocean and to make a run for Arabia.[324] There were never enough cruisers for sustained and systematic patrolling, and those struggling to do the job found their mobility and effectiveness reduced by having to remain within reach of coaling stations, and take captured vessels great distances to ports of adjudication.[325] Naval officers also had difficulty distinguishing slaves

318 Hertslet, *Commercial Treaties*, VII, p. 818. For a discussion of the events leading up to this treaty and the motives of both parties see Kelly, ch. 13; Nicholls, pp. 228 ff.
319 'Pirate chiefs', April–May 1847, Hertslet, *Commercial Treaties*, XI, p. 1184; Sohar, XI p. 715; Mukalla and Shuhr, 14 May 1863, XIII, p. 687. Rights to search in territorial waters were assumed by Britain, see *Instructions* 1865 and 1882 editions.
320 For the treaty of 4 March 1857, see Hertslet, *Commercial Treaties*, X, p. 947. This renewed an agreement of August 1851, which had been antedated by a *firman* of 1848 forbidding the slave trade by sea into Persian ports (but not granting Britain the right to search conceded in 1851, see *Instructions* 2). Slavers used the Persian flag in order to escape British interference after the signature of the treaty with Zanzibar. The overland route was not practical at this time but the Shah did not include it in the ban of 1848, as he felt the loophole, however unreal, would disarm opposition from Muslim clerics. Kelly, p. 599; Nicholls, pp. 205, 240.
321 Treaties of 8 Nov. 1844 and 3 June 1850, Hertslet, *Commercial Treaties*, VIII, p. 731, IX, p. 548.
322 Bonafooma, 20 Sept. 1854, *ibid.*, X, p. 36; Maroni, 29 July 1861, *ibid.*, XI, p. 2; Mohilla, 16 Sept. 1854, *ibid.*, X, p. 34.
323 Treaty of 27 June 1865, *ibid.*, p. 639. The Hovas only controlled part of the island, see below, pp. 109–10.
324 For a discussion of this whole subject see Kelly, pp. 585 ff.
325 Until 1866 there was no vice-admiralty court at Zanzibar, and ships had to go to

from legitimate passengers.[326] Slavers carrying a few victims who had the run of the ship or were dressed as sailors escaped arrest.[327] It was believed in the Foreign Office that ten to eleven thousand slaves a year were exported to Arabia and the Persian Gulf from East Africa in the late 1860s, of whom the British captured only five to six hundred.[328] In addition thousands were legally imported into Pemba and Zanzibar.

For many years, however, the treaties satisfied the British public, whose knowledge of, or interest in, the Arab trade and the traffic from Portuguese East Africa to the islands of the Indian Ocean was minimal.[329] In the 1860s, however, attention was to become focused on the East African slave traffic, mainly as a result of the revelations of David Livingstone.

On his lonely wanderings through Africa he saw the ghastly depredations of the slavers—the charred villages, devastated fields, the corpses and the pathetic trails of victims on their march to the coast. He described them in passages such as this one published in 1865:

> . . . a long line of manacled men, women, and children, came wending their way round the hill . . . the black drivers, armed with muskets, and bedecked with various articles of finery, marched jauntily in the front, middle and rear of the line; some of them blowing exultant notes out of long tin horns. They seemed to feel that they were doing a very noble thing, and might proudly march with an air of triumph. . . . Two of the women had been shot the day before for attempting to untie the thongs. This, the rest were told, was to prevent them from attempting to escape. One woman had her infant's brains knocked out, because she could not carry her load and it. And a man was despatched with an axe because he had broken down with fatigue.[330]

He had seen, he said, such sights as could not be described and would not be believed, and he estimated that the traffic was responsible for a vast loss of life, for not one victim in five ever became a slave:

> Besides those actually captured, thousands are killed and die of their wounds and famine, driven from their villages by the slave raid proper.

Bombay, Aden or the Cape. Under certain conditions they were allowed to destroy slavers rather than sail them to these ports.
326 In theory vessels could not be condemned unless the slaves were 'crowded and chained together' or had chains on board which was rare in the Indian Ocean.
327 Kelly, p. 621; G. L. Sullivan, *Dhow Chasing in Zanzibar Waters*, London, 2nd ed. 1968 (first published 1873), described the methods used to disguise slaves as crewmen or passengers and the impossibility of inexperienced naval officers, often without interpreters, detecting such fraud. Interpreters, too, were often unreliable and open to bribery, pp. 57 ff.
328 These figures were those accepted by a Foreign Office committee which investigated the question in 1870. For a discussion of this subject see Kelly, pp. 622–3.
329 Slaves were also exported from Mozambique to Brazil in the days of the Atlantic trade.
330 Livingstone, *Zambesi*, pp. 356–7. For further revelations see *Last Journals*.

Thousands perish in internecine war waged for slaves with their own clansmen and neighbours, slain by the lust of gain . . . The many skeletons we have seen, amongst the rocks and woods, by the little pools and along the paths of the wilderness, attest the awful sacrifice of human life, which must be attributed, directly or indirectly, to this trade of hell.[331]

Livingstone's appeal to bring Christianity, commerce and civilisation to counter this terrible state of affairs led not only to the sending of missionaries to Nyasaland, but also to a wave of further exploration to open routes into the heart of Africa, and the tale he had told with such revulsion was confirmed by those who followed him into the interior. As the decade progressed, public imagination was to be stirred by the story of his disappearance, by the journey of Henry Morton Stanley to find him, by his own intrepid efforts to discover the furthest sources of the Nile, and finally, most poignant of all, his lonely death far inland.[332] To a nation only too ready to believe in the 'white men's burden', Livingstone gave a great cause, sufficient for others to use to justify the penetration of Africa and the many acts of spoliation to which it was to give rise—the total suppression of the African slave traffic. He awakened a determination to continue his work in missionary, humanitarian and commercial circles and fired the imagination of the church-going public, who subscribed the money to support the missions.

The government was slow to respond to this new interest, however, and its hand was largely forced by Frere, a former Governor of Bombay, and now a member of the India Council, who was much concerned with what he regarded as the threat to Britain's position in the Indian Ocean and the Middle East.[333] Muscat had been separated from Zanzibar on the death of Sayyid Sa'id in 1856, and in 1861 the British, as the arbitrators in a dispute between his heirs, had secured their consent to an agreement by which Zanzibar remained independent but her ruler was to pay his brother Thwain in Muscat a subsidy to make up for the revenues he no longer received from the island.

By 1868 Thwain had been murdered by his son and the Sayyid[334] or, as the British now called him, the Sultan, of Zanzibar refused to continue these payments. The question was tied up with the suppression of the slave trade by the Sultan himself, for whenever he was asked to take more active steps

331 Livingstone, *Zambesi*, pp. 391–2
332 For a discussion of this subject see Oliver, *Missionary Factor*, p. 34.
333 For a discussion of Frere's motives and a brief discussion of the position at Muscat and Zanzibar, see Gavin, 'The Bartle Frere Mission', pp. 122–8. For an exhaustive enquiry into British policy in the Persian Gulf and the relations between Muscat and Zanzibar from British sources, see Kelly, p. 538 ff.
334 The correct title was Sayyid, but henceforth the title Sultan will be used since this became normal British usage and was the official title after Zanzibar became a British Protectorate in 1890.

against the traffic, he claimed that without the revenues from it he could not pay the subsidy and suggested that if he were relieved of this burden he might make concessions. In Oman British influence was at a low ebb. The new ruler was supported by Muslim zealots, the Mutawi'ah, many of whom descended on Zanzibar during the trading season of 1868, caused turmoil and carried off thousands of slaves. To stop this the Royal Navy carried out its first intensive patrolling against the Arab slave trade in 1869. The results were disappointing for less than a thousand slaves were freed and high-handed action by British crews, who plundered and perhaps arrested innocent dhows in search of loot or prize money, caused much irritation among the local traders.[335]

In London an interdepartmental committee[336] suggested the negotiation of a new treaty with Zanzibar to reduce the slave traffic to the islands gradually under the supervision of the British Consul. In return Britain was to pay the Muscat subsidy. At Zanzibar the consular staff was to be enlarged and a regular mail steamer service was to be subsidised to increase her influence and boost legitimate trade, much of which was in the hands of British Indians.[337] The expenses of these changes were to be shared by the British and Indian Governments.

The Treasury, however, flatly refused to sanction the necessary expenditure,[338] and the humanitarians objected to the idea of a limited slave trade under British supervision. Over two years passed in fruitless inter-departmental bickering. Meanwhile, Barghash ibn Sa'id had succeeded his brother as Sultan of Zanzibar, and relying on Mutawi'ah support, he refused to make any concessions on the slave traffic. In Muscat a friendly ruler had regained the throne but he needed the subsidy from Zanzibar to maintain himself in power.

It seemed to Frere imperative to take a firm line to restore British influence in Zanzibar, and entrench it at Muscat, especially as the Turks, now conquering Arabia, appealed to Arabs to look on the Ottoman Sultan as leader of the Muslim world and might ultimately call on Indian Muslims in the same terms.[339] He therefore launched an agitation through the Anti-

---

335 See N. R. Bennett, *Studies in East African History*, Boston, 1963, pp. 33–4.
336 The committee, appointed by the Foreign Secretary, consisted of representatives of the Foreign Office, India Office, the Admiralty and the Colonial Office.
337 This service would have the advantage of linking the Union Steamship Company's service to the Cape with the end of the telegraph cable in Aden and so reduce the time for communications between Britain and South Africa from 3–4 weeks to 17 days.
338 Much difficulty had already been experienced in getting the government of India to contribute to the costs of the anti-slavery campaign or to agree to relieve Zanzibar of the Muscat subsidy. When the Treasury refused to pay for the new plan, the India Office, which financed the Zanzibar agency, decided to prevent the Foreign Office sending instructions to its Consul in Zanzibar. Once in complete control of this consulate the India Office was unlikely to put much effort into the anti-slavery campaign.
339 Payment of the Muscat subsidy by Britain would give her control over the ruler,

Slavery Society to force the government's hand.[340] Aided by the publicity just being given to Stanley's search for Livingstone, he was eminently successful in making a wide public aware of the existence of the East African slave traffic and in getting the support of the press, the missionary societies and members of Parliament for his plans. Eventually the government, responding to this pressure, sent him to Zanzibar to solve the question and agreed to pay for the mail service, an increased consular staff in Zanzibar and the Muscat subsidy.[341] In November Frere sailed, armed with a clear mandate to suppress the slave trade in the Indian Ocean.

His mission was to have far-reaching repercussions. Barghash was at first adamant. Slaves were particularly needed to restore the prosperity of the islands, devastated by a hurricane in 1872. He feared the alienation of his subjects and needed the revenue from the export tax on slaves to rebuild his fleet, which had been destroyed in the storm. Eventually, however, he yielded to the threat of a naval blockade and accepted a new treaty forbidding all export of slaves from his dominions on the mainland of Africa, providing for the closure of slave markets on the islands and for the protection of freed slaves, and granting Britain the right to search all vessels under his flag on the high seas and in territorial waters, and to try suspected slavers.[342] It also prohibited the holding of slaves by Indians.[343]

To carry out her more comprehensive policing role Britain increased her naval forces. Where previously only two cruisers had normally covered the whole area from Natal to the Persian Gulf, the squadron was now reinforced by a gunboat and sloop, and the depot ship H.M.S. *London* and her cruising boats were stationed at Zanzibar. New and more stringent treaties were also signed with Muscat, Mukalla and Shuhr,[344] and the ruler of Johanna agreed to liberate all persons entering the island and to protect freed slaves.[345]

The role of British Indians in the slave traffic was also attacked. It was from them that the 'Arab'[346] dealers borrowed funds or trade goods to

see Gavin, 'The Bartle Frere Mission', p. 131. For Turkish moves in Arabia, see Kelly, ch. 15.

340 See Gavin, 'The Bartle Frere Mission', pp. 138 ff.

341 Britain and India were to share the Muscat subsidy and the increased costs in Zanzibar.

342 Treaty of 5 June 1873, Hertslet, *Commercial Treaties*, XIV, p. 414; Coupland, *Exploitation*, pp. 212–13. Slavers could be tried by the British Vice-Admiralty Court at Zanzibar, but offenders were punished by the Sultan.

343 This was illegal by Indian law, but the law had been evaded by those Indians who claimed the protection of Zanzibar. Kirk now released the slaves of the Indians in Zanzibar and Consul Elton travelled around the coast and islands releasing others. See J. F. Elton, *Travels and Researches among the Lakes and Mountains of Eastern and Central Africa*, London 1879, pp. 69 ff.

344 Hertslet, *Commercial Treaties*, XIV, p. 414, XIII, p. 2

345 Frere to Granville, no. 27, 12 March 1873, FO 84/1389

346 'Arab' is used here for want of a better term in the very loosest sense which, although strictly incorrect, has become common, to include all who owed allegiance to

equip their caravans. Kirk now warned them not to advance credit to slavers and hoped that the capital hitherto used in the trade would be diverted to legitimate commerce.[347]

The treaty of 1873 opened a new era in the history of both the East African slave trade and the Sultanate of Zanzibar, an era of close co-operation between Kirk and Barghash. This astute ruler had signed the treaty only when it was clear to his subjects that he was yielding to superior force.[348] A visit to England in 1875 convinced him of his weakness in the face of her power and when the Egyptians seized his northern ports of Kismayu and Brava on the Benadir or Somali coast and were forced by Britain to withdraw, he recognised the value of her support.[349] But this support had a price.

Kirk had been worried for some years by the increasing number of slaves being marched along the coast overland. The Benadir ports imported many from as far away as Kilwa, both for local use and for export to Arabia.[350] The treaty of 1845 had banned all transport of captives by sea north of Lamu[351] but as Galla-Somali feuding made the land route to the Benadir unsafe, they had continued to be smuggled north by boat, messengers on relays of camels bringing warning of British patrols in the area.[352] In 1869 the Sultan established a garrison at Kismayu which warded off the Galla, opened the land route to the Somali coast[353] and facilitated the passage of slave caravans. With the outlawing of all maritime transport of slaves this overland traffic increased all along the coast.[354] The Egyptian invasion gave Kirk his chance of closing the northern outlet. The price of the explusion of

the ruler of Zanzibar, whether Arabs from Arabia, coastal Swahili, or the black retainers who sometimes conducted their trading operations and some of whom were slaves.

347 This as will be seen opens a complex question as most caravans engaged in legitimate trade as well.

348 Kirk thought he would have been killed had he signed at once. As it was, the Consul thought that his power had been increased. Kirk memo., 2 Nov. 1889, KP BASC.

349 For the Egyptian expedition see p. 79. The population of the Benadir coast was predominantly Somali with small Arab and Indian trading communities in the ports which owed allegiance to the Sultan. The Galla and the coast Swahili Bajuni peoples lived to the south of them.

350 Salim, pp. 15 ff

351 The 1845 treaty, like that of 1822, defined maritime zones within which the trade could be legally conducted.

352 Kantzow to Heath, 10 Nov. 1869, enc. in Kantzow to Admiralty, 10 Nov. 1869, *PP* LXII, 1871, C-340.

353 Salim, p. 20.

354 Kirk had pointed out the danger to his government before they forced Barghash to sign the treaty of 1873. Kirk to Wylde, 13 Dec. (?) 1875, KP STE. For eye-witness accounts of this traffic see Elton, ch. 2; H. Greffulhe, 'Voyage de Lamoo à Zanzibar', *Bulletin de la Société de Géographie et d'Études Coloniales de Marseille*, II, 1878, pp. 209–17, 327–60, 333–5. One caravan met by Greffulhe was ravaged by small-pox. See also Coupland, *Exploitation*, pp. 221–2.

Egypt from Kismayu and Brava was the abolition of slavery itself on the Benadir coast. 'The Egyptian affair' was, he wrote, 'the most lucky thing ever happened' but he regretted that force had not had to be used against the Egyptians as this would have enabled him to ask the Sultan for the total abolition of the slave trade on land.[355] Nevertheless, as he said:

> The Somali market cut off is an immense thing for not only did they get a good supply of slaves, about 10,000, but the losses in getting there by land were so awful and the death rate on the way so high that thousands more had to be brought down to Kilwa to allow for the loss.[356]

He was sure, however, that Barghash would soon be in difficulties again and 'then I can secure another step'.[357] The opportunity indeed soon came. In face of persistent smuggling to Pemba and active slaving along the coast, the Sultan was induced in 1876 to forbid slave caravans to enter, equip in, or travel in his dominions. Furthermore, Indian financiers were warned that they would not be able to sue slavers who failed to pay their debts because their slaves had been seized.[358]

Inevitably such measures roused opposition[359] but the British were on hand to help suppress them. Kirk sent a warship and then went himself with over two hundred of the Sultan's troops to put down disturbances at Kilwa, the main port of export. Only the weather prevented him from hunting down slave caravans on land, Barghash having temporarily placed the whole area under his command.[360] The Sultan, Kirk explained, was no puppet but 'he knows his fate is in our hands and from honest conviction of sound policy takes a decided course'.[361] At Kirk's suggestion, Barghash also reorganised his army along European lines under a British naval officer,[362] thus acquiring a more efficient, if still tiny, instrument to extend his power

355 Together with the establishment of a settlement under British control to police the Juba river.

356 Kirk to Wylde, 13 Dec. (?) 1875, KP STE

357 Kirk to Wylde, 8 Feb. 1876, *ibid.*

358 Kirk to Wylde, 1 June 1876, *ibid.*

359 There were demonstrations at Kilwa and Mombasa and the *Liwali* of Merka and his troops were murdered on the Benadir coast, see Salim, p. 47.

360 Kirk to Wylde, 1 June 1876, KP STE. It should perhaps be noted here that Kirk who worked so indefatigably to suppress the export of slaves did so to his own pecuniary disadvantage. It was in his interest to have the traffic continue and to have slave dhows captured at sea, for, as he wrote in 1878, 'the few fees it brought to me for cases in court just made the difference between spending all my pay and getting a small surplus'; Kirk to Wylde, 7 July 1878, KP STE.

361 *Ibid.*, 'He is by no means . . . a puppet in my hands but I have taught him to see his interests from my point of view . . . I have done so much for him that he trusts me personally, but he never takes the course I indicate because I do so. I have to bring him to see it is, if not what he thinks right, at least a political necessity . . . he likes me . . . and he fears me too . . .'.

362 This officer became subsequently a general in the Sultan's forces. For his life and work see R. N. Lyne, *An Apostle of Empire: Being the Life of Sir Lloyd Mathews, K.C.M.G.*, London 1936.

and extirpate the slave trade. Those *liwali* or governors who connived at it were removed, a coastal guard was established on Pemba,[363] and the islanders were warned that if the traffic persisted the Sultan would yield to British pressure and abolish slavery.[364]

Barghash was assuming a degree of personal authority hitherto unknown for he had never been a territorial ruler in the European sense.[365] He was respected as a *primus inter pares* wielding influence rather than power. Even on the coast, which he claimed from the Ruvuma river to the Horn, his influence was limited to the cities, where he merely appointed governors and collected customs, his interest being mainly commercial. Zanzibar served as the emporium for the coast and the people of the towns benefited from the commercial outlets it furnished and enjoyed considerable local autonomy. The Africans who lived around the ports often had close relations with them but ruled themselves.[366] In the interior the few Arab settlements strung along the trade routes ran their own affairs, although they flew the Sultan's flag, and their African neighbours were independent. Barghash was now taking the first hesitant and unenthusiastic steps towards turning his commercial empire into a territorial one. They were steps along a slippery path of ever-growing dependence upon Britain. To Kirk the Sultan was the instrument of informal empire, the agent who would suppress the slave trade and promote legitimate commerce, and with it British influence, at little cost to the imperial treasury. 'We must strengthen him,' he wrote, 'or be dragged into the work ourselves and that would be more entangling still.'[367] However, Barghash could be sure of British support only as long as he was useful and co-operative. Ominously the measures now being forced on him were not in the economic interests of his own subjects, whose prosperity depended on a steady supply of slave labour.

Slaves were used on Zanzibar and Pemba as domestic servants, concubines, trading agents, sailors, fishermen, craftsmen, dockers and labourers, but the majority, particularly on Pemba, were agricultural workers producing the cloves and coconuts upon which the economy of the islands was based.[368] These plantation slaves led a harder life than the others but even they seem usually to have been relatively well treated.[369] There were, of

363 Renault, I, pp. 280–1; Coupland, *Exploitation*, ch. 11.

364 Kirk to Wylde, private, 6 March 1877, KP STE; Kirk memo. undated KP BASC

365 For the character of Omani rule see Coupland, *Exploitation*, pp. 2–7, ch. 12; R. Oliver and G. Matthew (eds.), *History of East Africa*, I, Oxford 1963, pp. 212 ff.; P. Ceulemans, *La Question Arabe et le Congo (1883–92)*, Brussels 1959, pp. 26 ff.; Norman R. Bennett, *Mirambo of Tanzania, 1840 (?)–84*, London and Toronto 1971, pp. 16 ff.; Salim, ch. 1.

366 Salim, ch. 1

367 Kirk to Wylde, 1 June 1876, KP STE.

368 Zanzibar also had an important entrepôt trade.

369 For the treatment of slaves and their work, see John Middleton, 'Slavery in Zanzibar', *Trans-Actions*, Jan./Feb. 1967, pp. 46–8 (henceforth 'Slavery') and *Land Tenure in Zanzibar*, London 1961 (henceforth *Land Tenure*); C. Russell, *General*

course, instances of brutality, but theoretically at least they were protected by Muslim law and masters had only limited powers of punishment. They lived in small villages on their masters' lands, often with others of their ethnic group, and they grew their own food, a proportion of which was taken by their owners. They were allowed a certain number of days each week to work on their own account[370] but could not grow cloves or coconuts. These crops they picked and tended for their masters. Since agricultural work was largely seasonal many of them were hired out as labourers, a large part of their earnings being handed over to their masters.[371] Household slaves had an easier life and, particularly if they became Muslim, often held positions of trust. They could make money for themselves and buy slaves of their own. Some were artisans set up in business by their masters who collected part of their profits. On the same basis some were hired out as porters for up-country expeditions[372] and a few even served as caravan leaders in charge of free porters and newly acquired or 'raw' slaves.[373]

The numbers of slaves on the islands are hard to estimate. A recent study suggests there were about twenty thousand in the late nineteenth century and that they outnumbered the Arab ruling classes who formed the bulk of the owners by two to one.[374] Kirk thought about half came from the Nyasa

Rigby, Zanzibar and the Slave Trade, London 1935, pp. 333–4. There is some evidence that treatment was worse on Pemba, further from official eyes and where escape was more difficult. It may have worsened after the treaty of 1873 limited supplies and made masters more exacting, Renault, I, pp. 18–19.

370 Sources vary as to whether this was two days or three and it was different at the time of the clove harvest, H. S. Newman, *Banani*, London 1898, p. 36; R. H. Crofton, *A Pageant of the Spice Islands*, London 1936, pp. 95–6; Russell, p. 334.

371 According to Richard Burton they kept only 2 out of 8 or 10 pice earned in a day when he visited Zanzibar, but they had a ration of rice and treacle if they worked loading and unloading European ships, *Zanzibar, City, Island and Coast* (henceforth *Zanzibar*), 2 vols. London 1872, I, p. 467. Rashid bin Hassani earned 8 pice a day as a builder and kept only 1 but was fed by his mistress, 'The Story of Rashid bin Hassani of the Bisa Tribe, Northern Rhodesia' in M. Perham (ed.), *Ten Africans*, Northwestern 1963 (first published London 1936), (henceforth 'Rashid'), pp. 81–119, p. 99.

372 How much of their earnings they kept depended on their masters. Jackson states that most of those working for him in 1886–7 expected to have all their earnings appropriated on their return although by Muslim law they should have been allowed to keep half (Frederick Jackson, *Early Days in East Africa*, London 1969 (first published 1930), pp. 137–8). Rashid bin Hassani kept half of his earnings (Perham, 'Rashid', p. 103) and this was considered normal by Euan Smith (Euan Smith to Salisbury, tel. no. 137, 4 May 1890, FO 84/2069).

373 Renault, I, p. 15

374 Middleton, 'Slavery', p. 46. A few Shirazi also owned slaves. Early in the century Indians also had them but, as has been seen, they were forced to release them. This estimate is in striking contrast to those from British contemporary sources. Kirk thought there were about 113,000 slaves in 1889 in a total population of over 450,000 and he believed there had been three times as many in 1844, Kirk memo. 4 Nov. 1889, FO 84/2005. Nicholls thinks there were probably 60,000 in the 1850s, Nicholls, pp. 287–8, which would put Middleton's figure at nearer the truth for the late nine-

area, nineteen per cent from the 'tribes behind the coast', and only a very few from the upper Congo and Uganda.[375] Interestingly those from the Manyema and Unyamwezi were considered superior and used as household slaves.[376] There were also some from Ethiopia and the Somali coast. According to the explorer Richard Burton, Galla and Somali were considered 'roguish and treacherous' but Amhara and Guragé boys were thought to be honest, intelligent and amiable.[377] There were also eunuchs and concubines from Ethiopia and some white girls, mainly in the Sultan's own harem. Barghash himself had many slaves, both in his household and on his estates.

Although evidence indicates that slaves were not normally overworked or ill-treated, the death rate was remarkably high and the reproduction rate surprisingly low, presumably due to the small number of women on the plantations, the high incidence of disease,[378] and some occupational hazards. Porters loading and unloading ships, for instance, although believed to be well treated, suffered a high mortality from heart trouble.[379] Among household slaves manumission was practised as usual in Muslim societies and the children of concubines were usually free.[380] These factors, together with a few escapes[381] and kidnapping of slaves by Omani traders, who sold them in the Middle East, meant that a steady supply of fresh victims was required to keep up the labour force upon which the prosperity of the islands depended. After 1875, increased clove and coconut production, the growing transhipment trade and the desire of the colonial powers for porters and soldiers all created additional demands for manpower.[382]

teenth century when slaves had to be smuggled in. See also various estimates in Cave to Lansdowne, 15 April 1901, *PP* Africa, no. 4 (1901), XLVIII, 1901, p. 173, C-593.
375 Kirk memo. October 1889, FO 84/2005
376 Middleton attributes this to the fact that Manyema and Nyamwezi leaders were allied to Arab traders, see 'Slavery', p. 46.
377 Burton, *Zanzibar*, I, pp. 467–8
378 Middleton, 'Slavery', p. 46 states that there were few women and slave marriages were rare. Most women became concubines and household slaves. For the incidence of disease, see Cave to Lansdowne, *PP* Africa, no. 15 (1901), XLVIII, 1901, p. 38, C-593. The low fertility rate was frequently remarked on. See for instance Russell, p. 334; Hardinge to Kimberley, 26 Feb. 1895, *PP* Africa, no. 6 (1895), LXXI, 1895, p. 143, C-7707. Burton believed it was because slave women were reluctant to have children and resorted to abortions, but conditions on Zanzibar do not appear to have been bad enough for this.
379 Kirk memo. undated KP BASC. Kirk cites a mortality rate of 12%–15% a year not counting deaths from epidemics. Thus a gang had to be replaced every 7–9 years.
380 This may not have been the case among all sects, but most Muslims on the islands were Orthodox Sunni.
381 Escape was difficult but not unknown. Occasionally groups would seize a vessel and try to sail away. On Pemba there were a few villages of runaways and in Zanzibar, some slaves escaped into the interior where they risked being enslaved by the Shirazi, Middleton, 'Slavery', p. 46.
382 The market fluctuated with the demand for cloves, Renault, I, p. 285, and other factors, such as epidemics. Slaves were not bought, for instance during the outbreak of

The capture of a slave dhow by the boats of a British ship in 1867

Enthusiastic support for an anti-slavery demonstration at Exeter Hall in 1863

The distance from the mainland was so short and the coast so full of creeks and inlets that it was a simple matter to sneak over to Zanzibar or Pemba in small craft with just a few captives. If a dhow had the misfortune to fall in with a naval patrol, 'raw' slaves, often intermingled with legitimate passengers, were frequently afraid to declare themselves, having been told that the white men would kill them. Cornered slavers sometimes escaped by beaching their vessel and scurrying into the bush with their human cargo, leaving the frustrated pursuer with an empty dhow, which he could destroy[383] but only at the risk of leaving victims stranded to die, perhaps, on a barren shore.[384] Captives were sometimes hidden under other cargo such as fish. Naval officers tried to detect them by sprinkling pepper through cracks in the deck.[385] Once on the islands the population was so overwhelmingly sympathetic that it was easy enough to evade detection by the Sultan's few officials. If caught, slavers lost dhow and cargo, but risked only a short term of imprisonment.[386] So heavy was the mortality rate for slaves on Zanzibar and Pemba and so simple the smuggling that Kirk believed in 1889 that nine tenths of the slaves had been imported illegally since 1873.[387] He estimated that some three thousand a year reached Pemba[388] and thought the navy never intercepted more than five per cent of those destined for the islands.[389] Nevertheless after 1873 the trade was much reduced from its former level.

Slaves were extensively used in the Sultan's coastal dominions, too, where economic development was also rapid in the nineteenth century, doubtless stimulated, as on the islands, by the measures taken against the export trade following the signature of the treaties of 1822 and 1845. These made more slaves available for domestic use at a lower price. Development may also have been largely financed from profits on slave and ivory caravans into the interior.[390]

---

cholera of 1870 but imports perhaps increased later to make up for this, Kirk to Wylde (?) 3 May 1870, KP STZ.

383 Provided evidence of slaving was sufficiently clear.

384 See instance cited in Elton, pp. 61–2, in which a dhow was beached between Ras Madraka and Ras Khasham on the waterless northern coast.

385 W. W. A. FitzGerald, *Travels in the Coastlands of British East Africa and the Islands of Zanzibar and Pemba: Their Agricultural Resources and General Characteristics*, London 1898, p. 610. FitzGerald writes that in 1892 after the islands became a British Protectorate some slave women disguised as concubines had come on the Sultan's own steamer from Zanzibar to Pemba, where they were worth four times as much.

386 See below, p. 217

387 Kirk memo. 20 Nov. 1889, KP BASC; Kirk to FO 20 Aug. 1889, FOCP 6010

388 Kirk memo. on the working of the treaty of 1873, KP BASC; Kirk to (?) Allen, 8 Feb. 1893, KP Misc. The Sultan himself continued to import eunuchs and concubines and was accused of sending contraband slaves retaken by his officials to his own extensive plantations, Renault, I, p. 291.

389 Kirk to FO, 20 Aug. 1889, FOCP 6010

390 F. Cooper, 'The Treatment of Slaves on the Kenya Coast in the 19th Century', *Kenya Historical Review*, i, 2, 1973, pp. 87–107, p. 91; Nicholls, pp. 203–17

In the cities, as on Zanzibar, slaves were servants, concubines, dockers, fishermen, sailors, craftsmen, caravan leaders and porters.[391] Many were hired out or worked on their own, giving a proportion of their profits to their masters and accumulating wealth themselves. The majority were agricultural labourers employed by the Arabs, Swahili and Somali on the farms and plantations which sprang up all along the coast, producing rice, millet, sesame[392] and other grains, fruits, coconuts and sugar cane for local consumption or for export. In some areas they also tended livestock and collected lichen from the forest for dye.[393] Many were settled in villages with their families and were merely visited from time to time by their masters, who left the farming entirely to them. Sometimes they worked in gangs under a head slave and the owner took all the crops but allowed them certain days a week to work on their own account.[394] In some areas they lived and worked side by side with free farmers and their life style was much the same. Some masters had few slaves and worked alongside them.[395] Others were men of substance who owned several estates[396] and perhaps hundreds of slaves and lived in town on the proceeds of their labour. The Mazrui Arabs had thousands, and valued them as retainers as well as instruments of production.[397] The amount of land a man could cultivate depended on the number of slaves he could command and so did his wealth and status.[398]

It was said that slaves were better treated on parts of the coast than on the islands,[399] and later European observers were sometimes struck with the license allowed them.[400] This was at a time when British administration

391 The following discussion is drawn from primary works as cited, from informant Husein Salim, and from the following secondary works: Salim, chs. 1, 3; F. J. Berg, 'Mombasa under the Busaidi Sultanate: The City and Its Hinterland in the nineteenth Century', Wisconsin Ph.D. 1971, pp. 151 ff.; W. McKay, 'Some Notes on the Southern Kenya Coast in the Nineteenth Century', unpublished seminar paper, University of Nairobi, 13 Sept. 1972; Marguerite Ylvisaker, 'Shamba na Konde: Land Usage in the Hinterland of the Lamu Archipelago 1865–1895', *ibid.*, Oct. 1971; M. W. Beech, 'Slavery on the East Coast of Africa', *Journal of the Africa Society*, 1915–16, pp. 146–9.
392 Also called sim-sim or oil seed.
393 Greffulhe, p. 212   394 FitzGerald, pp. 28 ff
395 European and African sources agree that on first sight one might not know a slave from a free man or even, in the case of small-scale owners, the master from his slave. Said Suleiman Mwagogo, interview, 26 Sept. 1972.
396 Some owners had estates on Zanzibar or Pemba as well as on the coast. Personal communication from Mr F. Cooper.
397 Cooper, pp. 93–4   398 FitzGerald, p. 22
399 Report by Sir A. Hardinge on the Condition and Progress of the East Africa Protectorate from its Establishment to 20 July 1897, *PP* Africa no. 7 (1897), LX 1898, p. 199, C-8683, cited in Berg, p. 169.
400 FitzGerald, pp. 32, 278–81; Hardinge wrote, 'Slaves, in fact, in this country do much as they please, to an extent which no one who is not actually acquainted with local conditions probably realises, and the tenacious attachment of the Mohammedan population to the institution of domestic slavery often appears to me to rest rather on

made it easier for them to abscond and made ill-treatment less likely.[401] However, it is worth mentioning as Giriama, who worked for wages side by side with slaves, thought they were abused but cited examples[402] which would not shock anyone nurtured on accounts of American plantation slavery which merely shows once more the subjectivity of such judgements.[403] Coastal slaves had one great advantage, however, over those on the islands. There sprang up nearby settlements of *watoro* or fugitive slaves, where malcontents could find a welcome and moreover there were also local rulers anxious to build up their following and hence ready to receive them.[404] One would expect that a master's self-interest would dictate good treatment particularly in the countryside where supervision was minimal and escape relatively easy.

Watoro colonies were established in the Shimba Hills, in the hinterlands of Mombasa, Malindi and Lamu and on the Juba river. At the outset they were often attacked by their former masters but some found a safe retreat, grew in numbers and ravaged the neighbourhood, carrying off crops, cattle and captives of their own.[405] In 1874, for instance, Greffulhe reported there were about five thousand of them at Balawa north-east of Lamu, terrorising the Swahili and allied to the nomadic Boni.[406] The multiplication of watoro settlements indicates that many slaves were unhappy with their lot, although their treatment, which varied with place, time, the work the slave was engaged in and the idiosyncrasies of his master, seemed good to outsiders. Some slaves may simply have wanted a more adventurous life or found their status demeaning.[407] From 1875 fugitives also found a haven in the Christian missions on the coast.[408]

sentimental and religious considerations, or on an indolent dislike for, and distrust of, new customs, than on any great material advantage accruing to the slave owner from his very limited rights and powers over his slaves.' Hardinge to Salisbury, no. 21, 4 Feb. 1899, *PP* Africa, no. 8 (1899), LXIII, 1899, C-9502.

401 For British policy see below, pp. 300–1.

402 Masters were said to have given them the dirtiest jobs and to have been inconsiderate about the quantity of water they used since they had slaves to carry it. Kayaa wa Katore, interview, 22 Sept. 1972.

403 For a discussion of this point see above, pp. 66–7. Some European observers on the coast also thought slaves were sometimes abused. Greffulhe, who lived in Lamu in the 1870s, found them badly fed, clothed and overworked, Greffulhe, p. 215. Jackson was horrified to see children on the island tied to heavy poles which they had to hold up to avoid strangulation, Jackson, p. 21.

404 Rulers such as the Sultan of Witu or the Mazrui Mbarak bin Rashid.

405 FitzGerald cites instances of this on the very outskirts of Mombasa in 1891, pp. 130–1; see also Haggard to Kirk, 25 Aug. 1884, enc. in Kirk to Granville, 23 Sept. 1884, FOCP 5165; Gissing to Kirk, 14 Sept. 1884, enc. in Kirk to Granville, 8 Oct. 1884, *ibid.*; Salim, p. 51; Husein Salim, interview, 26 Sept. 1972.

406 Greffulhe, p. 216

407 Mr Cooper's researches now in progress on the nature of slavery on the coast should throw more light on this subject.

408 For a further discussion of the harbouring of fugitives by missions see below, pp. 163 ff.

The number of slaves in the Sultan's coastal dominions in the 1870s and 1880s[409] is hard to gauge but the market was expanding, stimulated by a growing demand for agricultural produce and increased commercial activity as the coastal people developed their trade with the hinterland and sent caravans into the far interior. The demand for labour was kept high not just by the normal attrition due to death and manumission, which was practised as usual in accordance with Muslim law, but also by the large number of escapes.

The Sultan's decrees and the treaty of 1873 forced slavers to change their methods and affected the sources of supply for both the coastal and the island market. Where in the past slave caravans had marched boldly to the ports, they now left their captives in a *boma* (encampment) inland and the leaders came down to the coast to meet dhow captains and arrange shipment. A close watch was kept on the movements of British patrols and when all was clear victims were brought in and despatched quickly either up the coast or overseas.[410] Less obvious places of embarkation were used[411] and captives were hidden in coastal villages long enough to recover from the ravages of the journey and even to learn some Swahili so that they could pass more easily as domestic slaves and incidentally command a higher price.[412]

Fewer slaves now came from the Nyasa region or other distant places and more from the nearer hinterland, the actual sources of supply varying with wars,[413] famines, shifts in political power and changes in trading conditions.[414] African peoples on or near the coast, like the Digo[415] and

409 At the end of the nineteenth century Hardinge estimated there were some 26,000 slaves belonging to Arabs and Swahili in the ten mile wide strip recognised as belonging to the Sultan of Zanzibar. It was thought that there had been 8,000 more in 1890, Salim, pp. 101 ff., fn. 2. Whether these figures are reliable is not yet clear.

410 Giraud, the French explorer, came across such a boma in 1883 some 100 kilometres from Dar-es-Salaam, V. Giraud, *Les Lacs de l'Afrique Equatoriale*, Paris 1890, p. 92, cited in Renault, I, p. 283. Legitimate caravans also halted short of the coast while their leaders went ahead to find prospective buyers who would advance the goods or cash they needed to pay off the hired porters who had carried their merchandise down from the interior, Husein Salim, interview, 26 Sept. 1972.

411 According to oral traditions one of these was Watamu. Here victims, smuggled in by boat at night had no idea where they were and, with the sea on one side and a forest full of wild animals on the other, could be left unshackled without fear that they would escape, Husein Salim, interview 26 Sept. 1972. It is possible that this was only after 1890 when the British Consul-General in Zanzibar reported that slavers were using small ports on the British coast because of energetic German measures on the Tanganyika shore, Euan Smith to Salisbury, tel. conf. no. 214, 6 Aug. 1890, FO 84/2069.

412 Molyneux to Earle, 18 April 1880, FO 84/1574; Kirk to FO, 25 July 1884, FOCP 5155. Informants today point out villages and houses where slaves were kept, Husein Salim, interview, 26 Sept. 1972.

413 Victims of wars of succession in Usambara for instance came into Pangani from 1869, Coupland, *Exploitation*, pp. 137–8.

414 Caravans from the Kenya hinterland brought more slaves into Mombasa when

Giriama[416] sometimes both absorbed slaves themselves and sold them to the Arabs. It is worth noting in this connection that on occasion the tables were turned and Swahili were themselves captured, usually by watoro, and sold to the Galla and Somali.[417] By the late 1880s and early 1890s there was much small-scale local kidnapping and trickery was used to lure victims on to dhows.[418] Slaves taken locally were sent as far afield as possible to discourage escape[419] and captives from distant areas were used on the plantations and farms on the coast where close supervision could not be exercised and flight was easy.[420]

The effects of the Sultan's measures and of the 1873 treaty, however, were only slowly felt. For many years slaves from distant Nyasa still reached the islands and on the Benadir coast, Barghash never had the power, even if he had the will, to eradicate slavery.[421] Elsewhere along the coast slaves could still be legally acquired and the regulations against slave caravans could not be enforced and in any case were aimed principally at the export traffic.[422]

In the East African hinterland slaving continued unabated. Here the Sultan's followers had penetrated far into the interior, ranging over a vast area from north of Lake Victoria to south of Lake Malawi and westwards

they found they sometimes made the difference between profit and loss on a particular venture, Berg, pp. 235, 246.

415 Digo, for instance, sold both Digo and non-Digo to the Wasin islanders, personal communication, W. McKay.

416 According to oral sources the Giriama allowed their Swahili trading partners to use their villages as slaving bases, Husein Salim, interview, 26 Sept. 1972.

417 The watoro followers of the Sultan of Witu captured the inhabitants of mainland villages around Lamu and exchanged them with the Somali for cattle, Ylvisaker, p. 6; Salim, p. 51. Watoro around Mombasa kidnapped Swahili and sold them to the Giriama who traded them to the Galla, FitzGerald, pp. 130–1. Watoro also preyed upon the Giriama and Galla watoro, escaped from Somali masters, were reported in the late 1880s to be carrying off the women, children and livestock of their former owners, FitzGerald, p. 465.

418 Husein Salim, interview 26 Sept. 1972; Nzaro wa Ruwa, interview 28 Sept. 1972. Ngumbao wa Ngowa, interview 22 Sept. 1972; Kayaa wa Katore, interview 22 Sept. 1972.

419 Informants suggest, however, that in the days when all transport was on foot, knowledge of surrounding country was very localised and many victims were young children; they did not have to be taken far. One informant stated also that the conversion of a slave to Islam would prevent his wishing to escape. It would also, of course, increase the chances of his being integrated into Swahili society and of being well treated. However, the same informant thought that only the more tractable were converted and the rest were exported, Husein Salim, interview, 26 Sept. 1972.

420 *Ibid.*

421 Barghash maintained it no longer existed (see Euan Smith to Salisbury, no. 115, 28 Feb. 1889, FOCP 5867) but all he really could do was to refuse to return to their owners slaves from the Benadir who ran away to Zanzibar, and to tell his judges to reject any claims of masters over slaves. Kirk to FO 20 Aug. 1889, FOCP 6010; Kirk memo. 20 Nov. 1889, KP BASC.

422 Memo. by Kirk, undated, on the working of the agreements with Zanzibar and the Sultan's decrees of 1876, MSS BE s Lugard 41.

into modern Zaire. The character of their operations depended on individual merchants and local conditions.[423] Many of them were simply itinerant traders and in places like Buganda their activities were peaceful and their influence strictly limited. Elsewhere they fostered or intervened in local disputes. According to Livingstone the sight of their wares prompted the Yao to raid for the slaves needed to buy them.[424] They might stay several years in one place growing their own food and doing business with their African hosts,[425] who welcomed them for the cloth, beads and other barter goods, especially arms and ammunition, which gave their customers a military advantage over their neighbours.[426] Along some of the main trading routes they established a few small settlements such as Tabora in central Tanzania and Ujiji on Lake Tanganyika to serve as bases and centres of supply. These were surrounded by independent African peoples who sometimes became trading partners of their Arab neighbours and intermarried with them.[427]

West of Lake Tanganyika, in areas where African communities were small and weak, Arab penetration took a different form. Here a handful of merchant adventurers began to acquire large numbers of followers and wield political power. The greatest of them was Hamed bin Muhammed, known as Tippu Tip,[428] who carved out a veritable empire in the rich ivory bearing lands around the upper Congo and its tributaries, collecting tribute, settling disputes and exercising some of the rudimentary functions of government. Eventually he, his relations, henchmen and partners dominated Utétéla and Manyema and ranged far down the Congo, into Ituri and westwards almost to the Kasai. By the early 1880s this expansion was underway. The Arabs had solid bases such as Nyangwe and Kasongo which were peaceful centres and a number of outlying posts but their marauding

423 Many works throw light on these operations but see Coupland, *Exploitation;* Alison Smith, 'The Southern Section of the Interior, 1840–84' and David Low, 'The Northern Interior 1840–84', chs. 8 and 9 in Oliver and Mathew; Ceulemans, pp. 28 ff.; Renault, I, pp. 7 ff.; N. R. Bennett, 'The Arab Impact' (henceforth 'Arab Impact'); and E. A. Alpers, 'The Nineteenth Century: Prelude to Colonialism' (henceforth 'Nineteenth Century'), chs. 11 and 12 in B. A. Ogot and J. A. Kieran, *Zamani,* Nairobi 1968.
424 David Livingstone, *The Last Journals of David Livingstone in Central Africa from 1865 to his Death,* edited by H. Waller, New York 1875, p. 75.
425 Livingstone, *Zambesi,* p. 516
426 For the arms trade and its importance see below, pp. 182 ff., 198.
427 Relations varied according to the fluctuating power of Africans and Arabs, see Bennett, *Mirambo,* for relations at Tabora and also Renault, I, pp. 28 ff.
428 For the remarkable career of Tippu Tip who became ruler of Utétéla by invitation on the death of the African ruler in 1872, see his own account in 'Maisha ya Hamed bin Muhammed el Murjebi Yaani Tippu Tip' with English translation by W. H. Whitely, *Supplement to the East African Swahili Committee Journals,* nos. 28/2 July 1958, 29/1 Jan. 1959 (henceforth 'Hamed ya Muhammed'); H. Brode, *Tippoo Tib, The Story of his Career in Central Africa,* London 1907; Ceulemans, pp. 12 ff.; Renault, I, pp. 51 ff. and 301 ff.; Alison Smith, 'Southern Interior'; Vansina, *Kingdoms,* pp. 235–40.

expeditions ravaged far afield. Their followers were a motley collection of free mercenaries (*ruga-ruga*) hired as soldiers or hunters,[429] free and slave retainers, contingents furnished by allied African rulers and boys, who had been captured in war, incorporated into a band and brought up to a life of pillage. In the forests of modern Zaire,[430] these marauders often obtained ivory by raiding defenceless villages, seizing hostages and holding them to ransom until the desired booty was produced. Death and destruction marked their path. Sometimes only children were spared, the boys to join the band and the girls to serve as wives.

Slaves played an important if variable part in these Arab operations. On the southern routes from Lake Malawi to the Tanzanian coast profits depended on the export of captives as much as on the sale of ivory. Elsewhere they were incidental to the ivory trade but nevertheless essential to the trading pattern. A merchant might travel round the interior for months or even years picking up goods here and there and bartering them off again before acquiring the ivory and other commodities he finally carried back to the coast. In some areas slaves might be all that was offered him and since there was a large internal market for them,[431] he would buy them and sell them again in the course of his wanderings. Kirk described a typical journey to the Lake Malawi area where a trader might arrive with cloth, guns and other imports but not ammunition, and be offered only slaves. He would take these captives to Portuguese territory where he would exchange them for powder, which was cheaper there than at Zanzibar where the Sultan exercised a monopoly. He would then return up country to barter his ammunition for the ivory his African customers had refused to part with for the goods he had originally brought them.[432] Slaves were also used to pay for services. Tippu Tip, for instance, gave some to the Jiji for ferrying his ivory across Lake Tanganyika.[433] In regions where not enough free porters could be hired, male slaves were either bought or extorted as ransom for hostages, to carry loads,[434] and even women were sometimes used. The lesser traders or the retainers of the Arabs, who got little in the way of ivory, might depend for their profits on capturing and selling slaves.[435] Thus in East Africa, as in the Sudan, the slave traffic supplemented the ivory trade.

Barghash had no control over his followers in the interior. Arabs with property in or links with Zanzibar might heed his wishes but he had no means of supervising their operations in the hinterland or of enforcing obedience if they kept outside his territories. Even settlements in the interior

429 They hunted elephant for ivory and other game for meat.
430 For a useful summary of these operations see Renault, I, pp. 61 ff.
431 For a discussion of African slavery see below, pp. 118 ff.
432 Memo. by Kirk, enc. in Plens. to Salisbury, no. 12 STC conf. 25 Jan. 1890. FO 84/2101
433 Renault, I, p. 70
434 *Ibid.*, Alpers, 'Prelude', p. 246
435 Renault, I, pp. 80 ff.

which flew his flag were virtually independent[436] and the Arabs of the upper Congo commanded armies and wielded power themselves. It was not in Barghash's commercial interests to alienate any of these merchants. His decrees and the measures taken against the maritime slave trade, therefore, did not affect slaving in the interior, except in so far as they curtailed the export traffic and thereby channelled victims into the interior or coastal market.

The new policy of 1883 in East Africa

In 1882 the Foreign Office reconsidered its whole anti-slave trade policy in East Africa and the Red Sea. The question arose when the Treasury announced its reluctance to renew the subsidy to the British India Steam Navigation Company for the Zanzibar mail service, due to expire in December.[437] Foreign Office officials believed the service had been invaluable in expanding British trade and influence, and Kirk now wanted to extend it to mainland ports in order to enable him to watch the Sultan's officials more closely and to foster growing British interests.[438] The Foreign Secretary, Lord Granville, hinted that his case would be stronger if he could show that it was an economical way of carrying out British policy.[439] Kirk pointed out that the expenses of suppressing the slave trade appeared on a number of different departmental estimates so that economy on one of them, such as a reduction in the naval forces on patrol, could not be offset against expenditure on another. He suggested that the cost of all anti-slavery measures should now be considered together.[440] This cleared the way for a re-appraisal of the whole policy and enabled the Foreign Office to gain its object by juggling with figures. Kirk, together with Hill, began to build his case.

It was easy enough to show that the machinery set up after Frere's mission had been only very partially successful. The *London* and her boats, although commanded with great vigour, had clearly not stopped the smuggling of slaves to Zanzibar and Pemba, and it was believed that several thousand a year were still exported from Mozambique to Madagascar and the Comoros. Naval officers despaired of achieving better results. Reports revealed the disturbing fact that the slave traffic on the mainland was growing in spite of the reduction of the export trade and that slaves were increasingly employed on the coast itself to work the plantations that were

436 It caused a sensation at Tabora when he recalled the *liwali* in 1881 but he appointed no successor. The liwali in any case was really an agent with no means of enforcing his wishes on the Arab community and he had secured power by driving his predecessor from office, see Bennett, *Mirambo*, pp. 29–31, 48–9, 77–8, 150–1.
437 For the institution of this service in 1873, see above, pp. 33–4.
438 Kirk memo., 24 Jan. 1882, FO 84/1657
439 Granville minute on Treasury to F.O., 22 March 1882, no date, *ibid*.
440 Kirk memo., 1 May 1882, *ibid*.

springing up. Against this the British were powerless. Naval officers who landed and found caravans on the move or encamped could do nothing.[441]

In 1881 the Commander-in-Chief of the East Indies squadron had suggested that the navy be supported by a secret service ashore to give information about the movements of slavers, that the Sultan use his English-trained troops to establish posts along the slave routes into the interior and that in Madagascar the Hovas might be encouraged to extend their rule over the still independent slave dealing Sakalava on the west coast of the island. He believed that if the trade could be attacked at its 'fountainhead' on the mainland and its 'terminus' in Madagascar, Britain would soon be able to dispense with the expensive and not very effective naval establishment at Zanzibar, and legitimate trade would benefit from the greater protection offered by the Sultan's posts and by the increased power of the Hovas.[442]

These views accorded well with those of Kirk and Hill, who disliked the naval campaign, believing it was irritating dhow owners and driving them to seek French protection and was interfering with legitimate trade and undermining British influence. They drew up a plan whereby action at sea was to be superseded by increased surveillance of the slave trade on land.[443] Three 'travelling' vice-consuls were to be appointed to the principal ports of the mainland to watch the traffic and promote legitimate commerce. The mail subsidy was to be continued and the service extended to include fortnightly calls at the coastal ports. The cost of this was to be transferred from the Post Office estimates to the Foreign Office slave trade vote. The expenses of the Zanzibar Consulate, hitherto shared with the India Office, were to be taken over by the Foreign Office, thus preventing any interference in East African affairs by the government of India.[444]

These charges were to be met by the withdrawal from Zanzibar of the naval re-inforcements sent there after Frere's mission,[445] including HMS *London* and her boats, and by a change in the system of bounties paid to naval crews for each slaver successfully prosecuted.[446] As the *London* was rotten and badly in need of replacement, her withdrawal would

---

441 It was even doubtful whether legally they could land and give chase if a trapped dhow beached and hustled her slaves off into the bush. The Sultan agreed that between Songo Mnara and Tunghi they might be pursued. In fact the navy did it everywhere with his tacit consent.

442 The Hovas had told the admiral they could stop the traffic if they could take troops to St. Augustine's Bay and acquire a gunboat, see Jones to Admiralty, no. 457, 10 Oct. 1881, FO 84/1607. For the history of Madagascar and the pattern of Hova conquest see H. Deschamps, *Histoire de Madagascar*, Paris 1965, pp. 153 ff.

443 See Hill memo., 23 Aug. 1882, FO 84/1694

444 Kirk complained of the 'paralysing' effect of the government of India's policy, memo, 23 March 1883, FO 84/1694.

445 Hill based his calculations of what would be saved on the cost of these reinforcements because the Admiralty would not divulge how many ships were required for purely slave trade purposes.

446 Bounties were usually paid on tonnage. As slavers now carried few slaves this was proving wasteful and henceforth bounty was to be paid for each slave freed.

save £25,000 as well as cut down running expenses. It was further decided that the Consul-General at Zanzibar could use the mail service to transport himself and his subordinates about the coast and thus save buying the yacht for which he had been asking for some years to enable him to supervise the Sultan's officials.[447]

This plan, conceived by Kirk, must be seen in the light of events taking place in Zanzibar. Here, in the last few years, British activity had much increased. Missionaries had established a number of stations in the far interior and Indian merchants had extended their operations. But they were not alone in the field. The Roman Catholic Holy Ghost Fathers and White Fathers and French, German and other speculators and traders were also increasingly active and agents of King Leopold II of Belgium's African International Association were setting up posts in the interior. Kirk was seriously alarmed lest Britain be forestalled in the work of opening up East Africa to European penetration and nursed groundless fears of French designs on Zanzibar and the mainland.[448]

Coming home on leave late in 1881, he carried a letter from the Sultan offering Britain the regency should he be succeeded by a minor.[449] The government, however, had no desire to assume such responsibility and thought the proposal contravened the Anglo-French agreement of 1862 to respect the independence of Zanzibar. It was therefore rejected but Kirk was determined to maintain 'a paramount British influence to control and guide the native ruler.'[450] His plan was to replace unpopular naval action by consuls on the mainland, who would foster trade, attract settlers and bolster up the Sultan's officials, while watching the slave traffic. The mail subsidy would cover a service to mainland ports which would develop legitimate, hopefully British, trade on the coast and prevent France, a political and commercial rival, from getting a foothold in new markets.[451] The suppression of the slave traffic and the capture of these markets by Britain would thus proceed simultaneously.[452] An Admiralty proposal that the scheme should also be applied to the Red Sea, where the short crossing and difficulties of inshore navigation made naval action particularly ineffective, met with his warm approval.

The Foreign Office strongly supported Kirk's plans but the Treasury haggled over every penny of proposed expenditure, quibbled at the salaries of the vice-consuls and succeeded in whittling down the mail subsidy until

447 Kirk to Wylde, 28 Oct. 1879 and 10 Dec. 1879, KP STZ
448 See N. R. Bennett, 'Some Notes on French Policy in Buganda and East Africa, 1879–90', *Makerere Journal*, vi, pp. 1–18.
449 Coupland, *Exploitation*, p. 377
450 Kirk to Mackinnon, 17 Dec. 1882, MP/91 f. 25
451 The British steamers would collect goods for export direct from the coast regularly, whereas hitherto they were collected irregularly by native craft, calling only at certain seasons, Kirk to Mackinnon, 15 Jan. 1883, MP/92, f. 9 ff.
452 'I look on the regular supply of information as necessary to the S[lave] T[rade] work and likely to divert the rising legitimate trade of East Africa into our hands.' *Ibid.*

it covered only monthly calls at the East African ports where the consuls were to be based.[453] When all the haggling was over, the annual saving to the Imperial exchequer was estimated to be over £20,000[454]—so high that the Foreign Office was emboldened to ask the Treasury to allow the appointment of two extra vice-consuls, one at Suakin and one in the Nyasa area. By the summer of 1883, all was agreed and in October three new consuls were posted to the Sultan's mainland territories, to be sent wherever Kirk wished.[455] He was given power to divert the mail ships as he saw fit, so as to 'swoop down' anywhere in what was now being referred to in official circles as Kirk's 'protectorate'[456]—significant words.

At the same time a consul was sent to Nyasaland.[457] This was a curious appointment. There were no recognised authorities to whom he could be accredited and his consular district was not defined. The British missionaries had long wanted a consul in the area, both to deter the Portuguese from annexing it and to relieve them of the need to deal with reprobates in the communities which settled around their stations.[458] The re-organisation of 1883 enabled the Foreign Office to meet their wishes. The consul's job was to work with the traders and missionaries and try to prevent the slave trading operations of the local rulers, particularly the passage of slave gangs across Lake Nyasa.[459] He was to persuade Africans that they had more to gain from legitimate trade than from the slave traffic. It was an unenviable task. He had nothing concrete to offer, was not protected by any territorial power or naval force, and the only weapon at his disposal was 'influence'. With this he was expected to suppress a flourishing commerce. His was certainly a situation fraught with danger.

New treaties with the Comoro Islands

While Kirk had been battling to get his plan accepted by the Cabinet,[460] Consul Holmwood had negotiated new treaties with the various rulers of the predominantly Muslim Comoro Islands. These heralded a much greater

453 See correspondence in FO 84/1694. An example of the kind of backbiting that went on was the Treasury's insistence that the Admiralty certify that the money saved on the naval establishment at Zanzibar was to be a net saving on the naval estimates and not used for other purposes.
454 FO to Treasury, 22 June 1883, *ibid.*
455 The consuls were placed in fact where the British India Steam Navigation Company (with whose head, Sir William Mackinnon, Kirk was in close touch) wanted them and they were often company agents, personal communication from Dr Alan Smith.
456 Spring Rice to Lister, 9 May 1883, FO 84/1657. If the ships were diverted more than four times a year, however, the company had to be paid.
457 Hanna, pp. 62–5
458 For the problems facing the missionaries see *ibid.*, pp. 16 ff.
459 Anderson minute, 16 May 1888, FOCP 5896
460 The Mackinnon papers show the extent of Kirk's activity. He was in close touch not only with Mackinnon, but also with members of Parliament.

involvement in the affairs of the isles. Slave dealing was to stop at once, all slaves were to be registered and, most revolutionary, slavery was to end in 1889, the date when private dealing was to become illegal in the Sudan. Holmwood, it appeared, was an optimist, who hoped other Muslim states would follow the example of Egypt and the Comoros. Meanwhile British consuls were to supervise and protect the slaves on the islands. Holmwood had obtained these far-reaching concessions by threats and his reasons are interesting. He believed that the Comoros, particularly Johanna, were potentially rich, and was determined to facilitate the development of British enterprise. As he reported:

> There are many eligible sites for sugar plantations entirely unoccupied, where water is abundant and the climate far from unhealthy, but the question of free labour supply has hitherto proved a serious difficulty to English planters. That it should be so no longer has been one of the objects I have had before me and it is trusted that the treaty now concluded has established a basis on which while the emancipation of slaves is secured, the interests of the other classes need not be lost sight of. If this be the case, Johanna will shortly become a country where British capital may be safely and profitably employed.[461]

In fact there were British planters already established on Johanna, growing mainly sugar, and using slave labourers, hired from their Comoro masters in contravention of English law.[462] Holmwood found the ruler had the best estates and reported that his slaves were ill-treated.[463] On Mohilla, he also found an English-run sugar plantation employing hired slaves. Slaves were also used by Comorans as concubines and servants and Holmwood had had to assure the rulers that Britain would interfere as little as possible with their domestic arrangements.

The centre of the slave traffic at this time was Grand Comoro, where Holmwood found the reigning Sultan's brother had raised a rebellion and gained control of part of the island.[464] He was both importing Makua slaves from Mozambique and reducing free islanders to slavery. Many were sold to the neighbouring isles, or to French planters at Mayotte and Nossi Bé ostensibly as contract labourers but none of them had returned.[465] Holmwood recognised slave dealers, who had been tried in Zanzibar, in the rebel's entourage. He thought all the islanders were deeply implicated in the traffic and estimated that there were some 27,000 slaves in the Comoros, mostly on

461 Holmwood's report together with the treaties are enclosed in Holmwood to Granville, 29 Oct. 1882, enc. in Miles to Granville, no. 93, 18 Nov. 1882, FO 84/1623.
462 See below, pp. 150–1
463 This is in contrast to the evidence of the most important of the planters, William Sunley, who maintained in 1862 that slaves on the islands were well treated, see Coupland, *Exploitation*, p. 175.
464 The revolt was said to have been provoked when the ruler tried to obey the orders of his suzerain, the Sultan of Zanzibar, to suppress the slave traffic.
465 Memo enc. in Holmwood to Granville, no. 111, 5 Sept. 1881, FOCP 4626

Grand Comoro, who would be freed by his treaties in 1889, provided steps were taken to see that the agreements were carried out.[466]

However, his superiors were unwilling to take strong action. Kirk warned the Foreign Office that interference in the islands might drive France to annex the whole group.[467] Relations with France were so strained over the occupation of Egypt that the moment was not considered opportune even to protest against the *engagés* trade.[468] There was also the practical difficulty that the most suitable candidate for the post of British vice-consul was a planter who employed hired slaves and could not therefore be appointed.[469]

Britain and the Madagascan slave trade

Madagascar was another flourishing market for African slaves in the early 1880s. Most were shipped from the coast of Portuguese Mozambique. Here again there were complications with France. Britain recognised the Hova ruler of the Imerina kingdom as sovereign of the whole island. This enabled her to seize and try all slave vessels from Madagascar by virtue of her treaties with the Hovas.[470] Moreover, under British pressure the Hovas in 1877 had declared that throughout their dominions all slaves from Mozambique were free—a measure designed to stop the import of Africans by destroying the market.[471] In practice, however, the Hovas had little or

466 Holmwood to Granville, 29 Oct. 1882, enc. in Miles to Granville, no. 93, 18 Nov. 1882, FO 84/1623. Foreign Office officials were mystified that the Comoro rulers had agreed to such far-reaching treaties. Holmwood himself had little faith that either the Sultan of Mohilla or the pretender on Grand Comoro would take steps against the traffic. The ruler of Johanna had told him that the agreement would make him very unpopular and had asked Holmwood to show his support for him and provide a steam launch. Holmwood could not promise a launch but was present at a meeting at which the Sultan had proclaimed his eldest son his heir, thus giving an appearance of support. Holmwood estimated there were 5,000 slaves on Johanna and 2,000 on Mohilla.

467 Kirk memo. 29 Dec. 1882, FO 84/1623. The rebel on Grand Comoro gave the impression that he was under French protection and the French were said to have warned Zanzibar not to interfere in island affairs. The Sultan of Johanna had asked what he was to do if a French dhow started to load slaves, and Holmwood had replied that he should leave it alone but try to stop his own subjects from selling the slaves. It was clear the question might lead to difficulties with France.

468 Granville minute on Anderson's minutes of 12 and 15 March 1884, FO 84/1683. This trade provoked Anderson's minute on the wisdom of showing up the French, see above, pp. 37–8.

469 See below, pp. 150–1

470 Kirk to Granville, no. 10, 8 Jan. 1881, FOCP 4626. For earlier treaties see above, pp. 40n., 87.

471 There were, however, many indigenous slaves who remained in slavery. For an outline of the situation see 'L'esclavage à Madagascar', *Afrique explorée et civilisée*, 1881–2 3ème année, pp. 167–70, 190–6. See also sources cited in Renault, I, p. 104, which I have not been able to consult: E. André, *De l'esclavage à Madagascar*, Paris

no control over some of the most inveterate buyers of slaves, the Sakalava of the west coast, who, from naval reports, regarded slaves as necessary to their existence, treated them well and rarely sold them. Estimates of the size of this trade were contradictory. According to the highest, four to five thousand slaves a year were exported to western Madagascar north of Cape St. Vincent in 1880.[472] Some Sakalava were still not under Hova domination[473] and, as has been seen, the Hovas were eager to use the slave trade question to get British assistance in extending their rule over them. But by 1883 the French conquest of Madagascar had begun. Henceforth the slave traffic to the island was to be a French responsibility. The British-Hova treaty remained in force but interference in Madagascan affairs would clearly lead to trouble with France.[474]

The slave trade in the Red Sea area and Ethiopia

The same problem was now arising on the shores of the Red Sea. By the beginning of 1884, the revolt in the Sudan had reached such proportions that Britain, now in occupation of Egypt, decided the Egyptians must withdraw from the whole coast south of Suakin. This port was to be held in order to guard the route to India, but it was besieged by the followers of the Mahdi, led by 'Uthman Diqna, a local merchant who had suffered ruin and imprisonment for slave dealing.[475] The Egyptian withdrawal left a power vacuum along the western shore of the Red Sea, which Britain hoped the Turks and Somalis would fill. However, on the eve of the Berlin conference,

1899 and R. Ratsimamanga, 'De la condition de l'esclave à Madagascar', Law thesis, Montpelier 1933.

472 The source of this is Captain Foot, an officer of long experience on the coast, who based it on enquiries he conducted in Madagascar. O'Neill in Mozambique commenting on these figures and the contradictory report of another naval officer thought 2,500–3,000 were exported from Mozambique in 1880 and that they went to the west coast of Madagascar, the Comoros and the French colonies of Mayotta and Nossi Bé, the French importing them as *engagés*, O'Neill to Granville, no. 55, 31 Dec. 1880, FO 84/1565; Jones to Admiralty, 10 Oct. 1881, FO 84/1607. It may be mentioned here that in 1886 a separate slave trade sprang up in local people from around St Augustine's Bay on the south-west coast of Madagascar to supply the sugar planters on the French island of Réunion after the immigration of Indian coolies had been stopped by the Indian government. Correspondence on this subject is to be found in FO 84/1764. This traffic was conducted in European ships and the victims were shipped as contract labourers.

473 O'Neill reported that the Hovas held only one station on the 450 miles of Sakalava coast south of Cape St Andrew, O'Neill to Granville, no. 46, ST, 12 Sept. 1880, FO 84/1565.

474 The French occupied Tamatave in 1883 and in 1885 a treaty with the Hovas put the foreign affairs of the island under French control and ceded the Diègo Suarez area to France. Britain accepted the situation but did not recognise formally the French protectorate over the island.

475 Holt, *Mahdist State*, ch. 4

she herself occupied Zeila. France began to build up her base at Obock and to extend her rule around the Gulf of Tajura, while further north Italy expanded her territories from Assab.

These developments breached Britain's treaty network. She had no agreement with France, and the one with Italy did not apply to the Red Sea. Instead of being able to attack the slave traffic by pressure on pliant, or so it was hoped, rulers, the Khedive and the Sultan of Turkey, she was now faced with the task of gaining the co-operation of France and Italy. The latter, anxious for British support against France in the Mediterranean as well as for her own expansionist schemes, was willing enough to open negotiations[476] but it was one thing to sign a treaty and another to carry it out.

France, Italy and Britain were now competing for the very limited commerce of the hinterland, the caravan trade of Harar, Shoa and the rest of the Ethiopian highlands in which slaves were a staple commodity. Palmerston, hoping to stop their export, had sent a mission to Shoa. His envoy had found, however, that only easily transportable goods of high intrinsic value could stand the cost of the journey to the coast and had concluded that the suppression of the slave trade would kill the foreign commerce of the highlands.[477] In the 1880s exports were still very limited and the demand for Ethiopian girls had increased since the Russian conquest of the Caucasus had reduced the supply of Circassian concubines.[478] Galla girls were considered particularly attractive. Wylde described them in glowing terms:

> The women are very pretty, have good figures, small hands and feet, soon become most cleanly in their person and dress, pick up all the benefits of civilization, get fairly educated, make good servants, and are faithful and lovable . . . the mother of many an Egyptian or Turk in high position has hailed from the Galla country or Abyssinia.[479]

Ethiopia also exported boys but in fewer numbers and there was a small traffic in eunuchs.[480]

Slaves for export came mainly from the south and south-west of modern Ethiopia and were the by-product of endemic warfare between Galla and Sidama states[481] and of Shoan wars of conquest and raids.[482] Many came

---

476 By the Assab Bay Convention of 1882 Italy acceded to the anti-slavery convention between Britain and Egypt of 1877.

477 Gavin, 'Palmerston's Policy', pp. 102 ff.

478 The last Circassian stronghold fell to Russia in 1864, but some Circassians moved into Turkey. For the Ethiopian slave trade see M. Abir, pp. 53–70; R. Pankhurst, *Economic History of Ethiopia 1800–1935*, Addis Ababa 1968 (henceforth *Economic History*), ch. 3.

479 Wylde, II, pp. 249–50

480 Out of 204 slaves released from 3 dhows captured off Mocha point in 1888, 3 were eunuchs, Gissing to Fremantle, 18 Sept. 1888 enc. in Ad. to FO, 2 Nov. 1888, FOCP 5896.

481 Abir, pp. 54–6

482 M. Perham, *The Government of Ethiopia*, 2nd ed. Evanston 1969 (first published 1948) (henceforth *Government*), pp. 219 ff.

through the Muslim Galla monarchy of Jimma Abu Jifar and crossed the Christian kingdom of Shoa en route to the coast.[483] In the 1880s this important tributary state of the Ethiopian empire was under the rule of the future emperor Menelik II,[484] who was conquering the lands to the south and south-west. The bulk of the trade of these regions passed through Shoa. Coastal merchants came to its great markets to exchange cloth, beads, hardware and metals for the products of the highlands, including thousands of slaves, whom they sent to ports on the southern coasts of the Red Sea and Gulf of Aden. Smaller numbers went northwards into Tigre and were shipped from the shores of Eritrea. Slaves were also marched overland to the markets of the Sudan. The actual number exported is almost impossible to estimate[485] but observers saw large caravans heading for the coast. The traveller P. Soleillet watched two going to Beilul with over a thousand captives each in 1884 and believed that they came every three months.[486] Most of the slaves exported were young children under the age of sixteen. Escape was hardly conceivable and they appear to have been usually well treated on their march to the coast[487] and since they supplied a luxury market their destinies were generally not harsh. Most were victims of wars, raids or kidnappings but some criminals and other offenders were reduced to slavery, sometimes with members of their families.[488]

The export traffic, together with the long distance trade of Ethiopia was in the hands of Muslims. The Christian church prohibited its members from slave dealing and forbade the enslavement of fellow Christians and their sale to infidels.[489] However, Christians could own slaves, capture them in war

483 R. H. F. Darkwah, 'The Rise of the Kingdom of Shoa, 1813–89', London Ph.D., 1966; Assistant Political Resident Aden to Secretary to the Bombay Government, 8 Aug. 1888 enc. in I.O. to F.O. 6 Sept. 1888, FO 84/1927.

484 Menelik became King of Shoa in 1865 and was Emperor of Ethiopia from 1889 to 1913.

485 For the difficulties of reaching an estimate see R. Pankhurst, 'The Ethiopian Slave Trade in the Nineteenth and early Twentieth Centuries: a Statistical Inquiry', *Journal of Semitic Studies*, 9, 1964, no. 1, pp. 220–8

486 P. Soleillet, *Voyages en Ethiopie*, Rouen, 1886, pp. 311–13

487 Abir, pp. 57–9; Antoine d'Abaddie, *Les causes actuelles de l'esclavage en Ethiopie*, Louvain 1877, reprint from *Revue des Questions Scientifiques*, pp. 11–12. Almost all the slaves released off Mocha point in 1888 were young children in good condition. There were reports that slaves were 'fattened up', however, after their march of some 22 days to the Gulf of Tajura. Gissing to Freemantle, 6 Sept. 1888, enc. in Ad. to F.O., 31 Oct. 1888, and 18 Sept. 1888, enc. in Ad. to F. O., 2 Nov. 1888, FOCP 5896. E. W. Polson Newman, discussing this trade in the twentieth century, describes groups of pitiably emaciated children, who were shot if they tried to attract attention; see 'Slavery in Abyssinia', *Contemporary Review*, 148, Dec. 1935, pp. 650–7, p. 652. However, this may have been because by this time the trade was being suppressed and slavers feared exposure.

488 This penalty is said to have been particularly abused by some of the Muslim Galla rulers, who might kill the actual criminal but sell his family, d'Abaddie, pp. 9–10.

489 For the attitude of the Christian church see R. Pankhurst, *An Introduction to the*

The slave market at Zanzibar in 1872

Released slaves receiving wages
at a mission estate at Mbweni in 1882

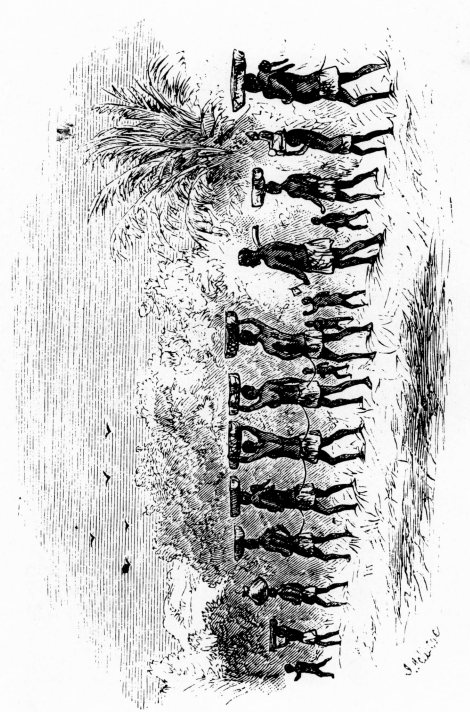

SLAVE GANG.

A slave gang in Katanga in 1875

and give them as tribute, dowry or gifts, all transactions which could disguise slave trading.[490] At least until the 1870s they enslaved fellow Christians,[491] and in the 1880s religion was no safeguard against export. Thus when the Royal Navy captured three dhows off Mocha Point in 1888 about half the two hundred odd slaves aboard were Christian and the rest Muslim.[492] Who captured them, however, is unknown.

In Shoa slavery was widespread. The ruler and his officials had large numbers of captives. King Menelik freely took them as prisoners of war or accepted them as tribute and gave many as presents to his followers.[493] Slavery was considered to be sanctioned by the scriptures[494] and the legal code laid down rules of conduct toward slaves which were very like those in Muslim law.[495] For instance, in theory slaves could not own property, but in fact they did so, and the children of a free man and a slave woman were free. Slaves were also often emancipated on the death of their owner, or after some years of service.[496] Travellers and other observers testified that

Economic History of Ethiopia from Early Times to 1800, London, 1961 (henceforth *Introduction*), pp. 372–3.

490 Newman, p. 652

491 Particularly Guragé, many of whom were kidnapped by Shoans, see J. L. Krapf, *Travels, Researches and Missionary Labours*, London 1860, p. 46. Guragé was conquered by Shoa between 1840 and 1889.

492 Gissing to Freemantle, 18 Sept. 1888, enc. in Ad. to FO, 2 Nov. 1888, FOCP 5896. This contradicts Darkwah's statement that only Muslims and other non-Christians were exported, p. 321. Commander Gissing visited Tajura, and found numbers of slaves awaiting export. He believed they were mainly Christians from Shoa, perhaps Guragé, obtained by stealing or purchase, see Gissing to Fremantle, 6 Sept. 1888 enc. in Ad. to FO, 31 Oct. 1888, FOCP 5896.

493 Darkwah, p. 321; Perham, *Government*, p. 219

494 *Report from the Government of Abyssinia to the League of Nations on the Question of Slavery* (henceforth *Report from the Government of Abyssinia*), communicated by Tafari-Makonnen (later Emperor Haile Selassie), 12 April 1924, Geneva, 14 May 1924, C.209.M.66, 1924, VI. The passage of the scriptures sanctioning slavery is Leviticus 25: 44. For Ethiopian slavery see *Slavery in Abyssinia, Annexe to the Note communicated by the French Government to the League of Nations*, published in 1923, A. 18. 1923 VI (henceforth *Slavery in Abyssinia*). In 1923 the slavery question was an obstacle to Ethiopia's entry into the League of Nations. This interesting document is a digest of information on slavery in Ethiopia from published sources, mainly the accounts of travellers and also an unpublished manuscript provided by the British Consul at Gore. See also W. C. Harris, *The Highlands of Ethiopia*, London 1844, III, p. 315, for the attitude of the priests who approved of the enslavement of non-Christians because it gave them the chance of being converted.

495 This code was the thirteenth-century *Fetha-Nagast*, which sanctioned the enslavement only of non-Christians taken in war, and recommended that slaves should be emancipated if they became Christian, see *Slavery in Abyssinia*; Pankhurst, *Introduction*, pp. 272–3.

496 Darkwah says that in Shoa prisoners of war *could* be emancipated after 7 years, p. 321. In *Slavery in Abyssinia* it is stated that in 1889 Menelik decreed that prisoners of war *had* to be emancipated after 7 years but not until 1924 did the emancipation of a parent free his child. Thus many persons must have been born into slavery, see *Report from the Government of Abyssinia*. Perham states that by customary law

on the whole they were well cared for although twentieth-century sources give the impression that they had little legal protection.[497] Some rose to high office, but most were employed on menial or domestic tasks or worked as agricultural labourers. Many were the retainers of princes and high officials. Large numbers of black slaves were obtained in wars and raids on Ethiopia's western borders but were generally not exported. They were valued for their strength, docility and the ease with which they could be distinguished if they escaped.

The Christian rulers of Ethiopia made a number of attacks on the slave trade in the nineteenth century, starting with the Emperor Teodros[498] who prohibited it. But the law was only enforced for a short time, and the traffic seems to have continued unhindered.[499] The withdrawal of Egypt from the Red Sea coast, however, gave Britain the chance to negotiate a treaty with Teodros' successor, Yohannes.[500] He had long wanted a port on the Red Sea, preferably Massawa, through which he might import European goods, particularly arms. Egypt had not only refused him access to the coast but had been most anxious to prevent him from acquiring arms.[501] Now, urged on by the Anti-Slavery Society, the British Government offered him free access to the sea in return for co-operation against the slave traffic. Two treaties were signed at Adowa on the same day in the summer of 1884. One assured Emperor Yohannes of free trade through Massawa[502] and the other was an agreement against the slave trade,[503] a matter on which it was said he wished to co-operate.[504] This latter was hardly likely to be successful particularly as no arrangement was made with Menelik of Shoa.

Menelik had already appreciated the propaganda value of taking action against the traffic. Hoping to get arms from Europeans at the coast he had issued a far-reaching edict in 1875 forbidding Christians from taking part in the trade and decreeing that all Muslim merchants crossing Shoa with slaves were to be imprisoned; but he did little to enforce the law and the trade may even have increased after it was passed.[505] There were good

captives of war should have been freed after 7 years but the law was not enforced and they were treated like other slaves. *Government*, p. 219.
497 See Perham, *Government*, p. 224; Newman.
498 Teodros (Theodore) II, 1855–68
499 Pankhurst, *Economic History*, pp. 92–5; Perham, *Government*, p. 219
500 Yohannes (John) IV, 1872–89
501 See correspondence in FO 1/30. Britain had hitherto supported Egyptian policy as she did not wish to jeopardise her relations with Egypt, Pankhurst, *Economic History*, pp. 588–9. For the arms traffic see below, pp. 185 ff.
502 Treaty between Britain, Egypt and Ethiopia, 3 June 1884, Hertslet, *Commercial Treaties*, XVII, p. 1, and Wylde, pp. 304–6.
503 Treaty between Ethiopia and Britain, 3 June 1884, Hertslet, *Commercial Treaties*, XVII, p. 1; Wylde, pp. 307–9
504 Hewett to Granville, no. 2, 9 June 1884, FO 1/31
505 R. A. Caulk, 'The Origins and Development of the Foreign Policy of Menelik II, 1867–96', Ph.D. London, 1966 (henceforth 'Menelik II'), pp. 23–4; Darkwah, pp. 327 ff.

reasons for this. The import tax on slaves provided a significant part of Menelik's revenue. Furthermore they were the most profitable goods exported and he believed that if he stopped the traffic traders from the coast would come less frequently to Shoa. He depended upon these merchants to bring him salt[506] and the European goods, over which he exercised a monopoly, as well as to export ivory, gold-dust, civet and musk, also royal monopolies.[507]

The French, Italian and British settlements on the coast faced the same difficulty. The prosperity of each small, poor colony depended upon its trade with the interior. By countenancing the slave traffic France or Italy could attract caravans to their territories. By suppressing it they might simply drive them away to the benefit of less scrupulous neighbours and, at the same time, alienate the people under their rule. The British at Zeila thus had a direct commercial interest in seeing that merchants were not able to find an outlet for their slaves through the French or Italian ports.

Ominously, the whole prosperity of Tajura, where the French were establishing themselves, was based on the slave traffic[508] and Beilul in the Italian sphere also flourished on it.[509] Dhow owners could now acquire French or Italian flags and as matters stood there was every inducement for them to do so since these colours protected them from molestation by British cruisers and profits on the slave trade were inordinately high. A naval officer, who visited Tajura in 1888, found that girls there cost $60–70, and boys $50, while across the Red Sea at Hodeida girls fetched $120–$130 and boys $70–$80. The cost of transport across the sea was only $5 a head.[510]

Even if France and Italy actively patrolled their coasts the odds were on the side of the slaver, for it was easy enough once a caravan had reached the

---

506 Salt was a currency as well as a necessity of life. For the salt trade see *ibid.*, pp. 314 ff.

507 *Ibid.*, pp. 307 ff. Abu Jifar, ruler of Jimma, told D'Abbadie that he would abolish the traffic but, unless neighbouring states did the same, caravans would cease to visit his dominions, p. 23.

508 Abir, pp. 61–5; report by Bougainville, 20 July 1889, FMM/BB4 1229

509 Soleillet, pp. 311–13

510 Gissing to Fremantle, 6 Sept. 1888, enc. in Ad. to FO, 31 Oct. 1888, FOCP 5896. These figures refer to Maria Theresa dollars. They may be compared with prices in Ethiopia. D'Abbadie, p. 14, writing in 1877, cites a case of a child originally kidnapped and sold on the frontiers of his own country for 19 francs (c. $4), resold at Gondar for 41 francs and probably worth 500–600 francs ($100–$120) at the coast. Darkwah, pp. 324 ff. states that in the 1870s and 1880s slaves sold in Kaffa for $2–$4, in Jimma Abu Jifar for $5–$15, in Shoa for $8–$30. Prices naturally fluctuated in accordance with the laws of supply and demand. On the Arabian coast in 1882 they ranged from $40–$150 and in 1884 from $70–$100, memo by Moncrieff, 19 Feb. 1882, enc. in Moncrieff to FO, no. 2, 20 Feb. 1883, FOCP 4914; Crowe to Molyneux, 9 Nov. 1884, cited in Renault, II, p. 53.

littoral to hide its young slaves among the sympathetic population[511] until the cruiser was out of sight and then to embark from any one of the many small ports or landing places and make a quick run for the Arabian shore. The crossing took only a few hours and in Turkish Arabia a welcome was always forthcoming. The outlook for the suppression of the Red Sea and Gulf of Aden slave trade was therefore hardly encouraging in 1884.

Britain's anti-slave trade policy and the scramble for Africa

It will have been observed that, generally speaking, the treaties made with African and Middle Eastern rulers fall into two categories—those aimed at cutting off the supply of victims for export and those aimed at closing the market. The countries which imported slaves were to be called in the Brussels Act of 1890 *pays de destination*.[512]

By the time of the Berlin Conference it was clear that these treaties had only partially succeeded. The great days of the export traffic to the Middle East and North Africa were over, but only the closure of the markets in the *pays de destination* could finally kill it. The treaties, backed as they were by inadequate naval power and consular vigilance, could not prevent the smuggling traffic which still brought several thousand or more Africans into these countries each year. Now that most captives who crossed the seas were transported in small craft and usually reached their destination in a few hours or were disguised as legitimate travellers, the navy's efforts had reached a point of diminishing return, and the most conscientious consul could do little without the loyal co-operation of the territorial authorities.

Here lay the crux of an important question. There were limits to the co-operation which an African or Middle Eastern ruler could give. The problem has to be seen in the wider context of their relations with European powers. Many of the so-called *pays de destination* were suffering from the effects of increasing European pressure, economic and political. Some had lost their independence, but in those which were still free this pressure was having a disintegrating effect on many of their institutions. The attack on the slave trade struck at the very roots of their way of life, heralding the end of slavery and inevitable changes in the labour systems and social organisation.

Co-operation against the traffic implied acceptance of the British concept that slavery was wrong. Most Africans and Middle Eastern peoples were still far from believing this. Since there had been no change of heart on the part of the population or of the religious leaders, the rulers of the *pays de destination* were placed in a peculiarly difficult position. Co-operation against

511 *Note Communicated to the League of Nations by the French Government* in 1923, section on the Somali coast, A.18.1923, VI.
512 Some countries, of course, both imported and exported slaves, i.e. Ethiopia, Zanzibar, Egypt and Cyrenaica.

the slave traffic would cost them popularity and the respect of their subjects. Those who tried did so mainly because they wanted British support or feared her attack. The pressure or inducement had to be very considerable. Some sought a way out of the dilemma by yielding only to an overwhelming show of force,[513] others asked for overt signs of pressure[514] or tangible support.[515] Only rulers of considerable personal prestige, such as Barghash in Zanzibar or Ismail in Egypt, could really risk putting the treaties into operation, and neither of them ended the smuggling traffic into their territories. They had not the administrative control to do so even if they had the desire.

Kirk's new arrangements for East Africa planned in 1882–3 were an acknowledgement that the limits of efficacy had been reached under the old system. They heralded a new era of greater British involvement on the mainland. British consuls watching for slave traders were also to supervise the Sultan's officials and bolster his power. A significant step had thus been taken towards domination of the sultanate. The moment had arrived when British interests demanded a more active policy. This had been achieved by juggling with the anti-slavery budget and was justified as an anti-slavery measure to the ever watchful Treasury and to Parliament. But such simple arrangements were no longer adequate in the new situation created by the scramble for Africa.

No longer could Britain pursue her traditional policy of suppression and defend her strategic and commercial interests by a combination of naval force and consular persuasion. She now had to stake out claims in Africa itself to prevent regions in which she had hitherto reigned supreme from falling to rival powers. Her anti-slave trade policy had always complicated her relations with African peoples but in the days when her supremacy was virtually unchallenged, except in limited regions, by France and to a lesser extent Portugal, it had posed no insuperable problems and had sometimes worked to her advantage. Now, however, it threatened to pose some real difficulties for her statesmen for it might not merely provoke a reaction from Africans determined to maintain their way of life and in some cases their livelihood but might actually drive them to seek the support of her colonial rivals and perhaps even to ask for their protection. The suppression of the slave trade might thus well become a pawn in the game of power politics in Africa.

513 Like Barghash in 1873
514 Like Ismail in 1872
515 Like the Sultan of Johanna in 1881

The Attack in Africa: Commerce, Christianity and 'Civilisation' versus the Slave Trade

African slavery

From the first Britain distinguished between the suppression of the export slave trade and the suppression of domestic slavery and the traffic which fed it. By domestic slavery, she meant the slavery practised by Africans.[1] Naval officers negotiating early treaties with West African rulers were ordered to:

> very clearly point out to them the distinction between the export of slaves which Great Britain is determined to put an end to and the system of Domestic Slavery with which she claims no right to interfere.[2]

Later treaties attempted to ban all slave dealing but they could not be enforced away from the coast or navigable rivers. It was hoped, however, that the slave trade of the interior and slavery itself would slowly succumb to the advance of Christianity, commerce and 'civilisation', the so-called three 'c's. Faith in this panacea was still widespread in the early 1880s. Readers of *The Times* were assured, for instance, that as merchants and missionaries taught Africans to produce goods for an export market, they would cease to sell their own people and put 'native muscles' to work at home.[3] As the foreign market for slaves shrank and the demand for other African products grew, so 'native muscles' were indeed more and more employed at home but they were largely recruited by means of the slave trade and forced to work by systems of slavery. However, the growth in African exports was only one of the factors which sustained the internal market for slaves and led to large scale slaving in the late nineteenth century.

African slavery took a number of forms and any discussion of the subject is bedevilled by the western terms 'slavery' and 'freedom', which while capable of different definitions,[4] usually convey to the European mind concepts arising out of the New World model of plantation slavery in which

---

1 Sometimes African slavery is called 'household' slavery. Neither the term domestic slavery nor household slavery is satisfactory.
2 *Instructions*, 1844 and 1866 editions
3 *The Times*, 21 Jan. 1882
4 The question of whether or not a definition of universal validity can be found will be discussed later.

the slave was an instrument of production, was not integrated into society and remained together with his descendants a chattel, who could be sold at will and had little legal protection.[5] The most stressed feature of this type of slavery was that the slave was the private property of another individual who thus 'owned' him. He could be bought, sold, and compelled to work for no reward—all against his will. A free man was not so 'owned'. Ideally he should be able to work if, when and how he pleases, go where he wishes, dispose of his earnings and possessions as he thinks fit, marry whom he wants, control his minor children and choose his own life style. In practice economic factors, social constraints and public (government) requirements may severely limit his actual liberty but if no one has acquired rights of ownership over him then he is not a slave.[6]

Nineteenth-century African concepts of freedom and slavery stressed different characteristics. Most Africans belonged to a lineage, clan or other kinship group[7] to which they owed clearly understood obligations and in which they had defined rights. This group protected them both spiritually and materially, and, was jointly responsible for their misdeeds. It often controlled property and rights to land. All full members of the community belonged to such a group and such rights as it had over them, which might

5 Western concepts are also based on slavery as practised in the ancient Mediterranean world and in medieval Europe, but the plantation model, the most publicised of the New World slave systems, is the one with which the European public is most familiar.
6 Some constraints may be held by some people to approximate to slavery—hence the Marxist concept of the 'wage slave'. Conscription, forced labour and imprisonment may reduce the individual to a state of virtual slavery but these are disabilities imposed by governments usually for limited periods and supposedly in the public interest and not for private purposes. Serfdom is distinct from slavery in that the serf is tied to the land and his relationship with his landlord imposes a system of mutual rights and obligations arising out of land use and tenure.
7 Most people still belong to such a group as well as to their nuclear family. For the purposes of this discussion a lineage will be taken to mean a group with some corporate functions in which each member can trace his descent through either the male line (patrilineal) or the female line (matrilineal) from a common ancestor. A lineage if it is large may be divided into branches or segments. A clan will be used to describe a usually larger group which may consist of a number of lineages who recognise common descent through either the male or female line but cannot trace it. For a discussion of this subject see A. R. Radcliffe-Brown, 'Introduction', pp. 1–86, in A. R. Radcliffe-Brown and Daryll Forde (eds.), *African Systems of Kinship and Marriage*, London 1950, pp. 39–43. The sources, however, often use these terms without clear definition, and Africans may use the same term to describe a kin group which operates on several different levels. For instance, the Iramba in Tanzania are grouped at the lowest level in exogamous lineages tracing descent from a common ancestor, whose members acknowledge joint responsibility for payment of fines, debts, bridewealth etc. These are part of a larger group which claims common descent and accepts corporate responsibility but is not exogamous. This in turn is part of a still larger and more dispersed group, claiming common descent but unable to trace it, which is not exogamous and does not acknowledge corporate responsibility. All are called by a word which has been translated as 'clan'. (I am indebted to Dr. Patrick Pender-Cudlip for this information.)

be extensive by western standards, arose out of their kinship relations. If a woman left the group to marry then payment (bridewealth) was necessary to compensate it for the loss of her services and, in the case of a patrilineal society, of her progeny. In the case of a matrilineal society her children belonged to her lineage and came under the jurisdiction of her eldest brother or maternal uncle.[8] A man's status depended largely on his position within this kin group, older males having most authority.[9] Prestige, within the society as a whole, increased with maturity and also with wealth and power, which grew in pre-colonial times with the number of wives, children and other dependents a man could command.

To a member of such a close-knit group the European concept of the 'free' or autonomous individual was meaningless, or when it was understood, might be deemed undesirable. The British missionary, W. P. Johnson, working among freed slaves in East Africa, found that in Yao the nearest equivalent to the word 'free' was 'of the family'.[10] Liberated captives generally thought the only real freedom lay in being returned to their own people. The Ila in Zambia described slaves as people 'who didn't know where their ancestors came from' and were not true kinsmen.[11] Among the Fulbe of far-away Fouta Toro in the Senegal Valley a slave was reminded of his status by a pun—a play on the word *Majjudo* which has the dual meaning of one who has lost his way and one who is ignorant of the traditions of society and has no legitimate social position.[12] James Vaughan, describing 'slavery' among the Marghi of Cameroon, stresses the fact that the slave is a resident alien integrated into society but only in a marginal way distinct from a true Marghi with his place in his lineage obtained by right of birth and ancestry.[13] A slave was not often distinguished from a free man by a difference in occupation or style of living, although these might vary, or even always by the fact that he was saleable, for free men might also sometimes be sold while some slaves never were. The difference most stressed was his different standing in a kinship group.[14] This is not to say that the slave was not kinless in America—he was. Nor is it suggested that concepts of private ownership of slaves did not exist in Africa—they did—but these were not

8 Descent systems are a complex subject. Some peoples have both patrilineal and matrilineal descent systems, but for the purposes of this discussion the question is reduced to its simplest terms.

9 In some cases there are rulers, in others authority is vested in groups of elders. Where age grade systems operate the oldest grade may yield power to the next senior grade and retire into an honourable old age.

10 W. P. Johnson, *My African Reminiscences 1875–95*, London 1924, p. 35. See also Duff MacDonald, *Africana*, 2 vols. London 1969 (first published 1882), I, p. 166.

11 A. Tuden 'Slavery and Stratification among the Ila of Central Africa' in A. Tuden and L. Plotnikov, *Social Stratification in Africa*, London and New York 1970, pp. 47–58 (henceforth 'Slavery and Stratification'), p. 51.

12 David Hanson, 'The Maccube of Futa Toro', M.A. Wisconsin 1971, p. 13.

13 James H. Vaughan, 'Marghi Mafakur', chapter in a forthcoming work on African slavery by Suzanne Miers and Igor Kopytoff (eds.).

14 This is not to say that all kinless people in Africa were slaves, however.

the predominant characteristics which distinguished the slave from the free.

Added to the difficulties of terminology, the historian dealing with African slavery is hampered by the inadequacy of the sources. Nineteenth-century European observers had the advantage of seeing slavery while it was still in full operation and slaves were being actively recruited[15] but they were usually untrained in the social sciences, often failed to understand the workings of African societies and were normally only incidentally concerned with the question. Their judgements were subjective[16] and coloured by the fact that they usually came from highly stratified societies with a great disparity in standards of living between rich and poor and had in mind the western model of plantation slavery. They often made vague generalities about treatment without establishing a clear frame of reference and they rarely analysed the real differences between the free man and the slave in the eyes of the Africans concerned. More recent investigators have been more scientific but are dealing with an institution which is usually either dead, moribund or much changed. They have to rely on oral evidence in which theory may predominate over practice and which may be limited by the reticence of informants unwilling to discuss a subject which has fallen into disrepute or afraid of embarrassing neighbours of slave descent. Moreover, the body of information is scattered and incomplete. It is a veritable hodge podge of observations made at different times by people with differing objectives and viewpoints, and evidence of historical change through time in response to internal and external pressures, which would be most revealing, is often scanty.

Nevertheless the sources are sufficient to show the many issues involved in any study of African slavery, which to be understood must be seen in the context of the power and kinship structures, the religious beliefs, ritual customs, judicial practices, systems of land tenure and usage, property rights, and inheritance laws as well as the economy of each individual society. With such fragmentary information only the merest sketch can be attempted here, based on a number of examples selected because each adds a new dimension to the subject. It is hoped that collectively they will serve as an introduction to the important, infinitely varied and little known institutions which have often been misnamed slavery.

Slavery in West Africa

In the largely Muslim states of the western and central Sudan slavery was widespread. Slaves were a by-product of the many wars which racked the

15 As the colonial occupation of African proceeded so the chances of seeing the institution in full operation decreased. The mere presence of a European administrator, believed to be sympathetic to the slave, might influence the whole situation even though little action was taken against slavery.

16 See above, pp. 66–7, 99.

area in the nineteenth century as well as being victims of raids[17] and small-scale kidnappings. Often captives were merely held as hostages until their kinsmen ransomed them with livestock and other goods but many thousands found themselves in lifelong bondage.

Since every Muslim had a duty to convert unbelievers, it was considered right and proper to enslave them, but the Faithful were also reduced to slavery, sometimes by their own rulers on the pretext that they were guilty of apostasy[18] or as the result of warfare between Islamic states or raids by one Muslim official into the territories of another.[19] Life was thus insecure for all alike over much of the Sudanic belt.[20] The majority of the captives were women and children. Men were more likely to die in the fighting and being more refractory were more likely to be killed or ransomed rather than kept. Slaves were also obtained by purchase and accepted as gifts or in payment of debts or bridewealth. People who committed serious crimes such as murder and persistent theft might also be enslaved sometimes with their kinsmen.[21] A number of slaves were traded northwards across the Sahara desert and others went south or west, some of them even reaching the New World, but the great majority were retained for local use.

Slavery was practised in accordance with Muslim law and local custom. Newly acquired slaves, whether bought or captured, were 'trade' slaves.[22]

17 The extent to which raids were launched for the purpose of capturing slaves is a matter of debate. For a brief discussion with further references see M. A. Klein, 'Slavery, the Slave Trade and Legitimate Commerce in Late Nineteenth Century Africa', *Études d'Histoire Africaine*, ii, 1971, pp. 5–28 (henceforth 'Legitimate Commerce'), pp. 7–8; see also M. Mason, 'Population density and "Slave raiding"—the case of the middle belt of Nigeria', *JAH*, x, 4, 1969, pp. 551–64.
18 Political insubordination and apostacy being classed as one, R. Cohen, 'Slavery among the Kanuri', *Trans-Actions*, Jan./Feb. 1967, pp. 48–50, p. 48.
19 E. A. Ayandele, 'Observations on Some Social and Economic Aspects of Slavery in Precolonial Northern Nigeria', *Nigerian Journal of Economic and Social Studies*, Ibadan, ix, 3, 1967, pp. 329–38 (henceforth 'Slavery in Northern Nigeria'), p. 335. Yeld states that in Northern Nigeria Muslim slaves could not be sold in the market or recaptured if they escaped, and they might be ransomed, but this may represent theory more than practice, E. R. Yeld, 'Islam and Social Stratification in Northern Nigeria', *British Journal of Sociology*, xi, pp. 112–128, p. 116.
20 For the insecurity of life in some areas see Mary Smith, *Baba of Karo*, London 1954, chs. 1, 2, 4; J. F. Schön, *Magana Hausa: the Life and Times of Dorugu*, London 1885.
21 Cohen, p. 49. The degree to which this was practised and the actual crimes punished in this way needs more investigation since the sources are particularly unsatisfactory. The spread of Islam with its prescribed penalties for certain offences probably reduced the incidence of enslavement as a punishment, see Fisher and Fisher, pp. 71–6.
22 They were called by the French *esclaves* or *captifs 'de traite'*. The information for this and the following section on slavery in the Sudan is taken from a variety of sources notably the reports of administrators in the French Sudan made around 1894 and collected in AOF K 14; M. G. Smith, 'Slavery and Emancipation in Two Societies', *Social and Economic Studies*, iii, 1954, pp. 239–90 (henceforth 'Slavery'); Mary Smith; Hanson; Cohen; Martin Klein, 'Slavery among the Wolof and Serer in

These were the real outsiders with the fewest rights and the least protection and were probably the hardest worked. They could be sold, pledged, bequeathed or given away. Their masters had complete control over their destinies and could punish them at will. Their treatment was probably worst while they were in the hands of dealers or captors and improved once they became the property of an owner who intended to keep them. The longer they remained with him the more likely they were to be at least partially integrated into society, to be given wives, and land to farm, and be allowed to own property. If a trade slave and his wife produced a child who belonged to his master he was even more likely to have these privileges[23] and less liable to be sold. If he accepted Islam[24] he became the ward of his owner, whose duty it was to see that he was instructed in the faith and suitably married. His chances of manumission also increased.

The children of trade slaves had quite a different status. Born in their master's household, they were considered part of his family and grew up as members of his social group, speaking his language, conversant with local traditions and initiated from the start into Islam. They were only sold in cases of extreme refractoriness[25] or in times of famine and then only as a last resort and perhaps to neighbouring peoples with the proviso that they might be bought back again when times improved.[26] Masters' powers of punishment were also limited. In Hausaland, for instance, they could not be sold or mutilated except by order of a court.[27] They were freer than their parents since escape was unlikely and owners were expected not only to arrange marriages for them but to set them up in their own living quarters. In some areas no more work was demanded of them than of 'free' unmarried men,[28] and usually they had, at least in theory, considerable free time. Some even lived and worked on their own, merely giving their master part of their

Senegambia', forthcoming in Miers and Kopytoff (henceforth 'Slavery in Sene-Gambia'); J. C. Froelich, 'Le commandement et l'organisation sociale chez les Foulbé de l'Adamawa', ch. 3, *Études Camerounaises*, nos. 45–6, Sept./Dec. 1954, and other sources as cited.

23 If the mother and father were slaves of the same master the child was the slave of that master but if the mother belonged to another owner then the child belonged to him too. By Islamic law a child could not be separated from his parents until he reached a certain age.

24 Ayandele ('Slavery in Northern Nigeria', p. 334) states that there is no record that slaves were urged to become Muslim, and Klein ('Slavery in Senegambia') writes that in Senegambia the *Tyeddo*, highly privileged warrior slaves, were not Muslim. However, the ordinary slave who accepted Islam could probably count on better treatment and in some areas he was not sold after a certain number of years' service.

25 Clapperton noted cases of this in Sokoto, see Clapperton, p. 214. He also recorded (p. 210) that slaves who did not work were sent to prison where treatment was such that they dreaded it but it was the same as that suffered by thieves.

26 This is reported for Fouta Toro, see Hanson, p. 7. The *commandant de cercle* of Bafoulabé thought the idea of selling such a slave unthinkable, report to Governor of Sudan, 15 May 1894, AOF K 14.

27 M. G. Smith, 'Slavery', p. 250   28 Klein, 'Slavery in Senegambia'

produce, earnings or working time, and had their own cattle and other possessions, including concubines and slaves. When they died, it is true, all of these went to their owner but in some areas he usually gave a proportion back to the widows and children.[29] Slaves might be richer than their masters. They might also have a say at family councils or, if an owner died leaving minors as heirs, they might take temporary charge of the household.[30] These second-generation slaves are usually referred to in the literature as 'domestic' slaves[31] and this term will be used to describe them henceforth. Some trade slaves also became sufficiently integrated into their master's society to be classed as domestic slaves.

Manumission was practised in accordance with Islamic law, but modified by local custom. Sources show that it was rare in some areas of the Sudanic belt.[32] A concubine's children by her master were usually free and she was free on his death.[33] This is the only form of manumission noted by Martin Klein for the Wolof and Serer regions of Senegambia but here, as among the Tuareg, slaves could change masters by committing some offence which would cause the injured party to demand the slave in compensation. They could, for instance, nick the ear of the desired master or his horse, or damage posts holding amulets in his courtyard.[34] In the Fouta Toro, where this was also practised, a slave could in addition gain his liberty by distinguishing himself in warfare as well as by the usual methods sanctioned in Islamic law, such as paying his master an agreed amount, or he could be freed by a Muslim court if he was ill-treated.[35]

Slaves had many uses in the western and central Sudan. The majority were agricultural workers since this was the main occupation and source of wealth. In some societies there was a great demand for extra hands to produce food, tend livestock, build houses and engage in handicrafts. Slaves increased a family's output and gave their owners time for other occupations. The Fulbe of Adamawa, for instance, used them to produce crops so that they themselves could remain purely transhumant pastoralists.[36] The Muslim peanut farmers of Senegambia invested their profits in guns and horses, which they used to capture slaves to work their fields while they

29 This was the custom in Fouta Toro, see Hanson, p. 14
30 See *inter alia* reports from Kita 6 March 1894, Medine 23 April 1894, Bafoulabé 15 May 1894, Kayes 8 July 1894 to the Governor of the Sudan, AOF K 14, and report from the Serer Provinces to the administrator at Thiès 27 April 1902, AOF K 27.   31 The French *captifs de case*
32 It was rare for instance in Bornu (Cohen, p. 50) and Fouta Toro (Hanson, p. 22).
33 This was in accordance with Muslim Maliki law.
34 Klein, 'Slavery in Senegambia'. For the Tuareg custom see above, pp. 74–5.
35 Hanson, p. 21—a slave could only engage in warfare with his master's consent except in the case of a *jihad* or holy war. Manumission for prowess in war was also practised among the Mende in modern Sierra Leone, John Grace, 'Slavery among the Mende of Sierra Leone during the Twentieth Century from 1900 until Abolition in 1927', forthcoming in Miers and Kopytoff.
36 Froelich, pp. 18–19

turned to war, politics and plunder.[37] Owners ranged from peasants or poor pastoralists with one or two slaves to rulers, high officials and rich men with several thousand, perhaps settled in slave villages in charge of a head slave, while the owner lived in town.[38] Villages belonging to rulers would produce food for the court. Systems of agriculture and land tenure varied but slave farmers usually divided their time between working on their own land and that of their masters and they also produced handicrafts.[39] Slaves were also used as concubines, domestic servants, porters, trading agents and artisans.[40]

Most important, however, were the slave warriors and officials. Rulers, office holders and members of the nobility kept large numbers of armed retainers to inspire respect from superiors as well as subordinates. Sometimes the majority of these and even their commanders were slaves. They were often formed into special detachments armed with firearms.[41] They might farm in peace-time but be ready to answer a call to arms when required. Royal slaves also served the rulers as officials, tax collectors, policemen, prison warders, messengers and even fief-holders in charge of whole regions. These soldiers and officials were sometimes a vital factor in the growth of royal power. In parts of the Fulani empire, for instance, they rendered the emirs independent of the aristocracy and protected them from rivals. Being dependent on their owners with no local lineage connections, they were more reliable and loyal than free men. A few wielded considerable power, sometimes isolating a ruler from his subjects, dominating him and influencing the succession.[42] Eunuchs were particularly prized as officials

37 Klein, 'Slavery in Senegambia'
38 Such villages were to be found from Bornu to the Fouta Jalon. Sometimes they were owned by more than one person—heirs perhaps of the original owner. Villages belonging to rulers might produce food for the court. Sometimes they were also regarded as repositories for slaves who could be exported if the occasion arose, as in Fouta Jalon in the eighteenth century, see Walter Rodney, 'African Slavery and Other Forms of Social Oppression on the Upper Guinea Coast', *JAH*, vii, 3, 1966, pp. 431–43, 436, 439–40, or as a source of domestic slaves, see Froelich, p. 21. Froelich discusses the various types of 'slave' villages in Adamawa, some of which were settlements of Kaka and Baya people who had been moved *en bloc* with their own rulers and belongings and resettled in fertile lands around Ngaoundéré. They paid taxes and supplied domestic slaves when required. Others were settlements of actual captives whose whole harvest went to the rulers, see pp. 21–3.
39 For example a French administrator in Fouta Toro in 1904 thought slaves worked for their masters for only one-third of their time, Hanson, p. 12; on the other hand Froelich says that some of the slaves of the Fulbe of Adamawa gave all their time to their master who in return clothed, fed and housed them, paid their taxes and provided wives, Froelich, p. 19. Women did farm work as well as men, and children scared away birds and herded animals.
40 In some areas smiths and certain other artisans belonged to hereditary castes but slaves, and freemen, could engage in other crafts.
41 For examples of this see Joseph P. Smaldone, 'Firearms in the Central Sudan: a Revaluation', *JAH*, xiii, 4, 1972, pp. 591–607.
42 For examples of the importance of slave officials and soldiers see Froelich, p. 22;

since they were unable to found a rival dynasty. They held office for instance in Bornu, Bagirmi and parts of the Sokoto empire.

Slaves played an important part in the political and economic development of parts of the western and central Sudan. In the economy they were a valuable export commodity and sometimes the only one.[43] For the trans-Saharan trade they had the advantage of having a high intrinsic value and being not too perishable, while they transported themselves. Elsewhere, they increased the production of goods which could be exported. In the Fulani empire, for example, they helped to produce surplus grain, hides and cotton, and to manufacture leather goods and textiles. But more significant than their contribution to the export trade was their role in the domestic economy. They supplied the local market with food crops and handicrafts. So great was the demand for slaves that in some areas they were used virtually as a currency, side by side with other forms of money, such as the Maria Theresa dollar, cowrie shells, cotton bands or copper weights. They served as barter goods and were widely used for paying off retainers as well as for taxes, tribute and dowry. A pilgrim on his way to Mecca might even take some with him and sell them off on the way to pay his expenses.

Most important, slaves were a convenient form of capital investment. In the conditions of the Sudan, where land was plentiful, population density low, where most households were almost self-supporting, and the role of credit was limited,[44] they were particularly useful since they were 'self-reproducing, self-supporting, and provided regular annual returns on investment'.[45] They could defend themselves against marauders, were readily saleable and could be bequeathed to one's heirs. Other possible forms of capital accumulation were either perishable and served a limited market like grain, or required food and protection like cattle, or brought in no return like cowries and cottons. Their versatility gave slaves considerable economic significance even when they were not put to immediate economic use.[46]

Slavery, however, served more than an economic function. In fact, the custom which usually prevented the sale of domestic slaves limited its

Klein, 'Slavery in Senegambia'; Yeld, pp. 49, 120–1; M. G. Smith, 'Historical and Cultural Conditions of Political Corruption Among the Hausa', *Comparative Studies in Society*, vi, 1963–4, pp. 164–94; M. G. Smith, *Government in Zazzau, 1800–1950*, London 1960 (henceforth *Zazzau*); S. F. Nadel, *A Black Byzantium*, London 1960, pp. 103–8.

43 Nachtigal, for instance, found they were the only significant export from Bagirmi. Nachtigal, II, pp. 668 and 688, cited Fisher and Fisher, p. 34.

44 Muslim law forbade the charging of interest on debts.

45 See M. G. Smith, 'Slavery', p. 266.

46 Nachtigal commented on the number of 'luxury servants' in Bornu, who did virtually nothing, and he marvelled at the ruler of Bagirmi and his followers who continued to demand tribute in slaves from their vassals at a time when they had not enough food for themselves and the market was glutted. Nachtigal, II, p. 652, cited Fisher and Fisher, p. 126.

economic value.[47] It was also a device by which extra people might be acquired and legally integrated into the society. Loyal supporters were often wanted for social and political, as well as economic, purposes. The border-lines are vague for the slave retainer might also farm, and a master's power and his wealth would therefore grow together. The basic requirement for every ambitious man was to increase his following and for each household was to enlarge its numbers.[48] The slave trade brought the individual to where he was required, and slavery integrated him into society. The integration began the day the trade slave found a permanent owner and the domestic slave was an established member of the social group, usually having a definite community of interest with the family to which he belonged. A slave's life style and occupation differed little from that of free men and depended simply on the type of master he served. Thus the slave of the poor nomad like his owner had a lower standard of living than the slave warrior who was of necessity highly privileged and had the opportunity to acquire captives of his own. However, the slave remained a dependent, socially not on a par with his master, rarely able to marry a free woman[49] and normally not eligible to inherit either possessions or position since he was not a full member of the lineage. On the other hand he was a recognised and protected member of the community with clear rights and obligations and some of the highest offices of state were open to him.

In non-Muslim West Africa slavery took many forms, only a few of which can be mentioned here. Slaves were widely used in the powerful states of Dahomey and Asante for instance. The former was a highly stratified society with a leisured class of princes, nobles and priests under a king, who wielded a degree of power unusual in Africa and exercised control through appointed officials chosen mainly from commoners.[50] He was thus not dependent upon hereditary chiefs or princely rivals or, unlike some Sudanic rulers, on slaves. In fact only slaves who had been freed could hold office.[51] Each king on his accession was enjoined to make the country greater and many wars were fought to enlarge the frontiers, secure trade routes and increase the population. Many slaves were victims of these conflicts and of special dawn raids launched for the capture of prisoners,[52] while others were bought and imported into Dahomey. Theoretically all

47 See M. G. Smith, 'Slavery'.
48 M. G. Smith, commenting on the assimilative character of Muslim slavery, points out that in the Fulani empire use of slaves as concubines enabled the ruling Fulani to increase more rapidly than the rest of the population, and this, together with their acquisition of numbers of slaves, made it more difficult for them to be overthrown. *Zazzau*, p. 83.
49 Free men, however, could usually marry slave women but this in itself made the women free by Muslim law.
50 See J. Lombard, 'The Kingdom of Dahomey' in D. Forde and P. M. Kaberry (eds.), *West African Kingdoms in the Nineteenth Century*, Oxford 1967, pp. 70–92.
51 Personal communication from Dr Boniface Obichere.
52 *Ibid.*

those taken in war were bought from their captors by the king.[53] Some were then given to nobles or favoured soldiers and some were sold to the Europeans, a traffic which continued into the 1890s when Dahomey supplied 'contract' labourers, captured for the purpose, to the Portuguese, Belgians and Germans in exchange for arms.[54] Most, however, were kept to work on the royal farms.

These estates produced food for the royal household and for sale in the market. Colonies of captives also processed palm products for export. This had been called plantation slavery and compared with the American model, since the slaves were wanted as instruments of production and forced to labour for long hours. This may have been true of the estates of the nobles, but recent research suggests that many of the royal farms were manned by whole villages of conquered peoples forcibly removed *en masse* to Dahomey who were allowed to remain together and even to worship their ancestral Gods, but were forced to pay tribute to the ruler, as were free Dahomeans.[55] They were not normally sold but they could not leave.[56]

The king kept several thousand women in the palace, the nerve centre of the kingdom. Some were his free wives, female officials or members of his bodyguard, but many were slave servants. A few Yoruba male captives, who had been castrated to give them greater strength,[57] were the only men in the palace and were used as guards and policemen.

Slaves had both social and political mobility. They served in the army in the nineteenth century and those who distinguished themselves in war or in other fields, such as hunting or weaving, were sometimes freed by royal edict.[58] Others were manumitted after years of good service. Slave women often became concubines of the ruler and their sons might sit on the throne. Both sexes could intermarry with the free and their children were free. The slaves of poor men lived much the same lives as their masters.

There hung a great shadow, however, over prisoners captured by Dahomey. They might be sacrificed on the death of the king or his nobles to accompany them to the next world[59] or as offerings to royal ancestors on state occasions. Victims were set aside and kept for this purpose. On important occasions, such as the annual Abomey festival, or 'customs', large

53 M. J. Herskovits, *Dahomey, An Ancient West African Kingdom*, 2 vols. New York 1938, I, p. 99; Coquery-Vidrovitch, pp. 110–12, suggests that this was symbolic and she questions the extent to which the king controlled even the traffic with Europeans.
54 Obichere, pp. 90–3; Annexe enclosed in Ouvary to Chimay, 5 March 1890, AEB/CAE/3 no. 112. See also above p. 29, below pp. 257–8.
55 W. J. Argyle, *The Fon of Dahomey*, Oxford 1966, pp. 142–5
56 Displaced agricultural colonies of this type seem also to have existed elsewhere—Adamawa, for instance. See Froelich, p. 21.
57 Personal communication from Dr Obichere.
58 The court was famous for its high standard of arts and crafts and certain of the women of the palace hunted to provide game for the royal table, see Lombard, pp. 73, 84.
59 *Ibid.*, pp. 85–6

numbers were dispatched, a practice which gave Dahomey an evil and blood-thirsty reputation in Europe.[60] Human sacrifice was widespread in Africa, and captives were obvious potential victims since they had no kinsmen and could be killed without causing tension in the society. Otherwise a slave's life was protected. No master could kill one without royal permission and on the death of an important man the king supplied the victims.

The second generation of slaves, the children of two slaves, were in a different category from their parents. Born in Dahomey, they were called *Dahomenou*, 'people of Dahomey', and could not be sold.[61] Those who belonged to commoners tended to be assimilated into their master's family intermarrying with them, while those whose parents worked on plantations usually stayed on these estates as domestic slaves, tending their own land, but owing labour or produce to their masters. Some were craftsmen who lived and worked on their own but paid dues to their owners. Often no more was required of a domestic slave than of the son of a household.[62]

Slaves were thus quickly assimilated and seem to have been wanted to swell the labour and fighting forces of the kingdom, depleted by constant warfare, and also to furnish an export commodity to sell to the Europeans.

Slavery as practised in Asante, a powerful Akan state in the hinterland of modern Ghana, had many similar features. Here the king, or *Asantehene*, was building up his power in the nineteenth century,[63] and, like the ruler of Dahomey, he relied on free-born officials, although some freed slaves held office. The army was composed of free men, including Hausa mercenaries. Interestingly even the court eunuchs were free boys offered to the Asantehene by their kinsmen in return for high reward. Nevertheless slaves were widely used.[64] Large numbers were presented to the ruler as tribute, many were taken in war and some were bought by private citizens in markets beyond the borders and imported. Persistent criminals who brought disgrace on their kinsmen and involved them in claims for compensation were also sold into slavery by their *abusua* or lineage.[65]

60 Obichere, p. 54.   61 Argyle, p. 144
62 In early colonial times slave weavers of upper Dahomey gave their masters 10/17ths of their earnings. Around Abomey half the produce of palm trees went to the cultivator whether he was the son of the owner or his slave, *Report by the French Government to the League of Nations*, 1924, A.25 (1924), VI.
63 Ivor Wilks, 'Ashanti Government', in Forde and Kaberry, pp. 206–38 (henceforth 'Ashanti Government'). Two separate systems existed at this time. The heart of the country was a confederation clustered around Kumasi under hereditary rulers owing allegiance to but not under the complete control of the Asantehene, while in Kumasi itself and the much larger conquered provinces the Asantehene was building up royal power.
64 The following discussion is based on personal communication from Dr Boniface Obichere and on Wilks; R. S. Rattray, *Ashanti Law and Constitution*, Oxford 1929, ch. 5; A. Norman Klein, 'West African Unfree Labour Before and After the Rise of the Atlantic Slave Trade', in Foner and Genovese, pp. 87–95; Meyer Fortes, 'Kinship and Marriage among the Ashanti', in Radcliffe-Brown and Daryll Forde, pp. 252–84.
65 *Abusua* is used for both lineage and clan.

Large numbers of captives together with free immigrants were settled by the Asantehene on land in Kumasi to build up the population of the metropolitan area. These people were rapidly absorbed and within a generation or two were indistinguishable from the free. It was even a capital offence to mention their servile origins.[66] The ruler also employed slaves in the gold mines and gave some to officials to grow food for their households. In addition, chiefs officially detailed by the Asantehene to engage in trade used them as agents.[67] These sometimes became rich and owned slaves of their own, although all their wealth was considered to belong to their masters who inherited it upon their deaths.[68] Slaves could manumit themselves by paying an agreed ransom and, as in Dahomey, their lives were protected. They could not be killed or mutilated without the permission of the central government.

A special category of slave, the *akyere*, however, could be sacrificed to the gods at funeral ceremonies. Persons who had been sentenced to death for crime were in this class and were often kept waiting until an opportunity for sacrificing them arose.[69] Sometimes they lived out their lives without paying the penalty, but their descendants in the female line inherited their unhappy position and thus formed a pool of people awaiting this grim fate.[70] Not surprisingly the akyere fled into the bush whenever a noble died.[71]

The Asante, unlike the Muslim peoples of the Sudan or the population of Dahomey, traced descent matrilineally. In such a society a man's offspring by a free woman belong to their mother's clan and come under the jurisdiction of their maternal uncles and the lineage can only expand at the rate that its daughters produce children. Failure to have offspring will result in extinction. In a patrilineal society on the other hand a lineage can be increased simply by its male members taking more wives whose offspring will swell its numbers. In matrilineal societies slavery provided a means not just of incorporating more people into a lineage but also of sidestepping the normal descent system. For if a man married a slave she was attached to his lineage, and so were her children. For this reason Asante men are said to have bought slave wives and to have preferred the children of these marriages, over whom they had complete authority[72] and who had no competing loyalties, to their free sons and daughters. Socially these children were treated as the equals of their other progeny and their servile origins

66 Wilks, 'Ashanti Government', pp. 229–30

67 Private economic enterprise by subjects of the Asantehene was discouraged in Asante, *ibid.*, p. 230.

68 Personal communication from Dr Boniface Obichere.

69 This was in contrast to Dahomey where criminals were either imprisoned, executed or exported.

70 Descendants in the female line only were involved since this was a matrilineal society.

71 Personal communication from Dr Obichere.

72 In lieu of their maternal uncles.

were not mentioned. However, they could not become lineage heads or have ancestor shrines and the rules of exogamy were not rigidly applied to them, at least for the first few generations. They were thus incorporated into the abusua but on a somewhat different basis from the free.[73] Male slaves were also bought by lineages short of men,[74] and the offspring of those who married free women were full, hence 'free', members of their mother's abusua in accordance with the normal rules of matrilineal descent.

Slavery was also practised by small-scale societies in West Africa like the Igbo of south-eastern Nigeria, who lived in acephalous villages consisting of a number of patrilineages of common descent. All free adult men participated in village decisions and the economy was based on subsistence agriculture. A few rich and able heads of households enlarged their following and hence their prestige and influence by accumulating numbers of wives and slaves. Surplus crops and palm products were traded to the Delta States and elsewhere in the region. Both free men and slaves collected palm nuts, repaired houses and fought when necessary but slaves also helped the women with cultivation.

They were captured in battles between groups of villages, which sometimes hired mercenaries to help them plunder and take prisoners.[75] They were also kidnapped or purchased. The Igbo sold not only persistent criminals but also difficult boys and abnormal children, who were considered a threat to society.[76] These sales had to be agreed to by both the maternal and paternal relations[77] although the Igbo practised patrilineal descent.

The judicial system was also a fertile source of slaves. Not only were persistent criminals sold but disputes were referred to the oracles of certain deities which served as courts of appeal.[78] People came from far and near to have their quarrels settled at famous oracles. Ostensibly the guilty disappeared. In fact they were often sold as slaves. The Aro who controlled one such shrine collected victims in this way. They were able traders[79] who travelled around the country, establishing settlements along the trade routes, perhaps fomenting local wars to get prisoners and taking away the criminals and unwanted children from the villages.

The Nike, the northern agents of the Aro, acquired a number of cap-

73 For a further discussion of this see Meyer Fortes.
74 Personal communications from Dr Obichere.
75 Victor Uchendu, 'The Institutions of Slavery in Southeast Nigerian Societies', unpublished paper read at the Central States Anthropological Meeting, St. Louis, Missouri, 28 April 1966 (henceforth 'Slavery in Southeast Nigerian Societies').
76 Custom varied but some people sold children who cut their upper teeth first, or who walked, talked or menstruated early.
77 Uchendu, 'Slavery in Southeast Nigerian Societies'
78 The settling of disputes through deities was a device for transferring the onus of difficult decisions to the spiritual world, see Victor Uchendu, *The Igbo of Southeast Nigeria*, New York 1965 (henceforth *Igbo*), p. 100.
79 For a brief discussion of the Aro see J. C. Anene, *Southern Nigeria in Transition*, Cambridge 1966, pp. 16–18.

tives.[80] They lived in regions where good and bad land was interspersed, and there was a tendency to sell surplus people in the poor areas and to accumulate slaves in the fertile ones. Nike slavery seems to have been unusually harsh. Slaves were chattels with theoretically no rights to land or goods, although in practice they acquired both.[81] There were no marriages between slave and free, and a man taking a slave concubine was ridiculed. Masters were responsible for the crimes of their slaves, who were permanent minors. If a man killed a free person he had to hang himself, but if a slave killed a free man his master was expected to hang himself. The killing of a slave was considered not murder but damage to property, and the culprit had to give the master another slave. Masters had powers of life and death over their own slaves and manumission did not exist.

As elsewhere, religion played a vital part in everyday life, villages being governed in accordance with law and custom believed to emanate from the spirit world and handed down from generation to generation. The village elders represented the ancestors and were the intermediaries between them and the living. A slave could neither be a village elder nor take part in the cult of the ancestors. He was valuable, however, for the performance of certain ritual functions. For instance, he could act as the diviner interpreting the will of the deity since a free man in this office might become too powerul.[82]

Thus, although slaves might in practice become rich and even have captives of their own, they remained always a caste apart, socially, economically and politically discriminated against. They were also liable to human sacrifice. Most slaves were used for agricultural work and Nike freemen ceased to demean themselves by performing the more arduous tasks. In this area there were also slave villages, planted in dangerous regions, whose duty it was to guard the frontiers for the Nike villages which owned them.

Among the central and southern Igbo there were cult slaves known as *osu*, who were dedicated to the service of the deity by their owners, on the advice of a diviner, or who accepted this bondage themselves to avoid being sold into slavery.[83] They were living sacrifices, hated and feared, residing as outcasts near their shrine, intermarrying among themselves and farming land apart from the village. They could not be ill-treated or forced to work and they might grow rich for they could steal with impunity as no one would risk the wrath of the god by harming them, but they were reviled by all and their children inherited their unenviable status.

Many Igbo were sold to the trading states of the lower Niger, the delta

---

80 For slavery in Nike see W. R. G. Horton, 'The Ohu System of Slavery in a Northern Ibo Village-Group', *Africa*, xxiv, 1954, pp. 311–36.
81 They could be evicted at will and in theory all their goods belonged to their masters.
82 In fact slave diviners were owned corporately by the village perhaps to ensure that no master became over powerful although Horton found no evidence that this was done consciously.
83 Sometimes children foiled their parents' attempt to sell them in this way.

and the coast to the east. Scattered along the shores and hinterland as far as Duala in modern Cameroon were a number of small independent communities primarily organised for trade.[84] Originally they supplied their European customers mainly with slaves but in the course of the nineteenth century they became major exporters of palm products collected from markets in the producing regions of the interior. Each state was different in its ethnic composition and its social and political structure. For example Bonny and New Calabar were monarchies founded by Ijaw groups, the various communities of Old Calabar were Efik and run by a cult society known as *Ekpe*, while Aboh was an Igbo kingdom on the lower Niger. Each state consisted of a number of trading corporations or Houses[85] usually composed of patrilineally related free people,[86] their dependent clients and slaves and ruled by a House Head.

Each House had its traders, farmers, fishermen, servants and canoemen, who manned the giant craft used for trade and war. Fierce competition sometimes erupted into open warfare between Houses and each sought to increase its productivity, wealth, power and security by acquiring slaves, who were incorporated into the group, often as children and who, like the free, engaged in all the activities of the House.[87] They might spend their lives on menial tasks and merely earn their keep, but with initiative and good fortune they could become traders. It was in the interest of the Head of a House to encourage the enterprising to buy captives and canoes and to build their own commercial networks. His wealth and generosity were measured by the number of affluent slaves he possessed. A prosperous slave commanded respect, was unlikely to be ill-treated and might be freed from menial tasks and sent out to work on his own, merely paying tribute to his master. His social mobility varied in each state. He could not usually hold royal office or the top political positions[88] but in some states, such as

84 See Dike; G. I. Jones; E. J. Alagoa, *The Small Brave City State*, Ibadan and Madison 1964; K. O. Ogedengbe, 'Aboh' and 'Clientship and Involuntary Servitude in Nineteenth Century Aboh', forthcoming in Miers and Kopytoff (henceforth 'Servitude'); R. A. Austen, 'Slavery and Duala Society', forthcoming in Miers and Kopytoff (henceforth 'Duala Slavery'); Robin Horton, 'Fishing Village to City State: a Social History of New Calabar' in Mary Douglas and Phyllis M. Kaberry, *Man in Africa*, New York 1971, pp. 38–60; Nair.

85 For convenience these corporations will be called Houses although their organisation varied and the term was not used in all the states.

86 In some states, like New Calabar and Bonny, children belonged to their father's lineage if he had paid a high bridewealth for their mother. Otherwise they belonged to their mother's lineage.

87 Certain states, like Duala and Old Calabar, also had entire villages of slaves working plantations away from town. This type of slavery was different from the House slavery described here.

88 Although there is oral evidence that if a slave was rich enough to pay membership dues for one of the expensive and exclusive societies which wielded political power, he would cease to be considered a slave. See Uchendu, 'Slavery in Southeast Nigerian Societies'.

Bonny and New Calabar, he might become head of his House or even found one. The famous Jaja of Opobo, erstwhile slave in Bonny, actually started his own state and built a commercial empire. Even the leaders of the least favoured slaves—the plantation labourers of Old Calabar, who lived in settlements away from the towns, sometimes wielded influence because of their large followings. One at least became the power behind the throne in Creek Town.[89]

Most slaves, however, were not so fortunate. They were hardworked and, although owners were expected to feed, clothe and house them suitably and find them wives, they had no means of forcing them to do so. Masters in fact had powers of life and death over them and there was no institutionalised manumission. They were often socially inferior. In Aboh, for instance, the women became concubines rather than wives and male domestic slaves could not offer sacrifices to the ancestral spirits.[90] Occasionally the fact that they were not full lineage members worked to their advantage, as in Old Calabar where the children of slaves could inherit their father's wealth whereas the riches of a free man were divided among his lineage.[91] But the slave was the most expendable member of the community, the most likely to be sold, although free people could be too, and the most likely to be sacrificed. In Aboh outsiders are said to have been bought specially for this purpose but in Old Calabar many plantation slaves suffered this horrible fate as Houses vied with each other in the lavishness of their funerals. However, free servants and wives were also killed to accompany the dead.[92] Slaves were also the most acceptable victims of conflicts. Thus, in Duala, brawls between Houses ended when sufficient slaves had been either killed or paid out in compensation to satisfy the honour of the participants.[93]

In short in the city states, a slave was not debarred from wealth or power but he led a more precarious existence than a free man and had a harder path to success, having to rely on ability and good fortune. But with these, even the trade slave, the lowest of the low, could rise to eminence.

Slavery in East and Central Africa

Slavery was equally widespread and varied in East and Central Africa. It was important, for instance, among trading peoples such as the Imbangala, Yao and Tio. To the first two, who were matrilineal, it offered, as in Asante, a means of side-stepping the normal rules of descent, allowing ambitious men to build up their following and lineages to increase their numbers.

89 Nair, p. 43   90 Ogedengbe, 'Servitude'   91 Nair, pp. 41–2
92 Nair, pp. 46–55. Human sacrifices were limited in Old Calabar by the 1880s owing to the formation of a slave association to protect their members and to missionary pressure.
93 Austen, 'Duala Slavery'

The Imbangala of modern Angola had been called upon by their ruler, the King of Kasanje, to supply victims for the Atlantic slave trade.[94] Rather than part with their kinsmen, they bought or captured *abika*,[95] slaves, who could be sent together with criminals to answer the royal summons. Each lineage retained as many as possible to build up its strength against the king, while he and his officials in their turn acquired them to increase their power *vis à vis* the lineages. With the end of the Atlantic trade the kingdom virtually disintegrated but lineages and officials anxious to gain local power continued to import abika until by the late nineteenth century they formed the majority of the population.

Ambitious men manipulated marriages to maximise their dependents. They married abika women to produce children under their own control in contrast to their offspring by free wives who belonged to their mothers' lineages and, were under the jurisdiction of their maternal uncles, with whom the boys went to live when they reached the age of puberty. They married their sisters to abika men to produce progeny who were full members of their matrilineages with the added advantage for their maternal uncles that they had no paternal kinsmen to compete for their loyalty or protect them in time of trouble.[96] The ambitious also married their own female abika to their male ones and their offspring swelled the number of lineage dependents. Once a man had acquired a big enough following, he could found his own village and live in relative independence of his kinsmen. Dependents were wanted not primarily for their labour, indeed the more productive males were often sold, but for the political power and social status that went with a large following. Slaves suffered few disabilities. Both slave and free could be pawned for trade goods and debt. Furthermore slaves were particularly valued by their owners, often their fathers, as loyal supporters, who might serve them as trading agents or officials.

The Yao of eastern Africa also acquired slaves for the same reasons.[97] A leader would establish a village with some kinsmen and they would proceed to exchange whatever goods they could produce, such as buckskin and baskets, for slaves. They would marry the women and give some

94 Joseph C. Miller, 'Slaves, Slavers and Social Change in Nineteenth Century Kasanje' in Frans-Wilhelm Heimer (ed.), *Social Change in Angola*, Munich (forthcoming).

95 Abika implies an alien residing in an Imbangala lineage. For Imbangala slavery see Joseph C. Miller, 'Imbangala Institutions', forthcoming in Miers and Kopytoff.

96 The loyalty of children to their father's kinsmen and the desire of men to control their own children is one of the causes of tension in matrilineal societies, see Mary Douglas, 'Is Matriliny Doomed in Africa?' in Douglas and Kaberry, pp. 123–37.

97 For Yao slavery see Duff MacDonald; E. A. Alpers, 'Trade, State and Society among the Yao in the nineteenth century', *JAH*, x, 3, 1969, pp. 405–20; J. C. Mitchell, *The Yao Village*, Manchester 1956; H. S. Stannus, 'The Wayao of Nyasaland', E. A. Hooton and N. I. Bates (eds.), *Varia Africana* iii, Harvard African Studies, Cambridge, Mass. 1922.

of the males to their sisters or daughters as husbands[98] and either use the rest of the men to work in the fields or sell them.[99] As the group proliferated raids were mounted to terrorise neighbouring peoples and capture slaves and other plunder.[100] Success attracted free followers and the process snowballed so that in the late nineteenth century some Yao leaders had gained control over a number of villages and founded small territorial chiefdoms.[101]

As among the Imbangala their slaves lived much as the free, and slave children were valued by their fathers for their loyalty and given office or sent out to trade. Free nieces and nephews were as likely to be pawned as slaves and Duff McDonald noted that Yao men regarded all their dependents, slave or free, as property with whom they could do as they wished.[102] Male slaves of the first generation were perhaps more insecure than others as they could be sacrificed for funerals and fugitives suffered harsh punishment; but, since most slaves were wanted as supporters and were sure of a welcome in other villages, their lot was usually good and some were said to be richer than their masters, although the latter could seize their goods if they wished.

Among the Tio of Stanley Pool slavery served not so much to incorporate aliens into Tio lineages, although it did this too, but to transfer Tio from one matrilineage to another.[103] The Tio were not strictly matrilineal as each man had rights and obligations towards both his mother's and his father's kinsmen and anyone who could attract a following could found his own village and might be joined by both maternal and paternal relations. The Tio equated wealth with having many dependents—wives, children and slaves—while poverty was to be kinless.[104] They had a ruler but he had little power in the late nineteenth century and able officials and commoners had plenty of incentive to increase theirs through the great Congo trading network.[105] The dice were loaded in favour of those who had plenty of dependents to pawn or sell for trade goods, to produce crops or to serve as

98 Such husbands had the advantage from the point of view of their owners that they had no outside loyalties like free husbands who would come to live in their wives' villages but would remain members of their own matrilineages.

99 MacDonald, I, p. 147

100 'Man Stealing' medicine was taken to ensure the success of these raids, Alpers, p. 412.

101 These were unstable, however, as junior kinsmen and village headmen were liable to break away sometimes sneaking off by night taking the slaves of others with them, MacDonald, I, p. 148.

102 MacDonald, I, pp. 168–9. In theory they could kill them as there would be no one to bring a case against them. In practice the paternal kinsmen of a free nephew would protest if he were killed. A slave, of course, had no relatives to protest and was therefore in an even weaker position.

103 For slavery among the Tio, see Vansina, *Tio*, pp. 365–71

104 *Ibid.*, pp. 306, 525, appendix no. 7

105 For this trade see above, pp. 52 ff.

trading agents, canoemen, soldiers or servants. Slaves were thus in great demand and, since the Tio freely sold their own people, most of them were Tio. They were easily obtained as conflicts and crime usually ended in the transfer of people from one matrilineage to another. Uncles disposed of their nephews, for instance, to pay fines or gave them in compensation for feuds, debts, adultery, murder or witchcraft.[106] Any kin-group who lost a member in this way immediately sought to replace him by buying a slave. Furthermore if a lineage was guilty of constant feuding its overlord might attack it and sell all its members into slavery. A steady supply of Tio slaves was thus generated in addition to outsiders captured in war, kidnapped or bought.

Although masters had powers of life and death over their slaves, ill-treatment was rare and most lived lives which differed little from those of the free. In fact their prospects were unusually good for on the deaths of their masters they were not only liberated but could inherit their riches and political office. There were instances of men being succeeded by their slaves because they had sold all their rightful heirs. With good fortune, therefore, an ex-slave could rise to eminence, power and wealth.[107] The women were usually married by their masters, some of whom had dozens of slave wives. Since they produced and marketed crops and pottery, Vansina believes that they were valued as a labour force rather than for the children they bore, particularly as these offspring, although belonging only to their father's lineage had more rights than slaves and were, therefore, less valuable to him.[108]

Patrilineal societies ranging from the great interlacustrine state of Buganda to small-scale societies like the Kamba and Giriama of modern Kenya also acquired slaves. Buganda, a strong centralised monarchy, lay at the northern end of the Zanzibari trading network and her ruler, the *Kabaka*, tried to prevent neighbouring states from dealing directly with the Arabs and acquiring trade goods, particularly arms. Since Buganda produced little ivory, she exacted it in tribute from neighbouring peoples, received it in gifts from their rulers or seized it in war. She was infamous for the raids which maintained her hegemony and netted quantities of cattle, tusks and slaves. The ivory and some slaves were sold to the Arabs but most remained in Buganda.[109] The majority were women and children for the men were

106 Vansina, *Tio*, pp. 365–71
107 For slaves and inheritance see *ibid.*, pp. 308, 367.
108 Vansina, *Tio*, pp. 466–7
109 J. W. Harrison, *A. M. Mackay—Pioneer Missionary of the Church Missionary Society in Uganda*, London 1890, p. 435. Perhaps, 2,000 were exported annually in the 1880s, see Gerald W. Hartwig, 'Slavery and State Formation in East Africa; the case of the Nyamwezi and Ganda', paper presented at the Southern Historical Association Annual Meeting, 20 Nov. 1971, at Houston (henceforth 'Nyamwezi and Ganda'). Only a very few reached Zanzibar, see Kirk memo. Oct. 1889, FO 84/2005, most being sold in the interior. The girls were much prized by the Arabs at Ujiji, see J. Becker, *La Vie en Afrique*, 2 vols., Brussels 1887, I, p. 221, and at Tabora, see Hartwig, 'Nyamwezi and Ganda'.

usually killed in battle. These captives made up the bulk of the slave population, although there were also some Ganda kidnapped in childhood or sold by their kinsmen to raise capital.[110]

All prisoners belonged to the Kabaka who distributed them to peasants and to chiefs who in turn gave some to their soldiers as the spoils of war.[111] Women acquired in this way could not be sold.[112] Most of the female slaves became wives, concubines or servants, who helped free women with agricultural and menial tasks. The males simply became the lowest class in the social scale, establishing households of their own, living on their master's land and paying him tribute in return for protection.[113] Theoretically masters had powers of life and death over them, could mutilate them, sell them and seize their possessions, even their wives and children. On the other hand a good chief was a generous one and a slave was often given cattle or a wife to start him off, particularly if he was a Ganda enslaved as compensation for some offence.[114] Most were valued retainers and the White Fathers trying to buy slaves to form their initial congregations in the 1880s, found few for sale.[115] Mobility was limited, however, as slaves did not normally become chiefs.[116] Girls who married their owners were free when they bore him a child, but their offspring although outwardly treated as full members of the clan were discriminated against when it came to such matters as inheritance.[117] Slaves were sometimes sacrificed on important occasions such as the ceremonies attendant on the birth of twins, but free people were also killed for state rituals.[118] Some slaves, either Ganda offered by their parents[119] or captives, were dedicated to the deity and worked around the temples. They might marry and their children inherited their status but they do not seem to have been reviled like the Nigerian osu.

Slavery was also practised in the nearby kingdom of Ukerebe where unlike Buganda it was not associated with raids and changed considerably as

110 John Roscoe, *The Baganda*, London 1965 (first published 1911), p. 14
111 Lucy P. Mair, *An African People in the Twentieth Century*, New York 1965 (first published 1934), p. 133.
112 Roscoe, pp. 92–3
113 F. D. Lugard, *The Rise of Our East African Empire*, 2 vols., London 1893, I, p. 172
114 Roscoe, p. 14; Mair, p. 18
115 Renault, I, p. 173
116 The way to advancement, however, was to serve the *Kabaka* as a court page and to catch his eye. Sometimes men sent slave boys rather than their own sons to court, fearing the former might fall foul of the ruler. In this way slaves sometimes became chiefs by winning royal favour, L. A. Fallers, 'Social Mobility, Traditional and Modern', ch. 4 in L. A. Fallers (ed)., *The King's Men*, London 1964.
117 Roscoe, pp. 14–15; Mair, p. 33. Among the Ganda the word for slave applied to anyone in a household who had not been born into the kin group and was therefore not a full clan member, Mair, p. 32.
118 Roscoe, p. 73; Mair, pp. 179, 233–4
119 Mair, p. 238. Sometimes a childless woman would offer a child to the deity if he granted her wish and made her a mother.

both long distance and local trade expanded in the nineteenth century.[120] Previously most slaves were victims of famines or other misfortune who were received into Kerebe patrilineages as an act of charity distinct from the hospitality accorded strangers who could fend for themselves; or they were Kerebe transferred from one lineage to another in compensation for an offence. All were encouraged to work hard and redeem themselves and by the third generation the descendants of those who had remained in servitude were considered full lineage members. From about 1870, however, the Kerebe began actively to search for slaves whenever neighbouring peoples were hit by famine. They wanted labour to help their wives in the fields and to produce a surplus, which could be traded or else given to the ruler in return for his protection against sorcery, cases of which began to proliferate as economic growth increased the tensions in Kerebe society and men began to accumulate wealth on an individual rather than a lineage basis.[121] More cases of sorcery also meant more people were enslaved for this crime. As a result of economic development therefore, slaves were more sought after, more valuable and less likely to be manumitted.

Among the Ila of modern Zambia, on the other hand, slavery does not appear to have been associated with trade.[122] They were organised in unstable petty chiefdoms constantly squabbling over fishing and grazing rights and cattle raids. Venereal disease, abortions, infanticide and a long post-parturition taboo on sexual intercourse kept down the birth rate and the Ila sought slaves for defence and survival—to fight, farm, tend their herds and keep up their numbers. Most were little girls bought from neighbouring and culturally similar peoples and easily assimilated. Some were captured or kidnapped or acquired in payment of compensation or debt. While basically patrilineal, the Ila had strong ties, rights and obligations towards their maternal kinsmen, hence village heads, seeking as elsewhere to enlarge their following, valued slaves for their lack of outside loyalties. Masters had unlimited powers over them[123] but ill-treatment was rare, as a malcontent could not only find a home in another village but could change masters by throwing ash on the owner of his choice, who would then demand him, presumably as compensation.[124] Some refractory men and older women were discriminated against but most slaves were rapidly

120 Gerald W. Hartwig, 'Servitude within Kerebe Society', forthcoming in Miers and Kopytoff (henceforth 'Servitude').
121 Gerald W. Hartwig, 'The Victoria Nyanza as a trade route in the nineteenth century', *JAH*, xi, 4, 1970, pp. 535–52 (henceforth 'Trade') and 'Long Distance Trade and the Evolution of Sorcery among the Kerebe', *African Historical Studies*, iv, 3, 1971, pp. 505–24 (henceforth 'Sorcery').
122 For Ila slavery see A. Tuden, 'Slavery and Social Stratification' and 'Ila Slavery', *Rhodes-Livingstone Journal*, xxiv, Dec. 1958, pp. 68–78; Edwin Smith and A. M. Dale, *The Ila Speaking Peoples of Northern Rhodesia*, 2 vols., New York 1968 (first published 1920), I, ch. 16.
123 Smith and Dale, I, p. 410
124 *Ibid.*, pp. 402, 411; for other instances of this custom see above, pp. 74–5, 124.

assimilated.[125] Theoretically they were full lineage members under the protection of the ancestral gods and thus manumission was impossible. In practice, however, the rules of exogamy did not apply to them and the girls were usually married.

The boys were brought up as Ila and given cattle and land. They could hold office and could intermarry with the free. However, since they had only one set of kinsmen, those of their master, they contributed less often to such things as bridewealth and received less in inheritances and when they died their owners inherited their possessions. If a slave married a free person from another lineage, his children automatically acquired another set of kinsmen and were thus a step nearer to the free as were the children of two slaves since the mere fact that they had been born in an Ila village made them to some extent kinsmen. Slaves could found their own patrilineages by buying other slaves. Sometimes free women bought girls, married them to their male kinsmen and started their own lineages.[126] Among the Ila clear distinctions between slave and free disappeared in a few generations.

A variant of this form of incorporative slavery was to be found among the Cokwe of modern Angola and Zaire. Originally a small matrilineal society, they began to prosper after the Portuguese lifted the government monopoly on the sale of ivory in the 1830s.[127] They now sold ivory and honey to passing caravans and bought women and children to incorporate into their lineages. They also acquired firearms. As their numbers grew so their hunters and raiders began to range over an ever-widening area, shooting elephant, plundering and taking prisoners. As more and more women and children were assimilated, the Cokwe homeland became overpopulated and lineage segments began to migrate outwards, village by village, sweeping into new areas like a tidal wave, overwhelming the inhabitants and marrying their women. Thus the Cokwe took over vast areas of the decaying Lunda empire and raided far and wide for slaves and ivory. Their expansion was in full progress in the early 1880s.

Pawning in Africa

A common custom in Africa was 'pawning' or offering the services of a person in return for a loan. A lineage or an individual faced with a heavy expense such as payments for bridewealth, ransom or fines, or a man needing credit for trade would pawn a dependent, who would then live

125 Tuden, 'Slavery and Social Stratification', pp. 51–5
126 This phenomenon of women buying slaves to start their own lineages occurred in other societies also.
127 For Cokwe slavery see Joseph C. Miller, *Cokwe Expansion 1850–1900*, occasional paper no. 1, African Studies Program, University of Wisconsin, Madison 1969, and 'Cokwe Trade and Conquest in the Nineteenth Century' in Richard Gray and David Birmingham (eds.), *Precolonial African Trade: Essays on Trade in Central and Eastern Africa before 1900*, London 1970, pp. 175–201.

with and work for the creditor until the loan was repaid. The kinship structure of the society, together with custom, determined who could be pawned. Thus in mainly patrilineal Dahomey a man could only pawn his own children.[128] Among the Igbo he could also offer his brothers and sisters.[129] In matrilineal Asante he could pledge his brothers, sisters, his sister's children and even his mother and the creditors were often their own husbands or fathers. In Asante, if a man's wife was also his pawn he could demand that she perform more household duties for him, go with him on trading journeys, tell him what property she had and share her profits with him.[130] Most pawns in Africa were children, usually girls who often ended up marrying the creditor, the bridewealth being adjusted to cancel the debt.

Pawnship was distinct from slavery. It was a fate which might overtake anyone in hard times, was only temporary and was not considered a disgrace. Even more important pawns did not lose their lineage affiliations. A slave was essentially a kinless person and as such was unprotected, there being no kin group to watch over his interests, but a pawn was only temporarily in the service of another lineage and his own kin retained the right to see that he was not ill treated. Sometimes there were special sanctions to ensure good care. Thus in Lagos[131] and Dahomey if the pawn died the debt was extinguished while in Asante it was cancelled if he or she committed suicide. Imbangala creditors recognised the obligation to return pawns safely and hastily transferred sick ones back lest they die without being properly installed among their own ancestors.[132]

Pawnship filled a great need in that it was a means of contracting and discharging a debt. Frequently it served to see lineages through an emergency by allowing them to raise the means to pay a fine, to ransom a kinsman or to survive a famine. Thus when food was short the Kamba and Girima of modern Kenya would offer a girl to neighbouring peoples in return for food and when the crisis was over they either redeemed her or she married into the creditor lineage, the bridewealth being adjusted to take account of the debt.[133] Sometimes Giriama men voluntarily placed themselves in pawnship to save their villages from starvation.[134] The transaction was

128 Dahomey is generally described as patrilineal and patrilocal but this is an oversimplification. Under certain circumstances children belong to their mother's family and may even live in their compound depending upon the type of marriage entered into. For a discussion of this complicated subject see Herskovits, I, pp. 300 ff.; for pawnship see pp. 82–5.

129 Uchendu, 'Slavery in Southeast Nigerian Societies'.

130 This does not mean that a man's wife would not normally look after him but simply that he could not expect it as a right. For pawning in Asante see Rattray, ch. 6, Claridge, *A History of the Gold Coast and Ashanti*, London 1964 (2nd edition), 2 vols., II, p. 178.

131 McIntyre, p. 61, fn 24

132 Miller, 'Imbangala Institutions'

133 Informant Nkeeki wa Mukewa, 17 Sept. 1972; informant Husein Salim, 29 Sept. 1972.

134 Informant Husein Salim, 29 Sept. 1972

quite distinct from the selling of persons into slavery in return for food, cases of which were also widely reported,[135] or the outright sale of a dependent to raise credit. Pawning was widely used in commerce also. Thus the first step on the path to success for an aspiring trader might be to pawn his nieces, nephews or some other dependent to buy goods.

The system probably functioned best when practised between closely related families living near each other, mitigated as Rattray suggests by 'the constant interplay of mutual social obligations'.[136] It was liable to abuse, however, for all too often the pawn was never redeemed. Itsekiri merchants, for instance, received many children from the Urhobo in return for trade goods. The debts often remained unpaid and many consequently became slaves of the Itsekiri.[137] In Dahomey children were sometimes pawned secretly far from home and never recovered.[138] In Lagos people were sometimes kidnapped and held as pawns to force a debtor to repay the loan.[139] It should perhaps be noted, however, that the system did not always work to the disadvantage of the pawn. Among the Yoruba, for instance, men aspiring to office sometimes gave extended loans in order to secure the political support of the debtor and his lineage and in such circumstances the pawns were exceptionally well treated in order to ensure their loyalty.[140]

The whole question was intimately connected with the slave trade because unredeemed pawns often ended up as slaves, because the credit raised by pawning was often used to buy slaves and other trade goods, and because slaves were frequently given as pawns and this provided yet another incentive to buy slaves. The expansion of trade in the nineteenth century increased incentives and opportunities for pawning and the British thought the institution invidious. It should be noted also that whereas some African societies distinguished between pawns and slaves and called them by different names others seem to have made no such distinction and perhaps regarded them as slaves.[141]

Mary Douglas, writing on pawnship among certain matrilineal peoples in central Africa, notes that it gave rise to dependent lineages[142] and she describes it amongst the Lele of modern Zaire. This is a matrilineal society in

135 Instances of the selling of children, often kidnapped, are reported from Egypt to Morocco and Nigeria to East Africa. Sometimes men enslaved themselves voluntarily to save their villages; for an example see Vaughan.
136 Rattray, p. 55
137 Ikime, pp. 61–2
138 Herskovits, I, p. 84
139 McIntyre, p. 61
140 P. Morton-Williams, 'The Yoruba Kingdom of Oyo,' in Forde and Kaberry, pp. 36–69, p. 51.
141 In the present state of research and terminology it is sometimes difficult to know whether slave or pawn is meant.
142 Mary Douglas, 'Matriliny and Pawnship in Central Africa', *Africa*, xxxiv, 4, Oct. 1964, pp. 301–13 (henceforth 'Pawnship').

which boys go to live with their uncles at puberty. The elders in each village try to attract their sister's sons in order to build up their following. Their main asset is the right to dispose of marriageable girls and they offer them to their nephews as wives. Most of these are pawns, or the descendants of pawns, acquired in compensation for debt or some serious offence, including murder and sorcery. They are distinct from slaves in that they still belong to their own lineages and the creditors heed the wishes of their true kinsmen. The status of pawn is hereditary in the female line as is that of creditor. The heirs of the original creditor thus control the marriages of girls of the second and subsequent generations while a male pawn is distinguished from other free men only because he has no rights over his sisters and their children. This prevents him from collecting bridewealth or building up a following by attracting his sister's sons back to his village. On the other hand his 'owner' pays his own bridewealth when he marries, as well as certain other debts, and he can also have pawns of his own. His position is therefore not particularly irksome.

The creditor on the other hand can increase his following by marrying his female pawns to his nephews and offering his male pawns wives from his own lineage so that they will not go off and live with their uncles. Pawnship like slavery was thus an institution which was manipulated to avoid the normal residence pattern and authority structure of this type of society and it existed with variations among many matrilineal peoples including the Imbangala, the Pende, the Cokwe and the Yao.[143]

Mary Douglas suggests that this institution provided a permanent incentive to press claims for injury. For instance charges of sorcery, in which guilt or innocence was established by the poison ordeal, were pursued to get pawns as compensation.[144] It also encouraged indebtedness, and was thus an invidious institution.

Definition and role of slavery in Africa in the nineteenth century

It is obvious that these various forms of servitude cannot all be called slavery. No satisfactory definition of the word, encompassing both western and other forms of servitude, has yet been formulated. The League of Nations decided that slavery was: 'The status or condition of a person over whom any or all of the powers attaching to the right of ownership are

143 Douglas, 'Pawnship' gives a map and reviews some of the evidence. Among the Asante this seems not to have happened as although a creditor disposed of a female pawn in marriage her children belonged to her lineage unless she was pawned to her husband in which case Rattray found her status unclear.

144 Douglas, 'Pawnship', pp. 303–4. Alternatively the nineteenth century may have seen an increase in charges of sorcery in a particular society because there was less security and less faith in the old methods of protection—as suggested by the Kerebe examples discussed above, see p. 139.

exercised'.[145] Although broad enough to include most of the depressed classes mentioned in this discussion, this was soon found to be unsatisfactory in relation to Africa since it did not distinguish between the different degrees of 'restrictive freedom' common on the continent[146] and, more important, it did not distinguish between so-called 'free' junior members of lineages and slaves. The problem is clear enough. The only real chattel slave in Africa was probably the trade slave in the hands of a dealer, for he was simply a saleable commodity like any other object of commerce. As soon as he found a permanent master his integration into society as a human being began. He might remain saleable but in fact have considerable freedom, power and responsibility or he might be poor and hardworked and forbidden to leave but be sold only as a last resort just as a free man might be.

It is beyond the scope of this work to try to produce a definition of universal validity, nor would it probably be very fruitful especially as the concepts 'slave' and 'free' are themselves, as has been pointed out, western concepts often without exact African equivalents. A study of the various words which have been translated as 'slave', however, would go far to show how Africans conceptualised slavery.[147] There were often distinctions between trade and domestic slaves, between pawns and slaves, between slaves acquired as children and those obtained as adults[148] and between the offspring of two slaves and the progeny of one slave and one free parent. Some societies used different names for prisoners of war and bought slaves, and some distinguished between slaves performing different functions. Sometimes the same word was applied to a slave as to a grandchild or child, or a poor dependent. All of these facts reveal something of the attitude to slaves within a particular community.

It is suggested, however, that from the standpoint of African society in the nineteenth century a man may be regarded as a slave if he had no valid position in his community except as a dependent of a master or kin group with whom he had no true kinship affiliations.[149] His actual condition was immaterial. He could be a high official, content to remain in servitude or he might be really oppressed. His master might have rights over him which amounted to little more than a nominal connection or were identical to

145 *International Convention with the Object of Securing the Abolition of Slavery and the Slave Trade*, Geneva, 25 Sept. 1926, Article 1
146 C. W. W. Greenidge, *Slavery*, London 1958, pp. 22–3
147 I am thinking here of the type of analysis and translation which E. E. Evans-Pritchard makes in his study of terms relating to Zande customs and beliefs; see *Witchcraft, Oracles and Magic among the Azande*, Oxford 1958 (first published 1937), pp. 8–12.
148 Sometimes, as in the western Sudan there were different terms for slaves of different ages, sexes and size which were mainly market terms describing them for sale. The Duala, however, call a slave obtained as a child by a different word from the adults and usually he was integrated into Duala households and assimilated faster than adults; see Austen, 'Duala Slavery'.
149 I except here clients and other voluntary dependents since these retained their kinship ties.

those of a father over his son or an uncle over his nephew or he might have unlimited rights over both his labour and life, or any combination of rights placing the slave in various degrees of dependency and deprived status between these extremes. Slavery thus encompasses a whole range of situations, not capable of any neat or water-tight definition.

Any form of servitude which created a demand for slaves and thereby encouraged the capture, sale and transfer of persons contributed to the slave trade and raids which Britain wished to eliminate, and therefore comes within the province of this discussion.[150] All the forms of slavery mentioned did this with the exception of Igbo cult or osu slavery and even this was indirectly connected with slaving as persons would dedicate themselves to the deity to avoid being sold to dealers. Pawnship although distinct from slavery was considered a form of servitude by the British and has therefore been included here with it. The various examples of servitude which have been described serve to show the complexity of the problem facing Britain when she attacked the slave traffic.

Slavery served a number of functions in nineteenth-century Africa. It integrated people into a society, swelling the numbers of a kin group or a community, giving them greater power or security as well as a larger labour force. It disposed of surplus population, unwanted criminals and abnormal children, who might otherwise have died or been killed. It served ritual needs by furnishing victims for sacrifice, often outsiders who could be used in this way without creating tensions within the society itself. It provided a means of settling conflicts. In a continent where land was usually plentiful and consequently not marketable, slaves were a convenient capital investment. They were also an important medium of exchange in a situation where other currencies were used but were often not fully interchangeable.[151] Slavery allowed a man to build up his following and gain political power. The slave traffic kept the institution alive and took farmers, labourers, craftsmen, soldiers, officials, porters, sailors, traders, children, concubines and even wives to where they were wanted. It also provided convenient trade goods where others were lacking.

This is not to suggest that slavery or the slave trade were necessary or that they were the only means of meeting these varied needs.[152] There is clear evidence that even societies which practised slavery also achieved the same ends by other means. There were other forms of labour. The Kerebe, for instance, used seasonal migrant cultivators from nearby Bukara, who came to their country and were allowed to farm in return for giving their hosts part of their harvest.[153] Migrant farmers also grew peanuts in

150 Including the capture of women and children for assimilation.
151 For interesting examples of this see Vansina, *Tio*, pp. 303–9.
152 For a discussion on why certain peoples had slaves and others, whose conditions of life appear much the same, did not, see B. J. Siegel, 'Some Methodological Considerations for a Comparative Study of Slavery', *American Anthropologist*, n.s. 47, 1945, pp. 357–92.   153 Hartwig, 'Kerebe'

Senegambia.[154] The Nyamwezi used hired labourers[155] on their fields and free porters were widely employed in East Africa. Mercenary soldiers served the Asante, the Igbo and the Nyamwezi. Loyal trading partners, if not agents, could be secured by entering into blood brotherhood relationships. Nomadic or transhumant pastoralists solved the man-power problem posed by the need to keep their animals scattered in distant regions by placing them with friends or stock associates.[156] Men could attach themselves to rulers as free retainers or clients. Children could be adopted and strangers and captives completely assimilated.[157] Alternative forms of capital investment existed and other currencies were widely used. Cattle and other goods could be and were used to settle conflicts.

Nevertheless as long as wars and disorders enabled slaves to be cheaply acquired[158] and fed into the trade network, slavery was a convenient way of fulfilling these various requirements. In areas where the institution and the traffic which maintained it had taken root, their elimination would require considerable readjustment and a change in the overall conditions of African life. It might necessitate, for instance, the development of other means of making labour mobile, other forms of capital investment, more satisfactory currency systems, changes in religious and social organisation and in the basis of political power, together with new methods of dealing with such things as famine,[159] crime and debt. African societies were of course altering all the time and the extension of slavery in the nineteenth century was itself a reflection of rapid economic development and political change. Its elimination would clearly provoke resistance and risked dislocating the economy.

Legitimate trade versus the slave trade

It must now be considered whether commerce, Christianity and 'civilisa-

154 Klein, 'Slavery in Senegambia'
155 A. C. Unomah, 'Vbandevba and Political Change in a Nyamwezi Kingdom: Unyanyembe during 1840–90', paper presented to the Social Sciences Conference of East Africa, University of Dar-es-Salaam, Dec. 1970.
156 See P. H. Gulliver, *The Family Herds: A Study of Two Pastoral Tribes in East Africa, the Jie and Turkana*, London 1955, pp. 196 ff.; John Lamphear, 'The Oral History of the Jie of Uganda', London Ph.D. 1972; Nicolaisen, p. 107.
157 Some peoples, such as the Kikuyu, assimilated unredeemed prisoners of war so completely that they were full lineage members and could only marry outside the lineage. They also welcomed strangers, such as victims of famine, and assimilated them completely. I am indebted to Dr Godfrey Muriuki for this information.
158 Acquisition might be cheap because slaves were the by-product of wars fought for other reasons, including the necessity of a young warrior to prove himself, or because the captors had such a clear military advantage over their victims that casualties were unlikely.
159 Certain peoples had methods of guarding against this, for instance, Nyamwezi rulers maintained grain banks, see Unomah.

tion' had proved effective weapons against the slave traffic by 1884. In the case of legitimate trade the theory, as has been seen, was that as innocent commerce grew Africans would find it more profitable to employ their fellow men at home. There is plenty of evidence that as the demand for African exports expanded, they mobilised the labour necessary to produce and distribute them. However, it is equally clear that in wide areas this mobilisation was achieved by means of the slave trade, either because lack of communications and other factors made it difficult to do it any other way or because the mechanisms already existed and the many disorders made victims readily available. While this was preferable to the export traffic, and therefore initially more acceptable to the humanitarians, it still gave rise to depredations, and the same heartrending scenes continued to be enacted as countless victims were driven along the footpaths of Africa to meet the new demand.

As new commodities were exported, so new peoples entered the slave market. A few examples will show how legitimate trade and the slave traffic might complement each other. Thus the development of the rubber trade from the east coast of Africa in the later nineteenth century, presented the Makonde, in whose country the vine grew wild, with new opportunities for legitimate trade. They were soon collecting the rubber, taking it to Indian merchants in the little ports between Lindi and the Ruvuma River and exchanging it for brass wire, cloth and gunpowder. On their return home they sold the cloth to passing Yao dealers for slaves. The Yao continued on their way and arrived at the coast shorn of all evidence of slave trading. The slaves were put to work on the fields of the Makonde, who now had more time for trading expeditions and rubber collecting. Far from displacing the slave traffic, the production of export goods merely created a new market in the interior. Missionaries at Masasi reported that they had never seen so many slave caravans on their way from Yao country to the coast and that most of them disposed of their slaves while still a few days' march in the interior.[160] Such slaves as did reach the coast found a ready market there, for the coastal peoples, as already noted, were buying small numbers to work their farms.[161] By 1881 naval officers were actually reporting that between Lindi and Cape Delgado, owners would only sell their slaves for export in times of scarcity.[162] Further south the British Consul in Mozambique had remarked the previous year on the rising production of oil seed, grown by mulattos using slave labour, in areas only two hours' march from the coast but beyond Portuguese control. He thought only half the slaves reaching the coast were destined for export.[163]

Moreover, there is evidence that at times the decline in the export of

160 Maples to Allen, 11 June 1883, ASS 63/24
161 Maples to Allen, 19 Oct. 1882, ASS 63/23 and 11 June 1883, ASS 63/24 and see above, pp. 97 ff.
162 Jones to Admiralty, no. 457 conf. 10 Oct. 1881, FO 84/1607
163 Hanna, pp. 58–9

slaves, as a result of the various treaties with Britain, stimulated slavery in the interior by lowering the price so that more could be bought by Africans. For instance in East Africa some of the Kamba, who traditionally had no slaves and either ransomed or mutilated their prisoners of war, grew prosperous enough in the mid-nineteenth century on the proceeds of selling ivory on the Swahili coast to buy slaves from coastal dealers, who were seeking a market in the hinterland for people they could no longer legally export to Arabia. The Kamba then used them as farmers and herdsmen.[164] The Swahili may also have kept more slaves on the coast as a result of the shrinking of the export market after the treaties of 1822 and 1845.[165]

Not only did the slave trade and legitimate trade often flourish side by side, but sometimes the innocent trader found the slave dealer had a clear advantage. Hijaz slave merchants, for instance, took light valuable goods, which were easy to carry, to the inland markets of the Sudan and bought slaves. They then bought from the legitimate trader the heavy goods with which he had struggled up country and used these to buy up, at a high price, the whole supply of such valuables as gold dust, musk, ivory and ostrich feathers. These were taken back to the coast by the slaves accompanied by a few camels bearing water and food. The innocent trader could only afford such heavy items as hides and gum which he had to get back to the coast by employing carriers with camels.[166] Back in the Hijaz, dealers could put their slaves to profitable use as coolies, boatmen or divers, sell them at a high profit, or hire out their services.

In certain areas legitimate commerce was said to be unremunerative unless complemented by the slave traffic. The ivory traders of the upper Nile and East Africa, for instance, often depended on slave dealing to pay off their retainers and to make a profit.[167] Menelik of Shoa perhaps had good reason to believe that if slave dealing was forbidden in the highlands, coastal traders would no longer visit his territories and the export of legitimate goods would end.[168] Viable alternative exports were often hard to find in regions where transport costs were high and capital was lacking for large-scale production.

If legitimate trade was to function as a weapon against the slave trade a mobile labour force would have to be created and capital would have to be attracted. As it was, in the 1880s African producers might make a small beginning in the production or collection of export goods but as soon as the enterprise assumed larger proportions the chances were that it would create

---

164 Krapf, pp. 357–8; J. E. Lamphear, 'The Kamba and the Northern Mrima Coast', Gray and Birmingham, pp. 75–101, pp. 90–1. My own impression from Kamba informants is that they thought it useless to take adult prisoners, even women, as they usually escaped, and those groups who did not take part in the ivory trade and hence had little opportunity of acquiring slaves from far away did not have them.
165 See above, p. 97.
166 Wylde, II, pp. 245 ff. For another example of a legitimate trader being undercut by slavers at Lagos see above, p. 49.
167 See above, pp. 77, 103.
168 See above, p. 115.

a demand for slave labour, as it had, for instance, among the Makonde, the Nyamwezi, the Tio and many others. Nor was the problem limited to the production of export goods. Those producing for a local market, such as the Kerebe, resorted to the same solution.

It is true that hired labour could sometimes be found but there were basic difficulties about recruiting on any scale. For instance, some people regarded it as a mark of servility to work for others, even for wages, perhaps because the only labour bought or sold was slave labour.[169] W. P. Johnson, a missionary working in Nyasaland, testified to the difficulty of persuading men that they could take such work and still regard themselves as free. Even when they accepted the idea it might seem less attractive than the more hazardous enterprise of going on a trading exhibition to the coast.[170] There is evidence of a similar aversion to wage labour on the part of the Kamba[171] and the Tio,[172] while those who had tasted the delights of slave owning often regarded manual labour as beneath them, an attitude found, for example, among the Ganda[173] and the Muslim peanut farmers of Senegambia.[174] In some societies agricultural work was done by women and was not considered suitable for free men, and slaves were therefore bought to assist the women in the fields.[175] In many areas also there was so little security that people had little inducement to work to accumulate possessions which would attract raiders.[176] Africans might, however, be persuaded to work for others if there was the prospect of getting a gun or perhaps some other much desired commodity, but they frequently stopped as soon as they had what they wanted.[177] As long as land was plentiful and most people lived at the subsistence level, they had little incentive to work for others unless offered some powerful attraction.[178]

Since over much of the continent in the 1880s the only labour readily available was slave labour there was a danger that the development of

169 This is suggested by Vansina, *Tio*, p. 303.
170 Johnson, pp. 157–8
171 Informant Nkeeki Wa Mukewa, 17 Sept. 1972
172 Vansina, *Tio*, p. 303
173 Robert W. Felkin, 'Notes on the Waganda Tribe of Central Africa', *Proceedings of the Royal Society of Edinburgh*, 13, 1886, p. 746, cited in Hartwig, 'Nyamwezi and Ganda'.
174 Klein, 'Slavery in Senegambia'
175 Conversely certain jobs were sometimes normally done by free men.
176 MacDonald, II, p. 307. MacDonald writing in 1882 commented on the lack of incentive to accumulate cattle or even to store grain against famine in the Lake Malawi area. A boy when asked if he would keep a cow when he grew up replied: 'As if I had three lives!'
177 The prospect of being able to get a gun brought labourers to the South African diamond fields in the early days. Similarly, Renault says, Manyema hired themselves as porters to Arab expeditions only until they achieved their aim of getting a gun, Renault, I, pp. 69–70.
178 Johnson recounted how the Nyasa people when asked to go away to work on the roads would ask, 'Who are going? For how long is it? What sort of work is it?' and only after that, and with far less interest, would they ask about wages, Johnson, p. 212.

legitimate trade both for export and for local markets might lead not just to an increase in slavery but also to a greater exploitation of the slave as an instrument of production and hence a deterioration in his condition.[179]

For the British the labour question posed particular difficulties which discouraged investment and enterprise in Africa. In regions where slavery existed they often could only get labour by hiring slaves from their owners and this was illegal for British subjects. The only way for it to be lawful was if the arrangement was made directly with the slave and the wages were handed over to him. Naturally slave owners were unwilling to allow this. In practice British planters, such as the Sunleys in the Comoro Islands, were driven to hire slaves from their masters and turn over three-fifths of the wages to these owners. The Sunleys were developing the resources of the islands and claimed that by treating slaves and free workers in the same way they were dealing a blow to slavery and opening the eyes of the people to a rival economic system and way of life. Their efforts were praised by Livingstone, Frere, Hill and Holmwood, and the long-term effects were appreciated in the Foreign Office,[180] but it was felt that their employment of slaves could not be condoned while Britain was protesting at the recruitment of *engagés* by French and Portuguese planters, and they were felons under the law.

British Indians in Zanzibar were caught in a similar trap. They had to accept plantations as security from Arabs to whom they advanced credit, and they complained that this collateral was valueless if they could not hire labour to work these estates and that if their debtors knew the position they would not worry about repaying them. Furthermore, they said that if the law was strictly enforced all their activities must come to an end, for they would not be able to find servants, or labourers, and would be at a grave disadvantage compared with other foreigners.[181]

Kirk felt the principle of the law was correct and tried to enforce it.[182] The humanitarians did not think it went far enough and were pressing for a more stringent slave holding act at the time of the Berlin Conference. They feared that, if Britons were allowed to hire slaves through their masters,

179 This danger had been foreseen in the Colonial Office in 1863 when Rogers wrote: 'So long as labour is worthless, slavery will be light. In proportion as slave labour becomes productive of profit, it will be grindingly exacted. Is there not, therefore, considerable fear lest, by encouraging legitimate commerce, we may turn serfdom, with its loose intermittent obligations, into that unrelenting methodized slavery which is inflicted by a master, who sees his way to making a profit on every hour of his slaves' labour.' Quoted in J. Gordon, 'The Development of the Legal System in the Lagos Colony, 1862–1905', London Ph.D., 1967.
180 Coupland, *Exploitation*, pp. 174 ff.; Frere to Granville, no. 27, 12 March 1873, FO 84/1389; Holmwood report enc. in Miles to Granville, no. 93, 18 Nov. 1882, FO 84/1623
181 Petition enc. in Euan Smith to Salisbury, no. 346, 20 Nov. 1888, FO 84/1910
182 Kirk memo. 6 Sept. 1888, FO 84/1927; if he heard of a slave having to pay most of his earnings to his master he applied to the Sultan for redress.

they might end up advancing the masters the money to buy more slaves so that they could employ them.[183] They even wanted to outlaw the use of contractors employing slave labour.[184] Even as it stood, the law was bound to hamper British enterprises in slave holding countries and to place them at a disadvantage with foreign business, unless other governments were prepared to adopt the same policy. In fact, it was largely ignored. The Sunleys continued to use their slave hirelings in the Comoros and at Zanzibar the law was reported in 1888 to have been in abeyance for some years.[185] Like so many of Britain's anti-slavery measures it was subscribed to in principle, but proved unenforceable in practice.

The redemption of slaves, that is buying them and giving them their freedom, might have been a means of resolving the labour difficulty but this was also illegal for British subjects. By 1880, the Foreign Office view was that it encouraged the slave traffic by increasing the demand for slaves.[186] British subjects who redeemed slaves were technically guilty of slave dealing.[187] As foreigners had no such scruples and there was a danger that foreign planters and traders would take to redeeming slaves to obtain labourers and porters, Kirk explained to his government that this could be cheaper than hiring them.[188] For instance, a German in the service of Leopold II bought twelve slaves for about $10 each and arranged that they should work for three years for nothing in return for their freedom. This was cheaper than getting workers from the coast, who cost $5 a month. Foreigners who did this would thus have a distinct advantage over Englishmen and would provide a new market for slaves.

The problems of capital investment and labour involved in the development of legitimate trade in Africa were clearly extremely difficult to resolve. It is true that the odd planter who settled in the interior, such as John Buchanan, who introduced coffee to Nyasaland in the 1880s, set an example which might be followed. The missionaries too, paying for food and services, enabled neighbouring peoples to obtain European goods without participating in the slave trade. The scale had hitherto been small for it was difficult to find Europeans willing to invest any considerable sums in tropical Africa, in areas outside of white control. Without government backing and without such investment, enterprise was necessarily limited. There was also little official help forthcoming for African producers. Thus in

183 Waller to Allen, 29 Oct. 1884, ASS C 69/28
184 Waller to Allen, 16 June 1888, ASS C 69/33
185 Euan Smith to Salisbury, no. 346, 20 Nov. 1888, FO 84/1910
186 This attitude was a surprise to Salisbury, who admitted in 1889 that he was 'hopelessly' puzzled by it. 'I used to think', he wrote, 'that the redemption of captives was a good work—but it now appears that giving a ransom is only one degree less criminal than receiving it', minute on Vivian to Lister, 27 Sept. 1889, FO 84/1946.
187 W. P. Johnson recalled that when he wanted to buy a slave boy in Zanzibar to save him from ill treatment he had to arrange for an Arab to actually do the transaction, p. 39.
188 Kirk to Granville, 29 March 1881, no. 240, FOCP 4626

the Nyasa region where the African Lakes company had established itself, providing an outlet by steamer for local produce, the British Consul found a rare African who showed some interest in growing coffee but complained that he had no money for the necessary initial outlay. When Consul Hawes asked the Foreign Office if it had any money to help him the answer was a firm negative.[189] The project therefore died on the spot.

In areas outside of European control such investment as had been made in tropical Africa had been on a limited scale and had all too often encouraged slaving. Thus Indian financiers backing Arab trading caravans had incidentally financed their slaving operations or those of their African partners and European traders on the West African coast advancing credit to African merchants had incidentally encouraged them and their suppliers to procure slave labour.

One of the great obstacles to the development of legitimate trade was the high cost of penetrating into the interior of Africa, which made the export of many products unremunerative. The search for navigable rivers, which had been the object of so much of the exploration of the continent, revealed that while some rivers were navigable for hundreds of miles in the heart of Africa, there were usually serious obstacles between the coast and the free stretches of water. The Niger delta was exceptional in that the region produced a cash crop and waterways by which it could be evacuated. Elsewhere camels and other beasts of burden could be used in some areas, but in huge stretches of country there was no alternative to carriage by porters. Apart from their obvious limitations, they were hard to recruit and liable to desert. Caravans were also beset by the difficulty of obtaining food from people who usually grew only enough to satisfy their own needs and were often unable even to do that, and by the exactions of rulers and other peoples who expected payment from those passing through their territories. Very small beginnings had been made by 1884 in the building or planning of roads[190] and railways,[191] and steamers were in use on some of the navigable rivers and lakes, but any serious extension of modern means of transport required heavy investment which only came after the establishment of political control.

The question was closely linked to the slave trade because lack of communications was an obstacle to both the growth of legitimate trade and the

189 Hanna, p. 74. Most Africans and Arabs in the area were reluctant to consider growing cash crops as they said no one would buy them, *ibid.*, p. 71.
190 Mostly in European protectorates in West Africa or in South Africa and in Egypt but an attempt had also been made to build a road linking Lake Malawi to Lake Tanganyika and Stanley had built one along part of the lower Congo. It must be remembered, as J. H. Bevin points out, that the cost of roads, and even of canoe traffic, might be too high for existing trade conditions, and that both roads and rivers tied their users to set routes on which tolls could be easily exacted whereas porters could evade such charges by taking other paths, 'Gold Coast Economy about 1880', *Transactions of the Historical Society of Ghana*, ii, pp. 73–86, p. 78.
191 In South Africa, Egypt, Senegal and the Congo

development of a mobile labour force and because it was believed that the need for porters to carry goods up and down from the coast to the interior was a stimulus to the slave traffic. The picture of long lines of slaves yoked together by slave sticks, driven on by the lash and sweating under the burden of huge tusks of ivory, was oft described and widely believed. Recent research has shown that much of the carrying of ivory was done by hired porters, but slaves, sometimes expressly acquired, were certainly also used for the job[192] in East, West and Central Africa and the hired porters were often domestic slaves.

Whether the use of slaves was exaggerated or not in contemporary literature, businessmen and humanitarians were at one in advocating the development of communications, and particularly of railways, as a means of both developing African production of export goods and of suppressing the slave traffic. At the very time of the Berlin Conference, Stanley, hoping to interest British investors, was busy writing a book urging the laying of some eight hundred miles of track to link navigable waterways to the sea and to by-pass cataracts. 'Until railways are constructed', he wrote, 'it is useless to suppose that any remunerative trade can be made', but, once they were completed, he forecast that a continent 'abounding in tropical produce, populated by eighty-one million of workable people' would be open to European enterprise.[193] Most of these plans were still only hatching at the time of the Berlin Conference.

In the years that followed, the acquisition of political power by the Europeans provided the necessary conditions for capital investment. The unresolved question was where the labour was to be found. The clear danger was that this investment and the consequent expansion of legitimate trade and production and building of communications would create demands for labour that could not be met by free recruitment and might in areas where the slave trade existed simply increase the slave traffic at least in the initial stages, perhaps in disguised form, unless the colonial powers could be persuaded to guard against it by effective legislation, honestly enforced.

Christianity versus the slave trade

The great blossoming of Protestant and then Catholic missionary activity in Africa in the nineteenth century was intimately connected with the abolition of the slave trade.[194] Missionaries worked with liberated captives

192 Renault, I, pp. 69–70. It was sometimes difficult to tell the two apart as hired porters were occasionally yoked to prevent their deserting.

193 H. M. Stanley, *The Congo and the Founding of its Free State*, 2 vols. (henceforth *Congo*), I, pp. ix–xi. No credence can be placed upon Stanley's population estimates, see Wm. R. Louis and J. Stengers, *E. D. Morel, History of the Congo Reform Movement*, Oxford 1968, pp. 253–4.

194 This missionary enterprise sprang from the religious revival of the eighteenth

in, for instance, Sierra Leone, Fernando Po, India, the Seychelles, Réunion and East Africa. They established churches among those who returned to their homeland in Nigeria and they sent out freed slaves as preachers to spread the gospel themselves.[195] Both Buxton and Livingstone had called on Christian churches to combat the slave trade and both calls had been answered. Furthermore missionary societies and the churches which supported them did much to rouse public opinion against the traffic and spur governments into action. By the early 1880s missionaries of many nationalities and various denominations had penetrated into the heart of Africa. They had preached for instance, on the Niger, the Congo, the Zambesi and the Great Lakes and in many parts of South Africa.

Everywhere they carried the message that the slave trade was wrong. Slavery, on the other hand, they were often forced to accept, although they deplored it. Already they were urging Africans to abandon the worship of their own deities, together with polygamy, human sacrifice, poison ordeals, the murder of twins and belief in witchcraft and sorcery. To add slave holding to the list of sins, merely increased the difficulty of converting the rulers and elders upon whom they often depended for protection or even to get a hearing. Early missionaries in Nigeria compromised and allowed their converts to keep slaves, arguing that only after the population had become Christian, could they be expected to renounce it.[196] By the 1880s opinion was hardening against this practice, but few Africans had been converted and slavery and the trade which fed it flourished even in areas such as the Lagos hinterland where Christianity had long been established.

In East Africa in the 1870s both Catholic and Protestant missions had settlements where they cared for captives released from dhows.[197] The Catholics unashamedly increased their numbers by buying slaves, mainly children, from dealers. The Holy Ghost Fathers married the adults and set them up in Christian villages radiating out from Bagamoyo.[198] The White Fathers,[199] arriving in the late 1870s, headed straight for the far interior and bought children as the nuclei of their settlements in Tanganyika.[200] They even appealed for funds to ransom orphans from dealers. They tried to do

century in Britain and America, see C. P. Groves, *The Planting of Christianity in Africa*, 4 vols., published London 1948, 1954, 1955, 1958, I, pp. 178 ff.
195 See Ajayi. The most celebrated of the liberated African missionaries was Ajayi, or Bishop Samuel Crowther, who was freed by the British from a Portuguese slaver in Lagos, as a boy, and taken to Sierra Leone and subsequently went back to spread the gospel in Nigeria. Freed slaves also returned to East Africa from India.
196 Even mission agents kept slaves and pawns in Abeokuta in 1879, see Ajayi, pp. 103–5, 165, 169, 237–8.
197 Oliver, *Missionary Factor*, pp. 50 ff.; Renault, I, pp. 140 ff.
198 Oliver, *Missionary Factor*, pp. 22–3; Renault, I, pp. 140–3
199 The White Fathers, founded in 1868 by Cardinal Lavigerie, Archbishop of Algiers, were known by different names at different times but the most usual one in the early days was the Société des Missionnaires d'Alger. See Renault for a detailed study of their early work.
200 Renault, I, pp. 188 ff.

the same in Buganda but found there were few suitable slaves for sale and better results were to be had among the free.[201] Catholic missionaries assumed proprietory rights over their redeemed slaves to the point of recapturing and punishing those who absconded without permission.[202]

The buying of slaves to make them into Christians was frowned on by the British who thought it encouraged slave dealing. The British missionaries who fanned out across East Africa did not buy slaves, except very rarely, usually to save their lives. However, they often became embroiled in the slavery question. Some made the fatal mistake of taking in fugitives or even, in the case of the ill-fated Universities Mission group which Livingstone himself guided to the Zambesi, releasing them from their captors.[203] This provided them with their initial congregation but earned them the hostility of surrounding peoples. This, together with the unsettled conditions of the area and heavy loss of life, led to their withdrawal. The Church of Scotland mission established at Blantyre over a decade later became a haven for fugitives and soon had seven villages settled around them before their policy was changed.[204] Missionaries soon learnt that they had to harden their hearts and return runaways to their masters or redeem them if they were to be welcomed by those in authority in the areas where they settled.[205]

Some of the mission posts, with their nuclei of freed slaves, fugitives and other adherents, blossomed into veritable little colonies with extensive plantations. They introduced a few thousand Africans to the rudiments of Christianity and western technical skills.[206] Before 1884 they usually provided at least a degree of security against raids and famine [207] and with it the incentive to improve houses, acquire tools and other possessions and produce surplus food.[208] Manual labour was considered fitting for free men and European cloth and other goods could be bought with food or services. But they attracted lawless elements and it was a constant struggle to prevent their adherents from indulging in slaving and all manner of other crimes. Attempts to maintain discipline involved the missionaries in the exercise of secular powers which sometimes led to acts of brutality and together with the settling of disputes cost many valuable hours which might have been

201 Renault, I, p. 173   202 Renault, I, pp. 142, 203
203 Oliver, *Missionary Factor*, p. 14; Livingstone, *Zambesi*, pp. 355–64
204 Hanna, pp. 26–7
205 For the feelings of the missionaries see MacDonald, II, pp. 198 ff. and Hanna, p. 35.
206 Oliver, *Missionary Factor*, pp. 60–4. These settlements often roused the admiration of visitors for their order and prosperity.
207 There were exceptions. The Universities Mission station at Masasi for instance was attacked in the early 1880s, as was the Church Missionary Societies settlement at Mombasa and the White Fathers' station at Rumonge in 1881. Such attacks were often provoked by the action of mission adherents or the harbouring of fugitive slaves or sheltering of rebellious subjects by missionaries.
208 Freed slaves at Masasi worked very hard at their own fields but grudged time spent on those of the mission. They thought the missionaries should be content to have them observe Sunday as a day of rest, W. P. Johnson, p. 52.

spent evangelising.[209] The missionaries also found that freed slaves expected to be provided for long after they should have been self-supporting.[210] The worst drawback, however, was that these settlements were self-sufficient and divorced from the surrounding population, although sometimes the boys married local girls and established some links. On the whole they were isles of Christianity, in a sea of peoples at worst actively hostile and at best virtually untouched by the spiritual message.[211]

Outside them, where the real future lay, progress had in general been extremely slow.[212] Beyond the borders of actual European territories, missionaries were hampered by the very conditions of African life, the constant threat of raids, wars, famine and epidemics, even the migrations of people practising shifting agriculture which could suddenly remove their incipient congregations. Poor communications, the religious beliefs, customs and social organisation of the people and sometimes the opposition of slave dealers, all compounded their difficulties. Too often people welcomed them as protectors or as a source of arms and were disappointed to find them of little service.[213] While in the unsettled conditions of the interior many came to them for refuge and not because they were attracted by Christianity. It is possible that these very factors gained them a hearing and brought them adherents they would not otherwise have had but these adherents were of necessity usually from the weaker peoples,[214] the victims rather than the perpetrators of the slave trade.

In sum by 1884 in widely scattered areas a significant but small beginning had been made. A few children had been introduced to new ideas in Christian schools and some peoples had found a new opportunity to acquire trade goods by selling their produce or services to the missions and a few converts had been gained. A seed had been sown, often in fertile soil, but in some places missionaries could get no hearing at all.[215] Sometimes

209 Oliver, *Missionary Factor*, pp. 64–5. For examples of brutality in missions, see Hanna, pp. 28 ff.

210 Renault, I, p. 182

211 Oliver, *Missionary Factor*, pp. 64–5; Renault, I, pp. 181 ff.

212 An exception in the early 1880s was Buganda where progress was made among the pages at the Kabaka's court but the precarious situation of the missionaries and their converts was soon made clear by events, see below, pp. 193 ff.

213 Johnson, for instance, recalled that Mataka hoped he would enter into partnership with him for hunting and raiding. Mutesa of Buganda initially invited missionaries hoping probably that they would be allies against the Egyptians threatening him from the north and assure him a supply of arms and ammunition, D. A. Low, *Religion and Society in Buganda 1875–1900*, East African Studies no. 8, Kampala 1968 (henceforth *Religion*), p. 1. Many further examples could be given of people in danger asking missionaries to live among them. See for instance, Renault, II, p. 187; Livingstone, *Zambesi*, p. 362.

214 In Buganda, however, converts came largely from the aspiring young men at court, see Low, *Religion*.

215 Johnson's discussion of his difficulties on the shores of Lake Nyasa well illustrates this point, pp. 57 ff.

Africans tolerated them and even paid lip service to the anti-slavery cause but found it more to their advantage to maintain links with the slave dealers who provided them with arms.[216] Missionary enterprise had been on too small a scale and too circumscribed by the insecurity of African life to make much progress in the major work of evangelisation and had certainly had little effect on either slavery or the slave trade.

Britain and the suppression of slavery

To the Victorian mind Christianity was the basis of 'civilisation' and legitimate commerce was expected to provide sufficient prosperity for it to flourish. The trader and the missionary each in his own way brought this civilisation to Africa but they often operated single-handed, far from home, and with no power to back them up. There were, however, the small British colonies in Africa from which it was confidently hoped that commerce, Christianity and civilisation would radiate outwards. These were solid bases where Britain was able in theory to enforce her will and set an example. In fact little headway had been made against slavery by 1884. Even the slave trade continued in some colonies and in neighbouring African territories it went unchecked. The difficulties which faced the administrators and the methods they adopted merit examination, particularly as their experience moulded British policy towards the abolition of slavery when it came to be discussed at Brussels in 1889.

Slavery was suppressed in British colonies after 1833 in various ways. In those settled by Europeans—the West Indies, South Africa and Mauritius—slaves were declared free, a system of apprenticeship[217] to cover the period of transition to a wage economy was introduced and slave owners were offered compensation. A decade later in India, dealing with non-European slave holders, Britain simply ended the legal status of slavery. No slave was encouraged to leave his master but, if he did so, he could not be recovered through legal action or forced to return, and no cases arising out of any obligations of slavery could be brought to court. The result was a long period of transition during which slaves only slowly became aware of the position and masters realised that slaves were no longer a worthwhile investment and that the onus lay with them to treat them well enough to retain their services. At least this was the theory. Only seventeen years later did it become an offence to have slaves.

In 1874, when Britain annexed the territories on the Gold Coast over which she had previously exercised an informal protectorate, she decided

216 Harrison, p. 432. Kabaka Mutesa of Buganda, for instance, assured the missionary A. M. Mackay that he did not deal in slaves but said his chiefs did and the Arab traders wanted them in exchange for guns and cloth.
217 The abuses of this system and of the various free labour schemes introduced are beyond the scope of this work.

to adopt this Indian method of abolishing slavery. The Colonial Secretary, Lord Carnarvon, against his better judgement and owing to humanitarian pressure,[218] sanctioned ordinances making it illegal for anyone to force another to work for him, and declared free all who entered, or were born in, the colony after November 5, 1874. Contracts recognising slavery were henceforth void, slave dealing was outlawed and pawning was also made illegal. The penalty for infringing the new laws was up to seven years imprisonment.[219]

In taking these steps Carnarvon was trying to please the humanitarians without disrupting local society. Compulsory emancipation was not introduced because it might cause hardship to the slave as well as the master.[220] Furthermore, in all conscience it could only be done if the owners were compensated. This was considered impracticable as the authorities had no means of knowing who was a slave and who was not and opportunities for fraud were therefore endless. Schemes for the government to buy slaves and use them on public works until they had earned their redemption were rejected. The governor argued that they would probably desert their jobs.[221] The solution was reasonable enough in theory. Those already enslaved could stay with their masters on a voluntary basis and the worst evils engendered by the institution, slave raiding and dealing, together with pawning, would all come to an end, while slavery itself would finish as existing slaves died off.

It was felt that the effect of the ordinances would be so slow as to be almost imperceptible.[222] The governor was sure that few slaves would leave their masters since they would find it hard to make a living until wage labour became more general.[223] Any sudden and rigorous application of the laws would, it was believed, diminish the powers and prestige of the chiefs and prevent them, through lack of control over labour, from producing the commodities needed for legitimate trade. It might also drive innocent traders away from the British colony for fear of losing their slave porters and servants who could claim their freedom when they set foot on British soil.[224] It was carefully explained to the chiefs that no slave would be encouraged to leave his master and that the emancipation of a pawn would not extinguish the debt.[225]

With so cautious an approach it is not surprising that the ordinances

218 R. Robinson and J. Gallagher, with Alice Denny, *Africa and the Victorians*, London 1963, p. 31
219 Hertslet, *Commercial Treaties*, XV, pp. 527 ff. ordinances, 17 Dec. 1874
220 G. E. Metcalfe, *Great Britain and Ghana, Documents of Ghana History 1807–1957*, London 1964, p. 373
221 *Ibid.*, p. 377
222 Griffiths to Knutsford, 26 Jan. 1891, conf. CO96 215
223 Metcalfe, p. 377
224 See below for the fugitive slave question, pp. 163–6.
225 Claridge, II, pp. 181–2

remained very largely a dead letter in the 1880s.[226] There were no Europeans in the interior to enforce them, and although it was known that certain chiefs were evading the laws, it was almost impossible to get evidence against them, and equally hard to secure convictions in African courts.[227] Such effects as were felt were not encouraging. The few slaves who left their masters were regarded by the authorities as the least desirable and they often drifted into crime.[228] On the other hand, chiefs used the ordinances as an excuse to avoid keeping up roads, or performing other tasks demanded of them, on the plea that they could no longer force their slaves to work. The governor had to accept the argument, well knowing that it was spurious, for these very masters were still practising slavery.[229] The Colonial Office soon concluded that the abolition of the legal status of slavery had been over hasty.[230]

Other colonies were also lax. For instance, in Lagos which was part of the Gold Coast from 1874 to 1883, no edict was issued against African slavery which flourished, and the slave traffic brought young children into the island to serve as domestic servants. No vigorous action was taken for fear of disturbing trade with the interior.[231] Slavery was also at times 'winked at' in Sierra Leone.[232]

Where possible British expansion took the form of protectorates rather than colonies. The main reason for this was that the former could be ruled through their own chiefs, with fewer officials and fewer services. They were cheaper. But there was another advantage in that slavery could be tolerated, for, strictly speaking, protectorates, unlike colonies, were not British soil.[233] They could, thus, be ruled with less fear of provoking African reaction and disrupting the local economy for it was widely believed that Africans would not work for such wages as could be offered to them. The lesson learnt on the Gold Coast by experience was that, where possible, the institution should be left alone. The slave trade, however, was in theory not tolerated in either colonies or protectorates. But as long as slavery existed, it was bound

226 Claridge's statement that traders were diverted away from British territory for fear of losing their slave porters must be treated with caution. The authorities were always careful not to encourage desertions and there is evidence that trade between Accra and Salaga increased in the 1880s. I am indebted to Mr D. H. Jones for this information.
227 Freda Wolfson, 'British Relations with the Gold Coast, 1843–88', London Ph.D., 1950, p. 331
228 Claridge, II, p. 183. Most remained with their masters. Claridge thought them a numerous and contented class in 1915.
229 Metcalfe, p. 400
230 *Ibid.*, p. 399
231 Gordon, ch. 5
232 Fyfe, *A History of Sierra Leone*, Oxford 1962, pp. 323, 429
233 For some of the correspondence on this subject, see Newbury, *Documents*, pp. 294 ff., 365 ff.; see also A. A. B. Aderibigbe, pp. 4 ff.; McIntyre; C. Fyfe, pp. 323, 428–9; Flint, *Goldie*, p. 49; Claridge, pp. 178–81; Wolfson, 'British Relations', p. 252.

to continue at least on a small scale unless close administrative control was established, and even then smuggling was hard to suppress.

The occupation of Egypt in 1882 gave Britain the opportunity to press the Khedive to abolish slavery there. Lord Granville indeed seriously considered doing so.[234] It would have been popular in England and Foreign Office officials believed it was the only way to kill the slave traffic.[235] But Sir Evelyn Baring, Consul-General in Cairo, who had the difficult task of supervising the Egyptian Government, vigorously opposed any such radical move.

He argued that slavery was already dying a natural death in Egypt, and that for the time being the slave trade bureaux established under the terms of the convention of 1877,[236] to which slaves could apply for freedom, were sufficient to prevent any abuses. He agreed that they were often deterred from applying for manumission by the difficulty of making a living as free men and women, but he proposed to introduce some system of helping them to find jobs. This problem was acute in Egypt where labour was organised into monopolistic guilds and there were few opportunities for freed slaves.[237] In fact the government could only confer a very limited degree of liberty on those fugitives it freed. It could try to ensure that they were allowed to live and work where they wished, but by Muslim practice they could neither marry nor inherit property without the consent of their masters. The women, therefore, were often driven into prostitution. Granville suggested a tax on male slaves might encourage the development of a free labour market[238] but Baring feared this would be extremely unpopular.[239] A tax on women slaves was not considered as this would mean invading the privacy of the harem to know how many there were. Baring carried the day and no further steps were taken to end slavery in Egypt for the time being.

The problem of freed slaves

The problem raised by this correspondence, of what to do with freed slaves, is worth considering, for it existed wherever the British were in a position to liberate them, and it often deterred a consul from helping them to obtain manumission. The matter depended upon the existence of a free labour market. In Zanzibar, this was developing by the 1880s, and the freed

234 Minute by Granville, 12 Sept. 1882, FO 84/1625
235 Minutes by Kirk and Hill on Admiralty to FO, 20 Dec. 1882, FO 84/1694
236 Several bureaux were established in different parts of the country to register manumissions and help find jobs for the freed, see Baer, pp. 433 ff.
237 *Ibid.*, p. 438; Baring to Salisbury, no. 10 Af., 2 April 1889, FO 84/1972; Baring to Salisbury, confidential and No. 5 Af., conf., 30 April 1890, FO 84/2057.
238 Granville to Baring, no. 3, 15 April, 1884, FOCP 5165
239 Baring to Granville, *memo.*, 6 June 1884, *ibid*. All direct taxes were unpopular but Baring thought this one would arouse particular resentment.

slave found a ready-made community of fellows whom he could join. The watchful eye of the Consul, backed by a co-operative Sultan, could ensure that he was not re-enslaved.[240]

In Egypt and Tripoli, on the other hand, the difficulties of fending for themselves often drove the slaves back to their masters, or their owners persecuted them into returning by trumping up charges against them in collusion with the police.[241] In Benghazi the problem was particularly bad. The labour market was glutted and slaves were at times shipped to other Ottoman ports ostensibly for their own good. In reality the officials who had 'freed' them sold them out of the country.[242] The Consul complained that the rest often lost their papers and were re-enslaved, or lounged around the street, unable to find work and afraid to venture into the fields.[243] In Tunis, women freed through the Consulate were left unmolested only because they were thought to be under British protection.[244]

In Egypt under British domination, steps were taken to ease the position. To prevent collusion between masters and officials, the bureaux were taken out of the hands of local governors and placed under a special department in Cairo and manumissions increased at once.[245] A home was opened to look after freed women, paid for mainly by subscriptions raised by the Anti-Slavery Society in England. Even the home could often only place them in harems where it was virtually impossible to be certain how they fared. Baring reported an incident which illustrates the point:

'Mrs. Sheldon Amos . . . made the most tremendous row about a white slave belonging to . . . the Khedive's sister. She said the woman was ill-treated, that she was pining for her liberty, that she could not get out of the harem, that she appealed to me for protection, etc.; I took the case up and it gave me an infinity of trouble. Eventually I performed the unparalleled feat of having a slave from the harem of one of the Khedivial family landed at my door in charge of the Khedive's Chief Eunuch. I cross-questioned her. She said she was never so happy in her life, that she had not been in any way ill-treated, and that she wished to return to the harem. I then sent for Mrs. Amos. She saw the woman without me and told me she was quite satisfied, and that the woman might return to the harem . . . Mrs. Amos afterwards told me that this particular slave

240 Kirk to Salisbury, no. 9, 8 Jan. 1886, FOCP 5459

241 Cookson to Granville, no. 26, 28 June 1881, FOCP 4626; Baring to Rosebery, no. 6 Af,. 9 June 1886, and enc. report by Schaefer, 9 May 1886, FOCP 5459; Wood to Rosebery, no. 2 Af., 10 June 1886, FO 84/1768.

242 Thus as the French Consul pointed out the British Consul was merely procuring slaves for Turkish officials, Ricard to D'Estrées, 22 Feb. 1889, enc. in D'Estrées to Spuller, 4 March 1889, no. 78, FMAE/CC/Trip., 45.

243 Cameron to White, 26 Dec. 1888, enc. in White to Salisbury, no. 3 Af., 1 Jan 1889, FO 84/1971

244 Reade to Granville, no. 2 Af., 2 Dec. 1884, FO./84/1673

245 Baring to Rosebery, no. 6. Af., 9 May 1886, FOCP 5459

had been bribed to lie, and that she was, when I left Cairo, murdered. There is nothing impossible in this . . .'.[246]

Outside areas of British control, Britain could only exhort the authorities to help freed captives.

The problem was not limited to Muslim countries. In 1887 in Madagascar, over three hundred Makua freed by British efforts appealed to the Consul for help, saying they had been better off as slaves, when they had only one master. Now they were subject, like all Malagasies, to forced labour without food or pay and were abused and robbed by all Hovas. Although sympathetic, the British Government replied that it could do nothing since they were not British subjects.[247] There was also the fear that any intervention in the island would lead to diplomatic complications with France.

Difficulties on a larger scale were posed by the freeing of captives from slavers. These were 'raw' slaves, who had usually to be nursed back to health and always to be re-orientated. To the European, a man was free when he was turned loose to fend for himself. To the African, as has been seen, he was only free when he was restored to his own kin. When liberated from a slaver, he often regarded himself as the slave of the white man who had 'freed' him. Many of those freed from Atlantic slavers were absorbed into the British colony of Sierra Leone. Some of these found their way home but others remained in the colony and were recruited, sometimes forcibly, into the forces or settled in villages where they were often enslaved by other freed slaves.[248] Nor did the British authorities, anxious to provide labour for their Caribbean colonies, always show too much concern for their welfare. Before 1861 many were sent as 'free' contract labourers to the British West Indies where they were oppressed by the planters.[249]

Those freed in the Indian Ocean in the early days were sent to India, Mauritius, Natal or the Seychelles where they often ended up in bondage again or were forced to work for planters in conditions analogous to slavery.[250] Such arrangements proved unsatisfactory and laid Britain open to the charge that she was freeing slaves to stock her colonies with labour while trying to stop other powers from importing workers into theirs.

A happier solution was provided when she began distributing them among the missions in East Africa and paid for their maintenance until they became self-supporting.[251] But this had its drawbacks too for the coastal

246 Baring to Anderson, 15 Nov. 1889, FOCP 5459
247 Knott to senior naval officer or Consul-General, Zanzibar, 17 Dec. 1887; enc. in Haggard to Salisbury, 17 Jan. 1888, FOCP 5896 and Ferguson to Salisbury, 19 July 1888, SP/Ferguson.
248 Fyfe, numerous references; Newbury, *Documents*, pp. 180 ff.
249 See Asiegbu, pp. 34 ff.
250 See Renault, I, pp. 120–4. For instance, in India the adults were employed in Indian families and often re-enslaved. In the Seychelles they were forced to work on plantations and often oppressed.
251 Oliver, *Missionary Factor*, p. 22

people saw them working on mission lands and concluded that the missionaries were getting slaves for nothing, the navy having stolen them from their rightful owners.[252] 'Freedom' was in any case something of a mirage for the inhabitants of these settlements since they could not leave without fear of being re-enslaved.[253] The Universities Mission tried to return one group to their homeland but they refused to go beyond Masasi a hundred miles from the coast and had to be settled there as a mission colony.[254]

This problem of how to protect freed Africans was, of course, faced by all countries who freed them and all too often 'freedom' merely meant slavery under new names, such as apprenticeship or contract labour, or the liberators simply required forced labour. At the time of the Berlin Conference the French were embarking on a policy of establishing freed slave villages in the wake of their conquering armies in the western Sudan to take care of their prisoners of war as well as of liberated slaves and fugitives. Euphemistically called *villages de liberté*, these were placed on the military supply lines and provided forced labour for the French army.[255]

The subject in its full dimensions[256] is beyond the scope of this work but suffice it to say that by 1884 a number of solutions had been tried and many freed slaves had been successfully rehabilitated and numbers, particularly in West Africa, had returned home. But experience had shown that the freeing of a slave often merely transferred him from one sort of bondage to another and in the past, Europeans, including the British, had been as guilty of abusing liberated captives as anyone else.

The fugitive slave question

A question which posed great problems for all the representatives of 'civilisation'—the governors of British colonies, the commanders of warships and missionaries—was the problem of fugitive slaves. In West Africa, where the British colonies were tiny enclaves in slave holding communities, much friction with local peoples had resulted when they found that slaves were deemed free the moment they touched British soil. Governors had tried to overcome the difficulty by returning the runaways but the home

252 Mackenzie to Euan Smith, 18 Oct. 1888, enc. in Euan Smith to Salisbury, 22 Oct. 1888, FOCP 5770
253 Oliver, *Missionary Factor*, p. 53
254 *Ibid.*, p. 39
255 For a discussion of the French *villages de liberté* see Bouche. A few such villages were established in Senegal after slavery was abolished in the French colonies in 1848 but they languished under threat of raids by Moors and their inhabitants were fortunate to be able to become free wage labourers in St. Louis. On the other hand free slaves settled at Libreville in the 1840s were forced to work for the administration, Bouche, pp. 48 ff.
256 These dimensions include not only the fate of freed slaves in each country where slavery was practised but also the use, and often abuse of alternative sources of labour.

government had disallowed this, saying that only criminals might be extradited. Masters regarded the harbouring of their fugitives as barefaced robbery. The problem was particularly bad in Lagos and in the 1880s the governors tried to prevent fugitives from reaching the colony, and reprimanded anyone who encouraged them to come.[257] If a runaway could not be returned from a colony, however, he could be sent away from a protectorate,[258] and this was another advantage of protectorates over colonies.

With the occupation of the African coast by other colonial powers the question was likely to pose further difficulties. The British were faced with the invidious choice of returning the slaves, which would raise a storm in England, or of keeping them and perhaps driving away traders, who would take their goods to colonies with less rigid policies rather than risk losing their porters. Apart from diverting trade, there was the danger that neighbouring peoples might decamp altogether. There was clearly a need for a common policy. Fortunately for Britain, the French faced the identical difficulty in Senegal after 1880 when they, too, ceased to return fugitives, as a result of questions asked in the Senate.[259] By 1882 the Governor was complaining that the new policy was not only embroiling him with his neighbours on both sides of the Senegal to the point of war, but was bringing a flood of criminals into French posts.[260] Protests availed him nothing. Like his English counterparts he was merely reminded that he was to liberate the fugitives without alienating their masters, or driving away the trade upon which the prosperity of the settlements depended.[261] Exactly how to perform this feat was left to him. The main concern of the home governments, French and British, was that no untoward event should arise which would provoke parliamentary criticism or precipitate a local crisis.

Fugitives also sought asylum at British Consulates, as has been seen. Generally in cases of ill treatment, the Consul would ask the local authorities to free the slave and the request was usually granted. If there had been no cruelty, however, the slave was sent back to his master on the assurance that he would not be punished.[262] Consuls were normally on reasonable terms with the local governments and could be counted upon to handle the matter with tact, and the number of slaves who gained their freedom in this way was usually small. However, an over-zealous consul could cause a great deal of trouble. In 1884 while Suakin was besieged by Mahdists, the com-

257 Gordon, ch. 5

258 Although it was said to be 'contrary to the spirit of English law, and not to be sanctioned', Grey to Winnier, 19 Sept. 1850, Newbury, *Documents*, p. 303.

259 Before this they were expelled as vagabonds, which amounted to returning them, Bouche, pp. 54–5. See also Yves Saint-Martin, *Une source de l'histoire coloniale du Sénégal: Les Rapports de la Situation Politique (1874–91)*, Dakar, 1966.

260 Governor of Senegal to Rouvier, 20 March 1882. AOF/K/12

261 Jauréguiberry to Governor of Senegal, 2 May 1882, *ibid*.

262 Wylde minute on Vivian to Derby, no. 8, ST, 17 March 1877, FO 84/1472

mander of the British forces complained that the Consulate was becoming a 'house of call' for domestic slaves, who wanted to annoy their masters, and that this was hampering his attempts to gain the confidence of the local population at a time when the town was beset by enemies.[263] The Consul was warned that 'the slavery business' was not the most important part of his work.[264] Further difficulties arose when slave crews on Jidda dhows took to deserting in Suakin and claiming refuge at the Consulate. The British authorities feared that dhow owners might take their trade elsewhere rather than risk losing their crews. It was a relief when it was decided that, unless the slaves had been ill treated, they must be returned to their masters. This was justified on the grounds that they were not being sold and therefore the conventions with neither Egypt nor Turkey were being contravened.[265]

Difficulties also arose when slaves sought asylum on British warships. This question came to a head in 1876 when the government of India was particularly anxious to retain the friendship of the maritime Arabs and feared that their pearl fishing industry would be ruined if fugitives discovered they could gain their freedom by reaching a British man-of-war.[266] Instructions were issued that slaves were not to be taken on board unless their lives were in danger. This caused such an outcry from the humanitarians that a Royal Commission examined the whole matter. It found that international usage varied. German, Italian and American ships did not surrender fugitives. Russian vessels did not allow them on board unless they were in distress. Portugal and Holland thought they should be surrendered on request. France left the question to the discretion of the ship's commander. The commission decided that while a slave was not to be refused asylum if he was in danger, and once on board he was never to be surrendered, naval officers were to be careful not to receive a fugitive just because he wanted to be free. It was their job to see that trouble did not arise, either by refusing to let him on the ship or by sailing beyond the reach of runaways.[267] This was, of course, not acceptable to the humanitarians.

By 1884, long experience of the fugitive slave question had resulted in a cautious approach. Governors, consuls and naval officers had all been warned to take precautions to see that they did not have to give asylum if it was likely to embroil them with slave-holding peoples. The lesson had also to be painfully learnt by the missionaries. Imbued as they were with a deep

263 Fremantle to chief of staff, Cairo, 13 Nov. 1884, enc. in Baring to Granville, 30 Nov. 1884, FOCP 5165

264 Baring to Baker, 30 Nov. 1884, private, FO 633/5 no. 26

265 Baring to Granville, no. 9 Af., 26 Nov. 1884, and encs, FOCP 5165

266 See correspondence in *PP* LXX (1876) C-1413, ST no. 1

267 Report of the Royal Commission on Fugitive Slaves, 30 May 1876, *PP* XXVIII (1876) C-1516. This followed the example of the *May Frere* in 1873, which put to sea when the commander realised that a fleet of pearl fishing boats was leaving their safe anchorage in rough weather for fear their slave crews would take refuge on the ship, Commander of HMS *May Frere* to Acting Political Resident, Persian Gulf, 6 Sept. 1875, enc. 4, in Malet to Tenterden, 9 March 1874, *ibid.*

hatred of slavery and the slave trade, they found it particularly difficult to turn fugitives away.[268] In the early days some in fact eagerly received them, sometimes paying compensation to irate owners. This practice was soon given up in Nyasaland when it was found that it not only earned the missions the hostility of surrounding tribes but also involved them in unwelcome problems of having to discipline undesirable adherents.[269] Nearer to the coast and to the protection of the Zanzibar authorities, Protestant missions continued to harbour runaways in their freed slave settlements, against the advice of the Consul-General. They were a thorn in the side of the Arab community and were intermittently threatened with attack by infuriated owners unable to retrieve their legitimate property.[270]

The clear lesson learnt by the time of the Berlin Conference was that, as long as slavery existed, British officials, officers, and missionaries would have to treat runaways with great circumspection and be guided by the dangers of the local situation, rather than by their humanitarian instincts or even by the laws of British colonies. It was also obvious that as such colonies and protectorates acquired more European neighbours the difficulties inherent in the situation were liable to increase, unless a common policy could be implemented.

268 Particularly in cases where sick slaves took refuge with them with the knowledge of their masters, who demanded them back only when they had recovered. The law in Zanzibar was changed to prevent a master doing this. He had either to reclaim the slave while he was ill or not at all. W. P. Johnson, pp. 37–8.
269 See Oliver, *Missionary Factor*, ch. 2; Hanna, ch. 1; MacDonald, II, pp. 26 ff. and particularly pp. 197–210.
270 Oliver, *Missionary Factor*, pp. 54–6, 82

Part Two

The Slave Trade
and the Scramble for Africa 1884–90

Chapter Four

Humanitarian Causes and the Berlin Conference

The slave trade

The train of events from the signature of the Anglo-Portuguese treaty in February 1884 to the convening of the Berlin Conference the following November, and the story of the conference itself, are too well known to need more than the barest outline here.[1] However, the humanitarian aspects of the meeting have received little attention and since these are important in the story of the Brussels Conference, it is essential to know how they came to be raised at Berlin.

They played a small but significant part in the rejection of the Anglo-Portuguese treaty.[2] The main opposition to this treaty came from business circles and was led by James Hutton and Sir William Mackinnon, both of whom were supporting the efforts of King Leopold of Belgium to create a state in central Africa. They believed that whereas Portuguese rule over the mouth of the Congo would hamper British trade, the King, if he was allowed to establish himself, would open up central Africa to the commerce of all nations and to missionaries of all denominations. They visualised the Congo, under a disinterested philanthropic monarch, an image of himself the King was careful to foster, becoming a vast field for British enterprise to the mutual benefit of Britain and its African inhabitants.

Portugal's poor record against the slave trade induced the Anti-Slavery Society to support this agitation and they were joined by Protestant missionaries, who feared they would be discriminated against if the area fell into Portuguese hands.[3] This gave the opposition a sounder moral basis than it would have had, had it consisted only of businessmen, open to the charge that their motives were dictated by purely pecuniary interests.

1 See S. E. Crowe, *The Berlin West Africa Conference 1884–1885*, London, 1942; for a recent study see Wm. Roger Louis, 'The Berlin Congo Conference', ch. 5 in P. Gifford and Wm. Roger Louis (eds.), *France and Britain in Africa*, New Haven 1971 (henceforth 'Berlin Conference'); for a study based on the Portuguese and French archives, see Pinto, pp. 211 ff.
2 For this whole subject see Anstey, *Congo*, ch. 6; Pinto, pp. 211 ff.
3 Anstey, pp. 122 ff.; King Leopold was himself a Catholic but he had both Protestants and Freemasons in his service.

The domestic agitation, however, merely delayed ratification of the treaty until the opposition of other powers and its rejection by Germany finally killed it.[4] In these international negotiations humanitarian questions played virtually no part. The issues occupying the attention of the powers in the summer of 1884, as the scramble for Africa gained momentum, were territorial and economic. King Leopold, having received American recognition for his nascent state, was consolidating his position on the ground. France was expanding in West and Central Africa and on the Red Sea coast, while Germany was establishing colonies in West and South-West Africa and Britain laid the foundations of her protectorates on the Lower Niger, in the Oil Rivers and Somaliland. These events brought much of the African coast under European rule and ended British influence in some of the areas which had long been under her informal domination.

Furthermore, Britain lost the initiative in the Congo question. This passed to Germany, when Bismarck suggested to France that together they call a conference to settle it.[5] Their aim was to maintain freedom of trade and navigation on the Congo and free navigation on the Niger, two rivers which up to now had been open to the commerce of all nations, and to agree upon a formula for future annexations on the African coast. To add weight to the decisions of the conference it was decided to invite not just the African colonial powers, Britain, Germany, France, Portugal, Spain, Turkey and Italy, but also Russia, Austria, the Scandinavian states, Holland, Belgium and the United States of America.

The conference arose, therefore, out of a British diplomatic defeat, the rejection of the Anglo-Portuguese treaty, and a Franco-German *rapprochement*, itself a disquieting departure for Britain at a time when her occupation of Egypt had earned her French hostility and made her dependent on the diplomatic support of the Germans and their allies, Italy and Austria. Britain had been worried by French colonial expansion and shaken by Germany's eruption on the African scene. Her colonial supremacy was being challenged. To some it seemed that her lead as a world power was endangered.[6] She had no objection in principle to a conference and recognised that free trade and navigation on the Congo were in her interest, but there was a real danger that she might lose control of the Niger.

On the lower Niger, however, George Goldie and his National African Company bought up or amalgamated with their French competitors and Britain's trade was, therefore, unchallenged, while the treaties signed with local rulers were laying the basis for political power.[7] The company expected to be given a charter to rule the region and Britain came to the conference determined to resist any plans for international control of the river.

How to retain pre-eminence on the Niger and to safeguard British trade

4 *Ibid.*, p. 162; Pinto, pp. 211 ff.
5 For all these negotiations see Crowe, pp. 24 ff; Pinto, pp. 232 ff.
6 See Louis, 'Berlin Conference' for views expressed in the press at this time.
7 See above, pp. 51–2.

on the Congo were the questions preoccupying the Foreign Office in the days before the conference. True to its traditions, however, the Anti-Slavery Society urged Granville to see that safeguards against slavery and the slave trade were written into any regulations framed for the Congo.[8] They were told that the matter would not 'be lost sight of'.[9] Britain was represented at Berlin by Anderson of the Foreign Office and her Ambassador to Germany, Sir Edward Malet. They were instructed to promote the advancement of commerce but not to forget the 'well-being of the native races'. Freedom of trade was not to 'degenerate into licence' and precautions were to be taken to see that such evils as the internal slave trade were ended.[10]

These were in fact platitudes. No concrete proposals were made and doubtless little result was expected, but the instructions would look well in a Blue Book and placate the humanitarians. There the matter might have rested had not the Permanent Under-Secretary had a brainwave on the eve of the conference. He wrote to Granville:

> This country, is not likely to gain or lose anything by the Conference. The 'éclat' of it, such as it is, will appertain to Germany. It has occurred to me that G[reat] Britain might carry off all the honours of the meeting by being the first to propose (on so fitting an occasion) an international Declaration in relation to the *traffic in slaves* (la Traite), as distinguished from the institution of Slavery, making it a crime against the *Law of Nations*.[11] . . . The Declaration might be 'La Traite des Esclaves est désormais un crime interdit par le Droit des Gens, et de la compétence des Tribunaux de tous les pays civilisés, quelque soit la nationalité de l'inculpé.'
>
> If the Powers sh[oul]d object to the generality of that Declaration, we might propose to restrict it to Africa.

But, and herein lay an important point:

> the honour and credit of proposing either Declaration, . . . should be reserved to this country—and . . . no time sh[oul]d be lost in apprising Prince Bismarck of our intention to propose such a Declaration, otherwise we may be forestalled.[12]

On this Granville minuted 'many thanks I quite agree'. A telegram was despatched in all haste to Malet, who was told to do 'what is needful' to see

8 BFASS to Granville, 5 Nov. 1884, FO 84/1814
9 FO to BFASS, 14 Nov. 1884, *ibid.*
10 Instructions to Malet, 7 Nov. 1884, no. 59, Af., *ibid.*, and *PP* Africa, no. 8 (1884), LV 1884–5.
11 Similar declarations had been made at congresses about the navigation of rivers, privateering, blockades and other subjects.
12 Pauncefote to Granville, minute, 14 Nov. 1884, FO 84/1814, italicised here where underlined in the original.

that he was first to make the proposal.[13] It was feared that he might be forestalled by the United States[14] where King Leopold's pose as an opponent of the slave trade had made a strong appeal.[15]

The proposal was far-reaching for it would brand the slave trade everywhere, by land and sea, as a crime 'cognizable by the tribunals of all civilized countries whatever the nationality of the accused'.[16] Britain did not suggest that it be considered piracy since pirates were liable to seizure no matter what flag they were flying, and this would never be accepted by the maritime powers.[17]

Bismarck thought the declaration too stringent and feared that the inclusion of the slave traffic on land would cause difficulties in Africa.[18] Pauncefote soon concluded that all Germany was prepared to sanction was a 'moral declaration' without legal force and consequently of no practical value.[19] However, Sir Travers Twiss, a jurist who attended the conference in an unofficial capacity, also suggested that an attack on the slave trade on land would disorganise the African social system.[20]

Finally Malet asked the conference to declare that the export slave trade (*la traite*—which technically meant only the maritime traffic) and the commerce which fed it, were offences against the law of nations which all powers must suppress. But the French, who had not envisaged discussing the question[21] and thought general statements of principle beyond the scope of the conference,[22] proposed instead that only governments with territories in the 'conventional basin' of the Congo should engage to act against the traffic.[23] The United States wanted them also to agree to expel slave traders, but this raised legal difficulties since it implied banishment without trial and necessitated changes in criminal law.[24]

In the end the Berlin Act declared that the maritime slave trade (*la traite*) was forbidden by international law, and that the operations which furnished slaves for it on land and water 'ought likewise to be regarded as forbidden'. The powers with territories in the conventional basin of the Congo stated that their dominions would not serve as markets or transit routes for this

13 Granville to Malet, 15 Nov. 1884, no. 82 Af., *ibid.*
14 Minute by Pauncefote, 14 Nov. 1884, *ibid.*
15 Crowe, p. 80
16 Granville to Malet, no. 85 Af., 18 Nov. 1884, FO 84/1815
17 Minute by Pauncefote on Allen to Pauncefote, private, 21 Nov. 1884, *ibid.* Both the Anti-Slavery Society and Italy wanted the traffic declared piracy.
18 Malet to Granville, no. 104 conf., Af., 24 Nov. 1884, *ibid.*
19 Minute by Pauncefote, 9 Dec. 1884, on Twiss to Pauncefote, 3 Dec. 1884; Pauncefote to Selborne, 8 Dec. 1884 and enc., FO 84/1816
20 Malet to Granville, no. 27 Af., tel., 26 Nov. 1884, FO 84/1815
21 Instructions to Plens., no. 140, 8 Nov. 1884, FMAE/CP/All./59
22 Courcel to FMAE, 6 Jan. 1885, FMAE/CP/All./61
23 This was the area defined by the conference in which free trade was to prevail, see map 5.
24 Banishment was not a recognised punishment in the penal codes of some signatories.

traffic and that they would employ 'all the means at their disposal' to end it and punish those engaged in it.[25] They also bound themselves:

> to watch over the preservation of the native tribes, and to care for the improvement of the conditions of their moral and material well-being, and to help in suppressing slavery, and especially the slave trade.[26]

This was, as Hill said, 'sadly milk and watery'.[27] It certainly fell short of Britain's hopes of branding the traffic in all its forms as an international crime, and the provisions had little real value for there was no machinery to see that they were carried out, no practical measures were suggested and no common action was agreed. Each power was left to take what steps it wished in its own good time. On the credit side, however, the slave trade on land had now been condemned in an international instrument in so far as it furnished slaves for export and so had domestic slavery in the Congo and the trade which supplied it. Furthermore, the principle that 'native welfare' was a matter of international concern had been embodied in the Act, thus carrying one step further the process haltingly begun at Vienna so many years before.

If the results were disappointing for Britain, one of her objects at least had been served, for as Hill said: 'The Protocols of the Conference will show that it is not our fault [the agreement] . . . is not more practical.'[28] If some newspapers commented unfavourably on the 'hollow humanitarianism' of the Berlin Act,[29] the Anti-Slavery Society at any rate seemed to think a step had been taken in the right direction.[30]

Britain continued, however, to sign treaties with individual powers against the slave traffic. At Berlin in return for German support on the Niger question, she determined to recognise King Leopold's Association as a state, the Congo Independent State, and exchanged declarations which included a clause binding the King to prevent the slave trade and suppress slavery.[31] On the Congo, at any rate, the attack had begun, at least on paper.

It will be noted that the *engagés* traffic was not mentioned in the Berlin Act. Granville, spurred on by the Anti-Slavery Society, had suggested that Malet should try to get the question raised, but if possible by another power, to disarm any French suspicions that he was trying to 'interfere' in French colonies. Malet replied, however, that it was beyond the scope of the conference.[32]

25 Article IX, Berlin Act, E. Hertslet, *The Map of Africa by Treaty*, 3 vols., London 1909, 3rd ed. (henceforth *Map*), II, p. 474.
26 Article VI, *ibid.*, p. 473
27 Minute by Hill, 7 Jan. 1885, on Malet to Granville, no. 5 Af., 5 Jan. 1885, FO 84/1819.
28 *Ibid.*   29 Louis, 'Berlin Conference', p. 218
30 Minute by Hill, 7 Jan. 1885, on Malet to Granville, no. 5 Af., 5 Jan. 1885, FO 84/1819.   31 Declaration of 16 Dec. 1884, Hertslet, *Map*, II, p. 574
32 Granville to Malet, no. 154 conf., 13 Dec. 1884, FO 84/1817; Malet to Granville, no. 69 Af., 31 Jan. 1885, FO 84/1820

The liquor traffic

The Berlin Conference gave Britain the chance to embark on a new international 'humanitarian' crusade: the restriction of the sale of spirits to Africans. In some areas, mainly in West and South Africa, cheap imported liquors, known as 'trade spirits', were staples of African commerce. In places such as on the lower reaches of the Niger, the Zambesi and the Congo, they were virtually a currency.[33] This trade was old and well established and the demand was constant and growing. But, since spirits were too bulky for easy transport, the trade, except in South Africa, was largely limited to the coast or regions within easy reach of navigable rivers. On the whole consumption was restricted to rulers and richer Africans, who alone could afford to buy imported liquor. The large Muslim populations, if they held strictly to the tenets of their faith, did not take any alcoholic beverages. Thus in 1884 large areas of the continent and the majority of the African people were still untouched by this traffic. Most non-Muslim peoples brewed their own intoxicants, but these were 'beers' rather than spirits.

Humanitarians, headed by the missionaries and the Aborigines' Protection Society, objected strongly to the traffic on the grounds that it was demoralising, unproductive and hindered the advance of civilisation. There was a widespread belief that Africans were more prone to drunkenness than white men and a tendency to ascribe all manner of evils to the influence of alcohol.[34] The Church Missionary Society, for instance, solemnly warned Granville that it excited 'uncultured savages' to extend their 'dreadful practices of human sacrifice and cannibalism.'[35] There was strong feeling in humanitarian circles that the traffic was one of the worst evils to emerge from the contact between African and European and that it should be prohibited. It must be remembered that the temperance movement[36] was also militant in Britain at this time and that those who supported it at home supported it abroad. Temperance societies existed all over the country and were strongly upheld by various churches.

To forbid trade in a staple of African commerce, however, was no easy matter, particularly as taxes on liquor were an important source of revenue, especially in the British West African colonies. Direct taxes, introduced in mid-century, had proved so unpopular[37] that administrators came to rely

33 See A. H. M. Kirk-Green, 'The Major Currencies in Nigerian History', *Journal of the Historical Society of Nigeria*, 1960, pp. 132–50; D. J. Rankin, 'The Peoples and Commercial Prospects of the Zambesi Basin', *Scottish Geographical Magazine*, ix, 1893, pp. 225–40; W. T. Hornaday, *Free Rum on the Congo*, Chicago 1887, pp. 71–2.
34 See E. A. Ayandele, *The Missionary Impact on Modern Nigeria 1842–1914*, London 1966, ch. 10.
35 Memorial from the Church Missionary Society, December 1884, FO 84/1818
36 This movement began in the United States early in the nineteenth century and spread to Britain.
37 David Kimble, *A Political History of Ghana*, Oxford 1963, chs. 4, 8; Fyfe, p. 388; N. A. Cox-George, *Finance and Development in West Africa*, London 1961, pp. 78 ff.

on customs duties for their revenues and these naturally fell heavily on spirits, which were in constant demand at a time when Africans wanted few European goods. To officials the traffic was a heaven-sent source of income, badly needed to develop their territories.[38] Furthermore, the tax was easily collected through the customs machinery and could be justified on moral grounds since it cut consumption by raising the price,[39] although humanitarians thought it immoral to raise revenue from such a source.

Duties, however, could not be too high while the West African colonies were tiny enclaves surrounded by independent African peoples. If they were, trade would simply be diverted into rivers and ports not under British control and the colonies would lose a valuable source of revenue and an important branch of their commerce. The latter might be disastrous since all trade tended to follow that in leading articles. Hence they risked losing their established markets and source of African exports. Within limits the situation had been controlled by the morally questionable device of establishing customs posts in areas which were not actually administered, thus widening the catchment areas without assuming the expense and responsibility of governing them.[40]

In South Africa where the colonies were bigger, the Cape and Natal charged much higher duties than the West African colonies[41] and controlled sales to Africans within their borders by licensing laws. Taxes on liquor produced locally, however, were lower and the colonies, competing fiercely with each other, with the Boer states and with the Portuguese for the trade of the interior, sold spirits beyond their frontiers with little compunction.[42] As in West Africa, restriction was only possible if all the states adopted a common policy.

As more and more of the African coast came under European control high duties on liquor or even control of the traffic came within the realms of practical possibility for the first time, providing all the powers adopted similar measures. But great stretches of the coast were still not under effective control in 1884 and therefore smuggling might defeat any steps taken.

Granville had chided Bismarck, when the Anglo-Portuguese treaty was still under discussion, for his unwillingness to agree to a tariff imposing duties of more than 10 per cent *ad valorem* on brandy. He said that most colonial powers taxed spirits 'with a view to preventing the demoralization . . . of the

38 Some, while using the revenue, deplored the traffic. Lugard was to emerge as one of these, see F. Lugard, 'Liquor Traffic in Africa', *The Nineteenth Century*, xlii, 1897, pp. 766–84.

39 Meade of the Colonial Office wrote to the Foreign Office: 'We consider spirits a fit subject for taxation and we desire to restrict its importation', 15 April 1885, PRO 30/29/147.

40 This was done, for instance, in Sierra Leone and at Lagos, see Fyfe, pp. 401–2, Aderibigbe, p. 62.

41 For a discussion of the actual level of duties see below, pp. 276, 282.

42 See below, pp. 273, 276.

native races.'[43] However, although the Berlin Conference provided a forum for the discussion of general African questions, there is no evidence that he intended to raise the matter on humanitarian or any other grounds when the meeting began. He simply told Malet, as an afterthought to his instructions, that he hoped it 'might be placed on a satisfactory footing', whatever that might mean.[44] In fact it was first mentioned in passing by Italy, supported by the United States.[45]

No serious proposals on the subject might have been made at all had not the British delegates, particularly Anderson, come under the influence of Goldie. Goldie was in Berlin to further the interests of his company and he lost no time in urging that the transit of spirits on the Niger be prohibited. He contended that the trade was harmful to Africans, served no economic purpose since it was basically unproductive and stimulated no demand for other European goods, and hence commerce would be placed on a better footing were it to be eliminated.[46] There is no doubt, however, that it was to his advantage to secure control of the liquor trade on the Niger.

On the lower river palm oil and kernels in quantity could only be had in exchange for spirits.[47] In this region, now under British protection, the government was determined to retain the power to impose what taxes it wished on trade. From Goldie's point of view this meant that he could charge high duties on spirits. The company, as the administrator of the area, would simply pay these duties to itself,[48] and thus have a great advantage over its rivals who would bear the full burden of the tax. The proposed Berlin Act, however, allowed free transit on the Niger. Competitors could thus force their way upstream through the company's territories and trade beyond them without paying customs duties. If Goldie could forbid the free transit of liquor, he could prevent this and at the same time both ensure himself a monopoly of the spirits trade should it spread up river and prevent any smuggling into his dominions. He could thus defeat the conference's declared intention of keeping the Niger open to the trade of all nations.

The actual form of the company's charter was still not settled at this time;[49] there is no evidence in that document that Anderson realised he was

43 Granville to Ampthill, no. 10 Af., 30 June 1884, FO 84/1812, and *PP* Africa, no. 7 (1884), LV, 1884–5.
44 Granville to Malet, no. 65 Af., 12 Nov. 1884, FO 84/1814, and *PP* Africa, no. 3 (1884), LV, 1884–5, C-4360
45 Protocol II, *PP* Africa, no. 4 (1884), LV, 1884–5
46 He put forward this argument in 1895, see K. K. D. Nworah, 'Humanitarian Pressure Groups and British Attitudes to West Africa 1895–1915', London, Ph.D. 1966, p. 153.
47 See Flint, *Goldie*, p. 79–80
48 For the system subsequently set up by the company and the juggling with the balance sheets which enabled it to benefit from customs to the disadvantage of its rivals even though the Anglo-German agreement of 1885 stated that it could only charge duties sufficient to meet the costs of administration, see *ibid*., pp. 112 ff.
49 For this subject see *ibid*., pp. 62 ff.

furthering Goldie's monopolistic aims.[50] He certainly argued the case with his superiors entirely on humanitarian grounds, saying that he had consulted Stanley,[51] Dr. Laws—a missionary in Nyasaland—German and Dutch traders and 'many others' before reaching his conclusions. His views are of interest for they were widely held at the time and they were to mould the proposals made at the Brussels conference of 1889.

He did not believe that the inhabitants of the coast could be protected against the spirits traffic. This was convenient for it meant that the established trade in the coastal areas need not come under attack. But the interior was still mainly 'uncontaminated'. In Central Africa, much of it reached by way of the Congo, most peoples brewed their own 'beers'. He thought these were not particularly harmful physically as large quantities were required to produce intoxication, but they caused moral degradation and those who drank them soon acquired a 'taste for drink' and took the more readily to imported spirits. Here lay the seeds of real trouble for:

> the effect on them, when they drink largely, is disastrous; they know no moderation; the excitement of the brain makes them quarrelsome and uncontrollable; diseases which were comparatively harmless become malignant, and liver complaints rapidly carry them off.[52]

It would be some time, Anderson believed, before the traffic spread far inland owing to the expense and difficulties of carriage, but if, as was confidently expected at Berlin, there was now a rapid expansion of trade and a consequent increase in the purchasing power of Africans, liquor would come within their reach and the processes of 'civilisation and demoralisation' would be simultaneous. Once having the taste for spirits, they would distil for themselves. In the Muslim regions of Lake Chad and the central Niger, where no alcohol was drunk and the people were 'highly civilised', it would be the more reprehensible if European penetration created this taste and reduced the population to 'barbarism'. Religion and custom would prove no barrier and the wealth of the area would 'facilitate'

50 Hill certainly does not seem to have understood the implications for he minuted that to charge high duties on spirits on the Niger would be 'in the interests of humanity and not to our advantage', minute on Malet to Granville, no. 214 Af., 12 Dec. 1884, FO 84/1817. The Foreign Office later did not officially support Goldie's monopolistic aims but in the long run did little to thwart them. For a discussion of this see Flint, *Goldie*, pp. 62 ff.

51 Described by the American delegate, Sanford, as a friend of Goldie's, Sanford to Mackinnon, 27 Dec. 1884, MP/203/34

52 Anderson memo, enc. in Malet to Granville, no. 263 Af., 22 Dec. 1884, FO 84/1818. The Belgian Plenipotentiary, on the other hand, believed that where South American Indians succumb 'physically to drunkenness, . . . the African succumbs morally', Protocol 5, Berlin Conference, Africa no. 2, *PP* LV 1884–5. It was also thought that Europeans who imbibed alcohol in the tropics were more liable to liver complaints than they were in Europe, see H. H. Johnston, 'Alcohol in Africa', *The Nyasa News*, August 1894, pp. 145–7.

its fall. If the transit of spirits were prohibited on the Niger some forty million Africans, wrote Anderson, would be saved from this disaster.[53]

The proposal was all the more acceptable to Granville because Goldie represented the only British interest established on the river and if he favoured it there was no reason to thwart him,[54] more particularly as the Foreign Office was fortified with the knowledge that most of the trade spirits sold in West Africa were not made in Britain. They were mainly continental potato or corn spirits sold at an extraordinarily low price, costing the trader around two shillings for an entire case of twelve bottles, including the containers.[55] Germany was the greatest producer, although quantities of cheap liquor also came from Holland and the United States.[56] Most British liquors were more expensive[57] and spirits were not listed in a Board of Trade catalogue of the main British goods exported to West Africa in 1883.[58] The liquor sold on the Niger, in particular, seems mainly to have been German, even though some of it was shipped from Rotterdam.[59]

Thus, although British traders, including Goldie himself, dealt heavily in trade spirits, no major British manufacturing interest stood to lose by restricting the traffic. It would be in effect a discriminatory move against foreign goods and if liquor were not available, it might be confidently expected that Africans would buy more British manufactures.

There was the additional advantage that any steps against the liquor trade would appeal to a section of the British electorate. Petitions from temperance societies made this clear[60] and perhaps spurred Granville on to

53 Memo. by Anderson, conf., 10 Dec. 1884, inc. in Malet to Granville, no. 214 Af., 12 Dec. 1884, FO 84/1817; memo. by Anderson, enc. in Malet to Granville, no. 263 Af., 22 Dec. 1884, FO 84/1818

54 The Colonial Office were ready to agree provided all the other powers did so too, so that they could be sure that British traders were not placed at a disadvantage against foreign competitors.

55 Twelve bottles represented $1\frac{3}{4}$ Imperial gallons. Lugard gives the price as 1s. $9\frac{1}{2}$d., *East African Empire*, I, p. 214; in 1889 the Colonial Office thought that the price of German gin shipped free at Hamburg was 2s. 4d a case, minutes of a meeting held in the Colonial Office, 8 Jan. 1890, FOCP 6197.

56 Cheap liquors were also made elsewhere, but these were the greatest suppliers to West Africa.

57 The cheapest British spirits sold in West Africa were presumably those sold in areas not under European control. In 1883 256,507 gallons were sent there with a declared value of £36,318—the average price for $1\frac{3}{4}$ gallons was therefore 4s. $11\frac{1}{2}$d. as against the German price of 2s., PRO Customs/9/93.

58 Office of the Committee of the Privy Council for Trade to FO, 5 Nov. 1884 FO 84/1814. Customs records show that 302,078 gallons of spirits of British manufacture were sent to West Africa in 1883, however, and that they were worth £43,999. They formed only 1.76% of the total value of British manufactures exported to West Africa, which came to £2,494,919.   59 Flint, *Goldie*, p. 83, note 1

60 A petition of 9 Dec. 1884 came from the Church of England Temperance Committee, the United Kingdom Alliance and the Committee of the National Temperance League. Other letters came later from the Cambridge Temperance Society, the Aborigines' Protection Society, the Church Missionary Society and the London Missionary Society. See FO 84/1816 and FO 84/1817.

suggest that the sale of spirits be prohibited on both the Niger and the Congo.[61]

He dropped this proposal, however, when Malet said that Germany and Holland would never accept it as it would lead to the closure of their factories,[62] and simply asked the conference to prohibit, on humanitarian grounds, the transit of spirits on the lower Niger.[63] Britain was supported by Italy, Belgium and the United States, but Germany absolutely refused to agree. She was determined to protect both her existing and her future markets. This was hardly surprising as Europe was in the throes of the great trade recession of the years 1878–84 and liquor not only formed some 48 per cent of her total exports to Africa in 1883[64] but the traffic was growing rapidly. The export of spirits from Hamburg to West Africa alone in 1884 was one and a half times the total sent to the whole continent the previous year and the value of the trade from this port to West Africa had risen by three million marks.[65]

The French supported the Germans, voicing common suspicions when their plenipotentiary wrote:

on peut supposer qu'un certain sentiment de concurrence commerciale fortifie les Anglais dans les principes d'humanité et de tempérance dont ils se font avec tant de persistance les défenseurs au profit des populations Africaines voisines du Niger.[66]

In the face of determined opposition, Britain had to be content with the mere expression of a wish by the conference that 'native' peoples would be protected from the evils of the liquor traffic by an agreement between the signatories which would reconcile human rights with basic commercial interests.[67] Germany made it plain that she would not allow this to serve as an excuse to hamper free trade or impose differential duties. Nevertheless

61 Granville to Malet, no. 146 Af., 10 Dec. 1884, FO 84/1817
62 Malet to Granville, no. 219 Af., 13 Dec. 1884, *ibid.*
63 Protocol no. V and annexes, *PP* Africa, no. 4 (1885), LV, 1884–5, p. 133, C–4361
64 The Board of Trade believed that 27,690,800 kilos, or 6,091,245 gallons, of spirits were exported from Hamburg alone in 1883. See Office of the Committee of the Privy Council for Trade to FO, 5 Nov. 1884, FO 84/1814. German sources state that the total spirits export to Africa in that year amounted to 230,506 Doppelcentner (D-Ctr.). This would come to 23,050,600 kilos or 5,070,523 gallons, see F. M. Zahn, *Der Westafrikanische Branntweinhandel. Erwiderung auf die Offene Antwort des Herrn Reichstagsabgeordneten A. Woermann* (Gütersloh 1886), pp. 11–12.
65 Zahn states that Hamburg sent 351,290 D-Ctr, to West Africa in 1884. This comes to 35,129,000 kilos, or 727,453 gallons. His figures were taken from the report of the 6th Reichstag commission and tally well enough with those from American consular records, which show 33,086,800 kilos, Hornaday, p. 90. 3,000,000 marks equalled £150,000. Spirits formed 66% of Hamburg's trade to West Africa in 1884.
66 They thought, however, that it was because foreign traders made more out of the spirits traffic than British merchants, Courcel to FMAE, 19 Dec. 1884, FMAE/CP/All. /60.
67 Declaration enc. in Malet to Granville, no. 263 Af., 22 Dec. 1884, FO 84/1818, and published in Protocol VI, *PP* Africa, no. 4 (1885), LV, 1884–5, p. 133, C–4361.

Anderson did not regard this as a complete defeat. He believed that the declaration left the door open for African rulers to ask for the prohibition of the traffic in their territories and that European governments would find it hard to refuse by insisting on free transit. He hoped that such requests might be forthcoming.[68] Furthermore, the conference had not challenged Britain's right to levy what duties she pleased on her Niger protectorate, so Goldie could impose high taxes on the lower Niger and defend them on humanitarian grounds, in keeping with the spirit of the Berlin declaration.[69]

On the Congo, however, the Berlin Act specifically forbade the imposition of transit and import duties in the whole of the conventional basin of the river.[70] When this question was later raised at Brussels, Britain was to say that she had favoured import rather than export duties,[71] but at Berlin she made a statement which reads more as a plea against both. Trade on the Congo had hitherto been unhampered by duties or restrictions, and she agreed with the German view that customs houses were costly and hindered commerce and hoped that 'the natural resources of the country' would provide 'resources' to defray 'those moderate charges for government which should amply suffice for the wants of the territories in question'—a reflection on current British thinking on the modest needs of colonial governments.[72] The Germans, however, preferred export duties, believing them less liable to be discriminatory, easier and less vexatious to collect and more suited to a barter economy.[73] It was admitted that some duties might be necessary and eventually the conference decided to ban transit duties permanently, but to prohibit import duties for twenty years[74] by which time the whole economy might have changed and the situation be in need of reviewing.[75]

This decision was unpopular in Britain, where merchants feared that high duties might be imposed at the end of this period. However, as the French

68 In due course one arrived from the Emir of the key state of Nupe on the Niger begging Queen Victoria to forbid imports into his territories, Emir of Nupe to Rev. C. Paul, 1886, enc. in Moloney to Holland, no. 32 conf., 30 August 1887, COCP African 381. Precedents existed—Siam had made such a request, for instance.
69 For his subsequent policy see below ch. 6.
70 The 'conventional' basin stretched right across the continent (see map 5) and eventually included British, German, Italian and Portuguese territories in East Africa as well as parts of the French and Portuguese dominions in West and Central Africa and the Congo Independent State. Portugal retained her rights to charge duties in her existing East African territories as did the Sultan of Zanzibar on the coast.
71 She saw 'economic objections' to export duties which tended to raise the price of African goods on the world market, while import duties were more easily passed on to the African consumer.
72 Memo. by Crowe, 1 Dec. 1884, enc. in Malet to Granville, no. 164 Af., 1 Dec. 1884, FO 84/1816.
73 Import duties meant that goods had to be unpacked and this caused delays, *ibid.*, and Protocol IV, annexe 2, *PP* Africa, no. 4 (1885), LV, 1884–5, p. 133, C–4361.
74 Article IV, Berlin Act, Hertslet, *Map*, II, p. 472
75 Memo. by Crowe, 1 Dec. 1884, enc. in Malet to Granville, no. 164 Af., 1 Dec. 1884, FO 84/1816

pointed out, King Leopold's Association, which had been recognised as a sovereign state while the conference was sitting, had signed treaties prohibiting import duties with a number of powers,[76] and his neighbours could hardly charge such duties without driving their trade away into his dominions.[77] Furthermore, the French made it plain that they considered that the Berlin Act banned differential duties in the conventional basin for all time. This assurance contented the British representatives, for the important point was not so much what duties were to be imposed but to be sure that they would not be discriminatory.[78]

Anderson thought that in spite of the ban on import and differential duties, the powers in the conventional basin of the Congo might still be able to control the retail sale of liquor within their territories by police and sanitary regulations. This would not prevent the import of spirits, however, nor their sale beyond the borders of these states, in regions still unoccupied.[79]

Results of the Berlin Conference

Britain could, on the whole, be well pleased with the results of the conference. She had retained undisputed control of the lower Niger. Her interests in the conventional basin of the Congo appeared to have been safeguarded by the Berlin Act, providing for free trade and navigation. Before the end of the meeting the Congo Independent State had been generally recognised and it adhered to the Act immediately it was signed. Britain could now look forward, it seemed, to the opening of Central Africa to British trade under the protection of the apparently benevolent king. In addition, the Act specifically enjoined that Christian missionaries of all denominations should be protected. The spread of Christianity and commerce was assured, the slave trade and slavery had been specifically condemned. On the other hand, the powers, in framing the rules for what might be considered 'effective occupation', had not challenged Britain's distinction between 'annexed' territories where domestic slavery could not be tolerated and protectorates where it need not be interfered with.[80] Britain had not only retained her leadership of the anti-slavery movement, but she had emerged as the protector of Africans against the evils of the liquor trade. If her efforts had been

76 Treaties had been signed with Britain, Italy, Germany, the U.S.A., the Netherlands, Austria and Spain. Similar ones were later signed with France, Russia, Belgium, Denmark, Portugal, Sweden and Norway, Hertslet, *Map*, II, pp. 543 ff.

77 Malet to Granville, no. 27 Af., conf., 10 Jan. 1885, FO 84/1819

78 Malet to Granville, no. 130 Af., 21 Feb. 1885, FO 84/1822, and *PP* Africa no. 2 (1885), LV 1884–5, C-4284

79 Memo. by Anderson, enc. in Malet to Granville, no. 263 Af., 22 Dec., 1884, FO 84/1818

80 These clauses applied only to future occupations on the coast anyway and most of the coastline had been appropriated, see Articles XXXIV, XXXV, Hertslet, *Map*, II, pp. 484–5.

thwarted, she could take pride in the fact that true to her traditions she had tried and failed to get co-operation on a matter of African welfare. She had scored a moral victory at least on the international stage.

The arms traffic

On one question, however, which was later to be put forward as a humanitarian measure, she had taken no steps. This was the restriction of the arms traffic to Africa. In the discussions over the Anglo-Portuguese treaty Granville had admonished Bismarck for his reluctance to impose special taxes on munitions. Most colonial powers, he said, did this in order 'to prevent the ... mutual destruction of the native races.'[81] A glance at Britain's own policy, however, will show that this was a euphemism.

Arms, like spirits, were a staple of African trade and this commerce had important political and economic repercussions on the continent. Arms were wanted for warfare, self-defence, hunting, protecting crops against animals and as barter goods. They were also fired on ceremonial occasions. Their possession could vitally affect the power and prosperity of a ruler, a group or people who, if they made effective use of them,[82] could dominate their neighbours. Rulers would often attempt to monopolise the trade in arms and ammunition to prevent any challenge to their power.[83] Africans would block trade routes to stop them from reaching their enemies or rivals,[84] or simply to control this valuable commerce. They would remain on friendly terms with those colonies[85] or traders through whom they could get munitions,[86] and would sometimes welcome missionaries in the hope that they would bring arms.[87] In some areas, such as on the Niger, they might

81 Granville to Ampthill, no. 10 Af., 30 June 1884, FO 84/1812; *PP* Africa, no. 7 (1884), LV, 1884–5, C-4205
82 For a tentative discussion of the importance of firearms in Africa see Gavin White, 'Firearms in Africa: an introduction', *JAH* xii, 2, 1971, pp. 173–84 and for discussion of particular areas see the collection of papers in *JAH* xii, 2 and 4; Smaldone.
83 Numerous examples can be cited. I will give a few from regions far apart: Sultan Yusuf of Wadai (1874–98) exercised a monopoly of powder, so did the Sultan Barghash of Zanzibar; Tswana chiefs tried to monopolise the arms trade, as did the ruler of Nupe.
84 Examples could be multiplied. For instance, the Egba and Ijebu and others tried to block the passage of arms from Lagos to the north, see Aderibigbe, p. 102 and S. A. Akintoye, 'The Ondo Road eastwards of Lagos *c.* 1870–95', *JAH* x, 4, 1969, pp. 581–598, and the Ganda tried to prevent their reaching Bunyoro, see above, p. 137. Both Dahomey and Asante prevented arms going north, R. A. Kea, 'Firearms and warfare on the Gold and Slave Coasts from the sixteenth to the nineteenth centuries', *JAH* xii, 2 1971, pp. 185–213, p. 201.
85 Samory Touré, for instance, took care to remain on good terms with Sierra Leone.
86 The Arab traders in East and Central Africa were welcomed by rulers like Mutesa of Buganda to whom they supplied arms.
87 Examples can be drawn from Buganda to South Africa.

demand them as 'dash' before they would give merchants permission to trade. The trade pattern might be centred upon a good market for guns, caps or powder.[88] In South Africa concessions were often paid for by presents of arms to rulers.[89]

European policy was affected as well as African. After the Asante war of 1873–4, for instance, Britain was anxious to annex the ports through which the Asante got munitions and this was an important factor in inducing her to open what proved to be abortive negotiations with France to divide West Africa into British and French spheres of influence.[90] In short the desire to acquire arms or to control the supply underlay much of the policy of both African rulers and the colonial powers.

By 1884, however, Britain had not developed any coherent policy towards the arms traffic. She had imposed occasional embargoes to prevent them from reaching her enemies, such as the Asante or the Zulu. These had merely shown the difficulty of restricting the trade as long as the colonies were small enclaves surrounded by independent African peoples and rival colonial powers or European traders were established in the neighbourhood. Attempts to cut off supplies to the Asante during and after the Asante-British war of 1873–4, for instance, merely diverted the traffic and with it much other trade, away from the Gold Coast to Assinie and other ports where French and British traders did flourishing business at the expense of law-abiding merchants on the Gold Coast.[91]

Equally, when Natal cut off shipments of arms to Portuguese-controlled Delagoa Bay in 1874, she found that, as the Cape did not follow suit, the only result was that she lost her markets[92] to commercial rivals from her sister colony. Efforts to stop the Zulu acquiring arms around the time of the Zulu war of 1879 showed the complexity of the problem. The main suppliers were Dutch and other traders established in Lourenço Marques, but arms also came from Nossi Bé and Tamatave in Madagascar, where they were obtained from a French firm and shipped in small craft to the mainland. The Portuguese restricted the traffic through Lourenço Marques, but representations to the French merely elicited the response that since the arms were bought in America and transported in American ships they had no means of interfering.[93]

In her West African colonies Britain imposed duties on munitions in

88 Arab traders in East Africa, for instance, would buy guns in Zanzibar, but get their gunpowder from Portuguese territories where it was cheaper, see above, p. 103.
89 See E. A. Walker, *A History of South Africa*, London 1928
90 Hargreaves, pp. 172 ff
91 Wolfson, 'British Relations', pp. 387 ff
92 She therefore lifted the ban from 1875 until the eve of the Zulu war, when it was re-imposed, but it was then said that she had not regained the markets lost in 1874, Bulwer to Hicks Beach, 3 April 1879, secret, and enc. report of the Attorney General, 5 March 1879, COCP African No. 190 (CO.879/15).
93 Lyons to Salisbury, 27 May 1879 enc. in FO to CO, 31 May 1879, COCP African No. 208 (CO 879/17).

order to raise revenue and her merchants bartered them to the peoples of the interior. She resisted French pressure to restrict the traffic in the 1870s and early 1880s. Not only did she think it impractical since much of the coast was either independent or, if it was claimed by a European power, was not effectively administered so that smuggling could not be prevented, but she also did not believe that any British or even humanitarian objective would be served.

The matter was debated in the Colonial Office in 1882, when the Colonial Secretary suggested that restriction might stop the petty wars in the interior which hindered the expansion of commerce. The Governor of Sierra Leone objected. Such wars, he said, had 'unceasingly prevailed' before the introduction of firearms and these weapons had shortened them and so lessened suffering.[94] An embargo would merely encourage those peoples who could get smuggled arms to raid defenceless neighbours. It would also seriously curtail the ability of Africans to resist European encroachment to the advantage of the French, whom he regarded as the only aggressors in West Africa. These arguments were accepted and France's proposal for restricting the traffic along the north-west coast of Liberia was dropped, to her disgust. She thought Britain was merely protecting a lucrative trade[95] which attracted caravans from the hinterland.

In South Africa, the Cape and Natal also taxed firearms and ammunition, and disarmed their African populations as a matter of policy, as did the Boer Republics.[96] However, duties on munitions were a lucrative source of revenue and arms were an important branch of the African trade of the interior, for which the British and the Boers competed fiercely with each other and with merchants from Portuguese territory. Throughout the decade of the 1870s, the British colonies imported large quantities of arms quite openly. Duty was paid upon them and they were traded all over southern Africa. They were smuggled through the Transvaal where there were virtually no authorities to stop them, and even reached the Zambesi.[97] Occasional embargoes were placed on sales to certain areas,[98] but no serious general attempt to stop the traffic was made. As in West Africa, it could only be ended by international agreement. Unilateral action would merely throw the trade into the hands of rivals.

94 Havelock to Kimberley, no. 1 conf., 24 Feb. 1882, COCP no. 381 African. The administrator of the Gambia argued that restriction would deprive weaker tribes of the means of using fire-power and good defensive positions to ward off superior numbers of assailants, Gouldsbury to Havelock, 11 Feb. 1882, enc. in *ibid*.

95 Jauréguiberry to Governor, Sénégal, 31 Feb. 1883 (?), AOF/K/12. The French had to repeal their restrictions in the Rivières du Sud in the face of protests from French traders that they were unable to compete with foreign rivals.

96 Walker, pp. 356, 359, 376, 386–7, 390.

97 Memo. by Dawnay, 12 Dec. 1888, enc. in Euan Smith to Salisbury, no. 372, 15 Dec. 1888, FO 84/1911.

98 For instance to Zululand in the late 1870s and to South-West Africa in the early 1880s where the Herero and Khoi-khoi were at war, Walker, p. 403.

On the shores of the Red Sea and Gulf of Aden, the British were more cautious. On this strategically important coast lying on the route to India, and from which Aden drew its food supplies, they were anxious to keep the peace. Egypt had tried to restrict the arms traffic here and had been particularly anxious to prevent the Ethiopian rulers in the interior from building up their military strength. Britain, mindful of her interests in Egypt, had supported her, turning a deaf ear to Ethiopian pleas for arms.[99] With the withdrawal of Egypt from the coast after the outbreak of rebellion in the Sudan, however, Britain regarded the Emperor Yohannes as a friendly Christian ruler, a counterpoise to the Mahdi, and signed a treaty in 1884 allowing him to import arms freely through Massawa.[100] As the Berlin Conference drew to an end, however, Italy occupied this port, encouraged by the British who feared French designs in the area. Within a few months Yohannes was protesting that the agreement was being broken. Italy made spurious denials but Britain took no action.[101]

On the Somali coast further south Britain was now established at Zeila and France and Italy were expanding from their bases at Obock and Assab. Each struggling precarious little colony hoped to attract caravans from the interior and arms were a powerful draw for the trade of Shoa where Menelik was building up his power.[102] British officials, however, were anxious that their Somali and Afar neighbours, among whom warfare was endemic, should not get firearms or even learn to use them,[103] for fear that the British enclave would be endangered and its trade hindered by fighting and slaving in the hinterland. They therefore forbade imports of munitions through British territory. Since this would clearly give the French and Italians an advantage in building up their trade and influence in the area,[104] the British tried to get their co-operation. France agreed to control the transhipment of arms in Aden[105] but this was of limited value[106] and Granville

99 Pankhurst, *Economic History*, pp. 587–92
100 See above, p. 114
101 Pankhurst, *Economic History*, pp. 592–3
102 For the internal power struggle in Ethiopia see R. A. Caulk, 'Firearms and Princely Power in Ethiopia in the Nineteenth Century', *JAH* xiii, 4, 1972, pp. 609–630 (henceforth 'Firearms').
103 Blair to Secretary, Bombay Government, 10 Oct. 1884, enc. in Godley to Pauncefote, 27 Nov. 1884, FOCP 5057; Hunter to Baring, 20 Nov. 1884, enc. in Baring to Granville, 29 Nov. 1884, *ibid.* The government of India was most unwilling to allow the Germans to recruit Somalis in 1889 for fear of the influence men trained in the use of arms would have on their return, Salisbury to Malet, no. 231 Af., conf., 31 May 1889, FO 84/1954.
104 British merchants complained that they had not the same facilities for importing arms as French and Italians using Obock and Assab, while officials feared a loss of influence in the area, Hunter to Baring, 20 Nov. 1884, enc. in Baring to Granville, 29 Nov. 1884, FOCP 5057.
105 Pankhurst, *Economic History*, pp. 590–1; Waddington to Granville, 29 Jan. 1885, FOCP 5149.
106 This agreement was particularly useful before port facilities were expanded on the

opened negotiations with Italy to stop the traffic on the coast itself, hoping France would agree to it.[107] France and Italy, however, were less worried about the local danger. The caravan routes to the highlands from their territories were now open to Europeans and their merchants were vying with each other for the trade of Shoa by supplying arms to Menelik. Both powers also wanted his friendship, the French because of their rivalry with England and the Italians because they had designs on Massawa and its hinterland which was controlled by Menelik's overlord Emperor Yohannis.[108] The talks had borne no results therefore by the end of the Berlin Conference.[109]

In sum, any steps hitherto taken by Britain to restrict the arms trade had been prompted not by humanitarianism but by political or fiscal considerations. Beyond the borders of her colonies and away from the strategically important Red Sea area, she was willing enough to sell munitions to Africans unless she was at war with them or feared attack or disorders. Her colonies counted on the traffic to provide customs revenues, attract trade and extend their influence in the hinterland. Her merchants regarded it as an important branch of their business, more perhaps for its power to draw other trade than for its actual value in pounds sterling which was comparatively small.[110] Its value cannot be measured in purely monetary terms for, in some areas, such as on the Niger above the palm oil belt, no trade could be done at all unless arms and ammunition were offered.[111]

Some indication of the value of the traffic to the British arms industry, as opposed to its value to individual traders, can be elicited from customs records which show that in 1883 sixteen per cent of the total exports of

coast as larger ships had to put in at Aden, but it did not close the door to shipments direct to the coast.

107 FO to IO, 13 Dec. 1884, FOCP 5057; IO to FO, 17 Dec. 1884, *ibid.*; Granville to Lumley, no. 275 conf. 29 Dec. 1884, *ibid.*

108 Pankhurst, *Economic History*, pp. 590–2; for Franco-Italian rivalry in Shoa see Caulk, 'Menelik II', pp. 61 ff.; for France and the arms trade see Agnès Picquart, 'Le commerce des armes à Djibouti de 1888 à 1914, mémoire de mâitrise', Sorbonne 1970; H. Brunschwig, 'Une colonie inutile, Obock, 1862–1888', *Cahiers d'études Africaines*, Paris 1968.

109 The Italians said they would consider an agreement provided France accepted it, Lumley to Granville, tel. no. 3, 5 Jan. 1885, and no. 8 conf. 13 Jan. 1885, FOCP 5149. By the end of the year, however, they were saying that to try to prevent arms reaching Ethiopia was as hopeless as trying to stop the introduction of cholera, Lumley to Salisbury no. 255, 18 Dec. 1885, FOCP.

110 The greatest proportion of British arms shipped direct to Africa went to 'western Africa—not particularly designated', that is the whole coast from Liberia to the Cape but excluding European colonies. In 1882 British customs returns show that the total value of all exports from Britain to this region was £1,078,794 of which only £85,650 (7.9%) was accounted for by arms and ammunition, PRO Customs/8/123. These figures are a rough guide only, since they take no account of British arms shipped from foreign ports or the proportion of foreign arms in the British export total.

111 Flint, *Goldie*, p. 80

British munitions were sent directly to Africa.[112] Of this a significant proportion went to the Niger and the Congo,[113] the two areas under discussion at Berlin. Arms formed only 8.7 per cent of the total value of British goods exported to this area,[114] but nevertheless for the arms manufacturers Africa, and particularly western Africa, was an important market,[115] and these figures take no account of British munitions sent via foreign ports.

There is no evidence that Granville considered these vested interests when formulating his policy towards the Berlin Conference, but it seems reasonable that no British minister would attack them unless certain of public support. In attempting to restrict the spirits trade, Granville had clear evidence that the temperance movement was behind him and he knew that no important British industrial interests were at stake. The arms traffic, on the other hand, consisted largely of British manufactures and only the humanitarians attacked it. Granville took no steps to raise the matter in Berlin. Other powers also showed no interest in the question. Malet

112 Total munitions exports in 1883 had a declared value of £1,575,618, of this £252,079 went to Africa, PRO/Customs/9/93. The actual breakdown is as follows:

Destination	Declared value in pounds sterling
West Africa, British	22,599
West Africa, Foreign settlements	15,031
Western Africa not particularly designated (including the Niger and the Congo) ..	109,339
South Africa, British	81,694
Egypt	7,070
Tunis	67
Algeria	95
Morocco	184
East Africa, Portuguese	5,486
East Africa, native states	10,514
	£252,079

See ch. 6 below for a further discussion of the arms trade and the export figures for 1889. Some of the arms imported into South Africa, as will be seen, were for European use. Presumably Zanzibar was the main East African importer. No direct trade with Ethiopia is shown.

113 £109,339 worth went to 'western Africa not particularly designated'. A large proportion of this must have gone to the Congo and the Niger, *ibid.*

114 Total exports of British manufactures to 'western Africa not particularly designated' came to £1,247,853, of which £595,438 was the value of cottons, PRO/Customs/8/124.

115 This must, of course, be seen in proportion to the total market for British munitions. In this context Africa was a much less important market than Australasia, which in 1883 took £333,516, and the U.S.A. which took £133,343. European countries also imported large quantities, PRO/Customs/9/93, some of which were re-exported to Africa. For further discussion of exports from Belgium see below, pp. 199n., 265n.

reported that the rising importance of the arms trade to Hamburg made it unlikely the Germans would consider restrictions.[116]

It may seem surprising that, on the eve of the European occupation of the continent of Africa, the colonial powers showed no real anxiety about a trade which was daily increasing African powers of resistance. However, a number of factors had up to this time prevented Africans from making the most effective use of firearms.

In the first place most of the arms sold to them were of such poor quality that gun-running was sometimes defended on the cynical grounds that Africans were abandoning effective spears for inferior weapons which often blew up in their hands.[117] To be efficient guns had to be properly maintained. They also had to be loaded with the correct ammunition and most African peoples found it difficult to get a steady supply. They showed much ingenuity in improvising. The Shona, for instance, used home-made powder and glass balls from soda-water bottles, telegraph wire and nails.[118] But the result was a great loss of fire-power. In the western Sudan Barth saw bullets made of light pewter bounce right off the wicker shields of intended victims.[119] Even if weapons were reasonably good and correct ammunition was used, methods of warfare had to be adapted to make the best use of firearms, and some peoples bought guns but failed to change their time-honoured ways of doing battle.[120] Others preferred their traditional weapons,[121] and in the remoter regions guns were expensive and rare.[122] The demand was great and growing, however. Even poor quality obsolete arms, wrongly loaded, could be valuable in war for they were noisy and frightening to uninitiated African villagers. They were also useful for ceremonies and were regarded as status symbols.[123] But they held no terrors for well-equipped Europeans.

At the time of the Berlin Conference a great change was in progress. A rapid series of technical improvements in the western world was putting a new complexion on the African arms trade. European armies had replaced flintlock muskets with percussion guns firing caps by the mid-nineteenth century. From the 1860s they were re-equipping with far superior steel-barrelled breech-loaders, using composite cartridges.[124] A decade later these

116 Malet to Granville, no. 207, Af., 10 Dec. 1884, FO 84/1817
117 This could also result from using the wrong ammunition or too much of it.
118 J. M. Chirenje, A. Atmore, and S. I. Mudenge, 'Firearms in South Central Africa', *JAH* xii, 4, 1971, pp. 545–56, pp. 553–4.
119 Barth, III, p. 223   120 The Zulu in the war of 1879, for instance.
121 The Masai, Kamba and Nyankole, for instance. See R. W. Beachey, 'The Arms Trade in East Africa in the Late Nineteenth Century', *JAH* iii, 3, 1962 (henceforth 'Arms Trade'), pp. 451–67, p. 452.
122 In the Central Sudan, for instance.
123 See Beachey, 'Arms Trade', pp. 451–2. Sir Garnet Wolseley believed the gun was the African's 'symbol of advancement', Wolseley to Hicks Beach, no. 76, 10 March 1880, COCP African no. 222.
124 i.e. Chassepots, Sniders, Martini-Henrys, see Beachey, 'Arms Trade', p. 452.

were outdated by the repeating or magazine rifle.[125] As western armies changed over to new weapons they unloaded obsolete models on the market. Belgian manufacturers, in particular, made a good business of buying these up, adapting or renovating them and selling them to English, German, Dutch, and to a lesser extent French, merchants trading to Africa.

As late as 1890 most of the weapons exported to the continent were still cheap percussion or flintlock guns, but breech-loaders were in growing demand,[126] and the demand was likely to be met as European armies sold their discarded weapons and unwanted black powder.[127]

The events of the next few years were to make this question a matter of international concern. They were also to give Britain an opportunity of returning to the attack on the slave and liquor trades.

125 i.e. Winchesters, Mannlichers, Lebels and Lee Metfords.
126 The Liège arms factories had 300,000–400,000 obsolete arms bought from various governments in stock in 1890 costing only 5–6 francs (4s.) each, and destined for the African market. They were mainly percussion guns and flintlocks. In some areas Africans found it easier to use flintlocks which did not require caps like percussion arms. New weapons of poor quality were also exported from Liège, including Sniders, Président du Syndicat des Fabrication d'Armes à Liège to Baron Whetnall, very conf., 15 Feb. 1890, no. 103, and Petition to Chimay, 17 Feb. 1890, no. 104, AEB/CAE/3.
127 Magazine rifles used smokeless powder.

Chapter Five

From Berlin to Brussels 1885–9

The scramble for East and Central Africa and the Arab reaction

The scramble for Africa gained momentum after the Berlin Conference. The next few years saw the appropriation of most of the still independent stretches of the coast and a race by the colonial powers to stake out claims in the interior. The Brussels Conference of 1889 arose directly out of the events in East and Central Africa.

Here, as has been seen, the Sultan of Zanzibar, controlled the east coast ports and exerted influence rather than wielded power over his followers in the interior. The few very hesitant steps he had taken, urged on by Kirk, towards assuming a more definite personal authority[1] had achieved little when he became aware of the European threat to his position. This was brought home to him late in 1882 after Tippu Tip arrived in Zanzibar at the head of a caravan of three thousand men with two thousand elephant tusks,[2] the fruits of twelve rapacious years in the interior. He informed Barghash that King Leopold's agents had asked for help in establishing a station in the interior and had offered in return to export his ivory down the Congo and supply him with the arms and ammunition vital for the maintenance of his power and for his trading operations.[3] The Belgians hoped with his co-operation to divert into their own hands the ivory trade of Central Africa and ship the spoils to Europe by way of the western coast. From 1879 Stanley had been establishing the necessary lines of communications along the Congo.[4] Late in 1883 he passed Arab posts and established his own station at Stanley Falls. He then took ten slave retainers of the Arabs back down

1 These amounted to very little. He established some posts on the route to Tabora and in 1881 recalled the liwali of Tabora and he ordered his flag to be flown at Ujiji, Renault, I, pp. 294 ff.
2 Bennett, *Mirambo*, p. 146
3 'Hamed ya Muhammed', para. 148; Norman R. Bennett, 'Captain Storms in Tanganyika', *Tanganyika Notes and Records*, 54, March 1960, pp. 51–63, pp. 52 ff. (henceforth 'Captain Storms').
4 Between 1879 and 1882 Stanley established stations on the Congo, built a road around the cataracts of the lower river and placed steamers on the upper river. Late in 1882 he began to sign treaties with Africans along the route prior to building a railway around the obstacles of the lower Congo, see Stanley, *Congo*, for his account of his activities.

river with him to see for themselves the power of the white man and the value of the new route.[5]

Barghash appreciated immediately the threat to the Arab commercial monopoly in East Africa and to his own revenues, drawn largely from monopolies on sales of ivory and gunpowder and from customs duties. He is believed to have deputed Tippu Tip to return to the Manyema and take over the whole Congo basin as far as the Atlantic in his name.[6] He thus opened the contest for power on the mainland between Arabs and Europeans. Supplied by the Sultan with munitions, Tippu Tip set out on his mission. In the next few years he, his partners, and their followers conquered large areas west of Lake Tanganyika and consolidated and extended their hold on the Upper Congo.

The task was not complete when the recognition of the Congo State by the great powers in 1884–5 cut the ground from under Barghash's feet. There followed the proclamation of a German protectorate in East Africa in the region just behind the coast, straddling the routes to the interior, and then the partition of the mainland into British and German spheres of influence. The British, French and Germans went on to delimit the Sultan's continental territories, conceding him only a strip ten miles wide along the coast from Tunghi Bay to Kipini and the Benadir ports.[7] In return for her consent France secured the recognition of her protectorate over the islands of Grand Comoro, Johanna and Mohilla giving her control of the whole Comoro group, over which the Sultan claimed suzerainty. In the eyes of Europe Zanzibar had ceased to be a power in the interior. Barghash acknowledged defeat and withdrew from the fray.[8]

It now lay with the colonial powers to turn their colonies to account. They all lacked resources. Public opinion in Britain and Germany was not yet converted to African empires, and King Leopold's Congo venture was a

5 Stanley, *Congo*, II, pp. 162 ff
6 The exact nature of Barghash's instructions are unknown but Tippu Tip later wrote that on hearing of the Belgian offer, Barghash urged him to hurry back to the Manyema, see 'Hamed ya Muhammed', para. 149. His subsequent actions and remarks to Europeans all point to his having been asked to take over the area for Zanzibar, Alison Smith 'Southern Interior', pp. 291–3; Bennett, 'Captain Storms', pp. 57–60; Renault, I, pp. 308 ff. As early as 1879 Kirk was commenting that the Arabs were now so far west that they might find it better to send their ivory down the Congo by steamer (see Kirk to Wylde, private, 16 April 1879, KP STE) and Barghash's hostility led King Leopold's agents to keep their aim of linking the upper Congo with the west coast secret in 1882, Bennett, 'Captain Storms', p. 52.
7 For an outline of the events of the partition see J. Flint, 'The Wider Background to the Partition and Colonial Occupation', *History of East Africa*, I (henceforth 'Partition'), ch. 10.
8 Alison Smith, 'Southern Interior', pp. 293–4; he said to Tippu Tip on his return to Zanzibar: 'Hamed, you must forgive me, but I really do not want the hinterland at all. The Europeans here in Zanzibar want to steal from me. Will it be the hinterland? Those who are dead, who see nothing of this are at peace . . .' 'Hamed ya Muhammed', para. 168.

pùrely personal one which Belgium neither financed nor particularly favoured. Britain and Germany handed over their territories to chartered companies, the Imperial British East Africa Company[9] and the Deutsch Ost-Afrika Gesellschaft. Both had to pay the Sultan rent for the lease of his coastal strip. Their power to raise revenue from customs dues was limited at the coast by his commercial treaties[10] and in the interior by the Berlin Act. Their only hope of immediate profit lay in the proceeds of the ivory trade. It was therefore vital to retain access to the far interior where the great herds of elephant roamed, and to the populous regions around the lakes, where markets might develop and exports be produced. No western boundaries for the British or German spheres had been agreed upon and for the next few years each company feared that its rival would cut off its routes to the interior and divert the ivory trade to its own ports.[11] Plans matured slowly, however, and it was 1888 before either company was ready to establish itself even at the coast.

Before the British company was even formed or chartered, its promoter Mackinnon, together with Hutton, had despatched an expedition to 'rescue' Eduard Schnitzer, better known as Emin Pasha,[12] who had been appointed by Gordon as Governor of Equatoria, the southernmost province of the Egyptian Sudan. Emin, cut off from Cairo by the Mahdi's rising, had managed to remain in control of much of his now isolated province. It was reputed to be rich in ivory and Mackinnon hoped that Emin and his men would hold the far interior for the British East Africa Company but King Leopold, anxious to obtain a foothold on the upper Nile himself, wanted him to govern the region for the Congo State. Stanley was engaged to lead this expedition and since he was still under contract to the King, the latter was able to insist that he go by way of the Congo thus opening up his route to the Nile.[13] Stanley carried with him offers to Emin from both Mackinnon and Leopold II inviting him to enter their service.

To protect his rear in this hazardous enterprise through unknown country, Stanley arranged in February 1887 that Tippu Tip, the real ruler of the upper Congo, should come part way with him and supply porters. In return Tippu Tip was to be appointed King Leopold II's governor at

9 See M. J. De Kiewiet, 'History of the Imperial British East Africa Company, 1876–95', London Ph.D., 1955; John S. Galbraith, *Mackinnon and East Africa 1878–95: A Study in the 'New Imperialism'*, Cambridge 1972.

10 These treaties limited import duties to 5 % except on spirits and fixed specific export duties.

11 The Anglo-German agreement of 1886 drew the frontier from the Indian Ocean to the east coast of Lake Victoria and in 1887 the 'hinterland' agreement ruled out annexation by either power in the rear of the other's sphere but this did not apply west of Lake Victoria.

12 See G. N. Sanderson, *England, Europe and the Upper Nile, 1882–99*, Edinburgh 1965, ch. 2. See Iain Smith, *The Emin Pasha Relief Expedition 1886–90*, Oxford 1972; Galbraith.

13 For this expedition see *inter alia* Iain Smith; Ceulemans, pp. 86 ff.; Ruth Slade, pp. 94 ff.; 'Hamed ya Muhammed', paras. 168 ff.

Stanley Falls. This suited all parties. The expedition could proceed safe from attack in the rear and the great Arab trader could continue his commercial operations, although he was enjoined to stop the slave traffic, while the king, desperately short of men and money for his Congo venture, could establish his nominal rule over the upper river and profit from the export of Arab ivory down the Congo.

Tippu Tip's co-operation was in fact vital to Leopold II for the European eruption into East and Central Africa had produced an Arab reaction. Until the late 1870s relations between Europeans and Arabs had usually been cordial enough. Neither were aiming at political power and the few missionaries and travellers were not regarded as a threat. However, as the former began to establish themselves in the interior Arab suspicions were aroused and in some places, such as Tabora, Ujiji and in Buganda, they were actively opposed, but on the whole they were well enough received.[14] A French trader who entered into direct competition with the Arabs was driven out of Tabora,[15] but the African Lakes Company further south found the Arabs willing enough to come and deal with them. However, as the danger from the Europeans came to be recognised, this hostility spread. The reaction began when Barghash deputed Tippu Tip to conquer the lands west of Lake Tanganyika and it increased as European political ambitions became plain. When the Sultan withdrew from the fray some of his followers in the interior began to aim at acquiring control themselves and at driving out the Europeans.

The movement was unco-ordinated but widespread and the Arabs had allies among the Africans associated with their trading system. All over East Africa Europeans soon found their situation precarious. In some places actual fighting broke out. At Stanley Falls in 1886, during the absence of Tippu Tip, the Congo State's post was attacked and the King's agents driven out.[16] Only the appointment of Tippu Tip as Governor when he returned in July 1887 restored King Leopold's nominal power. Arab hostility forced the White Fathers to abandon some of their stations around Lake Tanganyika.[17] In Buganda, Christians were intermittently persecuted, and the new young Kabaka grew increasingly suspicious of Europeans and Muslims alike. Finally the Muslims seized power, expelled the missionaries in 1888 and placed a candidate of their own on the throne.[18] Far to the south, at the northern tip of Lake Malawi, the African Lakes Company and some of the British missionaries became embroiled in 1887 in a war with Mlozi, an Arab freebooter trying to set himself up as a local ruler.[19]

14 Renault, I, pp. 301 ff
15 N. R. Bennett, 'Arab Power', pp. 121–4; Renault, pp. 302–3
16 Ceulemans, pp. 71 ff
17 Renault, I, pp. 210–12
18 *Ibid.*, I, pp. 315–16, 343–4; D. A. Low, 'The British in Uganda 1862–1900', Oxford D. Phil., 1957
19 Oliver, *Missionary Factor*, pp. 113 ff.; Hanna, pp. 79 ff

The wars and disorders attendant on the Arab conquests threw great numbers of slaves on the market, as wide regions were ravaged and terrorised. In places whole populations were sold into slavery and replaced by followers of the Arabs, thus ensuring control of trade routes.[20] From the time that Tippu Tip and his partners began their conquests around and west of the lakes, reports flowed back to Europe of increased slave raiding and trading. The political character of the Arab movement was appreciated by some observers[21] but it was the slaving that was particularly emphasised.

There were now more Europeans in the interior to report events and, whereas in the past, slavers had tended to keep their operations out of sight of the missionaries, in their new mood of defiance they paraded their wretched captives in full view.[22] Some missions were flooded with pathetic refugees from Arab attacks.[23] Travellers had grim tales to tell. The German, Hermann von Wissmann, for instance, found the country between the Lomami and Sankuru rivers 'literally consumed by slave hunters' in 1886–7. Whole villages had been wiped out and great tracts devastated. The only signs of life were in the great Arab encampments where human limbs, hanging in the trees, bore gruesome testimony to the 'fiendish passion' with which slave hunting was conducted.[24] The settlers in far-away Nyasaland recounted the horrible story of the events leading to the outbreak of their war against the Arabs at the north end of the lake, when Nkonde villagers were driven out of hiding by fire, gunned down as they emerged, and their medicine man was used as bait for crocodiles.[25] Examples of such wanton cruelties are easily multiplied. Nor was the slaving and raiding limited to Arabs. Many Africans also engaged in it.

These events reduced to nought Kirk's carefully laid plans to combat the slave traffic by consular supervision of the Sultan's officials on land. Fortuitously all the consuls on the coast had been withdrawn because of ill health and other reasons by the end of 1885.[26] But by this time the German eruption had shattered Britain's informal empire in East Africa and fatally weakened both her prestige and Barghash's capacity to exert influence on the mainland. In the uncertain political situation, the Sultan was hardly likely to risk alienating his subjects by strong action against the slave traffic or by taking Kirk's oft-repeated advice to abolish slavery in Zanzibar and

---

20 Renault, I, pp. 333–4
21 It was reported by O'Neill, Euan Smith and the consul in Nyasaland, Hawes.
22 Hawes to Salisbury, no. 3 Af., 16 Jan. 1888, FOCP 5896
23 Oliver, *Missionary Factor*, p. 113; Renault, I, pp. 196 ff
24 O'Neill to Salisbury, no. 35 Af., 30 May 1888, FOCP 5896. H. von Wissmann described his experience to the Royal Geographical Society in London on 25 June 1888, *Proceedings of the Royal Geographical Society*, n.s. X, 1888, pp. 525 ff., and recounted them in his book, *My Second Journey Through Equatorial Africa from the Congo to the Zambesi in the years 1886 and 1887* (translation), London 1891.
25 Hanna, pp. 79 ff
26 Owing to Foreign Office dilatoriness they had not even been appointed until the end of 1883.

Pemba.[27] Kirk suspected the Germans of compounding the problem by hinting to the Arabs that they would tolerate slave dealing in their territories.[28] Furthermore the withdrawal of the *London*[29] had not only weakened the preventive squadron[30] and lessened the risk of capture at sea but it had ominously also given the Arabs the impression that Britain had lost interest in the whole campaign against the slave trade.[31]

Thus at the very time that the Arab movement was producing a steady stream of slaves from the interior, Britain's line of defence against the export slave traffic had failed. By the spring of 1888, consuls in Zanzibar, Mozambique and on the west coast of Madagascar were all reporting an increase in this trade.[32]

War in Nyasaland

The Arab movement had also robbed Hawes, the Consul in Nyasaland, of any hope of reducing the traffic there. Initially he had collected useful information and been quite well received, but by 1887 he was openly defied by chiefs supplying slaves to the Arabs. He concluded that it would be 'unwise' to attack domestic slavery and that the export trade could only be stopped by military force.[33] The outbreak of war between the British settlers and the Arab freebooters, led by Mlozi, at the north end of the lake emphasised the futility of his position. He had neither power nor authority. He took part in the initial fighting but soon left for England urging the settlers to make peace.[34] They heeded him as little as had the Africans and Arabs.

The Foreign Office was relieved to see him. His presence in Nyasaland

27 Kirk to Salisbury, no. 200, 1 Aug. 1885, FO 84/1727, and no. 143, 1 July 1886, and Holmwood to Iddesleigh, no. 151, 25 July 1886, FOCP 5459
28 Kirk to Rosebery, no. 143, 1 July 1886, *ibid.*
29 See above, pp. 104–6 ff.
30 Euan Smith complained in 1888 that since the withdrawal of the *London* there were never enough men or boats for slave trade duties, Euan Smith to Salisbury, 8 May 1888, SP/A.79.
31 Lugard, *East African Empire*, I, pp. 61–2; O'Neill to Salisbury, no. 35 Af., 30 May 1888, FOCP 5859; Renault, I, pp. 299–301. The dismantling of the *London* was widely known in the Muslim world. Gordon's proclamation of February 1884 rescinding the provisions of the 1877 Convention forbidding the sale of slaves from family to family, due to come into force in 1889 (see above, p. 80), was also widely discussed and reinforced the impression that Britain had abandoned the campaign.
32 O'Neill to Salisbury, no. 2 Af., 3 Feb. 1888, no. 35 Af., 30 May 1888, Knott to Aitken, 21 March 1888, enc. in Aitken to Salisbury, 3 May 1888, Euan Smith to Salisbury, no. 26 tel., 21 April 1888, FOCP 5896; Euan Smith to Salisbury, 8 May 1888, SP/A.79.
33 Hanna, pp. 77–9
34 Hawes to Salisbury, no. 13. C.Af., 4 Feb. 1888, no. 14 C.Af., 18 Feb. 1888 and encs., FOCP 5896

was now positively dangerous since he had become involved in a dispute which he had no means of settling and, had he come to any harm, the government could hardly have avoided taking action.[35] No help, however, could have been sent to him except through Portuguese territory. Portugal had long been advancing claims to the whole Zambesi basin including Nyasaland and Matabeleland, and was hardly likely to be co-operative. His superiors could be thankful that he had returned. But what could they do with him now? To send him back was to invite trouble, but to withdraw him and close the consulate would cause an outcry in Scotland, the home of the Scottish missions working in Nyasaland and of the African Lakes Company.[36]

Already the company and the Scottish churches were trying to raise support by putting their case before the public.[37] Articles appeared in the press emphasising the slaving activities of the Arabs. As a correspondent informed the readers of *The Manchester Guardian* in a typical representation of the case:

> English trade, English influence, English Christianizing efforts are at stake. They are in present peril at the hands of an organized band of murderers—of depraved slave hunters—whose track is marked by deadly ruin.[38]

Meetings were held, a deputation waited on Salisbury, and questions were asked in Parliament.[39] The Anti-Slavery Society was naturally drawn into the fray. O'Neill, the British Consul in Mozambique, who had taken part in the early fighting against Mlozi, informed the Secretary that the settlers were being attacked by slave hunters bent on battering down western, and Christian, influence. Arab power, he said, was spread by means of the slave trade and a great revival of the traffic had begun.[40] The Society joined with the Aborigines Protection Society to demand that the government help the settlers in their struggle.[41]

But how was Salisbury to help them? Doubtless he was personally sympathetic. His daughter testified that the suppression of the slave trade

35 Minutes by Salisbury, 15 May 1888, and Anderson, Salisbury wrote: 'To please the missionaries, we send a Representative of the Government; to spare the taxpayers, we make him understand that he will in no case be supported by an armed force. The only weapon left him is bluster . . . I distrust bluster very much as a weapon. It is apt to end either in discredit or a deferred engagement for material action which has to be honoured.'
36 Minutes by Anderson, 16 May 1888, and Lister, 17 May 1888, *ibid.*
37 Oliver, *Missionary Factor*, pp. 122–3
38 *The Manchester Guardian*, 25 Feb. 1888
39 Oliver, *Missionary Factor*, pp. 121–2
40 O'Neill to Allen, 23 Jan. 1888, ASS/C 63.64. O'Neill was personally much involved and had been anxious to return to the fray in 1888 but Hawes had insisted that he should stay clear of it, since it was outside his consular jurisdiction.
41 BF ASS to Salisbury, 24 May 1888, FOCP 5896

was perhaps his only 'purely crusading impulse'.[42] He also believed that British subjects should not be excluded from areas they had pioneered. But his parliamentary position was weak, depending on the support of the Liberal Unionists, who opposed African adventures. If abandoning the settlers to their fate was liable to raise a storm in humanitarian circles, sending an expedition to their aid might bring down the government. He could not fall back on the device of claiming Nyasaland and chartering a company to rule it because the African Lakes Company was too insignificant, undercapitalised and mismanaged a business to be cast in such a role.[43] He therefore, had no means of financing or running a protectorate in Nyasaland.

Moreover, there was the added complication that help could only be sent through Portuguese territory, and Portugal, intent on extending her own borders, was doing her best to render the British position untenable. She seized a steamer belonging to the African Lakes Company, maintained that she had every right to close the Zambesi to free navigation and increased transit dues on the river. More serious still, she refused to let arms and ammunition be bought in Quilimane or sent through her territories to the settlers. They soon found themselves desperately short, particularly of ammunition. On the other hand Arab caravans heading for the interior had no difficulty getting stocks from the Portuguese.[44]

Salisbury did what he could in the circumstances. He did not send Hawes back to Nyasaland but the consulate remained open in charge of a settler.[45] While making it clear that no official military expedition would be sent there, Salisbury encouraged the settlers to defend themselves[46] and allowed the company to enlist volunteers from the forces.[47] He pressed the Portuguese to let munitions pass through their territories and firmly resisted their claims to the area,[48] while instructing Euan Smith in Zanzibar to urge the new Sultan, Khalifa, who had succeeded Barghash in the spring of 1888, to try to stop the war.

42 Lady G. Cecil, *Life of Robert, Marquis of Salisbury*, 4 vols., London 1932, IV, p. 342

43 Hanna, pp. 83 ff

44 Hanna, pp. 131 ff.; Hawes to Salisbury 28 Jan. 1888, African Lakes Company to Salisbury, 12 May 1888, O'Neill to Salisbury, 17 Aug. 1888, tel., FOCP 5896; Stevenson to Salisbury, 11 Aug. 1888, FO 84/1926. Stevenson said that the Arabs got arms from the 'convict population' of Quilimane with the connivance of Mozambique officials.

45 A settler, John Buchanan, had been left as acting consul when Hawes left.

46 They were told that they had a perfect right to do so, Oliver, *Missionary Factor*, p. 122. Lugard (later Sir Frederick, and then Lord Lugard), an army officer on leave, who took command for a while, was informed that the government would be pleased if he succeeded in driving out the slavers but that it could not help him, M. Perham, *Lugard*, I, London 1956, p. 114.

47 FO to War Office, 18 Aug. 1888, FO 84/1926

48 Hanna, pp. 131 ff., Robinson and Gallagher, pp. 224 ff.; Oliver, *Missionary Factor*, pp. 121 ff.

Results were mixed. Khalifa had not the prestige or influence of his predecessor and was beset by problems nearer home where the Germans were bullying him and the Italians, anxious to obtain a foothold on the Benadir coast, were busy picking a quarrel with him. Even if his efforts to end the Nyasaland war were sincere, they were doomed to failure. His emissary merely joined Mlozi and the fighting dragged on.[49] Continuous pressure on Portugal[50] finally induced her to let some arms and ammunition through to the settlers, but the situation was such that there were fears that she would occupy the region herself. The Arabs continued to be well supplied with arms.

The arms traffic in East Africa

Early in 1888, O'Neill had suggested restricting the sale of munitions in Zanzibar. He had advocated this not just to his superiors but also to the Anti-Slavery Society.[51] Pointing out that the Arabs were armed not just with trade guns but with repeating rifles.[52] By the summer, warnings were coming from Euan Smith in Zanzibar. The arms trade in East Africa, he said, was now reaching dangerous proportions. Where Kirk had estimated in 1880 that 30,000–40,000 stands went up-country annually from Zanzibar and Portuguese territory,[53] he reported that some 80,000–100,000 firearms a year and large quantities of ammunition were entering East Africa from the island alone, and there had been a significant improvement in their quality. Arms of precision and good breech-loaders were replacing old flintlocks and percussion guns and the extraordinarily low prices at which they were available would soon make their use widespread. A first class Snider rifle 'quite as good as new' now cost only thirteen shillings in Zanzibar.[54] Already magazine rifles as well as breech-loaders were reaching remote Buganda.[55] The danger of allowing a trade of such dimensions to continue uncontrolled on the eve of the European occupation of Africa and in face of clear Arab and African hostility was self-evident.

However, to restrict it required the co-operation of at least Germany, Zanzibar and Portugal, all of whom like Britain had a stake in the trade. German firms, for instance, were the largest importers of firearms into the island and the only suppliers of powder.[56] The Sultan raised revenue from

49 Hanna, pp. 100 ff
50 For a useful summary of British efforts see memo. by A. W. Clarke, 3 Feb. 1890, CAB/37/26 no. 6.
51 O'Neill to Allen, 23 Jan. 1888, ASS/C 63.64
52 O'Neill to Salisbury, no. 2 Af., 3 Feb. 1888, FO 84/1901
53 Coupland, *Exploitation*, p. 262
54 Euan Smith to Salisbury, no. 154, 28 June 1888, FO 84/1907
55 Mackay to Euan Smith, 18 April 1888, enc. in *ibid*. Mackay reported the delivery of a hundred Winchester, Snider and Martini-Henry rifles and nearly 20,000 rounds of cartridges.
56 Fritz F. Müller, *Deutschland-Zanzibar-Ostafrika*, East Berlin 1959, p. 411

taxes on munitions and, in addition, exercised a monopoly on the sale of gunpowder, which he bought from the Germans at thirteen dollars for a hundred pounds and sold to the British Indians for thirty dollars for the same quantity.[57] Restriction of the traffic would deprive him of revenue and exacerbate his relations with his subjects trading in the interior, whose power, influence and commercial operations depended upon their ability to get arms. Portugal also raised revenues from customs duties on arms and ammunition. In fact they provided one seventh of the revenues of Mozambique at this time.[58] But, in addition, owing to the Sultan's monopoly of gunpowder, Arab caravans often came to Portuguese territory to get their ammunition, which thus drew trade to the province.[59] Britain's own stake in the munitions traffic to East Africa is hard to assess.[60] It seems to have

57 Euan Smith to Salisbury, no. 154, 28 June 1888, FO 84/1907
58 O'Neill to Salisbury, 12 Dec. 1888, FOCP 5867
59 Memo. by Kirk, enc. in Plens. to Salisbury, no. 12 STC conf., 25 Jan. 1890, FO 84/2101.
60 Customs returns show the following values for exports of British munitions to East Africa:

				Native States	*Portuguese Possessions*	*Total*
1883	..	..	..	£10,514	£5,486	£16,000
1884	..	..	..	16,893	6,744	23,637
1885	..	..	..	32,404	4,725	37,125
1886	..	..	..	2,763	3,632	6,395
1887	..	..	..	4,882	3,099	7,981
1888	..	..	..	9,317	8,874	18,191

The break-down for 1883 "Native States" includes 6,000,000 percussion caps and 14,936 muskets, rifles and fowling pieces valued at £9,706. These figures from PRO Customs 8/124, 125, 126, 127, 128, 129, 9/93, 95 show surprising fluctuations. Perhaps research would reveal that the peak years are accounted for by the imports for the Sultan himself or in 1888 by imports for the British companies. The figures are hard to reconcile with Lugard's statement in his *East African Empire*, I, p. 215 that on his travels he found most of the guns in 'native' hands were British made. This may, however, be because they were re-exported from other countries or were wrongly stamped. Old arms of all kinds were remodelled by manufacturers in Liège, Belgium, who also imported British barrels and made them up with Belgian locks and stocks. They also quite legally stamped British marks, slightly misspelt, on their own weapons, see Gavin White, p. 176. More research is needed before conclusions can be drawn but in 1883 £10,293 worth of parts and 'undesignated' firearms were sent to Belgium together with 8,774 muskets, rifles and fowling pieces worth £10,990 (Customs 9/93). The average price of the latter weapons however is higher than that of British arms exported to East African 'native states' in 1883. South Africa also imported large quantities of British arms and the arms trade from South Africa to East Africa was said to have received considerable impetus from the establishment of the Zanzibar–Cape Town mail service in 1873, see report of the Attorney General, enc. in Bulwer to Hicks Beach, 3 April 1879, secret, COCP Af. 190. Arms could also have come via other countries. Germany, for instance, perhaps bought some of the weapons she imported into Zanzibar in Britain and British traders also bought arms in Belgium for shipment to Africa.

been relatively small but the British Indians did all the retailing of munitions in Zanzibar and were the actual suppliers of the Arab caravans.

Restriction of the trade would thus require considerable sacrifices in some quarters and in view of the great demand it could only be achieved by rigorous action loyally enforced by all the powers on the coast. There is no evidence, however, that Salisbury was moved by these considerations or even by the fact that well-armed Arabs and Africans could oppose the European occupation of Africa, when he decided to take no steps towards negotiating an arms agreement. The reasons he gave were quite different. He wrote:

> A combined movement for the exclusion of arms and ammunition from Africa ought not to be entered into without careful examination. The Slave Trade, which is reaching such gigantic proportions, is said to consist of the operations of a comparatively small number of Arabs and vast multitudes of an inferior race. It is probable that these Arabs are already armed. If they go backwards and forwards from the coast to the interior they are almost certainly armed. If so our humane efforts to prohibit the importation of arms will have the effect of disarming not them but their victims. They are irresistible notwithstanding their great inferiority in numbers, because they are exclusively in possession of arms, the same superiority which enabled Cortes and Pizarro to conquer in America. If we restrict the importation of arms we perpetuate their superiority—and consequently their power for evil. When we concluded the Sand River Convention we thought we had done a very humane and sagacious thing. But its main effect has been to enable the Boers, numbering only 40,000 to trample on and enslave some 800,000 blacks. If you read the account of their encroachments in Bechuanaland it is their inferiority in arms which makes the natives so helpless.[61]

In other words, he felt that restriction of the trade would only help the Arabs to establish their power whereas the uncontrolled traffic would keep the situation fluid. His minute was accepted in the Foreign Office[62] and there, for the moment, the matter rested.

By the summer of 1888 the British situation in East Africa was precarious. The British East Africa Company, lagging behind the Germans to the irritation of the Foreign Office,[63] expressed fears that the latter would

61 Minute by Salisbury, 1 Aug. 1888 on Euan Smith to Salisbury, no. 154, 28 June 1888, FO 84/1907, partially quoted in Oliver, *Missionary Factor*, p. 133, note 4. By the Sand River Convention with the Transvaal in 1852 Britain agreed not to allow arms to be sold to Africans near the Boer frontiers.
62 Officials referred to it later as furnishing reasons for not embarking on an attempt to restrict the arms traffic.
63 Irritation at Mackinnon's dilatoriness is a recurrent theme in Foreign Office minutes of this period, see for example minute by Anderson, on Euan Smith to Salisbury no. 59 conf., 8 April 1888, FO 84/1906, minute by Salisbury on Euan Smith to Salisbury no. 28 tel., 26 June 1888, FO 84/1912.

encircle its territories. Nothing had yet been heard of the Emin Pasha expedition. The interior was in turmoil and European lives endangered. The fate of the settlers in Nyasaland, hung in the balance. The only vestige of European authority in the far interior was that wielded in the name of King Leopold II by the great Arab slaver Tippu Tip. All evidence pointed to an increase in the slave trade and the arms traffic was known to be reaching unprecedented proportions. At home, although the supporters of the Scottish missions had launched a campaign to bring their plight before the country, Parliament showed no desire to spend money on an African empire and the government's hands were tied when it came to defending British interests on the continent.

Matters were at this stage when the Roman Catholic Cardinal Lavigerie, Archbishop of Algiers, made a sudden dramatic entry on to the international stage.

The Cardinal's crusade

Cardinal Lavigerie was the founder of the White Fathers, who had established missions around Lakes Victoria and Tanganyika.[64] As the Arab movement developed they were forced to give up two stations on Lake Tanganyika and to withdraw from Buganda. Their remaining posts were flooded with fugitives who settled around them as followers or *suivants*. At Mpala, one of King Leopold II's stations which they took over in 1885,[65] they inherited a veritable little kingdom, and it continued to grow until it was a hundred kilometres long with some six thousand inhabitants. Here the Fathers appointed and deposed African rulers, collected tribute, including slaves, settled disputes and dispensed justice. They gave flags to their adherents and sent out levies to fight those who attacked their protégés.

To relieve them of the exercise of such temporal powers which left little time for pastoral work, Lavigerie sent out a former papal *zouave*, Leopold Louis Joubert, in 1887, to run the lay affairs of the little state and organise its defence force. The situation was fraught with danger. Strong action by Joubert was liable to provoke attacks on the smaller more vulnerable posts at Karema and Kibanga.[66] The Fathers struggled to protect the fugitives from the pillaging and wars which raged around them, at risk of becoming

64 See above, pp. 106, 138. For the Cardinal's anti-slavery and missionary work in Africa see Renault; for his life and work see L. Baunard, *Le Cardinal Lavigerie*, 2 vols., Paris 1896, and P. L. T. G. Goyau, *Un Grand Missionnaire, le Cardinal Lavigerie*, Paris 1925; also relevant are C. M. Allemand-Lavigerie, *L'esclavage Africain*, Ghent 1891, and *Documents sur l'oeuvre anti-esclavagiste*, St. Cloud 1889, and J. Perraudin, 'Le Cardinal Lavigerie et Leopold II', *Zaire*, 12, 1958.
65 See Renault, I, pp. 271-5 for the reasons behind the transfer of Karema and Mpala from King Leopold's International African Association to the missionaries.
66 See Renault, I, ch. 6 for this whole discussion

embroiled themselves.[67] They watched helplessly when the crops of their *suivants* were destroyed and tried to buy back members of their flock who were enslaved. They ransomed some of the small children and the sick who trailed past their doors and lamented that they could not save more. The missions were armed camps, centres of refuge rather than of evangelism.

Lavigerie had long looked for a means of bringing them peace and security. He had asked the Pope many years before to lead an anti-slavery crusade, seeing the slave trade as a great obstacle to mission work which could not thrive in the face of wars, depopulation and the hostility of slavers.[68] He had searched for an African ruler to found a Christian kingdom.[69] He had tried to interest the Knights of Malta in carving out a Catholic domain in the heart of Africa.[70] At different times he had appealed to various powers to hold Barghash responsible for any harm done to their subjects in the interior.[71] So far all had been in vain. Finally, receiving the news of an attack on Kibanga,[72] following the martyrdom of Christians in Buganda, he determined on drastic action to save his whole missionary enterprise from possible ruin.[73]

He appealed to the Pope for support. The fortunes of the Roman Catholic Church were at a low ebb and he saw a chance of placing her at the head of one of the greatest humanitarian causes of the age.[74] The moment was in fact propitious as Brazil, a Catholic country and the only western state in which slavery was still legal, was on the point of abolishing it. The Pope gave his blessing and Lavigerie set out on a one-man crusade to inform the western world of the horrors of a traffic which he held responsible for his troubles in Africa. He appealed to public opinion to spur governments into action. 'L'opinion', he wrote, 'est la vraie reine du monde aujourd'hui.'[75]

He began in his homeland, France, having ascertained that the government was prepared to give moral but not practical support. In the church of St. Sulpice on 1 July 1888, he preached a deeply moving sermon to a packed congregation, describing the depredations of the slavers, the cruelties inflicted on their victims, and all the grim details of the traffic which he estimated cost nearly half a million deaths a year—a staggering figure.[76] Muslims, he said, were responsible for these atrocities[77] and he

67 The Arabs did not directly attack the missions but their followers sometimes did. Rumaliza explained that he could not control them, *ibid.*, I, pp. 381–2.

68 *Ibid.*, I, pp. 165–9   69 *Ibid.*, I, pp. 236 ff

70 *Ibid.*, I, pp. 255 ff   71 *Ibid.*, I, pp. 350 ff

72 This attack by a *ruga-ruga* force raiding neighbouring people was not a deliberate attack on the mission, but Lavigerie was not aware of this at the time, *ibid.*, I, pp. 381–2, II, p. 77.

73 For Lavigerie's crusade see *ibid.*, II, pp. 72 ff

74 *Ibid.*, II, pp. 75–8   75 *Ibid.*, II, p. 78

76 These figures are based on Cameron's estimate of 500,000 victims *including* those killed in raids. Lavigerie thought this was the number enslaved and that, if those killed were included, victims numbered 2,000,000, Renault, II, p. 83. For a discussion of the validity of estimates given by explorers and others see E. Glyn-Jones.

77 His picture of a handful of Arabs devastating Africa was inaccurate. Much of the

called on Christian Europe to rise up in wrath and send out crusaders to fight the infidel just as they had done in mediaeval times. Five or six hundred volunteers financed by public subscription could end this terrible evil. His congregation was stunned. The press, which he carefully courted, reported the incredulity with which the people of France received the news that the slave trade was still active. Newspapers hailed the Cardinal as a new Peter the Hermit and carried his message to a wider but equally shocked and on the whole sympathetic audience.[78] He had the full support of the Roman Catholic Church and priests all over the country supported his appeal. It was aimed, however, at Christians of all denominations.

On July 31st he was in London addressing a large and distinguished gathering in Princes Hall called by the Anti-Slavery Society, with Lord Granville, now a leading member of the Opposition, in the chair, the Roman Catholic Cardinal Manning on the platform and prominent humanitarians and churchmen of all denominations in the audience.[79] Catholics had been especially called on to support the crusade.[80] With his usual perspicacity, Lavigerie paid tribute to Britain's long struggle against the slave traffic and he now called on her to wipe slavery from the face of the earth in accordance with Livingstone's dying wishes. He was a great orator, 'magnifique et habile, pathétique et simple, tout en demeurant grand', and he received a great ovation. 'On l'applaudit sans fin', recorded his biographer.[81] Having fired his broadside, he paid a courtesy call on Salisbury, [82] was received by the Prince of Wales, the patron of the Anti-Slavery Society, in the absence of the Queen, and then left the country.

As in France the reaction was one of astonishment. The *Bradford Observer* reported:

> The horrors of the Central African slave trade are no new sensation but it is news and terrible news, to be told ... that the trade, instead of decaying, as we had fondly believed, is on the increase, and is 'eating the heart out of Africa'.[83]

Lavigerie had not said anything that explorers,[84] missionaries and consuls

slaving was conducted by Africans and much of the raiding was unconnected with the slave traffic.
78 There were some discordant notes. *La France*, 4 July 1888, for instance asked if the cardinal merely wanted money for the White Fathers and the left-wing press gave little coverage, Renault, II, p. 84.
79 The audience included Sir John Kennaway, M.P., a Conservative and lay head of the Church Missionary Society, Horace Waller and Bishop Smythies of the Universities Mission to Central Africa, F. W. Fox, a prominent Quaker businessman and member of the Aborigines' Protection Society, Kirk, and the explorer V. Lovett Cameron, as well as the officials of the Anti-Slavery Society.
80 See Manning's circular letter to all London churches, *Weekly Register*, 29 July 1888.
81 Baunard, p. 456. For his powers of oratory see Renault, II, pp. 79–81
82 Renault, II, p. 89   83 *Bradford Observer*, 1 Aug. 1888
84 On 25 June 1888 the German explorer, H. Wissmann, had lectured to the Royal

had not already reported but his fiery oratory had made a deep impression on all who heard him and the press relayed his appeal forcibly to a wider public. The sudden arrival of a high dignitary of the Roman Catholic Church, and a Frenchman at that, bearing the message that in the heart of Africa ghastly atrocities were being committed daily and hundreds of thousands of innocent people being slaughtered or condemned to lifelong bondage, caused something of a sensation and the appearance on the same platform of Christians of all denominations, united in their determination to end these horrors, was in itself a significant event. The Cardinal received good coverage in both the national and the provincial newspapers.[85]

The general reaction was predictably that Britain could never lag behind in the anti-slavery cause. Lavigerie, by presenting the slave trade as a desperate human problem in urgent need of solution, breathed new life into the movement, which had been at such a low ebb that the Anti-Slavery Society, its finances in the doldrums, had been considering amalgamation with the Aborigines' Protection Society.[86]

Opinion was divided, however, as to what should be done. The Cardinal's plan to send out volunteers who would train Africans to defend themselves found some favour. Manning supported it[87] and Horace Waller called on young Christians to go to Africa and shoot slavers rather than big game,[88] but the Anti-Slavery Society, dedicated as it was to the peaceful defeat of the traffic through the spread of commerce and Christianity, could not agree to it. The Princes Hall meeting, therefore, ignored Lavigerie's recommendations and simply passed a tame resolution urging the government to co-operate with the other colonial powers to end the trade. This was sent to Salisbury with a covering letter from the society reminding him that it behoved Britain, as the leader of the anti-slavery movement, to take the initiative.[89] In the press there was talk of a congress of colonial powers and a proposal that they should agree to suppress raids by using well-armed African forces.[90]

Public interest was reflected by questions in the House of Commons

Geographical Society, describing the horrors of the traffic between the Lomani and the Sankuru, see above, p. 194.

85 See ASS/J.52 for a useful box of press cuttings

86 The society had considerably strengthened its committee since 1884, adding Manning, Hutton, W. H. Wylde, Sir R. N. Fowler, M.P., and Alfred Pease, M.P., among others. But its finances had been in the doldrums and it only decided against amalgamation on July 6th, after the crusade began in France, on the grounds that the increase in the slave trade and the new acquisitions of the colonial powers made its work more necessary than ever. Lavigerie subsequently gave the society 50,000 francs (£1,975 2s. 3d.) out of the funds he received from the Pope for his crusade, Renault, II, p. 93; *Anti-Slavery Reporter*, IX, Jan./Feb. 1889, 1.

87 *The Times*, 1 Aug. 1888

88 *Christian World*, 2 Aug. 1888

89 BFASS to Salisbury, 10 Aug. 1888, and enc. petition, FO 84/1925.

90 *The Standard*, 1 Aug. 1888

asking the government what action it proposed to take. Already the with-drawal of the *London* was being criticised.[91] Sir James Fergusson, Parlia-mentary Under-Secretary to the Foreign Office, however, played down the whole issue by throwing, what he called, 'cold water' on anti-slavery motions.[92] He doubted that the slave traffic had increased, there were merely more European observers to report it, and he assured the House that as Britain and Germany took over their concessions the traffic would decline. He also said that the government was acting in common with other powers;[93] whatever that might mean, for no steps had, in fact, been taken. It was not until reports arrived of the Cardinal's sermon in Brussels in mid-August that the Foreign Office began to consider what might be done.

In Belgium Lavigerie was received by Leopold II. Each of these arch-manoeuvrers had his suspicions of the other.[94] The Cardinal thought the employment of Protestants and Freemasons by the Congo State was inimical to the spread of Catholicism while the King suspected that, as a Frenchman, Lavigerie might try to further the territorial ambitions of France at the expense of his own African venture. However, both were men of vast ambitions, slender resources and fertile minds, and they had reason to co-operate. Leopold II hoped to use the men and money provided by the anti-slavery crusade to occupy the lands west of Lake Tanganyika before he could be forestalled by other powers. He was determined, however, that the volunteers must be under his orders. Bands of quixotic knights could not be allowed to roam lands he claimed but did not control. Lavigerie's hopes of a truly independent and international order of military knights financed by Christians of all denominations began to fade and were later abandoned.[95] They agreed that the anti-slavery force under the aegis of the Congo State would take over the White Fathers' little army, relieving them of the exercise of temporal power and Joubert, their French commander, was to become a naturalised Congolese and enter the King's service. To facilitate communications a steamer was to be placed on Lake Tanganyika.[96] A *modus vivendi* established, Lavigerie set out to rally the Belgian public to the cause.

In a great sermon delivered in Ste. Gudule, with the fine cathedral

---

91 *Hansard*, CCCXXIX, 30 July 1888, col. 738, 3 Aug. 1888 col. 1398–9. The with-drawal of the *London* had also been criticised in the press, see *Manchester Guardian*, 25 Feb. 1888; J. Scott Keltie, 'British Interests in Africa', *Contemporary Review*, July 1888.
92 Minute by Fergusson, 27 Aug. 1888, FO84/1927
93 Hansard, 3 Aug. 1888, CCCXXIX, cols. 1398–9
94 No record was kept of this meeting. The discussion which follows is based on Renault, II, pp. 93 ff. See also Perraudin, pp. 165 ff., for the relations between king and cardinal.
95 The Vatican also objected to the formation of such an order and Lavigerie himself soon decided it would take too long to get one going.
96 It was not apparently clear who was to finance this. The King and Cardinal each hoped to tap the resources of the other, Renault II, p. 101.

crammed to capacity,[97] he berated the nation for not supporting her king's great humanitarian work in Africa. He deplored the slaving on the upper Congo, reminding his congregation that the Berlin Act condemned the terrible trade, but in deference to Leopold II he did not specifically condemn Tippu Tip.[98] He called for a hundred volunteers, a Christian militia,[99] supported by private donations to go to the western shores of Lake Tanganyika to combat the traffic. He also urged for the first time the restriction of the arms trade. The response was immediate. A Belgian Anti-Slavery Society was formed to enlist recruits and run the enterprise and too many volunteers came forward at once.[100] But funds came in more slowly and not from the richer sections of the community or, significantly, from the King himself.

His crusade now well under way, the Cardinal returned to France and began to launch the anti-slavery societies which he hoped would translate public sympathy into practical action against the slave traffic. This was to prove disheartening work, shattering any dreams of an international humanitarian movement. Organisations of various sorts were founded in Belgium, France, Germany, Switzerland, Spain, Portugal, Austria, and Italy, which the Cardinal visited at the end of November, and even Haiti.[101] Some were abortive or achieved little but all had to be formed along national lines and such activities as they sponsored often served national ends. The whole movement was to be bedevilled by factional and sectarian disputes, by personal jealousies, and by the Cardinal's own determination to retain its leadership in Catholic hands. Nevertheless, he had awakened considerable public interest and, while the most active of the societies, the French and Belgian, began planning their expeditions, the first official response to the crusade came from the Foreign Office in London.

British proposals for an anti-slave trade conference

Reading the reports of the sermon in Ste. Gudule, Hill, who thought action justified by the Berlin Act, opened the discussion by asking, albeit with little of the Cardinal's spirit:

W[oul]d Lord Salisbury consent to our consulting the Powers, parties to

97 The congregation included several ministers and members of the diplomatic corps.
98 He had originally wished to do so, however. Renault, II, pp. 101–2.
99 The number was reduced because he was thinking of the Congo only. In a subsequent letter to Bismarck on August 24 he stated that 500 men would be needed to suppress the traffic east of the lake, *ibid.*, II, pp. 104.
100 There were 680 applicants by the end of 1888—many quite unsuitable, *ibid.*, II, p. 194.
101 For the history of these societies and of other responses to the crusade see *ibid.*, II, pp. 105 ff. They all took different lines. Where the Belgians planned armed expeditions, for instance, the Italians collected information about the slave traffic and the German Catholics supported mainly missionary activity.

the Act of Berlin, as to their views on any possible action? It need not commit us, though it w[oul]d probably be of more use for a Blue Book than to the Africans.

Lister agreed that it might be well to give the Cardinal's crusade some public encouragement. Salisbury, however (with the volunteers in mind), replied:

I should have no objection to enter heartily into this scheme if there was a chance of the House of Commons backing it. But if we can give no help we had better hold our tongues.[102]

The matter was referred to Fergusson, who, perhaps disliking the role he had been playing in dampening anti-slavery ardour in Parliament, showed some enthusiasm.

He would have no difficulty, he said, in getting the matter raised in the House where a number of members not normally interested in the slave trade had asked questions on the subject. He need only choose the best man to do it. He had been maintaining that Britain could not undertake military operations in regions like Nyasaland where she had no base of operations; however, volunteers might perhaps be used, if carefully controlled, to prevent them from 'following courses like the Elizabethan freebooters'. If other governments were to be consulted about sanctioning such an expedition, it might be wise to get Belgium to call the conference and to organise the venture. This would allay any French or Portuguese suspicions that it was a British undertaking to promote British missions and settlements. He urged that the ambassador in Brussels, Lord Vivian, should sound out the Belgians at once so that he could tell Parliament when it reconvened in November that the matter was in hand.[103] Salisbury now reconsidered the question:

Before taking the step suggested by Sir J. Fergusson, I should like to make the precise plan of action clearer to my own mind. Do we contemplate freeing the slaves throughout Africa? or simply forbidding the sale of slaves? or the transport of slaves in caravans? or only kidnapping? There are four different degrees of completeness which the crusade may assume. Let us take the simplest and easiest—the prohibiting of kidnapping. How are you to prevent that, or any other crime, unless you are Governors of the country? And how is Africa to be governed by 100 Belgians with £40,000 in their pockets? They might be strong enough to block one particular slave-road; but the caravans would simply go a little to the north or a little to the south of them.

102 Minutes by Hill, Lister and Salisbury on Vivian to Salisbury, no. 30 Af., 16 Aug. 1888, FO 84/1895
103 Minute by Fergusson, 27 Aug. 1888, FO 84/1927

I do not doubt that a motion on this subject in the House of Commons would be popular, so long as it confined itself to generalities. But would the House of Commons vote the money necessary to support 100 men—£10,000 a year—for five years, and pass special Mutiny and Indemnity Acts to enable the commander of these 100 men to organize them, to punish mutiny, and to slaughter slave dealers ? I greatly doubt it.

What we really can deal with is the coast, and this generation will have done its part if it destroys the *export* slave trade. I think under the circumstances, Vivian might be instructed to sound the Belgians, whether they would be willing to summon a Conference of the Powers controlling the coast of Africa for this purpose. They would be Great Britain, Germany, Portugal, France, Italy, Turkey, Egypt, Spain, Morocco.[104]

Thus the idea of calling a slave trade conference in Brussels gradually took shape. In a situation in which the government believed that the public expected it to take the lead in accordance with Britain's traditional policy, this was as Lister said, the 'safest' course of action.[105] It was infinitely more practical and less hazardous than the Cardinal's idea of sending out small bodies of volunteers to fight in Central Africa and similar schemes being mooted by the supporters of the African Lakes Company and the explorer C. Lovett Cameron.[106] It might also enable Britain to take advantage of the favourable trend of opinion evoked by Lavigerie to enlist greater co-operation from France against the export slave trade.[107]

Vivian was instructed to inform the Belgians that Britain would continue to bear 'cheerfully' the burden of watching the coast of Africa but, in view of the changed political situation on the littoral, she felt that united

104 Minute by Salisbury, 1 Sept. 1888, FO 84/1927. Salisbury in common with others mistook Lavigerie's proposal and thought that he merely contemplated sending 100 men to Africa, whereas the cardinal envisaged 100 men each training a force of Africans to defend themselves, Renault, II, p. 106.
105 Minute by Lister, 29 Aug. 1888, FO 84/1927 Lister was a defeatist who felt that as 'the influence and dignity of every native depends upon the number of his slaves, and . . . the universal love of sport and fighting makes slave-raiding a pursuit in Africa even more important than partridge shooting in Norfolk', the cardinal's plans to put a stop to a 'state of things founded on religion, custom, profit and taste and handed down from time immemorial' by checking the import of arms and sending forth 100 Belgians were absurd. But he also thought legitimate trade useless as a short term panacea since it encouraged the use of slave labour, and he feared that increased vigilance at sea would merely inflict greater sufferings on the slaves hidden in the dhows.
106 The explorer Cameron was now also raising an agitation to get money to place stations from the mouth of the Shire to the north end of Lake Tanganyika. The agitation proved abortive, see Renault, II, pp. 235–41, but it aroused some public 'enthusiasm', a fact noted by the Anti-Slavery Society which dissociated itself from the venture, see *Anti-Slavery Reporter*, IX, 1, Jan./Feb. 1889, p. 37.
107 Minute by Lister on Vivian to Salisbury, no. 30 Af., 16 Aug. 1888, FO 84/1895

action by the powers was called for to close the export markets for slaves and to stop smuggling. King Leopold's great interest in African welfare encouraged her to hope that he would call a meeting of the coastal powers for this object.[108]

The King did not believe the conference would ever really meet, but, if it did, it suited him well that any gathering to advance the cause of civilisation in Africa should be held in Brussels, perhaps because his appointment of Tippu Tip as governor at Stanley Falls laid him open to strong criticism. A conference would enable him to recover any ground which his image as a philanthropist had lost and also would give him an opportunity to reach an agreement with Britain over Africa.[109]

Meanwhile Hill, reading that the Vatican might issue a circular on the subject of a conference[110] and characteristically afraid that this would rob Britain of the 'kudos of being first'[111] began, with Kirk,[112] to work out proposals for the conference. These included considerably more than the agreement against the export slave trade envisaged by Salisbury. But before any decisions had been reached even as to which powers should be invited, the whole plan was suspended because of the turn of events in East Africa.

The East African blockade

In the summer of 1888, in an atmosphere of deep mutual suspicion, the British and German East Africa Companies were preparing to take over their respective concessions. The Germans had early appreciated the propaganda value of stating their aims in humanitarian terms,[113] but, as the time drew near for them to assume the administration, the British Consul-General, Euan Smith, grew increasingly alarmed at their behaviour. Their harshness was making them unpopular and he feared they might drive away the labourers needed to exploit their territories. His German counterpart talked ominously of using a modified form of slavery to make Africans work and the director of their company had plans for compelling slave owners to put their slaves to work producing plantation crops. Furthermore,

108 Salisbury to Vivian, no. 15 Af., 17 Sept. 1888, FO 84/1895. Zanzibar was now included in the list of Powers to be invited.

109 Leopold II to Lambermont, 27 Sept. 1888, no. 333, Papiers Lambermont (henceforth PL), 1885–8, and Ceulemans, pp. 239–40

110 In *The Times*, 24 Sept. 1888

111 Minute by Hill, 24 Sept. 1888. The idea of a conference was bandied about in the press, see Renault, II, p. 133, and by late August it was being suggested that it might be held in Brussels, *Kolonial Zeitung*, 25 Aug. 1888, p. 267.

112 Kirk had retired from the Foreign Office but his advice was always sought on East African questions.

113 See Bennett, 'Arab Power', p. 139, citing Schweinfurth, who said that the aims of the *Gesellschaft für Deutsche Kolonisation* included the expulsion of slave trading Muslims and the prohibition of the arms and spirits traffics.

the Germans made large cash advances to the Arab contractors who were to supply labour and this encouraged the acquisition of raw slaves.[114]

The Germans took over their concession in mid-August and within a few weeks their high-handed actions roused widespread opposition and they were faced with a full scale rebellion aimed at ousting them from the mainland.[115] Hitherto Bismarck had shown little interest in the anti-slavery movement. Lavigerie had refused an invitation from German Catholics to attend their congress in Freiburg. He was afraid of offending public feeling in France if he visited the victors of the Franco-German war, and of arousing German susceptibilities;[116] but he had urged German Catholics to found an anti-slavery society[117] and had written to the Chancellor asking for his support. Bismarck did not reply[118] but after the outbreak of the revolt his attitude changed.[119] He realised that the rebellion had been largely provoked by the actions of the German East Africa Company,[120] but he found it convenient to lay all the blame on the slave trading Arabs, who he claimed were opposing German interference with their nefarious traffic. Initially his object was to get British support to prevent the British company rendering the German position untenable by fostering the revolt and attracting Arab traders away to their own sphere. He thought the British were encouraging Arab resistance[121] and he appealed for Salisbury's help, asking him to secure the Sultan's co-operation and to stop the British press from inflaming public opinion and fomenting an Anglo-German dispute over East Africa.

He suggested the slave trade issue might prove valuable propaganda: The animosity against our Treaty arrangement[122] is to be traced principally to the *slave dealers*. This circumstance, if properly turned to account in influencing public opinion in England, would afford that public opinion a motive for co-operating with us.[123]

---

114 Euan Smith to Salisbury, no. 59 conf., 8 April 1888, FO 84/1906; no. 117, 1 June 1888, FO 84/1907, 11 April 1888, SP/79
115 See G. S. P. Freeman-Grenville, 'The German Sphere, 1884–98', Oliver and Mathew (eds.), ch. 12, pp. 438 ff.; J. A. Kieran, 'Abushiri and the Germans', ch. 10 in B. A. Ogot (ed.), *Hadith* 2, Nairobi 1970.
116 Renault, II, p. 111
117 C. M. Allemand-Lavigerie, *Mémoire—en forme de lettre à M. le Président du congrès des Catholiques Allemands de Fribourg sur la création d'une société anti-esclavagiste*, 28 Aug. 1888, Paris 1888; Lavigerie to Bismarck, 24 Aug. 1888, *Weiss Büch*, 8 Dec. 1888; Renault, II, pp. 111, 225
118 Renault, II, p. 147
119 Müller, pp. 421–2; Renault, II, pp. 147 ff
120 Bennett, 'Arab Power', pp. 196–7; Leyden to Pauncefote, 8 Oct. 1888, FO 84/1894; Renault, II, pp. 154–5.
121 Malet to Salisbury, no. 70 Af. conf., 18 Sept. 1888, FO 84/1892
122 This referred to the Sultan's lease of part of the coast to the Germans.
123 Memo. by Berchem, 16 Sept. 1888, enc. in Malet to Salisbury, no. 70, Af. conf., 18 Sept. 1888, FO 84/1892

This was received with indignation in the Foreign Office, which had no control over the press and where officials did not believe the opposition came mainly from slave dealers.[124] But for diplomatic reasons Salisbury had no desire to quarrel with Germany.[125] He would have been glad enough to see her retire from the coast of her own accord but, failing this, he was ready to work with her. He urged the Sultan to mollify the Germans and he counselled patience and tact at Berlin.

By October the towns on the German coast were deserted, trade was at a standstill and a number of Europeans had lost their lives. The Sultan was unable to quell the revolt, even if he wanted to.[126] It was imperative for the Germans that there should be a display of Anglo-German solidarity to prevent Britain from taking advantage of the situation. The British, on the other hand, had no desire to incur unpopularity, just as they were establishing themselves in their concession, by co-operating with the hated Germans. Bismarck, however, forced Salisbury's hand by inviting him to join him in a blockade of the East African coast, ostensibly to restore the Sultan's authority and prevent the export of slaves and the import of arms.[127]

Salisbury was in a dilemma. There was little sympathy in Britain for the German East African venture and he knew that to accept would be thoroughly unpopular at home, quite apart from any adverse effects it might have on Britain's relations with the people of the coast. But he feared that if he did not join the blockade the Germans might end by taking Zanzibar. He was also worried by Italian designs in East Africa, and thought both the German and Italian Governments were 'very much excited' and unpredictable. He therefore decided, to the disgust of the missionary societies, the British East Africa Company and even some of his own staff,[128] to co-operate in the blockade in the hope that he might prove a restraining influence.[129] Italy also decided to join in and sent a ship to the coast.

124 Minute by Lister on Memo. by Berchem, 16 Sept. 1888, *ibid.*
125 See Wm. Roger Louis, 'Great Britain and German expansion in Africa, 1884–1919', ch. 1 in P. Gifford and Wm. Roger Louis (eds.), *Britain and Germany in Africa: Imperial Rivalry and Colonial Rule*, New Haven 1967 (henceforth *Britain and Germany*), I, pp. 11 ff.
126 Incriminating evidence against the Sultan was later found when the rebel leader Bushiri was captured.
127 He also inspired an article in the *Norddeutsche Allegemeine Zeitung*, 26 Oct. 1888, praising the Papal Brief of 1888 in which the Pope put himself at the head of the anti-slavery campaign. The article described the suppression of slavery as one of the civilising missions of the century, Renault, II, pp. 149–50.
128 Protests were received from some of the missionary societies and from the Imperial British East Africa Company. Hill, Euan Smith and Kirk also opposed the blockade. Kirk whose opinions usually carried weight wrote that he thought Salisbury was acting 'with full information but against the opinion of every competent advisor', Kirk to Fowell Buxton, private, 5 Nov. 1888, ASS/BEA/G 7.
129 Salisbury to Euan Smith, no. 48 tel., conf., 11 Oct. 1888, tel. no. 55, 18 Oct. 1888, FO 84/1912; Salisbury to Goschen, 15 Oct. 1888, SP/Goschen; Cecil, pp. 235–7;

Neither Salisbury nor Bismarck regarded the venture as primarily an anti-slavery measure[130] but it had the merit that it could be presented to the public in this guise and would perhaps be less unpopular in Britain on this account.

In the course of these negotiations, Salisbury had mentioned the projected slave trade conference to the German Ambassador[131] but it is possible that the latter did not pass on the message to his superiors, for Count Herbert Bismarck seemed unaware of the proposal in December.[132] But, once embarked on the blockade, Salisbury suspended discussion of the conference.

The blockade could be successfully enforced only if other maritime powers and the Sultan of Zanzibar co-operated, and Salisbury's trump card in presenting it as an anti-slavery measure and disarming English critics was that it gave Britain the right, which she had sought so long in vain, to search French ships. This took some manoeuvring, France herself suggesting the legal fiction by which it could be done.[133] The operation had to be undertaken in the name of the Sultan, who proclaimed a blockade of his own coast as though he were at war with his subjects, and forbade the import of munitions. The export of slaves was already illegal. He thus became the reluctant belligerent ally of Britain and Germany who undertook to 'help' him enforce his own laws.[134] He only agreed to this farce in the face of German threats and refused to contribute either men or ships to assist the operation. For convenience the blockade was extended to his whole coastline although much of it was not in rebellion.

Since the Sultan was technically at war his new allies, Britain, Germany and Italy, now had the right to stop vessels of all nations on the high seas and in territorial waters and search them for contraband of war. They could only look for slaves if this had been sanctioned by treaty,[135] but France was the only power likely to object to their doing so and her acquisition of the

L. W. Hollingsworth, *Zanzibar Under the Foreign Office*, 1890-1913, London, 1953, p. 29; D. R. Gillard, 'Salisbury's African Policy and the Heligoland Offer of 1890', *EHR*, lxxv, 297 (1960), pp. 631–53.

130 Salisbury to Goschen, 14 Oct. 1888, SP/Goschen, certainly neither Kirk, Euan Smith or Hill thought it would be effective against the slave traffic. Bismarck in a speech to the Reichstag said that the blockade had not been intended as a serious anti-slavery measure but as a gesture of Anglo-German solidarity, 26 Jan. 1889, *Stenographische Berichte über die Verhandlungen des Deutschen Reichstages*, VII, Legislature-periode III, Session 27, p. 619 (henceforth *Verhandlungen*).

131 Minute by Salisbury on Malet to Salisbury, no. 30 tel. conf., 6 Dec. 1888, FO 84/1893.

132 Malet to Salisbury, no. 30 tel. conf., 6 Dec. 1888, FO 84/1893

133 Beauclerk to Salisbury, no. 13 tel., 31 Oct. 1888, FO 84/1893; Greindl to Leopold II, 30 Oct. 1888, E.I.C. I.R.C.B. (723) correspondence Greindl no. 76/I; the French suggested following the precedent of their own blockade in Annam in 1863.

134 Salisbury to Euan Smith, no. 59 secret, 25 Oct. 1888, FO 84/1912

135 The Germans only had treaty rights acquired under the convention of 1841 and the Italians those acquired by the conventions of 1831 and 1833.

whole Comoro group and her hegemony over Madagascar had given slaves more opportunity to acquire her flag. The French, however, were in no mood to resist combined Anglo-German pressure.

They had been much embarrassed by an incident in August 1888, which had thrown the whole question unpleasantly into the limelight. A British cruiser had stopped a French dhow off Pemba but had had to release her as her papers were in order. A boat was sent after her, however, to watch her movements. Some hours later the naval interpreter reported that he had hidden in a tree and watched the disembarkation of seventy-five slaves, who were subsequently sold on the island.[136] This caused great indignation in Britain, where it was feared that the sight of an English warship standing by powerless while a French dhow unloaded her human cargo would stimulate the owners of vessels to take out French papers.[137] Strong representations were made to Paris[138] and a British cruiser was sent to patrol the Mozambique Channel. British protests were backed by the Germans, who also claimed they had evidence of slave trading under the French flag.[139]

The French made caustic comments about the doubtful evidence of interpreters skulking up trees. Their Consul-General in Zanzibar suspected that Britain and Germany were jealous of the commerce carried on by French dhows and thought they were using the slave trade issue to ruin it.[140] But for all this the French were thoroughly alarmed. The Ministry of Foreign Affairs suspected that their flag was in fact being abused[141] and had already urged the Ministry of Marine to increase their naval forces in the Indian Ocean,[142] which were manifestly inadequate to police their shipping.[143] They had for some time feared that Britain would use the slave traffic as a reason for interference in Madagascar where she had still not recognised the French protectorate.[144] By October 1888 they suspected that a British press campaign denouncing slave trading under French colours was a prelude to action in the island.[145] They therefore reinforced their

136 Admiralty to FO, 15 Oct. 1888, enc. Blaxland to Fremantle, 4 Nov. 1888, FOCP 5896
137 A little later Euan Smith reported that it had indeed had this effect.
138 Salisbury to Lytton, no. 171 Af., 29 Oct. 1888, FO 84/1886
139 Michahelles to Lacau, 12 Sept. 1888, *Weiss Buch*, 8 Dec. 1888
140 Lacau to Goblet, 14 Sept. (?) 1888, enc. in Goblet to Krantz, 20 Nov. 1888, FMM/BB 3 991.
141 Goblet to Krantz, 7 Sept. 1888, and 20 Nov. 1888, *ibid.*, and 26 Nov. 1888, FMAE/MDA/111
142 FMAE to FMM, 4 June 1888 and 11 June 1888, FMM/BB 3 990. For the divergence of views between the two ministries see Renault, II, pp. 160–3
143 Michel to FMM, 3 Jan. 1888, FMM/BB 4 1220; FMM to FMAE, 8 June 1888, FMAE/MDA/142
144 Instructions to Michel, 7 June 1887, FMM/BB 4 1199; FMAE to FMM 4 June 1888, FMAE/MDA/Af. 142; Le Myre de Villiers to FMAE, 20 July 1888 enc. in FMAE to FMM, 24 July 1888, FMM/BB 3 991
145 Jusserand to Goblet, 16 Oct. 1888, FMAE/MDA 111

naval squadron in East African waters, ordered more care to be taken in the issue of their colours and told their naval commander to keep patrolling off Madagascar and the Comoros and to maintain effective control over dhows flying the French flag.[146]

However, it was one thing for France to take active steps to police her own flag and quite another for her to grant Britain and Germany the right to search for slaves. Feeling still ran very high in France on the subject and the government energetically denied in the Chamber of Deputies that they had made any concessions.[147] Indeed they had merely agreed that within the limits of the blockade French dhows might be searched. If they had munitions on board they could be seized but if they were carrying slaves they were to be handed over to the nearest French authorities.[148] In practice, however, this meant that French slavers could be apprehended at last. Salisbury had certainly scored a point.

To make the blockade complete, Portugal undertook to forbid the import of munitions on her coastline and to take naval measures to enforce the embargo. If carried out this would also, of course, stop the export of slaves from Mozambique.

As a serious measure against the slave trade, the blockade was hampered at every turn by political considerations. For instance, the British undertook to patrol their own coast lest the Germans should alienate its population, and they refused to assist the Germans off Bagamoyo, having no desire to become involved in their operations against the rebels, or to share their unpopularity. To relieve pressure on the German navy, however, one British ship was sent to Lindi in the extreme south, where it was hoped she would attract little attention.[149] The result was a redeployment of the British fleet at the expense of its anti-slavery operations. Boats usefully stationed off Zanzibar and Pemba were withdrawn to the British coast from which few slaves were run, especially during the north-east monsoon when the blockade began, while the Somali ports from which slaves did come at this time of year were left unguarded through lack of ships. The lone cruiser stationed at Lindi from which slaves were exported to Madagascar at this season had the impossible task of watching over a hundred miles of shore

146 FMM tel. to consul Aden for commander of the ship *Estaing*, 9 Sept. 1888, and to Michel, 11 Sept. 1888 and 15 Nov. 1888, FMM/BB 4 1213; Michel to commander of the *Boursaint*, 10 Dec. 1888, FMM/BB 4 1220; Krantz to Goblet, 5 Dec. 1888, FMAE/MDA 111, pp. 333–4.
147 *Journal Officiel de la République Française* (henceforth *Journal Officiel*), 20 Nov. 1888. The British had hoped that Lavigerie's campaign heralded a softening of French feeling on the right to search and the Anti-Slavery Society had asked him to help secure this right but realising that it would alienate French public opinion he refused to interfere, Renault, II, pp. 159–60.
148 Waddington to Salisbury, 23 Dec. 1888, FOCP 5770
149 Euan Smith to Salisbury, no. 336 conf., 19 Nov. 1888, and no. 353 1 Dec. 1888 FOCP 5770

more than two hundred miles away from her coaling base at Zanzibar.[150] The Germans patrolling their own coast and covering the outlets of the main slave routes to Zanzibar were hampered by lack of ships and the need to give priority to their military operations.[151] Italian co-operation was sporadic and never very serious. Several hundred slaves were eventually released during the blockade but the British naval commander thought better results could have been obtained more cheaply by other methods.[152]

Even less success was achieved against the arms traffic. Munitions continued to arrive at Zanzibar in large quantitities[153] and as long as they reached the island they were easily smuggled to the mainland in dhows or canoes.[154] Arms, for instance, were placed in the sides or bottoms of these craft and boarded over, while ammunition was hidden in tins packaged up with identical tins of kerosene so that the fraud could not be detected by shaking. Thorough search at sea was always difficult and the odds were on the side of the smuggler.

Britain and Germany eventually forced the Sultan to forbid the import of munitions into Zanzibar, over-ruling his objections that he would lose revenue and many British Indians would be ruined.[155] But the prohibition could be enforced on foreigners only with the consent of their governments since the Sultan's treaties granted foreign consuls the right to try their own nationals. None of the powers objected at the time[156] but it was clear that permanent control of the arms traffic would require an international agreement. The Sultan was further bludgeoned into delegating to Britain and Germany the right to search for arms in his territorial waters.[157]

In spite of all these efforts, it was thought that arms were still smuggled

150 This vessel had also to keep any captures with her until she could tow them to Zanzibar since during the north-east monsoon the weather precluded their being sent on their own with a prize crew. All the British ships suffered from being far from base, but those on the British coast could hold slavers at Mombasa pending shipment to Zanzibar. For the naval difficulties and the Admiral's views on the effectiveness of the blockade see Fremantle to Admiralty, 2 Dec. 1888, enc. in Admiralty to FO 5 Jan. 1889, FOCP 5867.

151 They had to keep ships at Bagamoyo and Dar-es-Salaam and at one stage their vessels were patrolling the coast shelling at random trying to kill as many people as possible, Euan Smith to Salisbury 14 Jan. 1889, SP/A.79.

152 Fremantle to Euan Smith, conf. 22 Feb. 1889, and enc., FOCP 5867

153 By French and German steamers, Euan Smith to Salisbury, no. 28 tel., 22 Jan. 1889, FO 84/1924, and no. 58, 22 Feb. 1889, FO 84/1976

154 Euan Smith to Salisbury, no. 12, 3 Jan. 1889, FO 84/1975. On the island arms and ammunition were stored by British Indians in their houses, and there was no police force capable of keeping watch over them. Euan Smith to Salisbury no. 10, tel. 10 Jan. 1889, FO 84/1984.

155 Euan Smith to Salisbury, no. 58, 2 Feb. 1889, FO 84/1976

156 Those most concerned, France, Portugal and Austria, ordered their consuls to co-operate, memo. by Leyden, 7 Oct. 1889, FO 84/1961.

157 Territorial waters were defined to include the entire Zanzibar Channel, Euan Smith to Salisbury, no. 87, 3 March 1889, FO 84/1984. The British already had powers to search in territorial waters for slaves.

into the mainland and the results achieved by the blockading fleet were negligible. In March 1889, for instance, the British boarded over thirteen hundred dhows and took one gun from one passenger.[158] Some vessels, to the great annoyance of their crews, were visited several times over. It is small wonder that most observers thought the blockade was costly, laborious, unproductive and an irritant to the local population. It depressed trade without achieving worthwhile results.

The blockade had barely begun when the Germans began to talk of raising it. Its mere implementation had served Bismarck's main purpose and the German Consul-General in Zanzibar was keen to end it by March, before the coastal caravans normally left to trade up-country, fearing that if they carried news of it with them trade would be diverted from the German sphere perhaps for ever.[159] He also thought that by irritating the inhabitants of the coast it was making pacification more difficult.[160] The German navy disliked it from the start. Crews suffered much from sickness and the officers resented being used to restore the authority of the German East Africa Company.[161]

However, Salisbury refused to end it at the very time of year when it might begin to prove useful against the slave trade. He wrote:

> The whole affair would seem rather ridiculous if we had watched the coast carefully during the period when the prevailing winds were adverse to the trade—and left it just when the winds were becoming favourable.[162]

So it dragged on, heartily disliked by everyone. By May, German participation was negligible. The Imperial navy, which was secretly ordered to search for slavers only occasionally,[163] was supporting military operations against the rebels.[164] The British were still patrolling but with little heart for the job. However, as Salisbury said, the problem was to find some means of ending the whole thing 'with a flourish'.[165]

The anti-slavery decrees in Zanzibar 1889-90

In this dilemma, Euan Smith came to the rescue. From late in 1888, he found the Sultan less and less co-operative[166] and without his help and that

158 Fremantle to Ad., 10 April 1889 enc. in Ad. to FO, 11 May 1889, FOCP 5972
159 Malet to Salisbury, no. 138 Af. secret, 14 Dec. 1888, FO 84/1893
160 Euan Smith to Salisbury no. 55, 2 Feb. 1889, FO 84/1976
161 Euan Smith to Salisbury no. 12, 3 Jan. 1889, FO 84/1975, and no. 6, secret tel., 4 Jan. 1889, FO 84/1984, and 14 Jan. 1889, private, SP/A 79
162 Salisbury to Portal, 4 April 1889, private, SP/A.80
163 H. Loth, *Kolonialismus und 'Humanitäts' Intervention—Kritische Untersuchung der Politik Deutschlands gegenüber dem Kongostaat 1884–1908*, Berlin 1966, p. 51
164 Portal to Salisbury, 17 May 1889, SP/A.79
165 Salisbury to Portal, no. 121, tel. secret, 22 Aug. 1889 FO 84/1983
166 See Hollingsworth, pp. 30 ff

of his officials, the smuggling of slaves could not be prevented. The slave runners were well known in Zanzibar. Some had been convicted more than once but their punishment at the hands of a sympathetic ruler was little more than nominal.[167] Since profits were high and the risk of capture small, they had little to discourage them. A suggestion that they might be sent to Aden to serve their sentences was turned down by the India Office on the grounds that there was no room in the prisons for them.[168] The British imposition of a fine upon the Sultan when some slave traders escaped after killing a naval officer on the island of Pemba, merely aroused Khalifa's resentment instead of making him more co-operative.[169] Euan Smith feared that if the blockade was allowed to peter out without some decisive blow being struck at the slave traffic, the slavers would assume that the Europeans had done their worst and failed, and that their nefarious business could now continue indefinitely.

He strongly advocated the abolition of slavery on the islands as the logical ending to the blockade. He felt many of the leading Arabs realised that the institution was doomed and that as long as it continued, Zanzibar was at the mercy of any colonial power choosing to use it as an excuse for aggression. He recognised that to avoid hardship and the ruin of the economy, it would be necessary to institute a scheme for the immigration of free labourers, probably from India, and with British help. To Salisbury's objection that the slave owners would have to be paid compensation, he replied that this was unnecessary since most slaves, particularly on Pemba where the traffic was most active, had been illegally imported since 1873.[170]

For a while the whole question was a pawn in a political game being played out in Zanzibar. Euan Smith, who had lost all influence over the Sultan, was involved in an intrigue with leading Arabs to replace him by his brother, Sayyid Ali, who was pro-British and who made it clear he favoured abolition. Salisbury, however, discouraged these plans. The Germans knew nothing of the conspiracy and were suspicious of Sayyid Ali and he feared a *coup* would raise the thorny question of the future of Zanzibar and perhaps end in a joint Anglo-German protectorate or the division of the sultanate

167 Euan Smith to Salisbury, no. 66 v. conf., 8 Feb. 1888, FO 84/1976. Euan Smith said they served a short term of imprisonment under the best conditions. This is in striking contrast to other testimony about the terrible conditions in the Sultan's prisons.
168 IO to FO, 25 June 1889, FOCP 5896
169 Portal to Salisbury, 4 May 1889, SP/A.79. This fine of $10,000 was extorted from the Sultan, who was to recover it from the Arabs of Pemba. It was paid on 1 Feb. 1889. Eventually one of the culprits was arrested and a year later the Sultan unsuccessfully demanded his money back, Euan Smith to Salisbury, no. 33, tel., 12 Feb. 1890; Salisbury to Euan Smith no. 12, tel., 17 Feb. 1890, FO 84/2069.
170 Euan Smith to Salisbury, no. 360, 3 Dec. 1888, FO 84/1911, no. 201 tel. secret, 15 Dec. 1888, no. 206 tel. 20 Dec. 1888, FO 84/1913, private 3 Feb. 1889, SP/A.79, no. 66 v.conf., 8 Feb. 1889, and minute by Salisbury, no. 115, 28 Feb. 1889, FOCP/ 5867. Euan Smith's views were endorsed by Kirk and Hill.

between the two powers. Apart from any strategic value that it might have and the large British Indian interests involved, Britain could hardly see the Sultan, the titular ruler of her coastal concession, pass under German control. Salisbury was unwilling to precipitate the whole issue. Sayyid Ali also opposed the plot and the matter was dropped.[171]

However, Euan Smith, who thought the Sultan's political rights on the mainland should be ended,[172] was allowed to put his views to the Germans, when he visited Berlin privately in the summer of 1889, and Salisbury particularly endorsed his proposal that the Sultan should be forced to issue an anti-slavery decree as a condition of raising the blockade. This would not only be 'beneficial in itself' but would resolve the dilemma of Britain and Germany 'who have got a blockade on hand which they do not quite know what to do with, and which threatens to expire ungracefully'.[173]

Euan Smith found the Germans receptive.[174] Count Bismarck was prepared to go even further, suggesting that the Sultan should abolish slavery on the mainland, declare free all who entered his possessions after an agreed date and delegate permanently to Britain and Germany the right to search in his territorial waters.[175] The British were afraid, however, that abolition on the mainland would cause disturbances in their sphere and prove unenforceable.[176] Furthermore it might give rise to claims for compensation which could not be overridden, as they could be in the islands, on the grounds that the slaves had been illegally imported.[177]

The Sultan made a desperate effort to strengthen his own position by offering to abolish slavery within a set time if the blockade was lifted and he was guaranteed his throne and given a decoration.[178] But such a spontaneous gesture from the ruler of Zanzibar would have stolen the thunder from the British and Germans.[179] Finally, in return for the raising of the blockade, he was forced to declare that anyone entering his dominions after 1 November

171 For these discussions see: Euan Smith to Salisbury, no. 62 tel. most secret, 14 Feb. 1889, and tel. secret (no number) 17 Feb. 1889, tel. 20 Feb. 1889, tel. 25 Feb. 1889 FO 84/1984; Portal to Salisbury 3 Aug. 1889, 4 Aug. 1889, 12 Aug. 1889, SP/A.79; Salisbury to Euan Smith, no. 39, tel. secret, 15 Feb. 1889, FO 84/1973
172 Like Kirk, Euan Smith thought the sultanate had outlived its usefulness to Britain. For their views see Euan Smith to Salisbury no. 113 most secret, 25 Feb. 1889, FO 84/1973 and Kirk to Mackinnon 20 Mar. 1889, MP/98/42.
173 Salisbury to Malet, private, 3 July 1889, FO 343/3
174 Euan Smith to Salisbury, private, 19 July 1889, FOCP 5977
175 Salisbury to Portal, no. 121 tel. secret, 22 Aug. 1889, FO 84/1983
176 Portal to Salisbury, no. 224 tel. v. secret, 23 Aug. 1888, FO 84/1984; Kirk to Salisbury, 20 Aug. 1889, FOCP 6010; Euan Smith to Salisbury, no. 66 v. conf., 8 Feb. 1888, FO 84/1976.
177 Kirk to Salisbury, 20 Aug. 1889, FOCP 6010
178 Portal to Salisbury, tel. private, 21 July 1889, SP/A. 79
179 It would also have made it more difficult to oust the Sultan from the mainland if his throne had been guaranteed. Euan Smith advised against accepting his offer on both counts, Euan Smith to Salisbury, private, 26 July 1889, SP/A.79.

1889 would be free, and to delegate permanently to Britain and Germany the power to search in his territorial waters.[180]

In his agreement with the British he also conceded that all children born in his kingdom after 1 January 1890 would be free. The Germans, however, to the surprise of the British, did not want this included in their arrangement with him.[181] These declarations meant that slavery would end in the Sultan's dominions as existing slaves died.

The blockade was raised on 1 October 1889. It had lasted nine months and Salisbury could congratulate himself that politically it had served its purpose. He had avoided any collision with Germany or Italy over Zanzibar. Germany, who had sent out the explorer Wissmann as Imperial Commissioner to subdue the rebels and control the company, was now crushing the revolt and bringing the coast under control. Italy had reached an agreement by which the Sultan ceded the Benadir ports to the British East Africa Company which handed them over to the Italians.[182] The Sultan was still on his throne and looked entirely to Britain for protection against the Germans. In fact Portal reported a farcical but 'convenient' situation in which the Germans would ask him to compose their letters to the Sultan and the latter would ask for his advice before answering them.[183] To justify the blockade before public opinion, to please the humanitarians and to impress the Arabs, a declaration against slavery had been obtained from the Sultan, which it was hoped might end the institution in the islands within a decade.[184]

Need for an agreement against the maritime slave trade

On the other hand the experiences of the blockade had highlighted the need for an international treaty against the slave traffic. They had shown once more the inadequacy of naval measures unless supported by the territorial authorities and backed by an efficient intelligence service. The British admiral had advocated setting up a central bureau in Zanzibar to collect, collate and evaluate information about the movements of slavers.[185] The difficulties of suppressing the slave trade without a treaty with France, at a time when her interests and shipping in the Indian Ocean were on the increase had also been clearly demonstrated.

180 Portal to Salisbury, no. 233 tel., 13 Sept. 1889, FO 84/1984
181 Portal to Salisbury, no. 231, tel. secret, 7 Sept. 1889, and minutes by Salisbury, *ibid.*
182 R. L. Hess, 'Germany and the Anglo-Italian Colonial Entente', in Louis and Gifford (eds.), *Britain and Germany*, I, pp. 160 ff., summarises Italian policy.
183 Portal to Barington, 24 Sept. 1889, SP/A.79
184 In view of the short expectation of life amongst slaves on the islands, Portal to Salisbury, private, 13 Sept. 1889, FO 84/1984.
185 Fremantle to Euan Smith, conf. 22 Feb. 1889, and enc. FOCP 5867

The French Consul-General, Lacau, conciliatory at first,[186] soon decided that Britain was deliberately harassing French dhows in the hope of diverting their trade into the hands of British Indians or of coercing them to seek British protection.[187] There were disputes over the right to search in territorial waters, protests when the British exceeded their powers and seized French vessels[188] and arguments as to whether Africans found on board were slaves or passengers. This last cause of friction gave rise to an interesting experiment by Lacau, who introduced a system by which all *bona fide* travellers were given a linen bracelet sealed with his consular seal. Friction became so acute that British naval officers were increasingly unwilling to stop French dhows.[189] The Germans were suspected of fomenting the ill feeling.[190] All in all the experiences of the blockade were not calculated to make settlement of the vexed question of the right to search any easier.

With the Germans there were troubles of a different order. The British followed clear rules of procedure in dealing with suspects, handing them over for trial by their national authorities or bringing them before the Vice-Admiralty Court at Zanzibar. They took considerable care to see that justice was done. Naval officers were made to pay some of the expenses of anyone they wrongfully detained. Convicted slavers were imprisoned in Zanzibar where, as has been noted, their punishment was light.

The Germans were more ruthless and more casual. They hanged slave traders[191] and were found to be condemning them without trial. Portal reported such a case which boded evil in view of the fact that the Germans had had months of experience blockading the coast:

> Baron von Gravenreuth seizes a dhow under the British flag near Bagamoyo under suspicion of slave trading—without trial bags the dhow, puts a German flag on her, puts the crew in irons and sends me back the English flag in a napkin. . . . I remonstrate, 'Really my dear Baron, you must not condemn English dhows and their crews without trial, nor send me English flags in napkins, it won't do, really'! [sic] He is profuse in apologies, 'did not know it was irregular, but *que voulez-vous*? He is a soldier not a diplomatist! But what could he do to please me?' We then went through the case and examined the evidence carefully, and I then asked that he sh[oul]d send me the crew of the dhow, and the witnesses,

186 Fremantle to Ad., 3 Jan. 1889, enc. in Ad. to FO, 24 Jan. 1889, FOCP 5867
187 Lacau to FMAE, 17 March 1889, FMM/BB 3 1004
188 See, for example, Euan Smith to Salisbury, no. 56, 28 Jan. 1889, and enc. and no. 57, 2 Feb. 1889, and encs., FO 84/1975
189 Fremantle to Euan Smith, 15 March 1889, enc. in Euan Smith to Salisbury, no. 157, 18 March 1889, FO 84/1977
190 Euan Smith to Salisbury, no. 94 tel., 8 March 1889, FO 84/1984 and no. 96, 11 March 1889, FO 84/1977
191 Euan Smith to Salisbury, 3 Feb. 1889, SP/A.79, Portal to Salisbury, no. 319, 2 Sept. 1889, FO 84/1980

for trial in this Court. He agreed with effusion 'but what witnesses do you want?' I pointed out that by his and his officers' reports of the case, the chief and almost only witness on whom the case turned was an Arab proprietor named Salem—let him therefore send to this court the crew of the dhow and Salem. 'My dear fellow,' answer[ed] Baron von Graveneuth, 'I am too stupid, I am always making these mistakes from being only a soldier, I should have thought of this before, but as for Salem— I hung him yesterday! and if I had thought he might easily have come here first!'[192]

The seeds of future international disputes lay in such proceedings, quite apart from the danger of a miscarriage of justice. At the outset too, the Germans seemed to have little idea of what to do with the slaves they freed. The British feared that they were turned loose and inevitably re-enslaved or, just as ominous, that they were forced to work for the Germans.[193] These were doubtless the teething troubles of a new colonial administration but they emphasised the desirability of a common policy.

The blockade had also shown the need for an international treaty if the arms traffic was to be controlled. This was necessary both to limit the import of munitions into Zanzibar and to close the other avenues by which arms might reach East Africa. They were reported to be coming from the Comoros and Nossi Bé for instance,[194] as well as from Portuguese territory and they could clearly also come up the Congo. Obviously only a far-reaching agreement would have any chance of success.

First moves against the arms trade

From the outset of the blockade the Germans had put a higher priority on the suppression of the arms traffic than on the prevention of the slave trade. Their main aim was to stop arms reaching the rebels. Consequently Bismarck made the first tentative moves towards an international agreement by opening negotiations with individual powers. Particularly important was the attitude of Leopold II, who by offering arms to the Arabs could in one move give them the weapons to resist the German advance and divert the ivory trade down the Congo. Fortunately for Germany, however, it suited the King to co-operate. He had no desire to see the Arabs equipped with munitions for, although he was making use of Tippu Tip as his governor at Stanley Falls, this was a temporary expedient, the wisdom of which he had begun to doubt.[195] He did not trust him or his partners and wanted to keep them dependent upon himself for their arms supplies.

192 Portal to Barington, 3 Oct. 1889, SP/A.79
193 Fremantle to Ad., 16 Jan. 1889, enc. in Ad. to FO, 22 Feb. 1889, and 2 Feb. 1889, enc. in Ad. to F.O, 1 March 1889, FOCP 5867
194 Euan Smith to Salisbury, 28 Aug. 1888, FO 84/1908
195 For the King's relations with Tippu Tip see Ceulemans, pp. 98 ff. Lavigerie's revelations seem to have disturbed Leopold II for he asked his minister in Berlin to

In fact in 1885 he had forbidden the importation of arms of precision into the State but he was on difficult ground as this might be considered against the provisions of the Berlin Act. Indeed it had elicited a protest from the Portuguese.[196] He took the view that he could legally impose such restrictions for humanitarian and security reasons[197] but of course his measures were useless and merely risked driving trade away from the Congo as long as they were not also imposed in neighbouring French and Portuguese territory. Portugal agreed to take similar action in 1886 but there the matter rested and the ban appears to have been a dead letter, for by 1888 it was being openly violated on the upper Congo.[198] It did not apply to trade guns and trade powder.

The question was of commercial as well as political importance since the Congo State, itself trading in ivory on the upper river, was competing with three private companies, the French firm of Daumas, Beraud and Co., the Belgian Sanford Exploring Expedition and, most formidable of all, the Dutch Nieuwe Afrikaanse Handels-Venootschap. The last two had their own steamers and seriously threatened the King's commercial plans, particularly the Dutch house, which contracted to supply arms and ammunition to Tippu Tip in return for fifteen tons of ivory.[199] It was in his sermon in Brussels after his interview with the King that Lavigerie had suggested taking steps to disarm the Arabs[200] and Leopold II was soon dropping hints in German circles that he wanted to forbid the import of arms into central Africa.[201] In October he met the challenge from the Dutch company by forbidding the sale of precision arms on the upper Congo and its tributaries[202] and his agents seized the Dutch consignment on its way up the river.[203]

The King therefore welcomed Bismarck's invitation to take part in the struggle against the Arabs by measures against the arms and slave trades. He hinted that Germany might ask him to act against the slave traffic in the Bahr el-Ghazal thus giving him a humanitarian reason to move towards

sound out the views of the German explorer Schweinfurth as to whether it would be better to exterminate the Arabs or use them! Leopold II to Greindl, 1 Sept. 1888, EIC IRCB (723) No. 76/I.

196 Note by Van Eetvelde, 22 March (?) 1885, and undated protest from the Governor of Angola, EIC/AR (294) 375.

197 Note on the arms trade undated but prepared for the Brussels Conference, 1889, EIC Al. (1378).

198 *Ibid.*

199 Ceulemans, pp. 196 ff.; Sanford to Mackinnon, 10 July, 1887, MP 209/4

200 See above, p. 206

201 The King asked Greindl, the Belgian Minister in Berlin, to discuss it with the explorer Schweinfurth, Leopold II to Greindl, 1 Sept. 1888, EIC IRCB (723) no. 76/I.

202 *Bulletin Officiel de l'État Indépendant du Congo* (henceforth *Bulletin Officiel*), 1888, p. 286, decree of 11 Oct. 1888

203 Ceulemans, p. 198; C. Liebrechts, *Léopold II, fondateur d'empire*, Brussels 1932, p. 140

the upper Nile.[204] The Germans took the point and also helped him further by suggesting that he might forbid all trade in munitions in the Congo State, specifically mentioning the commerce of the Dutch firm.[205] The wily monarch complied with alacrity, prohibiting the trade in arms of precision throughout the Congo and dealings in munitions of all kinds on the upper river and its tributaries. To enforce these regulations he announced that all boats coming upstream would be searched.[206] This was in contravention of the Berlin Act but he counted on Bismarck's support.

The Germans went as far as to ask the Dutch to forbid the export of arms from Holland to the Congo.[207] The King and the Chancellor also approached France and Portugal, suggesting that they take measures to control the traffic. Portugal promised co-operation but many months later the King thought she had actually done little, while France had not responded to the overture.[208]

In April 1889, Germany proposed to Britain that they negotiate an international agreement to control the trade in precision weapons and their ammunition in all the African territories of the colonial powers.[209] Such an agreement would alleviate German fears that the British might arm the Arabs in East Africa and safeguard Germany's position in South West Africa where she had no military force and no means of ending the endemic warfare between the Herero and the Khoi-khoi or Namas. She had already accused Cape merchants of selling arms in her territories.[210]

The German proposal was not welcomed in Britain. Hill pointed out that it would be beyond her resources to prevent smuggling and ensure that all arms were registered and licensed throughout her African territories. Germany had a much smaller area to police. Moreover she could continue to allow munitions to be shipped from Hamburg while leaving to Britain the task of seeing that they were not sold in British territory. He thought an agreement would lead to constant German fault finding and also to the ruin of the British arms trade in Africa.[211] Salisbury agreed that the proposal was

204 Leopold II to Greindl, 8 Nov. 1888, EIC IRCB no. 76/I. For this whole subject see Ceulemans, pp. 136 ff.
205 Bismarck to Alvensleben, 20 Sept. 1888; *Weiss Buch*, 8 Dec. 1888, no. 41
206 Decree enc. in Vivian to Salisbury, 4 Nov. 1888, FO 84/1895; Decree 28 Jan. 1889, no. 3 March 1889, enc. in Vivian to Salisbury, 14 March 1889, FO 84/1945; Metternich to Bismarck, 5 Nov. 1888 and Van Eetvelde to Alvensleben, 30 Nov. 1888, *Weiss Buch* 8 Dec. 1888, nos. 40 & 42.
207 Rumbold to Salisbury, no. 3 Af., 24 Dec. 1888, FOCP 5770
208 Analyse CAE/AGR/VE/162, see below, p. 253, n. 110.
209 Memo. communicated by Hatzfeldt, 9 April 1889, FO 84/1960
210 The Cape leaders said they were taking precautions but they themselves complained that German traders were selling arms across the border, Rosebery to Malet, 27 March 1886, FO 84/1757; Note verbale, 30 April 1886, enc. in Malet to Rosebery, 1 May 1886, FO 84/1759; Note verbale 27 April 1888, enc. in Malet to Salisbury, 28 April 1888, FO 84/1892.
211 Minute by Hill on Hatzfeldt to Salisbury, 9 April 1889, FO 84/1960

'quite impracticable' and thought it would not be accepted by the Cape for whom Britain could not legislate and would be unwelcome in Natal.[212]

This raised an interesting question. In the mid-1880s the Colonial Office had been anxious to conclude an agreement with Portugal and Germany to restrict the munitions trade south of the 16th parallel, in order to protect the trade and revenues of Natal which were threatened by an arrangement between Portugal and the Transvaal by which goods in transit to the latter paid only a 3% transit duty at Delagoa Bay.[213] This was lower than duties charged in Natal and spirits, arms and even English woollens and cottons formerly imported through the colony were now going to Lourenço Marques.[214] Natal complained of loss of trade and revenue and protested that Africans along her borders were being 'demoralised' by cheap arms and spirits sold by the Boers.[215] The Colonial Office pressed for an agreement to limit the traffic in the two staples of this trade, spirits and arms, on humanitarian grounds.[216] By 1886, they also wanted to limit the import of munitions in West Africa, where the administrator of the Gambia claimed it would prevent the wars which hindered trade and agriculture in the hinterland.[217] But the question was shelved pending the outcome of similar discussions with Germany over the western Pacific.

By the time these had failed Salisbury was Foreign Secretary. He firmly opposed such schemes. He did not believe other powers would faithfully execute an agreement and the only effect would be to cause 'considerable' loss to the English gun trade and leave the Africans in British territories exposed to attacks from their enemies armed by other powers.[218] The Colonial Secretary, Sir Henry Holland, later Lord Knutsford, reluctantly agreed with him.

When the Germans made their proposals two years later, however, Knutsford had executed a *volte face* and no longer favoured an arms agreement for southern Africa. The Colonial Office had tried restricting the supplies to Africans in the interior, he said, but had given it up on finding the only result was that rulers unfriendly to the British, got their arms from the

212 Minute by Salisbury, *ibid.*
213 The Transvaal planned a railway link with Delagoa Bay.
214 Natal at the time gave no rebate on duties on goods in transit, to the irritation of the Boers.
215 Secretary, London Chamber of Commerce, South African Section, to Bulwer, 17 Feb. 1886 enc. in Bulwer to CO, 18 Feb. 1886, COCP African no. 381 CO 879/31.
216 CO to FO, 5 March 1886, and enc. Bulwer to CO, 23 Oct. 1885, *ibid.* Lord Granville who was the Colonial Secretary at the time did not believe that injury to the trade of Natal alone was sufficient grounds for negotiating an agreement.
217 Rowe to Granville, 4 June 1887, and enc. Hay to Rowe, 16 May 1886, *ibid.*, CO to FO, 11 Aug. 1886, *ibid.*
218 FO to CO, 23 March 1887, FO 84/1860. In 1887, 12.34% of the total exports of British munitions were sent directly from Britain to South Africa and western Africa, see returns in Customs 9/97. These totals include arms for government use. See below, pp. 262ff., for a fuller discussion of this point.

Starving slaves abandoned on the march

Sir John Kirk

Tippu Tip

Boers while friendly ones were left at the mercy of their enemies.[219] Knutsford was quoting Sir Hercules Robinson, the British High Commissioner in South Africa, and the question has to be viewed in the light of the situation in southern Zambesia.

Here Britain, impelled by the Cape was slowly extending her territories. In 1885 she had declared a protectorate over Bechuanaland up to the 22° parallel South and in 1888 she had proclaimed a British 'sphere of influence' up to the Zambesi, including Mashonaland and Matabeleland.[220] This was intended simply to warn off foreigners, for she had no semblance of an administration. The area was reputed to be rich in gold and both Portugal and the Transvaal protested.[221] The Portuguese themselves claimed Mashonaland, a raiding ground of the Ndebele. White freebooters and concession hunters ranged over the region unhindered. By 1888 their attention was focused on the court of Lobengula, ruler of the Ndebele. Underlying the international dispute lay fierce rivalry between different sets of white adventurers and endemic disputes between Africans whose territories had no boundaries in the European sense of the word. Khama, ruler of the Ngwato, for instance, whose dominions were bisected by the frontier of the Bechuanaland protectorate, was engaged in a border squabble with Lobengula.[222]

In this situation, it was essential for Britain to remain on friendly terms with Africans within her sphere of influence, and important that they look to her for the arms necessary to protect themselves against the encroachments of Boers, Portuguese or other foreigners.[223] In the spring of 1889 when the Germans made their arms proposals Khama was threatened with attack by the Boers and Lobengula feared the Portuguese. The Colonial Office had every desire to keep them friendly by supplying their needs.[224] Not only this but a few months earlier, Charles Rudd, the agent for the South African financier Cecil Rhodes, had obtained a concession for mining rights from Lobengula by promising him one thousand Martini-Henry rifles with ammunition, £100 a month and a steamboat. The King had been more interested in the guns than in the money.[225]

219 Draft of Knutsford to Loch, no date, enc. in CO to FO, 2 Nov. 1889, and Robinson to CO 18 Oct. 1889, FO 84/2005.
220 For a discussion of this and of the importance for South Africa of establishing British power up to the Zambesi see Robinson and Gallagher, pp. 221 ff.
221 See Knutsford memo. Feb. 1889, CAB/37/23 no. 9; Anderson memo. 6 Jan. 1890, CAB/37/26 no. 2. Germany also contested the region around Lake Ngami.
222 See P. Mason, *The Birth of a Dilemma*, London 1958, pp. 122 ff.; H. M. Hole, *Lobengula*, London 1929, pp. 125 ff.
223 In Bechuanaland arms were also wanted for hunting which was essential for African food supplies. For the situation in the area see memo. 30 Nov. 1888, CAB/37/22, no. 39.
224 CO to FO, 1 March 1889, FO 84/1990
225 Robinson to CO, 18 Oct. 1889, enc. in CO to FO, 2 Nov. 1889, FO 84/2005. J. G. Lockhart and C. M. Woodhouse, *Rhodes*, London 1963, pp. 144–5

This concession formed the basis of the claim upon which Rhodes got a charter to rule the lands both north and south of the Zambesi for his British South Africa Company. It was this company which was eventually to establish an administration in the 'sphere of influence'.[226] But in the spring of 1889 negotiations had only just begun, the company was still in embryo, there were no British authorities in the area and Lobengula was having second thoughts about the concession. Both the High Commissioner and the administrator in Bechuanaland supported Rhodes' schemes.[227] In this fluid and somewhat precarious situation they had no desire to be hampered by an international arms agreement, and their views prevailed in the Colonial Office.[228]

This accorded well with Salisbury's own distrust of such agreements. Only in the strategically important Red Sea area, where he had inherited the negotiations begun in 1885 with Italy, did he show any desire to restrict the arms traffic, and these negotiations had borne no fruit by 1889. British local officials had wanted an extensive agreement covering the whole Somali coast north of the possessions of the Sultan of Zanzibar, and including every kind of weapon, even daggers, bows and arrows.[229] The trade remained forbidden in the British Somali ports and strictly controlled at Aden;[230] while north of Massawa, Britain blockaded the coast to stop supplies reaching the Mahdists besieging Suakin.[231]

Italy, whose representative in Shoa, Antonelli, had undertaken in 1884 to supply Menelik with fifty thousand rifles and a million cartridges within a decade, had no wish to stop deliveries.[232] By 1886 British officials were

226 The company was to operate north and west of the Transvaal or South African Republic, west of Portuguese territory and north of Bechuanaland. No northward limits were fixed and Rhodes was aiming to extend his territories north of the Zambesi and to take over the Bechuanaland protectorate and Nyasaland.
227 The arms destined for Lobengula under the Rudd concession were subsequently taken quite openly through Bechuanaland by Jameson. When this was criticised both in the Cape Parliament and in Britain the High Commissioner defended it on the grounds that they could easily have been bought in the Transvaal and that he had agreed that the Bechuanaland Exploring Company should supply a roughly equivalent number of rifles to Khama, thus their forces were balanced. He maintained that it was necessary to treat all friendly rulers alike and that arms were needed for defence and hunting, see Robinson to CO, 18 Oct. 1889, FO 84/2005.
228 Draft of Knutsford to Loch, no date, enc. in CO to FO, 2 Nov. 1889, FO 82/2005
229 IO to FO, 18 May, 1887, and enc. FOCP 5467. Arms were defined as 'firearms, bayonets, swords, daggers, spears, spear-heads, bows, arrows, cannon, parts of arms and machinery for the manufacture of arms'. They also wanted to stop imports of sulphur, lead and ammunition.
230 At Aden the sale, export and transhipment of munitions were forbidden and imports of lead and sulphur for Arabia controlled.
231 Interestingly in 1885–6 the Mahdists were exporting arms (but not ammunition) and slaves in exchange for grain and cotton brought by blockade runners from Arabia, Jago to Rosebery, no. 2 Af., 15 April 1886, FOCP 5459.
232 Lumley to Granville, no. 8 conf., 13 Jan. 1885, and enc., FOCP 5149 and no. 255, 18 Dec. 1885, FOCP 5331.

worried lest arms sent to Shoa fell into the hands of Somali and Danakil tribesmen. Caravans could be plundered *en route* and the use of arms was becoming more common.[233]

Having had no luck with Italy, Britain made overtures to France. The French were ready to co-operate because they wanted an agreement with Britain over the frontiers of their respective Somali territories. They therefore banned the traffic through their ports in 1886[234] and the Anglo-French boundary convention of 1888 contained provisions against the arms trade as well as the slave traffic.[235] These measures aroused the resentment of French merchants and the opposition of the governor of Obock because they threatened the development of trade with Shoa.[236] The French Government tried in vain to get Britain to accept their interpretation of the agreement under which arms could enter their territories provided they were in transit to Menelik and were not sold on the coast.[237]

The only result of the Anglo-French embargo on the arms traffic was to increase Menelik's dependence upon the Italians, and French traders soon began to evade the regulations.[238] The Italians, who had occupied Massawa in 1885, had a brief change of heart after the outbreak of their war with the Emperor Yohannes in 1887. They blockaded the Eritrean coast and asked Salisbury to negotiate a tripartite agreement,[239] but when presented with a draft they did no more,[240] and continued to send arms to Menelik, who they were anxious should remain neutral in the war and dependent upon themselves for munitions. By the spring of 1889, the French were threatening to end their embargo[241] which was simply playing into Italian hands. Italy thereupon agreed to limit the private trade in arms only. This would enable her to continue to make Menelik 'presents' of munitions. While

233 Hogg to Gaspary, 19 Feb. 1886, enc. in Godley to Pauncefote, secret, 18 March 1886, FOCP 5331

234 Caulk, 'Menelik II', pp. 146 ff.; Pankhurst, *Economic History*, p. 593

235 Agreement of 2/9 Feb. 1888, Hertslet, *Map*, II, pp. 726–8

236 Caulk, 'Menelik II', pp. 190 ff.; Lagarde to Goblet, 11 Oct. 1888, FMAE/MDA/135

237 Note of 28 April 1888, *ibid.*, Lytton to Salisbury, no. 190, 28 March 1888, no. 289, 18 May, 1888, FO to IO, 6 April, 1888, FOCP 5659.

238 Caulk, 'Menelik II', pp. 196 ff., with the knowledge of the governor of Obock Picquart, pp. 146–7; Pankhurst, *Economic History*, pp. 593–4.

239 Caulk, 'Menelik II', pp. 205 ff.; FO to IO, 13 May 1887 FOCP 5467; Salisbury to Kennedy, no. 13. v. conf., 25 Jan. 1888, FOCP 5659; Catalani to Pauncefote, 8 Feb. 1888, *ibid.*

240 The draft was sent to them in June 1888; they did not accept it until February 1889 after France and Britain returned to the attack, Lytton to Salisbury, no. 51, conf., 2 Feb. 1889, FOCP 5794; Salisbury to Dufferin, no. 28, conf., 9 Feb. 1889, *ibid.*

241 Lytton to Salisbury, no. 51, conf., 2 Feb. 1889, FOCP 5794, French traders were evading it and the governor of Obock ignoring it and urging that it should be ended, Caulk, pp. 196 ff., Lagarde to Goblet, 2 Sept. 1888, FMAE/MDA/135, and 14 June 1889, FMAE/MDA/138, Stace to Portal, 23 Sept. 1888, enc. in Portal to Salisbury, no. 311, 2 Oct. 1888, FOCP 5752.

these negotiations languished,[242] events in Ethiopia changed the whole position.

In March Yohannes was killed in a battle against the Mahdists and Menelik embarked on his struggle for the throne. In May he signed the famous treaty of Wichale (Uccialli) with Italy, which delimited the Italo-Ethiopian boundaries, outlawed the slave trade and provided that munitions might be imported through Massawa; but only for himself and upon his making a regular application for them, and they were to be escorted to his borders by Italian soldiers. Article XVII stipulated that Ethiopian foreign relations *might* be conducted through Italy. In October Italy notified the powers of the existence of this article, thus virtually claiming a protectorate over Ethiopia, a pretension of which Menelik was unaware.[243]

The arms negotiations continued to drag on with both France and Italy making difficulties until finally Italy frankly stated that now she was in alliance with Menelik she wished to be free to send him arms.[244] Thus the negotiations had broken down on the eve of the Brussels Conference after five years of desultory talks. The arms question had been but a pawn in the political game being played out on the Red Sea and Somali coasts where Britain, France and Italy competed for trade and influence in the hinterland. The game had been played so far to the benefit of Italy. The arms embargo and the fact that Antonelli was on an official mission gave him an advantage over French traders,[245] who evaded the embargo but could not afford to supply such good weapons as their Italian rival. By the time the negotiations broke down the British local authorities had decided that they, too, would have to allow Menelik to import arms through their ports, for in the existing situation, not only were British traders placed at a disadvantage, but Menelik was forced to depend on the Italians or to deal with French merchants at Jibouti through the Abu Bekr family, who also traded in slaves.[246]

At the time of the Brussels Conference therefore, the dangers of an unrestricted trade in munitions were clear to all the colonial powers and some of them had been pressing for local agreements for some time, the

242 See correspondence in FOCP 5794 and 5883.
243 The Amharic text of the treaty was significantly different from the Italian one. An English translation of the Italian text is in Hertslet, *Map*, II, pp. 454–5. For a discussion of how the treaty was used by Italy to claim a protectorate see C. Giglio, 'Article 17 of the Treaty of Uccialli', *JAH*, vi, 2, 1965, pp. 221–31; S. Rubenson, 'The Protectorate Paragraph of the Wichale Treaty, *ibid.*, v, 2, 1964, pp. 243–83; 'Professor Giglio, Antonelli and Article XVII of the Treaty of Wichale', *ibid.*, vii, 3, 1966, pp. 445–57.
244 Dufferin to Salisbury, no. 44, tel., 22 Sept. 1889, no. 239, 28 Nov. 1889 and enc. Italian note of 4 Nov. 1889 FOCP 5883 and private letter, 28 Nov. 1889, SP/A.66.
245 Caulk, 'Menelik II', pp. 110–11
246 Walsh to Stace, 25 May 1889, Stace to Baring, 10 Nov. 1889, in Clarke to Salisbury, 20 Nov. 1889, FOCP 5883.

British on the Somali and Red Sea coasts, the French in West Africa, the Germans in East Africa,[247] and King Leopold on the Congo, but none had borne fruit. The conference was to give the interested powers the opportunity to bring the matter up as a humanitarian question.

Preliminaries of the Brussels Conference

Plans for a slave trade conference in Brussels were revived in the spring of 1889 when Germany came around to the idea. Meanwhile Bismarck had used the anti-slavery movement to good advantage, finding it popular and politically useful. In the autumn of 1888 public meetings in Cologne and Freiburg had passed resolutions calling for action against the East African slavers.[248] In November a Catholic anti-slavery society had been formed in Cologne[249] and another important meeting had taken place in Munich in December.[250] When Bismarck decided to send Wissmann out to suppress the rising in East Africa, he knew he would be opposed in the Reichstag by the Catholic Centre Party, whose leader, L. Windthorst, believed that Germany, situated as she was between two great military powers, should not dissipate her resources on colonial ventures. However, by linking the anti-slavery question to the suppression of the revolt, Bismarck was able to get Windthorst and his followers to give grudging support.[251]

In November Salisbury had published an unusually full Blue Book on the slave trade, including his letter asking Leopold II to call a conference. In December the Reichstag passed a resolution to the effect that it would support any measures agreed upon by the colonial powers for the suppression of the traffic, and the German press, particularly the Catholic organs began to discuss the proposal for a conference.[252] It became clear that the idea was popular in Catholic circles and might also appeal to the evangelical supporters of the older missions who disliked the Catholic complexion of

247 The Germans, unable to get British co-operation in a general arms agreement, continued their efforts to cut off supplies in East Africa where they feared the British company would capture the ivory trade by offering arms to the Arabs. The question was still unresolved when the conference opened. At Zanzibar the prohibitions on exports remained in force but the search for arms being smuggled to the mainland was abandoned when the blockade was lifted.

248 *Weiss Buch*, 8 Dec. 1888, nos. 24, 25

249 Renault, II, pp. 225 ff.; this was the *Afrika-Verein Deutscher-Katholiken*, which aimed at supporting missions as well as combating the slave trade. This gave it a somewhat different character from that intended by Lavigerie and made co-operation with the Protestants impossible. Moves were made towards the formation of an anti-slavery commission by Protestants in the *Deutsche Kolonial-Gesellschaft* but they seem to have come to little.

250 *Ibid.*, II, p. 229 note 1

251 *Ibid.*, II, pp. 152–6

252 Ceulemans, p. 241

Lavigerie's movement and did not regard the suppression of the East African rebellion as an anti-slavery measure.[253]

The British Anti-Slavery Society had been trying to get the matter discussed in the House of Commons all through the winter of 1888-9 but the government had fended them off,[254] presumably because Count Bismarck[255] had told the British Ambassador in December that he thought a conference unnecessary and undesirable as agreement would never be reached.[256] On 26 March however, the society through its supporters in both parties finally managed to get a debate and the House, unusually full for such an event, passed a resolution calling for a conference of all the powers who had signed declarations against the slave traffic.[257]

Count Bismarck was in London at the time. The idea now suited him well, for diplomatic as well as domestic reasons. France was trying to detach Italy from the Triple Alliance with Germany and Italy, and he thought that Italy, vulnerable as she was to French naval attack, might take heart from a display of Anglo-German solidarity. He was therefore prepared to work with Salisbury over Zanzibar, Samoa and the slave trade conference.[258] 'We want,' he explained, 'not only the reality of friendship but the occasional demonstration of it.'[259] He was even willing to take the initiative in calling the meeting himself and mentioned it to the French Ambassador.[260] But once Germany had agreed to the plan there was no further reason for delay and Salisbury gladly asked Vivian to set the wheels in motion once more.

This time he initially envisaged asking France, Germany, Portugal and Turkey, but strangely not Italy.[261] By the time he wrote to Vivian, however, Turkey had been omitted,[262] perhaps because he thought she would not help, while Italy had been added at the request of the Germans.[263] The Belgians began at once to propose additions. They established that the

253 Loth, p. 55; Renault, II, p. 283

254 *Anti-Slavery Reporter*, IX, 6, Nov.-Dec. 1888, pp. 233-5; Buxton to Allen, 10 Dec. 1888 and 17(?) Dec. 1888, ASS/53.54

255 Count Herbert Bismarck was the son of the Chancellor Prince Bismarck and was Secretary of State for Foreign Affairs.

256 Malet to Salisbury, no. 30 Af., conf., 6 Dec. 1888, FO 84/1893

257 For the occasion Sidney Buxton, a Liberal, enlisted the help of Sir John Kennaway, a Conservative, and the society congratulated itself that some hundred members of Parliament sat through the debate, see *Anti-Slavery Reporter*, IX, 2, March/April 1889, p. 55.

258 Salisbury to Queen Victoria, 29 March 1889, *Letters of Queen Victoria*, ser. 3, C. E. Buckle, (ed.), London 1930, I, pp. 483-4

259 Currie to Salisbury, 27 March 1889, SP/Currie

260 Salisbury to Malet, 30 March 1889, no. 148 Af., FO 84/1953, Malet to Salisbury, no. 87 Af., conf., 13 April 1889, FO 84/1957

261 Salisbury to Malet, no. 148 Af., 30 March 1889, FO 84/1953

262 Salisbury to Vivian, no. 17 Af., 17 April 1889, FOCP 5983. Vivian to Chimay, note verbale, 16 May 1889, no. 35, AEB/CAE/1.

263 Malet to Salisbury, no. 87, conf. Af., 13 April 1889 and minutes by Hill, 15 and 16 April 1889, FO 84/1957

Congo, accidentally omitted by Salisbury, would be included.[264] They wanted Spain to come since she was an African coastal power, Russia because she expected an invitation and Turkey so that the conference should not seem to be embarking on a Christian crusade against slavery.[265]

In fact, as the possibilities of the meeting dawned upon King Leopold, he determined to ask the powers to allow him to levy import duties in the Congo, on the plea that he would need the extra revenue to finance action against the slave traffic.[266] For this he needed the consent of all the signatories of the Berlin Act and of the U.S.A.,[267] who had a separate tariff agreement with the Congo state. It was clearly simpler if they all came to the conference and were associated in the anti-slavery campaign. There was much truth in the Belgian arguments that the signatories of the Berlin Act might be offended if they were not asked, and that their moral support was needed,[268] and the King won the point.

Against Salisbury's better judgement Persia was invited as she was a Muslim state, said to be co-operating against the traffic, whose support might therefore be valuable.[269] Egypt could not be asked as she was part of the Ottoman empire. Brazil, who had abolished slavery the previous year, and other minor powers were not included for fear the meeting would become too big and unwieldy. They could always be asked later to adhere to the decisions of the meeting if this proved necessary.

The British thought the Sultan of Zanzibar should be represented as a 'solace to his feelings' and to alleviate any damage to his prestige which might have resulted from his anti-slavery proclamation.[270] But the great difficulty was to find a representative. The Sultan would have liked Kirk but Britain feared this would excite German suspicions. It was eventually decided between Britain and Germany that the Sultan would send the members of a mission which he had fortuitously sent to Germany to congratulate the Kaiser on his accession. The German Chancellor was already highly cynical about the conference. 'There will hardly be any results,' he wrote, 'in England it is a matter of popularity and the more peculiar participants the more useful it will be.'[271]

264 Salisbury to Malet, 30 March 1889, no. 148 Af., FO 84/1953; Salisbury to Vivian, no. 22 Af., 30 April 1889, FOCP 5983
265 Vivian to Salisbury, no. 29 Af., 19 April 1889, no. 34, Af., 27 April 1889, no. 38, Af., 11 May 1889, no 42, Af., 8 June 1889, *ibid.*
266 Vivian to Salisbury, no. 36, Af., 4 May 1889, *ibid.*
267 The U.S.A. had signed but not ratified the Berlin Act.
268 Vivian to Salisbury, no. 42 Af., enc. Belgian note, 7 June 1889, FOCP 5983. The Belgian minutes and drafts are in AEB/CAE/1, nos. 37, 40, 41, 42.
269 The Belgians were sceptical about Persian co-operation. Minutes by Lister and Salisbury on Vivian to Salisbury, no. 87, Af., 17 Sept. 1889, FO 84/1946, and Salisbury to Vivian, no. 54, conf., 5 Oct., 1889, no. 76, 19 Oct. 1889, no. 107, Af. conf., 12 Oct. 1889, FOCP 5893.
270 Minute by Currie, 30 August 1889, FO 84/1955
271 Loth, pp. 54–5, 'Ergebnisse wird sie kaum haben, in England aber ist sie Popularitätssache, und je mehr sonderbare Teilnehmer desto wirksamer'.

However, when Count Bismarck saw the Sultan's emissaries, two 'respectable' Arabs and an interpreter, he warned Salisbury that they were not qualified for the job.[272] In London this was considered unimportant. It would 'look bad' if the Sultan sent no one and nominal representation was better than none. As Lister had said:

> The Sultanate of Zanzibar is at the present moment the most limited monarchy in existence and the merest dummy will do to represent the Sultan, but he should be a subject and co-religionist of the Sultan's. One of the impending mission in his native costume would do very well and Kirk might be asked to look after him and let him know what was going on.[273]

Happy as this solution would have been for Britain, it was not to be. The envoys, pleading cold, homesickness, old age and infirmity, begged to be excused. None of the powers felt they could interfere,[274] so to the astonishment of the British and the mortification of the Sultan, they simply fled to Marseilles and boarded the steamer for home.[275] Only when it docked did the Sultan find they were not at the conference which had opened nearly two weeks before. Britain and Germany eventually decided that the Sultan should be jointly represented by their own second plenipotentiaries, Kirk and Dr von Arendt, a former German Consul-General in Zanzibar.[276]

272 Malet to Salisbury, no. 142 Af., 30 Oct. 1889, FO 84/1958
273 Minute by Lister on Portal to Salisbury, no. 252 tel., 16 Oct. 1889, FO 84/1984 and minutes of 12 Oct. 1889 and 14 Oct. 1889 on Malet to Salisbury, no. 144 Af., 5 Oct. 1889, FO 84/1958
274 The matter was felt to be a delicate one since the Sultan had accepted the invitation and the Belgians expected the delegates. The Germans like the British wanted a Zanzibari to attend, Greindl to Lambermont, 7 Nov. 1889, no. 114, AEB/CAE 2.
275 From the start the mission had had its humorous side. Apparently the German Consul-General, acting on his own initiative, first proposed to the Sultan that he should send this mission and, to the consternation of the Foreign Office, Portal suggested they visit England. The French were taken by surprise by the arrival of the emissaries at Marseilles and the official sent to meet them found to his mortification that the German Consul-General had gone out to the ship in the Prefect's boat. To forestall him, he took the Health Inspector's launch and arranged for a prolonged sanitary inspection, while he greeted the envoys. He suspected the German of eavesdropping.
In Germany a 'great fuss' was made of the emissaries. In England they spent their time sight-seeing, were received by the Queen at Balmoral and looked after by both Kirk and Hill. But the visit was expensive and to avoid having to keep them until the conference met, Salisbury 'persuaded' them to leave for Brussels early. Euan Smith thought they confused it with far-away Brazil and were afraid to go. On their return to Zanzibar, however, the Sultan said they had hurried back to sell the perishable goods they had acquired. He made them give up all their presents and sit on stools outside his door, explaining that he would have punished them further had they not been to London and seen the Queen.
276 Before this decision was reached the King had tried to get Stanley appointed to represent Zanzibar. Stanley was on his way back from the Emin Pasha expedition and

King Leopold would have welcomed the attendance of a papal delegate. Lavigerie's anti-slavery societies were now organising themselves and the Cardinal had arranged an anti-slavery conference to be held in August in Lucerne at which the Pope was expected to play an important part. The Belgian society was enrolling recruits for the Congo and the King hoped that the Pope would contribute money but leave their operations under the control of the state.[277] However, relations between the Pope and Italy were too strained for them to be represented at the same meeting,[278] and it was agreed that instead of inviting the Pontiff the assembly should simply show some sign of deference to him.[279] At the King's suggestion the Brussels Conference was postponed until after Lavigerie's gathering so that it might take advantage of its deliberations, but the Lucerne meeting was adjourned at the last minute.[280]

After months of discussion the conference had been enlarged to include all the signatories of the Berlin Act, the Congo and Zanzibar, both of whom adhered to it, together with the United States of America and Persia. It was thus a far cry from the small meeting of coastal powers envisaged by Salisbury in March.

When the Belgians produced a draft invitation the British found to their astonishment that the maritime slave traffic was not even mentioned! The King was calling for a conference to deal with slave raiding and trading on land,[281] the only part of the traffic which concerned the Congo. This did not suit Salisbury, who insisted that the British public was primarily interested

---

the King feared he would work for the British unless he could lure him to Brussels. However, Stanley was not available and the British and Germans never considered his representing the Sultan.

277 Ceulemans, pp. 289 ff.; Leopold to Lambermont, no. 27, 13 July 1889 and no. 28, 17 July 1889, PL 1889–90

278 Italy had seized Rome and the Papal States in 1870. Relations had deteriorated with the coming to power in Italy of Signor Crispi in 1887.

279 In the closing session the delegates paid tribute to the Pope's contribution to the anti-slavery cause, which amounted to his initial support of Lavigerie, a donation to the movement and the issuing of a Brief putting himself at its head on 24 Oct. 1888. The Pope had hoped for a greater part in the conference and had prepared a plan to submit to it, Renault, II, p. 296.

280 Ostensibly this was because the Cardinal was ill and few French representatives were able to come because of the French elections. In fact Lavigerie was afraid that, as large numbers of Germans, Swiss and Austrians were proposing to attend, the leadership of the meeting might fall into Protestant hands, particularly as he was ill and could not preside over it. He feared also that controversial political and religious issues might be raised which would ruin his work. The conference was to discuss the formation of more anti-slavery societies, the raising of funds, the encouragement of missions, education and legitimate trade, the restrictions of the arms and spirits traffics, the use of force by governments and private agencies and the pressure to be exerted on Muslim states to secure the abolition of slavery. A conference was subsequently held in Paris in Sept. 1890. For this whole subject see *ibid.*, II, pp. 259 ff.

281 Draft enc. in Vivian to Salisbury, no. 61 Af., 2 Aug. 1889, FOCP 5983

in the export traffic and that this must be specifically stated to be an object of the meeting.[282]

Eventually, on 24 August, invitations were sent out asking the seventeen chosen powers to come to Brussels to discuss measures to end the slave trade by land and sea.[283] No limits were to be set on the field of discussion and delegates were to be free to suggest whatever practical measures they thought necessary. At the instigation of Germany the meeting was originally planned for October so that it might come soon after the raising of the East African blockade, but by an unfortunate clerical error the French did not receive their invitation until long after the other powers and they asked for a delay to collect information. The date was finally set for 18 November 1889.

Inevitably an invitation couched in such general terms and emanating originally from Britain aroused the deepest suspicions. France thought the whole thing a pretext for prolonging the occupation of Egypt on the grounds that it was necessary for the suppression of the slave traffic, and also a manoeuvre to force her to grant the right to search.[284] She was particularly suspicious because on the eve of the conference Britain signed a treaty with Italy granting mutual rights to search.[285] This convinced her that the British were trying to isolate her.[286] Portugal, engrossed in her territorial disputes with Britain and the Congo, foresaw the conference dividing Africa at her expense[287] and sought assurance that territorial questions would not be raised. Russia thought England and Italy might further their ambitions on the upper Nile.[288] The Turks feared they might be pressed to abolish slavery and were irritated by attacks on them in the humanitarian press, and they shared French fears that England was trying to get an international mandate to stay in Egypt.[289] The Americans were afraid of backing the

282 Salisbury even advanced the specious argument that the export trade was the main reason for the capture of slaves in Africa, Salisbury to Vivian, no. 36 Af., 10 Aug. 1889, *ibid.*

283 Various drafts and discussions of the invitation are in AEB/CAE/1 nos. 57 bis., 64, 66, 67, 68. The invitation as presented to Britain is in Solvyns to Salisbury, 26 Aug. 1889, FOCP 5983.

284 Bourée to Spuller, no. 14, 16 Aug. 1889, FMAE/CP/Belg.82; note by van der Straten, v. conf., 25 Sept. 1889, AEB/CAE/2; Vivian to Salisbury, no. 100 Af. conf., 6 Oct. 1889, memo. by Sanderson, 10 Oct. 1889, FOCP 5983; Salisbury had mentioned to Waddington that Britain hoped France would change her views on search as early as April, Salisbury to Lytton, no. 71 Af., 1 April 1889, *ibid.*

285 Anglo-Italian treaty, 14 Sept. 1889, Hertslet, *Commercial Treaties*, XVIII, p. 825. This was based on the treaty of 1841 with minor modifications.

286 Vivian to Salisbury, no. 108 Af., conf., 12 Oct. 1889, FOCP 5983; Bourée to Spuller, 26 Sept. 1889, FMAE/CP/Belg. 82

287 Moncheur to Chimay, 29 Aug. 1889, no. 81, 11 Sept. 1889, no. 98, AEB/CAE/1; Billot to Spuller, 29 Aug. 1889, no. 106, FMAE/CP/Port. 230

288 Leopold II to Lambermont, 22 Aug. 1889, no. 75, AEB/CAE/1

289 Borchgrave to Chimay, 24 Oct. 1889, no. 78, AEB/CAE/2; Bourée to Spuller, no. 14, 16 Aug. 1889, FMAE/CP/Belg. 82

cause of the colonial powers[290] while even the Danes had visions of being forced to accept unwelcome commitments.[291]

Nevertheless all the invitations were accepted. No power could risk the odium of failing to co-operate in a great humanitarian cause. In the weeks before the conference met, however, all the interested participants, including the instigators, were examining how best their national interests might be furthered or defended at the meeting. Baron Lambermont, the permanent head of the Belgian Foreign Ministry, did his best to allay suspicions and improve the atmosphere but it was uphill work and he had little hope that the gathering would have any important tangible results, for, as he sadly confided to Vivian, it seemed as if many of the powers were 'indifferent to the objects of the conference (and) others more or less hostile to it.'[292]

290 Emile Banning, *Mémoires politiques et diplomatiques*, Paris and Brussels 1927, p. 74
291 De Forgeur to Chimay, 24 Sept. 1889, no. 127, AEB/CAE/1
292 Vivian to Salisbury, no. 108 Af., conf., 12 Oct. 1889, FOCP 5983

Chapter Six

The Brussels Conference

The delegates

It was a gay and distinguished assembly which finally met in Brussels in the gloom of the Belgian winter of 1889–90. No efforts were spared to make it a glittering occasion. 'It is hard work,' Kirk reported, 'all the dinners, receptions and balls'.[1] Gathered together were a wealth of diplomatic talent and many of the leading experts on Africa, ostensibly bent on a great philanthropic work. Humanitarians hailed the meeting as the unique event it was and freely tendered their advice. A forked slave stick was on display for the edification of the delegates and much horrifying information about the slave traffic had been collected by the hard working members of the Belgian Foreign Ministry.

It had been decided to follow the model of the Berlin Conference so that each power was represented by one or two plenipotentiaries and as many delegates as were wanted to give technical advice. The size of the delegations directly reflected the importance placed upon the conference by the various governments. In most cases the chief plenipotentiary was the Ambassador or Minister in Brussels. The less interested powers sent no other representative.[2] Russia, however, also sent a noted jurist, M. de Martens, who was to do valuable work.[3] The United States added Henry S. Sanford to her delegation after the opening of the conference. He was a shareholder in a company trading on the upper Congo and had long been closely associated with King Leopold's African venture.[4] The Dutch professed little interest in the

1 Kirk to Wylde, private, 24 April 1890, FO 84/2103
2 Spain, Austria, Sweden and Norway, Turkey, and Persia sent only their Ministers in Brussels, Denmark her Consul-General in Antwerp.
3 They also sent their naval attaché in Paris.
4 Sanford, a former U.S. Minister in Belgium, had been instrumental in securing American recognition of the Congo state and had been an American delegate to the Berlin Conference where he had furthered the King's cause. In 1886, with some associates, he founded the Sanford Exploring Company to trade on the upper Congo. This company received concessions from the King but soon found that agents of the Congo State hampered its trading operations. By the end of 1889 the company had merged with the Belgian Société Anonyme Belge pour l'Industrie et Commerce du Haut Congo, in which Sanford was a minor shareholder, see James P. White, 'The

conference but significantly sent their Consul in Banana who was a manager of the Nieuwe Afrikaanse Handels-Venootschap. Congo trading interests were thus represented in these two delegations. Italy was represented by two diplomats. Germany was content to send her Ambassador in Brussels and Dr. von Arendt, formerly Consul-General in Zanzibar, an able man with a good grasp of East African affairs.[5] The small German and Italian delegations contrasted sharply with those of Britain, Portugal and France.

Britain was strongly represented by Vivian and Kirk, and by delegates from the Colonial Office, Foreign Office and the Admiralty.[6] The French Ambassador was assisted by a high official of the Foreign Ministry, as well as by a former colonial governor, the Consul-General in Zanzibar, Lacau, and representatives of the Naval and Colonial Department.[7] Portugal also sent a strong team. Her Ambassador was a former Minister of Marine and Colonies, appointed particularly so that he might represent her at the conference, and he had with him an ex-governor of Mozambique, a well-known explorer, a naval officer and the Consul from Newcastle who was well versed in the Anglo-Portuguese territorial dispute.[8]

The Congo was particularly favoured. Added to her own plenipotentiaries, two officials of the State, and two delegates who had worked in Africa,[9] she had the assistance of the particularly able Belgian plenipotentiaries, Lambermont, who presided over the conference[10] and Émile Banning, who drafted many of the proposals.[11] But, above all there was the cardinal factor of the royal presence. King Leopold watched every move like a hawk, bombarded Lambermont with suggestions, buttonholed delegates at parties or summoned them to the palace, where he exerted his charm to win them over to his views. He employed the art of flattery to the full and made the most of

Sanford Exploring Expedition', *JAH*, viii, 2, 1967, pp. 291–302, and Ceulemans, pp. 196 ff.

5 Von Arendt, who was now conveniently Consul-General in Antwerp, died during the conference and was replaced by C. Göhring, Consul-General in Amsterdam in the spring of 1890. The Germans also had a secretary.

6 Respectively A. E. Havelock, former Governor of Natal and Sierra Leone, E. Wylde, and Captain A. Moore, RN.

7 M. Corgodan, M. Ballay, Amiral Humann and M. Deloncle

8 The Minister was H. de Macedo. His colleagues were Brito Capello, Augusto de Castilho, a naval officer, and Batalha Reis, the author of pamphlets and articles on the Portuguese claims in Africa.

9 The delegates were Capt. Coquilhat and Lt. Charles Liebrechts.

10 After the Foreign Minister the Prince de Chimay had opened it and declined the Presidency. Lambermont was indefatigable in his 'behind the scenes' negotiations and he worked hard to carry out the wishes of the King. For his life and work see J. Willequet, *Le Baron Lambermont*, Brussels, 1971.

11 Banning was one of the most erudite men at the meeting. A high official of the Belgian Foreign Office, he had dreamed from childhood of the 'civilising' of Africa. He was to become increasingly disillusioned with his sovereign's Congo policy as the conference wore on. For his work at the conference see his own account in *Mémoires politiques et diplomatiques*, already cited and the article on him in *Biographie Nationale*, XXIX, Supplement I, Brussels, 1956, pp. 186–99.

his curious dual role of constitutional monarch of a minor power and autocratic ruler of vast African dominions. Typical of his methods was his remark to the French Ambassador: 'Tell your government that the King of the Belgians will not forget what you did for the sovereign of the Congo'.[12]

The King's vigilance was matched by the care with which Anderson and Salisbury followed the deliberations from London. The conference was also closely watched by humanitarian bodies and by the charter companies and other businesses interested in African trade. Some even sent observers to Brussels to press their views.[13] The motives of those concerned ranged from genuine humanitarianism to the narrowest self-interest.

The Conference and the scramble

Unfortunately for the harmony of the meeting, no detailed programme had been agreed upon by Britain, Belgium and Germany before it opened. Each had simply a rough idea of what the others would suggest. Lambermont looked to Britain to take the lead[14] but Salisbury decided that she should only propose measures for the suppression of the maritime slave trade, which he persisted in regarding as the main object of the conference, and for the restriction of the spirits traffic. On other matters her interposition was to be 'very sparing'.[15] King Leopold was determined to make proposals to end slave raids and the internal trade.[16] The Germans said they knew little about the slave traffic and would simply follow the British lead, but they would suggest controlling the arms traffic.[17]

The absence of an agreed detailed programme would have mattered little if the conference had been harmonious and the instigators had worked closely together. In fact it was bedevilled by increasing suspicion as the scramble for Africa continued and by the exigencies of the European diplomatic situation. Anglo-German cordiality, for instance, marked the first weeks. Vivian reported with satisfaction at Christmas:

It has evidently been the object of our German colleagues, who have acted most loyally towards us, to make this good understanding as patent as possible, but while acting with equal loyalty towards them, we have

12 Bourée to Goblet, no. 7, 7 March 1889, FMAE/CP/Belg.82
13 Members of both the Anti-Slavery Society and the Aborigines' Protection Society visited Brussels and saw the King and some of the delegates. Cawston attended for the British South Africa Company. Kirk was a director of the Imperial British East Africa Company.
14 Memo by Anderson, 22 Oct. 1889, FO 84/2005
15 Salisbury's comments on *idem.*, 30 Oct. 1889
16 *Ibid.*
17 Salisbury to Trench, no. 446 Af., 14 Nov. 1889, and minute by Currie, 12 Nov. 1889, FO 84/1955

carefully avoided giving the appearance of a coalition or combination which might tend to divide the Conference into two hostile camps and do irremediable mischief.[18]

It was impossible, however, to prevent the meeting from reflecting the existing European alignments and in general the Triple Alliance powers supported each other, while France maintained good relations with Russia, was careful not to alienate Turkey and was assiduously courted by the Portuguese. Other powers took little part and carried little weight, except for King Leopold, who worked closely with Britain.

By the spring of 1890 the Anglo-German entente had itself broken down as relations in East Africa deteriorated. The arrival of Stanley and Emin Pasha at the coast in December 1889 stimulated German enthusiasm for colonies. The treaty-making expeditions of both nations, ranging over the interior, increased British fears that they might be cut off from Uganda and the upper Nile, and German fears that Britain might block access to Central Africa. By May public opinion in both countries was inflamed and the governments opened negotiations for a general settlement of their differences in Africa.[19] These events did not make the course of the negotiations in Brussels any smoother.

Nor did the other serious territorial dispute of the time, the Anglo-Portuguese squabble over Nyasaland and Zambesia. In fact while the conference was sitting, Portugal lost this struggle. Britain made the treaties which laid the foundations of her rule in Nyasaland and Northern Rhodesia, and Portugal was forced, when Salisbury sent an ultimatum to Lisbon in January 1890, to keep her forces south of the River Ruo.[20] But the dispute led to some curious Portuguese antics in Brussels, which wasted the time of the conference. For instance, Portugal had been at pains before the meeting began to let it be known that she would not discuss territorial questions. But it no sooner opened before she furnished delegates with a list of stations from which she proposed to fight slave raiders and a map showing railways she intended to build to foster legitimate trade. This was a disguised way of claiming certain regions also claimed by Britain and the Congo State.[21] Portugal was sharply told that territorial questions did not come within the scope of the conference. Apparently she had hoped to draw other powers into her dispute with Britain to strengthen her hand.[22] She found little encouragement, but much time was wasted.

More serious was the leakage of information to the press. In view of the

18 Vivian to Salisbury, no. 52 STC, 21 Dec. 1889, FO 84/2011
19 For this see Sanderson, ch. 3; Galbraith, ch. 7.
20 See Hanna, pp. 138 ff.
21 Plens, to Salisbury, no. 10 STC, 23 Nov. 1889, and enc., FO 84/2011
22 Billot to Spuller, no. 137, 31 Oct. 1889; no. 146, 14 Nov. 1889, no. 162, 12 Dec. 1889, FMAE/CP/Port. 230, no. 6 tel., 8 Jan. 1890, FMAE/CP/Port. 231; Waddington to Ribot, no. 85, 21 March 1890, FMAE/CP/Brit. 847; De Grelle Rogier to Lambermont, 18 Jan. 1890, no. 79, AEB/CAE/3

suspicions and tensions which prevailed, the conference decided to keep its deliberations secret in case they gave rise to discussions in the newspapers which might impede agreement. But the main proposals were barely laid before the meeting when they were published, sometimes in garbled form, in, at first, the French and, later, the Belgian press.[23] This caused much irritation and heightened mistrust. After investigation, the Belgians decided the Portuguese were the culprits and that they had hoped by this manoeuvre to wreck the whole meeting.[24]

All these factors hampered the work of the conference. In addition there were the national susceptibilities which led France, Portugal and Turkey to play down evidence of slave dealing in their territories.[25] In fact few questions were considered on their merits. On the other hand, few of the proposals were entirely humanitarian and it soon became clear that none would be accepted if they conflicted with the interests of a great power. All in all the interested delegates settled down to hammer out a slave trade agreement in an unpromising atmosphere of mutual suspicion and with a determination to feather their own nests.

Measures against the maritime slave trade

The British, maintaining that the conference should concern itself primarily with the export slave traffic, which was all the powers had the means to suppress, brought forward proposals for a comprehensive agreement to replace their existing hodge-podge of treaties which were all different and largely out of date.[26] They suggested that within a specific 'slave trade zone' signatories should have the 'right of supervision, jointly and severally, whether on the high seas or in territorial waters, over all sailing vessels under any flag'.[27] The wording was carefully chosen to avoid alienating the

23 See for instance, *Journal des Débats*, 30 Nov. 1889; *Soir*, 8 Dec. 1889; *Indépendance Belge*, 10 Feb. 1890.
24 Banning, p. 80; Vivian to Currie, private, 8 Dec. 1890 FOCP 5983
25 A Belgian booklet, the *Livre Gris*, which contained a digest of information on the slave and munitions trades taken from the works of explorers, missionaries and naval officers and from information supplied by governments, had to be withdrawn and a modified version submitted. The French particularly objected to the statement that slave trading still went on in Sénégal, Gabon and at Tajura, see Banning, p. 77; Bourée to Spuller, tel. 30 Nov. 1889, FMAE/CP/Belg. 82.
26 Hill had wanted to negotiate a new general treaty as early as 1880, see minute, 18 June 1881, FO 84/1938. Spain had long been pressing for the revision of her treaties with Britain of 1817 and 1835, mainly because she wanted to abrogate the right to search which was no longer exercised in the Atlantic, see del Mazo to Salisbury, 2 Aug. 1888, FOCP 5896. The Russians were dissatisfied with the treaty of 1841, which listed as evidence of slave trading equipment found on ships carrying white emigrants, but contained no provisions for the protection of 'coloured emigrants'. Memo by Hill, 31 Aug. 1888, on Dering to Salisbury, no. 3 Af., 22 Aug. 1888, FOCP 5896.
27 Plens, to Salisbury, no. 19 STC, 30 Nov. 1889, FO 84/2011

Delegates to the 1889-90 Brussels Anti-Slavery Conference, including (seated second left) Sir John Kirk, with Lord Vivian on his left and Baron Lambermont, president of the conference, next to him

The sole survivor:
a village in East Africa after a slave raid

A cruelly ingenious method of securing a slave

French but what was being asked for was no less than the right to search not only on the high seas but also in territorial waters.[28]

The pill was sweetened by some concessions which it was hoped would enable France to swallow it. For instance, the right was limited to the zone in which the slave runners actually operated[29] and to the kind of craft they used which were usually not owned or operated by Europeans.[30] Furthermore slavers were to be brought before mixed tribunals representing at least five of the signatory powers, and offenders were to be turned over to their own national authorities for punishment under their own laws.

Signatories were to pass adequate legislation for the infliction of severe penalties.[31] They were also to see that their flags were not abused. A system was to be established whereby full information was to be exchanged not only on all matters which might lead to captures, but on such things as the sentences passed on slavers and detailed lists of ships permitted to fly each national flag.[32]

The French were not to be lured into accepting this. They produced a counter-project, designed to render the right to search unnecessary by stringent regulations to prevent abuse of national flags.[33] Each power was to police its own shipping, but its flag was only to be flown by indigenous vessels if they were owned and skippered by 'respectable' people, not previously convicted of slaving, who had sufficient funds to cover fines. The vessels were to be registered annually and to be clearly marked with their names and registration numbers.

No Africans might serve in the crew of a dhow or be carried as passengers unless they had been seen, listed and given identifying marks[34] on embarkation by the authorities of the power whose flag the vessel flew, or by the local territorial officials. Passengers and crew were equally to be seen and identified when they landed. Throughout Africa and the adjacent islands Africans might only board indigenous ships at ports where competent authorities existed and, in the zone, they might only disembark at such ports. No vessel was to carry a bigger African crew than she needed.

Vessels might only be visited within the slave trade zone, from which the

28 Proposals enc. in Plens. to Salisbury, no. 12 STC, 25 Nov. 1889, FO 84/2011
29 This started at Suez, ran down the African coast to 25° 5 S and then followed a line drawn around eastern Madagascar and from northern Madagascar to Baluchistan. It included both shores of the Red Sea and Persian Gulf and the whole Arabian coast.
30 Occasionally a European built vessel ran slaves from Madagascar.
31 This was aimed at forcing Turkey to pass adequate laws.
32 The British had in mind a system of international information offices or bureaux. To avoid repetition I have not included here the less controversial British proposals which were eventually incorporated into the Brussels act.
33 The proposals are enc. in Plens. to Salisbury, no. 7 STC, 21 Jan. 1890, FO 84/2101.
34 The French had in mind the system of linen bracelets sealed with the consular seal then being tried in Zanzibar.

Red Sea was excluded, and then only if they were indigenous craft and there was good reason to suspect they were not entitled to the colours they were flying. The visit was simply to verify the flag and it was to be conducted in accordance with the regulations of 1867. Neither crew nor passengers might be mustered and checked against the identification lists. But a dhow suspected of fraudulent use of her colours was to be handed over for investigation to the authorities of the nation whose flag she was flying. If she was not entitled to the flag she was to be handed back to her captor. Otherwise she was to be dealt with by her own national officials. There were to be indemnities for wrongful arrest and international tribunals were merely to settle the amount of the indemnity and to resolve any disagreement between the captor and the investigator.

It was clear that France had not moved from her basic position and was merely trying to whittle down Britain's powers so laboriously acquired by treaties with other nations. She was even trying to limit the right to verify the flag to indigenous vessels within a slave trade zone which excluded the strategic Red Sea area and this would have meant leaving Turkey, Zanzibar and Persia to police their own shipping. They did not have sufficient naval forces for the job nor did they have the complete control of their coastlines which, together with trustworthy local officials, was necessary to carry out the regulations governing passengers and crews and they were hardly likely to give enthusiastic co-operation.

Britain could clearly not accept such an arrangement but since the French proposals for the control of indigenous shipping flying European flags were a step in the right direction, it was decided that the Russian jurist de Martens would work out a formula safeguarding those British rights which were still required and incorporating the most valuable of the French suggestions. This became chapter III of the Brussels Act.[35]

All existing treaty rights to search, visit and detain ships at sea and in territorial waters, and to try slavers were confirmed but, and here the British made a concession, they were limited to the zone, as defined by Britain,[36] and to vessels of less than 500 tons—a provision which could be changed if it became necessary.[37] Within the zone vessels might be arrested for suspected slave trading, an important French concession, as well as for fraudulent use of the flag, but the rules for visiting French ships were still to follow the 1867 agreement. The French provisions for the issue of colours and for the registration of such vessels, and for control over African passengers and crew were all incorporated into the Act. Very small coastal

35 Although with some minor modifications. For the Brussels Act see Hertslet, *Map*, II, pp. 488 ff. The Act and Protocols of the conference were also published in *PP* L 1890, p. 41, C-6049, Africa, no. 8 (1890). See also below, Appendix I.

36 The southern limit on the African coast, however, was changed to a point near Quilimane to meet Portuguese objections that there was no slaving south of this point. The whole of Madagascar was still included.

37 It had been decided that it was unwise to limit the provision to sailing vessels since slaves might soon be run in steam launches.

craft which would find the regulations too vexatious were exempted,[38] but were to be specially licensed.

A suspected vessel was to be taken to the nearest authorities of the country whose flag she was flying and each power undertook to appoint competent authorities in the zone. These were to hold an enquiry in the presence of the captor. Compensation was to be paid for wrongful arrest. Suspected slave traders were to be tried by their national courts and according to their own laws.[39] This system did away with the need to send prizes back to European ports.[40] It was expected to be cheap and prompt[41] and to result in all slavers being tried in the zone. It was hoped that this would reduce the disparity in penalties.[42] Each power undertook to pass adequate legislation for the infliction of severe punishment.

The system of international tribunals was abandoned. Britain had put it forward to make the right of search more palatable to France and when she failed to get French agreement, she preferred to retain her existing quite satisfactory courts, rather than set up cumbersome international ones.[43]

All slaves detained on board a vessel against their will[44] were to be freed and disposed of according to the treaties with individual powers, or, if there was no agreement, they might be handed over to the territorial authorities[45] who would try to return them to their land of origin, or help them to resettle. Fugitive slaves taking refuge on a man-of-war were to be freed immediately but to remain answerable for any crimes they might have committed.

38 Vessels with a crew of up to ten men engaged in fishing or coastal trade within the territories of any one power, who never went more than five miles out to sea, were to be specially licensed.

39 Convicted vessels were to be lawful prizes to be given to the captors. If the case was not considered proven by the investigating authority the captor could appeal to the national court of the suspect. Consular courts could be set up to try these appeal cases.

40 The system under the treaty of 1841

41 Memo. by Vivian, Kirk and Wylde, 15 March 1890, enc. in Plens. to Salisbury, no. 61 STC, 15 March 1890, FO 84/2102

42 Plens. to Salisbury, no. 30 STC, Feb. 1890 and enc. notes FO 84/2101

43 Most captured vessels flew the Arab flag and could be tried in British courts, and there was also a large number of vessels under the British flag which Britain wished to try in her own courts, *ibid.*, Kirk to Anderson, 22 Jan. 1890, FO 84/2101, and Kirk memo. 9 Nov. 1889 on memorial from BFASS, 1 Nov. 1889, FO 84/2005. Kirk in fact opposed international courts. He thought that they would be a retrograde step. He had himself judged cases brought before him in Zanzibar and wrote: 'I have myself sat for 20 years and I am sure done better alone than I should have if hampered by a pack of miscellaneous colleagues—some ignorant, many prejudiced and others interested the wrong way. Although the French flag is abused still 99 in 100 of the slave vessels are under the Zanzibar flag and for the sake of trying the one Frenchman we should lose the advantage of dealing alone with the 99 Arabs. International courts are a clumsy contrivance.' Kirk to Allen, private, 5 Nov. 1889, K.P. AS. I am indebted to Dr D. O. Helly for this reference.

44 This wording covered slaves serving as members of the crew as well as slaves intended for sale.

45 The word 'might' left the matter to the discretion of the captor.

Merchant vessels were not allowed to free fugitives as this might give rise to dangerous incidents.

An international bureau was to be set up in Zanzibar to which the powers would send all information likely to be useful in suppressing the traffic, together with records of the conviction of slavers, specimens of the papers to be carried by all dhows in the zone and registers of vessels permitted to fly their flags. This information was to be available to naval, consular and judicial officers concerned with anti-slavery operations.

Britain wanted an auxiliary office in the Red Sea where the traffic was increasing,[46] but Kirk reported:

> the Turks backed by the Russians opposed us, Alvensleben[47] shook his head at us and not a man would help—we had not a friend and of course had to drop it . . .[48]

The proposal fell victim to international politics, a surprise Russo-Turkish rapprochement[49] and the deterioration in Anglo-German relations.

In the main, however, Britain was quite pleased with the maritime clauses of the Brussels Act. She had maintained all her existing powers and, in return for concessions[50] which she regarded as nominal,[51] she had persuaded France to agree to the arrest of suspected slavers and to strict rules to prevent the abuse of her flag. This was all that Salisbury had expected to achieve.[52]

Admittedly the system was far from foolproof. A French dhow, for instance, might still clear port with all her papers in order, pick up slaves at some out of the way spot, land them secretly at their destination and sail happily into port again having complied with all the regulations. If intercepted by a cruiser, search was not allowed, so her illicit cargo had only to be kept out of sight for her to escape detection. It was also true that it would be a long time before the regulations governing the transport of passengers could really be enforced.[53] Nevertheless an important step had been taken and results might be expected as European control of the coast tightened up. Kirk wrote jubilantly to the Anti-Slavery Society:

> I flatter myself we have on the maritime side got very much from France. No dhow can ship or land a native unless before a French official or failing that the *territorial authority*[,] as the French consuls are few, that

46 As against Zanzibar where it was believed it would soon die.
47 German Minister in Brussels
48 Kirk to Wylde, 14 May 1890, FO 84/2103
49 Banning thought it unaccountable, Banning, p. 110.
50 The restriction of search to the zone and to small indigenous craft
51 Anderson minute 25 Feb. 1890 on Plens. to Salisbury, no. 44 STC, 22 Feb. 1890, FO 84/2101
52 Salisbury memo. 30 Oct. 1889, FO 84/2005
53 Minute by Anderson on Vivian to Salisbury, no. 44 STC, 25 Feb. 1890, FO 84/2101

means the English and German officials will see every black passenger(?) board or land from a French dhow on the coast.[54]

The French were equally satisfied. Britain's willingness to give up the right to search outside the slave trade zone had taken them by surprise and dispelled their suspicion that she wanted the right in order to police the seas generally[55]—a common illusion in France. The Act left France in a privileged position *vis-à-vis* the other powers all of whom had treaties with Britain. Both Germany and Portugal had protested in vain against this.[56] The French delegates felt that France had finally emerged triumphant from her long struggle as the champion of maritime freedom against British pretensions. Her privileged position was guaranteed by international treaty, her policy vindicated and she stood as a shining example to other powers, who would now seek similar rights for themselves.[57] As Vivian said: 'le droit de visite vient de recevoir . . . un fort coup de canif.'[58]

Measures against the slave trade in the *pays de destination*

Since the only completely effective method of suppressing the export slave traffic was to close the markets, the conference turned its attention to the *pays de destination*, some of which had begun to take action before it ever met. The new decrees issued by the Sultan of Zanzibar on the eve of the conference have already been mentioned.[59] In Egypt, under British supervision and with the help of the Khedive, strict measures were being taken to prevent the import of slaves including those disguised as domestic servants and wives. Sales from family to family were now illegal and dealers were severely punished. The ease with which slaves could obtain their

54 Kirk to Allen, private, 21 June 1890, ASS/BEA/C 7
55 Bourée to Spuller, no. 19, 9 Feb. 1890, and private, 13 Feb. 1890, FMAE/MDA/114
56 Bourée to Spuller, no. 19, 9 Feb. 1890 *ibid.*; Greindl to Lambermont, 22 Feb. 1890, no. 57, AEB/CAE/4. The Germans also complained that as they had only signed the treaty of 1841 they had not the extensive powers to search and detain slavers which Britain had acquired, and they made it a condition of their agreement to the maritime clauses of the Act that Salisbury help them negotiate treaties similar to Britain's with Turkey, Persia, Egypt and other rulers in the zone. Salisbury agreed with regard to the three former but pointed out that Britain herself as the protecting power was responsible for the rulers of South Arabia, her Somali Coast and the Persian Gulf, Vivian to Salisbury, no. 82 STC, conf. 2 April 1890, Vivian to Curie, 25 April 1890, FO 84/2102; Salisbury to Vivian no. 104 Af., 29 April 1890, FOCP 6197; Leyden to Currie, 16 April 1890, and enc. FO 84/2036; Salisbury to Malet, no. 64 tel., 24 June 1890, FOCP 2034.
57 Bourée to Spuller, private, 13 Feb. 1890, FMAE/MDA/114; Bourée to Ribot, no. 33, 14 April 1890, FMAE/MDA/115. 'Nous sommes venus ici presque en accusés,' the French admiral told Banning, 'maintenent on nous rend justice'; Banning, p. 117.
58 Bourée to Ribot, no. 33, 14 April, 1890, FMAE/MDA/115
59 See above, pp. 216–19

freedom had made them a poor investment risk.[60] Baring reported in 1889 that slave dealing was rare and that Egyptians were gradually coming to believe that free labour was cheaper and slaves were a burden. Slavery was still legal but he did not recommend abolition as this would offend Muslim feeling, and the institution was already moribund.[61]

The Turks were sufficiently worried by the spectre of the conference to order all provincial governors to suppress the traffic and take more rigorous steps against the already small trade in the capital.[62] The first convictions against the slave dealers in the provinces were obtained and in Tripoli two of them were sentenced to a year's imprisonment although Ottoman law merely imposed a light fine.[63] Pressed by Britain, the Sultan issued a new law in December 1889 which enabled the convention of 1880 to be put into operation.[64] Prison sentences could now be legitimately imposed and the necessary identification papers for slaves serving on Ottoman vessels or travelling with their masters were issued. Furthermore British naval officers were authorised to attend the trials of captured slavers as 'private prosecutors' and were thus enabled to keep a close watch on the proceedings.

In Persia the Residency Agent at Lingah reported the publication of a notice threatening slave traders with severe punishment.[65]

In Tunis the question of slavery attracted some attention in the press at the time of the conference[66] and in May 1890 a new abolition decree was issued, requiring masters to furnish freedom papers to all slaves within three months and making slave dealers liable to prison sentences ranging from three months to three years.[67]

In Madagascar, where the British complained of an active slave trade some of it under the French flag in 1888 and 1889,[68] a new law was promul-

60 Ten thousand slaves had been freed since 1883.
61 Baring to Salisbury, no. 10 Af., 2 April 1889, and memo. by Clarke, 12 April 1889, FO 84/1972
62 Marinitch memos of 13 April 1889 and 6 July 1889, enc. in White to Salisbury no. 8 Af., conf., 13 April 1889 and no. 10 Af., conf., 8 July 1889 FO 84/1971; White to Salisbury, no. 12 Af., conf., 22 July 1889, *ibid.*
63 This was the opinion of the Minister of Justice and a fine was the only penalty imposed in Constantinople. The two convictions were obtained in Tripoli but the sentences were upheld in Constantinople, Hay to White, 1 July 1889, Marinitch memo. 20 Aug. 1889, enc. in White to Salisbury, no. 13 Af., *ibid.*
64 Imperial *Irade*, 4 Dec. 1889, translation enc. in White to Salisbury, no. 1 Af., 1 Jan. 1890, FO 84/2056
65 Residency Agent Lingah to Ross, 3 Feb. 1890 enc. in Wolff to Salisbury no. 68, 3 March 1890, FO 84/2040
66 *La Tunisie*, 28 Feb. 1890, 18 April 1890, 2 May 1890; C. Jobard
67 *Journal Officielle de la Tunisie*, 29 May 1890 enc. in Hay to Salisbury, no. 1 Af., 31 May 1890, FO 84/2029
68 Knott to Haggard, 26 Jan. 1888, FOCP 5896; Knott to Aitken, 21 March 1888, enc. in Aitken to Salisbury, 3 May 1888, *ibid.*; Knott to Aitken, 26 Nov. 1888, enc. in Aitken to Salisbury, 30 Dec. 1888, FOCP 6009; Knott to Sauzier, 20 July 1889, enc. in Sauzier to Salisbury, no. 39, 19 Aug. 1889, FOCP 6010; Knott to Sauzier, 15 Aug. 1889, enc. in Sauzier to Salisbury, no. 44, 18 Sept. 1889, FOCP 6052.

gated reiterating that all Africans from Mozambique who landed on the island were free,[69] and the French took steps to stop the abuse of their colours in East African waters.[70] Early in 1890, the Hovas attacked the Sakalava at Tullea where slaving had long gone unchecked. In the Comoros the French stated that slavery was abolished by virtue of the establishment of their protectorate and the Sultan of Johanna issued an abolition decree.[71]

On paper, therefore, considerable advances had been made towards closing the markets in the *pays de destination* but in practice, except in Egypt, little had changed. In the Red Sea and Gulf of Aden the slave traffic was in fact reported to be increasing while the conference was sitting, and to have the active support of both Ottoman and Egyptian officials.[72] In Libya it also continued, in spite of more vigorous Turkish action.[73] Slaves were still shipped across both the Mediterranean and the Red Sea disguised as domestic servants. Sometimes they had regular manumission papers fraudulently obtained.[74] But even if they had no papers, under the new law of 1889 owners could still escape prosecution if they could prove they were not slave dealers. A great difficulty was the lack of a clear understanding as to how long a slave had to be in servitude before he ceased to be a 'trade'

69 Lytton to Salisbury, 24 April 1889, no. 52 Af., FO 84/1950

70 Michel to Prouhet, 22 July 1889, copy of instructions from Resident-General Madagascar to Residents at Tamatave, Majunga and Nossi Bé, FMM/BB 4 1229; FMAE to Krantz, 9 Nov. 1889, FMAE/MDA/143; Fremantle to Admiralty, 18 March 1890, enc. in Ad. to FO, 18 June, 1890, FO 84/2079; Knott to Millan no. 21 private and conf., 20 May 1890 enc. in Sauzier to Salisbury, no. 32, 12 June, 1890, FO 84/2039

71 This decree, as the British pointed out, was unnecessary if in fact slavery had been abolished as a result of French protection, Salisbury to Lytton, no. 75 Af., 5 April 1889, FO 84/1949. The French were anxious that the British should not use Holmwood's treaty of 1882 as grounds for inquiry into the affairs of the islands, FMD to Goblet, 18 Dec. 1889, FMAE/MDA/120.

72 Report from Commander, *HMS Albacore*, 25 Dec. 1889, enc. in Ad. to FO, 24 Jan. 1890, FO 84/2073; Muhammad to Wood, 1 April 1890, enc. in Wood to Salisbury, no. 1 Af., 12 April 1890, FO 84/2056; Wood to Salisbury, no. 2, Af., 14 April 1890, *ibid.*; Muhammad to Wood, 29 April 1890, enc. in Wood to Salisbury, no. 3 Af., 4 May 1890, *ibid.*; Muhammad to Wood, 6 June 1890, enc. in Wood to Salisbury, no. 4 Af., 24 June 1890, *ibid.*; Stace to Bombay Government, 21 March 1890, enc. in IO to FO, 16 July 1890, FO 84/2086; Barnham to Salisbury, no. 1 Af., 15 May 1890, FO 2057; Brenton to Hoskins, 15 April 1890, enc. in Ad. to FO, 19 May 1890, and 29 April 1890, enc. in Ad. to FO, 29 May 1890, FO 84/2082; Hoskins to Ad., 8 June 1890, enc. in Ad. to FO, 23 June 1890, FO 84/2084; Brenton to Hoskins, 1 June 1890, enc. in Ad. to FO, 5 July 1890, FO 84/2085. British naval officers complained that Suakin itself was a headquarters of the slave trade and that Egyptian officials on the Sudanese coast were deeply implicated in the traffic while the Governor-General, a British officer, was unco-operative. The situation was aggravated by the fact that the British had insufficient ships in the Red Sea and neither the French nor Italians were effectively checking the traffic from their territories.

73 Hay to Salisbury, no. 1 Af., 3 April 1890, FO 84/2055; Marinitch memo. 5 June 1890, enc. in White to Salisbury, no. 5 Af., 7 June 1890, FO 84/2056

74 Marinitch memo., *ibid.*

slave and became a 'domestic' slave. In the absence of a ruling on this subject, newly acquired slaves on both sides of the Red Sea could be passed off as domestic slaves, even if they had been bought from a dealer only a month before, and clearly had been only recently captured.[75]

In Zanzibar, the Sultan had not promulgated his decree freeing all children born after 1 January 1890. He pleaded that it might lead to a massacre of new-born infants, and the proclamation freeing all slaves entering his dominions after November 1889 had only been displayed for a few hours.[76] The new measures which had been designed to impress the Arabs when the blockade ended were, therefore, virtually unknown. Sultan Khalifa died in February and his successor, Sayyid Ali, proved more co-operative and discussion of a new decree began while the conference was sitting.[77] Meanwhile, however, the traffic continued in spite of the efforts of the new Sultan and attempts by the French to exercise greater control over their dhows.[78]

French regulations for ensuring that slaves did not travel on their vessels were easily evaded. Slavers copied the linen bracelets stamped with the consular seal used to identify bona fide passengers.[79] Captains of slavers sent their crews, posing as free passengers, to get the necessary papers from French officials and then landed slaves in their place armed with these papers.[80] By the spring of 1890 evidence of such fraud led the French to forbid the embarkation of all African travellers on their dhows.[81]

Clearly as long as slavery existed slaves would continue by one means or another to reach the markets. To attack the slave traffic without attacking slavery was, as Lister said: 'Like permitting the consumption of meat while punishing the butchers.'[82] But this was just what the powers were doing. They were in no position to do otherwise. None of the colonial nations were prepared to tackle slavery in their own territories. The French, in fact, had just had to dis-annex some of their territories in Senegal in order not to have to liberate slaves, who could legally claim their freedom when they set foot on French soil. They had found that the slave-owning Peul and Wolof simply moved away from their settlements rather than risk losing their

75 Brenton to Hoskins, 1 June 1890, enc. in Ad. to FO, 5 July 1890, FO 84/2085; Barham to Salisbury, 28 May 1890, enc. in Baring to Salisbury, no. 6 Af., 5 June 1890, FO 84/2057
76 Euan Smith to Salisbury, tel. 23 Dec. 1889, FO 84/1984; BFASS to Salisbury, 25 March 1890, FO 84/2077; C-in-C. East Indies to Ad., 29 Jan. 1890, enc. in Ad. to FO, 11 March 1890, *ibid*.
77 Euan Smith to Salisbury, no. 173 tel. secret, 17 June 1890, FO 84/2069
78 Ad. to FO, 22 Aug. 1890, and encs., FO 84/2089
79 Euan Smith to Salisbury, no. 259, 16 July 1890, FOCP 6053
80 Bell to Salisbury, no. 3 Af., 24 April 1890 and enc., FO 84/2029
81 Euan Smith to Brackenbury, 8 June 1890, enc. in Ad. to FO, 22 Aug. 1890, FO 84/2089
82 Minute on memo. by Marinitch, 20 Aug. 1889, enc. in White to Salisbury, no. 13 Af., 31 Aug. 1889, FO 84/1971

captives.[83] Similar problems had arisen in Diego Suarez.[84] France made it clear before the conference began that she would not discuss slavery.[85] King Leopold equally had no desire to raise the matter.[86] Salisbury did not think that the institution could be dealt with on the African continent. It had not been abolished in Egypt, and all that he hoped for was that combined pressure at the conference might make the Muslim importing nations take more effective action to control the trade which kept the institution alive.[87]

The proposals which were put forward in Brussels were drafted by Banning and originally covered all the importing countries.[88] But France objected to any of her territories being described as *pays de destination*.[89] This was neatly solved by limiting the proposals to countries where slavery was still legal, thus exempting Tunisia and the Comoro Islands. Madagascar posed a difficult problem for here African slavery was outlawed but it was legal to have Malagasy slaves. However, France managed to get the island exempted also.[90]

The countries in which slavery was legal and to which African slaves were imported, agreed to prevent all import, export and transit of slaves and to exercise strict surveillance over ports and slave routes.[91] Persia was particularly bound to supervise her coast, and also, a new departure, to watch the inland caravan routes.[92] They were all to stop slave dealing and to impose adequate penalties on offenders, including those who mutilated males.[93]

All illegally imported slaves, and fugitives who reached their frontiers, were to be freed. Liberated slaves were to be furnished with manumission papers, and returned to their own country, if possible. Otherwise they were to be protected and helped to earn their living.[94] An office was to be established in Zanzibar to ensure the freedom of slaves liberated on the island.[95]

Full information about the slave traffic was to be exchanged between the signatories. Banning had proposed that the *pays de destination* should be

83 See Yves Saint-Martin, *Une source* . . . ; Governor of Sénégal to Minister, 5 Feb. 1889 and 18 Oct. 1889, AOF/K/12; Commandant Supérieur du Soudan Français to the Governor of Sénégal, undated but forwarded to Paris, 8 Jan. 1889, *ibid*.
84 Froger to Sous-Secrétaire, Ministry of Marine and Colonies, 17 May 1887, FMAE/MDA/142
85 Note by van der Straten of conversation with Bourée, 25 Sept. 1889, AEB/CAE/2
86 Leopold II to Lambermont, no. 14, 14 April 1889, PL 1889–90
87 Memo by Salisbury, 30 Oct. 1889, FO 84/2005
88 For Banning's draft see enc. in Plens. to Salisbury, no. 47, STC, 28 Feb. 1890, FO 84/2101.
89 Bourée to Spuller, no. 21, 28 Feb. 1890, FMAE/MDA/114
90 Bourée to (?) Spuller, private, 13 Feb. 1890, *ibid*.
91 Article LXII, Hertslet, *Map*, II, pp. 508–9
92 Article LXIX, *ibid*., p. 510
93 Articles LXII, LXVII, LXX, *ibid*., pp. 508–10
94 Article LXIII, *ibid*., p. 509
95 Article LXX, *ibid*., p. 510

bound to act on all intelligence supplied by the diplomatic agents and naval officers, of the other powers, and that slaves might appeal to these officials for help. However, the Turkish plenipotentiary, Carathéodory Effendi, a Greek Christian, who endeared himself to the conference by his good humour when other delegates overstepped the bounds of diplomatic courtesy in their denunciations of Muslim morals and the iniquities of harems,[96] managed to get this provision whittled down so that these agents were merely to 'assist' the local authorities and then only within the limits of existing conventions.[97] They could, however, attend as observers any trials they had been instrumental in instigating, a provision wanted by Britain to ensure that trials were properly conducted.[98] Carathéodory also insisted that the conference drop a proposal for a special system of surveillance for western Arabia. He maintained, in the teeth of British evidence to the contrary, that the traffic was not flourishing in the Red Sea and that slavery in the Ottoman empire had nothing to do with the slave trade. He even had a clause inserted in the Brussels Act praising the Turkish law of 1889 and accepting Ottoman assurances that Turkey would organise an active supervision of this coast and of the routes to her other dominions.[99] 'The Turk,' said Vivian, 'is making difficulties, and requires sitting upon . . . when asked for any concession he invariably refers us to the law and the Prophet.'[100] But Carathéodory could not be 'sat upon' because he found powerful supporters in France and Russia, particularly the latter, whose help in the closing weeks, coupled with the fact that Germany no longer backed Britain,[101] enabled him to defeat the British attempt to have an auxiliary slave trade information bureau in the Red Sea.[102]

To prevent trade slaves being transported under the guise of domestic slaves, Banning had suggested that all those not illegally imported or newly enslaved who were travelling with their masters or serving as sailors should carry identification papers issued at their place of residence which could be verified by officials in the ports and towns through which they passed. This would have ended a clear abuse. The proposal, however, was rejected by all the Christian powers, led by Britain. Although aware that slavery among Africans and in the importing Muslim countries was often what Carathéodory called 'a mild servitude' in which the slave sometimes had more security and privileges than the poor free man, they said the distinction between domestic and other forms of slavery was 'flimsy and futile'. In fact

96 'Allez-y, Messieurs, prenez-en à l'aise', he would say laughing; Liebrechts, p. 147.
97 It was thus no advance on the Anglo-Turkish convention of 1880.
98 Article LXXI, Hertslet, *Map*, II, p. 510
99 Article LXVIII, *ibid.*, pp. 509–10
100 Vivian to Barington, 14 June, 1890, SP/A.49
101 See above, p. 239
102 See above, p. 244. Russian influence was strong in Constantinople in 1889–90 and in the spring of 1890 the Turks with Russian and French backing were putting forward proposals for the British evacuation of Egypt.

they were not prepared to countenance it in an international instrument[103] as it implied a recognition of slavery as a legal status.

Because of the Turkish opposition, the clauses dealing with the *pays de destination* went little further than existing British treaties. There was no undertaking to end slavery, and no means was devised to end the import of trade slaves under guise of domestic slaves. However, the importing countries were now responsible to all signatories of the Brussels Act for ending the slave traffic and caring for freed slaves and punishing offenders.

The Muslim powers had hardly proved co-operative, except of course for Zanzibar, who had no independent voice. The Persian plenipotentiary spent little time at the conference, and the British believed this was because the Shah did not want 'troublesome engagements', which among other things might curtail his supply of eunuchs.[104] The Turks, far from being intimidated by the combined weight of Christian opinion, had found the powers divided. As Banning put it:

il est de plus en plus évident qu'un grand courant d'idées politiques et morales n'existe pas sur le terrain de la traite au sein des Puissances Chrétiennes, divisées entre elles et jalouses de leur influence particulière comme de leur intérêt exclusivement nationaux. Dès lors, on est désarmé *vis à vis* des Orientaux qui n'eussent cédé qu'à une pression unanime et énergique.[105]

Measures against the slave trade on land

The British were alone in considering that the suppression of the maritime slave trade was the major object of the conference. To the other colonial powers the most important measures to be discussed were those dealing with the suppression of *razzia*, the transporting of victims overland and their sale on the African continent. To this end the Belgians put forward a comprehensive set of proposals designed by King Leopold to foster the interests of his Congo State, some of which were so far-reaching and general that they gave an anti-slavery complexion to the whole occupation and exploitation of Africa.

The conference was to declare that the best means of suppressing the slave trade was by the 'progressive organization of the administrative,

103 They were also not prepared to recognise the validity of such papers should slaves pass through their territories armed with them, Banning, pp. 108–9; Plens, to Salisbury, no. 47, STC, 28 Feb. 1890, FO 84/2101. However, the Anglo-Turkish convention of 1880 had required identification papers and they were provided for by the Turkish law of 1889, which was praised in the Brussels Act, Hertslet, *Map*, II, p. 509, article LXVIII.
104 Drummond Wolff to Salisbury, no. 25 tel., 25 Jan. 1890, and Af. most conf., 1 May 1890, FO 84/2040
105 Banning, p. 109

judicial, religious, and military services' in the territories under their rule. They were to commit themselves to the gradual establishment of fortified posts on the coast and in the interior to serve as centres of refuge and civilisation where Africans would be organised to defend themselves, be taught farming and trades and generally be 'civilised' in order to eradicate such customs as human sacrifice and cannibalism. The colonial powers were also to foster trade and protect missionaries of all denominations, as well as explorers and others working against the slave traffic.

Roads and, particularly, railways were to be built to link the interior stations with the coast and give easy access to inland waterways. Steamboats were to be placed on the navigable rivers and lakes. Flying columns operating from the various posts were to protect these communications and to pursue slave caravans in their own territories and in lands not under European control.

Slave traders and raiders were to be prevented from leaving the coast for the interior. The heads of caravans going inland were to give adequate guarantees that they would not engage in slaving and they and their followers were to carry identity cards so that on their return the coastal authority could check the number and identity of all members of the caravan and free any captives.

Organisations were to be set up to care for freed slaves who, if possible, were to be returned to their place of origin. Otherwise they were to be rehabilitated. They could be settled on the lands of the nearest European station and adult males might, with their consent, be enrolled into the forces of the nation which had liberated them. The children were to be educated. A fugitive slave claiming protection at any post or on any ship belonging to the signatory powers was to be received but, if he came from people among whom slavery was legal, an indemnity might be paid to the master, provided he was not a slave dealer.

Within a year of the ratification of the Brussels Act the African colonial powers were to pass laws imposing uniform penalties for slave trading and raiding. Persons engaged in razzia were to be deemed guilty of premeditated murder and arson. Dealers and those who transported captives were to be considered accomplices in these crimes. Offenders caught redhanded might be tried on the spot by the heads of stations, captives of ships or commanders of columns. They were to have no right of appeal and the sentences were to be executed within twenty-four hours.

The powers were to co-operate with one another and to welcome, help and protect all associations and private agencies, including anti-slavery societies, which might wish to operate against the slave trade in their territories, but these were to be under the general control of the government.

The import of arms, especially of precision weapons,[106] and ammunition was to be prohibited for twenty-five years throughout the regions devastated

106 'Les armes rayeés et perfectionnées'

by the slave trade and the territories around them. This was defined as the whole area between latitudes 20°N. and 22°S. and stretching from the Atlantic to the Indian Ocean. In this zone each government was to have a monopoly on the import of munitions. However, in the coastal regions where the arms trade had long been established it might release ordinary (trade) powder and flintlocks and unrifled percussion guns[107] to persons furnished with special licences, provided the area was free of slave trading. Uniform penalties were to be prescribed for unlawful possession and trafficking in arms.[108] Signatories whose territories lay outside the slave trade zone were to prevent munitions, particularly precision arms and their cartridges, from crossing their frontiers in the direction of the zone, and they were to urge African states not represented at the conference to adhere to the arms clauses of the Brussels Act.[109]

The King's aims were clear enough. He wanted first and foremost an international mandate to suppress the slave traffic by establishing fortified posts in the interior. He proposed to site them in Katanga, on Lake Tanganyika, the Uele river and the Bahr el-Ghazal. They would thus straddle the important trade routes. But from his viewpoint he would have an international mandate to occupy what he claimed to be the furthest corners of his state. Having got the conference to accept this principle, he then proposed to ask the delegates to furnish him with the material means to carry out the plan, by allowing him to raise money through the collection of import duties, forbidden by the Berlin Act, and through the encourage-ment of his recruitment of men for his forces.[110] Such an increase in his resources would enable him to occupy these regions before other powers could do so. He had no desire whatsoever to commit the other signatories to moving into the interior. He simply hoped to forestall them,[111] and he planned to use the crusaders sent out by the Belgian Anti-Slavery Society for the job.[112]

Fortunately for the King the British, French and Germans had no intention of accepting a definite commitment to move into the interior.[113]

107 'Fusils à silex or à piston non rayés'
108 Beginning with confiscation of the weapons and fines of not less than £200 or six months imprisonment.
109 These proposals were presented as drafts for chapters I and II of the Brussels Act and are enc. in Plens. to Salisbury, no. 3 STC, 21 Nov. 1889 FO 84/2011 and no. 12 STC, 25 Jan. 1890, FO 84/2101.
110 Ceulemans, pp. 253 ff.; Leopold II to Van Eetvelde, 19 Sept. 1889, no. 8, AGR/VE/27; Leopold II to Lambermont, 14 April 1889, no. 14, 7 Oct. 1889, no. 49, PL 1889–90; Analyse du dossier de la conférence anti-esclavagiste (henceforth Analyse CAE), note by Leopold II 18 Sept. 1889 on Van Eetvelde to Leopold II, 17 Sept. 1889, AGR/VE/162, memo by Anderson, 22 Oct. 1889, FO 84/2005.
111 Ceulemans, pp. 259–60   112 Renault, II, pp. 205–15
113 Plens. to Salisbury, no. 22 STC, 30 Nov. 1889, FO 84/2011, and no. 28 STC, 4 Dec. 1889, *ibid.*, and no. 36 STC, 8 Dec. 1889, *ibid.*; Salisbury to Vivian, no. 21 tel., 9 Dec. 1889, FO 84/2010; Lambermont to Leopold II, 29 Nov. 1889, no. 61, APR/72 (i); Bourée and Cogordan to Spuller, no. 2 CAE, 23 Nov. 1889, FMAE/MDA/114.

The proposals surprised them[114] and together they set about whittling them down.

The declaration that the slave trade could best be suppressed by setting up a full administration, by building posts and establishing lines of communication, including railways, was accepted.[115] However, instead of being 'obliged' to suppress the traffic by these means, under Article III the powers merely undertook to 'proceed gradually, as circumstances permit, either by . . . [these] means . . . or by any other means which they may consider suitable, with the repression of the Slave Trade.'[116]

The Belgians, but not the King, complained that this rendered the declaration almost worthless.[117] There was no definite obligation to set up an administration to combat the slave trade.

The role of the interior posts to succour and civilise Africans, to foster trade, to ensure that labour contracts were legal and to protect missions was accepted.[118] However, the last gave rise to *contretemps* between France and Turkey. The French wanted protection limited to those missions which opposed slavery and the Turks protested that this discriminated against Muslim missions.[119] Eventually a clause was inserted in the protocol saying that missionaries whose doctrines were subversive to the aims of the conference would not be protected.

To avoid the possibility of territorial encroachment on the excuse that it was an anti-slavery operation, each power was to act only in its own dominions and territorial waters.[120] Private agencies fighting against the slave trade were to be protected provided their activities were authorised by the territorial powers.[121] The Belgian provision that fugitive slaves were

114 Lister minuted: 'I never read so stupid and mischievous a set of Articles. Should not our . . . [plenipotentiaries] be told to say at once that H[er] M[ajesty's] G[overnment] will not agree to any articles binding England to make rail-roads or ports or steamers [sic] or to maintain forces inland for suppressing S[lave] T[rade].' Minute filed after Plens. to Salisbury, no. 3 STC, 21 Nov. 1889, FO 84/2011.

115 Article I, Hertslet, *Map*, pp. 490–1; telegraphic communication was added to the list of desirables.

116 Article III, *ibid.*, p. 492

117 As Lambermont put it, 'le projet laisse aux Puissances une latitude qui les met très à l'aise. C'est pour ça que plus tard l'opinion critiquera peut-être le nouvel arrangement', Lambermont to Leopold II, 29 Nov. 1889, no. 61, and 1 Dec. 1889, no. 62, 8 Dec. 1889, no. 70, APR 72 (1).

118 Article II, Hertslet, *Map*, pp. 491–2, in addition those stationed in them were to try to prevent African wars.

119 Plens. to Salisbury, no. 174 STC, 17 June 1890, FO 84/2104. The French specifically mentioned the Sanusi. Interestingly the Belgian Ambassador in Constantinople reported that the Sanusi were buying slaves and sending them as missionaries to their homelands, or other areas of their choice in Africa. This was said to have been one result of the closing of Tripoli and Tunis to slave caravans, Borchgrave to Chimay, conf., 21 Oct. 1889 no. 6, AEB/CAE 6; while a Turkish newspaper reported plans to propagate Islam in Africa for political reasons, Banning, p. 145.

120 Articles II and III, Hertslet, *Map*, pp. 491–2

121 Article IV, *ibid.*, p. 492

to be received on board ship or at posts was accepted,[122] but private stations and merchant vessels were not to give asylum, for fear of provoking discontent among slave owning peoples. No compensation was to be paid to the masters of fugitives because the British thought compulsory compensation a bad principle. There were a number of other facets to this question apart from the obvious difficulty of finding the necessary funds. It might lead to collusion between masters and slaves or to the buying or even ill treatment of slaves by owners secure in the knowledge that if they fled compensation could be obtained.

The powers agreed to enact, or propose to their legislatures within a year of the signature of the Brussels Act, laws making all persons concerned in man-hunting and mutilation liable to punishment for 'grave offences against the person'[123] and dealers liable to penalties for infringing individual liberty. All offenders were also to be subject to extradition. Uniform penalties could not be agreed upon since this would infringe upon the right of each power to impose what it considered suitable punishment. But the powers were to tell each other what penalties they were imposing and hopefully this would reduce the existing disparity between them.[124] The Belgian proposals that slavers caught red-handed should be tried on the spot without the right of appeal and that sentences should be executed within twenty-four hours was rejected as too ruthless and liable to cause both international disputes and miscarriages of justice.[125]

The clauses relating to the supervision of trade routes and the interception and pursuit of slave caravans were accepted[126] but only in so far as the degree of administrative control enabled them to be carried out. In other words there was no obligation to set up posts to combat the slave trade. This was shied away from on the grounds of expense and because it might prove useless since slave routes could easily be diverted to avoid them.[127]

It was agreed that coastal powers should supervise the ports to prevent slaves being shipped out and should inspect caravans leaving for the interior or returning from it.[128] Any slaves who had been acquired in the course of their travels were to be freed. However, the clause requiring heads

122 Article VII, *ibid.*, p. 494
123 Article V, *ibid.*, p. 493. Unless of course their laws were already considered adequate.
124 Some idea of the existing anomalous situation may be gleaned from the fact that the British imposed maximum sentences of ten years on slave raiders and seven years on slave dealers. While courts in Suakin were sentencing them to five years in 1889, French courts to two years and Turkish courts to one year, the Germans were hanging them.
125 Anderson pointed out, as an example, that it would enable Portuguese naval officers to try and hang British-protected persons within 24 hours on the 'pretext' that they had been caught slave trading, minute, 22 Nov. 1889, on Plens. to Salisbury no. 3 STC, 21 Nov. 1889, FO 84/2011.
126 Articles XV, XVI, Hertslet, *Map*, II, pp. 497–8
127 Observations by Kirk and Havelock on chapter II, enc. in Plens. to Salisbury, no. 12 STC conf., 25 Jan. 1890, FO 84/2101
128 Article XVII, Hertslet, *Map*, II, p. 498

of caravans to furnish sufficient security as guarantee that they would not deal in slaves, together with the proposal that all members of caravans be issued with identity papers before they left the coast, which were to be inspected on their return, were considered unsuitable to the conditions of African trade. Caravans did not necessarily have a recognised 'head' throughout their journey nor were they always organised on the coast and even if they were their personnel was constantly changing.[129] An expedition might set out with hired porters who would perhaps be paid off after a while and new ones engaged. Slaves might be bought en route and sold again during the journey and the caravan would return with a completely different complement of hired porters from those who had set out with it and with no incriminating evidence even if it had engaged in large-scale slaving operations in the interior and slaves had been used to carry goods at some point in its peregrinations. Such regulations would be easily evaded by slavers but would hamper legitimate traders and be repugnant to African ideas and customs. They would also impose a great burden upon the administration which would probably find them unworkable. Havelock pointed out, for example, that during the dry season some fifty thousand traders from all over the western Sudan and elsewhere descended upon Freetown and that it would be quite impossible to identify each of them.[130]

It was agreed therefore that only such persons as had been convicted of an offence against the Brussels Act should be required to furnish guarantees of good behaviour, and then only if they wished to trade in areas where the slave trade was rife.[131] The provision that all members of caravans must have identity papers was dropped.

King Leopold had wanted powers to inspect caravans leaving the interior for the coast in order to be able to supervise trade going eastwards out of the Arab zone of the Congo. Lambermont warned him this would arouse suspicions as to his motives and that the right to pursue and intercept caravans suspected of having slaves was already sufficient for his purpose.[132] The proposal therefore was dropped. As the Act contained a clause providing for the inspection of coastal caravans on their arrival in the interior,[133] his powers of supervision were very complete.

The care of freed slaves

The conference agreed that each government would protect freed slaves, repatriating them where feasible and otherwise providing them as far 'as

129 Plens. to Salisbury, no. 26 STC, 5 Feb. 1890, FO 84/2101
130 Observations by Kirk and Havelock on chapter II, enc. in Plens. to Salisbury, no. 12 STC conf., 25 Jan. 1890, *ibid.*
131 Article XIX, Hertslet, *Map*, II, p. 498
132 Leopold II to Lambermont, no. 73, 13 Dec. 1889, PL 1889–90; Lambermont to Leopold II, 14 Dec. 1889, APR/72 (1) 73
133 Article XVII, Hertslet, *Map*, II, p. 498

possible' with the means of earning a living.[134] Abandoned children were to be educated. The obligation to set up an organisation to look after liberated persons was rejected. Salisbury objected that it committed Britain to an expense she had no wish to incur.[135] King Leopold's clause allowing men to be recruited voluntarily into the liberator's armed forces was relegated to a protocol. The French feared it might cause a storm in their press and they took care to point out the possible abuses which might arise from such a provision. However, it suited them to have it on record that such recruitment was not forbidden since the normal method of enlisting their *tirailleurs* in West Africa was by buying them and enrolling them on a three to four year contract,[136] or they conscripted 'freed' slaves.[137] Furthermore they gave women prisoners of war as 'free wives' to their soldiers.

Contract labourers and soldiers, the Congo and the scramble

The whole question of the recruitment of Africans for services abroad, whether as labourers or soldiers, which had so often been attacked as a disguised form of slave trading might well have been considered at the conference. Both Hill and Anderson had contemplated it.[138] King Leopold had been careful to link the question with the suppression of the slave trade by mentioning in the invitations that the recruiting of men to fight the traffic should be encouraged.[139] He was at the time having difficulty raising recruits. Both French and British colonial officials were reluctant to allow him to enlist in their territories.

The French grudgingly agreed that he might recruit men in Algiers, who had already served their time in the French forces, but only after the King had hinted that if he prevented slavers from reaching Lake Tanganyika the ivory which now went through East African ports would be diverted down the Congo to the French benefit as well as his own.[140] The British refused to allow him to recruit in Lagos or on the Gold Coast and protested when he turned to Zanzibar and Dahomey. They complained that advances paid

134 Articles VI & XVIII, Hertslet, *Map*, II, pp. 493, 498. The insertion of the phrase as far 'as possible' watered down the force of this part of the article.
135 Salisbury to Vivian, no. 36 Af., 31 Jan. 1890, FOCP 6197. The British already provided for freed slaves by paying the missions who accepted them for their keep until they became self-supporting. See also above, pp. 154–6, 162–3.
136 Lambermont to Leopold II, 11 Dec. 1889, APR/ (1) 71; Plens. to Spuller, no. 2, 23 Nov. 1889, FMAE/MDA/114; Intelligence Department to FO, 22 June, 1889, FOCP 5979
137 A. S. Kanya-Forstner, *The Conquest of the Western Sudan*, Cambridge 1969, pp. 272–3
138 Minutes by Hill and Anderson, 15 Oct. 1888 and 26 Nov. 1888, FOCP 5896
139 Solvyns to Salisbury, 26 Aug. 1889, FO 84/1947
140 The French Ambassador also believed that French industrialists would find their tenders accepted by Belgium if recruiting was allowed, Bourée to Goblet, 7 March 1889, no. 7, FMAE/CP/Belg. 82.

to the men tempted Zanzibar owners to force their slaves to enlist and provided them with the means to buy more,[141] and that the premium paid to Dahomey encouraged the king, Béhazin, to go raiding.[142] The Lagos government wanted to prosecute Leopold II's agent[143] for slaving and the Royal Navy illegally stopped and removed two men from a steamer carrying recruits from Zanzibar to the Congo.[144] Although the charges could not be substantiated at Lagos and the British apologised for the detention of the steamer off Zanzibar, the whole question attracted unwelcome publicity.

King Leopold had no desire for the conference to consider how to prevent the enlistment of slaves. Nor did he want signatories of the Brussels Act to have unlimited powers to recruit in each others' possessions, as this might one day be turned against him in the Congo, where it was believed the shortage of manpower was likely to be quite temporary.[145] What he hoped for was freedom to recruit a limited number of men abroad for a few years. He also wanted to ensure that the vessels carrying these recruits would not be interfered with on the pretext that they were slavers. He went to some trouble to enlist German[146] and British[147] support before the conference opened, and he and his officials toyed with various plans for bringing the question before the meeting.[148]

In the event, however, the limitation of the right to search to small vessels removed the fear that steamers carrying recruits would be apprehended at sea and the King decided that his interests would best be served by making individual agreements with other powers allowing him to recruit in their territories.[149]

The conference, therefore, never considered the question of preventing the recruitment of slaves to serve in European territories, or the protection

141 Euan Smith to Salisbury, no. 316 conf., 1 Nov. 1888, FO 84/1910, and no. 322, 17 Nov. 1888, *ibid.*, and tel. no. 22, 16 Jan. 1890, FO 84/2096
142 Vivian to Salisbury, no. 89 Af., 21 Sept. 1889, FO 84/1946. The French also complained that it endangered their settlements at Porto Nova and Kotonu. The money for recruits also enabled King Behazin to buy arms to build up his military power, Obichere, pp. 90–4.
143 CO to FO, 8 July 1889, and enc. FO 84/1999; Salisbury to Vivian, no. 49 Af., 20 Sept. 1889, FO 84/1944
144 See E. Vanderwoude, 'Het Incident Met De "Brabo" (1888)', *Africa-Tervuren*, ix, 1963, 3, pp. 63–76. The detention was illegal since the vessel was not carrying the men into slavery but was transporting 'free' recruits.
145 Memo by Van Eetvelde, 17 Sept. 1889, no. 117 bis, AEB/CAE/1; note by Leopold II on memo. on Analyse CAE, AGR/VE/162
146 Leopold II to Lambermont, 16 Aug. 1889, no. 30, PL 1889–90; Chimay to Greindl, 22 Aug. 1889, no. 74, and Greindl to Chimay, 28 Aug. 1889, no. 80, AEB/CAE/1
147 Euan Smith to Salisbury, 12 July 1889, SP/A. 79; Anderson memo., 22 Oct. 1889, FO 84/2005
148 Coquilhat to Lambermont, 9 Oct. 1889, no. 12 AEB/CAE 3; note annexed to Van Eetvelde to Lambermont, 11 Oct. 1889, no. 17, *ibid.*
149 Leopold II to Lambermont, 1 Dec. 1889, no. 55, *ibid.*, and no. 63, 30 Nov. 1889, PL 1889–90

of African recruits and contract labourers. The only mention of the matter in the Brussels Act was the stipulation that the authorities at posts in the interior should ensure that African contracts of service were legal.[150] When the British Government was questioned in Parliament about the forced enlistment of slaves in Zanzibar, it merely replied that the matter was not within the scope of a conference against the slave trade.[151] Technically of course the men were not being consigned to slavery. Behind the scenes, however, Salisbury protested to the Congo that advances paid to the owners encouraged slave-running to the island.[152]

Salisbury had every reason not to hamper the Congo's recruiting operations, particularly those for the armed forces, for the King to forestall the Portuguese who had announced they were occupying regions claimed by the Congo and the British South Africa Company,[153] decided not to miss a golden opportunity to checkmate them with British help. He asked Salisbury to let him recruit eight hundred men in British colonies to 'annihilate' the Portuguese and establish bases from which to fight the slave traders. These posts were to run along his western frontier from Lake Victoria to the Zambesi, from the territories of the Imperial British East Africa Company to those of the British South Africa Company. He envisaged that they would eventually be handed over to Britain,[154] forming a vital link in the much talked of 'all red (British) route' from the Cape to Cairo.[155] They would also block the German advance into the rich ivory lands of Central Africa and relieve Mackinnon of his great fear that the Germans might encircle his company's dominions.[156] Mackinnon was, of course, a party to the plan

150 Article II, Hertslet, *Map*, II, p. 492
151 *Hansard*, CCCXLI, Col. 209; CCCXLIV, Col. 255–6. The answer drafted by Salisbury is in FO 84/2083, together with a minute reading: 'Lord Salisbury will remember that the Belgians are touchy about this: while there is reason to fear that the system is far from satisfactory.'
152 Vivian to Salisbury, no. 25 Af., 12 May 1890, FOCP 6053
153 The Portuguese territorial claims advanced at the conference, and ruled out of court, are enclosed in Plens. to Salisbury, no. 10 STC, 23 Nov. 1889, FO 84/2011.
154 Within days of the Portuguese announcement, Leopold II wrote to Lambermont suggesting an approach to the British: 'Il faut leur offrir de défendre nos droits en commun. L'occasion est magnifique et unique' and in another letter of the same day: 'Ce serait pour moi une immense économie, une grande sécurité. Éviterait une guerre certaine avec le Portugal', 24 Nov. 1889, nos. 57 and 58, PL 1889–90. Talks began with Vivian immediately, Vivian to Currie, 24 Nov. 1889, FO 84/2010. The King wanted to maintain the force of 800 men for six years.
155 This idea, pressed by Cecil Rhodes among others, found favour in the British press in the summer of 1889, Robinson and Gallagher, pp. 227–8. For its origins see R. Oliver, *Sir Harry Johnston and the Scramble for Africa*, London 1957, pp. 141 ff.
156 For Mackinnon's fears of encirclement and desire to get access to Lake Tanganyika and link up with the British South Africa Companies territories see Mackinnon to Nicol, 1 Aug. 1889, quoted in R. O. Collins, 'Origins of the Nile Struggle: Anglo-German Negotiations and the Mackinnon Agreement of 1890', ch. 4 in Louis and Gifford (eds.), *Britain and Germany*, pp. 119–51, pp. 130–1.

and the King urged him to help by persuading Stanley to take command of the force and pressuring Salisbury to allow recruiting in British colonies.[157]

Mackinnon added his pleas to those of Leopold and at the same time asked the Foreign Office for recruiting facilities for his own company to help drive the Arab slavers from Uganda.[158] Salisbury responded with an unusually strong letter to the Colonial Secretary:

> I wish the Colonial Office would cultivate some cosmopolitan philanthropy on the subject of Houssas and Elminas. If anything is to be done against the internal slave trade, or against the Portuguese who are nearly as bad, it is essential that the Congo State should have a fairly trustworthy black force. When the King of the Belgians asks for Houssas, we reply that we look upon every Houssa baby as a contingent Lagos policeman, and we will not spare him a man. This is bad enough but then he asks for some Elminas: and we reply that their moral nature is so susceptible, that if they served as soldiers in the Congo State for a few years, they would return to us bereft of the gentle and childlike nature they now possess.
>
> I think this is a very sad case of departmental selfishness. If we mean to do any good in this matter we must not be restricted by the emotions of Lagosian patriotism.[159]

In the end permission was given for the Congo to recruit in Swaziland, the Gold Coast and even Egypt where Baring initially opposed it.[160] The results, however, were disappointing. No Swazi or Gold Coast men were forthcoming and in the last months of the conference the King was again pressing the French to allow him to recruit in the Comoro Islands.[161]

The King's plans, however, blossomed into the Mackinnon Agreement of 24 May 1890, by which the King obtained access to the upper Nile and in return recognised the Imperial British East Africa Company's rights to a

157 Leopold II to Mackinnon, very conf. 28 Nov. 1889, MP/82/83, and private and v. conf., 12 Dec. 1889, MP/82/87. Stanley was not willing to take command.
158 Mackinnon to Leopold II, 7 Dec. 1889, MP/82/85. Pressure was also exerted by Kirk, a director of the British East Africa Company, Kirk to Mackinnon 24 Dec. 1889, MP 99/21, FO minute, 28 Nov. 1889, FO 84/2007.
159 Salisbury to Knutsford, 10 Dec. 1889, SP/D31/38, vol. 9
160 With great difficulty the Imperial British East Africa Company also obtained permission to recruit in India, but they were not allowed to enlist Punjabis as the government of India did not want them to learn to handle modern firearms. IO to FO 29 April 1889, FO 84/1992; Sir Owen Bourne to General Hutchinson, 25 Jan. 1890, MP/65/3. They were subsequently refused permission to recruit Zulu and only after a long battle did Baring agree to their recruitment of Sudanese, Galbraith, p. 163.
161 He had first asked for this in November 1889, Leopold to Lambermont, no. 62, 28 Nov. 1889, PL 1889–90; Van Eetvelde, to Leopold II, 6 May 1890, AGR/VE/27. The King also opened negotiations with the British South Africa Company to allow him to enlist 800 men in their territories and put out feelers, hoping he would be allowed access to Lake Nyasa through British territory, see memo. by Hertslet, 2 June 1890, FO 84/2083; Leopold to Salisbury, private, 22 June 1890, SP/A.49.

strip of territory linking Lake Albert to Lake Tanganyika. Thus the link in the Cape to Cairo route coveted by Rhodes and Mackinnon, was assured through territories behind the German possessions.[162]

The whole affair is of some interest as it shows how King Leopold took advantage of the conference to further his territorial ambitions, on the pretext that he needed men and was establishing posts to combat the slave traders. Salisbury does not appear to have taken the 'Cape to Cairo' dream particularly seriously but he was willing enough to accommodate the King and Mackinnon.[163] Indeed, his eagerness to do what he could for the Congo led him to turn a blind eye through the early months of the conference to the enlistment of domestic slaves in Zanzibar, in spite of the protests of Euan Smith[164] and questions in Parliament.[165]

Restriction of the arms traffic

The arms traffic proved to be the most troublesome one raised at the conference. All the interested powers tried to make capital out of it. King Leopold's proposals would not only have given him a monopoly of the arms traffic in the Congo but would also have enabled him to stop and search boats in his territorial waters without laying him open to the charge that he was infringing the Berlin Act. In the same way that the right to pursue and search caravans for slaves enabled him to supervise the trade along his eastern frontiers, so the arms clauses would give him greater powers over the commerce going westwards. These powers were wanted not just to prevent the smuggling of arms into the upper Congo, but to enable the King to stop the evasion of export duties. As matters stood traders avoided taxes on goods coming from the upper Congo by the simple device of obtaining a certificate to say that their wares had come from French territories and were simply in transit through the Free State. The King was careful not to say so in so many words but the arms clauses of the Brussels Act were so framed as to allow him to search boats and caravans and stop such fraud.

162 For the agreement and the negotiations leading to it see Galbraith and Collins. This agreement was transformed into the Anglo-Congolese treaty of 1894 after King Leopold's troops had appeared unexpectedly on the upper Nile. However, the clause which assured the Cape to Cairo link was cancelled when the Germans protested against the treaty, see Louis, 'Sir Percy Anderson'.
163 Collins, pp. 140–1; Robinson and Gallagher, pp. 246 ff
164 Euan Smith complained that the King's agents were paying large advances to recruits, which were appropriated by their owners. Euan Smith to Salisbury no. 22 tel. 16 Jan. 1890 and no. 126, tel. 24 April, 1890, and minutes by Anderson amended by Salisbury, 24 April 1890, 29 April 1890, FO 84/2069.
165 Question by Buxton, 13 Feb. 1890 (*Hansard*, CCCXLI, col. 209) and further questions asked by Pease on 6 May 1890 (*ibid.*, CCCXLIV col. 255–6) led to representations in Brussels. Vivian to Salisbury no. 25 Af., 12 May 1890, FOCP 6053.

If accepted, he would be able to set up customs posts and charge duties on exports from the upper Congo.[166]

The Germans were as eager as the King to control the arms traffic but they carried an amendment under which munitions, instead of being a government monopoly, were to be placed in bonded warehouses and sold only with official permission. Trade guns, defined as flintlock unrifled guns, and 'common' powder might only be purchased in approved areas where there was no slave trading. Precision arms—rifles, magazine-guns or breech-loaders—and their ammunition were only to be delivered to persons who gave guarantees that they were for their own use or to travellers holding certificates from their governments stating that they were intended for their personal defence. These arms were to be registered, stamped and licensed. Traders were to furnish the authorities with full information on all sales of munitions. The signatories were to exchange information on the traffic, on licences granted and on the repressive measures they had taken. Each state was to retain, of course, the right to arm its own forces and 'organize its defence', a vaguely worded clause enabling it to arm those people whom it wished to see strong. The German amendments were accepted without great argument and became articles IX and XI of the Brussels Act.[167]

A long and acrimonious battle was fought, however, as to the extent of the region to which they were to apply. France, supported by Portugal, tried to get them extended to the entire African continent. Her reasons are interesting. It was not, as might have been expected, that she wanted North Africa included in the zone in order to facilitate her advance across the Sahara.[168] Not at all. Her real reason was that she had been much piqued by the recent rejection in the Newfoundland Parliament of an Anglo-French fisheries agreement and wanted, as a point of principle, to force Britain to take responsibility for her South African colonies.[169] At this time the Cape was self-governing while Natal had representative institutions but not full responsible government. France contended that unless the restrictions covered the whole of Africa, arms would still percolate into regions afflicted by the slave traffic and a lucrative trade would have been sacrificed in vain.[170]

166 Van Eetvelde memo., 17 Sept. 1889, no. 117 bis, AEB/CAE/1; Analyse CAE, AGR/VE/162; Leopold II to Lambermont, no. 63, 30 Nov. 1889, and no. 73, 13 Dec. 1889, PL 1889–90; Note by Leopold II, 17 Nov. 1889, no. 40 and minute by Lambermont, 1 Dec. 1889, no. 56, AEB/CAE/3; Lambermont to Leopold II, 14 Dec. 1889, APR/72 1/73.   167 Hertslet, *Map*, II, pp. 494–6
168 In fact the North African states controlled the arms traffic but France had frequent cause to complain that the Turks did not prevent the landing of contraband, see for instance, D'Estrèes to Goblet, no. LV, 9 July 1888, FMAE/CC/Trip. 45, and D'Estrèes to Goblet no. LXXXI, 13 Oct. 1888, FMAE/CP/Trip. 26; D'Estrèes to Spuller, no. LXXX, 12 March 1889, FMAE/CC/Trip. 45.
169 Bourée to Spuller, no. 5 tel., 29 Jan. 1890; Spuller to Bourée, no. 7 tel., 30 Jan. 1890, FMAE/MDA/114
170 Lambermont to Leopold II, 11 Dec. 1889, APR/72 (1) 72; Spuller to Bourée, no. 24 17 Jan. 1890, FMAE/MDA/114; Plens. to Salisbury, no. 15 STC, 27 Jan. 1890, FO 84/2101

Privately Salisbury agreed with this argument. He wrote:

My impression, is that an absolute prohibition would be impracticable; that it cannot be extended to all the littoral of Africa; and that, unless it is so extended, prohibition on one stretch of coast will only amount to conferring a monopoly on some other part of the coast.[171]

However, he maintained that he could not legislate for the South African colonies, and the Colonial Office remained as adverse as ever to any restrictions on the traffic to Bechuanaland and the regions to the north. That is, any restrictions imposed by an international agreement. They were ready enough to control the traffic themselves by insisting that arms only pass through British Bechuanaland with the permission of the Administrator and only for chiefs who were friendly and amenable to British tutelage, or whom it was politic to arm.[172] The Ndebele ruler, Lobengula, they told Salisbury, was having second thoughts about accepting British protection. He would resent any attempt to interfere with his arms supplies and could always get them from the Transvaal[173] where they were locally manufactured. Furthermore they feared it would be a long time before the British South Africa Company was in a position to enforce any restrictions which Britain undertook to impose.[174]

Salisbury was not particularly impressed by these arguments. He realised that the time had come for some restrictions on the arms traffic. It was being pressed by other powers, was necessary to cripple Arab powers of resistance to the European penetration of East and Central Africa[175] and the humanitarians wanted it. In fact, there had been much written on the subject in the English press since 1888, and the Aborigines' Protection Society was carrying on an agitation for the limiting of the arms and spirits traffics, which culminated in an important meeting at the Mansion House in January 1890.[176] Furthermore Goldie wanted to restrict the arms trade on

171 Salisbury memo., 30 Oct. 1889, FO 84/2005
172 The passage of arms sent under the Rudd concession had attracted attention in the Cape where questions were raised in Parliament and it was agreed that in future the Administrator should take responsibility for all arms sent through Bechuanaland, Robinson to CO 18 Oct. 1889, enc. in CO to FO, 2 Nov. 1889, with other minutes and enc. FO 84/2005.
173 They suggested the Transvaal be invited to Brussels, but Salisbury informed them it was too late and the Boers could be asked to adhere to the Brussels Act later, FO to CO, 28 Feb. 1890, FO 84/2076.
174 CO to FO, 21 Feb. 1890 FOCP 6197, for the British South Africa Company's subsequent forcing of their protectorate on Lobengula see Mason, pp. 135 ff.; T. O. Ranger, *Revolt in Southern Rhodesia 1896–7*, London 1967, pp. 88 ff.
175 Salisbury memo., 30 Oct. 1889, FO 84/2005
176 According to Banning this meeting was inspired by the government which wanted support to overrule the protests of the arms manufacturers, Banning, p. 87. The Anti-Slavery Society would not support the Aborigines' Protection Society in this campaign fearing that it might jeopardise the real aim of the conference—the suppression of slave traffic, see Allen to Fox Bourne, 20 Dec. 1889, 13 Jan. 1890, ASS/C.150; Fox Bourne to Allen, 14 Jan. 1890, and 20 Jan. 1890, ASS/51.52.

the Niger as this would give him a monopoly of all foreign commerce above the palm-producing regions.[177]

Against this of course, had to be set the South African difficulty, Salisbury's own reluctance to include Egypt in the zone of restriction for fear this would give other powers an opening to interfere in Egyptian internal affairs,[178] the protests of British arms manufacturers[179] and the problem of the Ndebele. Britain decided to accept the zone proposed by the Belgians,[180] the limits of which, 22° South to 20° North, ran north of Bechuanaland and south of Egypt.

177 Goldie had asked for such a monopoly in 1886 and been refused, Flint, *Goldie*, pp. 79–80.
178 Minute by Anderson, 17 Feb. 1890, on Vivian to Salisbury, no. 37 STC, 15 Feb. 1890 FO 84/2101; Salisbury to Vivian, no. 52 Af., 24 Feb. 1890, FOCP 6197.
179 Banning testified that the government were worried by the protests of the arms manufacturers, Banning, p. 87.
180 It would be interesting to know how far this decision was also influenced by commercial factors. Customs figures in 1889 (PRO Customs 9/99) show that the total exports to Africa of British munitions exported directly from British ports were valued at £330,981 and of this £180,050 (54.4%) went to South Africa. To discover how much of this trade was endangered by the Brussels Act, however, the type of arms exported must be considered. The South African figures contain a very high proportion, £151,687 worth, of 'rockets and other ammunition' (*not* including percussion caps, gunpowder, shot and shells which are all separately listed). Presumably these were not for African use and would therefore have been unaffected by the Brussels Act. Many of the guns sent to South Africa may also have been too expensive for the African market. For instance the Cape and Natal took 3,951 'muskets, rifles and fowling pieces' worth £13,416—giving an average price of £3 8s. a weapon compared with an average price of 8s. 5d. for weapons sent to 'western Africa not particularly designated' (59,107 weapons worth £24,781). The trade in British made munitions to North Africa was only worth £9,055. These figures seem to indicate that limiting the zone was of little help to the English gun manufacturers. These figures, however, do not include arms sent to South Africa via other countries nor arms transhipped in England. The Liège arms manufacturers informed their government in 1890 that they sold 'assez bien d'armes' to English firms for the Cape, and Natal (and for the Transvaal by way of Lourenço Marques. These arms included discarded military weapons and cheap new ones. English manufacturers may have supplied parts for the latter but the total value of British 'other firearms and parts' which are listed together as having been sent to Belgium in 1889 was only £6,236 (this excludes, muskets, rifles and fowling pieces—only 606 of which went to Belgium—and various other weapons not within the range of this discussion). The stake of British manufacturers in this trade may therefore not have been very important. However, the Belgians thought that British traders—as against British manufacturers—had sufficient interests involved to comment, when asking if South Africa was included in the zone of restriction, 'les Anglais lorsque leur commerce est intéressé se soucieront du Congrès comme un poisson d'une pomme.' Président du Syndicat des Fabrications d'Armes à Liège to Baron Whetnall, very conf., 15 Feb. 1890, no. 103, AEB/CAE/3.
To establish the full extent of the munitions trade of the South African colonies beyond their frontiers, it would be necessary to know the total arms imports from all sources into the colonies, the size of the local market amongst whites and the amount of munitions manufactured in the colonies.

This meant the restrictions applied to Matabeleland and Mashonaland but this was inevitable since they were in contact with, if not within, the area infested by the slave trade. Salisbury could not admit in an international conference that Britain had as yet no power there. This would have cut the ground from under her feet in her dispute with Portugal, whose claims she had long opposed because they were not backed by effective occupation. He therefore had to overrule Colonial Office objections and accept responsibility and restrictions on the arms traffic. The Ndebele difficulty was, in any case, taken care of because the Brussels Act allowed governments to supply arms to anyone in their territories 'for state purposes'. In fact it strengthened Britain's hand in that she could protest if any other signatory supplied arms to Lobengula.

Only with great difficulty were the French persuaded to agree to the zone wanted by the British and Belgians.[181] But finally because they themselves wanted Madagascar and the Comoros excluded from the restrictions and this, in itself, established the principle that there should be a zone and not continent-wide control, they gave way.[182] When the whole question seemed resolved Germany brought it all up again demanding an assurance from Britain that the Cape and Natal would not allow munitions to enter German South-West Africa.[183] Relations between Britain and Germany were particularly acrimonious at this point and Kirk believed she was baiting some trap. However, she was contented with a British promise to call the attention of the colonies to the Brussels Act and all she seems to have wanted was some text to show that she had tried to hold Britain responsible for her colonies. Privately she told the Belgians she was sure arms would continue to cross her frontiers.[184]

The Germans had been particularly anxious to include Madagascar and the Comoros in the arms zone, to prevent their serving as bases from which munitions were smuggled into East Africa. They also wanted shortened percussion guns and their caps treated as trade guns and trade powder in East Africa, on the grounds that these weapons were required for the defence of caravans and that, cut down as they often were to make them more portable and frequently loaded with the wrong ammunition, they were not

181 The Belgians also had to face protests from their arms manufacturers who claimed that their trade to Africa was worth an average of 2,279,706 francs (£91,188) a year, that the USA and Africa were their biggest markets and that the American market was now being restricted by duties. They had stocks on hand in 1890 of 300,000 to 400,000 guns which could only be sold in Africa, and restriction of the trade would cause unemployment. See letter from the Liège arms manufacturers to Chimay, 17 Feb. 1890, no. 104, AEB/CAE/3.
182 Bourée to Spuller, no. 15, 3 Feb. 1890, FMAE/MDA/114
183 Plens. to Salisbury, no. 101 STC, 26 April 1890, FO 84/2102
184 Greindl to Lambermont, 30 April 1890, no. 125, AEB/CAE/3. Good quality arms were apparently plentiful in South-West Africa at this time, see Shula Marks and Anthony Atmore, 'Firearms in Southern Africa: a Survey', *JAH*, xii, 4, 1971, pp. 517–30, p. 521.

precision arms.[185] France, Britain and the Congo all contended that they were the very weapons most used by slave traders and were highly dangerous. The two latter were reluctantly prepared to let the Germans have their way.[186] The matter most nearly concerned Germany and anyway she could always issue permits for such arms if she wished.

The French objected, however, as they thought the public would take it amiss if the regime for West Africa, where their territories lay, was different from that for East Africa.[187] The question was settled by some horse-trading. Germany gave up her demand and agreed to exclude Madagascar and the Comoros from the arms zone provided France declared that she would see that munitions from the islands were not exported to *German* territory.[188]

Britain had not recognised the French protectorate in Madagascar and at a moment when her own relations with Germany were strained, she found herself faced with an obvious Franco-German rapprochement and one that had implications far beyond the scope of the conference, as Kirk put it:

> The direct recognition of German possessions (as German not Zanzibari) on the coast of Africa by France coupled with that of France as the disposer of Madagascar was the first surprise prepared for us.[189]

Negotiations for a general settlement of Anglo-German differences in Africa were already under way and the German Ambassador had suggested to Anderson that Germany buy her coastal concession from the Sultan and had dismissed 'lightly' the latter's reminder that France, as a party to the agreement of 1862 recognising the independence of Zanzibar, would have to be consulted. Faced with an evident Franco-German understanding in Brussels, Salisbury merely asked France to extend her declaration to the whole East African coast. Privately Vivian told the French Ambassador that he believed this implied the recognition of the French right to speak for Madagascar.[190] Some weeks later when the terms of the Anglo-German agreement of 1 July 1890, giving Britain a protectorate over Zanzibar and Pemba and providing for the German purchase of her concession, were known, France complained that she had not been consulted and demanded compensation. Kirk, however, told Salisbury that

> it is quite understood here that our acceptance in Conference of the French declaration as to the prevention of the export of arms from

185 Many were discarded military weapons, often rifles, which were refurbished and shortened mainly at Liège, German note, 23 Jan. 1890, no. 86, AEB/CAE/3.
186 Salisbury minute, on Plens. to Salisbury, no. 16 STC, 30 Jan. 1890, FO 84/2101; Leopold II to Lambermont, no. 86, 9 Feb. 1890, PL 1889–90
187 Plens. to Ribot, no. 27, 27 March 1890, FMAE/MDA/114
188 Munster to Ribot, 23 April 1890, FMAE/CP/All./95. The wording had to be carefully chosen since France could not actually legislate for the Hovas, Ribot to Plens., no. 55, 15 May 1890, FMAE/MDA/115.
189 Kirk to Wylde, private, 10 May 1890, FO 84/2103
190 Bourée to Ribot, no. 33, 28 May 1890, FMAE/MDA/115

Madagascar to the British *possessions and protectorate* in East Africa implies a reciprocal acknowledgement of rights.[191]

The arms zone as defined at Brussels,[192] 20° North to 22° South, was a diplomatic victory for Salisbury. Furthermore outside the limits of the zone he would only concede that territories in contact with it would prevent 'at least' precision arms from crossing their frontiers in the direction of the zone.[193]

The Colonial Office, however, was far from happy with the arrangement. The zone included all the West African colonies and the fear was that their trade and revenues would suffer, as neither the 'impecunious and feeble' republic of Liberia nor the still independent peoples of Dahomey[194] and the Ivory Coast could be relied upon to carry out the Act even if they agreed to it. Arms would therefore probably be smuggled into West Africa and trade diverted away from the British territories. The Colonial Office wanted the agreement limited in the first instance to five years in order to assess its effect on the prosperity of the colonies.[195] The Belgians had asked for twenty-five years. In the end a compromise was reached. The arms clauses of the Brussels Act were to remain in force for twelve years.[196]

On the Niger, Britain played a trump card. The river was included within the arms zone but it also came within the free navigation agreement of the Berlin Act. Restriction of the traffic therefore required special handling. The Royal Niger Company had established its strangle-hold on trade by charging crippling duties and license charges, such as two hundred per cent *ad valorem* on war materials traded above Lokoja where without arms no trade could be conducted.[197] But they were being challenged by a German trader, perhaps an *agent provocateur*,[198] who had found other obstacles put in his way besides the heavy taxes which the company merely paid to itself, and had tried to defeat Goldie's monopoly by going to Nupe and encouraging the Emir to say that he was not under the company's

191 Kirk to Salisbury, 22 June 1890, SP/Kirk. This is hard to reconcile with Salisbury's statement to the French Ambassador in London that he had forgotten that France was a party to the agreement of 1862, and should be consulted, Waddington to Ribot, no. 54 tel., 21 June 1890, FMAE/CP/Bret./80. The matter was resolved by the Anglo-French declarations of 5 Aug. 1890, by which France recognised the British protectorate over Zanzibar and Pemba in return for the recognition of her domination of Madagascar and of vast territories in the Sudanic belt stretching from Algiers to Say, Hertslet, *Map*, II, pp. 738–9.
192 Article VIII, Hertslet, *Map*, II, p. 494
193 Article XIII, *ibid.*, p. 497
194 The French made it clear at the conference, however, that they intended to rule Dahomey and war actually broke out in February 1890 while the conference was still sitting. The conquest was completed in 1894. See Obichere, pp. 51 ff.
195 CO to FO, 2 Nov. 1889 and enc. and minutes, FO 84/2005 and minutes of a meeting in the Colonial Office, 8 Jan. 1890, FOCP 6197
196 Article XIV, Hertslet, *Map*, II, p. 497
197 See above, p. 182 and Flint, *Goldie*, pp. 96–7
198 For a full discussion of this subject see *ibid.*, pp. 112 ff

protection. If this was so, the company could not interfere with traders going there or charge duties on their goods and the German Government demanded that transit to Nupe be free.

This threatened Goldie's whole position as his profits depended upon keeping a monopoly of the Niger trade, and he claimed not only Nupe but also all the navigable water on the Niger and Benue and refused to allow traders to stop, even for supplies, without paying taxes. Matters came to a head in 1888 when German pressure forced the British Government to inquire into the whole question of the Niger Company's administration. The Brussels Conference met before the investigator's report had been received.

When King Leopold issued his decrees limiting the arms traffic on the upper Congo in 1888, Anderson had watched the proceedings with interest. Not knowing that they were inspired by Bismarck, he had commented: 'This, if not met with a German or a French protest, will be useful to us on the Niger.'[199] The conference now gave Britain an opportunity to take similar action on the Niger. She declared that, for humanitarian reasons, no arms of precision would henceforth be allowed to pass up the river[200] provided France would give a similar undertaking for the upper Niger. These declarations were duly made by the English and French in Brussels, thus strengthening the Niger Company's political and commercial hold on its territories.

Britain also made use of the conference to try to help her settlers and traders in Nyasaland. The Arab war had actually ended on the eve of the Brussels Conference. Consul Johnston, on the treaty-making expedition, which laid the foundations of British Nyasaland and North Eastern Rhodesia, had found the British down to their last cartridges and their opponents ravaged by smallpox and reduced to eating 'rats, leather and roots' and had negotiated a precarious peace.[201] The African Lakes Company still needed ammunition, however, for defence and to supply African hunters who shot game for ivory and meat, and the Portuguese were still blocking supplies.[202]

Britain contended that, as a point of principle, those who represented civilisation and were combating the slave trade in the interior should not be endangered by disputes between a power at the coast and one in the hinterland.[203] She therefore tried to introduce a clause into the Act to force coastal authorities to allow munitions to cross their territories in transit to a signatory in the interior with no direct access to the sea. This met with vigorous opposition from Portugal, who not only regarded it as an attempt to force her to allow munitions to reach Nyasaland, Mashonaland and

199 Anderson minute on Vivian to Salisbury, 4 Nov. 1888, FO 84/1895
200 The suggestion was Anderson's. Anderson memo, 22 Oct. 1889, FO 84/2005.
201 Hanna, p. 152
202 Johnston to Salisbury, no. 12 Af., 16 March 1890, FO 84/2051
203 Plens. to Salisbury, no. 16 STC, 30 Jan. 1890, and enc., FO 84/2101; Salisbury to Vivian, no. 90 Af., 23 April 1890, FOCP 6197

Matabeleland, where they might be used against her, but also considered that her ability to block such supplies was one of her most potent weapons in her territorial dispute with Britain.[204] She had not abandoned hope that the quarrel would be settled with the help of the other powers but meanwhile she had no intention of giving up what would be an important bargaining point if she had eventually to negotiate directly with Britain.

However, other powers had their objections too. France thought it an infringement of national sovereignty that any nation should have to agree to arms traversing its territories against its will. Germany feared the clause might be invoked against her in East Africa. Thinking it over, Kirk had early pointed out that it might be turned to Britain's disadvantage by adventurers like the German Karl Peters,[205] then engaged in a race to reach Uganda before the agents of the British East Africa Company. Salisbury, with the Zambesi in mind, considered making only transit by water compulsory but Anderson feared France might force Britain to allow arms to pass up the Niger.[206]

Salisbury decided to compromise. The coastal power, he agreed, might 'exceptionally and provisionally' refuse transit for arms of precision and their ammunition if it felt that their despatch threatened its own safety. Portugal complained that this would be no protection because she was so weak that Britain could always force her to give way if she ever refused transit no matter how good her reason.[207]

A successful diplomatic struggle took place to isolate her. France was won over when Britain agreed to allow arms to pass through Lagos to Porto Novo to be used for her war against Dahomey.[208] Germany agreed to support Britain when Anderson raised the matter in Berlin during the course of the negotiations for the treaty of 1 July 1890.[209] The transit clause was eventually accepted[210] but Portugal made it clear that she would not allow transit to territories in dispute, thus, she hoped, ruling out Nyasaland[211] and retaining her bargaining point.

204 Plens. to Ribot, no. 27, 27 March 1890, FMAE/MDA/114; De Grelle to Lambermont, 18 April 1890, no. 122, AEB/CAE/3 also enc. in Vivian to Salisbury, very conf., no. 96 STC, 25 April 1890, FO 84/2102
205 Anderson memo, 22 Oct. 1889, FO 84/2005
206 Minute by Anderson, 23 Feb. 1890, on Vivian to Salisbury, no. 43 STC, 21 Feb. 1890, FO 84/2101
207 De Grelle to Lambermont, 18 April 1890, no. 122, AEB/CAE/3
208 Bourée to Ribot, no. 47, 20 April 1890, FMAE/MDA/115; Waddington to Salisbury, no. 49, 4 June 1890, FMAE/CP/Bret./850; Vivian to Barington, 4 June 1890, private, and Vivian to Salisbury, 5 June 1890, SP/A 49. The British squirmed a little, saying that the French operations in Dahomey were warlike and that Porto Novo had access to the sea, but the French insisted, saying that surf rendered access impossible.
209 Anderson to Currie, private, 3 May 1890, FOCP 6146; Anderson to Malet, 3 May 1890, enc. in Malet to Salisbury, no. 47 Af., 3 May 1890, FO 84/2031
210 Article X, Hertslet, *Map*, II, p. 496
211 Plens. to Salisbury, no. 191, STC, 24 June 1890, FO 84/2104

Britain could be reasonably contented with the arms clauses of the Brussels Act. She had limited both the zone of their application and the duration of the agreement to suit her particular interests and had secured a declaration which strengthened her hand on the Niger and an arms transit clause which might help her settlers in Nyasaland.

Taken all in all, if faithfully carried out, the arms agreement strengthened the hands of the colonial nations and was bound to cripple Arab and African resistance to European occupation of the regions within the arms zone. The slave trade conference had thus given the powers the opportunity of presenting in humanitarian guise a set of measures wanted for political or commercial reasons.

Italy and Ethiopia

Italy tried to use the arms agreement to further her protectorate in Ethiopia. Just before the conference opened, she had notified the powers of Article XVII of the treaty of Wichale, distorting its sense to imply that Menelik had accepted her protection.[212] In the early weeks of the conference she made much of the treaty, claiming that it prevented her from restricting the arms traffic to Ethiopia and she tried to introduce a stipulation providing that colonial powers should ask African countries bound to them by alliance, or under their protection or influence, to accept the arms clauses of the Brussels Act.[213] In the spring of 1890 she announced that Menelik had asked her to represent him at the conference.[214]

Russia strongly objected. She had approached Turkey and France soon after receiving the Italian communication about the treaty of Wichale, asking if it infringed on Turkish territorial claims[215] and complaining to the French that Ethiopia was a geographical expression, that Menelik was not in control of all of it, that Italy had not established a protectorate, that she and Britain were trying to dominate the Red Sea, and that France had been over hasty in acknowledging the Italian communication.[216] The Turks do not appear to have felt strongly on the subject but they followed the Russian

212 Giglio, p. 229

213 Plens. to Spuller, no. 10, 12 Dec. 1889 and Bourée to Spuller, no. 5 tel., 29 Jan. 1890, FMAE/MDA/114; Plens. to Salisbury, no. 15 STC, 27 Jan. 1890, FO 84/2101

214 Tornielli to Salisbury, 15 March 1890, FOCP 6197

215 The Turks had not acknowledged the Italian annexation of Massawa in 1885. Their claims did not apply to Ethiopia however.

216 De Giers to De Nelidon, 17 Oct. 1889, conf. and note of Russian views communicated to Spuller, FMAE/MDA/138; Laboulaye to Spuller, no. 108, 11 Dec. 1889, FMAE/CP/Russ. 286. France had acknowledged the Italian communication without comment since the text of the treaty of Wichale was not communicated to her.

lead.[217] The French had no basic objection to an Italian protectorate over Ethiopia as long as it did not include Harar.[218]

The question was badly handled by the Italians and caused a veritable storm in a tea-cup. Russia and France took the view that Italy was trying to manoeuvre them into accepting her protectorate over Ethiopia and was therefore raising a territorial issue and involving the conference in the delicate question of her relationship with Menelik.[219] They already knew that he had no desire to come under Italian protection and had not agreed to the protectorate.[220] Germany, placing increasing reliance on the Triple Alliance after the fall of Bismarck in March 1890, gave Italy whole-hearted support and urged England to follow suit. She hoped to use the incident to create 'a bond between Italy and Britain' and drive 'a wedge between Italy and Russia'.[221] Salisbury was willing to back Italy but counselled moderation. Russia was backed by France and Turkey, neither of whom seemed to feel strongly on the subject themselves.

Why Russia did remains something of a mystery. All sources agree that she was interested in maintaining the links between the Ethiopian Coptic and the Orthodox Russian Church. Collections were apparently made for the Ethiopian Church in Russia,[222] and Russia was the protector of the Holy Places of the Orthodox Church in Jerusalem, where the Ethiopians had a convent.[223] Russia certainly mentioned the danger of Roman Catholic Italy 'penetrating' the Holy Places[224] and she was said to regard the Ethiopians as under her 'moral protection'[225], whatever that was. Certainly a

217 Imbert to Spuller, no. 263 tel., 27 Nov. 1889 and no. 265 tel. 30 Nov. 1889, FMAE/CP/Turk. 489; Laboulaye to Spuller, no. 103, 28 Nov. 1889, FMAE/CP/Russ. 286; Bourée to Ribot, no. 34, 24 April 1890, FMAE/MDA/115. Bourée said the Turks opposed Italy but did not want to involve themselves in any responsibilities, presumably on the western shore of the Red Sea, and they, therefore, sheltered behind the Russians and French.

218 Étienne to Spuller, 23 Oct. 1889, FMAE/MDA/138. Harar was in the French sphere of influence as delimited by the frontier agreement with Britain in 1888 and both powers had agreed not to annex it themselves while retaining the right to oppose its annexation by a third party, see Hertslet, *Map*, II, p. 726.

219 Note, 9 April 1890, re Ethiopia, FMAE/MDA/138

220 In December Savouré arrived with a letter from Menelik which he delivered to the French President, asking for arms, offering to protect French traders and saying that trade could be diverted through Jibuti. He was clearly not conducting his relations through Italy. Savouré said he wanted to open a railway from Jibuti to Harar and Shoa, note on Savouré's audience with Carnot, 6 Dec. 1889, FMAE/MDA/138. The Russian traveller, Machkov had also brought back the news that Menelik did not want an Italian protectorate, Lagarde to Spuller, tel., 10 Dec. 1889, *ibid.* Menelik, however, was apparently unaware of the Italian pretensions until after the end of the Brussels conference, Caulk, 'Menelik II', p. 332.

221 Norman R. Rich, *Friedrich von Holstein*, Cambridge 1965, 2 vols., I, p. 328

222 Morier to Salisbury, no. 2 Af., 28 April 1890, FO 84/2055

223 Borchgrave to Chimay, 2 May 1890, AEB/AG de B/Adhes. I

224 Note, 9 April 1890, FMAE/MDA/138

225 Borchgrave to Chimay, 2 May 1890, AEB/AG de B/Adhes. I

Russian traveller in Ethiopia in 1889 had made much of the religious link and the Emperor Yohannes had sent representatives to the nine hundredth anniversary of the Russian Church in Kiev the previous year. Ironically Menelik did not take the overtures very seriously, although he sent a letter to the Tsar, and the Ethiopian clergy objected to any Russian pretensions to interference.[226]

But whether Russian policy sprang from the desire, as the French Ambassador reported, to cement the ecclesiastical link against the day when Russia might establish naval bases in Egypt and the Red Sea,[227] or whether it was part of an attempt to put pressure on Italy to detach her from the Triple Alliance, or was dictated by Russian internal politics[228] or arose from jealousy over the Holy Places as the Turks suggested,[229] was not established during the conference. Russia objected also to Menelik's assumption of the title of 'Emperor' of Ethiopia, saying that the Tsar could not accept this[230] and that to allow Menelik, who had only so far been recognised as King of Shoa, to appear at an international conference under a title still in dispute would open the way for a similar step by the Prince of Bulgaria, whom Russia had not recognised,[231] and set a dangerous precedent.

Italy was ready enough to represent Menelik as his delegate and not his protector, thus removing the political implications of the question, but she could not give up all idea of representing him without great loss of face. At one point it looked to the Belgians as though either Russia or Italy might leave the conference, but to everyone's relief eventually a solution was found. Menelik was not to be represented in Brussels but after the end of the conference Italy was to notify the other signatories that he had adhered to the Brussels Act. This procedure was duly followed and both Russia and France accepted the notification, but with reservations as to its political implications.[232]

The liquor agreement

Britain took advantage of the Brussels Conference to return to the attack on the liquor trade. Anderson had suggested this in 1888, but in terms which indicate that he had lost some of the humanitarian fervour which had so marked his despatches from Berlin. He wrote,

226 Caulk, 'Menelik II', pp. 304–5
227 Laboulaye to Spuller, 22 Jan. 1890, FMAE/CP/Russ. 287
228 The Italians suggested this, Rumbold to Salisbury, no. 14 Af., very conf., 15 May 1890, FOCP 6197.
229 Note for Lambermont by Borchgrave, 22 Feb. 1890, AEB/AG de B/Adhes. I
230 Vauvineux to Laboulaye, no. 36, 17 April 1890, FMAE/CP/Russ. 286
231 Bourée to Ribot, no. 34, 26 April 1890, FMAE/MDA/115
232 Renzis to Chimay, 28 Aug. 1890, Giers to Vink, 25 Sept. 1890, Ribot to Beyens, 16 Oct. 1890, AEB/AG de B/Adhes. I, Menelik, folder II

The spirits traffic, only promotes the Slave Trade like cannibalism by demoralizing the natives, but if there is a conference all the English philanthropists, who are absolutely illogical, will urge the introduction of the question as they did at Berlin. It is therefore a question whether it is politic to anticipate them by suggesting its discussion; the suggestion will not be accepted by France and Germany, but we might get credit for the effort.[233]

Salisbury had no doubts that the subject must be raised. Although it might 'require some ingenuity' to bring it within the scope of a slave trade conference it was 'a matter with which the British Representatives cannot possibly omit to deal.'[234]

His attitude to the question was markedly different from his views on controlling the arms trade. He had been ready enough in 1887, for instance, to negotiate a spirits agreement for South Africa, where Natal complained that she had lost trade and revenues as a result of the Delagoa Bay agreement between Portugal and the Transvaal.[235] He had been prepared to do the same for West Africa, where the Royal Niger Company was pressing for high uniform duties from Senegambia to the Cameroons together with high license charges for the sale of spirits.[236] These negotiations were never opened, however, because in the Cape the ministers opposed the idea,[237] while Natal solved the problem by lowering her transit duties,[238] and the West African governors feared that the only results of a treaty would be to divert their trade to areas beyond their control.[239]

In 1889, Anderson, pursuing the line he had begun at Berlin, suggested that Britain should leave the trade of the coastal regions alone. He thought the people of these areas had taken to spirits to such an extent that they were 'in a hopeless condition' and would either resort to smuggling or distil for themselves if their supplies were cut off. Anyway Britain could not interfere with the customs arrangements of her colony at the Cape and it would be difficult to harmonise the various tariff systems in force along the coast.[240] On the other hand the Muslim peoples of the western Sudan, reached by way of the Niger, and the 'heathen tribes' of the interior, who were mainly in the conventional basin of the Congo, were still 'uncontaminated' by European spirits and should be protected.

233 Memo. by Anderson, 26 Oct. 1888, FOCP 5896
234 Memo. by Salisbury, 30 Oct. 1889, FO 84/2005
235 See FO to CO, 1 June 1887, FO 84/1864, in which Salisbury states his views and also above, pp. 175, 224.
236 FO to CO, 1 June 1887, *ibid*.
237 Minute from the ministers to the governor, 19 Aug. 1887 enc. in Robinson to Holland, 24 Aug. 1887, conf., COCP African no. 381 (CO 879/31)
238 Havelock to Holland, conf., 12 Sept. 1887, *ibid*.
239 Moloney to Holland, no. 32 conf., 30 Aug. 1887 and Griffin to Holland, conf. 24 March 1888, *ibid*.
240 For the different rates of duties charged in different British colonies, see below, pp. 276–6.

With regard to the first of these, England had 'a good card to play'. Anderson proposed that she declare her readiness to prohibit the passage of spirits beyond the confluence of the Niger and the Benue and to maintain heavy duties on the lower river, and that she ask the other powers to agree that free transit of liquor on the lower Niger be absolutely forbidden.[241]

This would help the Royal Niger Company defeat the German challenge to its monopoly. Goldie now charged a duty of two shillings a gallon on spirits imported into the lower river and another two shillings on liquor traded above Lokoja, and, in addition to the normal charge of £100 for a license to trade in company territory, he charged an extra £100 for permission to deal in alcohols. This was naturally resented by the Germans who claimed that the tariff was discriminatory and complained moreover that the company while forbidding the import of spirits into part of its northern territories was bringing them in itself and, that it also did a roaring trade elsewhere in liquors at the expense of its competitors whom it burdened with the full weight of its crippling taxes.[242]

Anderson pointed out that a declaration such as he proposed would serve a dual purpose:

Such a resolution, if carried, or even if lost, must bring credit to England. It would have the incidental advantage, if carried, of getting rid of our Niger difficulties with Germany, who if the Hamburg spirit trade is stopped, would possibly cease to trouble her head about the river.[243]

The French he thought would make a similar declaration for the upper Niger. For the protection of the uncontaminated 'heathen tribes' of Central Africa, he suggested that there should be a prohibition on the import of all liquors above a certain strength into the conventional basin of the Congo and the signatory powers on the coast should agree to see that spirits did not reach the interior through their territories. He believed that this undertaking would weigh most heavily on the Portuguese, and would please the Scottish missionaries and the African Lakes Company, who complained of the sale of spirits from Mozambique in the Zambesi basin.[244]

Salisbury agreed to the Niger and Congo proposals but rejected Anderson's suggestion that the liquor trade on the coast be left alone. He determined to press for customs duties high enough to check the consumption of imported liquors along the whole African coast, and suggested the South African taxes of nine shillings a gallon in Natal and ten at the Cape be taken as a model. He was not worried about smuggling. Spirits, he said were

241 Anderson's proposals are in a memo. of 22 Oct. 1889, FO 84/2005.
242 See Flint, *Goldie*, pp. 96 ff
243 Anderson memo. 22 Oct. 1889, FO 84/2005, Anderson does not seem to have been aware that the company was buying large quantities of spirits in Hamburg, see Flint, *Goldie*, p. 118.
244 Anderson memo., 22 Oct. 1889, FO 84/2005. The African Lakes Company did not deal in spirits, see Lugard, *East African Empire*, I, p. 213.

less portable than arms and if Mozambique, or any other territory, was lax in enforcing payment of duties, it would not seriously lower the cost of spirits in the far interior. He did not think the danger of Africans distilling for themselves was as yet a serious one. Curiously, initially he seems really to have believed that the conference might accept a duty such as he proposed.[245]

It is clear that he felt strongly on the subject, perhaps from personal conviction that the traffic was harmful, or not in Britain's economic interests,[246] but doubtless also because a high tax would please those members of the electorate who supported the temperance movement. Temperance societies were more vocal than they had been at the time of the Berlin conference. A new one, the United Committee for the Prevention of the Demoralisation of Native Races by the Liquor Traffic, had been formed in 1887 with members in both Houses of Parliament,[247] and, together with the Aborigines' Protection Society,[248] it drummed up support for the restriction of the spirits trade. Meetings were held up and down the country, culminating in the Mansion House meeting of January 1890, already mentioned in connection with the arms question. Petitions came in not only from the missionary and humanitarian societies normally concerned with Africa but also from such organisations as the Band of Hope Union, the National Temperance League, the British Women's Temperance Association, the temperance organisations of the various churches and even from the inhabitants of Norwich.[249] Salisbury was reminded that he had promised in 1888 that he would not cease to press the matter 'in season and out of season' in the cause of human happiness.[250]

Petitions were also sent to Brussels once the conference opened. There was certainly an element of official inspiration in this, for both the Aborigines' Protection Society and the United Committee sent representatives to Brussels to canvass King Leopold II and members of the various delegations, and they were advised by Vivian to collect as many petitions for the conference as they could get.[251] They were subsequently encouraged to go

245 'I do not see,' he wrote, 'why a general duty of 10s. a gallon over the whole coast of Africa, upon all spirits over 45 degrees proof should not be enacted, and to a great extent carried out,' memo. 30 Oct. 1889, FO 84/2005.
246 He may have felt that Africans might more profitably have been investing in productive British goods such as tools, see above, pp. 176–7 for Goldie's views. Kirk thought it might be 'replaced by more legitimate and civilizing forms of barter', Kirk to Fox Bourne, 14 Dec. [?] 1895, KP Misc.
247 Its chairman was the Duke of Westminster, its vice-chairman Sir John Kennaway, MP. For the latter, who also actively supported the anti-slavery cause, see above, pp. 31, note 142, 230, note 257.
248 The Secretary of the Aborigines' Protection Society told the Anti-Slavery Society that he was getting 'expressions of opinion from proper organizations in England,' Bourne to Allen, 29 Oct. 1889, ASS/C 51/52.
249 These are conveniently printed and collected in FOCP 5983.
250 British Women's Temperance Association to Salisbury, 26 Aug. 1889, FOCP 5983
251 F. W. Fox to Fox Bourne, 2 Dec. 1889, ASS/C151/41.

to Berlin where they urged the German Colonial Department and members of the Reichstag, as well as the secretaries to the Emperor and Empress, to co-operate in saving the Africans from the ravages of the liquor traffic.[252] The humanitarians were thus used to show the Germans how strongly the British public felt on the subject.

Eventually a hundred and fifty-five petitions arrived in Brussels; all but five of them were British and the vast majority were from temperance societies. Most claimed that the spirits and the arms traffics were evils attendant on the slave trade, but one from the French Société Contre l'Abus du Tabac said that smoking was just as demoralising as alcohol and should also be stopped.[253]

If Salisbury's desire to impose a duty on spirits heavy enough to check consumption pleased the humanitarians and the temperance societies, it found no favour with the Colonial Office, which sent the strongest possible protests. He was informed that although the duties charged in South Africa, nine shillings a gallon in Natal and ten at the Cape, were high, they merely applied to spirits sold in the colonies. Only nominal taxes were levied on liquor for sale beyond their borders. Furthermore considerable quantities of spirits were also distilled in the colonies. They paid virtually no excise tax and were freely 'distributed by traders among the tribes of the interior'. Liquors were also manufactured in the Transvaal and the Orange Free State and these industries would receive a great impetus if the Cape and Natal gave up their system of rebates.[254]

In West Africa, the Colonial Office was ready enough to have the conference agree on a high rate of duty if it could be sure that other powers would carry out their treaty obligations. But the administrative staff in both the French and German colonies was, it said, 'of the slenderest proportions' and would be quite unable to prevent smuggling, nor could Liberia do so. It would be difficult to prevent even in the British colonies, where there were more customs officers. Furthermore many of these officials were Africans and might be tempted by the bribes which high duties would encourage traders to offer. None of the colonies, British or foreign, or Liberia could afford to increase their customs services to the level necessary to enforce a high scale of duties.

252 The Rev. J. Grant Mills of the United Committee and F. W. Fox, a prominent Quaker businessman representing the Aborigines' Protection Society, went to Berlin, having been briefed on the exact state of the negotiations in Brussels by Kirk and Vivian. Grant Mills saw the Dutch Foreign Minister, and Fox also saw the Dutch delegate in Brussels, see report by Grant Mills, 16 April 1890, FO 84/2081; Fox to Fox Bourne, 28 April 1890, ASS/C 151/143; Fox to Currie, 30 April 1890, enc. Fox to Vivian, 14 April 1890, FOCP 6197.
253 These petitions are filed in AEB/CAE/18 and 19. One is Belgian, one Dutch, one Swiss and two French.
254 CO to FO, 13 Nov. 1889 and 16 Nov. 1889, and minutes, FO 84/2007; minutes of a meeting in the Colonial Office, 8 Jan. 1890, and CO to FO, 11 Jan. 1890, and enc. memo. by Havelock, 26 Nov. 1889, FOCP 6197.

The only result of such a tax therefore would be to divert, perhaps for ever, the trade of the British colonies. The Colonial Office even suggested that foreign powers might be tempted to agree to a duty of ten shillings a gallon knowing that Britain would enforce it, and hoping that, by allowing smuggling in their own territories, they could attract the commerce of the British colonies.[255] Such a tax would also encourage Africans to distil for themselves in areas outside of British control, thus competing with a European industry. This had already begun in the Zambesi valley,[256] where interestingly Dr. Rankin reported that locally made spirits were as strong as the imported variety but did not have 'the flavouring ingredients to excite their [the African] palate and thirst like those so cunningly manufactured in Rotterdam, Hamburg and Marseilles'.[257]

Any massive diversion of trade resulting from a high duty on liquor would deal a fatal blow to the revenues of some of the West African colonies. At this time, for instance, the Gold Coast and Lagos raised the bulk of their revenues from taxes on spirits[258] and the great difficulty would be to find another source of income. Other trade goods might not be able to stand higher taxation without a decrease in consumption and there was the additional consideration that the liquor tax was in effect a differential duty on foreign products.

The Colonial Office was much in favour, however, of an agreement to impose a moderate uniform tax on spirits along the West African coast to prevent the trade of the British colonies from being diverted to neighbouring territories where the duties were lower. Already the Gold Coast, which charged a tax of two shillings and sixpence a gallon had had to lower the duty to one shilling east of the Volta River, because her trade was going to German Togo where the duty was only a penny halfpenny a gallon.[259] Knutsford suggested that Britain should propose to the conference a two

255 FOCP 6197. In connection with the fears of the Colonial Office one may note that by the Anglo-French frontier agreement of 10 Aug. 1889, Britain only accepted the proposed frontier for the Gold Coast on condition that the French charged duties at Assinée on spirits of from 40 to 100 francs a hectolitre (1s. 6d. to 3s. 9d. a gallon) depending on their strength, Hertslet, *Map*, II, p. 731. In November 1889 the Governor of Senegal informed the Colonial Department that he had only 55 customs agents to cover French posts from Senegal to the Slave Coast and asked for more, 5 Nov. 1889, AOF/2B 63.

256 Anderson memo. 22 Oct. 1889, FO 84/2005

257 Rankin, p. 238. Rankin does not mention Réunion or Mauritius as sources of supply although trade spirits came into Zanzibar at this time from both of them, see Euan Smith to Salisbury, no. 65 conf., 14 April 1888, FOCP 5673.

258 Memo by Anderson, 22 Oct. 1889, FO 84/2005; CO to FO, 11 June 1889, FOCP, 5979. The Gold Coast raised nine tenths of its revenues from taxes on liquor.

259 Newbury, *Slave Coast*, pp. 119-20. Newbury here quotes a source which gives the impression that duties east of the Volta were not reduced until 1890. They may in fact have come into force in that year but the correspondence at the time of the conference gives the impression that they had been reduced before the end of 1889.

shillings and sixpenny duty and, if the system worked well, she could try to get it raised later to a level high enough to check consumption.[260] Salisbury grumbling that 'it is very inconvenient to have to negotiate in partnership with the Colonial Office . . . they resemble Molière's Étourdi more than anything else.'[261] modified his plans. It was already clear in any case that a high duty would not be accepted by other powers. Even King Leopold, who welcomed the chance to impose an import tax denied him by the Berlin Act, and would have liked it to be higher, believed that it was unwise to try to get a duty higher than about 1s 10d. The Germans, he was sure, would agree to no more.[262] This proved to be over-optimistic.

Germany was most reluctant to come to grips with the matter at all. At the time she produced over two million hectolitres (forty-four million gallons) of spirits a year from more than twenty-six thousand distilleries.[263] Her taxes on liquor consumed at home were markedly lower than those of most of the other powers.[264] She imposed no duty on spirits in South-West Africa and only very small ones in Togo and the Cameroons.[265] The question involved the protection of German agriculture and shipping as well as of the trade of Hamburg.[266] British consular reports showed a steady rise, in the 1880s, in the commerce between Hamburg and West Africa, and an increase in the tonnage of German ships engaged in this traffic. For volume and value, Hamburg's exports to West Africa took fourth place

260 CO to FO, 11 Jan. 1890, FOCP 6197. 2s. 6d. was higher than the duty in most of the British West African colonies. Their rates were as follows:

Gold Coast	2s. 6d. a gallon
east of Volta	1s.
The Gambia—Rum	2s.
—Gin	2s.
Sierra Leone	2s.
Lagos	6d.
Oil Rivers—no duty	
Niger below Lokoja	2s.
above Lokoja	4s.

Ibid., and memo. on West African liquor traffic, COCP Af. (West) no. 503.
261 Minute by Salisbury, on CO to FO, 11 Jan. 1890, FO 84/2072
262 Leopold II to Lambermont, no. 61, 26 Nov. 1889, PL 1889–90. The Congo had no wish to prohibit the spirits traffic as this would deprive the state of a means of raising revenue by imposing import duties, although officials believed that drinking spirits encouraged idleness amongst Africans, see Note, undated and unsigned, in EIC/A1 (1378).
263 Banning, p. 127
264 The highest German spirits tax was 34 francs a hectolitre compared to Britain's 477 francs, Holland's 252 francs, America's 245 francs, Belgium's 200 francs, France's 156 francs 25 centimes, and Italy's 150 francs.
265 In Togo the tax was 1½d. a gallon and in the Cameroons *c*. 6d.
266 The State of Hamburg, but not the port, had been absorbed into the Zollverein only in 1888.

in her non-European trade in 1888 and nearly half of them were spirits.[267]

There was some support in the Reichstag for limiting the spirits traffic[268] and Germany had not objected to a duty of 25% in Zanzibar where there was as yet little demand for liquor.[269] She would also, doubtless, have been glad to raise her own duties in Togo and the Cameroons. But there were her vested interests to consider.

Bismarck was thought to be negotiating with the Hamburg dealers at Christmas[270] but apparently nothing came of this for when the conference reconvened he clearly wanted to delay discussion of the question at least until after the Reichstag elections in February. He was in the invidious position of having either to appear to favour alcoholism or to risk alienating Hamburg and the landowners, manufacturers and merchants interested in the exports of spirits.[271] He tried to get Salisbury to drop the whole issue but was told feeling ran too high in England for this.[272] By the time the Reichstag elections were over, he was involved in the crisis which ended in his dismissal.

Britain, finding that she could not reach an agreement with Germany, eventually made her proposals to the conference in March 1890.[273] She declared herself willing for humanitarian reasons to see that no spirits were sold north of Lokoja provided other powers would agree to end free transit on the Niger and the French would take similar steps for the upper river.

267 The total exports from Hamburg to West Africa in 1888 came to 1,121,605 cwt. Of this 652,130 cwt. were spirits (c. 7,373,789 gallons) and big increases were expected. The only more important non-European markets for Hamburg's trade were U.S.A., Brazil and Argentina, see report enc. in Dundas to Salisbury, no. 26 commercial, 12 Oct. 1889, FO 64/1219.

268 There were debates on the subject on 14 May 1889, and on 27 Nov. 1889, when members asked that the traffic to the German colonies be restricted. F. W. Fox, a member of the Aborigines' Protection Society, visited members of the Conservative, National Liberal and Advanced Liberal Parties in Berlin in April 1890 and was assured that 'a large majority' of the German people were in favour of restrictions. However, they do not appear to have made any great impact on the government; Fox to Fox Bourne, 28 April 1890, ASS/C 151/43.

269 Britain and Germany had wanted a 25% tax on spirits of more than 20% alcohol entering the Sultan's dominions, but France had objected because it would weigh unfairly on the better quality French products imported into Zanzibar and already costing about 50s. a dozen bottles, see Euan Smith to Salisbury, 14 Aug. 1888, FOCP 5673. Germany was still prepared to accept this tax in 1890 see Fox to Vivian, 14 Apri 1890, enc. in Fox to Currie, 30 April 1890, FOCP 6197.

270 Pogson to Anderson, private, 28 Dec. 1889, FO 84/1959. Kirk was going to meet the Germans during the Christmas recess to try to come to an arrangement but he was delayed in London by the development of the Anglo-Portuguese dispute and Lord Salisbury's illness of January 1890. As a result the favourable moment for settling the matter, while relations were cordial and before the Reichstag elections were imminent, passed.

271 Greindl to Lambermont, 5 Feb. 1890, no. 15 and 6 Feb. 1890, no. 16, AEB/CAE/7

272 Salisbury to Vivian, no. 50 Af. 10 Feb. 1890, and Currie minute, FO 84/2100

273 Plens. to Salisbury, no. 60 STC, 15 March 1890 and enc. FO 84/2102

She proposed that elsewhere in the arms zone, 20° North to 22° South, the import of spirits should be prohibited in regions where they were not already consumed, and distillation for local consumption should be forbidden. Small quantities might be allowed for the use of foreigners only. In the regions of the zone where the trade was already established, she asked for import duties of 50 francs a hectolitre or 1s 10d a gallon, and an equivalent excise tax on locally made liquor. The colonial governments were also to prevent spirits from reaching the 'uncontaminated' areas from their territories. The restriction and duties were only to apply to the arms zone in order to exclude the South African colonies.

The provisions for the Niger were accepted. So were those for the other 'uncontaminated' regions. Since each power was to define these for itself and there were no established markets at stake, this part of the agreement caused little difficulty. Local distillation in these areas was also forbidden.[274] However, a great battle was waged over the fifty franc duty. The main protagonists were the Dutch, who bore much of the odium of the struggle, but were solidly backed by the Germans. The Dutch delegate, Mr. de la Fontaine Verwey, who was the Dutch company's agent at the mouth of the Congo and Dutch Consul at Banana, made a spirited defence of the liquor traffic, claiming that its evils were much exaggerated, that it stimulated African production, that, if it ceased, Africans would stop bringing their goods for trade and the European stations might need government protection.

He claimed that spirits were essential trade goods but were not the most important or profitable articles of trade and that they were watered down by both European traders and African middlemen so that they got progressively weaker as they were traded inland, and, at a distance from the coast, they contained only 'faint traces of alcohol'.[275] As evidence that the traffic was not demoralising he cited the fact that the very areas where the traffic was established were those which produced the greatest quantity of goods for export. He asked for a moderate tax and the preaching of temperance so that the traffic might decrease gradually without dislocating trade, or encouraging smuggling and African distillation.

274 Articles XC and XCI, Hertslet, *Map*, II, pp. 514–15. Kirk suspected that King Leopold had had visions of setting up distilleries on the upper Congo, ostensibly to produce liquor for export but really to supply a local market, Kirk minute, 27 Dec. 1889, in Plens. to Salisbury, 20 Dec. 1889, FO 84/2011. The Portuguese and Germans had no wish to suppress local distilleries, Plens, to Salisbury, no. 72 STC, 27 March 1890, FO 84/2102.

275 The Dutch statement is enclosed in Plens. to Salisbury, no. 64 STC, 18 March 1890, FO 84/2102. The total Western African traffic amounted they said to some 8,000,000 gallons a year costing 9d. a gallon and comprising from 1/8th to 1/10th of the total trade. Far more important in value was the trade in textiles. However, as has been shown above traders maintained that the sale of spirits attracted African cusomers and the Dutch claimed that if they refused to sell them they might need protection from irate customers. He also suggested that with the end of slavery Africans might cease to produce goods for export if denied the spirits they wanted.

What duty did the Dutch suggest? Amid great hilarity they rose with infinite reluctance from 6 francs 25 centimes a hectolitre to 6 francs 50 centimes and finally 7 francs 50 centimes rising in three years to 15 francs (7*d* a gallon). This they said was their ultimate limit. All the other powers except the Germans supported the British proposal of 50 francs a hectolitre. The Germans agreed with the Dutch that this would be prohibitive.[276]

Strong diplomatic representations were made in Berlin and the Hague. Dutch ministers, however, were under pressure from the Rotterdam traders interested in the Congo.[277] The Dutch Foreign Minister, 'an honourable man', winced when the British Ambassador smugly informed him that Britain 'unlike others' regarded trading interests as a secondary matter,[278] but he remained firm.

Eventually a compromise was agreed upon. An initial duty of 15 francs a hectolitre was to be imposed on all imported spirits of up to fifty degrees centigrade for the first three years after the Brussels Act came into force. After this the duty might, but did not have to, be raised to 25 francs for a further three years and at the end of this period the question was to be reconsidered with a view to imposing, if possible, a higher minimum duty throughout the zone.[279] Powers outside the conventional basin of the Congo could, of course, always impose a higher tax if they wished to do so. The Act did not apply to beers or fermented beverages. An excise tax not lower than the minimum duty was to be charged on all distilled liquors manufactured in the zone.[280] Signatories with possessions in contact with the zone were to prevent the smuggling of liquors across their inland frontiers.[281] Information about the spirits trade in their territories was to be exchanged by the colonial powers.[282]

This was a far cry from Salisbury's hopes of getting a tax high enough to cut consumption, and once he realised that defeat was inevitable, he concentrated on making sure that Britain's struggle to get a high duty would clearly emerge in the published protocols of the conference. 'Will the proceedings as ultimately published show all this controversy—or only the ultimate outcome of it?' he asked Vivian.[283] Reassured on this point, he made doubly certain that his government would get credit for its efforts by having Vivian declare that Britain only accepted the solution in order that advantage might be taken of the more valuable parts of the Brussels Act, but her efforts to get a tax high enough to check consumption would remain on

276 Plens. to Salisbury, no. 72 STC, *ibid.*
277 Rumbold to Salisbury, no. 8 Af., conf., 18 April 1890, and no. 10 Af., 23 April 1890, FOCP 6197
278 Rumbold to Salisbury, no. 11 Af., conf., 25 April 1890, *ibid.*
279 Article XCII, Hertslet, *Map*, II, p. 515
280 Article XCIII, *ibid.*
281 Article XCIV, *ibid.*
282 Article XCV, *ibid.*
283 Salisbury minute on Malet to Salisbury, no. 9 tel. 18 April 1890 and draft to Vivian 23 April 1890, FO 84/2035

record and would, she hoped, serve as the basis for more successful future negotiations.[284] She considered this agreement to be purely temporary.

The limiting of the spirits tax and restrictions to the arms zone did not go unchallenged. France wanted them applied to the whole continent for the same reason as she had tried to get all Africa included in the arms zone and because her government hoped they would get credit at home for their humanitarianism.[285] The Portuguese wanted the zone extended to South Africa, presumably to embarrass Britain, as they seemed to think the evil effects of alcoholism in Africa much exaggerated.[286] However, Britain successfully kept the restrictions to the zone, and fended off a German attempt to force her to declare that she would use her good offices to get the Cape and Natal to stop spirits from entering South West Africa. Britain was fortunate that the real position in South Africa was never revealed. She was able to claim that the high duties charged in the colonies were evidence of their co-operation and that most of the liquor exported to the interior was destined for the Boer Republics.[287] Privately the Germans complained of British hypocrisy[288] but apart from demanding the declaration over South West Africa they did not pursue the point.

At the last minute when the spirits question seemed to be settled, the American plenipotentiary, Sanford, asked the conference to forbid the sale of 'noxious' spirits in Africa. This raised an interesting question for there was much talk about the harmfulness of trade spirits. When the West African Governors were consulted about the British proposals for the Brussels Conference, they had said that trade rums and gins, or genevas, were poisonous and should be prohibited.[289] This view was widely held. The Germans and Dutch denied the charge and claimed that tests had shown that they were not injurious to health. Belgian tests bore this out.[290]

284 Salisbury minute on Plens. to Salisbury, no. 99 STC, 26 April 1890, FO 84/2102; Salisbury to Vivian, no. 105 Af., 29 April 1890, FO 84/2100; Vivian to Salisbury, no. 136 STC, 20 May 1890, FO 84/2103.

285 Banning, p. 118; Lambermont to Greindl, 9 April 1890, no. 33, AEB/CAE/7

286 Bourée to Ribot, no. 37, 3 May 1890, FMAE/MDA/115, Bourée though they were perhaps supporting Germany in return for German support in the Anglo-Portuguese dispute.

287 Plens. to Salisbury, no. 146 STC, 27 May 1890, FOCP 6197. This was based on a letter from the Colonial Office saying that it would be as impossible to 'cut off the supply of liquor from the hotels of Johannesburg and Pretoria as from those of Algiers and Cairo', CO to FO, 20 May 1890, *ibid.*

288 Greindl to Lambermont, 16 April 1890, no. 40 AEB/CAE/7

289 Minutes of a meeting in the Colonial Office, 8 Jan. 1890, FOCP 6197

290 Dutch statement, 15 March 1890, enc. in Plens. to Salisbury, no. 64 STC, 18 March 1890, FO 84/2102. The Dutch said tests had been conducted at St. Thomas's Hospital in London in 1888, and by the government of the Cameroons. Banning prints the results of tests made in Belgium for the Congo government in 1888. These showed that 58% of the spirits were pure and that the rest contained only infinitesimal quantities of toxic substances, pp. 138–9.

The proposal was anyway highly unwelcome. As Vivian complained:[291]

That wretched old Sanford has sprung upon us a proposal ticketted with his Gov[ernmen]t's stamp to exclude and confiscate all noxious spirits imported into Africa. It is sufficiently plausible and with the Temperance Societies watching over our proceedings, it was impossible to scotch it as the Conference would have wished, but I doubt the practicability of the project, while to introduce a contentious question, which it would take weeks to settle, at this late hour just as the conference had finished its labours is really too bad. We hope you will be able to squash it.

The proposal was Sanford's own, but it received the full approval of his government which strongly supported restrictions on the liquor traffic.[292] Britain, supported by Germany, opposed the motion fearing to re-open the liquor question and believing that it was impractical to insist that the country of origin should examine all spirits exported to Africa and supply a certificate of purity. The matter was 'decently buried' in a protocol, which merely recorded that the conference was sympathetic to the proposal and the powers would 'give their attention' to the matter at the ports of import and export.[293] At the eleventh hour the United States attempted to get the liquor duties raised but it was too late to bring the matter up again.[294]

America also wanted the conference to recognise the independence of Liberia in return for her acceptance of a new tariff agreement for the Congo,[295] where no import duties could be imposed without her consent. She had not ratified the Berlin Act but had a treaty with the Congo State

291 Vivian to Wylde, 25 May 1890, FO 84/2103
292 Sanford proposed his amendment in a plenary session of the conference on 24 May 1890 but he had suggested it to his government on 3 April 1890 and it was approved on 25 April 1890, Sanford to Blaine, 3 April 1890, US M-193, Roll 27; Blaine to Sanford, 25 April 1890, Belg. 2, pp. 588 ff., US M-77, Roll 20. The timing is of some importance as the Belgians suspected Sanford of trying to delay the conference in order to allow an opposition group to form to defeat King Leopold's eleventh-hour proposal to apply import duties in the Congo. See below, p. 286, Banning, pp. 137–8. But Sanford was not aware of the King's plans until 5 May 1890, although he suspected the suggestion might be made, see Sanford to Blaine, 14 May 1890, US M-193, Roll 28.
293 Plens. to Salisbury, no. 144 STC, 24 May 1890, and minutes, FO 84/2103; Sanford to Blaine, 6 June 1890, US M-193, Roll 28
294 The United States had from the first complained of the inadequacy of the proposed liquor duties. The temperance issue seems to have been more important than the protection of her trade. 700,000 gallons of trade spirits a year were exported to Africa, see Blaine to Terrell no. 54, 9 April 1890, and tel., 10 June 1890, Belg. vol. 2, pp. 584, 595–6, US M-77, Roll. 20.
295 Blaine to Terrell, tel. 10 June 1890, Belg. vol. 2, pp. 595–6, US M-77, Roll 20. The United States had already emphasised her special relationship with Liberia by suggesting she use her 'friendly influences' to get Liberia to adopt the measures agreed to in Brussels to restrict the liquor traffic; see Blaine to Sanford, 18 April 1890, *ibid.*, p. 585.

specifically ruling out such taxes.[296] The American proposal was believed in Brussels, to be simply an electoral move[297] and was rejected on the grounds that territorial questions were outside the province of the conference.[298] The United States did not press the point but wanted her position clearly recorded, presumably to get credit for her efforts. Liberia, it was agreed, could adhere to the Brussels Act.[299]

From the British point of view the spirits clauses of the Act were quite satisfactory. The humanitarians and the temperance societies could be well pleased with the prohibition of the traffic in 'uncontaminated' areas. This was viewed as a major philanthropic achievement while no existing material interests had been sacrificed. The Royal Niger Company's monopoly was secured and the trade of the Cape and Natal untouched. The duties in coastal regions while too low to cut consumption or even to protect the revenues of the West African colonies, were nevertheless a step in the right direction, and not so high as to alarm the Colonial Office. In fact Salisbury had steered an ingenious course, which enabled Britain to pose as the champion of African welfare, while leaving it to others to whittle down the duties to a level which would not ruin her West African possessions. Kirk summed up the situation:

> We are very pleased with what we have got seeing the Gov[ernmen]t never expected to get more than the credit of showing how far we were willing to go.[300]

The bureaux in Brussels and Zanzibar

An integral part of the whole British plan for the suppression of the slave trade had been the establishment, not only of local bureaux to collect and collate information on the maritime slave traffic, but also of a central bureau in Brussels. This office was to correspond with the signatories, and gather and disseminate the information about the traffic, which they were bound to supply. All the parties to the treaty were to be represented on it and it was to supervise the working of the Brussels Act, control the bureau in Zanzibar, and any others which might be established, examine the facts sent to it and recommend any changes in the Act which might facilitate its execution.[301] It was to oversee the Zanzibar branch to prevent that bureau from becoming too independent or falling under the domination of the most influential

296 See Declarations of Washington, 22 April 1884, Hertslet, *Map*, II, p. 603.
297 Banning, p. 149
298 Terrell to Blaine, tels. 13 June and 14 June 1890 and no. 103, 15 June 1890, US M-193, Roll 28
299 *Ibid.*, and Blaine to Terrell, tel., no date, 1890, Belg. vol. 2, p. 597, US M-77, Roll 20.
300 Kirk to Wylde, private, 25 May 1890, FO 84/2103
301 Salisbury to Vivian, 28 March 1890, no. 74 Af., FOCP 6197

local official,[302] who the British feared might be a German.[303] The Brussels bureau could, of course, perform the same functions for the arms and spirits traffic as for the slave trade.

However, the Turks, Portuguese, Italians, Russians and French all objected to the Brussels bureau having the right to criticise, comment on or even draw conclusions from the information presented to it. Such powers would enable it to castigate any signatories who failed to carry out their obligations.[304] A bureau of this type might infringe the national sovereignty of its members. The French disliked the whole idea. In the spring of 1890, the Germans had called a conference in Berlin to regulate the conditions of work in factories and mines[305] and the same type of supervisory bureau had been suggested. The French had objected, particularly as it was to be established in Berlin. Now they said that if they accepted the British proposal the Kaiser would think it discourteous. They could hardly explain this to the conference and they hoped Salisbury would drop the project.[306] He agreed to change the character of the bureau, but was determined the French should take the blame. He wrote to Vivian:

> They cannot afford to practise more than a certain amount of obstruction in this particular conference: and if you force them to expend a portion of their allowance upon this matter, they will have less at their disposal for other subjects.[307]

The Brussels bureau was whittled down therefore until it was simply an information office attached to the Belgian Foreign Ministry, with the duty of collecting, exchanging and publishing whatever information on the slave, arms and liquor traffics the various powers sent it.[308] The British insisted that the protocol, however, should clearly record the type of bureau they had had in mind and their hope that it could be established in the future.[309]

The Zanzibar bureau was to centralise material on the slave trade in the maritime zone and to keep archives for the use of naval or consular officers or other interested officials. It was to draw up annual reports on its opera-

302 The Belgians had suggested the Zanzibar bureau might be independent, Kirk memo, 15 April 1890, *ibid.*; Vivian to Salisbury, 16 May 1890, SP/A. 49.
303 Vivian to Salisbury, 16 May 1890, SP/A. 49. This was before the future of Zanzibar had been decided. In the event the island became a British protectorate.
304 Ribot to Plens. no. 46, 24 April 1890 and Bourée to Ribot, no. 35, 27 April 1890, FMAE/MDA/115
305 Interestingly Salisbury had opposed the idea of regulating the working conditions of adult males. He considered it an infringement of their liberty and thought only women and children should be protected, Waddington to Spuller, 25 Feb. 1890, tel., FMAE/CP/Bret. 847.
306 Salisbury to Lytton, no. 90 A. Af., 14 May 1890, FOCP 6197
307 Salisbury to Vivian, private, 14 May 1890, SP/A. 49
308 See Articles LXXXII–LXXXIX, Hertslet, *Map*, II, pp. 5131–4
309 Vivian to Salisbury, no. 139 STC, 22 May 1890, and enc., FO 84/2103

tions[310] but, like its Brussels counterpart, it had no power to supervise the working of the treaty and was thus of very limited value.

The Congo import duties

The last weeks of the conference were taken up with King Leopold's struggle to get the right to levy import duties of up to 10 per cent *ad valorem* in the conventional basin of the Congo. The United States objected to this on technical grounds. It was a modification of the Berlin Act, which she had not ratified, and she could not, therefore, have an amendment to that Act written into the Brussels treaty. This was easily overcome by drawing up a separate declaration allowing import duties to be signed by all signatories of the Berlin Act, while the United States agreed to negotiate a new treaty with the Congo giving up her right to import goods without paying duties. This was on the understanding that she would have the same privileges as the other powers throughout the conventional basin.[311]

This solution, however, was not reached without much diplomatic activity. Sanford had his own grievances against King Leopold[312] and roundly denounced the Congo government in his despatches home. The King, he said, was a liberal philanthropist eager to make money and was liable 'in the name of civilisation' to run into 'excesses of the heart and perhaps of the head'. His government in the Congo was 'utterly irresponsible' without constitutional checks or balances and his agents were competing with private traders and hampering their operations. The rubber and ivory exports of certain regions were being reserved to the State, the adminstrative system was expensive, the King's ambitions kept growing and his military expeditions were unnecessary. The Arabs could easily be weaned away from slaving to ivory dealing without a fight.[313]

Sanford wrote that the commerce of a vast region 'is to be taxed because one man has been extravagant and exceeded his calculations—if he ever had any'.[314] He thought that in the long run the financial outlook for the Congo was excellent. A large trade would develop when the railway to the upper river was completed and the King already had power to levy export

310 See Articles LXXIV–LXXXI, Hertslet, *Map*, II, pp. 511–12
311 For these negotiations see Blaine to Terrell and Sanford, tel., 24 June 1890, vol. 2, p. 599, US M-77, Roll 20; tel., 28 June 1890, vol. 3, p. 1, US M-77, Roll 21; Terrell to Blaine, no. 105, 17 June 1890, no. 113, 2 July 1890, US M-193, T-28. The United States treaty of 1884 gave her the privilege of importing goods duty free into the Congo Free State only, see Hertslet, *Map*, II, pp. 602–3.
312 For his involvement in the Congo see pp. 222, 236. Among Sanford's complaints was the King's unwillingness to encourage the immigration of free blacks from the United States into the Congo. He thought the King was afraid they would spread republican ideas, Sanford to Blaine, conf., 3 June 1890, US M-193, Roll 28.
313 Sanford to Blaine, 14 May 1890, conf., 3 June 1890, 19 June 1890, US M-193, Roll 28. For these expeditions see Ceulemans, pp. 269 ff.
314 Sanford to Blaine, conf., 3 June 1890, US M-193, Roll 28

duties, the conference had agreed to a tax on liquor and Leopold was himself dealing in ivory. He urged his government to ask for a delay pending an inquiry into the revenues of the Congo. This would give time to try to get concessions in return for renouncing the privilege of importing goods duty free in a region where America might hope to build up a large trade exchanging her cheap cottons for ivory, coffee, rubber and other products. [315] Basically, however, the United States did not want to see the slave trade conference fail. Nor did she want to risk other powers in the conventional basin of the Congo charging differential duties on her goods if she was not a party to the Brussels arrangement. She therefore accepted the King's proposals.

The Dutch, however, waged a longer and more bitter battle against them, which threatened the whole work of the conference. The Nieuwe Afrikaanse Handels-Venootschap were the major traders on the Congo and they had suffered heavily in 1889 from the competition of the Congo State whose officials had bought up quantities of ivory which they had hoped to purchase. They complained that they had established themselves and placed a steamer on the river at great expense and now that they hoped to make profits they found themselves competing with the King, who could pay higher prices. [316] They were sure that import duties would not raise enough revenue to cover the cost of collection and that Leopold II simply wanted to drive them out of business. [317] The Congo State would, of course, have the advantage of merely paying the tax to itself and could use the duties to subject Dutch traders to vexatious formalities. For instance, instead of landing goods, as they now did, at convenient places along the coast, all their imports might have to be cleared through Banana and they would have to build a large warehouse there and pay duties on goods they were re-exporting to French and Portuguese territories. [318] Holland suggested higher export duties as an alternative, or the imposition of direct taxes, but the Belgians replied that the former would raise the price of African merchandise on the world market to too high a level while the latter would weigh heavily on private traders. [319] In the King's view import taxes were far preferable for they were borne by the consumer. [320] But the Dutch insisted that their trade would be ruined.

315 The concessions Sanford had in mind were the exemption of certain goods from import duties and limits on the export duties on rubber and ivory. Sanford to Blaine, 20 June 1890, *ibid*.
316 De la Fontaine Verwey to Hartsen, 5 Sept. 1889, MBZ 106 H1, 1889–90
317 Minister of Communications, Trade and Industry to Foreign Minister (Hartsen), 14 May 1890, *ibid*.
318 *Idem*; Rumbold to Salisbury, no. 15 Af. conf. 28 May 1890, and enc. article from *Nieuwe Rotterdamsche Courant*, 25 May 1890 (translation), FOCP 6197; Sanford to Blaine, 18 June 1890, US M-193, Roll 28; Plens. to Salisbury no. 171 STC, 14 June 1890, and enc., FO 84/2104.
319 Plens. to Salisbury, no. 171 STC, 14 June 1890, FO 84/2104
320 Leopold II to Lambermont, no. 166, 10 Sept. 1890, PL 1889–90

They were not alone in their views. Both French[321] and British merchants[322] opposed the import duties, and Salisbury was questioned about them in Parliament.[323] The Congo State's trading operations and its treatment of private firms were also attacked.[324] None of the major European colonial powers, however, wished to put obstacles in the King's way, although at Berlin they had raised the same objections to import duties as the Dutch had brought forward. In fact they were committed to supporting King Leopold. They also had territories in the conventional basin of the Congo and stood to gain from the measure,[325] although Salisbury does not seem to have realised that the proposal covered the whole free trade area.[326] He seems simply to have been willing to fall in with the King's wishes.[327] The French had vain hopes that they could get Leopold II to give up ivory trading in return for concessions on import duties.[328]

In any case, none of the powers wished to see the conference fail because of a minor issue and the King not only stood firm, he virtually held a pistol at their heads. He announced that unless he got his way he would not sign the Brussels Act—to do so would be dishonest, as he had not the resources to implement it. Furthermore, he insisted that the Act and the Declaration went together, no power could sign one without the other, except for the United States, who had to do so. The King's advisers were appalled to find that he was willing to risk the whole slave trade treaty, won after so many months of gruelling labour, for a pecuniary question, but they failed to shake his resolve.[329] Realising that he might never again be presented with such a golden opportunity of increasing the revenues of the Congo and, perhaps, even more important, of adding to his powers of control, he had no intention of yielding.

321 Daumas and Co., to FMAE, 31 June 1890, FMAE/MDA/118
322 Incorporated Chamber of Commerce, Liverpool to Salisbury, 16 May 1890, 26 June 1890, FOCP 6197. See also note 3, p. 292 below.
323 Questions were asked on 15 May 1890 and 20 May 1890, Hansard, CCCXLIV, cols. 947, 1403.
324 See, for instance, Spuller to Bourée, :28 Sept. 1889 and Bourée to Spuller, no. 16, 2 Oct. 1889, and enc., FMAE/CP/Belg. 82; Daumas & Co., to FMAE, FMAE/MDA/118; Vivian to Salisbury, conf., no. 23 Af., 3 May 1890, FO 84/2024; Banning, p. 157.
325 Britain, Germany, France, Portugal, Italy and Zanzibar had territories in the conventional basin. Zanzibar could charge what duties she liked, but in fact her commercial treaties limited import duties to 5%. It could be argued that the King's proposals would enable her to revise these treaties.
326 Vivian to Salisbury, private, 29 June 1890, SP/A.49.
327 He had agreed to it in principle when the King first raised the question in September 1889, see Vivian to Salisbury, no. 88, Af., conf., 20 Sept. 1889 and Salisbury to Vivian, no. 53, Af., 30 Sept. 1889, FOCP 5983. Kirk approved the proposal because it would enable the British East Africa Company to raise revenue and because he wanted to 'help the poor King'; Kirk to Wylde, 25 May 1890, FO 84/2103; Kirk to Mackinnon, 23 June 1890, MP/99/39.
328 Ribot to Étienne, 26 June 1890, FMO/A VI, 80a; Banning, pp. 157 ff
329 Banning, pp. 141 ff

The Dutch were equally adamant. They asked for a delay and an inquiry into the Congo's financial needs.[330] This was naturally rejected by the King, who was unwilling even to give the conference a clear statement of the State's revenues.[331] The Dutch objected strongly to King Leopold's misuse of a humanitarian conference to further his own ends and deeply resented his refusal to let them sign the slave trade treaty alone. In fact they demanded to do so,[332] but the King would not hear of it.[333] The conference thus had to choose between letting the whole slave trade effort come to naught or signing the treaty without one of the signatories of the Berlin Act, a course that would nullify the liquor and arms clauses which could only be modified with the consent of all signatories of the Berlin agreement.

The conference was held together with difficulty while these negotiations dragged on. Their real work finished, members became increasingly irritated at the Dutch attitude. It was hard to believe that Holland would hold out against the concerted efforts of the Great Powers, in defence of a company which was prosperous enough to pay the tax[334] and was not considered particularly important. The Dutch stand was attributed to the shaky position of the government which needed the support of the Liberal Party and feared parliamentary attacks if it did not seem to be defending Dutch trading interests. It was expected that Holland would eventually give way but not before the end of the parliamentary session.[335]

For a brief moment at the end of June, all seemed solved. The Dutch plenipotentiary, anxious for a settlement, announced that he could sign both Act and Declaration having made a counter-declaration of his own reserving full liberty in subsequent negotiations.[336] The conference congratulated him and jubilantly called a special session for the signature of the treaty and the King invited all members to a banquet to celebrate the successful conclusion of the great humanitarian work. But to the consternation, and

330 Plens. to Salisbury, no. 171 STC, 14 June 1890, FO 84/2104

331 He told Lambermont when he read a draft article to be inserted in the press that it was better not to give an exact figure but to say that his revenues were 'a few hundred thousand francs' a year. See Leopold II to Lambermont, no. 110, 2 June 1890, LP 1889–90. The conference was given the same information, Plens. to Salisbury, no. 179, STC, 20 June 1890, FO 84/2106.

332 Plens. to Salisbury, no. 45 STC., tel., 28 June 1890, FO 84/2106

333 Banning, p. 158

334 The company declared a dividend of 13% in 1889.

335 The position of the Dutch Government was reported by both French and Belgians, see Anethan to Lambermont, 8 June 1890, no. 102 and 26 June 1890, no. 141, AEB/CAE/8; Legrand to Ribot, no. 40, 29 May 1890, and no. 44, 6 June 1890, FMAE/CP/Hol. 685. Further research in Holland would be necessary to establish the truth of this assertion. However, the Minister of Foreign Affairs, Hartsen, favoured accepting the duties and the Ambassador in Brussels advised doing so as he found himself isolated, but the Minister of Communications, Trade and Industry strongly opposed it, because of the views of the Dutch Company, see Gericke van Herwynen to Hartsen, 18 May 1890 and Minister of Communications, Trade and Industry to Hartsen, 14 May 1890, MBZ 106 H1, 1889–90.

336 Gericke van Herwynen to Hartsen, tel. 27 June 1890, *ibid.*

amidst the sympathy, of his colleagues, the wretched Dutchman had to withdraw his statement. He had exceeded his instructions. Holland would not sign. The banquet was cancelled and all was once more thrown into the melting pot.[337]

At this stage Salisbury compounded the situation. To the great mortification of his plenipotentiaries he announced that Britain could not agree to a modification of the Berlin Act over the head of one of its signatories. If Holland would not sign, neither would Britain. Furthermore, he wanted assurances from the Congo powers that the money from duties would be used only to combat the slave trade. Salisbury's qualms were reasonable enough in view of the objection to the duties raised by English traders and the obviously bad precedent which would be set if an international treaty were altered without the agreement of all parties. But Holland was now less likely to give way. Kirk rushed back to England to explain the position and Vivian pleaded with Salisbury to accept a French compromise by which all the powers but Holland and the United States would sign both the slave trade treaty and the Congo Declaration.[338] The Americans would sign the former only and a separate tariff agreement with the Congo State. The protocols of both Act and Declaration would remain open for six months for the Dutch to sign.

It would certainly have been an anti-climax if England had failed to sign the slave trade treaty and Salisbury decided to accept this solution. He safeguarded his position, however, by placing it on record that Britain only agreed to the import duties as an anti-slavery measure—only for so noble a cause would she accept restrictions on free trade. Furthermore he made it plain that the treaty would not come into force until all the signatories of the Berlin Act had signed it.[339] To the immense relief of the participants this brought the work of the conference to a conclusion.

All but the Dutch, and the Turks who were merely late receiving their instructions, signed the Brussels Act on 2 July 1890. They also signed, with the additional exception of the United States, a declaration providing that import duties of up to 10 per cent *ad valorem* might be imposed by the powers with possessions in the conventional basin of the Congo, the preamble making it clear that the duties were necessary to raise the money to fight the slave traffic. The powers who had ratified the Berlin Act were to negotiate an agreement on the system of customs to be established. There were to be no differential duties, and customs formalities were to be kept as simple as possible. This agreement was to run for fifteen years, the remainder of the time for which import duties had been forbidden under the

337 Hartsen to Gericke van Herwynen, tel., 28 June 1890, *ibid.*; Vivian to Salisbury, private, 29 June 1890, SP/A.49; Plens. to Salisbury, no. 200 STC, 29 June 1890, FO 84/2104; Banning, p. 161
338 Plens. to Salisbury, no. 200 STC, 29 June 1890, FO 84/2104; Vivian to Salisbury, private, 29 June 1890, SP/A.49
339 Salisbury to Vivian, no. 56 Af. tel., 1 July 1890, FO 84/2106

Berlin Act. At the end of fifteen years, unless a new treaty had been negotiated, the Berlin Act was to remain in force, but duties of up to 10 per cent could still be imposed.[340] The United States signed a separate agreement with the Congo State relinquishing her free trade privileges, on the understanding that she was to enjoy the same rights throughout the conventional basin of the Congo as the powers who had ratified the Berlin Act.[341]

The great work was at last completed. The King held his celebration banquet on 3 July and received telegrams of congratulations from both Queen Victoria and Lord Salisbury. He could be well pleased with his work. He had won his battle for import duties and safeguarded his recruiting operations. He had enhanced, at least in the eyes of a gullible public, his image as a philanthropist, and, on the strength of it, he had managed to negotiate a loan for his Congo enterprise from Belgium. Moreover the great majority of the members of the conference had expressed their sympathy and support for his African venture. The establishment of an administration and the crushing of the Arabs now had the general blessing of the powers.

Germany, too, could congratulate herself on having achieved an agreement on the arms trade and on managing to keep the liquor taxes to a minimum. The French were happy with the maritime solution and pleased that import duties could now be raised in the conventional basin of the Congo. The Turks, far from being overawed by the combined weight of Christian opinion, had made few concessions and had found powerful friends. The Portuguese had gained little but neither had they lost anything. The Italians had posed as the protectors of Menelik at the conference and although this had not been accepted there were no difficulties when they announced his adhesion later.

Britain, of course, could be happiest of all. She had at last managed to bind all the great powers, and some of the minor ones, in that comprehensive act against the slave trade which she had so long sought in vain. Furthermore she had concluded an agreement against the liquor traffic which, if it fell short of ideal, at least was a basis for further negotiations. Her reputation as the leader of humanitarian causes could only be enhanced by the Brussels Act and at the same time her own particular interests had been defended. Certain sacrifices, it is true, were being required of her traders and manufacturers by the agreement to impose import duties in the Congo and by the restrictions on the arms trade, but, on the whole, the extension of orderly government in Africa could only be to her advantage since it could be expected to bring in its wake a growing demand for British manufactures. Taken as a whole, the treaty was most satisfactory. As Kirk said, 'We have got a very good act.'[342]

340 For this declaration see Hertslet, *Map*, II, pp. 517–18
341 Her previous treaty was with the Congo State only so that this extended her rights to a much greater area, while abrogating the provision allowing free imports, Gosselin to Salisbury, no. 209 STC, 6 July 1890, FO 84/2104.
342 Kirk to Wylde, 25 May 1890, FO 84/2103

Epilogue

The Brussels Act
and its Aftermath 1892–1919

The suppression of the slave trade and slavery

It was nearly two years before the Brussels Act came into force. The Dutch played out their drama to the bitter end, signing the treaty only at the last possible moment. Observers thought this was because the government found their stand popular[1] and wanted it clear that they had done all they could to defend Dutch interests in the face of the combined opposition of the other powers.[2] Although only the Netherlands resisted King Leopold's import duties, merchants of other nationalities objected to them too.[3] The last six months of 1890 were enlivened by a press campaign between the Dutch company and King Leopold, who inspired articles and letters in British, Dutch, French and Belgian papers and even sent a representative to England to try to win over the business community.[4] After all the fuss it is something of a surprise to find that the resolution for the ratification of the Act eventually passed the Dutch Parliament by an overwhelming majority.[5]

1 Legrand to Ribot, no. 40, 29 May 1890, no. 44, 6 June 1890, no. 55, 5 July 1890, no. 58, 19 July 1890, no. 65, 5 Sept. 1890, FMAE/CP/Hol. 685, and no. 83, 14 Nov. 1890, FMAE/CP/Hol./686; Rumbold to Salisbury, no. 64 Af. v.conf., 8 Dec. 1890, FOCP 6122; Anethan to Lambermont, private, 15 July 1890, No. 4, AEB/CAE/12; Anethan to Chimay, 4 Aug. 1890, no. 18, *ibid.*

2 It was believed too that they waited until sure that the Opposition would not use the issue to attack them in Parliament. The influence of the Queen Regent was also mentioned as a possible factor in their capitulation, Rumbold to Salisbury, no. 64 Af. v.conf., 8 Dec. 1890, FOCP 6122; Legrand to Ribot, no. 101 tel., 17 Dec. 1890, FMAE/CP/Hol./686; Greindl to Chimay, 10 Dec. 1890, no. 47 AEB/CAE/15; Anethan to Chimay, 11 Dec. 1890, no. 63, *ibid.*; Willequet, p. 104.

3 See, for instance, Liverpool Chamber of Commerce to Salisbury, 26 June 1890, FOCP 6197; Birmingham Chamber of Commerce to Salisbury, 22 July 1890, FOCP 6122; FO to Leeds Chamber of Commerce, 26 Aug. 1890, *ibid.*; *Report of Proceedings of the Conference of African Merchants on the Congo Free State Import Duties held in the London Chamber of Commerce Rooms 4 November 1890*, Manchester 1890 (copy in AEB/CAE/16). Even the Society of Friends protested that the duties would hamper legitimate trade and therefore militate against the anti-slavery cause, Solvyns to Chimay, 10 Dec. 1890, AEB/CAE/15. See also above, p. 288.

4 There is much correspondence on this in the Belgian Archives, see particularly AEB/CAE/13.

5 *Nieuwe Rotterdamsche Courant*, report of session of 28 May 1891

Honour had apparently been satisfied although nothing concrete had been gained.

While these negotiations were proceeding, the powers with territories in the conventional basin of the Congo sent technical commissions to Brussels to fix uniform tariffs for their dominions. Britain, Germany and Italy had reached agreement on import duties of 5 per cent for the eastern zone.[6] The negotiations of France and Portugal with Leopold II, however, were bedevilled by the King's determination to monopolise the ivory and rubber exports of his state. No sooner had the Brussels Conference ended than he imposed heavy duties on elephant tusks and prohibited private traders from entering large tracts of the Congo on the pretext that he could not protect them.[7] French merchants promptly complained, and their government used the negotiations to try to force the King to modify his policy.[8] However, in February 1891 it was finally agreed that maximum import duties in the western zone of the conventional basin of the Congo were to be 6 per cent except on salt, arms and ammunition, which were to pay 10 per cent, and spirits, the rate for which was laid down in the Brussels Act.[9]

An unforeseen and serious difficulty was the refusal of the French Chambre de Députés to accept certain provisions relating to the maritime zone, the detention of suspects and the verification of the flag[10] on the grounds that the right to search was being restored, that French shipping would be harassed and the honour of the nation had been sacrificed. The British would not allow these clauses to be dropped[11] and, as no one wanted the treaty abandoned, France was simply allowed to ratify the rest of the pact while the other powers ratified it all. The solution was unusual in diplomatic history and left France in a privileged position, but little was lost in practice as her government agreed to abide by the regulations of 1867 and to put into operation the new rules for the issue of French colours.[12]

6 See correspondence in FOCP 6122 and agreement in Hertslet, *Map* II, p. 518. This matched the duties which Zanzibar might impose on the coastal strip.

7 Lytton to Salisbury, no. 166 Af., conf., 26 Nov. 1890, FOCP 6122; Vivian to Salisbury, no. 76 Af., 18 Dec. 1890, *ibid.*

8 Vivian to Salisbury, no. 273 STC conf., 14 Nov. 1890, no. 275 STC, 15 Nov. 1890, *ibid.*, British delegates to Salisbury, no. 8, 19 Nov. 1890, *ibid.*; Lytton to Salisbury, no. 166 Af., conf., 26 Nov. 1890, *ibid.*, and other correspondence in the same confidential print.

9 They also agreed to impose export duties of 10% on rubber and ivory except for exports from the reserved areas of the Congo which were to pay more. The agreement is in *BFSP* 84, p. 447.

10 The articles to which they objected were articles XXI–XXIII and XLII–LXI, Hertslet, *Map*, II, pp. 409, 504–8.

11 Salisbury thought the British public would object to their government's accepting such a proposal and he wanted the onus of dropping them to rest on France. He wrote: 'It is, I think, important in every sense, and for every purpose, that we should to the utmost extent possible fix on France in the public eye the whole responsibility for the obstruction which she is offering to the suppression of the slave trade.' Salisbury to Vivian, private, 4 Dec. 1890, SP/A.49.

12 Hertslet, *Map*, II, p. 525

These and other difficulties[13] finally overcome, the Brussels Act came into operation on 2 April 1892. It remained in force until 1919. Its subsequent history is beyond the scope of this work but a brief outline will be given here to round off the story.

After 1890 the colonial powers extended their rule over all of Africa, except Liberia and Ethiopia, gradually establishing effective control and delimiting their frontiers in a series of agreements between themselves. Many of the more important slavers actively resisted them and were defeated in war. Thus the Congo State crushed the Arabs in the Manyema,[14] the British overcame Mlozi in Nyasaland and the Emirs in Nigeria, while the French conquered Dahomey and defeated Samory Touré in Guinée and Rabeh in Chad. In addition small campaigns were fought against less powerful opponents. This was all part of the process of conquest and cannot be attributed to the Brussels Act. Nevertheless this treaty and the conference which produced it had their importance. They had focused attention on the slavery issue and helped to rally support to the imperialist cause. These wars waged in their homelands against people who were victims of European aggression, were largely justified on the grounds that it was the white man's mission to bring civilisation to darkest Africa and not least among its blessings was the suppression of slaving. As Joseph Chamberlain, who was British Colonial Secretary from 1895 to 1903, remarked in connection with Nigeria:

> sooner or later we shall have to fight some of the slave dealing tribes and we cannot have a better *casus belli* ... public opinion here requires that we shall justify imperial control of these savage countries by some serious effort to put down slave dealing.[15]

That the British public, or a vocal and important section of it, took the commitments of the Brussels Act seriously was amply demonstrated when the Imperial British East Africa Company announced in 1892 that it must withdraw from Uganda for financial reasons. The Liberal government of the day was prepared to let the territory go but the issue was carried to the electorate in a widespread press and propaganda campaign which resulted in a spate of petitions urging its retention largely on the grounds that the slave trade and slavery should be abolished. Other reasons such as economic advantages and the need to save the Christian missions were also cited but the biggest single consideration was the suppression of the slave traffic.[16] The popularity of this issue was a mixed blessing for British policy makers. It could be, and was, used to support their actions. The war against the Aro

13 See correspondence in FOCP 6262 for the various difficulties raised by other powers before they ratified the Act.
14 Tippu Tip, however, with his usual perspicacity, withdrew to Zanzibar before the fray.
15 Minute, 5 April 1900 on Moor to Chamberlain, no. 1 conf., 28 Jan. 1900, CO 520/1
16 D. A. Low, *Buganda in Modern History*, Berkeley and Los Angeles 1971, pp. 76 ff

in Nigeria, for instance, was fought for political and economic reasons, but the fact that they were notorious slavers was considered useful justification.[17] On the other hand it might force administrators to take steps which they did not consider to be in the best interests of Britain. Self-interest dictated, for instance, that they end slave raiding with its attendant disorders and depopulation as well as the export slave trade which carried workers away from their African territories. However, the advantages of suppressing local slave dealing, the import of slaves or slavery itself, were not always as clear and these issues were often tackled more hesitantly, and sometimes only in response to humanitarian pressure.

Large-scale slave raiding generally died out in areas under European control around the turn of the twentieth century. It was still rife in Northern Nigeria, for instance, and thousands of victims were still paid annually in tribute when Britain took over the government from the Royal Niger Company in 1900,[18] but as effective administrations were established it disappeared. Equally the export traffic declined to small proportions as the coasts, the sources of supply, as well as Zanzibar, Pemba, Madagascar, the Comoros and the North African markets came under European rule. A smuggling trade continued, however, into the second half of this century. Initially some of the loopholes in the Brussels Act were exploited. Thus for some fifteen years after it was signed the French, anxious to retain influence in Muscat, issued their colours to Omani dhows and failed to stop slaving under their flag.[19] Victims were smuggled into Oman on French dhows from as far away as Mozambique. This eventually ended when the question was submitted to the Hague International Tribunal in 1905 and the court decision curtailed the French right to grant colours.[20]

The export trade to the Middle East, however, continued while the markets lasted.[21] The last country to abolish slavery was Saudi-Arabia in 1962,[22] and in 1958 it was said that in this oil-rich land a male slave sold for £150 and an attractive girl for as much as £700.[23] For many years victims were smuggled across the Red Sea or Indian Ocean in dhows. Ethiopia was for long a fertile source of supply.[24] Slaves were also smuggled in disguised as pilgrims or as their wives, children or servants. They came from as far

17 Minute by Moor to the Under-Secretary of State for the Colonies 5 June 1900, CO 520/6; minute of 3 Aug. 1901 on Probyn to Chamberlain, no. 200, 6 July 1901, CO 520/8. For the part of the Aro in the slave trade see above, pp. 131–2.
18 Lugard to Chamberlain, 2 Nov. 1899, minutes and memo. by Lugard, CO 446/8 30397; Lugard to Chamberlain, no. 166, 21 July 1900, CO 446/10 26964.
19 B. C. Busch, *Britain and the Persian Gulf 1894–1914*, Berkeley and Los Angeles 1967, pp. 154–86
20 *Ibid.*, pp. 183–4   21 It is sometimes said to continue today.
22 Mohamad Awad, *Report on Slavery*, New York 1966, p. 123. This report was produced for the United Nations.
23 Greenidge, p. 52
24 This was a smuggling traffic so information is hard to come by. The last dhow was captured in the Red Sea in 1923 but the traffic is thought by Pankhurst to have been active in the 1930s, see *Economic History*, p. 123.

away as Mauretania or Nigeria and had been tricked,[25] kidnapped or perhaps sold by poverty-stricken parents either to save the rest of the family or in hopes of giving them a future brighter than their own. Some were also sold by pilgrims in financial straits along the route or in the Holy cities.[26]

The European contract labour traffic, which had not been tackled at all in Brussels, also continued to cover slaving operations. In 1906 for instance workers were still bought in Bihé, transported sometimes in shackles to the coast of Angola, furnished with a five-year contract and shipped against their will to serve out their lives on the plantations of São Tomé and Principé. Conditions were said to have improved by 1915 but this traffic was still sporadically denounced in the 1920s.[27] Moreover a League of Nations commission reported as late as 1931 that the methods used to recruit labourers in Liberia for Spanish Fernando Po and French Gabon differed little from slaving.[28]

On the African continent the slave trade also flourished far into the present century. In regions beyond European control it was openly conducted. At Kufra, in the Libyan desert, for instance, slaves were said to be freely sold in 1929.[29] Ethiopia continued to import and export slaves and raiding went on within her borders and along her frontiers up to the time of the Italian conquest in 1936 although by this time the measures taken by Empereror Haile Selassie, and the greater control of outlying areas aided by the use of aeroplanes, had driven the traffic underground and reduced it in scale.[30] Even in some European territories the traffic still existed on the eve of the Second World War. Sometimes this was in remote districts. Thus in the Mandara mountains on the borders of Nigeria and Cameroon, slavers dodged back and forth over the Anglo-French frontier, keeping on the move and taking advantage of the floods which cut off the country for much of the year and of good cover in the uninhabited lands around Lake Chad.[31]

25 In Yola in the 1920s for instance, the British reported men were applying for passports to go on pilgrimages with as many as eight children. If they were strangers and slave dealing was suspected these applications were rejected, see Secretary, Northern Provinces, to Chief Secretary, Lagos, 10 March 1926, NAN/50127/vol. 1. In Burundi in 1961, informants suggested that dealers might arrive in an area with a wife, settle down and marry three more local girls and then take them on a pilgrimage from which they never returned.
26 Greenidge, pp. 52–4
27 H. W. Nevinson, *A Modern Slavery*, London 1906; Duffy, *Slavery*, pp. 226–9
28 Greenidge, London 1958, p. 188
29 K. Holmboe, *Desert Encounter*, London 1936 (trans.), pp. 187–8. The oasis was later occupied by the Italians.
30 For the Ethiopian slave traffic and the measures taken against it first by Menelik II and then by the present emperor see Pankhurst, *Economic History*, pp. 99 ff. See also McLoughlin, pp. 371–2 for Ethiopian raids into the Sudan and Kenya in the 1920s and 1930s.
31 For this traffic see Secretary, Northern Provinces, to Chief Secretary, Lagos, 18 March 1933, NAN/50127 vol. I, and 26 March 1934, 23 Feb. 1935, 5 March 1936, NAN/50127 vol. II; Commissioner Northern Provinces to Chief Secretary, Lagos, 10 April 1937, 21 March 1938, and 29 March 1939, *ibid*.

Sometimes, however, the traffic was conducted under the eyes of British officials. Berta from western Ethiopia, for instance, were brought into the Anglo-Egyptian Sudan in the 1920s and sold to cattle-keeping nomads across the White Nile for use as concubines and servants. The victims were mainly little girls who believed the British would ill-treat or even eat them.[32] Such a traffic in young children discreetly conducted was hard to detect. Likewise girls from Adamawa were secreted into Kano. A slaver would buy two or three and stay a year or more in the Cameroons, teaching them Hausa and treating them well so that betrayal was unlikely, before he smuggled them into Kano, taking care to keep their origins secret.[33] In this case British officials actually thought the children were better off than they would have been in their homelands but since they were procured as slaves efforts were made to stop the traffic.[34] Similar cases could be cited for other areas and sometimes children were bought for adoption. They might, of course, truly become full members of their new kin group but the practice was open to abuse and liable to encourage dealers to procure slaves.[35]

Small-scale slaving of this sort could only be put down with African co-operation. This often took years to win and misunderstandings were common. Thus the French found that Senegalese chiefs who arrested slave caravans in the 1890s fully expected to keep the slaves they had liberated.[36] Lugard reported from Northern Nigeria that when he freed some fifty children and put them in the care of 'respectable families' the Africans thought that he had merely confiscated their property to give it to his own

32 I am indebted to the Rev. Dr. A. J. Arkell for allowing me to use papers in his possession on this subject and for discussing it with me. He was responsible for the arrest in the late 1920s of dealers involved in this traffic.

For a long time detection was thwarted because the victims were unwilling to admit that they were Berta since this carried with it connotations of slavery. Even when their origins were known the traffic was hard to trace. One of the principals concerned lived in Ethiopia and kept a wife in the Sudan who received the children and then forwarded them on as the opportunity presented itself. See also McLoughlin, pp. 360 ff. for this traffic and other instances of slaving in the Sudan in the 1920s and 1930s.

33 Harris to Resident, Kano, 24 Jan. 1922, NAN/50127, vol. I

34 *Ibid.*; Secretary, Northern Provinces, to Chief Secretary, Lagos, 23 March 1922 and minute by Clifford, 6 April 1922, NAN/50127, vol. I.

35 The British regarded such adoption as slaving, while recognising that it might cause little hardship, see Resident, Bauchi, to Secretary, Northern Provinces, 22 Dec. 1921, NAN/50127, vol. I. A Serer informant in Senegal in 1964, Monsieur Jean Senghor of Djiloré, remembered his father buying children to rescue them from a dealer and subsequently bringing them up as members of his family to the point that they were unaware of their origins for many years.

36 Administrator, Sine-Saloum, to Directeur des Affaires Politiques no. 262, 27 Sept. 1893, no. 313, 21 Dec. 1893, no. 348, 6 Feb. 1894, AOF/K/13. The French feared they might seize legitimate travellers and pass them off as slaves they had freed, Directeur des Affaires Politiques to Administrator, Sine-Saloum, no. 1203, conf., 2 Aug. 1893, and conf., 21 Sept. 1893, *ibid.*

employees.[37] Sometimes such misapprehensions arose out of the actions of the colonial officials themselves. Thus, French efforts against the slave trade in the western Sudan could hardly be taken seriously in the period of conquest when they distributed prisoners to their own soldiers and allies and settled freed slaves in what were euphemistically called *villages de liberté* where they seemed to be little more than slaves of the white administrators.[38] Moreover, colonial authorities were often slow to act against the traffic. Thus in 1899 the Governor of the French Sudan warned his subordinates not to interfere with local slave dealing but to limit their efforts to preventing the export of captives,[39] and as late as 1908 only cases of slaving which involved kidnapping were prosecuted in Guinée.[40] In British Sierra Leone until 1926 the laws against slave dealing did not preclude owners who bought slaves in neighbouring Liberia from keeping them unless the authorities could prove that they were for sale.[41] Sometimes it was hard to define the parameters of slaving. Thus in the Mandara mountains girls were given in marriage to neighbouring peoples in times of famine for very low dowries. Such brides were despised and often changed hands frequently for low bridewealth but the people concerned did not consider this slave dealing. In fact it seems to have been nearer to pawning for they often tried to redeem their daughters when times improved. But the British regarded it as approximating to slaving and tried to stop it.[42] Similar problems arose in East Africa when the Giriama sold their daughters to Muslims on the Swahili coast and claimed, when the British prosecuted them, that they were merely betrothing them early in accordance with their customs.[43] Gradually, however, African co-operation might be won where good faith was established or perhaps rewards offered.[44]

37 Lugard to Chamberlain, no. 143, 16 June 1900, CO 446/10
38 G. Deherme, Rapport de mission sur l'esclavage en Afrique Occidentale Française, 1906, pp. 112, 174, AOF/K/25
39 Lt. Gov. Trentinian to the *commandants de cercle* of the Soudan, circular 87, 27 Jan. 1899, AOF/15/G/162
40 Report on slavery in Guinée by Inspector Saurin, 20 Feb. 1908, AOF/K/29. The Governor of Guinée in 1902–3 ordered his administrators to tell Africans that they might buy slaves in neighbouring colonies and import them if they wished. This was countermanded by his superior but it did the cause no good. Governor, Guinée to *commandants de cercle*, Boke, Benty, Boffa and Friguiagbe, tel., 6 Dec. 1902, no. 736, AOF/K/28; Governor, Guinée, to Administrator, Koussi, no. 374, 13 March 1903, *ibid*.
41 For slaving in Sierra Leone see Slater to Thomas, 20 June 1924, and encs. *Sierra Leone Sessional Paper no. 5*, 1926.
42 Secretary, Northern Provinces, to Chief Secretary, Lagos, 23 Feb. 1935, *ibid*.
43 R. F. Morton, 'The Shungwaya Myth of Miji Kenda Origins: A Problem of Late Nineteenth-Century Kenya Coastal History', *The International Journal of African Historical Studies*, v, 3, 1972, pp. 397–423, pp. 412–13.
44 Thus the Resident at Yola complained in 1922 that chiefs were sympathetic to slavers but reports for subsequent years showed a steady increase in cooperation, see Resident, Yola, to Secretary, Northern Provinces, 14 June 1922, NAN/50127, vol. I;

In the last resort, however, the traffic could not be stamped out as long as there was a market for slaves and this market was only gradually whittled down by a combination of legislative action and changing economic conditions. The Brussels Act did not commit signatories to definite action against slavery and in fact measures varied not only with each power but in each colony. In general British administrators believed that African slavery was not particularly oppressive and they were careful not to precipitate the wholesale desertion of slaves, fearing that this would dislocate the economy, drive masters to emigrate, cause a breakdown in law and order, and end either in slaves being left landless and without means of support or in their mass exodus back to their homelands. They thought the institution would die a natural death as a wage economy developed and that the wisest course was not to speed its demise but to end the worst abuses by stopping the slave trade and protecting slaves who left their masters. The measures actually taken depended on local circumstances, on the policy of the local administration and on the degree of humanitarian interest aroused in Great Britain.

Thus in Zanzibar and Pemba, the government, fearing the clove industry would be ruined if deprived of slave labour, only reluctantly abolished the legal status of slavery under humanitarian pressure in 1897[45] and paid compensation to masters whose slaves claimed their freedom. Concubines were not included in this emancipation for fear of disrupting domestic life.[46] Kirk had advised against compensation in case it lead to a general rush for liberation and to collusion between masters and slaves to defraud the Administration.[47] Since he believed that most slaves had been imported since 1873 and were therefore illegally held, he regarded it as an unnecessary concession. In the event emancipation proceeded slowly. Work was plentiful and the freed were immediately resettled with new employers or remained as paid workers with their former masters,[48] but many preferred to remain in servitude perhaps because they were afraid of losing their homes, land, the master who cared for them in time of need or the com-

Secretary, Northern Provinces to Chief Secretary, Lagos, 17 Dec. 1923 and 23 April 1925, *ibid*. Greater cooperation was reported in the Cameroons Mandate generally in 1927, see Secretary, Northern Provinces, to Chief Secretary, Lagos, 25 Feb. 1927 and 10 Aug. 1927, *ibid*., and in Bornu from 1928, see Secretary, Northern Provinces, to Chief Secretary, Lagos, 27 March 1928, and 14 June 1930, *ibid*., and 26 March 1934, NAN/50127, vol. II.
45 See memorials from the Anti-Slavery Society to Salisbury and other correspondence in ASS/BM/8155 h. 9.
46 There were cases, however, of concubines being freed, Farler to Mathews, 26 Jan. 1900, enc. no. 2 in Hardinge to Salisbury, no. 3, 9 April 1900, *PP* Africa, no. 4 (1901), XLVIII, 1901, p. 173, C-593.
47 Kirk to Lugard, 30 Oct. 1896 and 10 Sept. 1897, Lugard Papers, 41, MSS BE s 70. Kirk no longer had a permanent official position but he was consulted on East African affairs.
48 Farler to Mathews, 26 Jan. 1900, enc. no. 2 in Hardinge to Salisbury, 9 April 1900, *PP* Africa, no. 4 (1901), XLVIII, 1901, p. 173, C-593.

panionship of their fellows.[49] Some, having tasted the joys of freedom, asked to be re-enslaved and were disgusted to find the British unable to help them. Nevertheless the islands suffered a severe labour shortage and the abolition of the legal status of slavery ironically led to the introduction of forced labour. Vagrancy laws were also passed to prevent the freed from wandering around living by petty crime.[50]

The Kenya coast was torn by revolts in the 1890s and the British government, which took over the administration from the Imperial British East Africa Company in 1895, resisted humanitarian pressure to add to its problems by abolishing slavery.[51] Many slaves had left their masters during the rebellions[52] and many more decamped in the years that followed. They found refuge in the Christian missions or earned a living in the British Protectorate behind the Sultan's coastline where slavery was not recognised and there was also work to be had on projects like the Uganda railway.[53] Flight was made easier in the late 1890s when the British decided that police could no longer be used on the coast to find and return fugitives.[54] Slaves also obtained freedom through the normal working of Muslim law and custom[55] and through an important decree issued by the new Sultan, Ali, in 1890 allowing them to bring cases to court and to purchase their freedom for a reasonable sum and stipulating that only the lawful children of their masters could inherit them.[56] Moreover the declaration Britain had forced on the reluctant Sultan Khalifa at the end of the Anglo-German blockade, freeing all children born after 1 January 1890 was finally promulgated in 1898.[57] The British took no active steps to liberate these children,

49 Last to Mathews, 22 Feb. 1900, enc. no. 1 in Hardinge to Salisbury, 9 April 1900, *ibid*. Freed slaves sometimes asked to be returned to servitude after a few months of freedom. Archdeacon Farler reported that upon being asked their reasons 'they reply that they do not like this regular every-day work that they have now to do to maintain themselves. They find life dull and monotonous; they miss the old feudal tie which bound them to some large plantation, where they shared in the weddings and feasts of the family, and if they are sick or in trouble they have no one to go to; in fact the life of a freed slave is too prosaic for them. They seem much surprised, and somewhat disgusted, when they are told that no power exists to return them to slavery again.' Farler to Mathews, 26 Jan. 1900, enc. no. 2 in no. 3 Hardinge to Salisbury, 9 April 1900, *ibid*.
50 Farler to Mathews, 26 Jan. 1900, enc. no. 2 in Hardinge to Salisbury, 9 April 1900, *ibid*.; Middleton, *Land Tenure*, p. 53
51 Salim, p. 108
52 *Ibid*., pp. 101–2
53 Report by Monson on slavery and free labour in the British East Africa Protectorate, 14 April 1903, enc. in Eliot to Lansdowne, 2 May 1903, FO 2/712.
54 Salim, pp. 102–5; Hardinge to Salisbury, no. 19, 4 Feb. 1899, and Salisbury to Hardinge, tel., 11 Feb. 1899, *PP* Africa no. 8 (1899), LXIII 1899, p. 303, C-9502.
55 See above, p. 60
56 Decree of 1 Aug. 1890, Lugard, *East African Empire*, I, pp. 562–3
57 See above, p. 219. This decree had been kept such a secret that Sultan Khalifa's two immediate successors knew nothing about it, Hardinge to Salisbury, no. 1, 13 June 1898, *PP* Africa, no. 8 (1899), LXIII, 1899, C-9502.

however, as they had no means of supporting them.[58] By 1907 as a result of all these changes and of the declining prosperity of the slave owning classes, already feeling the pinch of severe labour shortage, slavery was much attenuated and the time was considered ripe to end it.[59] An ordinance therefore declared that henceforth all slaves were legally free and masters could claim compensation if they wished to do so.[60] As in Zanzibar concubines were not counted as slaves for the purpose of this ordinance.

In Northern Nigeria, Lugard, at the outset of his administration, abolished the legal status of slavery without offering compensation to owners but then illogically declared free all children born after 1 April 1901. The result was that all persons born before this date were still considered slaves and, although slavery was not recognised by British law, cases involving slaves were dealt with in the Native Courts under Muslim law.[61] Slaves could, however, bring cases to court or appeal to British political officers and they now could ransom themselves. Lugard hoped thus to ameliorate their lot without unduly precipitating the demise of slavery.[62] In fact many captives had left their masters during the disturbances of the period of conquest and the majority of those who had remained with them stayed on, perhaps because they were bound by social and economic ties or because they could not find the ransom money and did not care to risk the uncertainties of flight.[63]

In the Niger Coast Protectorate the legal status of slavery was also abolished in 1901 but here everyone was considered free irrespective of his date of birth. However, the Governor of the day was as anxious as the authorities in Zanzibar and Northern Nigeria to keep slaves from leaving their masters and dislocating the existing social and economic structure of society. He, therefore, produced an original solution. Using the trading Houses of the Niger Delta States as his model,[64] he introduced the Native House Rule Proclamation which legalised the obligations owed by House members to House heads and he extended this system to chiefs in areas where Houses were unknown. To ensure a steady supply of recruits to these Houses, he also produced a Master and Servant Proclamation which enabled them to procure children as apprentices.[65] These measures, intended

58 Hardinge to Salisbury, no. 10, 17 Oct. 1898, and enc. no. 1 Hardinge to Craufurd, 17 Oct. 1898, *ibid*.
59 Salim, pp. 109–10
60 In Zanzibar on the other hand masters were compensated if their slaves claimed their freedom and slaves who did not do so were considered to be still in servitude.
61 In non-Muslim areas slavery was not recognised
62 Lugard to Chamberlain, no. 166, 21 July 1900, CO 446/10
63 Minute by Grier, 26 May 1924, on memo. on slavery for NAN/CSO 26/2 1 11799 vol. I
64 See above, pp. 132–3 ff
65 Moor to the Under-Secretary of State for the Colonies, 3 Aug. 1900, CO 520/6. Moor to Chamberlain, 26 Feb. 1902, and minute, 2 April 1902 by H. A. Butler, CO 520/13. See also S. M. Tamuno, 'The Development of British Administrative Control of Southern Nigeria, 1900–12', London Ph.D. 1962, pp. 115 ff.

to be temporary to bridge the gap between a slave and a wage labour system, provoked humanitarian protests a decade later when a boy was punished for leaving his House without the permission of its head. The subsequent enquiry revealed that the British had legalised a system very akin to African slavery and that officials wished to retain it because it enabled them to call on chiefs or heads of Houses to provide forced labour.[66] The House Rule Proclamation was subsequently amended to allow House members to buy their freedom and in 1914 it was repealed.[67]

In the Protectorate of Sierra Leone slave dealing and all transfers and bequests of slaves were outlawed in 1896, slaves were given the right to redeem themselves for a fixed sum of money, and masters could not claim slaves in British courts. In theory, therefore, the government did not recognise the institution or use its power to uphold it. In practice the British recognised it and their policy served to maintain it.[68] The inheritance of slaves continued.[69] Under vagrancy and other laws, slaves were not allowed to leave their masters without permission and cases of fugitives and disputes about ownership were dealt with by British officials in their executive but not their judicial capacity. The degree of oppression to which this gave rise is debatable but slaves certainly suffered under serious disabilities.[70] They could not, for instance, own property without the consent of their masters and those who bought their redemption risked losing their land and possessions. Their children could be married without their consent and slave marriages, not being recognised in African law, could be broken up. Moreover the redemption provisions were abused by persons 'redeeming' girls to use them as concubines or simply buying them under guise of freeing them. Even the slave dealing laws were faulty, as has been seen, for owners who brought slaves into Sierra Leone from Liberia could keep them unless the authorities could prove they were for sale and this was virtually impossible.

By 1924 the wheel had come full circle. The Governor of the day no longer wanted to maintain the rights of masters. He believed that slavery was retarding the economic development of the country since slaves had little incentive to work and owners regarded manual labour as beneath them.

66 Thorburn to Crew, conf. 15 Oct. 1910, with minutes and memoranda, CO 520/95; Egerton to Harcourt, conf. 19 Oct. 1911, and encs. and minute by Harcourt, 31 Dec. 1911, CO 520/107.
67 Tamuno, pp. 339 ff
68 A useful summary of the history of the question is contained in Slater to Thomas, 20 June 1924, and encs., *Sierra Leone Sessional Paper no. 5*, 1926. Unless otherwise indicated this is the source used here. See also J. Grace, *Domestic Slavery in British West Africa*, London, forthcoming.
69 A bequest was held to be different from straight inheritance. Had this not been the case slavery would have died out with the demise of masters living in 1896.
70 See Grace for a discussion of this question.

This, together with mounting criticism, led to the declaration that all slaves were to be free on the death of their existing owners. More drastic steps had to be taken, however, when the Court of Appeal decided that it was still legal for masters to recover fugitives by force.[71] This caused an outcry in Britain and the legal status of slavery was finally effectively ended from 1 January 1928.

From these examples it will be clear that Britain's pragmatic policy gave rise to anomalies ranging from the legalisation of slavery under another name in the Niger Coast Protectorate to its open continuance in Sierra Leone. Abolition of the legal status of slavery, called 'blessed words' in the Colonial Office because they satisfied public opinion[72] could mean much or little depending on administrative policy. It mattered little, for instance, if British courts took no cognizance of slavery as long as slave cases could be tried in Native Courts or settled by executive officers and while fugitives were returned to their owners, or forced to buy their redemption. Britain's cautious handling of the abolition of slavery, however, was neither in contravention of the Brussels Act nor unique to her. The policy of each of the other colonial powers was different but they tended to be equally reluctant to end the institution.[73]

Fugitive slaves, however, were often dealt with in contravention of the Act. They brought the whole slavery question into the open and sometimes forced British officials to throw their principles to the winds. Thus, although the intention behind the abolition of the legal status of slavery was to make it possible for discontented slaves to leave their masters,[74] Lugard, fearful of provoking social and economic discontent if wholesale desertions took place, carefully instructed officials in Northern Nigeria to discourage those who absconded without 'good reason'. The authorities, for instance, were to refuse to help them find jobs or give them land to cultivate. If possible they were to be made to ransom themselves. A fugitive who had been ill treated was always to be freed but if this was liable to provoke popular resentment, an officer might connive surreptitiously at his escape, thus settling the matter without encouraging other desertions or upsetting the masters.[75] These orders illustrate the dilemma of the colonial administration and in some dependencies, such as the Kenya coast until 1899 and Sierra Leone until 1928, fugitives were handed back to or could be seized by their owners. The British, of course, were not the only offenders. In the early days the

71 *Sierra Leone Royal Gazette*, 1927; Grace
72 Minute by Antrobus on Moor to Chamberlain, conf. no. 1, 28 Jan. 1900, CO 520/1.
73 The Germans for instance allowed it to continue unchecked in the Cameroons and the French in West Africa and Gabon did not abolish it until 1905. In Guinée early in the twentieth century they went as far as to punish slaves who refused to work for their masters.
74 Minute by Bailey (?) 14 Sept. 1899 on Lugard to Chamberlain, 12 Sept. 1899, CO 446/8 24433; F. D. Lugard, *Political Memoranda*, 1906
75 Lugard, *Political Memoranda*, 1906

French also sometimes returned runaways unless they had been ill-treated.[76]

This raises the interesting question of how far it was possible to 'free' a slave by administrative action. If an ex-slave stayed in his master's society, he often found the stigma of slavery remained with him. Cases are recorded of men who obtained their liberty from the British or French and then went back and paid ransom so that they might really be free in their master's eyes and their own.[77] In some areas, such as Southern Nigeria and the Cameroons, the British authorities issued freedom certificates, illegally since slavery was not a legal status, as an act of kindness to ex-slaves who would insist on paying a fee which they handed over to their former masters thus apparently regularising the position.[78] Governments could liberate slaves from their obligations to their owners but they could not give them social equality.

However, gradually, African slavery was less and less widely practised. Its demise was hastened by the outlawing of slave raiding and trading which drastically reduced the supply of slaves and their value as capital assets since they could no longer be freely sold. Important too was government protection of the slave and the introduction of a new judicial system which did not recognise either slavery or the transfer of persons in settlement of conflicts. Equally vital were the economic, social and political changes of the colonial period. The development of a wage economy and a modern communications system made it increasingly easy for slaves to leave their masters and in some areas for the latter to find other sources of labour. New forms of capital accumulation and the acceptance of a fully interchangeable currency provided useful alternatives to the use of slaves; while the influence

76 See for instance Administrator, Medine, to Governor of the Soudan, 23 April 1894, AOF/K/14, Commandant de Cercle de Kayes to Governor of the Sudan, 8 July 1894, *ibid.*; Governor of Guinée to Administrator, Faranah, 13 Aug. 1900, no. 338, AOF/K/28; circular from Ponty to administrators and *commandants de cercle* in Senegambia-Niger, no. 535, 11 Oct. 1903, AOF/K/15. In Guinée as late as 1911, the Governor-General of French West Africa had to order the Governor of Guinée to allow freed slaves to go home if they wished, Governor-General, A. O. F., to Governor, Guinée, 11 July 1911, AOF/K/29.

77 There are many recorded cases of this from areas far apart, see for instance report from Podor, 22 Feb. 1904, AOF/K/18; Secretary, Southern Provinces, to Chief Secretary, Lagos, 28 Jan. 1925, NAN/CSO 26/2 1 11799 vol. I; minute by Governor, Southern Provinces, enc. in Secretary, Southern Provinces to Chief Secretary, Lagos, 14 Feb. 1925, *ibid.*, Resident, Cameroons Province, to Secretary, Southern Provinces, 31 Jan. 1925, *ibid.* In Zanzibar slaves as well as masters were said to look down on those who obtained their freedom from the British, Last to Matthews, 22 Feb. 1900, enc. no. 1 in Hardinge to Salisbury, no. 3, 9 April 1900, *PP* Africa, no. 4 (1901), XLVIII, 1901, C-593. In Guinée slaves sometimes found the population so hostile to their gaining their freedom that they asked for another master rather than for liberty, G. Deherme, Rapport de mission sur l'esclavage en Afrique Occidentale Française, 1906, AOF/K/25.

78 Minute by Governor, Southern Provinces, enc. in Secretary, Southern Provinces, to Chief Secretary, Lagos, 14 Feb. 1925, NAN/CSO 26/2 1 11799 vol. I.

of western education and ideas and the appearance of new status symbols, such as motor cars in Ethiopia, also played their part in hastening the demise of the institution.

Nevertheless in some areas it lingered on right through the colonial period and is not completely dead in Africa today. Neither is pawning. In areas of subsistence economy, where life has changed little, slavery is said to be still practised.[79] Elsewhere slave origins are often remembered but perhaps not mentioned for fear of embarrassing a neighbour, who may be quite unaware of his servile ancestry. Slave descent can still be of importance in determining the rights of an individual over a plot of land or his eligibility to titles or office. It may also be a factor in deciding whether a marriage is permissible, as the rules of kin group exogamy may or may not apply to members of slave origin. In some areas slaves still form a distinct social class and do not readily intermarry with the free.

If slave trading as well as slavery outlasted the Brussels Act, the other three main issues of the Brussels conference, the arms and spirits traffics and freedom of trade and navigation in the conventional basin of the Congo, also had a long history.

The arms traffic

Between 1892 and 1919 by far the most important of these questions was the arms trade, which gave rise to charges and counter-charges as the various colonial powers accused each other of failing to carry out the provisions of the Brussels Act. In the first decade of this century, for instance, the French in Chad and the British in the Sudan were worried about the import of arms into Turkish Tripoli.[80] British traders complained that King Leopold's officials gained an edge over them by exchanging arms for ivory on the Uele and for food in the Lado enclave, and consuls reported that quantities of arms were being imported into the Congo.[81] The French

79 Vaughan, for instance, writes that as late as 1959–60 the Marghi did not seem to be aware that slavery had been outlawed.
80 Cambon to Bourgeois, 30 July 1906, MFO/AOF VI Affaires Politiques, carton 2719 dossier 1; Ministry of Foreign Affairs to Ministry of Colonies, 14 Aug. 1906, *ibid.*; memo. from Cambon, 21 Jan. 1907, FOCP 9185; Cromer to Grey, no. 21 sec., 31 Jan. 1907 and encs. Governor, Kordofan, to Cromer, sec., 3 Jan. 1907 and Owen to Rumbold, 3 Dec. 1907, *ibid.* Cotton, arms and camels were reputedly taken to Kufra and there exchanged for slaves and ivory. Many of the arms, which were said to have been shipped from Greece, reached Wadai and the British feared their import into Kordofan. Italy, who had designs on Libya which she was eventually to conquer, was also concerned at this traffic, see minutes of preliminary meeting of French, British and Italians re the arms conference of 1908, 6 April 1908, FOCP 9333; Hardinge to Grey, no. 6 Af., 10 Jan. 1909, *ibid.*
81 Hertslet to Grey, no. 1 Af., 4 Jan. 1906, FOCP 8908; CO to FO, 29 March 1906, and minute FO 367/34; CO to FO 1 March 1907, and enc. petition from Congo traders, FOCP 9185.

were concerned at smuggling into their territories from Spanish Rio Muny[82] and the crews of British Elder Dempster line ships were accused of selling arms in Liberia[83] where German traders were suspected of importing gunpowder.[84]

But the traffic which caused the greatest concern was that to Arabia and the Somali coast. Britain and Italy constantly accused France of failing to control the flow of arms through Jibouti. Jibouti lived by its commerce and a large part of its revenues came from taxes on arms.[85] The French feared that measures against the arms traffic would drive trade away to rival British or Italian ports and alienate both their Danakil subjects and the Ethiopians in the interior. Their colony was small and the population sparse and they seem to have been less concerned than the British and Italians at the possibility of the arms being used against them or for inter-tribal fighting in their territory, which at times reached serious proportions. They simply failed to carry out the provision of the Brussels Act and of a subsequent agreement with Britain and Italy reached in 1906.[86] Jibouti, therefore, served as a distributing centre from which arms reached the Sudan and Uganda as well as Somali and Danakil country.

Given that the French had no desire to stop the trade, it soon became clear that there were serious loopholes in the Brussels Act. For instance arms were quite legally landed at Jibouti and re-exported to Arabia which was not in the arms zone. Many of these weapons were then smuggled back into Africa. Caravans also legitimately left Jibouti carrying rifles, ostensibly for their own defence, but in reality for sale. Lastly, the provision which allowed an interior power to demand free transit of munitions across the territories of coastal signatories enabled Ethiopia to import large quantities tax-free through Jibouti. Not only did French officials, who were sometimes

82 Commissioner-General, French Congo to Minister of Colonies, 10 May 1906, MFO/AOF VI, Affaires Politiques, carton 2719 dossier 3.
83 Wallis to Grey, no. 15 Af. conf., 17 Feb. 1906, FOCP 8908; Hardinge to Grey, conf. 17 April 1908 and minute, 21 April 1908, FO 367/122. The British believed that Elder Dempster crews were indeed guilty in 1908 but they did nothing as they thought it would provide them with a lever to force the French to revise the arms agreement.
84 Wallis to Grey, no. 33 Af. conf., 4 May 1906, FOCP 8908
85 Picquart, pp. 160–2. The actual percentage varied but between 1902 and 1911 the lowest was 26 % in 1903 and the highest 55 % in 1911. In addition to taxes imposed on munitions, Jibouti revenues gained from the taxes on other items brought by caravans attracted to the port because arms were available there. The importance of the traffic to the port is very clear from the French documents, see particularly the minutes, of a French interdepartmental committee which considered the question FMAE/AQG/NS 23; Ministry of Colonies to Ministry of Foreign Affairs, 9 June 1908, FMAE/AQG/NS 26.
86 The agreement of 1906 granted mutual rights to search in territorial waters on the Red Sea and Somali coasts and the signatory powers agreed to make representations to Menelik II about the arms traffic to Ethiopia, Grey to Clerk, no. 1 Af., 13 Dec. 1906, FOCP 8908.

bribed,[87] fail to ensure that requests for transit rights really emanated from the Ethiopian Government, but the Ethiopians connived at an illicit traffic. Originally this was said to be because Menelik II wanted his people armed for defence against expected attack from the colonial powers,[88] but by 1908 he was incapacitated, the country was politically unstable and corruption was rife. Slaves and ivory were freely exchanged for arms and members of the government from the heir to the throne, Lij Iasu, downwards were said to be profiting from the traffic. An estimated fifty per cent of the weapons imported for official use were sold within a few months and replaced by new imports.[89]

Muscat was another important distributing centre. Arms imported into the port were not only believed to be smuggled back into Africa but also went up the Persian Gulf and, to the consternation of the British, reached Afghanistan and the North-west frontier of India.[90] This traffic also flourished under French protection for, by her treaty of 1844 with Sayyid Said, France was guaranteed free trade with Muscat and about half the arms traffic of the Sultanate was in the hands of French merchants, some of whom had their headquarters at Jibouti.[91]

Britain, fearing the repercussions of this trade on her position in India, the Sudan and Somaliland, called a conference in 1908 to revise the Brussels Act. She was supported by Italy, worried about its effects in Eritrea and Italian Somaliland, by the Turks eager to cut off the trade to restless Arabia and by Persia, concerned at the traffic in the Persian Gulf. She was opposed by Belgium, anxious to protect the Liège arms industry and, of course, by France.[92] The French made no bones about their position. They were being asked to give up not only a valuable commerce, but the major source of revenue for their Somali colony, which would consequently have to be supported by the motherland. They were prepared to make this sacrifice and even to allow Britain to take over Muscat, if she wished, but at a price.

87 Picquart, p. 127
88 Report from the Italian *chargé d'affaires*, Addis Ababa, to the Foreign Minister, communicated to the British Government, 5 March 1908, FOCP 9333.
89 Doughty Wylie to Grey, no. 64 sec., 24 Aug. 1911, FOCP 10053; Thesiger to Grey, 12 Feb. 1912, FOCP 10134 and no. 94, 11 Dec. 1912, FOCP 10326; Picquart, pp. 32, 40–1, 123 ff., 166. Soldiers also sold their arms, and cartridges were said to be in use as small change, CO to FO, 9 Jan. 1907, FOCP 9185; Hohler to Grey, no. 1 Af., 22 May 1907, *ibid*.
90 See *inter alia* IO to FO, 11 Feb. 1907 and enc., FOCP 9185; IO to FO, 4 March 1907 and encs., 27 March 1907 and enc., FOCP 9185; Busch., pp. 270 ff.
91 There is a considerable correspondence on this subject in both the British and the French archives. Secondary works include Picquart who focuses on Jibouti and Busch, who deals with Muscat.
92 For the attitude of the powers see memo. by Clarke, 28 Jan. 1908, FOCP 9333. The bulk of the arms sold in Muscat came from Belgium and many of the rest from Britain and, by 1911, from Germany but the traffic was largely in the hands of French traders, IO to FO, 12 Aug. 1910, and enc. Government of India to Morley, tel., 11 Aug. 1910, FOCP 9868; IO to FO, 27 Nov. 1911, FO 367/266.

They demanded the cession of the Gambia which they had long coveted.[93] This was more than Britain was prepared to pay. The arms conference failed[94] but negotiations dragged on[95] until Britain finally settled the question at Muscat by blockading the coast and getting the Sultan to stipulate that all arms were to be kept in a special customs house from which they could only be withdrawn for an approved destination. France accepted these regulations and Britain paid compensation to French merchants.[96] Arms leakages through Jibouti, however, continued and were still disturbing the British on the eve of the First World War.[97]

The spirits traffic

Compared with the arms traffic the spirits trade was far less important as an international issue. Duties on liquor nevertheless continued to provide a high proportion of the revenues of some of the West African colonies and the temperance societies kept up their campaign. The British usually imposed higher duties than their neighbours and the old worries about smuggling or driving away trade to rival colonies persisted. Hoping to get a minimum duty of 3s. a gallon imposed all along the West African coast, Britain called a conference, which met in 1899, to revise the Brussels Act.[98] Results were predictably disappointing. All that could be agreed upon was a rise to 2s. 5½d. or 70 francs a hectolitre, and even this was not obtained for Togo or Dahomey.[99] A further conference in 1906 succeeded in bringing

93 A lengthy French correspondence on this subject is in FMAE/AQG/NS 23 and 24 and subsequent volumes. British documents are in the FO 367 series, with interesting additional material in the papers of Sir Edward (later Viscount) Grey (FO 800/113) and in Cabinet Papers. For the proposals made at the arms conference of 1908 see memo. by the British plenipotentiaries, 22 June 1908, FOCP 9333. For earlier negotiations for an exchange of the Gambia see Hargreaves, *Prelude*, pp. 151 ff.

94 The conference did, however, prohibit the arms traffic in parts of equatorial Africa at Germany's instigation, see protocol signed Brussels 22 July 1908, Treaty Series 29, (1908), *PP* CXXIV, 1908, p. 5, C-4320.

95 Many alternatives were put forward. It was suggested, for instance, that an alternative *quid pro quo* might be the rectification of the frontier of Pondicherry or the cession of the right bank of the Gambia to France or settlement of the Newfoundland and New Hebrides disputes or rectification of the Wadai-Darfur frontier. The French hoped for the Gambia as late as 1912.

96 See Busch, pp. 300–1. All but one were successfully bought out and the matter was more or less concluded in 1914, Grey to Cambon, 24 Dec. 1913, FOCP 10451; Grey to Bertie, no. 52, 4 Feb. 1914, FOCP 10899; memo. by Slade on the political position in the Persian Gulf at the end of the war, 31 Oct. 1916, annexe to the Committee of Imperial Defence sub-committee on territorial changes, 3rd interim report, 28 March 1917, Milner Papers 124, folder 182–300.

97 Thesiger to Grey, no. 3, 1 Jan. 1914, FOCP 10899

98 CO to FO, no. 8, 4 May 1896 and no. 15, p. 58, 15 Dec. 1896, West Africa (1897), *PP* LXII, 1897, p. 795, C-8480; FO to CO, no. 16, 30 Jan. 1897, *ibid*.

99 The documents of the 1899 conference are in FO 2/261 and 262. They are printed in CO 879/58/586 African (West) 1901, and some were published in *PP* CV, 1900, C-103. 60 francs was all that could be obtained for Togo and Dahomey.

the minimum duty up to 100 francs a hectolitre, or 3s. 7d. a gallon, but concessions had to be made to Portugal and Italy. The former insisted on a lower rate in Angola where there were distilleries, which she claimed were changing over to sugar production; while the latter wanted to avoid the expenses of preventing smuggling in Eritrea, where she said the traffic was very small.[100] By 1908, Germany had joined Britain in pressing for higher duties and also wanted the zones of total prohibition, which each power had drawn independently, to be made contiguous in neighbouring colonies.[101] A conference called to implement these proposals in 1912, however, proved abortive. By this time governors in both French and British colonies were sounding warnings that high duties on imported spirits encouraged Africans to make palm wine, and this was damaging the trees which produced palm oil and kernels for export.[102] It should be noted that while the agreed minimum duty was still only 100 francs a hectolitre at the outbreak of war in 1914, some colonies, acting separately, had raised duties well above this level while each power had defined areas of total prohibition in accordance with the Brussels Act.

The abrogation of the Brussels Act

The First World War changed the African colonial scene. When it ended, all Germany's colonies had been conquered. The victorious British, French and Belgians emerged from the conflict determined to be rid of the Berlin and Brussels Acts which gave their former enemies and neutrals, most of whom had little interest in Africa, a say in their affairs.[103] They considered

100 A drawback was allowed for those Angola distilleries which were converting to sugar production and a duty of 70 francs a hectolitre was agreed upon for Eritrea. For the 1906 conference see documents in FO 367/34 and 35; and in FOCP 8908. The agreement was published in Treaty Series no. 46 (1907), *PP* CXXIV, 1908, p. 15, C-3856. Since Britain's aim was to impose higher duties in West Africa, the concessions to Portugal and Italy mattered little to her, see minute by Antrobus, 23 Oct. 1906, FO 367/35 35710.

101 Revision of the 1906 agreement was desired by Germany and Britain at the 1908 arms conference but was objected to by Portugal, France and Spain. British temperance groups actively pressed the question. Negotiations finally led to the conference of 1912. See plenipotentiaries to Grey, no. 15 arms conference, 29 May 1908, FOCP 9333, and no. 18 arms conference, 16 June 1908, enc. in Hardinge to Grey, no. 138 Af., 16 June 1908, *ibid.*; De Salis to Grey, no. 124 Af., 19 Dec. 1908, with encs.; FOCP 9504; Hardinge to Grey, no. 16, 17 Dec. 1909, and no. 181 Af., 29 Dec. 1909, FOCP 9695; Kinderlen Waechter to Goschen, 22 Nov. 1910, enc. in Goschen to Grey, no. 52 Af., 28 Nov. 1910 FOCP 9868; and subsequent correspondence in FOCP 10049.

102 CO to FO, 10 March 1911, FOCP 10049; report of Governor-General of French West Africa, 26 July 1911, MFO Affaires Politiques, carton 2722.

103 The revision of the Berlin and Brussels Acts form the subject of a voluminous correspondence. Discussions began as early as 1916 and continued for the next three years. Particularly useful are the following documents: Board of Trade to FO,

that the commercial clauses infringed on their sovereign powers by limiting their right to control their own tariffs, and the Belgians claimed the provisions regarding freedom of navigation interfered with the proper policing of Congo waterways. Furthermore the treaties had manifestly failed to achieve some of their objects. The Berlin Act had not prevented the establishment of highly monopolistic regimes in Northern Nigeria and the Congo Independent State in the early days of colonial rule, and its neutrality clauses had not kept the war from spreading to tropical Africa. The Brussels Act had not provided a satisfactory solution to either the arms or the spirits traffic, while the slave trade, had been reduced to such small proportions that the colonial powers thought the treaty was no longer necessary.

However, if the agreements had failed in many respects and were now considered obsolete, the humanitarian principles embodied in them, together with the free trade and navigation clauses had become in a sense sacred. The public, particularly in Britain and America, firmly believed in them. They were very much in keeping with the spirit which inspired the League of Nations and the colonial powers hesitated to dispense with them. Such a step would have cost them vital American support and alienated sections of their own electorates as well as interested neutrals. It would also have prejudiced their claims to be entrusted with the administration of the German colonies, which were to be mandates held under the authority of the League of Nations and ruled for the benefit of their inhabitants and of mankind in general.

The colonial powers, therefore, took advantage of the general peace settlements to sweep away the Brussels and Berlin Acts and replace them with three new treaties, which suited their purposes better but still retained the model and many of the principles agreed to in Brussels some thirty years earlier. These conventions were signed by Britain, her Dominions and India, France, Belgium, Portugal, Italy the United States of America and Japan at St. Germain-en-Laye on 10 September 1919.[104]

One of them dealt with the spirits traffic and applied to all African dependencies except those in North and South Africa. Since German and Dutch trade had been completely disrupted by the war and the West African colonies had found their revenues from taxes on trade spirits much

---

12 Feb. 1916, FO 368/1849 f. 27933; note communicated to FO by Cambon, 2 March 1918, FO 371/3470 f. 40216; CO to FO, 14 Sept. 1918, with enc. memo. and minutes by Percy, Hurst and others, FO 371/3470 f. 26138 157491; memo. by Long, 16 Nov. 1918, Cab. 24/70 GT 6333; CO to FO, 3 March 1919, FO 608/218 3459; minute by Strachey, 27 Jan. 1919, FO 371/4322 f. 31762; memo. by Strachey, 3 March 1919, FO 608/219 f. 803/2/1 3574; memo. entitled 'suppression des servitudes internationales du passé', undated, AEB AF 1–2 in folder marked 'annexe à la lettre du Ministère des Colonies du 23 Dec. 1918'.
104 The English versions of these conventions are in CMD. 414, 477, 478, *PP* LIII, 1919.

depleted, the ideal moment had come to deal this commerce a final blow. The Anti-Slavery and Aborigines' Protection Society, [105] temperance societies in England and abroad,[106] certain West African groups[107] and British businessmen[108] all urged its total prohibition. No real evidence that these liquors were more harmful than more expensive brands had ever been produced, nor was it now believed in official and trading circles that Africans were more prone to drunkenness than Europeans.[109] The real objection to these trade spirits was that they were cheap enough to supply the African market, and in this sense they were perhaps injurious, and the bulk of them came from Germany and Holland.[110] The British naturally believed that already slender African purchasing power would be better expended on British manufactured goods,[111] while the French and Portuguese, whose wines were not classed as trade liquor, had no reason to protect this foreign trade. Merchants were quick to point out that it had laid the basis for the German palm oil and kernel industry and for the prosperity of German shipping lines running to West Africa.[112] They urged speedy action, as the Dutch were said to be sending out large consignments to recapture their lost markets and shipments of American rum, which had been widely sold during the war, were also expected.[113]

The liquor convention, therefore, entirely prohibited trade spirits, but

---

105 AS & APS to Balfour, 14 Feb. 1919, and enc. FO 608/219, f. 802/1/1 2336. The Aborigines' Protection Society which had occupied itself with the spirits question and 'native' welfare generally was amalgamated in 1909 with the British and Foreign Anti-Slavery Society to form the Anti-Slavery and Aborigines' Protection Society, henceforth AS & APS.

106 United Committee on Native Races and the Liquor Traffic to Read, 24 April 1919, FO 608/219 f. 799/2/1; Fédération Internationale pour la Protection des Races Indigènes contre l'Alcoolisme, to Secretary, English branch, *ibid*.

107 Clifford to Milner, 7 March 1919, containing the resolution passed by 'influential educated natives' of the Gold Coast, FO 608/219, f. 808/1/1 7600; Boyle to CO, tel. 21 Jan. 1919, transmitting resolution of the Lagos community, enc. in Hardinge to Strachey, 29 March 1919, FO 608/219 f. 799/2/1.

108 Association of West African Merchants to Milner, 22 Feb. 1919, FO 608/219 f. 799/2/1 5833, and 14 April 1919, *ibid*., 9686.

109 For the views of merchants see Association of West African Merchants to Milner, 14 April, 1919, FO 608/219 f. 799/2/1 9686. For those of the Colonial Office see memo. by Long, 18 Dec. 1918 CAB. 24/72/1 & 2. British officials in West Africa also frequently declared that there was little drunkenness and that much of what there was was due to the consumption of palm wine and other African brews.

110 Some cheap British spirits were sold in Africa and were also objected to but the trade was not important.

111 *Liverpool Journal*, 10 Jan. 1919, enc. in United Committee on Native Races and the Liquor Traffic to Read, 24 April 1919, FO 608/219 f. 799/2/1 8564.

112 Association of West African Merchants to Milner, 14 April 1919, *ibid*., 9686

113 Tyrell to Balfour, 1 July 1919, *ibid*., 14232. American rum was not considered as bad as German and Dutch trade spirits but it was cheap enough to supply the African market, see minute by Acting Treasurer, Sierra Leone, enc. in Wilkinson to Milner, 14 Feb. 1919, *ibid*., 5833.

left each territory free to define these liquors for itself.[114] Other spirits were to pay customs duties of at least 800 francs a hectolitre.[115] They were not to be manufactured in the colonies or sold in areas where the traffic was not already established, except in small quantities for 'non natives'. This introduced an invidious distinction between local peoples and foreigners which had already been tried in Northern Nigeria where Africans from 'contaminated' areas in the south were allowed to buy liquor for their own consumption and were said to regard this as a status symbol.[116] However, the colonial governments did not think it was their duty to enforce abstinence on either white men or on those Africans who were used to imported spirits and who mixed with the European community.[117] The new convention further provided that a bureau should be established under the League of Nations to collect and circulate information on the spirits traffic and each signatory was to publish reports on the trade in their territories and the amount of tax levied.

A second treaty dealt with the arms traffic. This trade, which had been a source of such anxiety before the war, now threatened to become a major issue as erstwhile belligerents prepared to sell surplus stocks.[118] However, the British hoped for co-operation from the French who now appeared anxious to prevent arms and ammunition from entering their colonies and from the Americans, eager to keep them out of the 'more turbulent' states of the New World.[119] A far-reaching convention was, therefore, signed forbidding the export of all modern arms and artillery and war materials except to signatories for their own use. The powers thus accepted an obligation not to export these weapons unless they could be sure of their ultimate destination. Furthermore, no arms of any sort were to be sent, except with

114 This of course opened the way to discrimination and the regulations as applied in Sierra Leone in the early 1920s discriminated against Dutch spirits irrespective of quality.

115 Again an exception was made for Italian colonies where the tax was to be 600 francs.

116 Boyle to Milner, 21 Jan. 1919, FO 608/219 f. 799/2/1 5833. It was even suggested that sometimes Africans began to drink for this reason.

117 Strachey minute, 22 March 1919, on AS & APS note on article 19 of the League of Nations Covenant, 18 March 1919, FO 608/219 f. 803/2/2 4876. This question arose in connection with the regulations to be applied in territories which were League Mandates. West African governors in the discussion bearing on the St. Germain convention protested against any discrimination between Africans and Europeans on racial grounds, see Clifford to Milner, 26 Jan. 1919, FO 608/219 f. 799/2/1 5833; Cameron to Milner, 3 Feb. 1919, *ibid.*; Boyle to Milner, 21 Jan. 1919, *ibid.* The AS & APS also opposed it and unlike the governors they favoured prohibition for all, see AS & APS to Balfour, 14 Feb. 1919, and enc., FO 608/219 f. 802/1/1 2336.

118 The British negotiators were worried lest their own Ministry of Munitions was selling arms and they believed the French would follow suit, Hurst to Spicer, 18 Feb. 1919, and enc. tel. Balfour to War Cabinet, 18 Feb. 1919, FO 371/4317 f. 2411 27498; memo (?) 21 Feb. 1919, *ibid.*, 29221; report of inter-dept. meeting on arms traffic convention 24 and 28 Feb. 1919, *ibid.*, 33137.

119 Memo. (?) 21 Feb. 1919, *ibid.*, 29221

permission, to a zone, which included all of Africa (except Algeria, Libya and South Africa), the offshore islands, the Arabian peninsula, Persia, Transcaucasia, Gwadar and the former Ottoman territories in Asia. In addition, within a defined maritime zone, which covered the Red Sea, the Persian Gulf and the Gulfs of Oman and Aden, arms were not to be carried in 'native' vessels of under 500 tons and were to be imported only at specified ports and under government control. No right of search was accorded as the French attitude had not changed[120] but the flag might be verified and suspected gunrunners were to be handed over to their own national authorities for trial. Compensation was to be paid for wrongful arrest and rules were laid down for the issue of colours. The clause which allowed a power in the interior to demand transit rights for munitions across the territories of coastal signatories was retained. However, the arms traffic to Ethiopia had not only furnished a bad precedent, but was still a matter of grave concern. Political instability continued and the British feared both Italian and French designs. They wanted Ethiopia to remain independent and hence recognised that she needed arms for defence, but they wished to be sure that these were for government use alone.[121] The treaty therefore stipulated that transit rights would be withdrawn if they were abused and that guarantees of good faith were to be furnished. A central office under the League of Nations was to receive reports on the arms traffic and it was hoped that all members of the League of Nations would adhere to this convention thus closing loopholes.

The last convention signed at St. Germain-en-Laye revised the commercial clauses of the Berlin and Brussels Acts. France, Belgium and Britain were all anxious, as has been seen, to end international control over their customs in the conventional basin of the Congo.[122] The agreement, therefore, gave them the right to fix their own tariffs and navigation dues. The clauses against differential duties in the conventional basin, however, were retained for the commerce of all members of the League of Nations who adhered to the convention as well as for signatories. By the 1930s this was regretted by both France and Britain, who found their products

120 Note of Ministry of Marine, 17 March 1919, MFO Affaires Politiques, 38. This states that as the French parliament had twice rejected treaties containing the right to search, France could not accept it now.

121 Britain's concern was to keep the course of the Blue Nile, which was vital for the prosperity of both Egypt and the Sudan, from coming under French or Italian control. It is true that her agreement of 1906 with France and Italy had provided that if Ethiopia was divided Britain would have control of the river but she had no desire to see Ethiopia broken up in 1919 nor to see either France or Italy establish a mandate, see minute on Wingate to FO, 5 Jan. 1919, FO 371/4317 f. 2411 2619; minute 21 Jan. 1919, *ibid.*, 1304; minute by Spicer, 7 Feb. 1919, FO 608/218 1781; Thesiger to Sperling, private, 7 March 1919, and minute by Spicer, 10 April 1919, FO 608/218 6789; memo. by Milner, 30 May 1919, Milner Papers, 152 folder 'Mandates B and C'; memo. by Thesiger, 31 May 1919, FO 608/218 11417; memo. by Dodds, 19 Aug. 1919, FO 608/218 21281.

122 See documents cited above, pp. 309–10, note 103.

undersold by cheaper Japanese manufactures. It was further stipulated that there was to be no discrimination in the treatment of nationals of any of the signatories and all religious, cultural, scientific and charitable enterprises were to be protected. Free navigation on the Niger and on the waterways of the Congo basin was also retained.

What of the slave trade? This was dismissed in a single article which read:

> The Signatory Powers exercising sovereign rights or authority in African territories will continue to watch over the preservation of the native population and to supervise the improvement of their moral and material well-being. They will in particular endeavour to secure the complete suppression of slavery in all its forms, and of the slave trade by land and sea.[123]

All the practical measures of the Brussels Act had disappeared, including the information bureaux, which had ceased to function during the war. The minor place of the slave trade in this treaty is an indication of the small priority attached to it by 1919.

The issue was not dead, however, for it was envisaged that all humanitarian causes would be taken up by the League of Nations and in 1926 the League, having collected much information, negotiated a far-reaching convention against slavery, trying to cover all its forms, not only in Africa but elsewhere. A committee of experts was established in 1932 to try to supervise the working of the agreement and reports were regularly asked for from member states. The issue eventually passed to the United Nations after the Second World War.[124]

The spirits and arms questions were also taken up by the League in the 1920s. The arms agreement of St. Germain-en-Laye never came into full operation for neither it, nor a subsequent convention signed by members of the League in 1925, were ratified by all signatories. However, the colonial powers applied restrictions on the import of munitions into their territories. The spirits convention on the other hand had a long history. The old Brussels slave trade bureau was reactivated in 1922 as the Central International Office for the Control of the Liquor Traffic in Africa and lived on, first under the auspices of the League and then after the Second World War, as a United Nations Office. The Belgians resisted attempts to transfer it to Geneva as they wished to retain control of it and later, supported by the other colonial powers, they prevented its removal to New York, fearing that this would leave it open to American pressure. It finally seems to have petered out in the mid-1950s.

123 Article 11, Convention of St. Germain-en-Laye, CMD 477, *PP* LIII, 1919
124 See Greenidge, pp. 190 ff

Conclusion

Looking back over the long history of Britain's campaign against the slave trade, the Brussels Act can be seen as the culmination of her efforts. Here at last was the comprehensive international treaty which had been sought in vain by Castlereagh and Palmerston. It was no accident that it was signed as the European powers were preparing to take over large areas of Africa for it was also an incident in the scramble for the continent. It arose, as has been seen, from Cardinal Lavigerie's attempt to force the colonial powers to take action against the wars and raids which were impeding his missionary enterprise. His appeal fell on fertile ground because the British wished to remain at the head of the anti-slavery movement. Lord Salisbury and Foreign Office officials believed that the public expected them to take the initiative. It is clear that their motives were not entirely humanitarian. They sought credit for their government at home and abroad, they wanted to make sure that whatever forces the Cardinal mustered were channelled into lines that were not inimical to British interests, and they had good reason, given Britain's commitment to the cause, to want to bind other colonial powers to share the onus of attacking the slave trade and to resist the temptation of attracting caravans to their territories by countenancing it; to be sure, in fact, that others did not profit from a traffic they had outlawed. Furthermore, once the Brussels Conference met, the British, in common with other participants, did not hesitate to use it to further their own interests.

Nevertheless it would be over-cynical to condemn British policy as hypocritical. Having embraced the anti-slavery cause early in the nineteenth century, the British public as a whole seem to have regarded it as primarily a humanitarian venture upon which they were prepared to sanction the expenditure of a certain amount of public money and some diplomatic and naval effort. They continued to support it long after the end of the Atlantic traffic and in areas in which Britain had few interests. They do not seem to have expected or received any substantial return, although they clearly hoped that Britain would gain from the growth of the legitimate trade which was confidently expected to replace the slave traffic. Moreover, the leadership of the anti-slavery movement doubtless enhanced their belief in the civilising agency of British rule.

Given this basic attitude on the part of the electorate, the cause was there for interested parties to turn to account. Missionaries and traders sometimes tried to use it to get government and public support for their particular purposes. Ministers, Foreign Office officials and other public servants did the same thing. Since the cause was popular and money for Britain's other African interests strictly limited, they were constantly tempted to use it to extract money from Parliament or to rouse support or allay criticism for a particular policy. Thus the seizure of Lagos, the granting of the East African mail subsidy and the blockade of the Sultan of Zanzibar's mainland coast were all justified before the electorate as anti-slave trade measures although this was not their primary aim. The Brussels Conference furnished a further example of this, an important one since it served the purpose of all the colonial powers. Not only did it give them an opportunity to further specific aims such as limitation of the arms traffic or the raising of import duties in the Congo but it also harnessed popular sympathy behind the occupation of parts of Africa.

The fact that Foreign Office officials and ministers used the cause does not mean that they were any less convinced of the need to suppress the traffic than members of the public. It was simply that a policy which both dealt a blow at the slave traffic and served at the same time some other British interest had a particular appeal for them. Thus Kirk, whose personal dedication to suppression is beyond question, but who also wished to advance the British position in East Africa, more than once congratulated himself on the fact that the Brussels Act went far beyond its ostensible aims. Such an attitude is after all to be expected of men whose job it was to protect British interests abroad. Just as it can be shown that they sometimes used the slavery issue to further other aims, it is also clear that they pursued it quite consistently, although it often complicated British relations with European, Asian and African peoples, placed their traders at a disadvantage and hampered British enterprise in areas where only slave labour was available. It would have been much simpler, for instance, for Britain to recognise Egyptian sovereignty over the Red Sea coast without demanding a convention against the slave trade. She might with advantage to their pockets have allowed her subjects to participate in slaving and to hire slave labour from their masters. Her patrolling of the African coast, while it showed the flag and allowed her to dominate certain waters, was often uneconomic in that there were sometimes no obvious British interests to protect and where there were she could always have acted without engaging in anti-slavery operations. The harbouring of fugitive slaves in her consulates abroad and on her warships at sea exacerbated her relations with local peoples and brought no obvious advantage, and her anti-slavery policy was a clear irritant in her dealings with other European powers.

A fair question, however, is whether Britain did all that she could to suppress the traffic. Here, it must be remembered that while the public embraced the cause, it was never more than a secondary issue for which only limited funds were available. Policy-makers therefore worked under severe constraints. They were limited also by the pacific character of the leadership of the Anti-Slavery Society, which served as a watchdog for public opinion but which did not advocate the use of force, and they had to consider the attitude of the other maritime powers with their deep-seated suspicions of British motives. Lastly there were the inescapable realities of the situation in most of Africa. As late as 1890 Britain had little power beyond the coast and navigable rivers. The British reaction to Lavigerie's crusade furnishes a clear example of the effect of these various limitations. Salisbury, with one eye on Parliament and the other on the international scene, whittled down the more far-reaching plans suggested by his sub-ordinates and decided to limit British efforts to the calling of a conference. This was cautious but infinitely practical. It pleased the British public, gratified European opinion generally, enhanced the imperialist cause and maintained Britain's position as leader of the anti-slavery movement, and it produced the long desired treaty, which was regarded as a primarily humanitarian instrument. His attempt to limit the conference to dealing with the much diminished maritime slave trade, however, although true to British traditions, seems on the face of it to have been wanting in both zeal and realism. However, it reflected his uncertainty as to how far the British electorate was really prepared to embark on African adventures. Essentially Britain still considered herself a naval power and was unwilling to under-take commitments to action on land from which it might be difficult to extricate herself.

In sum it may be said that British efforts to suppress the slave traffic waxed and waned through the nineteenth century. A minimum of naval and diplomatic effort was constantly expended but the sudden bursts of activity which led to such measures as the launching of the Niger expedition, the forcing of the treaty of 1873 on Zanzibar or the calling of the Brussels Conference usually owed their inspiration to the activities of one individual, whose motives might be primarily humanitarian like Buxton's, strategic like Frere's, or religious like Lavigerie's. An individual who appealed to the humanitarian, if parsimonious, instincts of the British people could usually get action. Government reaction was determined by the personal pre-dilictions of ministers, by their parliamentary position and by the inter-national situation. Palmerston, for instance, was more responsive, rasher and more inclined to use the slave trade issue himself than Salisbury but he faced a less complex international scene. If one can generalise at all in discussing a policy pursued over many decades in constantly changing circumstances and led by a whole succession of individuals, it is perhaps fair to suggest that Britain remained faithful to the anti-slavery cause and made certain sacrifices to further it but that she did not sacrifice any im-portant national interest and she sometimes used it for other than humani-tarian purposes. But when all is said and done she did more than any other power.

If the Brussels Act was the culmination of her attempts to commit all the maritime nations as well as the *pays de destination* to take active measures against the traffic, it remains to discuss its value as an anti-slavery measure. The treaty has been called by Europeans the Magna Carta of the African people. It was no such thing. It had defects even as an instrument for the suppression of the slave trade, while African slavery, and the various devices, such as forced or contract labour, by which the white man made Africans work for him were beyond its scope. Nevertheless the Act cannot be written off as a failure. It focused attention on the slave traffic and bound the powers to take action. If they often dragged their feet, they had subscribed to the principle and were sensitive to the charge that they were failing to carry out their obligations, and during the period that the treaty was in force the traffic died down. In fact in 1958 the secretary of the Anti-Slavery Society claimed that it had been the most successful of the agreements against the trade and he deeply regretted its abrogation, believing that with the dismantling of its machinery the trade to Arabia had revived.[1]

Ironically one of the most important results of the Act arose out of the very clauses the British had whittled down—those which enjoined the colonial powers to set up effective government and develop communications in the heart of Africa. No definite commitments had been undertaken, it is true, but these provisions were the basis upon which it was claimed that the British Government should subsidise a railway to Uganda and indeed that it had a moral obligation to keep Uganda. Equally those who wished to see colonial rule a reality and to sweep away such devices for the evasion of responsibility as the 'sphere of influence' or the charter company claimed that the Act morally committed Britain to establish an administration in for instance, Bechuanaland, Nigeria and the Gambia. At a time when there was strong opposition in Britain to the extension of Imperial rule and responsibilities this proved useful. In fact in so far as it furnished moral justifications for wars of conquest against slaving peoples and gave added ammunition to colonial enthusiasts and to administrators anxious to extend their control, the Brussels Act may be called the Magna Carta of the colonial powers.

It also furthered their cause by limiting the arms traffic in Africa. However, it has been seen that it had serious loopholes as far as this commerce was concerned and indeed as an experiment in international cooperation on African problems it proved generally disappointing. The necessity to call a conference which had to reach unanimous decisions hampered the colonial powers in their efforts to limit the arms and spirits traffics. They found it quicker and easier to reach agreements separately with their immediate neighbours and in fact subsequent conferences tended

1 He also claimed that its abrogation without the consent of all signatories (only some of whom were parties to the conventions of St. Germain) was illegal. There appears to have been some doubt in the Foreign Office on the point also, see Greenidge, pp. 178–9, 202.

only to be called when independent negotiations had failed and when none of them achieved the desired result.

In the development of the doctrine of international trusteeship the Brussels Act was a landmark. Where the Berlin Act embodied the principle that 'native welfare' was an international responsibility, the Brussels Act reaffirmed the principle and took the practical step of binding signatories to combat the slave trade and limit the traffic in arms and spirits. It also set up for the first time international machinery of a sort, the 'slave trade bureaux' to facilitate the execution of the treaty. It was thus one step nearer to establishing standards of international morality by which the colonial powers might judge each other and the rest of the world judge them.

The Act was a triumph for the humanitarian pressure groups who had long urged governments to take such action, and who could no longer be ignored in an age when Europeans, with a profound belief in their civilising mission, sought to justify their invasion of Africa on the grounds that they were promoting the moral and material welfare of its inhabitants. Many of the statesmen who assembled in Brussels in 1889 used the anti-slavery movement to further their own ends, but they were forced to pay at least lip service to a high ideal. The Act largely failed both as an instrument for the promotion of 'native welfare' and as an experiment in international co-operation. Nevertheless the ideal had been voiced and the responsibility accepted, and the principles embodied in it were adopted by the League of Nations and eventually passed to the United Nations. They were principles above the sordid and selfish aspirations of individual powers. The Act therefore left a firm imprint on the history of Europe in Africa. Its creators saw it as primarily a humanitarian instrument, but they made sure that it served their purpose. As Kirk so aptly said, it was 'a very good Act'.

Unpublished Documentary Sources

Official Archives

Great Britain
Foreign Office Public Record Office, London:

FO 84 Slave Trade, 1816–92, correspondence of the Foreign Office with its agents abroad, other government departments, private organisations and individuals. This series has been the major source for this work. Highly selective use has been made of the volumes before 1880 to gather information on particular topics not available in printed works. More extensive use has been made of the series for the 1880s and particularly for the years 1888–90 and the case files of the Berlin Conference. Exhaustive use has been made of the case files for the Brussels Conference.

Foreign Office Confidential Prints, Slave Trade, 1858–92 (PRO FO 541 or FO 881). Selected correspondence printed by the Foreign Office for official use. This series has been widely used, it contains in addition to much useful information on the slave trade, case volumes on the Brussels Conference. It is particularly valuable as it brings together material from many different sources but it has been used in conjunction with the original documents in FO 84 and other series as it does not contain all the documents and only rarely has the invaluable comments minuted by officials on the original documents. This series is numbered FO 541 in the Public Record Office but since copies are available elsewhere the numbers used in the footnotes are the ones on the prints themselves.

Foreign Office Confidential Prints, Africa (PRO FO 403 or FO 881). Selected correspondence printed by the Foreign Office for its own use. Like the FO 541 series noted above it contains correspondence from a number of sources. It has been widely used. The number FO 403 is used in the Public Record Office only and as there are copies elsewhere the numbers used in the footnotes are those on the documents themselves.

Foreign Office Confidential Prints, Traffic in Arms (PRO FO 428). This series contains selected correspondence on the arms traffic after 1907 with some documents on the liquor trade and has been selectively used for the epilogue only.

FO 1 Abyssinia (Ethiopia), 1808–1905, used only for the correspondence with the Hewett Mission 1884.

FO 2 General Correspondence Africa, 1825–1905, used selectively for the epilogue and contains some case files on the liquor conference of 1899.

FO 64 Germany, 1781–1905, used for the consular reports from Hamburg for 1889–90.

FO 367 General Correspondence Africa 1906–13, used selectively for the epilogue, contains case files on the arms and liquor traffics.

FO 368 Commercial. Foreign Office commercial correspondence after 1906, used in connection with the revision of the Brussels Act in 1919.

FO 371 Political, 1906–43. Foreign Office political correspondence after 1906, used in connection with the revision of the Brussels Act in 1919.

FO 608 Peace Conference 1919–20, used in connection with the revision of the Brussels Act in 1919.

Colonial Office Public Record Office, London:
CO/147 Lagos, correspondence of the Colonial Office with the Governor. Used for the year 1900 when the abolition of slavery in the protectorate was under discussion.

CO/446 Northern Nigeria, correspondence of the Colonial Office with the Governor. This series has been used for the year 1900 when the abolition of slavery in the protectorate was under discussion.

CO/520 Southern Nigeria, correspondence of the Colonial Office with the Governor. This series has been used for the years 1900–2, in connection with the abolition of slavery and the Aro war, and 1906–11 in connection with the House Rule Ordinance.

Colonial Office confidential prints Africa (CO 879)
CO African nos. 190, 208, 222, 381 correspondence relating to the arms and liquor trades in Africa, 1879–1889, between the Colonial Office, the Governors of the West and South African colonies and the Foreign Office.

Customs Records, Public Record Office, London:
Customs 8, lists of British manufactures exported from British ports, listed by the country of destination. These have been used for the years 1882–9.

Customs 9, lists of British manufactures exported from British ports, listed by article. These have been used for the years 1882–9.

Cabinet Papers, Public Record Office, London: These contain reports and digests for cabinet use and valuable summaries of British policy.
CAB 37, cabinet papers 1880–1916, used for the years 1880–90.

CAB 24, memoranda 1915–39, used in connection with the revision of the Brussels Act in 1919.

Belgium

Ministère des Affaires Étrangères, Brussels: *Correspondance et Documents (Afrique):*
Conférence anti-esclavagiste de Bruxelles, 1–19, this series contains the archives of the conference, conveniently collecting together all the correspondence of the Foreign Ministry with the various delegations, with King Leopold II, with its agents abroad and all other persons, together with the papers of the commissions of the conference and the petitions presented to it. This series has been a major source for this work.

Acte Général de Bruxelles, documents on the ratification and publication of the Act and adhesions to it.

Exécution de l'Acte Général de Bruxelles, correspondence concerning the execution of the Brussels Act.

Traite des esclaves, 1839–91, contains documents on the slave trade, on recruiting in Zanzibar and the searching of the ship 'Brabo' by the British.

Traite des esclaves, trafic d'armes et de spiritueux, Conférence anti-esclavagiste (1890), miscellaneous documents 1876–1926.

Conférence des Spiritueux 1899–1917, documents on later history of the liquor question, consulted for the epilogue.

Conférences des Armes 1908–13, vols. 1–6, documents on later history of the arms question, consulted for the epilogue.

AF 1.7 contains documents on the revision of the Brussels Act from 1916.

Extraits de Presse, 64: contains press cuttings on the Brussels Conference; *235:* contains press cuttings on the slave trade 1890–1900.

Former Ministère des Colonies, Place Royale, Brussels:

État Indépendant du Congo and *Institut Royale Coloniale Belge* (EIC–IRCB). These are the archives of the Congo State containing King Leopold's correspondence with his officials and notes on the policy and trade of the Congo. It has been used highly selectively to throw light on the King's policy during the early discussions of the conference. Correspondence on the Brussels Conference is in series AI (Affaires Indigènes) but the correspondence with the King's officials and representatives abroad is filed by correspondent.

France

Ministère des Affaires Étrangères, Paris:

Mémoires et Documents, Afrique: this correspondence of the Ministry with its agents abroad, other government departments and private organisations, includes the case files of the Brussels conference (M & D Afrique 114–19) and correspondence with agents in Madagascar, Zanzibar and the Congo.

Correspondance Politique: general diplomatic correspondence of the Ministry with its agents abroad. Used extensively for the years 1888–90 particularly the correspondence with French Ambassadors in Britain, Belgium, Portugal, Holland, Germany, Russia and Turkey.

Correspondance Commerciale: correspondence of the Ministry with its consular agents used for the years 1888–90.

Archives Nationales, Section d'Outre-Mer (archives of the former Ministère de la France d'Outre-Mer), Paris:

Afrique VI, Affaires Diplomatiques, correspondence relating to the Brussels Conference is in vols. 80 and 81, much of it duplicated in the Foreign Ministry. Correspondence on the Brussels Act is in vol. 89.

Afrique Occidentale Française (AOF XIV) contains reports on the application of the Brussels Act. Consulted for the Epilogue only

Affaires Politiques, correspondence on later history of Brussels Act and the slave, arms and liquor questions in the twentieth century, consulted for the Epilogue.

Ministère de la Marine, Paris:

Series BB 3: correspondence with the Foreign Ministry, much of it duplicated in that Ministry, consulted for the years 1887–90.

Series BB 4: correspondence with French naval officers in the Levant and Indian Ocean squadrons, consulted for the years 1887–90, contains much valuable information on the French attitude to the right to search and suspicions of Britain as well as on the French dhow traffic and the slave trade in the Indian Ocean and Red Sea.

Holland

Ministerie van Buitenlandsche Zaken, Algemeen Rijksarchief, The Hague:
Series A-106H, correspondence of the Foreign Ministry on the Brussels conference, used very selectively only.

Senegal

Archives of Afrique Occidentale Française (AOF) Dakar:
Series K: correspondence on slavery and slave trade questions of the Governor-General of the A.O.F. with his subordinates and with Paris and that of the various provincial governors. This series is invaluable and contains interesting reports of French officials from various parts of French West Africa when inquiries on slavery and the slave trade were launched in 1893–4 and in the years after 1900, as well as the Deherme report of 1906.

Nigeria

National Archives of Nigeria, Ibadan:
CSO 26, correspondence between the Chief Secretary, Lagos, and the Residents of the various provinces, used very selectively for the suppression of slavery and the slave trade.

United States of America

Department of State, National Archives, Washington, D.C.:
General records of the Department of State, RG 59, diplomatic instructions, Belgium II and *despatches from U.S. Ministers to Belgium:* these two series contain all the correspondence between the Department and its delegates at the Brussels Conference and were used for the years 1889–90 only. They are available on microfilm in the National Archives in Washington, D.C. and the footnote references refer to the numbers on the microfilms.

Collections of Private Papers

Anti-Slavery and Aborigines' Protection Society in Rhodes House, Oxford: There is much relevant material in this large collection of papers of both the British and Foreign Anti-Slavery Society and the Aborigines' Protection Society, which amalgamated in 1909. It was used primarily for the correspondence of the British and Foreign Anti-Slavery Society at the time of the Brussels Conference.

Evelyn Baring, 1st Lord Cromer: private correspondence in the Public Record Office, London (FO 633). This was used in connection with Egypt in the 1880s.

Robert Cecil, 3rd Marquess of Salisbury: private correspondence, in Christ Church, Oxford, with agents abroad and other members of the government and private individuals. This has been extensively used for the years 1888–90 and proved a valuable source.

Sir Edward Grey, Viscount Grey of Fallodon: private papers in the Public Record Office, London (FO 800), used selectively for the Epilogue only.

Sir John Kirk: private correspondence in the possession of Mrs Foskett, his granddaughter. These papers yielded some useful information but were on the whole disappointing.

George Granville Leveson Gower, 2nd Earl Granville: private correspondence in the Public Record Office, London (PRO 30/29). This source has been used for the period 1884–5 only.

Baron Lambermont: private correspondence in the Ministère des Affaires Etrangères in Brussels. This correspondence, mainly with King Leopold II, has been used for the years 1888–90. Much of it is in the archives of the Belgian Foreign Ministry.

King Leopold II: private correspondence in the Palais Royal, Brussels, this has been used for the years 1888–90.

Frederick, Lord Lugard: private correspondence in Rhodes House, Oxford. These papers were useful for the Epilogue.

Sir William Mackinnon: private correspondence in the Library of the School of Oriental and African Studies, London. This valuable source has been used for the years 1882–90.

Sir Edward Malet: private correspondence in the Public Record Office, London (FO 343). This is useful for the years 1888–90 when Malet was then British Ambassador in Berlin.

Alfred Milner, Viscount Milner: private papers in Bodleian Library, Oxford. These papers were used highly selectively in connection with the revision of the Brussels Act in 1919.

E. Van Eetvelde: private papers in the Archives Générales du Royaume, Brussels. Van Eetvelde was the Administrator General of the Congo Independent State and represented the State at the Brussels Conference. The papers have been used for the years 1888–90.

Published
Documentary Sources

Official Publications
British

Parliamentary Papers: there are a large number of Blue Books relevant to this work but since it is always more profitable to use the FO 84 series in the Public Record Office a select list used for particular topics is given here.

Correspondence respecting the Reception of Fugitive Slaves on Board Her Majesty's Ships, Slave Trade no. 1 (1876), LXX 1876, p. 257, C-1413

Report of the Royal Commission on Fugitive Slaves, XXVIII 1876, p. 285, C-1516

Report on Slavery and the Slave Trade in Morocco, Slave Trade no. 4 (1883), LXVI 1883, p. 535, C-3700

Correspondence with Her Majesty's Ambassador at Berlin Respecting the West African Conference, Africa no. 2 (1885), LV 1884-5, p. 117, C-4284.

Further Correspondence respecting the West African Conference, Africa no. 3 (1885), LV 1884-5, p. 127, C-4360.

Correspondence respecting the West African Conference, Africa no. 7 (1884), LV 1884-5, p. 449, C-4205.

Further Correspondence respecting the West African Conference, Africa no. 8 (1884), LV 1884-5, p. 449, C-4241.

Protocols and General Act of the West African Conference, Africa no. 4 (1885), LV 1884-5, p. 133, C-4361

Protocols and General Act of the Slave Trade Conference held at Brussels 1889-90, with annexed Declaration, Africa no. 8 (1890), L 1890, p. 41, C-6049. Translation, p. 657

Correspondence respecting Slavery in Zanzibar, Africa no. 6 (1895), LXXI 1895, p. 143, C-7707

Papers relative to the Liquor Trade in West Africa, West Africa LXII 1897, p. 795, C-8480

Correspondence respecting the abolition of the Legal Status of Slavery in Zanzibar, Africa no. 6, LX 1898, p. 559, C-8858

Report by Sir A. Hardinge on the Condition and Progress of the East Africa Protectorate from its Establishment to the 20th July, 1897, Africa no. 7 (1897), LX 1898, p. 199, C-8683.

Correspondence respecting the Status of Slavery in East Africa and the Islands of Zanzibar and Pemba, Africa no. 8 (1899), LXIII 1899, p. 303, C.9502

International Convention respecting the Liquor Traffic in Africa, signed at Brussels, 8 June 1899. Treaty Series no. 13, 1900 CV 1900, p. 1, Cd. 103.

Correspondence respecting Slavery and the Slave Trade in East Africa and the Islands of Zanzibar and Pemba, Africa no. 4 (1901), XLVIII 1901, p. 173, C.593

International Convention Respecting the Liquor Traffic in Africa. Signed at Brussels 3 Nov. 1906. Treaty Series no. 46, 1907, CXXIV 1908, p. 15, Cd. 3856

Protocol between the United Kingdom, the Independent State of the Congo, France, Germany, Portugal and Spain, prohibiting the Importation of Firearms, Ammunition, etc. Within a Certain Zone in Western Equatorial Africa. Signed at Brussels, 22 July 1908. Treaty Series no. 29, 1908, CXXIV 1908, p. 5, Cd. 4320.

Convention Revising the General Act of Berlin, February 26, 1885, and the General Act and Declaration of Brussels, 2 July 1890. Signed at St.-Germain-en-Laye, 10 Sept. 1919. Treaty Series no. 18, 1919 LIII 1919, p. 553, Cmd. 477.

Convention relating to the Liquor Traffic in Africa and Protocol. Signed at St.-Germain-en-Laye, 10 Sept. 1919. Treaty Series no. 19, 1919 LIII 1919, p. 569, Cmd. 478.

Convention for the Control of the Trade in Arms and Ammunition, and Protocol. Signed 10 Sept., 1919. Treaty Series no. 12, 1919 LIII 1919, p. 705, Cmd. 414.

Sierra Leone: Sessional Paper no. 5 1926

Hansard, *Parliamentary Debates*, used mainly for the period 1888–90

British and Foreign State Papers.

F. Lugard, *Political Memoranda*, 1906, confidential instructions to political officers in Northern Nigeria.

Instructions for the Guidance of H.M. Naval Officers Engaged in the Suppression of the Slave Trade.

This very useful source was published in 1844, 1865, 1882, 1892. It is available in the Foreign Office Library, London.

German

Weiss Buch, December 1888.

Stenographische Berichte über die Verhandlungen des Deutschen Reichstages, 1888–90.

League of Nations

1923 A 18 VI	Question of Slavery, information communicated by certain governments.
1924 A 25, A 25(a) VI	Reports received from various governments on the question of slavery.
1924 C 209 M 66 VI	Temporary Slavery Commission. Report from the Government of Abyssinia.
1925 A 19 VI	Temporary Slavery Commission. Report adopted July 13–25, 1925.

Collections of Documents

ALLEMAND-LAVIGERIE C. M.	*Documents sur l'oeuvre anti-esclavagiste*, St. Cloud 1889
HERTSLET, E.	*The Map of Africa by Treaty*, 3rd edition, London 1909, 3 vols.
HERTSLET, L. and E.	*Commercial Treaties*, London 1840–1924, 30 vols.
METCALFE, G. E.	*Great Britain and Documents of Ghana History 1807–1957*, London 1964.
NEWBURY, C. W.	*British Policy Towards West Africa, Select Documents, 1786–1874*, I, Oxford 1965, II, *1875–1914*, Oxford 1971.

Periodicals

The Anti-Slavery Reporter, the journal of the Anti-Slavery Society, is a most valuable source and was extensively used for the period 1880–90.

L'Afrique explorée et civilisée, a monthly journal published in Geneva, has been used for the period 1879–83 and contained some useful articles.

Newspapers

No systematic study of the press was undertaken but the various diplomatic archives contain some useful cuttings and there are press files covering the Brussels conference in the Belgian Ministry of Foreign Affaires and cuttings on Cardinal Lavigerie's crusade in the papers of the Anti-Slavery Society in Rhodes House.

Published Primary Works

d'ABADDIE, Antoine	*Les Causes actuelles de l'esclavage en Ethiopie*, Louvain 1887 (reprint from *Revue des Questions Scientifiques*)
ALLEN, C. H. and CRAWFORD, J. V.	*Morocco Report to the Committee of the BFASS*, London 1886
ARNOT, F. S.	*Garenganze or Mission Work in Central Africa*, 3rd edition, London 1889 (first published 1889)
AUBIN, E.	*Morocco of Today*, London 1906, translation
BAIKIE, W. B.	*Narrative of an Exploring Voyage up the Rivers Kwora and Binnie (commonly known as the Niger and Tsadda) in 1854*, London 1856

BAKER, S. W.   *Albert N'Yanza, Great Basin of the Nile*, London 1866, 2 vols.

BANNING, E.   *Mémoires politiques et diplomatiques*, Paris and Brussels 1927

BARTH, H.   *Travels and discoveries in North and Central Africa*, London 1957, 3 vols. (first published 1857)

BECKER, Jerome   *La Vie en Afrique*, Paris 1887, 2 vols.

BURTON, Richard F.   *Zanzibar City, Island and Coast*, London 1872, 2 vols.

The Lake Regions of Central Africa, New York 1961, 2 vols. (first published 1860)

BUXTON, T. F.   *The African Slave Trade*, London 1839
The Remedy: Being a Sequel to the African Slave Trade, London 1840, reissued 1968 as *The African Slave Trade and its Remedy* with an introduction by G. E. Metcalfe

CAMERON, V. L.   *Across Africa*, London 1877, 2 vols.

CLAPPERTON, H.   *Journey of a Second Expedition into the Interior of Africa from the Bight of Benin to Soccatoo*, London 1966 (first published 1829)

CLAPPERTON, H. and DENHAM, D.   *Narrative of Travels and Discoveries in Northern and Central Africa in the Years 1822–1823, 1824*, London 1826

COILLARD, François   *On the Threshold of Central Africa*, 2nd ed., London 1902 (first published 1897)

COLOMB, Captain   *Slave Catching in the Indian Ocean*, London 1873.

COQUILHAT, Camille   *Sur le Haut-Congo*, Paris 1888

CRAWFORD, J. V.   See ALLEN, C. H.

CROW, H.   *Memoirs*, London 1970 (first published 1830)

DENHAM, D.   See CLAPPERTON, H. and DENHAM, D.

DOUGHTY, C. M.   *Travels in Arabia Deserta*, London 1888, 2 vols.

ELTON, J. F.   *Travels and Researches among the Lakes and Mountains of Eastern and Central Africa*, London 1879

FELKIN, Robert W.   'Notes on the Waganda Tribe of Central Africa', *Proceedings of the Royal Society of Edinburgh*, 13, 1886

FITZGERALD, W. W. A.   *Travels in the Coastlands of British East Africa and the Islands of Zanzibar and Pemba*, London 1898

GIRAUD, V.   *Les Lacs de l'Afrique Équatoriale*, Paris 1890

GREFFULHE, H.   'Voyage de Lamoo à Zanzibar', *Bulletin de la Société de Géographie et d'études Coloniales de Marseille*, II, 1878

HAMED bin MUHAMMED (Tippu Tip)   'Maisha ya Hamed bin Muhammed el Murjebi Yaani Tippu Tip', *Supplement to the East African*

Swahili Committee Journals, nos. 28/2 July 1958 and 29/1 January 1959, translated by W. H. Whiteley

HARRIS, W. C. — *The Highlands of Ethiopia*, New York 1844

HARRISON, J. W. — *A. M. Mackay—Pioneer Missionary of the Church Missionary Society in Uganda*, London 1890

HILL, G. B. (ed.) — *Colonel Gordon in Central Africa 1874–79*, London 1884

HINDE, S. L. — *The Fall of the Congo Arabs*, London 1897

HORE, E. W. — *Tanganyika: Eleven Years in Central Africa*, London 1892

HORNADAY, W. T. — *Free Rum on the Congo*, Chicago 1887

HURGRONJE, C. Snouck — *Mekka in the Latter Part of the Nineteenth Century*, London and Leyden 1931, translation

JACKSON, Frederick — *Early Days in East Africa*, London 1969, (first published 1930)

JOBARD, C. — *L'esclavage en Tunisie*, Tunis 1890

JOHNSON, Samuel — *The History of the Yorubas from the Earliest Times to the Beginning of the British Protectorate*, Lagos 1956 (first published 1921)

JOHNSON, W. P. — *My African Reminiscences, 1875–95*, London 1924

JOHNSTON, H. H. — 'Alcohol in Africa', *The Nyasa News*, August 1894

KELTIE, Scott J. — 'British Interests in Africa', *Contemporary Review*, July 1888

KRAPF, J. L. — *Travels, Researches and Missionary Labours*, London 1860

LAIRD, Macgregor and OLDFIELD, R. A. K. — *Narrative of an Expedition into the Interior of Africa by the River Niger in the Steam Vessels Quorra and Al Burka in 1832, 1833 and 1834*, 2 vols., London 1971 (first published 1837)

LANE, E. W. — *Manners and Customs of Modern Egyptians*, London 1954 (first published 1836)

LIEBRECHTS, C. — *Léopold II, fondateur d'empire*, Brussels 1932

LIVINGSTONE, David — *Missionary Travels and Researches in South Africa: including a Sketch of Sixteen Years' Residence in the Interior of Africa*, London 1857

The Last Journals of David Livingstone in Central Africa from 1865 to his Death, 2 vols., ed. by H. Waller, London 1874

LIVINGSTONE, David and Charles — *Narrative of an Expedition to the Zambesi and its Tributaries: and of the Discovery of the Lakes Shirwa and Nyassa 1858–64*, London 1865

LUGARD, F. D. — *The Rise of Our East African Empire*, London 1893, 2 vols.

	'Slavery Under the British Flag', *The Nineteenth Century*, xxxix, 1896
	'Liquor Traffic in Africa', *The Nineteenth Century*, xlii, 1897
	The Dual Mandate in Tropical Africa, 5th edition, London 1965 (first published 1922)
MACDONALD, Duff	*Africana*, 2 vols., London 1959 (first published 1882)
MACKENZIE, Donald	*The Khalifate of the West*, London 1911
MAPLES, Chauncy	*The Life of Bishop Maples*, London 1897
McCOAN, J. C.	*Egypt as It Is*, London 1877
NACHTIGAL, G.	*Sahara und Sudan Ergebnisse sechsjähriger Reisen in Afrika*, Vol. I, 1879, Vol. II, 1881, Berlin, Vol. III, 1889, Leipzig, Vol. III, Wadai and Darfur translated by A. G. B. and H. J. Fisher with introductory notes, London 1971
NEWMAN, H. S.	*Banani*, London 1898
OLDFIELD, R. A. K.	See LAIRD, Macgregor
RANKIN, D. J.	'The Peoples and Commercial Prospects of the Zambesi Basin', *Scottish Geographical Magazine*, ix, 1893, pp. 225–40
ROSCOE, John	*The Baganda*, London 1965, (first published 1911)
RUSSELL, Mrs. Charles (ed.)	*General Rigby, Zanzibar and the Slave Trade*, London 1935
SCHÖN, J. F.	*Magana Hausa: The Life and Times of Dorugu*, London 1885
SCHWEINFURTH, George	*The Heart of Africa*, 2 vols., translation, New York 1874
SLATIN, Rudloph C.	*Fire and Sword in the Sudan*, London 1896
SOLEILLET, P.	*Voyages en Ethiopie*, Rouen 1886
STANLEY, H. M.	*Through the Dark Continent*, 2nd edition, London 1899, 2 vols. (first published 1878)
	The Congo and the Founding of its Free State, London 1885
SULLIVAN, G. L.	*Dhow Chasing in Zanzibar Waters*, London 1969 (first published 1873)
SWANN, A. J.	*Fighting the Slave Hunters in Central Africa*, London 1910
THOMSON, Joseph	*To the Central African Lakes and Back*, London 1968, 2 vols. (first published 1881)
TIPPU TIP	See Hamed bin Muhammed

TUCKER, A. R.   *Eighteen Years in Uganda and East Africa*, London 1911

WARD, Herbert   *Five Years with the Congo Cannibals*, London 1890

WHITELEY, W. H. (translator)   See Hamed bin Muhammed (Tippu Tip)

WISSMANN, H. von   *Proceedings of the Royal Geographical Society*, n.s. x, 1888, pp. 525 ff.

                                    My Second Journey through Equatorial Africa from the Congo to the Zambesi in the Years 1886 and 1887, London 1891, translation

WYLDE, A. B.   *'83 to '87 in the Sudan*, London 1888, 2 vols.

ZAHN, F. M.   *Der Westafrikanische Branntweinhandel. Erwiderung auf die Offene Antwort des Herrn Reichstagsabgeordeneten A. Woermann*, Gütersloh 1886

Published Secondary Works

Note: works mentioned only once in the text have been omitted unless they are of particular interest and a few works not mentioned but particularly relevant have been included.

ABIR, M.   *Ethiopia in the Era of the Princes*, London 1968.

AJAYI, J. F. Ade   *Christian Missions in Nigeria 1841–1891*, London 1965

AJAYI, J. F. Ade and SMITH, Robert   *Yoruba Warfare in the Nineteenth Century*, Cambridge 1964

AKINTOYE, S. A.   *Revolution and power politics in Yorubaland 1840–93*, London 1971

                                    'The Ondo Road Eastwards of Lagos, 1870–95', *Journal of African History*, x, 4, 1969

ALPERS, E. A.   'Trade State and Society among the Yao in the Nineteenth Century', *Journal of African History*, x, 3, 1969, pp. 405–20

                                    'The East African Slave Trade', *Historical Association of Tanzania*, paper no. 3, 1967

ANENE, J. C.   *Southern Nigeria in Transition 1885–1906*, Cambridge 1966

ANSTEY, Roger   *Britain and the Congo in the Nineteenth Century*, Oxford 1962

                                    'British Trade and Policy in West Central Africa between 1816 and the early 1880's, *Transactions of the Historical Society of Ghana*, iii, 1, 1957, pp. 47–71

	'Capitalism and Slavery: a Critique'. *The Economic History Review*, 2nd Series, xxi, 2, 1968
	'A Re-interpretation of the Abolition of the British Slave Trade, 1806–7', *English Historical Review*, lxxxvii, April 1972, pp. 304–32
	'The Volume and Profitability of the British Slave Trade, 1761–1807' in Engerman and E. Genovese (eds.), *Race and Slavery in the Western Hemisphere Quantitative Studies*, Princeton, forthcoming
ARGYLE, W. J.	*The Fon of Dahomey*, Oxford 1966
ASCHERSON, Neal	*The King Incorporated*, London 1963
ASIEGBU, J. U. J.	*Slavery and the Politics of Liberation 1787–1861*, London 1969
ATMORE, A., CHIRENJE, J. M. and MUDENGE, S. I.	'Firearms in South Central Africa', *Journal of African History*, xii, 4, 1971, pp. 545–56
AYANDELE, E. A.	*The Missionary Impact on Modern Nigeria 1842–1914*, London 1966
	'Observations on some Social and Economic Aspects of Slavery in Pre-colonial Northern Nigeria', *Nigerian Journal of Economic Studies*, Ibadan, ix, 3, 1967
AUSTEN, R. A. and SMITH, W. D.	'Images of Africa and British Slave-Trade Abolition: The Transition to an Imperialist Ideology', *African Historical Studies*, ii, 1, 1969
AWAD, Mohammed	*Report on Slavery* (for the United Nations), New York 1966
BAER, G.	'Slavery in Nineteenth Century Egypt', *Journal of African History*, viii, 3, 1967, pp. 417–41
BAUNARD, L.	*Le Cardinal Lavigerie*, 2 vols., Paris 1896
BEACHEY, R. W.	'The Arms Trade in East Africa in the Late Nineteenth Century', *Journal of African History*, iii, 3, 1962, pp. 451–67
	'The East African Ivory Trade in the Nineteenth Century', *Journal of African History*, viii, 2, 1967, pp. 269–90
BENNETT, N. R.	*Mirambo of Tanzania, 1840 (?) –84*, London and Toronto 1971
	Studies in East African History, Boston 1963
	'Some Notes on French Policy in Buganda and East Africa, 1879–90, *Makerere Journal*, vi, pp. 1–18
	'Captain Storms in Tanganyika', *Tanganyika Notes and Records*, 54, March 1960, pp. 51–63
BETHEL, L.	*The Abolition of The Brazilian Slave Trade*, Cambridge 1970

'The Mixed Commissions for the Suppression of the Trans-Atlantic Slave Trade in the Nineteenth Century', *Journal of African History*, vii, 1, 1966, pp. 79–93

BEVIN, J. H. 'Gold Coast Economy about 1880', *Transactions of the Historical Society of Ghana*, ii, pp. 73–86

BIRMINGHAM, David See Richard Gray and David Birmingham

BOAHEN, A. A. *Britain, the Sahara and the Western Sudan, 1778–1861*, Oxford 1964

BOOTH. Alan R. 'The United States African Squadron 1843–61', in J. Butler (ed.), *Boston Papers in African History*, I, Boston 1964, pp. 79–117

BOUCHE, Denise *Les villages de liberté en Afrique noire française (1887–1910)*, Paris 1968

BOVILL, E. M. *Golden Trade of the Moors*, Oxford 1957

BIOBAKU, S. O. *The Egba and their Neighbours 1842–72*, Oxford 1957

BRODE, H. *Tippoo Tib: The Story of his Career in Central Africa*, London 1907

BRUNSCHVIG, R. 'Abd', *Encyclopaedia of Islam*, I, 1960

BRUNSCHWIG, Henri *L'avènement de l'Afrique noire du XIXᵉ siècle à nos jours*, Paris 1963

BUSCH, B. C. *Britain and the Persian Gulf 1894–1914*, Berkeley and Los Angeles 1967

CAULK, R. A. 'Firearms and Princely Powers in Ethiopia in the Nineteenth Century', *Journal of African History*, xiii, 4, 1972, pp. 609–30

CECIL, G. *Life of Robert, Marquis of Salisbury*, London 1932, 4 vols. IV

CEULEMANS, P. *La question arabe et le Congo (1883–1892)*, Brussels 1959

CHIRENJE, J. M. See Atmore, A., Chirenje, J. M. and Mudenge, S. T.

CLARIDGE, W. W. *A History of the Gold Coast and Ashanti*, 2nd edition, London 1964, 2 vols.

COHEN, R. 'Slavery among the Kanuri', *Trans-Actions*, Jan./Feb. 1967, pp. 48–50

COLLINS, R. O. 'Origins of the Nile Struggle: Anglo-German Negotiations and the Mackinnon Agreement of 1890', in P. Gifford and Wm. Roger Louis (eds.), *Britain and Germany in Africa: Imperial Rivalry and Colonial Rule*, I, New Haven 1967, pp. 119–51

COOPER, F. 'The Treatment of Slaves on the Kenya Coast in the Nineteenth Century', *Kenya Historical Review*, July 1973

COLLISTER, Peter — *The Last Days of Slavery: England and the East African Slave Trade 1870–1900*, Nairobi, Dar-es-Salaam, Kampala 1961

COQUERY-VIDROVITCH — 'De la traite des esclaves à l'exportation de l'huile de palme et des palmistes au Dahomey: XIXe', in C. Meillasseux (ed.), *The Development of Indigenous Trade and Markets in West Africa*, Oxford 1971, pp. 107–23

CORWIN, A. F. — *Spain and the Abolition of Slavery in Cuba 1817–1886*, Texas 1967

COUPLAND, R. — *The British Anti-Slavery Movement*, London 1933

East Africa and its Invaders, London 1938

The Exploitation of East Africa, 1856–1890, London 1939

CROFTON, R. H. — *A Pageant of the Spice Islands*, London 1936

CROWE, S. E. — *The Berlin West African Conference, 1884–1885*, London 1942

CURTIN, P. D. — *The Image of Africa*, Wisconsin 1964

'Epidemiology and the Slave Trade', *Political Science Quarterly* 83, 1968

The Atlantic Slave Trade: A Census, Wisconsin 1969

'The Slave Trade and the Atlantic Basin: Intercontinental Perspectives', in N. I. Huggins, Martin Kilson and Daniel M. Fox (eds.), *Key Issues in the Afro-American Experience*, New York 1971, pp. 74–93

CURTIN, P. D. and VANSINA, Jan — 'Sources of the Nineteenth Century Atlantic Slave Trade', *Journal of African History*, v, 2, 1964, pp. 185–208

DAGET, S. — 'L'abolition de la traite des noirs en France de 1814 à 1831', *Cahiers d'Etudes Africaines*, 1971, pp. 15–58

DAVIS, David Bryon — *The Problem of Slavery in Western Culture*, Cornell 1966

DEBBASCHE, Y. — 'Poésie et traite: l'opinion française sur le commerce négrier au debut du XIXe siècle', *Revue Française d'Histoire d'Outre-Mer*, xlviii, 1961, pp. 311–52

DeJONGHE, E. — *Les formes d'asservissement dans les sociétés indigènes du Congo Belge*, Brussels 1949

DESCHAMPS, H. — *Histoire de la Traite des noirs de l'antiquité à nos jours*, Fayard 1971

DIKE, K. Onwuka — *Trade and politics in the Niger Delta 1830–85*, Oxford 1966 (5th edition)

DOUGLAS, Mary	'Is Matriliny Doomed in Africa ?', in Mary Douglas and Phyllis M. Kaberry (eds.), *Man in Africa*, New York 1971, pp. 124–37
	'Matriliny and Pawnship in Central Africa', *Africa*, xliv, 4, 1964, pp. 301–13
DUFFY, J.	*A Question of Slavery*, Harvard 1967
DUNN, Ross	'The Trade of Tafilalt: Commercial Change in Southeast Morocco on the Eve of the Protectorate,'
	African Historical Studies, iv, 2, 1971, pp. 271–304
EMERIT, M.	*La Revolution de 1848 en Algérie*, Paris 1949
EVANS-PRITCHARD, E. E.	*The Sanusi of Cyrenaica*, Oxford 1949
	Witchcraft, Oracles and Magic among the Azande, Oxford 1958 (first published 1937), pp. 10 ff.
FISCHER, H.	'The Suppression of Slavery in International Law', part I, *The International Law Quarterly*, 3, Jan. 1950, pp. 29–43
FISHER, A. G. B. and H. J.	*Slavery and Muslim Society in Africa*, London 1970
FISHER, H. J. and ROWLAND, V.	'Firearms in Central Sudan', *Journal of African History*, xii, 2, 1971, pp. 215–39
FLADELAND, Betty	'Abolitionist Pressures on the Concert of Europe 1814–22', *Journal of Modern History*, 38, 4, 1966
	Men and Brothers: Anglo-American Antislavery Co-operation, Illinois 1972
FLINT, John C.	*Sir George Goldie and the Making of Nigeria*, London 1960
	'The Wider Background to the Partition and Colonial occupation', in R. Oliver and G. Mathew (eds.), *History of East Africa* I, Oxford 1963, chapter 10
FONER, L. and GENOVESE, E. D.	*Slavery in the New World*, New Jersey 1969
FORTES, Meyer	'Kinship and Marriage among the Ashanti', in A. R. Radcliffe-Brown and Daryll Forde (eds.), *African Systems of Kinship and Marriage*, Oxford 1950, pp. 252–84
FORDE, Daryll and RADCLIFFE-BROWN, A. R.	*African Systems of Kinship and Marriage*, 1950
FREEMAN-GRENVILLE, G. S. P.	'The German Sphere 1884–98', in R. Oliver and G. Mathew (eds.), *History of East Africa*, I, Oxford 1963, pp. 434–53
FROELICH, J. C.	'Le commandement et l'organisation sociale chez les Foulbés de l'Adamawa', chapter 3, *Études Camerounaises*, nos. 45–6, Sept./Dec. 1954
FYFE, C.	*A History of Sierra Leone*, Oxford 1962

GALBRAITH, John S.	*Mackinnon and East Africa 1878–95: A Study in the 'New Imperialism'*, Cambridge 1972
GALLAGHER, J.	'Fowell Buxton and the New African Policy, 1838–1842', *Cambridge Historical Journal*, x, 1950, pp. 36–58
GASTON-MARTIN	*Histoire de l'esclavage dans les colonies françaises*, Paris 1948
GAVIN, R.	'The Bartle Frere Mission to Zanzibar, 1873', *The Historical Journal*, v, 1962, pp. 122–48.
GENOVESE, E. D.	See FONER, L., and GENOVESE, E. D.
GIFFORD, P. and LOUIS, Wm. R. (eds.)	*Britain and Germany in Africa: Imperial Rivalry and Colonial Rule*, New Haven and London 1967
GIGLIO, C.	'Article 17 of the Treaty of Ucciolli', *Journal of African History*, vi, 2, 1965, pp. 221–31.
GILLARD, D. R.	'Salisbury's African Policy and the Heligoland Offer of 1890', *English Historical Review*, lxxv, 1960, pp. 631–53
GOYAU, P. L. T. G.	*Un Grand Missionnaire, Le Cardinal Lavigerie*, Paris 1925
GRAY, Richard	*A History of the Southern Sudan, 1839–1889*, London 1961
GRAY, Richard and BIRMINGHAM, David	*Precolonial African Trade: Essays on Trade in Central and Eastern Africa before 1900*, Oxford 1970
GREENIDGE, C. W. W.	*Slavery*, London 1958
HAMILTON, David	'Imperialism Ancient and Modern; A Study of English Attitudes to the Claim to Sovereignty to the Northern Somali Coastline', *Journal of Ethiopian Studies*, v, July 1967, pp. 9–35
HAMMOND, Richard J.	*Portugal and Africa 1815–1910*, Stanford 1966
HANNA, A. J.	*The Beginnings of Nyasaland and North Eastern Rhodesia 1859–95*, Oxford 1956
HARGREAVES, John D.	*Prelude to the Partition of West Africa*, London 1963
HARTWIG, Gerald W.	'Long Distance Trade and the Evolution of Sorcery among the Kerebe', *African Historical Studies*, iv, 3, 1971, pp. 505–24
	'The Victoria Nyanza as a Trade Route in the Nineteenth Century', *Journal of African History*, xi, 4, 1970, pp. 535–52
HERSKOVITS, M. J.	*Dahomey, An Ancient West African Kingdom*, 2 vols., New York 1938
HESS, R. L.	'Germany and the Anglo-Italian Colonial Entente', in P. Gifford and Wm. R. Louis (eds.), *Britain and Germany in Africa: Imperial Rivalry and Colonial Rule*, i, New Haven 1967, pp. 153–78

HILL, G. B. (ed.)   *Colonel Gordon in Central Africa, 1874–1879* (2nd edition), London 1884.

HILL, R.   *Egypt in the Sudan, 1820–81*, Oxford 1959

HOLLINGSWORTH, L. W.   *Zanzibar under the Foreign Office 1890–1913*, London 1953

HOLT, P. M.   *A Modern History of the Sudan*, New York 1961

The Mahdist State in the Sudan, 1881–98, Oxford 1958

HOPKINS, A. G.   'Economic Imperialism in West Africa: Lagos 1880–92', *Economic History Review*, xxi, 1968, pp. 580–606

An Economic History of West Africa, London 1973

HORTON, Robin   'Fishing Village to City State: A Social History of New Calabar', in Mary Douglas and Phyllis M. Kaberry, *Man in Africa*, New York 1971, pp. 38–60

HORTON, W. R. G.   'The Ohu System of Slavery in a Northern Ibo Village Group', *Africa*, 24, 1954, pp. 311–36

HOWARD, Warren S.   *American Slavers and the Federal Law 1835–62*, Berekeley and Los Angeles 1963

HUGGINS, N. I., KILSON, Martin and FOX, Daniel M.   *Key Issues in the Afro-American Experience*, New York 1971

HYDE, F. E., PARKINSON, B. B. and MARRINER, S.   'The Nature and Profitability of the Liverpool Slave Trade', *Economic History Review*, 2nd series, v, 1953

IKIME, Obaro   *Niger Delta Rivalry*, London 1969

JOHNSON, Douglas   *Guizot*, London and Toronto 1963

JONES, G. I.   *The Trading States of the Oil Rivers*, London 1963

KABERRY, Phyllis M.   See DOUGLAS, Mary

KANYA-FORSTNER, A. S.   *The Conquest of the Western Sudan*, Cambridge 1969

KEA, R. A.   'Firearms and Warfare on the Gold and Slave Coasts from the Sixteenth to Nineteenth Centuries', *Journal of African History*, xii, 2, 1971, pp. 173–84

KELLY, J. B.   *Britain and the Persian Gulf 1795–1880*, Oxford 1968

KIERAN, J. A.   'Abushiri and the Germans', ch. 10 in B. A. Ogot (ed.), *Hadith* 2, Nairobi 1970

KILSON, Martin   See HUGGINS, N. I., KILSON, Martin and FOX, Daniel M.

KIRK-GREEN, A. H. M.   'The Major Currencies in Nigerian History', *Journal of the Historical Society of Nigeria*, 1960, pp. 132–50

KLEIN, Martin A. — 'Slavery, the Slave Trade and Legitimate Commerce in Late Nineteenth Century Africa', *Études d'Histoire Africaine*, ii, 1971, pp. 5–28.

KLEIN, Norman A. — 'West African Unfree Labour before and after the Rise of the Atlantic Slave Trade', in Foner and E. D. Genovese (eds.), *Slavery in the New World*, New Jersey 1969, pp. 87–95

KLINBERG, F. J. — *The Anti-Slavery Movement in England*, New Haven 1926.

KNIGHT, F. W. — *Slave Society in Cuba during the Nineteenth Century*, Wisconsin 1970

LAMPHEAR, J. E. — 'The Kamba and the Northern Mrima Coast', in Richard Gray and David Birmingham, *Precolonial African Trade: Essays on Trade in Central and Eastern Africa before 1900*, Oxford 1970, pp. 75–101

LANGER, W. L. — *European Alliances and Alignments 1871–90*, New York 1931

LEVY, Reuben — *The Social Structure of Islam*, Cambridge 1957

LLOYD, C. — *The Navy and the Slave Trade*, London 1949

LOMBARD, J. — 'The Kingdom of Dahomey', in D. Forde and P. M. Kaberry (eds.), *West African Kingdoms in the Nineteenth Century*, Oxford 1967, pp. 70–91

LOTH, H. — *Kolonialismus und 'Humanitäts' Intervention—Kritische Untersuchung der Politik Deutschlands gegenüber dem Kongostaat 1884–1908*, Berlin 1966

'Great Britain and German Expansion in Africa, 1884–1919', in P. Gifford and Wm. Roger Louis, (eds.), *Britain and Germany in Africa: Imperial Rivalry and Colonial Rule*, I, New Haven 1967, pp. 3–46

LOUIS, Wm. Roger — 'The Berlin Congo Conference', P. Gifford and Wm. Roger Louis (eds.), *France and Britain in Africa: Imperial Rivalry and Colonial Rule*, II, New-Haven 1971, pp. 167–220

'Sir Percy Anderson's Grand African Strategy 1883–96', *English Historical Review*, lxxxi, April 1966, pp. 292–314

LOW, David A. — 'The Northern Interior 1840–84', in R. Oliver and G. Mathew (eds.), *History of East Africa*, I, Oxford 1963, pp. 297–351

LYNE, R. N. — *An Apostle of Empire: Being the Life of Sir Lloyd Mathews K.C.M.G.*, London 1936

MAIR, Lucy P. — *An African People in the Twentieth Century*, New York 1965 (first published 1934)

MANNING, Patrick — 'Slaves, Palm Oil and Political Power on the West African Coast', *African Historical Studies*, ii, 2, 1969, pp. 279–88

MARRINER, S.   See HYDE, F. E., PARKINSON, B. B. and MARRINER, S.

MARTEL, A.   *Les Confins Saharo-Tripolitains de la Tunisie (1881–1911)*, Paris 1965

MASON, M.   'Population Density and "Slave Raiding"—the case of the Middle Belt of Nigeria', *Journal of African History*, xli, 1969, pp. 551–64

MASON, Philip   *The Birth of a Dilemma*, London 1958

MATHIESON, W. L.   *Great Britain and the Slave Trade 1839–65*, London 1929

MAUGAT, E.   'La traite clandestine à Nantes au XIXe siècle', *Bulletin de la Société Archéologique et Historique de Nantes*, 1954, pp. 162–9

McINTYRE, W. D.   'Commander Glover and the Colony of Lagos, 1861–73', *Journal of African History*, iv, 1, 1963, pp. 57–79

MCLOUGHLIN, P. F. M.   'Economic Development and the Heritage of Slavery in the Sudan Republic', *Africa*, 23, Oct. 1962, pp. 355–91.

MEILLASSOUX, Claude (Editor)   *The Development of Indigenous Trade and Markets in West Africa*, Oxford 1971

MIDDLETON, John   'Slavery in Zanzibar', *Trans-Actions*, Jan./Feb. 1966, pp. 46–8

     Land Tenure in Zanzibar, London 1961

MIEGE, J. L.   *Le Maroc et L'Europe (1830–94)*, 4 vols., Paris 1961

MILLER, Joseph C.   *Cokwe Expansion 1850–1900*, Occasional Paper no. 1. African Studies Program, University of Wisconsin, Madison 1969

     'Cokwe Trade and Conquest in the Nineteenth Century', in Richard Gray and David Birmingham, *Pre-Colonial African Trade: Essays on Trade in Central and Eastern Africa Before 1900*, Oxford 1970, pp. 175–201

     'Slaves, Slavers, and Social Change in Nineteenth Century Kasanje', in Frans-Wilhelm Heimer (ed.), *Social Change in Angola*, Munich 1973 (forthcoming)

MITCHELL, J. C.   *The Yao Village*, Manchester 1956

MUDENGE, S. I.   See ATMORE, A., CHIRENJE, J. M. and MUDENGE, S. I.

MÜLLER, F. F.   *Deutschland-Zanzibar-Östrafrika*, East Berlin 1959

NADEL, S. F.   *A Black Byzantium*, Oxford 1960

NAIR, Kannan K.   *Politics and Society in South Eastern Nigeria 1841–1906*, London 1972

NEWBURY, C. W.   *The Western Slave Coast and Its Rulers*, Oxford 1961

	'North African and Western Sudan Trade in the Nineteenth Century: A Re-evaluation', *Journal of African History*, vii, 2, 1966, pp. 233–46
NEWITT, M. D. D.	'Angoche, the Slave Trade and the Portuguese *c.* 1844–1910', *Journal of African History*, xiii, 4, 1972, pp. 659–72
NICHOLLS, C. S.	*The Swahili Coast: Politics, Diplomacy and Trade on the East African Littoral, 1798–1856*
NICOLAISEN, J.	'Slavery among the Tuareg in the Sahara', *KUML*, 1957, pp. 107–13
OBICHERE, B. I.	*The West African States and European Expansion*, New Haven 1971
O'FAHEY, R. S.	'Slavery and the Slave Trader in Darfur', *Journal of African History*, xiv, 1, 1973, pp. 29–43
OLIVER, R.	*The Missionary Factor in East Africa*, 2nd edition, London 1965
	Sir Harry Johnston and the Scramble for Africa, London 1957
OLIVER, R. and MATHEW, G. (eds.)	*History of East Africa*, I, Oxford 1963
PANKHURST, R.	*Economic History of Ethiopia 1800–1935*, Addis Ababa 1968
	'The Ethiopian Slave Trade in the Nineteenth and Early Twentieth Centuries: A Statistical Inquiry', *Journal of Semitic Studies*, ix, 1, 1964, pp. 220–8
PARKINSON, B. B.	See HYDE, F. E., PARKINSON, B. B. and MARRINER, S.
PARSONS, F. V.	'The North-West African Company and the British Government, 1875–95', *Historical Journal*, I, 2, 1958, pp. 136–53
PERHAM, Marjorie	*Lugard—The Years of Adventure 1858–1898*, London 1956
	Lugard—The Years of Authority 1898–1945, London 1960
	The Government of Ethiopia, 2nd edition, Evanston 1969
	Ten Africans, Evanston 1963, first published London 1936
PERRAUDIN, J.	'Le Cardinal Lavigerie et Léopold II', *Zaire*, 12, 1958
PINTO, F. Latour da Veiga	*Le Portugal et le Congo au XIXe siècle*, Paris 1972
POLANYI, Karl	*Dahomey and the Slave Trade*, London 1966

PORTER, Dale H.	*The Abolition of the Slave Trade in England 1784–1807*, Archon 1970
POTSON, Newman E. W.	'Slavery in Abyssinia', *Contemporary Review*, 14, Dec. 1935
PRIESTLEY, Margaret	*West African Trade and Coast Society*, London 1969
QUENEUIL, H.	*La Conférence de Bruxelles et ses résultats*, Paris 1907
RADCLIFFE-BROWN, A. R.	See FORDE, Darryll
RAMM, A.	'Great Britain and the Planting of Italian Power in the Red Sea, 1868–85', *English Historical Review*, lix, 1944, pp. 211–36
RATTRAY, R. S.	*Ashanti Law and Constitution*, Oxford 1929
RENAULT, Francois	*Lavigerie, l'esclavage Africain, et l'Europe*, 2 vols., Paris 1971
RICE, Duncan C.	'Critique of the Eric Williams Thesis—the Anti-Slavery Interest and the Sugar Duties 1841–53', The Trans-Atlantic Slave Trade from West Africa, Cyclostyled Paper of the Centre of African Studies, University of Edinburgh 1965
ROBERTS, Andrew	'Nyamwezi Trade', in Richard Gray and David Birmingham, *Precolonial African Trade: Essays on Trade in Central and Eastern Africa before 1900*, Oxford 1970, pp. 75–101
ROBINSON, R. and GALLAGHER, J., with DENNY, Alice	*Africa and the Victorians*, London 1963
RODD, F. R.	*People of the Veil*, London 1926
RODNEY, Walter	'African Slavery and Other Forms of Social Oppression on the Upper Guinea Coast', *Journal of African History*, vii, 3, 1966, pp. 431–43
ROSS, David A.	'The Career of Domingo Martinez in the Bight of Benin 1833–64', *Journal of African History*, vi, 1, 1965, pp. 79–90
RUBENSON, S.	'The Protectorate Paragraph of the Wichale Treaty', *Journal of African History*, v, 2, 1964, pp. 243–83
	'Professor Giglio, Antonelli and Article XVII of the Treaty of Wichale', *Journal of African History*, vii, 3, 1966, pp. 445–57
SAINT-MARTIN, Yves	*Une source de l'histoire Coloniale du Sénégal: les rapports de la situation politique (1874–91)*, Dakar 1966
SALIM, A. I.	*Swahili-Speaking Peoples of Kenya's Coast 1895–1965*, Nairobi 1973
SANDERSON, G. N.	*England, Europe and the Upper Nile 1882–1899*, Edinburgh 1965
SCHNAPPER, B.	*La Politique et le Commerce français dans le Golfe de Guinée de 1838 à 1871*, Paris 1961

SHUKRY, M. F.	*The Khedive Ismail and Slavery in the Sudan (1863–79)*, Cairo 1939
SIEGEL, B. J.	'Some Methodological Considerations for a Comparative Study of Slavery', *American Anthropologist*, n.s., 47, 1945, pp. 357–92
SMALLDONE, Joseph, P.	'Firearms in the Central Sudan: A Revaluation', *Journal of African History*, xiii, 4, 1972, pp. 591–607
SMITH, Alison	'The Southern Section of the Interior, 1840–84', in R. Oliver and G. Mathew (eds.), *History of East Africa*, I, Oxford 1963, pp. 254–96
SMITH, Edwin W. and DALE, A. M.	*The Ila-Speaking Peoples of Northern Rhodesia*, 2 vols., New York 1968 (first published 1920)
SMITH, Mary	*Baba of Karo*, London 1954
SMITH, M. G.	'Slavery and Emancipation in Two Societies', *Social and Economic Studies*, iii, 1954, pp. 239–90
	Government in Zazzau 1800–1950, London 1960
	'Historical and Cultural Conditions of Political Corruption among the Hausa', *Comparative Studies in Society and History*, vi, 1963–4, pp. 164–94
SMITH, Robert	See AJAYI, Ade and SMITH, Robert
SOULSBY, H. S.	*The Right of Search and the Slave Trade in Anglo-American Relations, 1814–62*, Baltimore 1933
STANNUS, H. S.	'The Wayao of Nyasaland', *Harvard African Studies*, III, Cambridge, Mass. 1922 (eds. E. A. Hooten and N. I. Bates)
TEMPERLEY, Howard	*British Antislavery 1833–1870*, London 1972
TUDEN, A.	'Ila Slavery', *Rhodes-Livingstone Journal*, xxiv, Dec. 1958, pp. 68–75
	'Slavery and Stratification among the Ila of Central Africa', in A. Tuden and L. Plotnikov, *Social Stratification in Africa*, London and New York 1970, pp. 47–58
UCHENDU, Victor	*The Igbo of Southeast Nigeria*, New York 1965
VANDERWOUDE, E.	'Het Incident Net de Brabo 1888', *Africa Tervuren*, ix, 3, 1965, pp. 63–75
VANSINA, J.	*Kingdoms of the Savanna*, Wisconsin 1966
	The Tio Kingdom of the Middle Congo 1880–92, Oxford 1973
VERGER, Pierre	*Flux et reflux de la traite des Nègres entre le Golfe de Benin et Bahia De Todos os Santos du XVIIe au XIXe Siècles*, Paris and The Hague 1968
WALKER, E. A.	*A History of South Africa*, London 1928
WARD, W. E. F.	*The Royal Navy and the Slavers*, London 1969

WEBSTER, C. K.	*The Foreign Policy of Castlereagh*, I, 1812–15, London 1931
	II, 1815–22, London 1947
WHITE, Gavin	'Firearms in Africa: an Introduction', *Journal of African History*, xii, 9, 1971, pp. 173–84
WHITE, James P.	'The Sanford Exploring Expeditions', *Journal of African History*, viii, 2, 1967.
WILKS, Ivor	'Asante Policy towards Hausa Trade in the Nineteenth Century', C. Meillassoux, *The Development of Indigenous Trade and Markets in West Africa*, Oxford 1971, pp. 124–41
WILLEQUET, Jacques	*Le Baron Lambermont*, Brussels 1971
WILLIAMS, Gomer	*History of the Liverpool Privateers and Letters of Marque with an Account of the Liverpool Slave Trade*, London and Liverpool 1897
WILLIAMS, Eric	*Capitalism and Slavery*, Chapel Hill 1944
YELD, E. R.	'Islam and Social Stratification in Northern Nigeria', *British Journal of Sociology*, xi, pp. 112–28

Unpublished Dissertations and Theses

ADERIBIGBE, A. A. B.	'Expansion of the Lagos Protectorate, 1863–1900', London Ph.D. thesis 1959
BENNETT, N. R.	'The Arab Power of Tanganyika in the Nineteenth Century', Boston Ph.D. thesis 1961
BERG, F. J.	Mombasa under the Busaidi Sultanate: The City and Its Hinterland in the Nineteenth Century', Wisconsin Ph.D. thesis 1971
CAULK R. A.	'The Origins and Development of the Foreign Policy of Menelik II, 1867–96', London Ph.D. thesis 1966
DARKWAH, R. H. F.	'The Rise of the Kingdom of Shoa, 1813–89', London Ph.D. thesis, 1966
GAVIN, R. J.	'Palmerston's Policy towards East and West Africa 1830–65', Cambridge Ph.D. thesis 1958
GILLARD, D. R.	'Lord Salisbury's Foreign Policy, 1888–92, with Special Reference to Anglo-German Relations', London Ph.D. thesis 1952
GLYN-JONES, E.	'Britain and the End of Slavery in East Africa', Oxford B.Litt. thesis 1956
GORDON, J.	'The Development of the Legal System in the Lagos Colony, 1862–1905', London Ph.D. thesis 1967

HANSON, David — 'The Maccube of Fouta Toro', Wisconsin M.A. 1971

HERRINGTON, Elsie I. — 'British Measures for the Suppression of the Slave Trade from the West Coast of Africa 1807–33', London M.A. thesis 1923

HOPKINS, A. G. — 'An Economic History of Lagos, 1880–1914', London Ph.D. thesis 1964

DE KIEWIET, M. J. — 'History of the Imperial British East Africa Company, 1876–95', London Ph.D. thesis 1955

LEVEEN, E. Philip — 'British Slave Trade Suppression Policies 1821–65: Impact and Implications', Ph.D. Chicago (Economics) 1971

LOW, D. A. — 'The British and Uganda 1862–1900', Oxford Ph.D. thesis 1957

MACKENZIE, K. — 'Great Britain and the Abolition of the Slave Trade by the Other Powers (1812–22)', Oxford B.Litt. 1952

NWORAH, K. K. D. — 'Humanitarian Pressure Groups and British Attitudes to West Africa 1895–1915', London Ph.D. thesis 1966

OGEDENGBE, K. O. — 'The Aboh Kingdom of the Lower Niger c. 1650–1900', Wisconsin Ph.D. thesis 1971

PICQUART, Agnès — 'Le commerce des Armes à Djibouti de 1888 à 1914', Sorbonne Mémoire de Maïtrise 1970

SMITH, Alan B. — 'History of the East African Posts and Telecommunications Administration 1837–1967', Nairobi Ph.D. thesis 1971

STILLIARD, N. H. — 'The Rise and Development of Legitimate Trade in Palm Oil with West Africa', Birmingham M.A. thesis 1938

SWAISLAND, H. C. — 'The Aborigines' Protection Society and British Southern and West Africa', Oxford Ph.D. thesis 1967

WOLFSON, Freda — 'British Relations with the Gold Coast, 1843–88', London Ph.D. thesis 1950

WOZENCROFT, G. — 'The Relations between England and France during the Aberdeen-Guizot Ministries (1841–6)', London Ph.D. thesis 1932

Unpublished Papers

ADEFUZE, Ade 'Palwo Economy, Society and Politics'. Paper presented at Makerere University, 22 April 1972

MCKAY, William 'Some Notes on the Southern Kenya Coast in the Nineteenth Century'. Seminar paper, University of Nairobi, 13 Sept. 1972

UCHENDU, Victor 'The Institutions of Slavery in Southeast Nigerian Societies'. Paper read at the Central States Anthropological Meeting, St. Louis, Missouri, 28 April 1966

UNOMA, A. C. 'Vbandevra and Political Change in a Nyamwezi Kingdom: Unyanyembe during 1840–90'. Paper presented to the Social Science Conference of East Africa, University of Dar-es-Salaam, Dec. 1970

YLVISAKER, Margarite 'Shamba na Konde: Land Usage in the Hinterland of the Lamu Archipelago 1865–1895'. Seminar paper, University of Nairobi, Oct. 1971

General Act for the Repression of African Slave Trade*

(*Brussels, 2 July 1890*)

[*Translation*]

IN THE NAME OF GOD ALMIGHTY . . .

[*The list of the heads of the signatory States follows*]

Being equally actuated by the firm intention of putting an end to the crimes and devastations engendered by the traffic in African slaves, of efficiently protecting the aboriginal population of Africa, and of securing for that vast continent the benefits of peace and civilization;

Wishing to give fresh sanction to the decisions already adopted in the same sense and at different times by the powers, to complete the results secured by them, and to draw up a body of measures guaranteeing the accomplishment of the work which is the object of their common solicitude;

Have resolved, in pursuance of the invitation addressed to them by the Government of His Majesty the King of the Belgians, in agreement with the Government of Her Majesty the Queen of Great Britain and Ireland, Empress of India, to convene for this purpose a conference at Brussels, and have named as their plenipotentiaries: . . .

[*The names and titles of the Plenipotentiaries follow*]

Who, being furnished with full powers, which have been found to be in good and due form, have adopted the following provisions:

Chapter I. Slave-Trade Countries—Measures to be taken in the Places of Origin

Article I

The powers declare that the most effective means of counteracting the slave-trade in the interior of Africa are the following:

1. Progressive organization of the administrative, judicial, religious, and military services in the African territories placed under the sovereignty or protectorate of civilized nations.

2. The gradual establishment in the interior, by the powers to which the territories are subject, of strongly occupied stations, in such a way as to make their protective or repressive action effectively felt in the territories devastated by slave hunting.

3. The construction of roads, and in particular of railways, connecting the advanced stations with the coast, and permitting easy access to the inland waters, and to such of the upper courses of the rivers and streams as are broken by rapids and cataracts, with a view to substituting economical and rapid means of transportation for the present system of carriage by men.

4. Establishment of steam-boats on the inland navigable waters and on the lakes, supported by fortified posts established on the banks.

* This translation differs in wording but not in meaning from that published in Hertslet, *Map, II*, referred to in footnotes.

5. Establishment of telegraphic lines, insuring the communication of the posts and stations with the coast and with the administrative centres.

6. Organization of expeditions and flying columns, to keep up the communication of the stations with each other and with the coast to support repressive action, and to insure the security of high roads.

7. Restriction of the importation of fire-arms, at least of those of modern pattern, and of ammunition throughout the entire extent of the territory in which the slave-trade is carried on.

Article II

The stations, the inland cruisers organized by each power in its waters, and the posts which serve as ports of register for them shall, independently of their principal task, which is to prevent the capture of slaves and intercept the routes of the slave trade, have the following subsidiary duties:

1. To support and, if necessary, to serve as a refuge for the native population, whether placed under the sovereignty or the protectorate of the State to which the station is subject, or independent, and temporarily for all other natives in case of imminent danger; to place the population of the first of these categories in a position to co-operate for their own defence; to diminish intestine wars between tribes by means of arbitration; to initiate them in agricultural labour and in the industrial arts so as to increase their welfare; to raise them to civilization and bring about the extinction of barbarous customs, such as cannibalism, and human sacrifices.

2. To give aid and protection to commercial enterprises; to watch over their legality by especially controlling contracts for service with natives, and to prepare the way for the foundation of permanent centres of cultivation and of commercial settlements.

3. To protect, without distinction of creed, the missions which are already or that may hereafter be established.

4. To provide for the sanitary service and to extend hospitality and help to explorers and to all who take part in Africa in the work of repressing the slave-trade.

Article III

The powers exercising a sovereignty or a protectorate in Africa confirm and give precision to their former declarations, and engage to proceed gradually, as circumstances may permit, either by the means above indicated, or by any other means that they may consider suitable, with the repression of the slave-trade, each State in its respective possessions and under its own direction. Whenever they consider it possible, they shall lend their good offices to such powers as, with a purely humanitarian object, may be engaged in Africa in the fulfilment of a similar mission.

Article IV

The States exercising sovereign powers or protectorates in Africa may in all cases delegate to companies provided with charters all or a portion of the engagements which they assume in virtue of Article III. They remain, nevertheless, directly responsible for the engagements which they contract by the present act, and guarantee the execution thereof. The powers promise to encourage, aid and protect such national associations and enterprises due to private initiative as may wish to co-operate in their possessions in the repression of the slave-trade, subject to their receiving previous authorization, such authorization being revokable at any time, subject also to their being directed and controlled, and to the exclusion of the exercise of rights of sovereignty.

Article V

The contracting powers pledge themselves, unless this has already been provided for by laws in accordance with the spirit of the present article, to enact or propose to their respective legislative bodies, in the course of one year at the latest from the date of the signing of the present general act, a law rendering applicable, on the one hand, the provisions of their penal laws concerning grave offences against the person, to the organizers and abettors of slave-hunting, to those guilty of mutilating male adults and children, and to all persons taking part in the capture of slaves by violence; and, on the other hand, the provisions relating to offences against individual liberty, to carriers and transporters of, and to dealers in slaves.

The accessories and accomplices of the different categories of slave captors and dealers above specified shall be punished with penalties proportionate to those incurred by the principals.

Guilty persons who may have escaped from the jurisdiction of the authorities of the country where the crimes or offences have been committed shall be arrested either on communication of the incriminating evidence by the authorities who have ascertained the violation of the law, or on production of any other proof of guilt by the power in whose territory they may have been discovered, and shall be kept, without other formality, at the disposal of the tribunals competent to try them.

The powers shall communicate to one another, with the least possible delay, the laws or decrees existing or promulgated in execution of the present Article.

Article VI

Slaves liberated in consequence of the stoppage or dispersion of a convoy in the interior of the continent, shall be sent back, if circumstances permit, to their country of origin; if not, the local authorities shall facilitate, as much as possible, their means of living, and if they desire it, help them to settle on the spot.

Article VII

Any fugitive slave claiming, on the continent, the protection of the signatory powers, shall receive it, and shall be received in the camps and stations officially established by said powers, or on board of the vessels of the State plying on the lakes and rivers. Private stations and boats are only permitted to exercise the right of asylum subject to the previous consent of the State.

Article VIII

The experience of all nations that have intercourse with Africa having shown the pernicious and preponderating part played by fire-arms in operations connected with the slave-trade as well as internal wars between the native tribes; and this same experience having clearly proved that the preservation of the African population whose existence it is the express wish of the powers to protect, is a radical impossibility, if measures restricting the trade in fire-arms and ammunition are not adopted, the powers decide, so far as the present state of their frontiers permits, that the importation of fire-arms, and especially of rifles and improved weapons, as well as of powder, ball and cartidges, is, except in the cases and under the conditions provided for in the following Article, prohibited in the territories comprised between the 20th parallel of North latitude and the 22nd parallel of South latitude, and extending westward to the Atlantic Ocean and eastward to the Indian Ocean and its dependencies, including the islands adjacent to the coast within 100 nautical miles from the shore.

Article IX

The introduction of fire-arms and ammunition, when there shall be occasion to authorize it in the possessions of the signatory powers that exercise rights of sovereignty or of protectorate in Africa, shall be regulated, unless identical or stricter regulations have already been enforced, in the following manner in the zone defined in Article VIII:

All imported fire-arms shall be deposited, at the cost, risk and peril of the importers, in a public warehouse under the supervision of the State government. No withdrawal of fire-arms or imported ammunition shall take place from such warehouses without the previous authorization of the said government. This authorization shall, except in the cases hereinafter specified, be refused for the withdrawal of all arms for accurate firing, such as rifles, magazine guns, or breech-loaders, whether whole or in detached pieces, their cartridges, caps, or other ammunition intended for them.

In seaports and under conditions affording the needful guarantees, the respective governments may permit private warehouses, but only for ordinary powder and for flint-lock muskets, and to the exclusion of improved arms and ammunition therefor.

Independently of the measures directly taken by governments for the arming of the public force and the organization of their defence, individual exceptions may be allowed in the case of persons furnishing sufficient guarantees that the weapon and ammunition delivered to them shall not be given, assigned or sold to third parties, and for travellers provided with a declaration of their government stating that the weapon and ammunition are intended for their personal defence exclusively.

All arms, in the cases provided for in the preceding paragraph, shall be registered and marked by the supervising authorities, who shall deliver to the persons in question permits to bear arms, stating the name of the bearer and showing the stamp with which the weapon is marked. These permits shall be revocable in case proof is furnished that they have been improperly used, and shall be issued for five years only, but may be renewed.

The above rule as to warehousing shall also apply to gunpowder.

Only flint-lock guns, with unrifled barrels, and common gunpowder known as trade powder, may be withdrawn from the warehouses for sale. At each withdrawal of arms and ammunition of this kind for sale, the local authorities shall determine the regions in which such arms and ammunition may be sold. The regions in which the slave-trade is carried on shall always be excluded. Persons authorized to take arms or powder out of the public warehouses, shall present to the State government, every six months, detailed lists indicating the destinations of the arms and powder sold, as well as the quantities still remaining in the warehouses.

Article X

The Governments shall take all such measures as they may deem necessary to insure as complete a fulfilment as possible of the provisions respecting the importation, sale and transportation of fire-arms and ammunition, as well as to prevent either the entry or exit thereof via their inland frontiers, or the passage thereof to regions where the slave-trade is rife.

The authorization of transit within the limits of the zone specified in Article VIII shall not be withheld when the arms and ammunition are to pass across the territory of the signatory or adherent power occupying the coast, towards inland territories under the sovereignty or protectorate of another signatory or adherent power, unless this latter power have direct access to the sea through its own territory. If this access be wholly interrupted, the authorization of transit can not be withheld. Any application for transit must be accompanied by a declaration emanating from the government of the power having the inland possessions, and certifying that the said arms and ammunition are not intended for sale, but are for the use of the authorities of such power, or of the military forces necessary for the protection of the missionary or commercial stations, or of persons mentioned by name in the declaration. Nevertheless, the territorial power of the coast retains the right to stop, exceptionally and provisionally, the transit of improved arms and ammunition across its territory, if, in consequence of inland disturbances or other serious danger, there is ground for fearing lest the despatch of arms and ammunition may comprise its own safety.

Article XI

The powers shall communicate to one another information relating to the traffic in fire-arms and ammunition, the permits granted, and the measures of repression in force in their respective territories.

Article XII

The powers engage to adopt or to propose to their respective legislative bodies the measures necessary everywhere to secure the punishment of infringers of the prohibitions contained in Articles VIII and IX, and that of their accomplices, beside the seizure and confiscation of the prohibited arms and ammunition, either by fine or imprisonment, or by both of these penalties, in proportion to the importance of the infraction and in accordance with the gravity of each case.

Article XIII

The signatory powers that have possessions in Africa in contact with the zone specified in Article VIII, bind themselves to take the necessary measures for preventing the introduction of fire-arms and ammunition across their inland frontiers into the regions of said zone, at least that of improved arms and cartridges.

Article XIV

The system stipulated in Articles VIII and XIII, shall remain in force for twelve years. In case none of the contracting parties shall have given notice twelve months before the expiration of this period, of its intention to put an end to it, or shall have demanded its revision, it shall remain obligatory for two years longer, and shall thus continue in force from two years to two years.

Chapter II. Caravan Routes and Transportation of Slaves by Land

Article XV

Independently of the repressive or protective action which they exercise in the centres of the slave-trade, it shall be the duty of the stations, cruisers and posts, whose establishment is provided for in Article II, and of all other stations established or recognized by Article IV, by each government in its possessions, to watch, so far as circumstances shall permit, and in proportion to the progress of their administrative organization, the roads travelled in their territory by slave-dealers, to stop convoys on their march, or to pursue them wherever their action can be legally exercised.

Article XVI

In the regions of the coast known to serve habitually as places of passage or terminal points for slave-traffic coming from the interior, as well as at the points of intersection of the principal caravan routes crossing the zone contiguous to the coast already subject to the control of the sovereign or protective powers, posts shall be established under the conditions and with the reservations mentioned in Article III, by the authorities to which the territories are subject, for the purpose of intercepting the convoys and liberating the slaves.

Article XVII

A strict watch shall be organized by the local authorities at the ports and places near the coast, with a view to preventing the sale and shipment of slaves brought from the interior, as well as the formation and departure landwards of bands of slave-hunters and dealers.

Caravans arriving at the coast or in its vicinity, as well as those arriving in the interior at a locality occupied by the territorial power, shall, on their arrival, be subjected to a minute inspection as to the persons composing them. Any such person being ascertained to have been captured or carried off by force, or mutilated, either in his native place or on the way, shall be set free.

Article XVIII

In the possessions of each of the contracting powers, it shall be the duty of the government to protect liberated slaves, to return them, if possible, to their country, to procure means of subsistence for them, and, in particular, to take charge of the education and subsequent employment of abandoned children.

Article XIX

The penal arrangements provided for by Article V shall be applicable to all offences committed in the course of operations connected with the transportation of and traffic in slaves on land whenever such offences may be ascertained to have been committed.

Any person having incurred a penalty in consequence of an offence provided for by the present general act, shall incur the obligation of furnishing security before being able to engage in any commercial transaction in countries where the slave-trade is carried on.

Chapter III. Repression of the Slave-Trade by Sea

Section I. General provisions

Article XX

The signatory powers recognize the desirability of taking steps in common for the more effective repression of the slave-trade in the maritime zone in which it still exists.

Article XXI

This zone extends, on the one hand, between the coasts of the Indian Ocean (those of the Persian Gulf and of the Red Sea included), from Beloochistan to Cape Tangalane (Quilimane); and, on the other hand, a conventional line which first follows the meridian from Tangalane till it intersects the 26th degree of South latitude; it is then merged in this parallel, then passes round the Island of Madagascar by the east, keeping 20 miles off the east and north shore, till it intersects the meridian at Cape Ambre. From this point the limit of the zone is determined by an oblique line, which extends to the coast of Beloochistan, passing 20 miles off Cape Ras-el-Had.

Article XXII

The signatory powers of the present general act,—among whom exist special conventions for the suppression of the slave-trade, have agreed to restrict the clauses of those conventions concerning the reciprocal right of visit, of search and of seizure of vessels at sea, to the above-mentioned zone.

Article XXIII

The same powers also agree to limit the above mentioned right to vessels whose tonnage is less than 500 tons. This stipulation shall be revised as soon as experience shall have shown the necessity thereof.

Article XXIV

All other provisions of the conventions concluded for the suppression of the slave-trade between the aforesaid powers shall remain in force provided they are not modified by the present general act.

Article XXV

The signatory powers engage to adopt measures to prevent the unlawful use of their flag, and to prevent the transportation of slaves on vessels authorized to fly their colours.

Article XXVI

The signatory powers engage to adopt all measures necessary to facilitate the speedy exchange of information calculated to lead to the discovery of persons taking part in operations connected with the slave-trade.

Article XXVII

At least one international bureau shall be created; it shall be established at Zanzibar. The high contracting parties engage to forward to it all the documents specified in Article XLI, as well as all information of any kind likely to assist in the suppression of the slave-trade.

Article XXVIII

Any slave who has taken refuge on board a ship of war bearing the flag of one of the signatory powers, shall be immediately and definitely set free. Such freedom, however, shall not withdraw him from the competent jurisdiction if he has been guilty of any crime or offence at common law.

Article XXIX

Any slave detained against his will on board of a native vessel shall have the right to demand his liberty. His release may be ordered by any agent of any of the signatory powers on whom the present general act confers the right of ascertaining the status of persons on board of such vessels, although such release shall not withdraw him from the competent jurisdiction if he has committed any crime or offence at common law.

Section II. Regulation concerning the use of the flag and supervision by cruisers

1. Rules for granting the flag to native vessels, and as to crew lists and manifests of black passengers on board

Article XXX

The signatory powers engage to exercise a strict surveillance over native vessels authorized to carry their flag in the zone mentioned in Article XXI, and over the commercial operations carried on by such vessels.

Article XXXI

The term 'native vessel' applies to vessels fulfilling one of the following conditions:
1. It shall present the outward appearance of native build or rigging.
2. It shall be manned by a crew of whom the captain and a majority of the seamen belong by origin to one of the countries on the coast of the Indian Ocean, the Red Sea, or the Persian Gulf.

Article XXXII

The authorization to carry the flag of one of the said powers shall in future be granted only to such native vessels as shall satisfy at the same time the three following conditions:
1. Fitters-out or owners of ships must be either subjects of or persons protected by the power whose flag they ask to carry.
2. They shall be obliged to prove that they possess real estate situated in the district of the authority to whom their application is addressed, or to furnish *bona fide* security as a guarantee of the payment of such fines as may be incurred.
3. The above-named fitters-out or owners of ships, as well as the captain of the vessel, shall prove that they enjoy a good reputation, and that in particular they have never been sentenced to punishment for acts connected with the slave-trade.

Article XXXIII

This authorization granted shall be renewed every year. It may at any time be suspended or withdrawn by the authorities of the power whose colours the vessel carries.

Article XXXIV

The act of authorization shall contain the statements necessary to establish the identity of the vessel. The captain shall have the keeping thereof. The name of the native vessel and the amount of its tonnage shall be cut and painted in Latin characters on the stern, and the initial or initials of the name of the port of registry, as well as the registration number in the series of the numbers of that port, shall be printed in black on the sails.

Article XXXV

A list of the crew shall be issued to the captain of the vessel at the port of departure by the authorities of the power whose colours it carries. It shall be renewed at every fresh venture of the vessel, or, at the latest, at the end of a year, and in accordance with the following provisions:

1. The vessel shall be visaed at the departure of the vessel by the authority that has issued it.

2. No negro can be engaged as a seaman on a vessel without having previously been questioned by the authority of the power whose colours it carries, or, in default thereof, by the territorial authority, with a view to ascertaining the fact of his having contracted a free engagement.

3. This authority shall see that the proportion of seamen and boys is not out of proportion to the tonnage or rigging.

4. The authorities who shall have questioned the men before their departure shall enter them on the list of the crew in which they shall be mentioned with a summary description of each of them alongside his name.

5. In order the more effectively to prevent any substitution, the seamen may, moreover, be provided with a distinctive mark.

Article XXXVI

When the captain of a vessel shall desire to take negro passengers on board, he shall make his declaration to that effect to the authority of the power whose colours he carries, or in default thereof, to the territorial authority. The passengers shall be questioned, and after it has been ascertained that they embarked of their own free will, they shall be entered in a special manifest, bearing the description of each of them alongside of his name, and specially sex and height. Negro children shall not be taken as passengers unless they are accompanied by their relations, or by persons whose respectability is well known. At the departure, the passenger-roll shall be visaed by the aforesaid authority after it has been called. If there are no passengers on board, this shall be specially mentioned in the crew-list.

Article XXXVII

At the arrival at any port of call or of destination, the captain of the vessel shall show to the authority of the power whose flag he carries, or, in default thereof, to the territorial authority, the crew-list, and, if need be, the passenger-roll previously delivered. The authority shall check the passengers who have reached their destination or who are stopping in a port of call, and shall mention their landing in the roll. At the departure of the vessel, the same authority shall affix a fresh *visé* to the list and roll, and call the roll of the passengers.

Article XXXVIII

On the African coast and on the adjacent islands, no negro passengers shall be taken on board of a native vessel, except in localities where there is a resident authority belonging to one of the signatory powers.

Throughout the extent of the zone mentioned in Article XXI, no negro passengers shall be landed from a native vessel except at a place in which there is a resident officer belonging to one of the high contracting powers, and unless such officer is present at the landing.

Cases of *vis major* that may have caused an infraction of these provisions shall be examined by the authority of the power whose colours the vessel carries, or, in default thereof, by the territorial authority of the port at which the vessel in question calls.

Article XXXIX

The provisions of Articles XXXV. XXXVI, XXXVII, and XXXVIII are not applicable to vessels only partially decked, having a crew not exceeding ten men, and fulfilling one of the two following conditions:

1. That it be exclusively used for fishing within the territorial waters.
2. That it be occupied in the petty coasting trade between the different ports of the same territorial power, without going further than five miles from the coast.

These different boats shall receive, as the case may be, a special licence from the territorial or consular authority, which shall be renewed every year, and subject to revocation as provided in Article XL, the uniform model of which licence is annexed to the present general act and shall be communicated to the international information office.

Article XL

Any act or attempted act connected with the slave-trade that can be legally shown to have been committed by the captain, fitter-out, or owner of a ship authorized to carry the flag of one of the signatory powers, or having procured the licence provided for in Article XXXIX, shall entail the immediate withdrawal of the said authorization or licence. All violations of the provisions of Section 2 of Chapter III shall render the person guilty thereof liable to the penalties provided by the special laws and ordinances of each of the contracting parties.

Article XLI

The signatory powers engage to deposit at the international information office the specimen forms of the following documents:

1. Licence to carry the flag;
2. The crew-list;
3. The negro passenger list.

These documents, the tenor of which may vary according to the different regulations of each country, shall necessarily contain the following particulars, drawn up in one of the European languages:

1. As regards the authorization to carry the flag:
(*a*) The name, tonnage, rig, and the principal dimensions of the vessel;
(*b*) The register number and the signal letter of the port of registry;
(*c*) The date of obtaining the licence, and the office held by the person who issued it.
2. As regards the list of the crew:
(*a*) The name of the vessel, of the captain and the fitter-out or owner;
(*b*) The tonnage of the vessel;
(*c*) The register number and the port of registry, its destination, as well as the particulars specified in Article XXV.
3. As regards the list of negro passengers:
The name of the vessel which conveys them, and the particulars indicated in Article XXXVI, for the proper identification of the passengers.

The signatory powers shall take the necessary measures so that the territorial authorities or their consuls may send to the same office certified copies of all authorizations to carry their flag as soon as such authorizations shall have been granted, as well as notices of the withdrawal of any such authorization.

The provisions of the present article have reference only to papers intended for native vessels.

2. *The stopping of suspected vessels*

Article XLII

When the officers in command of war-vessels of any of the signatory powers have reason to believe that a vessel whose tonnage is less than 500 tons, and which is found navigating in the above-named zone, is engaged in the slave-trade or is guilty of the fraudulent use of a flag, they may examine the ship's papers.

The present article does not imply any change in the present state of things as regards jurisdiction in territorial waters.

Article XLIII

To this end, a boat commanded by a naval officer in uniform may be sent to board the suspected vessel after it has been hailed and informed of this intention.

The officers sent on board of the vessel which has been stopped shall act with all possible consideration and moderation.

Article XLIV

The examination of the ship's papers shall consist of the examination of the following documents:

1. As regards native vessels, the papers mentioned in Article XLI.

2. As regards other vessels, the documents required by the different treaties or conventions that are in force.

The examination of the ship's papers only authorizes the calling of the roll of the crew and passengers in the cases and in accordance with the conditions provided for in the following article.

Article LXV

The examination of the cargo or the search can only take place in the case of vessels sailing under the flag of one of the powers that have concluded, or may hereafter conclude the special conventions provided for in Article XXII, and in accordance with the provisions of such conventions.

Article XLVI

Before leaving the detained vessel, the officer shall draw up a minute according to the forms and in the language in use in the country to which he belongs.

This minute shall be dated and signed by the officer, and shall recite the facts.

The captain of the detained vessel, as well as the witnesses, shall have the right to cause to be added to the minutes any explanations they may think expedient.

Article XLVII

The commander of a man-of-war who has detained a vessel under a foreign flag shall, in all cases, make a report thereof to his own government, and state the grounds upon which he has acted.

Article XLVIII

A summary of this report, as well as a copy of the minute drawn up by the officer on board of the detained vessel, shall be sent, as soon as possible, to the international information office, which shall communicate the same to the nearest consular or territorial authority of the power whose flag the vessel in question has shown. Duplicates of these documents shall be kept in the archives of the bureau.

Article XLIX

If, in performing the acts of supervision mentioned in the preceding articles, the officer in command of the cruiser is convinced that an act connected with the slave-trade has been committed on board during the passage, or that irrefutable proofs exist against the captain, or fitter-out, for accusing him of fraudulent use of the flag, or fraud, or participation in the slave-trade, he shall conduct the arrested vessel to the nearest port of the zone where there is a competent magistrate of the power whose flag has been used.

Each signatory power engages to appoint in the zone, and to make known to the international information office, the territorial or consular authorities or special delegates who are competent in the above mentioned cases.

A suspected vessel may also be turned over to a cruiser of its own nation, if the latter consents to take charge of it.

3. Of the examination and trial of vessels seized

Article L

The magistrate referred to in the preceding article, to whom the arrested vessel has been turned over, shall proceed to make a full investigation, according to the laws and rules of his country, in the presence of an officer belonging to the foreign cruiser.

Article LI

If it is proved by the inquiry that the flag has been fraudulently used, the vessel shall remain at the disposal of its captor.

Article LII

If the examination shows an act connected with the slave-trade, proved by the presence on board of slaves destined for sale, or any other offence connected with the slave-trade for which provision is made by special convention, the vessel and cargo shall remain sequestrated in charge of the magistrate who shall have conducted the inquiry.

The captain and crew shall be turned over to the tribunals designated by Articles LIV and LVI. The slaves shall be set at liberty as soon as judgement has been pronounced.

In the cases provided for by this article, liberated slaves shall be disposed of in accordance with the special conventions concluded, or to be concluded, between the signatory powers. In default of such conventions, the said slaves shall be turned over to the local authority, to be sent back if possible, to their country of origin; if not, this authority shall facilitate to them, in so far as may be in its power, the means of livelihood, and, if they desire it, of settling on the spot.

Article LIII

If it shall be proved by the inquiry that the vessel has been illegally arrested, there shall be clear title to an indemnity in proportion to the damages suffered by the vessel being taken out of its course.

The amount of this indemnity shall be fixed by the authority that has conducted the inquiry.

Article LIV

In case of the officer of the capturing vessel does not accept the conclusions of the inquiry held in his presence, the matter shall be turned over to the tribunal of the nation whose flag the captured vessel has borne.

No exception shall be made to this rule, unless the disagreement arises in respect of the amount of the indemnity stipulated in Article LIII, and this shall be fixed by arbitration, as specified in the following article.

Article LV

The capturing officer and the authority which has conducted the inquiry shall each appoint a referee within forty-eight hours, and the two arbitrators shall have twenty-four hours to choose an umpire. The arbitrators shall, as far as possible, be chosen from among the diplomatic, consular, or judicial officers of the signatory powers. Natives in the pay of the contracting Governments are formally excluded. The decision shall be by a majority of votes, and be considered as final.

If the court of arbitration is not constituted in the time indicated, the procedure in respect of the indemnity, as in that of damages, shall be in accordance with the provisions of Article LVIII, paragraph 2.

Article LVI

The cases shall be brought with the least possible delay before the tribunal of the nation whose flag has been used by the accused. However, the consuls or any other authority of the same nation as the accused, specially commissioned to this end, may be authorized by their Government to pronounce judgement instead of the tribunal.

Article LVII

The procedure and trial of violations of the provisions of Chapter III shall always be conducted in as summary a manner as is permitted by the laws and regulations in force in the territories subject to the authority of the signatory powers.

Article LVIII

Any decision of the national tribunal or authorities referred to in Article LVI, declaring that the seized vessel did not carry on the slave-trade, shall be immediately enforced, and the vessel shall be at perfect liberty to continue on its course.

In this case, the captain or owner of any vessel that has been seized without legitimate ground of suspicion, or subjected to annoyance, shall have the right of claiming damages, the amount of which shall be fixed by agreement between the Governments directly interested, or by arbitration, and shall be paid within a period of six months from the date of the judgement acquitting the captured vessel.

Article LIX

In the case of condemnation, the squestered vessel shall be declared lawfully seized for the benefit of the captor.

The captain, crew, and all other persons found guilty shall be punished according to the gravity of the crimes or offences committed by them, and in accordance with Article V.

Article LX

The provisions of Articles L to LIX do not in any way affect the jurisdiction or procedure of existing special tribunals, or of such as may hereafter be formed to take cognizance of offences connected with the slave-trade.

Article LXI

The high contracting parties engage to make known to one another, reciprocally, the instructions which they shall give, for the execution of the provisions of Chapter III, to the commanders of their men-of-war navigating the seas of the zone referred to.

Chapter IV. Countries to which Slaves are sent, whose Institutions Recognize the Existence of Domestic Slavery

Article LXII

The contracting powers whose institutions recognize the existence of domestic slavery, and whose possessions, in consequence thereof, in or out of Africa, serve, in spite of the vigilance of the authorities, as places of destination for African slaves, pledge themselves to prohibit their importation, transit and departure, as well as the trade in slaves. The most active and the strictest supervision shall be enforced at all places where the arrival, transit, and departure of African slaves take place.

Article LXIII

Slaves set free under the provisions of the preceding article shall, if circumstances permit, be sent back to the country from whence they came. In all cases they shall receive letters of liberation from the competent authorities, and shall be entitled to their protection and assistance for the purpose of obtaining means of subsistence.

Article LXIV

Any fugitive slave arriving at the frontier of any of the powers mentioned in Article LXII shall be considered free, and shall have the right to claim letters of release from the competent authorities.

Article LXV

Any sale or transaction to which the slaves referred to in Articles LXVIII and LXIV may have been subjected through circumstances of any kind whatsoever, shall be considered as null and void.

Article LXVI

Native vessels carrying the flag of one of the countries mentioned in Article LXVII, if there is any indication that they are employed in operations connected with the slave-trade, shall be subjected by the local authorities in the ports frequented by them to a strict examination of their crews and passengers both on arrival and departure. If African slaves are found on board, judicial proceedings shall be instituted against the vessel and against all persons who may be implicated. Slaves found on board shall receive letters of release through the authorities who have seized the vessels.

Article LXVII

Penal provisions similar to those provided for by Article V shall be enacted against persons importing, transporting, and trading in African slaves, against the mutilators of male children or adults, and those who traffic in them, as well as against their associates and accomplices.

Article LXVIII

The signatory powers recognize the great importance of the law respecting the prohibition of the slave-trade sanctioned by His Majesty the Emperor of the Ottomans on the 4th (16th) of December, 1889 (22 Rebi-ul-Akhir, 1307), and they are assured that an active surveillance will be organized by the Ottoman authorities, especially on the west coast of Arabia and on the routes which place that coast in communication with the other possession of His Imperial Majesty in Asia.

Article LXIX

His Majesty the Shah of Persia consents to organize an active surveillance in the territorial waters and those off the coast of the Persian Gulf and Gulf of Oman which are under his sovereignty, and on the inland routes which serve for the transportation of slaves. The magistrates and other authorities shall, to this effect, receive the necessary powers.

Article LXX

His Highness the Sultan of Zanzibar consents to give his most effective support to the repression of crimes and offences committed by African slave-traders on land as well as at sea. The tribunals created for this purpose in the Sultanate of Zanzibar shall rigorously enforce the penal provisions mentioned in Article V. In order to render more secure the freedom of liberated slaves, both in virtue of the provisions of the present general act and of the decrees adopted in this matter by His Highness and his predecessors, a liberation office shall be established at Zanzibar.

Article LXXI

The diplomatic and consular agents and the naval officers of the contracting powers shall, within the limits of existing conventions, give their assistance to the local authorities in order to assist in repressing the slave-trade where it still exists. They shall be present at trials for slave-trading brought about at their instance, without, however, being entitled to take part in the deliberations.

Article LXXII

Liberation offices, or institutions in lieu thereof, shall be organized by the governments of the countries to which African slaves are sent, for the purposes specified by Article XVIII.

Article LXXIII

The signatory powers having undertaken to communicate to one another all information useful for the repression of the slave-trade, the Governments whom the present chapter concerns shall periodically exchange with the other Governments statistical data relating to slaves intercepted and liberated, and to the legislative and administrative measures which have been taken for suppressing the slave-trade.

Chapter V. Institutions Intended to Insure the Execution of the General Act

Section I. Of the international maritime office

Article LXXIV

In accordance with the provisions of Article XXVII, an international office shall be instituted at Zanzibar, in which each of the signatory powers may be represented by a delegate.

Article LXXV

The office shall be constituted as soon as three powers have appointed their representatives.

It shall draw up regulations fixing the manner of exercising its functions. These regulations shall immediately be submitted to the approval of such signatory powers as shall have signified their intention of being represented in this office. They shall decide in this respect within the shortest possible time.

Article LXXVI

The expenses of this institution shall be divided in equal parts among the signatory powers mentioned in the preceding article.

Article LXXVII

The object of the office at Zanzibar shall be to centralize all documents and information of a nature to facilitate the repression of the slave-trade in the maritime zone. For this purpose the signatory powers engage to forward within the shortest time possible:

1. The documents specified in Article XLI;
2. Summaries of the reports and copies of the minutes referred to in Article XLVIII;

3. The list of the territorial or consular authorities and special delegates competent to take action as regards vessels seized according to the terms of Article XLIX;

4. Copies of judgments and condemnations in accordance with Article LVIII;

5. All information that may lead to the discovery of persons engaged in the slave-trade in the above mentioned zone.

Article LXXVIII

The archives of the office shall always be open to the naval officers of the signatory powers authorized to act within the limits of the zone defined by Article XXI, as well as to the territorial or judicial authorities, and to consuls specially designated by their Governments.

The office shall supply to foreign officers and agents authorized to consult its archives, translations into a European language of documents written in an oriental language.

It shall make the communications provided for in Article XLVIII.

Article LXXIX

Auxiliary offices in communication with the office at Zanzibar may be established in certain parts of the zone, in pursuance of a previous agreement between the interested powers.

They shall be composed of delegates of these powers, and established in accordance with Articles LXXV, LXXVI, and LXXVIII.

The documents and information specified in Article LXXVII, so far as they may relate to a part of the zone specially concerned, shall be sent to them directly by the territorial and consular authorities of the region in question, but this shall not exempt the latter from the duty of communicating the same to the office at Zanzibar, as provided by the same article.

Article LXXX

The office at Zanzibar shall prepare in the first two months of every year, a report of its own operations and of those of the auxiliary offices during the past twelve months.

Section II. Of the exchange between the Governments of documents and information relating to the slave-trade

Article LXXXI

The powers shall communicate to one another, to the fullest extent and with the least delay that they shall consider possible:

1. The text of the laws and administrative regulations, existing or enacted by application of the clauses of the present general act;

2. Statistical information concerning the slave-trade, slaves arrested and liberated, and the traffic in fire-arms, ammunition, and alcoholic liquors.

Article LXXXII

The exchange of these documents and information shall be centralized in a special office attached to the foreign office at Brussels.

Article LXXXIII

The office at Zanzibar shall forward to it every year the report mentioned in Article LXXX, concerning its operations during the past year, and concerning those of the auxiliary offices that may have been established in accordance with Article LXXIX.

Article LXXXIV

The documents and information shall be collected and published periodically, and addressed to all the signatory powers. This publication shall be accompanied every year by an analytical table of the legislative, administrative, and statistical documents mentioned in Articles LXXXI and LXXXIII.

Article LXXXV

The office expenses as well as those incurred in correspondence, translation, and printing, shall be shared by all the signatory powers, and shall be collected through the agency of the department of the foreign office at Brussels.

Section III. Of the protection of liberated slaves

Article LXXXVI

The signatory powers having recognized the duty of protecting liberated slaves in their respective possessions, engage to establish, if they do not already exist, in the ports of the zone determined by Article XXI, and in such parts of their said possessions as may be places for the capture, passage and arrival of African slaves, such offices and institutions as may be deemed sufficient by them, whose business shall specially consist in liberating and protecting them in accordance with the provisions of Articles VI, XVIII, LII, LXIII, and LXVI.

Article LXXXVII

The liberation offices or the authorities charged with this service shall deliver letters of release and shall keep a register thereof.

In case of the denunciation of an act connected with the slave-trade, or one of illegal detention, or on application to the slaves themselves, the said offices or authorities shall exercise all necessary diligence to insure the release of the slaves and the punishment of the offenders.

The delivery of letters of release shall in no case be delayed, if the slave be accused of a crime or offence against the common law. But after the delivery of the said letters an investigation shall be proceeded with in the form established by the ordinary procedure.

Article LXXXVIII

The signatory powers shall favour, in their possessions, the foundation of establishments of refuge for women and of education for liberated children.

Article LXXXIX

Freed slaves may always apply to the offices for protection in the enjoyment of their freedom.

Whoever shall have used fraudulent or violent means to deprive a freed slave of his letters of release or of his liberty, shall be considered as a slave-dealer.

Chapter VI. Measures to Restrict the Traffic in Spirituous Liquors

Article XC

Being justly anxious concerning the moral and material consequences to which the abuse of spirituous liquors subjects the native population, the signatory powers have agreed to enforce the provisions of Articles XCI, XCII and XCIII within a zone extending from the 20th degree of North latitude to the 22nd degree of South latitude, and bounded on the west by the Atlantic Ocean and on the east by the Indian Ocean and its dependencies, including the islands adjacent to the mainland within 100 nautical miles from the coast.

Article XCI

In the districts of this zone where it shall be ascertained that, either on account of religious belief or from some other causes, the use of distilled liquors does not exist or has not been developed, the powers shall prohibit their importation. The manufacture of distilled liquors shall be likewise prohibited there.

Each power shall determine the limits of the zone of prohibition of alcoholic liquors in its possessions or protectorates, and shall be bound to make known the limits thereof to the other powers within the space of six months.

The above prohibition can only be suspended in the case of limited quantities intended for the consumption of the non-native population and imported under the regime and conditions determined by each Government.

Article XCII

The powers having possessions or exercising protectorates in those regions of the zone which are not subjected to the regime of the prohibition, and into which alcoholic liquors are at present either freely imported or pay an import duty of less than 15 francs per hectolitre at 50 degrees centigrade, engage to levy on such alcoholic liquors an import duty of 15 francs per hectolitre at 50 degrees centigrade, for three years after the present general act comes into force. At the expiration of this period the duty may be increased to 25 francs during a fresh period of three years. At the end of the sixth year it shall be submitted to revision, the average results produced by these tariffs being taken as a basis, for the purpose of then fixing, if possible, a minimum duty throughout the whole extent of the zone where the prohibition referred to in Article XCI is not in force.

The powers retain the right of maintaining and increasing the duties beyond the minimum fixed by the present article in those regions where they already possess that right.

Article XCIII

Distilled liquors manufactured in the regions referred to in Article XCII, and intended for inland consumption, shall be subject to an excise duty.

This excise duty, the collection of which the powers engage to secure, as far as possible, shall not be less than the minimum import duty fixed by Article XCII.

Article XCIV

The signatory powers having possessions in Africa contiguous to the zone specified in Article XC engage to adopt the necessary measures for preventing the introduction of spirituous liquors within the territories of the said zone via their inland frontiers.

Article XCV

The powers shall communicate to one another, through the office at Brussels, and according to the terms of Chapter V, information relating to the traffic in alcoholic liquors within their respective territories.

Chapter VII. Final Provisions

Article XCVI

The present general act repeals all contrary stipulations of conventions previously concluded between the signatory powers.

Article XCVII

The signatory powers, without prejudice to the stipulations contained in Articles XIV, XXIII and XCII, reserve the right of introducing into the present general act, hereafter and by common consent, such modifications or improvements as experience may prove to be useful.

Article XCVIII

Powers who have not signed the present general act shall be allowed to adhere to it.

The signatory powers reserve the right to impose such conditions as they may deem necessary to their adhesion.

If no conditions shall be stipulated, adhesion implies acceptance of all the obligations and admission to all the advantages stipulated by the present general act.

The powers shall agree among themselves as to the steps to be taken to secure the adhesion of states whose co-operation may be necessary or useful in order to insure complete execution of the general act.

Adhesion shall be effected by a separate act. Notice thereof shall be given through the diplomatic channel to the Government of the King of the Belgians, and by that Government to all the signatory and adherent states.

Article XCIX

The present general act shall be ratified within the shortest possible period, which shall not in any case exceed one year.

Each power shall address its ratification to the Government of the King of the Belgians, which shall give notice thereof to all the other powers that have signed the present general act.

The ratification of all the powers shall remain deposited in the archives of the Kingdom of Belgium.

As soon as all the ratifications shall have been furnished, or at the latest one year after the signature of the present general act, their delivery shall be recorded in a protocol which shall be signed by the representatives of all the powers that have ratified.

A certified copy of this protocol shall be forwarded to all the powers interested.
Article C

Article C

The present general act shall come into force in all the possessions of the contracting powers on the sixtieth day, reckoned from the day on which the protocol provided for in the preceding article shall have been drawn up.

The India Act (V. of 1843)
Abolishing the Legal Status of Slavery

An Act for declaring and amending the law regarding the condition of slavery within the territories of the East India Company.

I. It is hereby enacted and declared, that no public officer shall, in execution of any decree or order of the Court, or for the enforcement of any demand of rent or revenue, sell, or cause to be sold, any person, or the right to the compulsory labour or services of any person, on the ground that such person is in a state of slavery.

II. And it is hereby declared and enacted, that no rights arising out of alleged property in the person and services of another as a slave shall be enforced by any Civil or Criminal Court or Magistrate within the territories of the East India Company.

III. And it is hereby declared and enacted, that no person who may have acquired property by his own industry, or by the exercise of any art, calling, or profession, or by inheritance, assignment, gift, or bequest, shall be dispossessed of such property, or prevented from taking possession thereof, on the ground that such person, or that the person from whom the property may have been derived, was a slave.

IV. And it is hereby enacted, that any act which would be a penal offence if done to a free man, shall be equally an offence if done to any person on the pretext of his being in a condition of slavery.

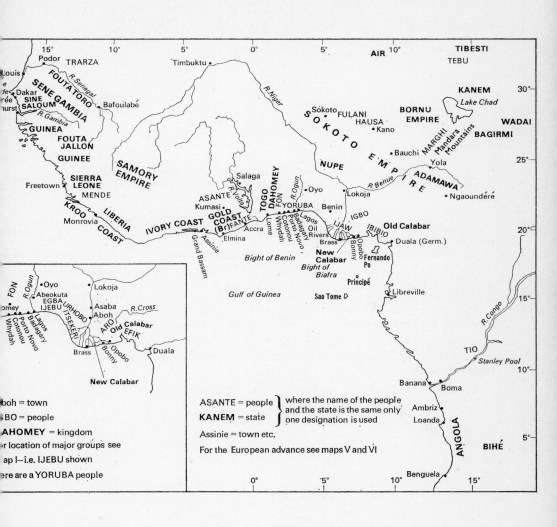

TIBESTI
TEBU

15°   10°   5°   0°   5°   AIR   10°

Podor TRARZA   Timbuktu •

L'ouis •
e   KANEM   30°
ée   • Dakar   FOUTA TORO   R. Senegal   Lake Chad
rée   SENE GAMBIA   Sókoto FULANI   BORNU
hurst   SINE   • Bafoulabé   • Kano   HAUSA   EMPIRE   WADAI
        SALOUM   R. Gambia   BAGIRMI
    GUINEA   • Bauchi   MARGHI Mandara
        FOUTA   Mountains   25°
        JALLON   • Yola
        GUINEE   SAMORY   NUPE   ADAMAWA
                            EMPIRE   R. Benue
    SIERRA   Salaga   • Oyo   Lokoja   • Ngaoundéré
Freetown • LEONE   ASANTE   R. Volta YORUBA Benin
        MENDE   Kumasi TOGO DAHOMEY FON
    KROO   GOLD FANTE   Lagos IGBO
        LIBERIA   COAST   Accra Lome   Oil Old Calabar   20°
Monrovia COAST IVORY COAST (Br) Elmina Whydah Rivers IBIBIO Duala (Germ.)
                    Assinie   Cotonou Brass New
                    Grand Bassam   Porto Novo   Opobo Bonny Calabar
                        Bight of Benin   Bight of Fernando
                                              Biafra Po
                            Gulf of Guinea   Sao Tome ▷ Príncipé
                                                                          15°
                                                      • Libreville

FON   R. Congo
        • Oyo   • Lokoja
R. Ogun Abeokuta   TIO
omey   EGBA URHOBO Asaba   Stanley Pool 10°
    IJEBU ITSEKERI Aboh R. Cross
Lagos   Banana
Porto Novo ARO Old Calabar   • Boma
Badagary   EFIK
Whydah   Brass Opobo   Duala   Ambriz •
            Bonny   Loanda ANGOLA   5°
    New Calabar
                                                  BIHÉ

boh = town
BO = people   ASANTE = people ⎫ where the name of the people
AHOMEY = kingdom   KANEM = state ⎬ and the state is the same only
r location of major groups see Assinie = town etc. ⎭ one designation is used
ap I—i.e. IJEBU shown
ere are a YORUBA people   For the European advance see maps V and VI

        0°   5°   10°   15°
                                          Benguela •

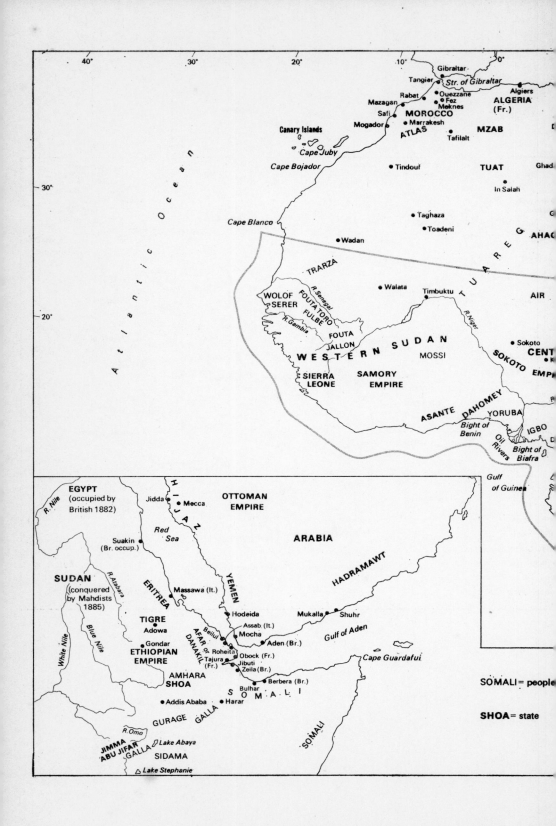

Gibraltar
Str. of Gibraltar
Tangier
Algiers
Ouezzane
Rabat
Fez
Meknes
Mazagan
ALGERIA
Safi
MOROCCO
(Fr.)
MZAB
Mogador
Marrakesh
Canary Islands
ATLAS
Tafilalt
Cape Juby
Tindouf
TUAT
Ghad
Cape Bojador
In Salah
Cape Blanco
Taghaza
AHAC
Toadeni
Wadan
TRARZA
TUAREG
WOLOF
Walata
Timbuktu
AIR
SERER
FOUTA TORO
R. Senegal
FULBE
R. Niger
R. Gambia
FOUTA
WESTERN SUDAN
Sokoto
JALLON
SOKOTO
CENT
MOSSI
EMP
SIERRA
SAMORY
LEONE
EMPIRE
ASANTE
DAHOMEY
YORUBA
Bight of
IGBO
Benin
Oil
Rivers
Bight of
Gulf
Biafra
of Guinea

EGYPT
HIJAZ
Jidda
OTTOMAN
EMPIRE
(occupied by
Mecca
R. Nile
British 1882)
Red
ARABIA
Suakin
Sea
(Br. occup.)
SUDAN
HADRAMAWT
(conquered
R. Atabara
YEMEN
by Mahdists
ERITREA
Massawa (It.)
1885)
TIGRE
Mukalla
Shuhr
Hodeida
Adowa
Blue Nile
Assab (It.)
Beilul
Mocha
Gulf of Aden
Gondar
ETHIOPIAN
AFAR
Aden (Br.)
EMPIRE
DANAKIL
Cape Guardafui
White Nile
Roheita
Obock (Fr.)
AMHARA
Tajura
Jibuti
SHOA
(Fr.)
Zeila (Br.)
SOMALI
Berbera (Br.)
Bulhar
SOMALI = people
Addis Ababa
Harar
R. Omo
GURAGE
GALLA
SOMALI
SHOA = state
JIMMA
Lake Abaya
ABU JIFAR
GALLA
SIDAMA
Lake Stephanie

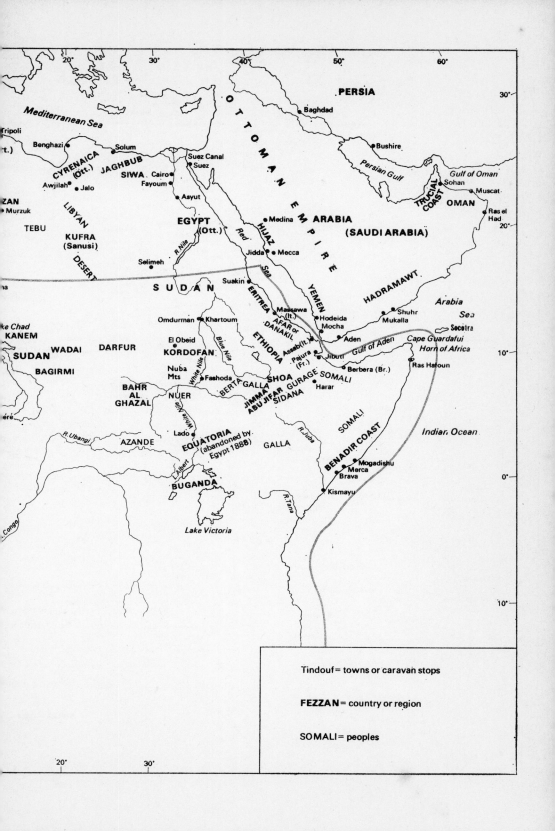

Tindouf = towns or caravan stops

FEZZAN = country or region

SOMALI = peoples

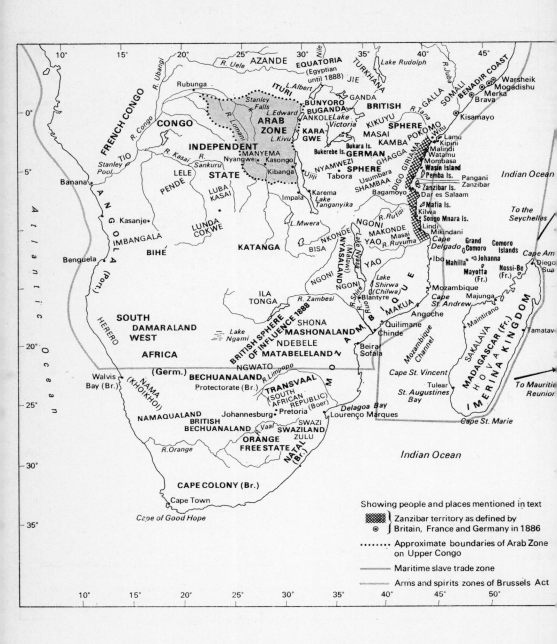

Showing people and places mentioned in text

▨} Zanzibar territory as defined by
⊙} Britain, France and Germany in 1886

•••••• Approximate boundaries of Arab Zone
on Upper Congo

〰〰 Maritime slave trade zone

〰〰 Arms and spirits zones of Brussels Act

R. Bomu 25°   Boundary 1885   30°   Lado
Juba

R. Uele   EQUATORIA   White abandoned by   JIE   L. Stephanie
                                                                                          (Egyptian)
                                                                                          Nile Emin Pasha 1888   TURKHANA   L. Rudolph
la   CONGO
ongo   R. Aruwimi   INDEPENDENT   L. Albert   BUNYORO   R. Juba   SOMALI   ITALIAN PROTECTORATE 1889
                                                                            L. Kyoga   Warsheik
Stanley Falls   STATE   BUGANDA   R.Tana   GALLA   Kisamayo   SOMALI   Mogadishu
                                                                GANDA   Merka
              L. Edward   ARAB ZONE   ANKOLE   Lake Victoria   BRITISH SPHERE   KAMBA   GALLA   BENADIR   Brava   0°
MANYEMA   RUANDA   Bukara   Anglo-   MASAI   KIKUYU   POKOMO   COAST
              L. Kivu   KARAGWE   Bukerebe   German   WITU. Protectorate
UTETELA   Nyangwe   BURUNDI   Is.   border 1886   Witu   claimed by
Kasongo   Rumonge   KEREBE   Shimba   GIRIAMA   Germany 1889
                    Kibanga   CHAGGA   Hills   DIGO   Lamu Is. (Zanzibar)
                              Ujiji   NYAMWEZI   IRAMBA   USAMBARA   Kipini
                              (Arab   Tabora   GERMAN   SHAMBAA   Malindi
R. Lualaba   L. Tanganyika   settlement)   (Arab   SPHERE   Pangani   Watamu
                    Karema   settlement)   Wasin Is.   Freretown
              Mpala   Bagamayo   Pemba Is.   Mombasa
KATANGA   L. Mweru   L. Rukwa   Zanzibar Is.   5°
                                          NGONI   Dar es Salaam   Zanzibar
              L. Banguelo   NKONDE   Karonga   R. Rufisi   Indian Ocean
                    Karonga   Lake   R. Rufusi   Mafia Is.
R. Luapala   Nyasa   R. Rufusi   Kilwa Kivinge
BISA   (Malawi)   Songo Manara Is.
              R. Luangwa   YAO MAKONDE   Masasi   Lindi
NGONI   Kota   MAKUA   Mikindani
              Kota   German-   R. Ruvuma   Cape Delgado
                    Portuguese   Tunghi Bay   Grand Comore
                    YAO   border 1886   Ibe Is.
              NGONI
ILA   Zumbo   L. Shirwa (Chilwa)   Mozambique   15°
TONGA   Tete   Blantyre   MAKUA
                    R. Ruo
                                          Angoche Is.
MOZAMBIQUE   Quilimane
              Chinde

ALLA = peoples   territory recognised as   Frontiers claimed by
UGANDA = states   belonging to Zanzibar by   Congo Independent State
                                  Britain, France and   according to the
= approximate area of   Germany 1886   Declaration of Neutrality
Arab Zone on Upper Congo-   1885
arrows indicate raiding grounds

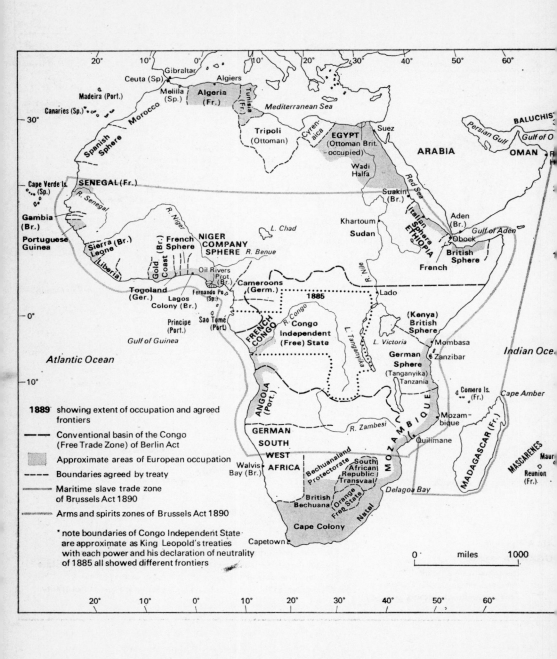

20° 10° 0° 10° 20° 30° 40° 50° 60°

Gibraltar
Ceuta (Sp)   Algiers
Madeira (Port.)   Melilla   Algeria   Tunisia
                   (Sp.)   (Fr.)   (Fr.)   Mediterranean Sea
Canaries (Sp.)   BALUCHIS
— 30°   Morocco   Persian Gulf   Gulf of O
          Spanish   Tripoli   Cyren-   EGYPT   Suez   OMAN
          Sphere   (Ottoman)   aica   (Ottoman Brit.
                                                                 -occupied)   ARABIA
Cape Verde Is.   Wadi
  (Sp.)   SENEGAL (Fr.)   Halfa
— 30°   R. Senegal   Suakin   Aden
Gambia   Khartoum   (Br.)   (Br.)   Gulf of Aden
(Br.)   R. Niger   Italian
Portuguese   Sierra   NIGER   Sudan   Sphere   Obock
Guinea   Leone (Br.)   French   COMPANY   ETHIOPIA
                Liberia   Sphere   SPHERE   R. Benue   British
                Gold   Oil Rivers   French   Sphere
                Coast (Br.)   Prot.   R. Nile
Togoland (Ger.)   Fernando Po (Sp.) Cameroons   1885   Lado
Lagos Colony (Br.)   (Germ.)
          Principe (Port.)   (Kenya)
          Sao Tomé (Port.)   FRENCH   R. Congo   Congo   British
— 0°   Gulf of Guinea   CONGO   Independent   Sphere
                                                    (Free) State   L. Tanganyika   Mombasa
Atlantic Ocean   L. Victoria   Zanzibar
                                                                   German   Indian Oce
— 10°   Sphere
                                          ANGOLA   (Tanganyika)
                                          (Port.)   Tanzania   Comoro Is.
1889 showing extent of occupation and agreed   (Fr.)   Cape Amber
      frontiers   GERMAN   R. Zambesi   Mozam-
                                         SOUTH   bique
---- Conventional basin of the Congo   WEST   Quilimane   MASCARENES
      (Free Trade Zone) of Berlin Act   AFRICA   Walvis   Bechuanaland   South   Maur
      Approximate areas of European occupation   Bay (Br.) Protectorate   African   Reunion
- - - Boundaries agreed by treaty   British   Republic   (Fr.)
      Maritime slave trade zone   Bechuana   Orange Transvaal   Delagoa Bay
      of Brussels Act 1890   Free   Natal
      Arms and spirits zones of Brussels Act 1890   Cape Colony State
                                                                                 miles
  * note boundaries of Congo Independent State   Capetown   0   1000
    are approximate as King Leopold's treaties
    with each power and his declaration of neutrality
    of 1885 all showed different frontiers

20° 10° 0° 10° 20° 30° 40° 50° 60°

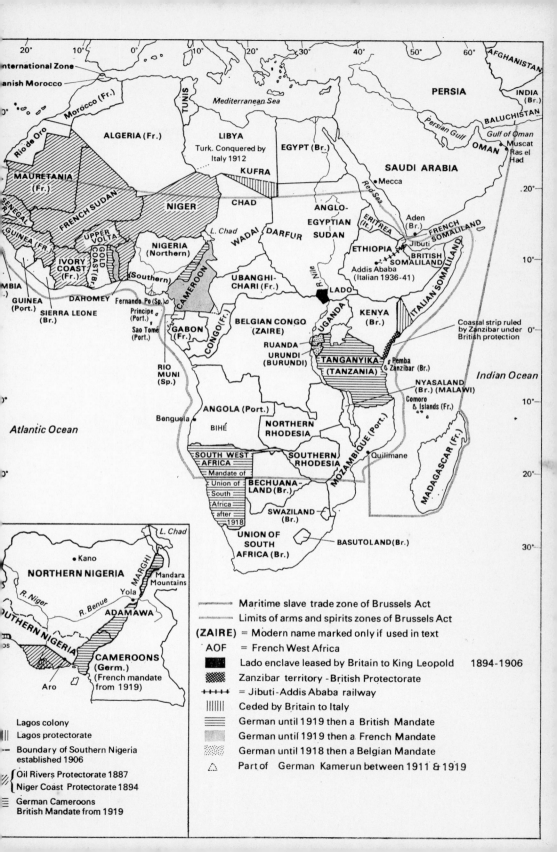

20°   10°   0°   10°   20°   30°   40°   50°   60°

AFGHANISTAN

International Zone
Spanish Morocco

Morocco (Fr.)   TUNIS   Mediterranean Sea   PERSIA   INDIA (Br.)

BALUCHISTAN

Rio de Oro   ALGERIA (Fr.)   LIBYA   EGYPT (Br.)   Persian Gulf   Gulf of Oman

Turk. Conquered by Italy 1912   SAUDI ARABIA   OMAN   Muscat Ras el Had

MAURETANIA (Fr.)   KUFRA   .20°

FRENCH SUDAN   NIGER   CHAD   Red Sea   Mecca

SENEGAL   L. Chad   WADAI   DARFUR   ANGLO-EGYPTIAN SUDAN   ERITREA (It.)   Aden (Br.)   FRENCH SOMALILAND

GUINEA (Fr.)   UPPER VOLTA   NIGERIA (Northern)   Jibuti   BRITISH SOMALILAND   10°

GAMBIA   IVORY COAST (Fr.)   GOLD COAST (Br.)   ETHIOPIA   ITALIAN SOMALILAND

GUINEA (Port.)   DAHOMEY   (Southern)   CAMEROON   Addis Ababa (Italian 1936-41)   SOMALILAND

SIERRA LEONE (Br.)   Fernando Po (Sp.)   UBANGHI-CHARI (Fr.)   R. Nile   LADO

Principe (Port.)   CONGO (Fr.)   BELGIAN CONGO (ZAIRE)   UGANDA   KENYA (Br.)   Coastal strip ruled by Zanzibar under British protection

Sao Tomé (Port.)   GABON (Fr.)   RUANDA URUNDI (BURUNDI)   Pemba   0°

RIO MUNI (Sp.)   TANGANYIKA (TANZANIA)   Zanzibar (Br.)

Indian Ocean

NYASALAND (Br.) (MALAWI)   10°

ANGOLA (Port.)   Comoro Islands (Fr.)

Benguela   BIHÉ   NORTHERN RHODESIA   MOZAMBIQUE (Port.)

Atlantic Ocean

SOUTH WEST AFRICA   SOUTHERN RHODESIA   Quilimane   MADAGASCAR (Fr.)

Mandate of   BECHUANA-LAND (Br.)   20°

Union of South Africa after 1918   SWAZILAND (Br.)

UNION OF SOUTH AFRICA (Br.)   BASUTOLAND (Br.)   30°

L. Chad

• Kano

NORTHERN NIGERIA   MARGHI   Mandara Mountains

R. Niger   Yola

R. Benue   ADAMAWA

SOUTHERN NIGERIA

Aro   CAMEROONS (Germ.) (French mandate from 1919)

Lagos colony
Lagos protectorate
Boundary of Southern Nigeria established 1906
Oil Rivers Protectorate 1887
Niger Coast Protectorate 1894
German Cameroons British Mandate from 1919

Maritime slave trade zone of Brussels Act

Limits of arms and spirits zones of Brussels Act

(ZAIRE) = Modern name marked only if used in text

AOF = French West Africa

Lado enclave leased by Britain to King Leopold   1894-1906

Zanzibar territory - British Protectorate

+++++ = Jibuti-Addis Ababa railway

||||| Ceded by Britain to Italy

German until 1919 then a British Mandate

German until 1919 then a French Mandate

German until 1918 then a Belgian Mandate

△ Part of German Kamerun between 1911 & 1919

Index